W9-AQL-967

THE ROUGH GUIDE TO

Trinidad & Tobago

This sixth edition updated by

Polly Thomas

ROUGH GUIDES

roughguides.com

Contents

Introduction to
Trinidad & Tobago

Sitting pretty just off the coast of the South American mainland it was once part of, the twin-island republic of Trinidad and Tobago (often shortened to "T&T") is one of the Caribbean's most diverse and underexplored destinations. The islands boast spectacular rainforests, waterfalls, savannahs and reefs, and the endless undeveloped beaches are some of the prettiest in the region, from palm-lined white sand fringed by limpid waters to secluded, wave-whipped outcrops. As the home and heart of West Indian Carnival and the place where calypso, soca and steel pan were invented, T&T is a cultural pacemaker for the Caribbean and a fantastic place to party.

Trinidad and Tobago's economy is the most diversified and industrialized in the English-speaking Caribbean, with an average of 151,000 barrels of oil and 40 billion cubic metres of natural gas produced here each year. Because gas and oil are the main economic earners, both islands remain largely unfettered by the more noxious elements of Caribbean tourism, and are well suited to independent travellers without being fully fledged resorts. Visitors are not generally corralled in all-inclusives or holed-up on private swathes of sand and the beaches are enjoyed by locals and foreigners alike, with visitors often in the minority. Sun and sea are by no means the only draw here, however: no other Caribbean island offers such a variety of **wildlife and habitats** in so compact an area (roughly half the size of Hawaii Island). In Trinidad, there are tropical rainforests of mahogany and teak patrolled by howler monkeys and ocelots, wetlands harbouring manatees and anacondas, and **remote beaches** where giant leatherback turtles lay their eggs, while Tobago is best known for its stunning **coral reefs**, favoured by manta rays and shoals of brightly coloured tropical fish. Both islands also offer some brilliant opportunities for birdwatching; with more than 430 recorded species T&T has one of the richest concentrations of birds per square kilometre in the world.

ABOVE BLUE AND YELLOW MACAW **OPPOSITE** HAULING IN A SEINE NET, CHARLOTTEVILLE

The crowded and dynamic **towns and cities** are equally engaging, with fretworked "gingerbread" homes sitting side by side with temples, mosques, Catholic cathedrals and Anglican churches. The many ethnic groups brought to labour in the islands after slaves were freed in 1834 have given rise to a remarkably varied populace, hailing from India, China, Portugal and Syria as well as Africa, England, France and Spain. Though racial tensions are inevitably present, Trinbagonians (as they're collectively known) generally coexist with good humour, and are proud of the multiculturalism that has so enriched the islands. This easy-going mentality is best expressed in the local propensity for "liming" – taking time out to meet friends and talk, usually over food and a beer or glass of rum.

Both islands share a party-hard ethic, and Trinidad has an electrifying **music scene** that rivals even that of Jamaica. T&T is the birthplace of calypso and the more fast-paced soca, as well as that quintessential sound of the Caribbean, the steel pan; you'll hear plenty of all three year-round, but especially during the republic's most famous party, its annual pre-Lenten **Carnival**. During this unique and explosive event, the no-holds-barred debauchery of the Jouvert "dirty mas" parades is followed by two days of pure joy as 5000-strong bands of intricately costumed revellers take to the streets in a celebration of life.

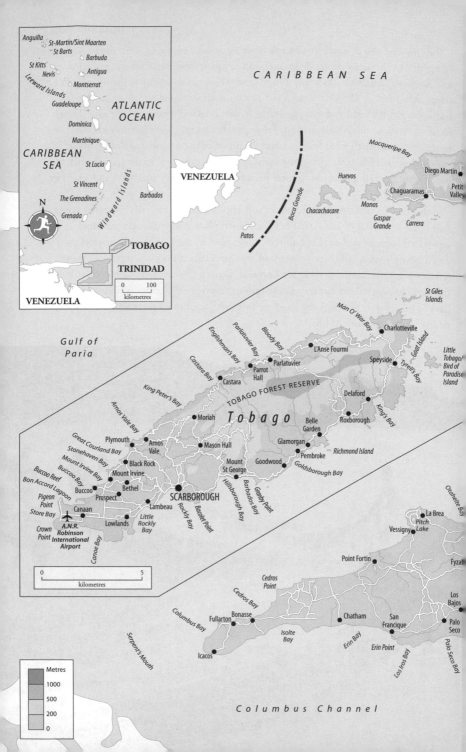

Anguilla
St-Martin/Sint Maarten
St Barts
Barbuda
St Kitts
Nevis
Antigua
Leeward Islands
Montserrat
Guadeloupe
ATLANTIC OCEAN
Dominica
CARIBBEAN SEA
Martinique
St Lucia
St Vincent
The Grenadines
Barbados
Windward Islands
N
Grenada
TOBAGO
TRINIDAD
VENEZUELA
0   100
kilometres

CARIBBEAN SEA

VENEZUELA

Macqueripe Bay
Diego Martin
Huevos
Chaguaramas
Petit Valley
Boca Grande
Chacachacare
Monos
Gaspar Grande
Carrera
Patos

Gulf of Paria

St Giles Islands

Man O' War Bay
Charlotteville
Goat Island

Englishman's Bay
Parlatuvier Bay
Bloody Bay
L'Anse Fourmi
Little Tobago/ Bird of Paradise Island
Castara Bay
Parlatuvier
Speyside
Parrot Hall
Tyrrel's Bay
Castara
King Peter's Bay
TOBAGO FOREST RESERVE
Delaford
King's Bay
Arnos Vale Bay
Moriah
Tobago
Roxborough
Belle Garden
Great Courland Bay
Plymouth
Arnos Vale
Mason Hall
Glamorgan
Richmond Island
Stonehaven Bay
Mount Irvine Bay
Black Rock
Pembroke
Mount Irvine
Mount St George
Goodwood
Goldsborough Bay
Buccoo Bay
Bethel
Buccoo Reef
Buccoo
Lambeau
Bon Accord Lagoon
Prospect
SCARBOROUGH
Pigeon Point
Store Bay
Canaan
Little Rockly Bay
Crown Point
Lowlands
A.N.R. Robinson International Airport
Canoe Bay
Rocky Bay
Bacolet Point
Hillsborough Bay
Barbados Bay
Granby Point

Ortoire Bay

La Brea
Pitch Lake
Vessigny
Point Fortin
Fyzal
Cedros Point
Los Bajos
Cedros Bay
Chatham
San Francique
Palo Seco
Columbus Bay
Fullarton
Bonasse
Isolte Bay
Erin Bay
Erin Point
Los Iros Bay
Palo Seco Bay
Serpent's Mouth
Icacos

Columbus Channel

Metres
1000
500
200
0

0   5
kilometres

FACT FILE

• Standing at about 1.34 million, T&T's **population** is around 40 percent Indian, 39 percent black, 18 percent mixed-race, 0.6 percent white and 0.4 percent Chinese. Its population is theologically diverse, too: with 26 percent Roman Catholic, 25 percent Protestant, 23 percent Hindu, 6 percent Muslim, 3 percent Presbyterian and 6 percent adhered to African-based **religions** such as Spiritual Baptist and Orisha.

• Go into almost any bar in the world and you'll see a bottle of **Angostura bitters**, produced in Trinidad and an essential ingredient of many classic cocktails. Its aromatic blend of herbs, spices and alcohol is such a guarded secret that no single person is permitted to know the full recipe.

• Trinidad is one of the world's most important nesting sites for the giant **leatherback turtle**. Grande Riviere on the north coast sees one of the world's highest density of nests, with some 500 turtles visiting per night at the height of the season.

• The peculiar **Pitch Lake**, at La Brea on Trinidad's southwestern coast, is the world's largest natural reservoir of asphalt.

• In 2006, T&T became the smallest nation ever to qualify for the **World Cup**, though the Soca Warriors didn't manage to score a goal in the tournament, drawing one match and losing two more before being knocked out.

• T&T lie outside the region's **hurricane** belt, and haven't suffered a big blast since Flora in 1963, though minor **earthquakes** occur at an average of one per month.

• Native to southern Trinidad, the **Moruga Scorpion** is officially the second hottest pepper in the world, notching up two million units on the Scoville heat scale, just a fraction less than the Carolina Reaper.

Where to go

Bound together for the convenience of the British Empire, Trinidad and Tobago are vastly different places. Trinidad offers culture, ethnic diversity, music, clubs, great food, pristine rainforest and a wealth of undeveloped beaches. Tobago is more of a conventional Caribbean resort, its southwest replete with busy strips of white sand and hotels of every stripe, as well as plenty of bars, restaurants and places to dance under the stars. The rest of the island is relatively undeveloped, with plenty of fantastic small-scale guesthouses, but nowhere in Tobago will you find the high-rise hotels and slick resort areas of other islands in the region. It's impossible to get a full picture of T&T without visiting both Trinidad and Tobago, and regular and inexpensive plane and ferry services between the two make it easy to see the best of each even during a short stay.

A visit to **Trinidad** will inevitably begin in **Port of Spain**, the vibrant capital which, with its restaurants, nightlife and accommodation, is a natural base from which to explore the rest of the country. To the west, **Chaguaramas** is the capital's playground, with a newly redeveloped waterfront at Williams Bay and the zip line, walking and mountain biking trails, golf course and great beach of Tucker Valley. Chaguaramas is also the jumping-off point for boat trips to the rocky, wooded islands of the **Bocas**. A sweeping curve of powdery sand and powerful waves, **Maracas Bay** is the first of many lovely beaches along the **north coast**, some reachable by road, others only on foot. Inland, the densely forested peaks of the **Northern Range** offer excellent hiking and birdwatching opportunities. South of the hills, the **East–West Corridor** provides access to caves,

OPPOSITE SCARLET IBIS; WATERFALL, NORTH TOBAGO

Author picks

Our authors have travelled the length and breadth of Trinidad and Tobago, shimmying through the streets at Carnival, body-surfing at the beaches and sampling the best of the islands' cuisine. Here are their highlights.

Carnival time Arrive in time to check out the panyards and party at the fetes, then cover yourself in mud and chip along to a rhythm section for Jouvert, and bring out the bling to play mas in the main parades – simply the most fun you will ever have. (pp.259–262)

Tropical birdlife Whether you get up close and personal with hummingbirds (p.127), see the scarlet ibis at Caroni Swamp (p.152) or spend an afternoon spotting the mindboggling number of colourful species at Asa Wright (p.124), T&T's rich birdlife is not just for the hardened twitcher.

Street food From a hot cup of corn soup to a filled-to-bursting roti dressed with curried mango, plus early morning chickpea doubles and paper bags of pholouri dipped into spicy tamarind sauce, T&T's street food is ridiculously moreish. (p.28)

Go cocoa loco Indulge in some chocolate tourism, exploring the cocoa groves at Velaja Estate (p.164), Brasso Seco (p.121), San Antonio (p.160) or Tobago Cocoa Estate (p.238), and take a taste of T&T home via a bar, a box of divine chocolates or some brewing cocoa and nibs.

Swim in a waterfall From floating in cool water under a rainforest canopy, to getting a watery massage, waterfalls are a highlight of T&T; Rio Seco (p.138) to Argyle (p.237), Sombasson (p.134), and Paria (p.119) are four of the best.

The deep south There's much more to the south than the Pitch Lake, from beachside palm groves and gorgeous wetlands at Columbus Bay and Icacos to history and culture at Moruga – plus a friendly, hospitable and uniquely southside vibe. (pp.180–184)

Our author recommendations don't end here. We've flagged up our favourite places – a perfectly sited hotel, an atmospheric café, a special restaurant – throughout the guide, highlighted with the ★ symbol.

CARNIVAL

Trinidad's **Carnival** is all about participation: rather than watching from the sidelines as in Rio – whether young or old, big or small, anyone with a willingness to "wine their waist" and "get on bad" is welcome to sign up with a masquerade band, which gets you a costume and the chance to dance through the streets alongside tens of thousands of fellow revellers. Preceded by weeks of all-night outdoor fetes, as parties here are known, as well as competitions for the best steel bands and calypso and soca singers, the main event starts at 4am on Carnival Sunday with **Jouvert** (pronounced "jou-vay"). This anarchic and raunchy street party is pure, unadulterated bacchanalia, with generous coatings of mud, chocolate, oil or body paint – and libations of local rum, of course – helping you lose all inhibitions and slip and slide through the streets until morning in an anonymous mass of dirty, drunken, happy humanity, chipping along to steel bands, sound-system trucks or the traditional "rhythm section" percussionists. Once the sun is fully up, and a sluice down with a hose has dispensed with the worst of the mud, the masquerade bands hit the streets, their costumed followers dancing along in the wake of the pounding soca. Monday is a mere warm-up for the **main parade** the following day, however, when full costumes are worn and the streets are awash with colour. The music trucks are back in earnest and the city reverberates with music, becoming one giant street party, until "las lap" and total exhaustion closes proceedings for another year.

swimmable rivers and waterfalls, the Yerette hummingbird centre, and the oldest Benedictine monastery in the Caribbean at Mount St Benedict.

The flat agricultural plains of **central Trinidad** provide a fascinating contrast to the north. From the ethereal Waterloo Temple in the Sea and the nearby Hanuman Murti statue to the busy market town of **Chaguanas**, Indian culture predominates; there's plenty of natural allure too, from the scarlet ibis that inhabit the mangrove labyrinth of **Caroni Swamp** to the manatees and monkeys in the protected wetlands at **Nariva**. Endless swathes of fine brown sand lined by groves of coconut palms make **Manzanilla** and **Mayaro** favourite spots for some beach time. The burgeoning city of **San Fernando** is a friendly base from which to explore the largely unvisited "deep south", where modern oil towns such as **Fyzabad** contrast with the spectacular coastline and wetlands around **Cedros** and **Icacos**.

Most people travelling to **Tobago** head for the translucent waters, coral reefs and excellent facilities around **Crown Point** on the low-lying southwestern tip. The vibrant capital, **Scarborough**, with its market and historic fort, offers a more genuine picture of local life, while the rugged windward (or Atlantic) coast is best known for the waterfall and cocoa estate at **Argyle** and the island's finest snorkelling and scuba diving at **Speyside**. The leeward (or Caribbean) coast promises some superb beaches, kicking off with the clear green waters of **Mount Irvine** and the wide sweeps of sand at **Stonehaven Bay** and **Turtle Beach**; further afield there's the twin bays at **Castara** to the palm-lined swathe of **Englishman's Bay**. On the northeast tip, the pretty village of **Charlotteville** has the sublime Pirate's Bay as well as the none-too-shabby Man O'War Bay.

When to go

Though T&T's **temperatures** remain tropical year-round, most people visit between January and March, when **Carnival** explodes into life, the trees are in bloom and the

OPPOSITE SPEYSIDE LOOKOUT POINT

CLIMATE IN PORT OF SPAIN

	Jan	Feb	Mar	Apr	May	Jun	Jul	Aug	Sep	Oct	Nov	Dec
AVERAGE DAILY TEMPERATURE												
Max/min (°C)	31/21	31/20	32/20	32/21	32/22	32/22	31/22	31/22	32/22	32/22	32/22	31/21
Max/min (°F)	87/69	88/68	89/68	90/69	90/71	89/71	88/71	88/71	89/71	89/71	89/71	88/69
AVERAGE RAINFALL												
mm	69	41	46	53	94	193	218	246	193	170	183	125

climate is at its most forgiving – the sun shines, rain is rare and the nights are cool. By May, the lack of rain has parched the formerly lush landscape: greens turn to yellow, dust clouds put the views into soft focus and bush fires rage through Trinidad's hills. Around the end of May, the **rainy season** begins, and the skies open up with dramatic deluges that can last all day. The wet season lasts until November, but there's usually a respite from the downpours in September, a period of hot sunshine and blue skies known as the **petit carem**. It's an excellent time to visit, with flights at low-season rates, though you'll find the resorts a little quiet. Some Tobago hoteliers raise rates during the **high season** (Dec 15–April 15), and those in Trinidad's Grande Riviere do the same during the turtle-laying season (March–Sept), but most of the smaller hotels charge the same year-round in both islands. During Carnival week, however, all Port of Spain hotels and guesthouses boost their rates.

15

things not to miss

It's not possible to see everything that Trinidad and Tobago have to offer in one trip – and we don't suggest you try. What follows gives a taste of the islands' highlights: gorgeous beaches, thrilling nightlife, fine food and exotic wildlife. All highlights have a page reference to take you into the Guide, where you can find out more. Coloured numbers refer to chapters in the Guide section.

1

1 NORTH COAST DRIVE

Page112–118

The drive along Trinidad's northern coastline provides glimpses of innumerable rainforest-smothered headlands, and stopoffs at some fantastic beaches.

2 HIKING IN THE NORTHERN RANGE

Pages 122 & 135

Trinidad's Northern Range hills offer excellent hiking, with hundreds of trails through the lush forest.

3 CARAPICHAIMA

Page 155

Carapichaima provides a great introduction to Indo-Trinidadian culture, from the Temple in the Sea at Waterloo to the gigantic Hanuman Murti statue.

4 PANYARDS

Page 74

Take a pre-Carnival tour of Port of Spain's panyards to hear practice sessions for the coveted Panorama prize.

5 TURTLE-WATCHING

Pages 137, 142 & 216

Visit in season and you can watch leatherback turtles lay their eggs in the sand or see the hatchlings make their way to the sea.

6 ESCAPISM AT GRANDE RIVIERE
Page 141
Close to swimmable rivers and rainforest hikes, this remote and unspoiled coastal village is a fabulous place escape the crowds any time of the year.

7 PORT OF SPAIN NIGHTLIFE
Page 88
From jumping up at an outdoor fete to dancing the night away at a club or bar, there are few reasons to go to bed early in the nation's capital.

8 TRINBAGO CUISINE
Pages 27–32
From curry crab and dumplin' at Store Bay to gourmet Creole dishes at *Chaud*, T&Ts rich pot-pourri of influences has created a delicious and unique cuisine.

9 BIRDWATCHING AT ASA WRIGHT
Page 124
This standout nature centre is one of the best places in T&T for a spot of birdwatching.

10 CRUISING ALONG TOBAGO'S COAST
Page 202
A boat ride along the island's Caribbean coast provides a spectacularly different perspective on Tobago's scenery.

9

10

11

12

11 **TRINIDAD'S EAST COAST**
Pages 164–169
Enjoy some Trini-style beach time or explore the fantastically diverse forests and wetlands of Nariva Swamp.

12 **TOBAGO'S BEACHES**
Pages 213 & 232
From the emerald waters of Mount Irvine to the often-deserted Englishman's Bay, Tobago's beaches offer plenty of variety beyond the palm-trees-and-white-sand scene.

13 **HUMMINGBIRDS AT YERETTE**
Page 127
Witness these magical little birds flitting around the sugar-water feeders of a private garden in the Maracas–St Joseph valley.

14 **SPEYSIDE DIVING**
Page 241
With intricate reefs patrolled by shoals of colourful fish, the waters offshore of Speyside are a delight.

15 **CARNIVAL**
Pages 259–262
Whether you're watching the parade go by or joining a mas band, Carnival is T&T's ultimate party.

Itineraries

The itineraries here are designed to give you a taste of Trinidad and Tobago's many and varied attractions. Our week-long tours take in beaches, birdwatching, nature and culture, ticking off the islands' highlights as well as a few lesser-known sights. We've also mapped out an adrenaline-fuelled itinerary, featuring surfing, mountain biking and many other exhilarating experiences across both islands.

A WEEK IN TRINIDAD

❶ Port of Spain From Independence Square, walk up bustling Frederick Street to the National Museum. After lunch at *Chaud*, stroll around the Savannah to the Botanical Gardens, and sample Ariapita Avenue's restaurants and bars after dark. See pp.50–93

❷ North coast beach Enjoy sun, sea and surf at Maracas, or take to the calmer waters of Las Cuevas. Recharge with a slap-up dinner at *Buzo Osteria Italiana*. See p.113, p.115 & p.87

❸ West coast Make an early start to see the Indian temples at Carapichaima, head south to walk on the weird and wonderful Pitch Lake, and then watch scarlet ibis roost at Caroni. See pp.152–159

❹ Yerette and Mount St Benedict Spend the morning surrounded by dazzling hummingbirds at Yerette, then check into *Pax Guest House* at Mount St Benedict for old-world charm and fantastic views. See p.127 & p.128

❺ Asa Wright Nature Centre Head into the Northern Range for easy-access birdwatching, swimming in a natural pool and some lovely walks through the forest. See p.124

❻ Northeast Trinidad Drive around Trinidad's eastern tip and walk to Rio Seco Waterfall for a swim. Drive on to Grande Riviere via Toco and Galera Point, and spend the night in a beachside hotel. See pp.136–145

❼ East coast Take a scenic drive along the east coast, past sweeping Mayaro and Manzanilla beaches and the Cocal palm grove, and explore the amazing Nariva Swamp. See pp.164–169

A WEEK IN TOBAGO

❶ Crown Point Kick off your holiday at Pigeon Point, enjoying lunch and cocktails right on the sand. End the day with a gourmet dinner at *Kariwak Village*. See p.202 & p.208

❷ Mount Irvine After a morning on the beach, get active with a round of golf or a horseback ride through the sea at nearby Buccoo. See p.205 & p.213

❸ Castara Take the Northside Road through the precipitous village of Moriah and view the unravelling coastline from Mount Dillon. Check in to a Castara guesthouse and have sunset cocktails and dinner at *Castara Retreats* hotel. See pp.226–232

❹ Rainforest and Englishman's Bay Take a guided walk into the Tobago Forest Reserve, then spread your towel under a coconut palm. See p.234 & p.232

❺ Scarborough and the windward coast Check out fabulous views from Fort King George, have lunch at the *Blue Crab*, then

ABOVE SCUBA DIVING IN LITTLE TOBAGO

sample chocolate at Tobago Cocoa Estate and swim at Argyle Waterfall. **See p.219 & p.237**

❻ **Speyside** Hop on a glass-bottom boat to see (and snorkel among) pristine reefs and walk on Little Tobago. After lunch at *Jemma's Treehouse*, take in the view at Flagstaff Hill en route to a Charlotteville guesthouse. **See pp.240–243**

❼ **Charlotteville** Spend the morning exploring the village, then cool off with a swim at Pirate's Bay after lunch. **See pp.243–247**

ADRENALINE TOUR

❶ **Port of Spain** Try your hand at wakeboarding in the Gulf of Paria, then swing through the treetops at the Tucker Valley zip line. Return to the capital for a workout on the dancefloor. **See p.80 & p.100**

❷ **Blanchisseuse–Matelot bench trail** Hike this age-old trail along undeveloped coastline, and take a swim at the gorgeous beach and waterfall at Paria before hopping in a boat back to Blanchisseuse and checking into a seaside guesthouse. **See p.119**

❸ **Guanapo Gorge hike** Follow the road through the rainforest to walk and swim through the cool confines of this narrow gorge of 30m-high rocks, then hole up at *Pax Guest House*. **See p.134**

❹ **El Tucuche** From the Maracas–St Joseph Valley, trek through mist-drenched elfin and montane forest to the top of Trinidad's second-highest mountain, or rise to the challenge of mountain biking halfway to the summit. **See p.127**

❺ **Surfing at Mount Irvine** Hop on the ferry to Tobago and check out the breaks at the "Office", the undisputed capital of T&T's surf scene: take a lesson or ride the waves with the locals. **See p.213**

❻ **Tobago mountain biking** Hook up with a cycling guide to explore the flatland trails around Arnos Vale, or test your skills on adrenaline-charged downhill rides from precipitous Moriah. **See p.205**

❼ **Northeast Tobago drift diving** Head east to fly like a bird past walls of coral at Sisters Rocks, or let the currents take you through Charlotteville's famous "London Bridge". **See p.241**

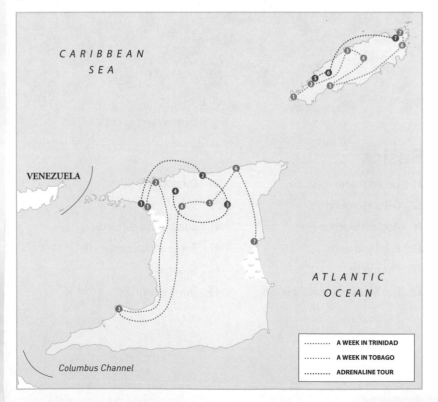

CARIBBEAN SEA

VENEZUELA

ATLANTIC OCEAN

Columbus Channel

·········· **A WEEK IN TRINIDAD**
·········· **A WEEK IN TOBAGO**
·········· **ADRENALINE TOUR**

FRUIT VENDOR, ARGYLE WATERFALL

Basics

Getting there

Though they don't get as many budget services as more touristic Caribbean islands, Trinidad and Tobago are served by regular international flights from the UK, US and Canada, as well as South and Central America and the rest of the Caribbean. And because Trinidad and Tobago are linked by inexpensive twenty-minute domestic services (see p.25), it's worth researching flights to both islands, even if you only plan on spending time on one of them.

If you're planning to visit just Tobago, booking a **package** might be your best option. There are legions of specialist companies (see p.22) who can arrange these, often at a lower rate than you'd get booking flight and accommodation independently. As Trinidad is less geared towards tourists, there are fewer deals available beyond birdwatching or Carnival packages, though Tobago-oriented companies sometimes give the option for a few days in Trinidad.

Fares peak during the winter high season (Dec–March) and before and after Carnival (see p.134), and also rise during the summer school holidays.

Flights from the US and Canada

To Trinidad, national carrier Caribbean Airlines fly from Miami (7 weekly), New York (21 weekly), Toronto (up to 21 weekly), Orlando (1 weekly) and Fort Lauderdale (7 weekly). American Airlines operate twice-daily nonstop flights from Miami, while United fly from Newark (5 weekly) and Houston (7 weekly). Budget carrier Jet Blue also offers daily flights from New York and Fort Lauderdale.

To Tobago, Caribbean Airlines operate direct flights from New York three times a week (Thurs, Fri & Sun).

High-season **fares** from Miami average at around US$550; low-season fares are around US$100 less. Add around US$100 if you're connecting from other

US cities or flying direct from Atlanta. From Canada, you'll pay around Can$600 in low season, Can$1150 in high season.

Flights from the Caribbean and Central/South America

It is possible to visit T&T in conjunction with a trip to another Caribbean island or the South/Central American mainland. Liat and Caribbean Airlines offer a wide range of **inter-island flights**. **From Venezuela** to Trinidad, Caribbean Airlines operate up to ten flights weekly, and Aerotuy seven per week, while Caribbean Airlines and LIAT have daily flights **from Guyana**. **From Suriname**, Caribbean Airlines and Suriname Airways both have four flights a week to Trinidad.

Flights from the UK and Ireland

To Trinidad, Caribbean Airlines fly nonstop three times weekly, while British Airways offer five weekly flights (with a stopoff in St Lucia); both operate out of Gatwick. From Gatwick **to Tobago**, **British Airways** fly once or twice weekly depending on the season (usually Mon and Fri), as do **Virgin** (Sun in summer, Tues & Sat in winter); both airlines make a short stop in St Lucia before continuing on to Tobago.

Fares to both islands start at around £650 year-round, but hike up to £800–1000 during school holidays, Christmas and Carnival season. Budget-airline services with Monarch to Tobago offer by far the cheapest fares, from around £500.

Note that there are no flights to T&T from Ireland: the best option is to take a flight to London or the US and then travel onward with one of the operators listed above.

Flights from Australia and New Zealand

The Caribbean is no bargain destination from **Australia** or **New Zealand**. There are no direct flights to Trinidad and Tobago, so you'll have to fly

---

A BETTER KIND OF TRAVEL

At Rough Guides we are passionately committed to travel. We believe it helps us understand the world we live in and the people we share it with – and of course tourism is vital to many developing economies. But the scale of modern tourism has also damaged some places irreparably, and climate change is accelerated by most forms of transport, especially flying. All Rough Guides' flights are carbon-offset, and every year we donate money to a variety of environmental charities.

to one of the main US gateway airports, and pick up onward connections from there. Air New Zealand and Qantas have regular services from major cities in Australia and New Zealand to Los Angeles, with connecting flights to New York or Miami on American Airlines or United: return **fares** start at around Aus$1700 or NZ$2000.

AIRLINES

Aerotuy ⓦ tuy.com.
Air New Zealand ⓦ airnewzealand.com.
American Airlines ⓦ aa.com.
British Airways ⓦ britishairways.com.
Caribbean Airlines ⓦ caribbean-airlines.com.
JetBlue ⓦ jetblue.com.
Liat ⓦ liat.com.
Monarch ⓦ monarch.co.uk.
Qantas Airways ⓦ qantas.com.au.
Suriname Airways ⓦ flyslm.com.
United Airlines ⓦ united.com.
Virgin ⓦ virgin-atlantic.com.

AGENTS AND OPERATORS

Caradonna US ☎ 1800 330 6611, ⓦ caradonna.com. Diving packages to Tobago.
Caribbean Destinations Australia ☎ 1800 354 104, ⓦ caribbeanislands.com.au. Comprehensive range of tailor-made Caribbean holidays, including a choice of accommodation packages.
Caribbean Journey US ☎ 1866 236 1924, ⓦ caribbeanjourney .com. Tailor-made hotel and villa holidays on Tobago.
Caribtours UK ☎ 020 7751 0660, ⓦ caribtours.co.uk. Specialist operator offering luxurious packages to both Trinidad and Tobago.
CV Villas UK ☎ 020 7563 7999, ⓦ cvvillas.com. Good value for villa holidays in Tobago, as well as a few small properties.
Geodyssey UK ☎ 020 7281 7788, ⓦ geodyssey.co.uk. Specialist in T&T and Venezuela, offering excellent tours that take in the cultural and natural highlights of both Trinidad and Tobago.
IGLU Tropical UK ☎ 020 8544 6620, ⓦ iglutropical.com. Cruise and accommodation packages.
Just Tobago UK ☎ 01373 814 234, ⓦ www.justtobago.co.uk. Specialist company offering flexible packages to Tobago with a range of prices and themes.
Kuoni Worldwide UK ☎ 0800 092 4444, ⓦ kuoni.co.uk. Flexible package holidays and good family deals to Tobago.
Mot Mot Travel UK ☎ 01327 359 622, ⓦ motmottravel .com. Excellent tour operator, with knowledgeable staff and some great tours on both islands, from nature-based trips to birdwatching and diving.
Newmont Travel UK ☎ 020 8920 1155, ⓦ newmont.co.uk. Caribbean flight specialist offering the best deals out of the UK.
North South Travel UK ☎ 01245 608 291, ⓦ northsouthtravel .co.uk. Friendly, competitive travel agency, offering discounted fares worldwide. Profits are used to support projects in the developing world, especially the promotion of sustainable tourism.

Regal Holidays UK ☎ 01353 659 999, ⓦ regal-diving.co.uk. Specializes in diving packages to Tobago, including eco-friendly packages, as well as live-aboards.
STA Travel UK ☎ 0333 321 0099, US ☎ 1800 781 4040, Australia ☎ 134 782, New Zealand ☎ 0800 474 400, South Africa ☎ 0861 781 781, ⓦ statravel.co.uk. Worldwide specialists in independent travel; also student IDs, travel insurance, car rental, rail passes, and more. Good discounts for students and under-26s.
Travel CUTS Canada ☎ 1800 667 2887, US ☎ 1800 592 2887, ⓦ travelcuts.com. Canadian youth and student travel firm.
USIT Ireland ☎ 01 602 1906, Australia ☎ 1800 092 499, ⓦ usit.ie. Ireland's main student and youth travel specialist.
Wildwings UK ☎ 0117 965 8333, ⓦ wildwings.co.uk. Excellent birdwatching and eco-tour packages in both Trinidad and Tobago.

Getting around

Public transportation around Trinidad and Tobago can at first seem chaotic and unpredictable, but once you've got the hang of it, getting around these two compact islands is relatively straightforward.

Buses, maxi taxis and route taxis serve most places mentioned in the Guide, though a few of the more rural areas have only infrequent services. In populated areas, buses and maxi/route taxis run from around 6am until late evening, but outside commuter hours the waits can be long and having your own car is infinitely more convenient. Private taxis are always available. Avoid travelling at peak hours (6–8am & 3–6pm), when urban roads are clogged with heavy traffic and maxis and taxis heave with people. The water taxi service between San Fernando and Port of Spain, and Port of Spain and Chaguaramas, offers a relaxed alternative to Trinidad's busy roads.

Note also that many of the islands' tour operators (see p.38) offer airport transfers and general transportation, say from Port of Spain to Grande Riviere or Crown Point to Charlotteville.

By bus and maxi taxi

Bus services in Trinidad and Tobago are divided between large public buses (run by the Public Transport Service Corporation, **PTSC**; ⓦ ptsc.co.tt) and private services (most often minibuses) called maxi taxis. All public buses and most maxi taxis in **Trinidad** leave from and terminate at **City Gate** – sometimes referred to as South Quay in official literature – in Port of Spain, the country's main transportation hub. Maxi and bus services between

PTSC "KNOW YOUR COUNTRY" TOURS

In addition to standard bus services, PTSC offers tours to some of Trinidad's most popular attractions. The **"Know Your Country" Tours** are designed primarily for locals (though tourists are welcome), and are an excellent and very cheap way of getting to some of the more inaccessible parts of the island. **Prices** range from TT$50 to TT$150, not including entrance fees and meals. The most popular trips are listed below, but the PTSC website (ⓦ ptsc.co.tt) details many other options.

Departing from **City Gate** in Port of Spain, there's a visit to **Los Iros** (stopping at Penal and the Divina Pastora church in Siparia), **Blanchisseuse** (stopping at the Asa Wright Nature Centre and passing through Morne La Croix and Brasso Seco, and with a swimming stop at Las Cuevas), **Mayaro** (stopping at Manzanilla Beach) and the **Pitch Lake** (stopping at Vessigny Beach). Starting from the PTSC terminus in San Fernando (though you could pick it up in the capital), there's also a tour to **Port of Spain**, taking in the National Museum and heading on to **Maracas** Beach. For more information, call ☏ 623 2341, ext 234 or 371.

Port of Spain and Arima are especially quick due to the **Priority Bus Route**, which runs along the course of the old railway line through Trinidad's east–west corridor. In **Tobago**, all buses leave from the Sangster Hill Road terminal, off Milford Road in Scarborough, and cover the entire island.

Buses and maxis are viable transport options for visitors, and riding in a maxi can often be an entertaining experience as well as a chance to chat to locals; it's also fun to try and spot the most unusual of the "names" splashed over the top of the windscreen – popular standards include the likes of "Problem Child" or "Wotless", perhaps in honour of the notoriously cavalier driving habits of their owners.

By bus

There are several types of **public bus** in Trinidad, with both urban and national services, all are air-conditioned and reasonably comfortable. **Bus stops** are often small concrete shelters on the side of the road, or sometimes just a sign on a telephone pole. **Tickets** must be bought in advance, either from the main City Gate terminus in Port of Spain, Scarborough's Sangster Hill Road bus terminal or from small general stores around the country – you cannot simply board a bus and buy your fare. Weekly and monthly travel cards are available. **Fares** run from TT$2 to TT$8, and services operate from 4.30am to around 9pm. **Bus information** can be obtained online, in person at the bus terminals, or by ringing ☏ 623 2341 (Trinidad) and ☏ 639 2293 (Tobago).

By maxi taxi

Maxi taxis carry anything from ten to thirty people, and are privately owned but run according to set routes and fares; each area has a different colour-coded stripe, or band. In Trinidad, **yellow-band** vehicles work from in and around Port of Spain to Diego Martin and the western tip; **red bands** in the east; **green-bands** in the centre and south; **black-bands** in and around Princes Town; and **brown-bands** from San Fernando to the southwest. **Blue-band** maxis operate in Tobago and there is only one set route, from Scarborough to Charlotteville (the rest are for schoolchildren and private tourist charters). Maxis adhere to no fixed **timetable**, though services are at their most frequent from 6–10am & 3–8pm; after 8pm you can expect a longer wait. Some maxis run intermittently through the night, especially along the east–west corridor and in the major towns. Importantly, maxis can be hailed anywhere along their route – just stick out your hand and if they have space they will pick you up – but it's often quicker to go to a main stand; since maxis wait until they are full before leaving, they may not have free seats until they reach their destination. Once aboard, they will let you off at any point; press the buzzers by the windows to stop the bus. **Fares** range between TT$4 and TT$10; ask fellow passengers if you're not sure, or just give the driver a TT$10/20 note and wait for your change.

By route taxi and private taxi

Private cars operating as shared taxis, **route taxis** follow similar rules to maxis, departing on set routes from stands in all sizeable towns. They can hold four to five passengers in addition to the driver and, apart from their H number plates, are indistinguishable from private cars (which have P number plates – although note that some P-licensed cars also operate as route taxis and are best avoided, as you could be getting into anyone's car), and come in various states of repair. Route taxis don't leave their stand until they're full, but are usually quicker (and slightly more expensive) than maxis as they stop less frequently.

To stop a taxi en route, hail it with a wave of your hand. There is a widely accepted code of hand signals among locals catching taxis; point left or right to indicate which direction you want to take at the next major turn-off. When entering the car, it's normal to greet other passengers with a "good morning" or a "good afternoon". To stop the taxi, just tell your driver you want to get out as you approach your destination – in Trini-speak, "nex corner drive". As with maxis, if you're not sure what you should be paying, just hand over a TT$20 note and wait for change; you're unlikely to be overcharged.

Like anywhere, **private taxis** take you directly to your destination, but are **unmetered**, so a price must be agreed beforehand, and they easily work out just as expensive as a cab in Britain or the US. As with route taxis, they have an H number plate. It is often possible – and more economical – however, to bargain with a route taxi driver to drop you where you want. Phone-A-Taxi (❶628 TAXI) offers the cheapest 24-hour, island-wide service in Trinidad; in Tobago, drivers hang out at the airport and all hotels and guesthouses will be able to recommend a driver.

By car

Driving in T&T requires **patience** and constant **alertness**: you simply cannot take your eyes off the road for one moment, and the packed one-way streets of downtown Port of Spain can seem a nightmare at first. Though Trinbagonian drivers are generally courteous, often stopping to let other drivers pull out or offering parking advice, they also habitually stop at short notice, turn without indicating and will happily block traffic to buy a snack or chat with a friend. The best thing to do is accept it; beeping your horn out of irritation will only get you withering stares; **horns** are more frequently used as a thank-you gesture for a courtesy or indication of an intention to overtake. Expect maxis/taxis to pull over at any moment, and always drive defensively.

Some drivers also take to the road at night with only one headlight/taillight, and keep full-beam headlights on all the time; keep your eyes to the left verge to avoid being dazzled. Hand signals are also frequently used: an up-and-down movement indicates that a driver is about to stop (or an

instruction for others to stop due to a hazard ahead); if pulling out into traffic, some still stick out an arm to indicate their intent. Whatever the motivation, slow down if faced with a hand signal. Driving on main highways can feel hair-raising – a favourite Trinbagonian habit is a high-speed weaving technique which looks as though it ought to cause a multiple pile-up (sadly, it often does so); left-hand overtaking is also commonplace. Always take extra care, and slow right down in the tropical rains.

Traffic lights can be confusing: as well as the usual red/amber/green sequence, you'll see flashing red or yellow lights at junctions; both mean "proceed with caution"; yellow means it's primarily your right of way, red that it's someone else's.

Seat belts are compulsory, but not always used. Drinking and driving is also illegal, though the attitude towards it is more laidback in T&T than most other countries. The law also demands that drivers be properly attired; men can be charged for driving without a top on ("bareback"), so always keep a T-shirt handy. **Road signs** are based on the English system (although distances and speed limits are in kilometres), and you must drive on the **left**. In Trinidad, the **speed limit** is 80kmph on highways and 55kmph on main roads in built-up areas. Tobago's speed limit is 50kmph.

A valid international **driving licence** or one issued in the US, Canada, UK, Germany or the Bahamas is required for driving both cars and motorcycles for up to ninety days. Apply to the Licensing Division on Wrightson Road, Port of Spain (❶625 1031), if you intend to drive in T&T for longer than three months.

Car rental

All companies require you to be 25 or over and hold a valid **driving licence**; most ask for a deposit guaranteed by a credit card imprint, though some smaller firms, especially in Tobago, accept a cash deposit of around US$170. You'll be offered a collision damage waiver at extra cost (usually US$5–15/day); without one, you will be liable for damage, but note that you may well be able to arrange CDW cover through your home insurance before you arrive in T&T, which often works out to be much cheaper. Rental prices vary, so shop around; they tend to start at around US$30 per day for the smallest vehicle, inclusive of third-party insurance and unlimited mileage. Check tyres (including the spare) before you drive away, and make sure you're present when existing scratches and bumps are noted.

CAR RENTAL FIRMS

Econo-Car Trinidad and Tobago Ⓦ econocarrentalstt.com
/trinidad-car-rentals.html
Europcar Trinidad Ⓦ europcar.co.tt
Hertz Trinidad Ⓦ hertz.com
Sheppy's Tobago Ⓦ tobagocarrental.com
Sherman's Tobago Ⓦ shermansrental.com
Singh's Trinidad and Tobago Ⓦ singhs.com/about.html
Thrifty Trinidad and Tobago Ⓦ thrifty.com

Motorcycle and bicycle rental

Renting a **motorcycle** isn't advisable in Trinidad
because of the volume of traffic and unpredictable
driving, but a bike can be a good way of getting
around Tobago's quieter roads. You can rent
bicycles on both islands, though for the same
reason they're not great for getting around Trinidad,
other than for exploring quiet areas such as Tucker
Valley in Chaguaramas.

MOTORCYCLES

Sheppy's Tobago Ⓦ tobagocarrental.com

BICYCLES

Easy Goers Airport Rd, Crown Point, Tobago ☏ 681 8025 or
☏ 787 0685, Ⓦ easygoersbikes.com.
Geronimo's 15 Pole Carew St, Woodbrook, Trinidad ☏ 622 2453,
Ⓦ geronimocycle.com.
Mike's Bikes 21 O'Connor St, Woodbrook, Trinidad ☏ 624 6453,
Ⓔ info@caribbeancycling.net.

By water taxi

Trinidad's **water taxis** (☏ 624 5137, Ⓦ nidco.co.tt)
save time and stress on the roads between Port of
Spain and San Fernando (45min; TT$15; see p.79 &
p.178), and are a quick and easy way to get from the
capital to Chaguaramas (15min; TT$10; see p.101).
The Port of Spain terminal is on Wrightson Road,
adjacent to the Tobago ferry terminal.

Travelling between Trinidad and Tobago

There are two options available if you wish to
travel between the islands – the plane, quick
and relatively inexpensive; and the ferry, a bit
slower and a lot cheaper, but a rough ride that's
notorious for seasickness. The air bridge is the
more pleasant experience, though it does mean
that you have to get to and from Piarco airport,
which can be a lengthy journey at rush hour; the
ferry, by comparison, departs from central Port
of Spain.

By ferry

Fast **catamarans**, *T&T Spirit* and *T&T Express,* make
the journey between the islands in around three
hours (though ongoing engine problems mean
that journey time is often longer). In Trinidad,
ferries arrive and depart from the **Ferry Terminal**
opposite the Twin Towers on Wrightson Road in
Port of Spain; in Tobago, the terminal is on Milford
Road in central Scarborough. There are usually
around six sailings per day, but it's best to call in
advance or check the Inter-Island Ferry Service
website, Ⓦ https://ttiferry.com which lists current
schedules. Bear in mind that the journey can be
rough due to strong currents in the Bocas (less so
from Tobago to Trinidad); take seasickness tablets,
and sit in the middle of the boat rather than the
back or the front. Seasoned ferry passengers travel
with a sheet or wrap to cover the sometimes less-
than-clean seats.

One-way **tickets** cost TT$50; standard car prices
are TT$150 one-way (though few rental outfits
will let you take their cars on the ferry). Note that
you can't book seats or buy tickets on the phone
or online. For same-day tickets only, the Port
of Spain and Scarborough terminal ticket offices
are open Monday to Thursday 7.15am to 3pm,
4.15 to 6pm & 7 to 10.30pm, Friday 7.15am to
3pm; be prepared to join the queue at least
three hours before the boat leaves. Otherwise,
you have to buy in advance (essential for busy
periods like Carnival, Easter or Great Race) in
person from travel agencies and authorized
vendors – check the website for a full list. For
further information, call ☏ 625 4906 in Trinidad,
☏ 639 2416 in Tobago.

By plane

National carrier Caribbean Airlines (☏ 625 7200,
Ⓦ caribbean-airlines.com) makes the twenty-
minute **flight** between Trinidad and Tobago up to
twenty times a day each way. **Tickets** cost US$24
one-way and US$48 return; you can book and pay
for an e-ticket online, or visit a ticket office in
person. The latter are at Piarco Airport (daily
4.15am–7pm), and at Nicholas Towers, Independence Square, Port of Spain (Mon–Fri 8am–4pm,
Sat 8am–noon); in Tobago, there's an office
opposite departures in Crown Point Airport
(daily 5.45am–9.45pm; ☏ 660 7200). Note that all
tickets are flexible: once you've paid, you can
change the date and time of your flight online,
by phone or at ticket offices; this, however,
seems likely to change in the future so check
before you book.

Accommodation

Though Trinidad and Tobago aren't the most tourist-oriented islands in the Caribbean, there's no shortage of places to stay. Tobago has numerous luxury resorts, cosy guesthouses and private villas, with the largest concentration in the Crown Point area. In Trinidad, there is plenty of accommodation in Port of Spain – owing mostly to the annual Carnival invasion and regular business travellers – as well as guesthouses and hotels near most of the better beaches along the north coast. Trinidad's centre and south is less promising; with the exception of Mayaro Bay in the southeast, most options are expensive and geared towards oil workers and business travellers.

Accommodation in T&T is **cheaper** than you might expect for a Caribbean destination – ranging from as little as US$30 (£20) per night for a basic room with a fan in Port of Spain to US$60–80 (£35–55) for an air-conditioned unit with cable TV, and US$200/£120-plus for the top-notch places. Rates at most places in Trinidad change only at Carnival time, though business-oriented hotels often charge more in the week than at weekends. In Tobago, most places have two rates; one for the summer **low season** (mid-April to mid-Dec) and another for the winter **high season** (mid-Dec to mid-April). Many local hoteliers are open to a bit of haggling, however, particularly in the shoulder seasons (mid-April to July and Sept to mid-Dec), or if you plan to stay for more than two weeks. Trinbagonians always get rooms at a lower rate; this is normal practice, ensuring that resorts get a mix of local people and tourists. There are a couple of hidden extras to watch out for: **room tax** (ten percent) and **service charge** (ten percent) are added to quoted room rates at more expensive hotels, though not at guesthouses. Throughout the Guide, we have taken tax and service charges into account when quoting prices, but it's worth checking whether these charges have been included each time you rent a room. Note that we have also quoted high-season rates for accommodation in Tobago. It's also worth noting that while online accommodation sites such as ⓦbooking .com purport to offer discounted rates, their high surcharges often mean that small properties bump up their base rate for the site, and you'll

often get a cheaper stay by cutting out the brokers and booking directly.

Though it's advisable to **book ahead** during the busy times of Carnival (see p.34) – and Easter on Tobago – at other times you should have no problem finding suitable accommodation once you've arrived; staff at Tourist Office desks at Piarco and Crown Point airports (see p.78 & p.197) can direct you to a place that suits your plans and budget, and many hotels in Tobago offer free airport pick-ups.

Hotels

Most of T&T's resort-type **hotels** cluster around Tobago's better beaches, such as along the coast between Buccoo and Plymouth, where you'll find expansive, landscaped enclaves with private beaches, as well as ecohotels and holistic retreats. In between these are no-nonsense concrete blocks dedicated to the needs of the package tourist, and legions of eight- to-twelve-room properties with pastel decor, loud bedspreads and a pool. Thankfully, the all-inclusive trend that's swept through the rest of the Caribbean hasn't really caught on here. Though some larger properties offer all-inclusive plans, you can also stay on a room-only basis. You may be offered the option of a meal plan – the most common are CP (Continental; room and breakfast), MAP (Modified American; room, breakfast and dinner) or FAP (Full American; room and all meals including snacks and tea).

On both islands, large-scale hotels meet international standards in terms of **facilities**: air conditioning, TV (usually cable or satellite), telephone, wireless internet access, private bathroom with hot water and maybe a balcony, as well as restaurants, bars and sometimes a pool on site. However, most of the smarter Trinidad hotels cater largely to business travellers, so you won't find much in the way of organized entertainment or a holiday atmosphere – something that you'll find in abundance in Tobago.

ACCOMMODATION ALTERNATIVES

Useful websites that provide alternatives to standard hotel and hostel accommodation.
CouchSurfing ⓦcouchsurfing.org.
Vacation Rentals by Owner ⓦvrbo.com.
Airbnb ⓦairbnb.com.

Guesthouses, host homes and B&Bs

T&T's myriad small **guesthouses** are often great value for money and friendly places to stay. It's not compulsory for any guesthouse to be registered with the tourist board and many perfectly good ones are not; however, those that are have been inspected and approved according to labyrinthine standards. Being anything from a couple of rooms tacked on to a private home or a smoothly run nine-room establishment, guesthouses generally have less facilities than at hotels; many don't have a pool, and you could get a fan instead of air conditioning. There may also be no hot water, a shared bathroom, homelier decor and more of a personal touch. Prices at more basic options are lower than at hotels, though more upmarket ones often cost as much.

Many guesthouse (and even hotel) rooms include a kitchen or kitchenette (the latter consisting of a hot plate, fridge and sometimes a microwave) for roughly the same rate as a standard room. Most provide utensils; make sure that an inventory is taken in your presence to ensure that you are not held liable for breakages that occurred before you arrived.

Private **host homes** and **B&Bs** are inexpensive and generally excellent; neither charge room tax or VAT, and you may get more insight into local lifestyles and attitudes than you'd experience elsewhere. Both host homes and B&Bs are monitored and inspected by the Tourism Development Company (TDC), which also produces a list of registered establishments (see Ⓦ gotrinidadand tobago.com). You can also find places listed in the classified sections of local papers (see p.32), all of which are available online as well as in print. What you get for your money varies enormously; some offer air conditioning and an en-suite bathroom, whereas others are much more basic; and owners are often open to a bit of bargaining.

Villas, beach houses and long-term rentals

Most **holiday villas** rented to tourists are in Tobago and tend to have full staff and facilities such as a kitchen and pool. These options can actually be quite cost-effective if you're travelling in a group; plan on paying US$150 per night for the most basic villa to as much as US$1000 per night for something in the lap of luxury – those around the Mount Irvine golf course, for example. Most are privately owned but represented by websites or agencies such as Ⓦ vrbo.com; in Tobago, contact Island Investments, 30 Shirvan Rd, Scarborough (❶639 0929, Ⓦ islreal.com). You can also check the TDC website Ⓦ gotrinidadandtobago.com.

In Trinidad, **beach houses** are available in areas such as Mayaro and the Toco coast – generally geared to locals on a weekend break (you may have to bring your own bed linen and so on) – though you can get some real bargains by scanning the local papers. If you are planning to stay in Trinidad for a month or more, consider a furnished apartment, again best found via the newspaper classified ads.

Food and drink

A unique and addictive blend of African, Indian, Chinese, European and Latin American influences, the fantastic cuisine of Trinidad and Tobago is a highlight of any visit to the islands. It's hard to overemphasize the centrality of food to local culture; a true Trinbagonian would never lime (the local word for socializing) without a full stomach, and many leisure activities – beach days, river limes – revolve around the preparation and consumption of food and drink. It's rare to visit a private home without being offered something to eat, and you may be regarded as rude if you refuse, though it's not very likely that you'll want to.

Even in T&T's larger hotels and international-style restaurants, Trinbagonian cuisine hasn't been dumbed down for visitors, and you're likely to be offered dishes from the vast array of **local food**. Due to the islands' diverse heritage, "local" can mean anything from **Indian curry** and **roti** to **Creole coocoo** and **oil down** or Spanish and South

---

TAX AND TIPPING

The addition of a **tax** (up to fifteen percent) and **service charge** (usually ten percent) to your restaurant bill is standard, and is not usually included in prices given for individual dishes, making what seems a moderately priced meal considerably more expensive. If the service charge is included, you don't need to leave a tip.

American-style **pastelles** (cornmeal patties filled with ground meat or fish, olives and raisins, wrapped in a banana leaf and traditionally eaten at Christmas time).

Cooks in T&T have a far lighter hand with hot peppers than you might expect, preferring the delicate flavours of fresh herbs such as chives (aka spring/green onions), thyme and the ubiquitous coriander-like **chadon beni**. Heat is usually added later at the table, in liberal dashes of fiery **hot-pepper sauce**. If you don't like things too hot, remember to say so when buying takeaway, or your meal may be automatically smothered with pepper sauce. If you like things just a little spicy, ask for "slight pepper".

Eating out

There's a burgeoning **restaurant culture** in **Trinidad**'s urban areas, with Port of Spain and San Fernando in particular replete with everything from casual diners to world-class gourmet establishments, as well as some stylish places to enjoy Indian, Creole, Chinese and international cuisine. You'll also find a huge lunchtime variety in Trinidad's larger shopping malls, where food courts offer delicious curries, roti, Chinese staples, macaroni pie and lentil peas, potato or green-fig salad, Creole-style fish, chicken and the ubiquitous pelau alongside burgers, grilled meats and sandwiches.

In **Tobago**, Crown Point has a decent spread of restaurants, from Italian pizza joints to seafood, Creole cooking, curry and roti. If you're here in the low season (mid-April to mid-Dec), bear in mind that many kitchens close at around 9pm, or even open up for bookings only. Away from the southwest, most restaurants are small-scale affairs serving strictly seafood and Creole cuisine, though hotels do hold some more upmarket places to eat.

Breakfast

Breakfast is traditionally a hearty meal, designed to stand you in good stead for a hard day's work. Staples include spicy **fried fish**, **smoked herring** cooked up with onions and peppers (and sometimes egg), or **buljol**, a delectable blend of flaked saltfish, fresh onions, tomatoes, lime juice and sweet peppers, usually eaten with avocado and a couple of light, airy rolls called hops, or with coconut bake, a flat round bread made with grated coconut. It's ideally washed down with a steaming mug of sweet **chocolate tea**: fresh cocoa, spiced up with nutmeg, cinnamon and sugar. The most popular breakfast on the go, however, is doubles (see below): vendors do a brisk trade from as early as 5am.

Street food

T&T offer the best **street food** in the Caribbean, with everything from Indian specialities to gyro wraps, fried chicken and, of course, roti (see p.30); and as vendors are subject to stringent hygiene checks, eating on the hop doesn't constitute a health risk. In Trinidad, Port of Spain's street-food hotspots (all best after dark) are the Western Main Road in St James, Ariapita Avenue, the Queen's Park West end of the Savannah and Independence Square. In Tobago, there are a few doubles and roti vendors in Crown Point and Scarborough.

The most popular Indian snack is **doubles**, two pieces of soft, fried **bara** bread sandwiching a runny channa curry that's dressed with cucumber, pepper sauce and *kucheela* mango chutney, and usually sold in the mornings from streetside stalls noticeable for their long queues and stripy umbrellas. **Aloo pies** (flattened fried doughballs filled with spiced potato) are another popular snack, as are cheese, beef or fish versions. A little less substantial are the addictive **pholouri** (fried split-pea-flour doughballs served with tart and tasty tamarind curry sauce) or **sahina**, a ground channa and dasheen leaf fritter. Port of Spain's Savannah and most junctions along the Eastern Main Road are flanked by vendors selling small local **oysters**, served in a cup with a peppery, vinegary tomato sauce.

Creole street delicacies include **corn soup**, a thick and satisfying split-pea broth with vegetables, chunks of sweetcorn and mini dumplings. **Accra** is a peppery saltfish fritter, while **bake and shark** (see opposite) is available far beyond its traditional home, Maracas Beach.

TOP 5 STREET SNACKS

Corn soup Fortifying and delicious, great after a night out.

Doubles Delectable chick-pea delights, best at breakfast time.

Gyros Wraps of meat, fish or falafel are ubiquitous to the street-food scene.

Pies Filled with potato, beef or fish, and dressed with Trini chutney.

Pholouri Addictive doughballs with a spicy dipping sauce.

SHARK TALES

One of T&T's most popular street foods has long been **bake and shark**, slices of seasoned shark meat, served hot in a floaty fried bake and slathered in delicious chadon beni, tamarind and garlic sauces, and topped with fresh pineapple and salad. The bake and shark capital of Trinidad is Maracas Beach, where scores of vendors compete with stalwart operator *Richard's* to draw in the queues. Delicious as shark and bake may be, however, you might want to think twice before tucking in. Sharks are increasingly rare in Caribbean waters, as they are globally. Trinidad and Tobago hold the dubious honour of being the sixth-largest exporter of shark fins in the world, while overfishing and the practice of landing juvenile sharks has pretty much decimated the shark population in local waters. Sharks play a vital role in the already fragile ecosystems of the Caribbean Sea, and the decrease in their numbers is having dire consequences for the region's reefs and its fish populations. For this reason, T&T's environmentalists advocate asking for more **sustainable fish** with your bake: flying fish, mahi-mahi, carite and tilapia are all sound choices.

Fast food

Though international fast-food chains – particularly *Subway*, *Pizza Hut*, *Burger King* and *McDonald's* – are part of the scenery, **local outlets** still manage to draw the crowds: chicken chains *Japs* and *Royal Castle* are the Trinbagonian *KFC* equivalent, using a tasty blend of spices and herbs in the batter and serving flying-fish sandwiches and veggie burgers. *Joe's Pizza* (Trinidad only) is another good option, and also delivers.

Creole cooking

In T&T culinary terms, **Creole** refers to African-style cooking which has picked up many other influences along the way. Often served with coleslaw and a slice of *zaboca* (avocado), **pelau** is a classically Creole chicken dish, utilizing the "browning down" tradition of caramelizing meat in burnt brown sugar. Rice, pigeon peas, garlic, onions and pumpkin are then added and cooked down in coconut milk to delicious effect.

Browning is also used to make traditional **Sunday lunch** of baked chicken, usually served with rice, stewed peas, macaroni or potato pie and potato, pasta or green fig (banana) salad. Another Creole staple is **callaloo**: chopped dasheen leaves cooked with okra, pumpkin, coconut milk and occasionally crab meat, into a tasty, pleasantly slimy mixture that's sometimes puréed. It's often served with **coocoo**, a kind of cornmeal polenta flavoured with okra. Two dishes not for the squeamish are the highly spiced local **black pudding**, and **souse**, pigs' or chickens' feet marinated in lime juice and peppers, and served cold. A classic accompaniment to main meals is **oil down**: vegetables (particularly breadfruit or cassava) stewed in coconut milk and flavoured with pig tail.

Though increasingly rare these days, "**wild meat**" such as iguana, agouti, lappe, manicou, tattoo and quenk are considered a delicacy, and end up in the pot where available. Though a 2013–2015 hunting ban made it temporarily illegal to kill, eat or sell wild meat, it was still sold illicitly throughout the banned period; and though you could theoretically try it once the hunting season is reinstated, as it's slated to be in 2015, you might bear in mind that as many of these animals are endangered, it's more ethical to steer well clear.

Creole soups include **corn soup** (see opposite); **san coche**, a lentil soup cooked with pig tail; and cow-heel soup, thick with split peas and slowly cooked meat. **Fish broth** is a thin and delicious fortifying soup padded out with boiled green bananas and dumplings, while **pacro water** is similar but substitutes pacro (a mollusc known as chip-chip in Trinidad) for fish, and is touted as a strong aphrodisiac. Soups made from pumpkin, callaloo or pulses (red peas, black-eyed peas etc), often flavoured with pig tail, are also classic Creole creations.

Seafood is extremely popular and unfailingly good: from thick steaks of dense and delicious kingfish, grouper, tuna, cavalli, carite, barracuda and mahi-mahi/dolphin (the fish also known as "dorado", not the mammal), to smaller fillets of "red fish": moonshine, snapper, parrotfish, flying fish and tilapia. (Note that of these, mahi-mahi, flying fish, carite and tilapia are the most sustainable choices.) Creole-style fish is usually fried or stewed in a peppery tomato-based marinade of onion, sweet and hot peppers and garlic, while **curry crab and dumplin'** (crab cooked in its shell with a coconut curry sauce and served with boiled dumplings) is a marvellous Tobago speciality. Local **lobster** is usually doused in a lemon, garlic or herb butter, or sometimes curried.

Indian cooking

Though the obvious staple of Indo-Trinidadian cooking is **curry**, the T&T version is somewhat different to that served in India, using fresh hot peppers rather than chilli paste and a blend of curry powder that's unique to the islands. One of the most popular curry dishes is **duck**, which forms the centrepiece of the ever-popular Trini tradition of a "curry duck lime". Another mainstay is the vast array of **chutneys**, ranging from super-sweet to tart or peppery. Sweetly curried mango or *pomme cythere* on the seed, peppery **anchar** and **kucheela**, a hot mango pickle, are universally plopped into rotis, doubles and aloo pies.

Roti

The unofficial national dish, **roti** is a stretchy flat bread ("skin") used to wrap curried meat, vegetables or fish, a style of preparation that originated in Trinidad but is now popular across the Caribbean. There are several variations of **roti skins** including basic **dhalpuri** (with seasoned split peas layered into the dough); **sada** (more like a flatbread, it's cooked on a hot griddle, usually in the early morning, and served with sauteed fresh tomato or aubergine "choka"); and **buss-up-shut**, a thin, tasty shredded skin that resembles a torn cloth shirt and is used to spoon up mouthfuls of curry sold in "snackboxes". **Paratha** or **dosti** is a plain roti skin.

Roti fillings range from curried chicken and beef to conch, goat and shrimp. Most vendors include meat on the bone – if you don't fancy sucking out the marrow as the locals do, ask for "boneless". Common vegetarian fillings (also used to complement the meats) are channa (curried chickpeas) and potato, sweet pumpkin, bodi (green beans) and *bhaji* (local spinach). In a restaurant, you may be offered a bowl of peppery lentil dhal as an accompaniment.

Good roti shops abound in the capital, but most locals agree that the best roti is to be found in the Indian heartlands of Central or South Trinidad.

Fruit and vegetables

Local **fruit and vegetables** are plentiful and cheap, particularly if you buy from large markets. Some unusual local fruits include the super-sweet and extremely popular **sapodilla**, grey-brown and globular with gritty, sweet pulp, while cherry-sized chenets (also called guinep) have smooth green skin and a large seed with sweet, slightly acidic flesh. The knobbly green-and-brown skin of the **soursop** surrounds a delectable milky white pulp, often made into ice cream; its smaller cousin the **sweetsop** is less common. Look out also for the scrumptious **kymet**, a round, deep purple fruit with seeds that form a star shape when the fruit is cut in half. The round **pomme cythere** (or "pomsitae") is sweet and yellow when ripe, but is often eaten green with salt and hot pepper as "**chow**" – as is the star-shaped **carambola** (five finger), pineapple and unripe mango.

Green-skinned with a soft, aromatic orange flesh, **pawpaw** (papaya) is best eaten with a squeeze of fresh lime, while **bananas** (often called figs – look out for the tasty, tiny finger variety or young green bananas boiled and eaten as a savoury), **watermelon** and **pineapples** are all very common. **Citrus** is ever popular; you'll see lemons, limes and exceptionally sweet oranges and grapefruit, while **portugals** are easy-peel, thick-skinned mandarins.

Many varieties of **mango** grow profusely in rural areas, perfuming whole communities with the distinctive aroma of rotting fruit from April till August. The most popular (and expensive) type is the rosy, medium-sized julie, while the long stringy mango is best avoided unless you have dental floss handy.

The most frequent vegetables seen on the Creole dinner plate are boiled **root vegetables** (known as **blue food** or **ground provisions**) such as yam, the chewy, purple-tinted dasheen, the softer, white-coloured eddoe and cassava as well as sweet potato and regular potatoes. Dasheen leaves are cooked up with okra (ladies' fingers) to make callaloo (see p.29). You'll also see aubergine (locally called melongene or baigan), **christophenes** – pear-shaped and light green with a bland, watery taste similar to marrow – green **bodi** string beans and **breadfruit**, green and thick-skinned with clothy white flesh that can be baked, boiled or fried. **Plantain** is a popular accompaniment, a larger, denser member of the banana family; deliciously sweet when ripe, it's usually served fried or boiled, or as plantain chips, a healthier alterative to potato crisps.

Thanks to the **Indian influence**, pulses (referred to as peas) are widely used in the form of split-pea dhal; green lentils cooked with pumpkin and coconut; curried chickpeas (channa); and black-eyed peas or fresh and green pigeon peas cooked with rice and coconut milk.

Desserts and sweets

Though there are plenty of fantastic local puddings, from nutmeg-laced cassava **pone** to the classic **black cake** – a ridiculously rich, rum-soaked Christmas speciality – most restaurant dessert menus concentrate on serving international staples. Home-made **ice cream** is ubiquitous and delicious, however, with flavours such as cherry-sorrel or barbadine sold everywhere from street stalls to supermarkets.

As for sweets, look out for **bene balls**, tooth-crunching globes of sesame seeds and sugar, and **coconut cake**, a slab of shredded coconut boiled in sugar syrup and pink food colouring. **Tamarind balls** take a little getting used to, combining the tart taste of tamarind with sugar and salt, as do **salt prunes** (seasoned, sweet-and-sour prunes rolled in a dusty red colouring, often dropped into white rum) and **red mango**, which is green mango, well seasoned with spices and sugar and doused in bright red colouring. Other candies include **toolum**, a sticky ball of grated coconut, molasses and ginger, **pawpaw balls** (shredded green papaya boiled in sweet syrup and rolled in sugar) and gingery **fudge**, while there are hundreds of often sickly sugared and fried **Indian sweets**; kurma (sweet fried doughballs) are probably the most popular.

Drinking

Given T&T's capacity for consumption of beer, it's hardly surprising the national brews go down smoothly. The market leaders are **Carib**, a light, golden lager, and **Stag**, a little more robust and marketed as "a man's beer". Both taste best drunk very cold straight from the bottle (women are usually offered a straw), and both are available on draught. **Carib Pilsner Light** is a bearable if rather insipid lower-alcohol alternative. **Guinness** is brewed in Trinidad but, though bitter and refreshing, it bears little similarity to versions elsewhere. The sweeter Royal Extra or Mackeson **stouts** are excellent local alternatives.

Rum

Produced in Laventille by the House of Angostura, T&T's dark (or "red") and white **rum** are downed with equal enthusiasm, the white tending to be less abrasively strong than the overproof brands of other islands; regular rums are 43 percent alcohol. The most popular brands are the clear **White Oak** and its dark counterparts **Black Label** and **Royal**

Oak, all perfectly drinkable but best when mixed into a cocktail or with a chaser. Trinbagonian **rum punch** is delicious, using blended fruits, syrup, a sprinkle of ground nutmeg and, of course, a splash of the delectable **Angostura bitters**, also a worthy addition to any mixed drink. Most bars also offer the usual range of fruity cocktails – frozen margaritas are particularly good.

At 75 percent alcohol, the eye-watering **Forres Park puncheon rum** is perhaps best avoided, though it does add a kick to a rum cocktail.

Of the more high-end **aged rums**, **Angostura Single Barrel** matures in oak casks for five years and is a decent sipping or mixing rum; the bourbon casks used for **Single Barrel Premium** produce an agreeably buttery rum, and there's a very smooth seven-year-old in the range, too. The white **Reserva** is aged for three years and is a great cocktail base. Moving up a notch, **Angostura 1919** is a premium aged rum in a distinctive squared bottle; its counterpart, **Angostura 1824**, is heavy with molasses and is great drunk neat or over ice. Look out, also, for the fantastic **El Dorado** aged rums, produced in Guyana but widely available in T&T. If you're in T&T around Christmas, you might be offered **poncha crema**, an eggnog boosted with plenty of rum.

Wine

Sweet and strong **home-made wines** – cashew, banana, aloes, hibiscus and so on – are excellent if you can get your hands on them; **imported wine** is widely available by bottle and, less expensively, by box: larger supermarkets carry standard selections of Pinot Grigio, Chardonnay and Sauvignon Blanc; as well as Cabernet, Merlot and the like. Expect to pay a little more than you would at home, particularly if you order by the glass in a restaurant.

Soft drinks

Local soft drinks include the energy-boosting **Ginseng-Up**; delicious **Carib Shandy**, in sorrel and ginger varieties; **LLB**, a mix of lime, lemon and bitters that makes a good mixer for spirits; and **Bentley**, a refreshing bitter lemon soda. The best thing for the heat, however, is mineral-packed fresh **coconut water**, sold in water or jelly varieties. Vendors chop off the outer husk to expose a drinking hole (use a straw as the juice stains clothing), and then hack the nut in two so you can scoop out the delicious jelly. You can also buy bottles of fresh coconut water in supermarkets.

Made from boiled tree bark, cloves and aniseed, reddish-brown (sometimes yellow) **mauby** is a wonderfully bitter still drink. Other unusual options include tart, deep cerise **sorrel**, enjoyed at Christmas with a dash of rum. **Sea moss**, a white and glutinous preparation made from sea moss and milk, is widely believed to enhance sexual performance; other stamina-inducing potions are the "bomb", a blended concoction of Guinness, nutmeg and condensed milk or a carton of Supligen energy drink. Cinnamon- and nutmeg-infused carrot juice and **peanut punch**, blended with condensed milk, are a meal in themselves, sold from punch stalls across the islands.

The media

Dipping into the local media is an excellent way to acclimatize yourself with the nation's cultural and political life. Outspoken columnists, scurrilous newspaper headlines and the local programming available on TV all offer a fascinating picture of Trini society – especially during Carnival, when local stations preview costumes, road march songs and fetes, and the papers hotly debate the merits of the year's calypsos.

Print and online

Trinidad's main **daily newspapers** are the *Trinidad Guardian* (Ⓦ guardian.co.tt), a vaguely high-brow tome with a traditionally conservative attitude, the *Express* (Ⓦ trinidadexpress.com) and *Newsday* (Ⓦ newsday.co.tt); the latter two are picture-dominated with plenty of space for their sometimes outspoken columnists – look out especially for B.C. Pires's brilliant Friday column in the *Guardian*, and Kevin Baldeosingh's writing in the *Express*. All of the dailies have fat weekend editions with extended music, lifestyle and children's features, and salacious weekend **scandal rag** *Sunday Punch* remains very popular. **Tobago** boasts only one paper, *Tobago News* (Ⓦ thetobagonews.com), which is published on Fridays and concentrates on local sports, events and entertainment.

Sold at Piarco and Crown Point airports, supermarkets and book stores, **foreign magazines** – *Time*, *Newsweek*, *Cosmopolitan* and the like – are easy to find, but foreign newspapers – except for *USA Today* – are practically nonexistent. Of the **local glossies**, lifestyle and culture magazine

Mako is worth a look, while Carnival souvenir magazines provide a good insight into T&T's biggest festival; all are sold in pharmacies and supermarkets. Newspapers are sold at petrol stations, supermarkets, pharmacies and by street vendors.

Some of T&Ts most insightful and funny bloggers post stories at Ⓦ globalvoicesonline.org (search for Trinidad and Tobago); there's also plenty of good stuff online at Ⓦ meppublishers.com, home of the award-winning Air Caribbean inflight mag *Caribbean Beat*.

TV and radio

Trinidad and Tobago have several **TV stations**: TV6, TIC, ieTV, CNMG-TV and CMC TV, tending to show American soaps, sitcoms and game shows alongside educational and homegrown programmes. The main **local news** (with some international stories) is shown on TV6 and CNMG at 7pm and 10pm. The best local programming comes from the brilliant if cash-strapped **Gayelle**, which broadcasts only locally produced material: great if you can deal with the occasionally low production values. Cable TV is universally available (and where it isn't Direct TV satellites step in) showing a huge range of American channels and BBC World.

Radio is hugely popular, keeping the nation tapping its collective feet and serving as a source of information on upcoming events and parties. From November until Ash Wednesday, most stations are entirely devoted to soca and calypso, but after Carnival the mood switches abruptly and you'll hear reggae, R&B, hip-hop, rock and the inevitable "slow jams". The best stations for **contemporary local music** are Boom Champions 94.1 (Ⓦ boom championstt.com) Red 96.7 (Ⓦ red967fm.com), WEFM (Ⓦ 96wefm.com) With Energy For Music; (has a great breakfast show) and Slam 100.5 (Ⓦ slam1005 .com) while numerous others broadcast East Indian music, chutney and chat. Tobago's Radio Tambrin – 92.7FM – (Ⓦ tambrintobago.com) is an excellent way of keeping informed.

Festivals and public holidays

Trinbagonians have a well-deserved reputation for partying. No religious event passes without festivity, and on

the thirteen public holidays, banks and workplaces close and many take the opportunity to enjoy the country's beaches. Concerts are organized, shops have holiday sales and the newspapers are full of events and articles relating to the celebrations.

Public holidays embody T&T's cultural and ethnic diversity, acknowledging Hindus, Muslims, Baptists, Roman Catholics, trade unions and people of African and Indian descent. Every year there is a debate whether the Chinese should be given a day for Chinese New Year, and frequent discussion, too, as to whether the country has too many days off – but no politician is likely to risk offending a sector of the community by cancelling one. Though not officially recognized as a public holiday, **Carnival** functions like one: everything shuts down for the main days (the last Monday and Tuesday before Lent), and to a lesser degree for Ash Wednesday as well.

For more on what's on, visit ⓦ gotrinidadand tobago.com and ⓦ visittobago.gov.tt.

Festival calendar

JANUARY

Carnival season Trinidad and Tobago The festivities swing into action with the season's first fete, usually Soca in Moka in early Jan, and the fetes, calypso tents, steel pan competitions and general buzz build in intensity as the main days approach.

Harvest Festival Tobago ⓦ visittobago.gov.tt. Feasting and partying in Pembroke, Parlatuvier, Spring Garden and Mount Pleasant.

FEBRUARY

Harvest Festival Tobago ⓦ visittobago.gov.tt. Feasting and partying in Hope, Adelphi, Buccoo and Bon Accord.

Carnival The country's most famous festival (see pp.259–262), celebrated nationwide with fetes, pan and calypso competitions and costumed street processions. Dates are as follows: 2016 Feb 8–9; 2017 Feb 27–28; 2018 Feb 12–13; 2019 March 4–5.

MARCH

Harvest Festival Tobago ⓦ visittobago.gov.tt. Feasting and partying in Mount Saint George, Mason Hall and Roxborough.

Phagwah (see p.154) Celebrated in March or early April to honour the Indian tradition of Holi, which celebrates the arrival of spring, Phagwah is best experienced in central Trinidad. It's not a public holiday, but many Trinis of all backgrounds participate.

Goat Races Tobago (see p.212). Held at Mount Pleasant on Easter Monday, with the main event at Buccoo the following day, Tobago's goat races are one of the highlights of T&T's festival calendar.

Tobago International Game Fishing Tournament (ⓦ tgft .com). Big boats go after big fish from Charlotteville.

Shouter Baptist Liberation Day March 30. A relatively new public holiday in recognition of the African-based religion (see p.253) that suffered persecution in colonial Trinidad.

Turtle Season Trinidad and Tobago The leatherback laying season (see p.142) officially opens on March 1, with guided viewing sessions at Grande Riviere, Matura and Tobago's Turtle Beach.

Easter Weekend Trinidad As well as attending church and baking hot cross buns, Trinidadians indulge in the "beating of the bobolee", which involves pummelling an effigy of Judas Iscariot or, more usually these days, of any politician or public figure who's seen to deserve a good pounding. The skies above Port of Spain's Savannah also glitter with kites on Easter weekend, with a competition for the biggest and best.

APRIL

Harvest Festival Tobago ⓦ visittobago.gov.tt. Feasting and partying in Goodwood.

La Divina Pastora Held on the third Sunday after Easter in Siparia in southern Trinidad. The Black Virgin statue is carried in a procession through the town, while locals, decked out in new clothes, celebrate the event with feasting and merrymaking (see p.185).

PUBLIC HOLIDAYS IN T&T

Note that the Monday and Tuesday of Carnival as well as Ash Wednesday are also observed as public holidays. The dates of Hindu and Muslim festivals vary according to phases of the moon and other astronomical observations. When a public holiday falls on a Sunday, it is observed on the Monday, and when two holidays fall on the same date the following day is also given.

Jan 1 New Year's Day
March 30 Shouter Baptist Liberation Day
March/April Good Friday & Easter Monday
May 30 Indian Arrival Day
May/June Corpus Christi
June 19 Labour Day
Aug 1 Emancipation Day

Aug 31 Independence Day
Aug/Sept Eid ul Fitr
Sept 24 Republic Day
Sept/Oct/Nov Divali
Dec 25 Christmas Day
Dec 26 Boxing Day

CARNIVAL CALENDAR

Carnival and its associated events shift around each year depending on the days of the main parade, which takes place on the last Monday and Tuesday before Lent; **upcoming Carnival dates** are as follows: Feb 8 & 9 2016; Feb 27 & 28 2017; February 12 & 13 2018; March 4 & 5 2019; Feb 24 & 25 2020. The tourist board website ⓦgotrinidadandtobago.com has a fairly up-to-date **calendar of events**; the list below represents the main events, which appear in rough order of occurrence; Carnival season traditionally begins on January 1.

Opening of Calypso Tents Calypsonians battle it out in the "tents" – regular buildings, these days – for a place in the Calypso Monarch finals. The best-known tents are Calypso Revue, SWWTU Hall, Wrightson Road; Kaiso House, Queen's Park Savannah, at Dundonald Street; Klassic Russo, Port of Spain City Hall, Knox Street. Venues for Kaiso House and Klassic Russo are subject to change; contact the Trinbago Unified Calypsonians Organization (☎623 9660, ⓦtucott.com).

Panorama Steel pan bands play their composition of choice on the Savannah stage as they compete for the prestigious first prize. The semi-finals are the biggest deal, held on the Saturday two weeks before Carnival and featuring the "Greens" liming spot (entry fee applicable) as well as the actual pan competition. The finals take place on Carnival Saturday.

National Chutney Soca Monarch The best of Trinidad's popular chutney performers compete for the annual crown.

Kiddies' Carnival The children's costumes and characters rival those of the adults. There are three parades: the Red Cross Children's Carnival, held at the Savannah ten days before Carnival; the smaller St James Kiddies' Carnival on the following day; and the Junior Parade of the Bands from South Quay to the Queen's Park Savannah on Carnival Saturday.

Traditional/Individual Mas Held on the Sunday preceding Dimanche Gras, and the last Friday before Carnival Monday, with parades throughout the day and evening from South Quay to Adam Smith Square on Ariapita Avenue; this is the best place to see traditional Carnival characters such as Blue Devils, Dame Lorraine, Burrokeets, Fancy Sailors and Firemen. There are also traditional mas parades in St James (outside the Amphitheatre, Western Main Rd); check the press for dates and timings.

International Soca Monarch "Fantastic Friday" (the Friday before Carnival) sees the cream of the region's soca stars sing for the prestigious International Soca Monarch and Groovy Soca Monarch titles to a huge and packed crowd in the National Stadium.

Dimanche Gras Parades by the King and Queen of Carnival and the Calypso Monarch, finals staged at the Queen's Park Savannah on the Sunday before the main parades. Calypsonians go all-out with theatrical presentations of their compositions, while the sheer size of the King and Queen costumes, and the skill, sequins and special effects expended makes an amazing spectacle.

Jouvert (pronounced "joovay", from the French "Jour Ouvert", the break of day). Marking the beginning of the festivities, Jouvert is "dirty mas": raw, earthy and energetic. Wear as little as possible (no jewellery), join an organized band and expect to be covered in mud, paint, chocolate or even oil.

Carnival Monday Parade of the Bands Parades through the streets of Port of Spain from noon till dusk; most masqueraders don't wear their costumes on this day, instead getting creative with skimpy "Monday Wear".

Carnival Tuesday Parade of the Bands The full display of all the costumes. The route is the same as Carnival Monday; if you're not in a band, you can view the bands from the stands at the Queen's Park Savannah (for which you pay an entry fee), at the bleachers set up at the judging points at South Quay, Victoria Square on Park Street and Adam Smith Square on Ariapita Avenue at the Socadrome (see p.261) or anywhere along the parade route. Starts 7am.

Ash Wednesday The huge cooldown parties usually held at Maracas and Manzanilla have been scaled down in recent years; check the press for details of what's on, or follow the crowds and escape to Tobago.

Pont Fortin Borough Day More a series of events than a day, from exhibitions, parties and concerts to beauty pageants, all of which culminate in a Jouvert (see opposite) and mas (masquerade) on the streets in early May, followed by a beach cooldown the next day.

Pan in the 21st Century Steel band competition with a final held in the Jean Pierre Complex, Port of Spain.

Tobago Jazz Experience Ⓦ tobagojazzexperience.com. International and local artists performing at several venues across Tobago; recent performers have included John Legend, Randy Crawford, George Benson, Trey Songz, Chaka Khan and Emeli Sandé.

Bocas Lit Fest Ⓦ bocaslitfest.com. Brilliant literary festival, with workshops, readings, film screenings, open-mic sessions and book-signings across Port of Spain, plus the presentation of the coveted Bocas Prize.

MAY

Harvest Festival Tobago Ⓦ visittobago.gov.tt. Feasting and partying in Whim, Delaford, Belle Garden and Mason Hall.

Indian Arrival Day May 30. This public holiday commemorates the 1845 arrival of the first indentured Indian labourers in Trinidad.

JUNE

Harvest Festival Tobago Ⓦ visittobago.gov.tt. Feasting and partying in Lambeau and Bloody Bay.

We Beat Ⓦ webeat.org. Held in and around the Amphitheatre on Western Main Road in St James, Port of Spain, with concerts, parties and other events – expect lots of pan, too.

Corpus Christi June 10. A Catholic public holiday, celebrated with processions in small villages, though a quiet day in urban areas.

Labour Day June 19. A public holiday held in recognition of trade unions and workers. It is most publicly celebrated in Fyzabad in southern Trinidad, where the powerful Oil Workers' Union was established.

St Peter's Day June 29 (or nearest weekend). Celebrated in fishing communities throughout T&T, with huge fetes on the beaches and pots of fish broth sustaining hours of dancing. Charlotteville Fisherman's Fete at Man O'War Bay beach, Tobago, is the wildest all-night bash.

JULY

Harvest Festival Tobago Ⓦ visittobago.gov.tt. Feasting and partying in Castara and Black Rock.

Tobago Heritage Festival Ⓦ visittobago.gov.tt. Held in the last two weeks of July all over the island. Festivities include a traditional calypso competition, an "old-time" Tobago wedding ceremony and sports events.

AUGUST

Great Fete Tobago. Huge beach parties and concerts at Pigeon Point and other venues around the island.

Harvest Festival Tobago Ⓦ visittobago.gov.tt. Feasting and partying in Speyside.

Emancipation Day August 1. The 1834 abolition of slavery is commemorated with a procession through Port of Spain.

Great Race Speedboats navigate the dangerous currents of the Dragon's Mouth in a race from Trinidad to Tobago. It starts from Chaguaramas in the morning, but the festivities take place at the finishing line at Store Bay in Tobago in the afternoon.

Santa Rosa Festival Held the last week in August in Arima in Trinidad. Celebrates the culture and tradition of indigenous Amerindians with musical and acrobatic performances as well as obligatory feasting and street parties.

Independence Day August 31. Independence from Britain in 1962 is celebrated with flags and bunting on all public buildings, banks and institutions, while fetes and street parties feature soca and dub artists.

SEPTEMBER

Trinidad & Tobago Film Festival Ⓦ trinidadandtobago filmfestival.com. Held over two weeks, with films from all over the Caribbean, plus arthouse cinema from around the world, screened at MovieTowne Port of Spain, Chaguanas and Tobago.

San Fernando Jazz Festival Takes place over two days in late September on the San Fernando Hill

OCTOBER

Harvest Festival Tobago Ⓦ visittobago.gov.tt. Feasting and partying in Patience Hill.

Steel Pan Jazz Festival Ⓦ steelpanjazzfestival.com. Held at Port of Spain's Queen's Hall, this series of concerts and workshops at the beginning of the month features a fusion of foreign jazz masters and the hottest Trini steel bands.

Diwali (see p.155). An end-of-month festival honouring Mother Lakshmi, the Hindu goddess of light, via the lighting of deya candles throughout T&T. The National Council of Indian Culture stages nine days of shows, stalls and events.

Taste T&T Trinidad Culinary festival staged at the Hasely Crawford Stadium in Port of Spain, with cooking demonstrations, rum, wine and food tastings and live music.

Blue Food Festival Bloody Bay, Tobago. Held in celebration of the starchy tubers – yam dasheen, eddoes and the like which feature so heavily in Tobago cuisine, and which are cooked up in many imaginative and delicious ways: don't miss the dasheen ice cream.

NOVEMBER

Hosay (see p.73). This religious festival changes date every year according to the Islamic calendar, and is occasionally staged twice annually. The biggest event takes place in the Port of Spain suburb of St James, though it is also celebrated in Curepe, Tunapuna, Couva and Cedros.

Harvest Festival Tobago Ⓦ visittobago.gov.tt. Feasting and partying in Plymouth, Les Coteaux, Moriah and Scarborough.

DECEMBER

Parang season A tradition of nativity songs sung in Spanish with a mix of French patois dating from colonial days; performed by Parang groups (Oct–Dec) in bars, nightclubs and door to door, filling the streets with rich, haunting music.

Outdoor activities

A far cry from your average sun-sand-and-sea Caribbean destination, T&T offers plenty to do beyond the beach. The hugely rich natural environment affords many opportunities for birdwatching, hiking and freshwater swimming, either in rivers or in the pools below waterfalls, while offshore pursuits include an impressive range of watersports.

Birdwatching

Trinidad and Tobago ranks among the world's top ten countries in terms of **bird species** per square kilometre, boasting a diversity unmatched in the Caribbean: more than 430 recorded species and around 250 known to breed. Migrant species from South America are most common between May and September, while birds from North America visit between October and March. The dry months (Jan–March or April) are traditionally the most popular time for birders to visit; during the wet season, however, birds grab whatever chance they can to feed between showers, so you'll still see a lot of activity.

The best place to start in Trinidad is the Northern Range at the acclaimed **Asa Wright Nature Centre** (Ⓦasawright.org; see p.124); workers there assert that even on a relatively short visit you can see as many as 150 species. Other stops include the **Caroni Swamp** (see p.152), where you can take an afternoon boat tour to see the flocks of scarlet ibis, the national bird and most arresting of the 156 species that live in this swampland. The **Point-a-Pierre Wildfowl Trust** (see p.158) is an important waterfowl conservation centre nestling amid an industrial wasteland, with a successful breeding programme and the opportunity to see ibis up close.

The best **book** to bring is Richard French's encyclopedic *Guide to the Birds of Trinidad and Tobago*, which describes calls as well as plumage, habitats and behaviour. Online, visit Trinidad Birding (Ⓦtrinidadbirding.com). Plenty of tour companies and guides specialize in birding tours (see pp.38–39 for details). A short list of **good places to go birdwatching** in Trinidad include the Aripo Savannahs and Arena Dam, just south of Arima, (p.162); Mount St Benedict (p.128); Brasso Seco, off the Arima–Blanchisseuse Road (p.121); Nariva Swamp on the east coast (p.167); and Oropuche Lagoon in the southwest (p.181). Note that permits are needed for some of these sites; the guides listed on pp.38–39 can arrange these for you.

In Tobago, head for Little Tobago (or Bird of Paradise Island) on the windward coast (see p.241) to see sea birds in their natural environment; the Bon Accord Lagoon (see p.203), Adventure Farm (p.218) and the Grafton Caledonia Bird Sanctuary (p.216) are also fine birdwatching sites. At the protected Tobago Forest Reserve (see p.234), there are plenty of well-trained guides to accompany you.

Hiking

Trinidad and Tobago are ideal for **hiking**, despite the heat – the best plan is to start early and cover plenty of distance before midday, or choose a hike that goes through forest. You don't have to be supremely fit for most trails, nor do you need special equipment. In Trinidad, there is excellent hiking to be had in the forests of the Northern Range especially around Paria and Brasso Seco (see p.122); or the Chaguaramas hills. Of the numerous waterfall hikes, Guanapo Gorge (see

---

TOP 5 WATERFALLS

Argyle, Tobago (see p.237). Tobago's best waterfall, with several tiers and some nice swimming pools, and just a short walk from the coast road to boot.

Avocat, Trinidad (see p.118). One of Trinidad's most accessible falls, with a twelve-metre drop and a sizeable pool for swimming.

Guanapo Gorge, Trinidad (see p.134). A thirty-metre-high gorge carved out of the granite with numerous little falls along the way.

Paria, Trinidad (see p.119). A couple of hours' walk along the coast from Blanchisseuse takes you to pristine Paria beach, with a pretty cascade just inland in which to wash off the salt.

Rio Seco, Trinidad (see p.138). A forty-minute walk through stunning forest, Trinidad's most beautiful waterfall offers a deep emerald-green pool swathed by lush foliage.

p.134) is particularly spectacular. The best hiking in Tobago is to be had in the rainforest reserve (see p.234).

Don't hike alone. In addition to incidents of robberies on remote trails, there is no one to provide assistance should you run into problems; experienced local hikers always set out with two or more people. Plenty of tour companies provide private hiking trips (see p.38), but another, less expensive option is to join one of the excellent **local groups** on their regular weekend jaunts into rural areas, such as Hike Seekers (check hikemaster Laurence Pierre's Facebook group for details): you assemble at 7am, pay around TT$50 and set off. The group can normally arrange transport for you if you don't have your own (call ahead), though you must provide your own food and water. Bear in mind, though, that group sizes can be large. Many other groups set out each weekend; scheduled hikes are posted in the "what's on" sections of the daily newspapers, including those by the hundred-year-old Trinidad and Tobago Field Naturalists' Club (☎687 0514, ⓦttfnc.org), a slightly less visitor-friendly group that hike on the last Sunday of each month, leaving from Lower St Vincent Street in Port of Spain at 6.30am (TT$30). Their *Trail Guide* (see p.278) makes essential reading, describing fifty walks in minute detail. You could also check out **hashing**, a kind of cross-country race (which can be done as a walk) with lots of beer and rum drinking; if you want to have a go, contact the Port of Spain Hash Harriers (ⓦposhhh.org).

Be sure to abide by **hiking etiquette**: stick to paths and trails wherever possible, which avoids soil erosion and safeguards you from getting lost; bring rubbish – including cigarette butts – home with

TOP 5 TOBAGO DIVE SPOTS

Japanese Gardens, Speyside (see p.241). Gorgeous hard and soft corals.

Kelliston Drain, Speyside (see p.241). Home to the world's largest brain coral and frequented by manta rays.

London Bridge, Charlotteville (see p.241). Underwater arch with whooshing currents and lots of fish.

M.V. Maverick, Mount Irvine (see p.241). Purposely sunk in 1997, and home to spectacular coral and bonito.

Sisters Rocks, Parlatuvier (see p.233). Exciting drift diving and large pelagic fish including hammerheads.

you, and bury used toilet paper; do not discard matches or cigarettes and make sure any fires are completely extinguished; and finally, don't collect plant or wildlife specimens.

In terms of equipment, **sturdy shoes** with good grip will suffice if you don't have boots, though trainers work as a last resort; and always wear socks to protect against blisters and ticks. If hiking along a river-course, stout sandals are your best bet. Wear long trousers or leggings to protect against nettles, razor grass and insects (tuck trousers into socks); a long-sleeved shirt may also be advisable. A **hat** is good protection against sun and rain, and a light **waterproof** is useful in rainy season. Jeans are best avoided as they quickly become uncomfortable if wet. A dip is very often on the agenda, so wear **swimming gear**; a set of spare clothes left in the car is a good idea for when you finish walking.

T&T'S BEACHES

Maracas is Trinidad's most popular beach thanks to excellent facilities and a swathe of fine yellow sand and cool, clear green water; several more stunning places to swim lie a few miles down the road at **Las Cuevas** and **Blanchisseuse**, though all are sometimes subject to rough seas and undertows. Away from the oil refineries, many parts of the south coast offer fabulous swimming as well, while the east coast boasts the fabulously scenic **Manzanilla** and **Mayaro**. Most agree, though, that T&T's best beaches are in Tobago, where the water is calmer and tourist infrastructure more developed. The epitome of a Caribbean seashore, **Pigeon Point** is the queen of them all, with crystal-clear water, white sand and pretty palm-thatched gazebos, though its overt commerciality rather mars the spot. Nearby **Store Bay** and **Mount Irvine** are also lovely, but the undeveloped allure of **Castara**, **Parlatuvier**, **Englishman's Bay** and **Pirate's Bay** on the leeward side are far more stunning.

Bear in mind that undertows and strong currents make many of Trinidad's (and some of Tobago's) beaches risky; yellow and red flags indicate safe areas, in their absence, don't swim until you've checked with someone local.

Watersports

While **snorkelling** and **scuba diving** are popular on both islands, they are far better in **Tobago**, where the water is clearer away from the sediment-heavy currents from the South American mainland. The best dive spots are centred around Speyside on the windward coast, where you can see pristine reefs and a host of fish, including deep-water manta rays and the odd shark. Other top spots are offshore Charlotteville and the Sisters Rocks on the leeward side, as well as the Shallows or Flying Reef at Crown Point; Buccoo Reef remains popular, as the disintegrating coral sadly reveals. Everywhere, you'll see a dazzling variety of fish, from barracuda and grouper to angel, parrot, damsel and butterfly fish as well as spiny sea urchins and lobster nestled among the coral. Throughout the Guide, we have listed reputable dive operators (most of whom also rent snorkelling gear); for more details on **prices**, see p.241.

Most of the larger Tobago hotels have all you need in the way of **watersports** – kayaks, small sailboats, windsurfing and so on, and there's an excellent watersports outlet, Radical Sports, at Pigeon Point beach. In Trinidad, Chaguaramas is the main watersports area, where you can kayak and stand-up paddleboard, while there's also the option of wakeboarding, waterskiing and wakesurfing offshore of Port of Spain.

During the winter, big breakers – especially around Mount Irvine in Tobago and Toco in Trinidad – make ideal conditions for **surfing**. You can rent boards in Tobago, but in Trinidad you'll probably need to bring your own; check with the Surfing Association of Trinidad and Tobago (🌐 surftt.org) for details and further contacts.

T&T also boasts excellent **sport fishing** at around US$300 for a half day and US$600 for a full day – though not cheap, many boats accommodate up to six, and rods, tackle and bait are included. You're pretty much guaranteed some excitement; main catches include marlin, sailfish, tuna and dolphin. Boats for charter are listed throughout the Guide wherever available, and if you want more information about sport fishing, contact the Trinidad and Tobago Game Fishing Association (🌐 ttgfa.com).

Tour operators in Trinidad and Tobago

Tour companies' offerings range from eco-oriented hiking, **birdwatching trips** and kayaking

to more conventional **driving tours** of the islands' "highlights": the list below represents the very best of the bunch. We've specified whether each company is based in Trinidad or Tobago; most offer trips primarily in their home island, plus a few basic options in their sister isle. Note that you'll often get a reduced rate if you book in groups of four or more; some operators will not set out with less than four in any case. In addition to those listed below, try Cristo Adonis (☎664 5976 or ☎488 8539), whose Carib descent has ensured a thorough knowledge of Amerindian culture as well as medicinal plants and mountain trails.

Additional tour operators in Tobago are detailed on pp.202–203.

TOUR OPERATORS

TRINIDAD

Avifauna Tours Port of Spain ☎ 633 5614 or ☎ 477 2650, 🌐 rogernecklesphotography.com. Trini-English owner Roger Neckles is one of T&T's most respected wildlife photographers, and his tours – from Asa Wright to Nariva and Aripo Savannah, and Tobago – are conducted in a comfy a/c SUV and are excellent for ornithologists, photographers and amateur birdwatchers alike. US$100–150 per person.

Banwari Experience Bourg Malatress, Lower Santa Cruz, Trinidad ☎ 675 1619, ☎ 681 2393 or ☎ 223 1657, 🌐 banwaricaribbean.com. Wide-ranging company offering sightseeing throughout Trinidad and Tobago, plus a few novel options – Carnival, river limes, sports, beach picnics, shopping, hikes and waterfalls. From US$80.

Caribbean Discovery Tours c/o Stephen Broadbridge, 9b Fondes Amandes Rd, St Ann's, Port of Spain ☎ 620 1989 or ☎ 339 1989, 🌐 caribbeandiscoverytours.com. Entertaining, informative hikes plus safaris aboard a Land Rover, all with a birdwatching and animal-spotting slant. One of the best for Nariva, as well as Brasso Seco/Asa Wright and Northern Range waterfalls/hikes, nights in host homes and Paramin. Central Trinidad options include Caroni Swamp, birdwatching and rare-plant spotting at Aripo Savannah, as well as the usual Pitch Lake trip in south Trinidad there's an Icacos tour with visits to small-scale soap and coconut-oil makers, and wetland birdwatching. Day tours US$100 per person, including lunch and transfers.

Chaguaramas Development Authority Airways Rd, Chaguaramas ☎ 634 4364 or ☎ 634 4349, 🌐 chagdev.com. Waterfall and walking tours around Tucker Valley, as well as trips "down the islands", including Gasparee caves and hiking on Chacachacare. Transport to and from Chaguaramas and lunch/refreshments aren't included. Tours cost TT$30–220; see p.95 for more details.

Ieri Nature Adventures Arima ☎ 667 5636 or ☎ 685 6206, ✉ ierinatureadventures@hotmail.com. Dynamic guide Ivan Charles is a former national road cyclist, and offers both relaxed road trips and more hardcore mountain biking, plus tours covering most of Trinidad's natural attractions, from expert hiking adventures to Northern Range peaks and waterfalls, Tamana caves, kayaking at Caroni Swamp and visits to turtle-nesting beaches (including a two-night camp on a nesting beach). All-inclusive full-day trips from US$80 per person.

Indiversity Tours Port of Spain ☎ 743 1604, ✉ indiversity @gmail.com. As well as running a destination management company, owner Jalaudin Khan offers thoughtful historical and heritage tours that offer insight into cultural sights islandwide, especially Hindu temples, mosques and out-of-the-way places in the underexplored south. Hiking, birding and arts-based trips are also available. Full-day tours from US$80.

In-Joy Tours 2 Himorne Court, Hibiscus Drive, Petit Valley ☎ 633 4733 or ☎ 753 2775, ⓦ injoytours.com. Great option for "down the islands", trips take in Gasparee caves plus swimming and relaxation at Chacachacare or Monos islands. Other possibilities include Trinidad's National Museum and Maracas Bay; panyard tours, the Pitch Lake and other things south; and a day-trip to Tobago. Carnival packages available. Tours US$40–100.

Island Experiences 11 East Hill, Cascade, Port of Spain ☎ 621 0407 or ☎ 756 9677, ⓦ islandexperiencestt.com. Lively and knowledgeable eco-cultural tours led by charming, knowledgeable guides who provide an excellent insight into Trinidadian life; groups are kept small and itineraries personalized. Great for mas camps and panyards at Carnival, and evening and daytime city tours that provide a thorough grounding in the art of liming, including live calypso and steel pan, as well as bars and clubbing if the mood takes you. Daytime excursions combine stock stopoffs such as Asa Wright or Caroni with more unusual places such as a steel pan maker to see the instruments being produced, or to St James for roti and a bar lime. Other tours include the Pitch Lake and San Fernando, or Chaguanas markets and Felicity pottery. German- and English-speaking guides available. Half-day and evening tours US$45, full-day from US$80.

Limeland Tours Old Plum Rd, Manzanilla ☎ 668 1356 or ☎ 774 3438, ⓦ limeland-tours.com. Tours are led by a very personable former sport fisherman turned wildlife lover who lives near Nariva and has an exhaustive knowledge of the area's trails and wildlife – one of the best for the area, with the option to look for whatever wildlife you're interested in, be it manatees or monkeys. Also offers trips to Tamana caves and around the Manzanilla area. Full-day tours from US$95.

Paria Springs Tours 1 Mar Che Rd, St Ann's ☎ 620 8240, ⓦ pariasprings.com. Excellent and well-informed birdwatching and eco-adventure tours with experienced naturalist, Courtenay Rooks. Options include birdwatching all over Trinidad, Northern Range waterfalls, Tamana bat caves, adventurous and soft mountain-bike excursions (with tuition if needed), plus lovely kayak paddles "down the islands" and to Caroni Swamp. For the more adventurous, there's wakeboarding, waterfall rappelling and rock climbing, too. From US$85 per person.

TOBAGO

NG Nature Tours ☎ 660 5463 or ☎ 754 7881, ⓦ newtongeorge.com. A fantastic birding guide, Newton George offers tours for both serious birdwatchers and those with just a passing interest, pointing out hard-to-see birds with the aid of a light

pen. Trips cover the Forest Reserve, Little Tobago, Bon Accord Lagoon, Grafton Caledonia Bird Sanctuary and the Magdalena Grande wetlands, and there are also some ornithological Trinidad options. Full-day tours US$75–95.

Peter Cox Wildlife Tours ☎ 751 5822 or ☎ 294 3086, ⓦ tobago naturetours.com. One of the top birding guides on Tobago, with Main Ridge walks that include a night-time option (great for seeing nocturnal creatures such as armadillos and owls) and trips tailored for children in which you explore forest rivers and pools home to wabeen and crayfish. All the birding hotspots are covered too, from Little Tobago to the Magdalena Grande wetlands, as are Argyle Falls and the Tobago Cocoa Estate, Scarborough market and Fort King George, round-the-island sightseeing and turtle-watching during the laying season. Full-day tours US$90–115.

Yes Tourism ☎ 357 0064, ⓦ yestourism.com. A reliable all-round operator, offering sightseeing tours around Tobago (Caribbean coast, rainforest walks, Speyside glass-bottom boat to Little Tobago, Tobago Cocoa Estate etc plus waterfalls and shopping trips). Full-day tours US$95–125.

Sports

Sport is as much a national pastime as liming, and Trinbagonians are justifiably proud of their country's sporting achievements, in cricket, track and field – and football, since the Soca Warriors competed in the 2006 World Cup.

Cricket

Cricket is a national passion in T&T and the source of much debate; when the West Indies team is playing, radios everywhere are tuned in, regardless of the Windies' uninspiring performances of recent years. As long as you're not foolish enough to criticize legendary batsman Brian Lara, the "Prince of Port of Spain", mentioning cricket to any Trinbagonian is pretty much guaranteed to break the ice.

Big matches, from Tests to One-Day events, take place at the **Queen's Park Oval** in Port of Spain, and are great fun even if you're not a cricket fan; soca blares in the intervals, plenty of cold Carib gets downed, and fans are animated to say the least. Tickets are available from the Queen's Park Cricket Club, 94 Tragarete Rd, Port of Spain; those that like to party as they watch head for the all-inclusive "Trini Posse" stand (☎622 2295, ⓦqpcc.com). Match schedules are advertised in the media; for further information, contact the Trinidad and Tobago Cricket Board at Couva (☎636 1577, ⓦ ttcb.co.tt).

THE RULES OF CRICKET

The basic rules of cricket are by no means as complex as the official twenty-page rule book suggests. There are two teams of eleven players. A team wins by scoring more runs than the other team and dismissing the opposition; a team could score many more runs than the opposition, but still not win if the last two enemy batsmen doggedly stay "in" (ensuring a draw). The match is divided into innings, when one team bats and the other team fields. One-day matches have one innings per team, Test matches have two.

The aim of the fielding side is to limit the runs scored and get the batsman "out". Two players from the batting side are on the pitch at any one time. The fielding side has a bowler, a wicketkeeper and nine fielders. Two umpires adjudicate whether a batsman is out. Each innings is divided into **overs**, consisting of six deliveries, after which the wicketkeeper changes ends, the bowler is changed and the fielders move positions.

The batsmen score runs either by running up and down from wicket to wicket (one length = one run), or by hitting the ball over the boundary rope, scoring four runs if it crosses the boundary having touched the ground, and six runs if it flies over. A batsman can be dismissed by being "clean bowled", where the bowler dislodges the bails of the wicket; by being "run out", when one of the fielders dislodges the bails with the ball while the batsman is running; by being caught out, when one of the fielding side catches the ball after the batsman has hit it; or by "LBW" (leg before wicket), where the batsman blocks with his leg a delivery that would otherwise have hit the stumps.

These are the rudiments of a game whose beauty lies in its **skills and tactics**. The captain, for example, chooses which bowler (spin or fast) to play and where to position his fielders to counter the strengths of the batsman, the condition of the pitch and a dozen other variables. Cricket also has a poetry in its **esoteric language**, used to describe such things as fielding positions ("silly mid-off", "cover point", etc) and types of bowling delivery ("googly", "yorker" and the like).

Football

Football (soccer) is extremely popular in T&T, with fanatical support for the national team, the Soca Warriors (W socawarriors.net) since the team's spirited performance at the 2006 World Cup in Germany. Major matches take place at the National Stadium on Wrightson Road, Port of Spain; for more information, contact the T&T Football Federation (T 623 9500, W ttffonline.com).

Basketball

Basketball is also a major sport, with US games screened regularly on TV and several local teams that compete in the National Championships. Games are held at the National Stadium – check the website (W nbftt.net) or Facebook page of the National Basketball Federation of T&T for more info.

Other activities

T&T boasts some lovely **golf courses**, most with in-house caddies and carts for rent. In **Trinidad**, the best is St Andrew's in Moka, Maraval (T 629 2314, W golftrinidad.com). The only public course is the nine-hole Chaguaramas Golf Course,

Bellerand Road, Chaguaramas (T 634 4227, W chagdev.com). In **Tobago**, there's the pristine 18-hole course operated by the *Magdalena Grande* hotel (T 387 0288, W magdalenagrand.com) on the wind-blown Atlantic coast; and the eighteen palm-dotted holes attached to the *Mount Irvine* hotel (T 639 8871, W mtirvine.com). All but the Chaguaramas course host professional and amateur tournaments. For more information, contact the Trinidad and Tobago Golf Association (T 629 7127, W ttgolfassociation.org).

Cycling is very popular; for details email the Trinidad and Tobago Cycling Federation (E ttcyclingfederation@yahoo.com), or check their Facebook page. Major **horse racing** meets take place at the Santa Rosa Race Track, Arima (W arimaraceclub.com). Highlights of the racing calendar include the Midsummer Classic, run on the first Saturday in July, and the Derby Stakes, run in August or September. Fitness freaks will find Trinidad well equipped with **gyms** (packed in the run-up to Carnival, so people look good in the skimpy costumes). **Tennis courts** are to be found at the *Hilton*, *Cascadia* and *Crowne Plaza* hotels in Port of Spain and the *Mount Irvine*, *Turtle Beach*, *Crown Point Beach* and *Grafton* hotels in Tobago; the latter has air-conditioned squash courts, as does the *Cascadia* in Port of Spain.

Culture and etiquette

Despite the wild bacchanalia of Carnival, T&T is generally a friendly but conservative society. As a foreigner you will be treated politely and the same will be expected in return.

Outside the cities, it's usual to acknowledge people passing on the street with a nod of the head, "good day" or just "alright". Before starting any conversation, whether in a shop or asking for directions, local custom is to say "good morning" or "good afternoon"; the same goes when entering, say, a maxi. Everything is slowed down in T&T; people take longer to interact, to converse and to serve you in a shop or a diner. If you arrange to meet someone, be prepared to wait – being on time in T&T may well mean being 30–45 minutes after the time originally arranged, with no apology. Don't get frustrated; be flexible and tolerant and you will save yourself a lot of stress. Inevitably, though, if you follow suit and turn up late, you'll confront an irritated Trinbagonian who's made the effort to comply with "foreign" timekeeping.

Religious faith holds strong in T&T, especially in Tobago, and this affects islanders' day-to-day behaviour. Though you may see overtly sexual dancing and hear lewd lyrics, local people are still quite morally conservative; public drunkenness, for example, is very much frowned upon. Couples in T&T tend to be very undemonstrative in public, and the highly erotic-looking dancing ("wining") you'll see is usually between friends or couples. As a foreigner you may well be asked to dance by a stranger, but there's no necessity to demonstrate your wining skills unless you choose to – and twerking against several new acquaintances in one night will probably raise a few eyebrows. Note also that while local women may accept a dance with a stranger, she may just give him a "small wine", dancing for a while so as to be polite but breaking off after a minute or so. Of other social conventions, beachwear is restricted to the beach; nude and topless bathing is not allowed. Bear in mind also that camouflage clothing is illegal in T&T (a law passed following the 1990 coup in an attempt to prevent civilians from impersonating the military). The ban is most often enforced at airport arrivals halls, where offending items are confiscated, but camo (even a bikini or kids' hat) shouldn't be worn outdoors and is best left behind. Using obscene language in public is illegal and though the law is not often enforced, it is nevertheless important to be aware of it.

Finally, it is illegal to **smoke** in all enclosed public spaces in T&T– something adhered to rigidly.

Crime and personal safety

Despite the dire (and massively overblown) warnings on government travel advisories, most visits to Trinidad and Tobago are trouble-free – crime is far more of an issue for those living here than it is for tourists. There is the odd incident involving visitors in Tobago, but as long as you choose secure accommodation and use your common sense – not walking alone on deserted beaches or exploring downtown areas by night – there's no reason to feel intimidated.

In Port of Spain, Independence Square and the area east of Charlotte Street around the market are the most raucous parts of downtown, while there is more **crime** – much of it violent – further east in the hillside suburb of Laventille and nearby Morvant and Beetham than in any other part of the country. These are not places for the casual visitor and should usually be avoided. In Tobago, there have been **robberies** over the years, some of them violent, at villas and guesthouses – especially in Buccoo, but also Mount Irvine and Charlotteville; wherever you stay, make sure you lock up properly at night and don't sit on open verandas well into the wee hours.

If you use your common sense, and take the same precautions you would in any strange

---

TIPPING

Private- and route-taxi drivers in Trinidad don't expect a tip, but in Tobago, where many make their living from tourists, a ten-percent tip is standard. Restaurants often add a service charge into the bill; if this is the case, a tip is not necessary but will always be welcomed – if it's not included, 10–15 percent is the norm. If you're staying in a hotel, you might consider leaving some dollars for the chambermaid.

environment, you should find that the prospect of trouble is minimal wherever you are in T&T. **Avoid walking alone** or in small groups late at night or on deserted beaches and forest trails, keep flashy jewellery to a minimum (especially during Carnival), think twice before accepting lifts from strangers and don't go telling everyone where you're staying – or letting new acquaintances into your hotel room. Carry only as much cash as you need, get small notes when changing money so that you don't have to pull out wads of hundreds, and never leave belongings unattended on a beach or in a car. Have your **valuables** locked in the safes that many hotels have in their guest rooms.

In rural areas, you have little to fear – doors are still sometimes left unlocked in the countryside – but as a foreigner you may be a target. If you're unlucky enough to be the victim of theft or other offences, report the incident immediately, as you'll need a police report to make any insurance claim. Local officers are generally happy to help, though things will take longer than you're used to. To call the police in an **emergency**, dial ❼999; for fire ❼990, and ambulance ❼811.

Harassment

Proud to hail from a Caribbean nation that doesn't depend on holidaymakers for the bulk of its revenue, Trinidadians are far more likely to avoid tourists than hassle them; even in more touristy Tobago, **harassment** hasn't reached the proportions you encounter in more established Caribbean destinations. Many Tobagonians nonetheless make their living from foreign visitors; you'll be approached on the beach by vendors selling crafts or boat trips, but most are polite and rarely pushy if you're not interested.

Women travellers

Like other Caribbean countries, T&T has a predominantly **macho culture**. Trinbagonian women usually go out in groups or with their partners, so be prepared to meet surprised reactions if you're a woman travelling on your own. As independent travellers are still a novelty in the country, visiting solo will lead to a greater degree of attention than in Europe, the US or Australia – usually verbal comments or innuendo and rarely threatening: it's customary in T&T to be friendly to strangers, acknowledge people passing in the street and even make small talk. As a woman you'll be expected to be flattered by this "sweet talk", and comments are often humorous – though also very direct and perhaps somewhat lewd. Foreign women, of all ethnicities, usually get more of this attention.

The ritual of women visiting the Caribbean to find romance (or, more prosaically, "hot tropical sex") is so entrenched that solo female travellers may well be approached by men with this in mind – unsurprisingly, given many foreigners fly in (particularly to Tobago) with just this in mind. If sex is not on your agenda, simply say no and mean it.

Drugs

Visitors to the Caribbean often assume that all West Indians move around in a permanent haze of marijuana smoke. Though many islanders do of course indulge, this stereotype is hardly the reality. **Cannabis** (weed, herb, ganja) is illegal to grow or possess in Trinidad and Tobago, and penalties are severe. Tourists caught in possession are likely to be deported without a moment's notice, and jail sentences and fines are frequently imposed; the excuse that "it's OK at home to carry a little marijuana for personal use" is not acceptable. Local people who smoke do so with caution, shutting windows and doors and lighting incense. You probably will be offered weed (sometimes ready-rolled), particularly in Tobago. If you don't want it, refuse politely and firmly.

Many visitors do choose to indulge, of course, and if you do, bear in mind that in Tobago particularly, you will need to be extremely discreet. Don't light up in the street, or in nightclubs and popular beaches, and never leave paraphernalia lying around your hotel room.

Marijuana is not the only illegal drug with a following; powder and, particularly, **crack cocaine** are common in T&T. Geographically well placed as a trans-shipment point from South America, both Trinidad and Tobago have been badly affected; narcotics police patrol stretches of coastline, and there are "crack blocks" in every large town. You are more likely to be offered the drug in Tobago, where some visitors' taste for cocaine has provided a lucrative market.

Finally, do not consider smuggling drugs in or out of the country under any circumstances; customs officers have seen all the methods of concealment before and the chances are that you will be caught and imprisoned.

Shopping

Trinidad and Tobago offer a wide variety of souvenirs and products to suit every budget, from woven palm hats to expensive jewellery in Port of Spain's malls. Local artists create fine woodcarvings, shell and bead jewellery, paintings and beaten copper pieces, as well as lovely leather sandals. T&T also produces great music and has exceptionally talented writers – purchasing a few books and CDs will enable you to carry a little local culture back home.

Port of Spain and San Fernando have Trinidad's widest variety of **shops**, but there's a lot less on offer in Tobago, where you should head for Lowlands Mall or central Scarborough. Opening hours are generally Monday to Friday 8am to 5.30pm and Saturday 8am to 5pm; malls are usually open from 10am until 8 or 9pm, while supermarkets open 8am–8pm daily. Opening times are often variable, depending on the individual shop and mood of the shopkeeper.

Prices are generally higher in Tobago than in Trinidad. Paintings and woodcarvings may seem expensive in comparison with other local produce, but these works of art are unique and prices are far lower than in art galleries back home. For bargains, check out streetside vendors and small backstreet shops – souvenir shops, boutiques and malls have higher prices. Bargaining is conducted to a certain extent with street and beach vendors, but not in shops.

T&T's rich musical culture (see pp.263–268) has spawned an astonishing variety of styles – steel pan, calypso, soca, rapso, chutney, dub and parang – and produced many marvellous songs with strong lyrics and powerful rhythms. The best places to buy **music** are in Trinidad: in Port of Spain try Crosby's, at 54 Western Main Rd in St James, or Rhyner's, 54 Prince St (Wrhyners.com), while roadside vendors sell inexpensive pirate copies of popular reggae and soca tracks. In Tobago, try the stalls lining Wilson and Milford roads in Scarborough. You can also buy Trini music online at Wtrinidadtunes.com.

Local **book stores** are usually full of US titles and schoolbooks, though there are some decent stores in Port of Spain (see p.92). Many Trinbagonian authors are published in Britain and the US, however, so if you want to get a taste of T&T's culture it may be best to buy their work before you come.

T&T has some of the best-quality **cocoa** in the world, and **chocolate** made locally from Trinitario fine flavour beans is a burgeoning industry in T&T (see p.238). In Trinidad, you can buy exquisite chocolates by Cocobel (see p.92) from the workshop and a couple of gourmet shops, while Soular's delicious bars, nibs and cocoa powder (as well as their delectable muffin mix and dried bananas) are available at Tobago's Shore Things and at the M Store at Piarco Airport. The Tobago Cocoa Estate's award-winning bars are available only at the estate (see p.238), though their **cocoa balls** are more widely available, as are other brands. These are solid spheres or sticks of cocoa and spices, which you grate and boil up with milk and sugar to make traditional chocolate tea. Local **coffee**, which comes in a variety of flavours such as coconut and rum, can be bought in supermarkets and souvenir shops.

It's said that the reason the island's White Oak **rum** (see p.31) is not well known worldwide is because the locals keep it to themselves and consume the total production. Trinidad's famous Angostura Brewery (see box, p.76) produces a wide range of excellent rum as well as their ever-popular bitters, all readily available in shops throughout the islands. Both airports in Trinidad and Tobago have a selection of duty-free goods, though prices at Piarco in Trinidad are lower.

Arts and crafts

Locally made **arts**, **crafts** and unusual **souvenirs**, like carved calabashes, woven palm grasshoppers, shell jewellery and carved driftwood, are usually sold on or near the more popular beaches and in souvenir shops. Ornate carvings are also sold in art galleries and at individual stalls that occasionally appear on country roads. The road- and beach-side stalls are run by local craftspeople and artists who sell good-quality handmade goods at reasonable prices. You'll often see Rastafarians selling handmade leather sandals from stalls or on the street – try Port of Spain's Independence Square.

In **Tobago**, the widest variety is sold at the huts adjacent to Store Bay Beach, but you'll get better deals in Scarborough, at the vendors' mall and the stalls that line Milford and Wilson roads around the market square.

In order to protect local endangered animals, avoid buying products made from turtle shell, black coral, conch or bird feathers.

Travel essentials

Costs

Though no Caribbean island could be considered a budget place to visit, Trinidad and Tobago is undoubtedly one of the **cheapest Caribbean destinations** due to its strong oil and manufacturing-based economy. If you are prepared to take the least expensive accommodation, eat at budget cafés and street stalls and travel by public transport, you can get by on TT$500/US$80/£50/€61 a day. If, however, you opt for fancier accommodation and eat at more formal restaurants, you will need at least TT$1000/US$160/£100/€122 a day. Renting a car is obviously an added expense, with rates starting at TT$350/US$55/£33/€43 per day.

Costs vary around T&T, Tobago – where the already-imported goods from Trinidad have to be imported all over again – is generally more costly than Trinidad. Accommodation is cheaper outside Port of Spain, San Fernando and Tobago's Crown Point area. Restaurants vary greatly in price: fine dining establishments, recognizable by their plush decor, charge TT$150/US$25/£14/€18 and up for a main course; the more basic restaurants, with plastic tables and buffet-style service, offer huge meals from around TT$50/US$8/£5/€6.

During **Carnival season** all accommodation rates in Port of Spain jump by anywhere from 20 to over 100 percent, depending on the hotel. Carnival season often sees increases in other prices, such as drinks, taxi fares and club covers. And then there are the Carnival fetes (parties), which start at TT$100/US$16/£10/€12 for basic cooler parties (where you bring your own drinks) to TT$700/US$110/£55/€75 for a high-end all-inclusive event.

The **minimum wage** in T&T is currently TT$15/US$2.35/£1.45/€1.80 an hour; you might want to bear this fact in mind when negotiating taxi fares to off-route destinations and prices for other goods and services.

Electricity

Currents run on 110 or 220 volts, 60 cycles. The current is often sluggish around peak times, particularly in Tobago, making everything run a little less efficiently than at home. Plug pins are flat two-pronged, sometimes with a third, round pin too. Many hotels have generators, as power outages are common. Unplug appliances when not using, as power surges after shutdowns can damage electrical goods.

Entry requirements

Citizens of European Union countries (as well as Switzerland and Norway), the US and Canada do not require a **visa** for stays of less than three months. Nationals of Australia, New Zealand and South Africa all need visas before entering the country. You can apply for visas through the offices listed below or else have your travel agent obtain one on your behalf. On arrival, you will have to provide an **address** where you will be staying (hotels and guesthouses are acceptable; take any address from the Guide text if you're not yet sure), and, occasionally, proof that you have adequate finances for the length of your stay and a return or onward ticket. Your passport must be valid for six months beyond the period of your proposed visit.

Visa extensions are usually for an extra three months, but this depends on your reasons for wanting to stay; they are issued by the Immigration Office, 67 Frederick St, Port of Spain (Mon–Thurs 7am–4pm, Fri 7am–3.45pm; ☎625 3571, ⓦimmigration.gov.tt). You must first make an appointment to see an immigration officer; a one-week wait is typical. Bring your passport and, if you have one, a return ticket, as well as the TT$50 visa fee and TT$100 extension fee. Note that the policy regarding visa extensions is subject to change, and a lot can depend on the individual officer dealing with your case.

Embassies and consulates

UK
High Commission 42 Belgrave Square, London SW1X 8TNT ☎ 020 7245 9351, ⓦ tthighcommission.co.uk.

US
Embassy 1708 Massachusetts Ave, NW, Washington, DC 20036-1975 ☎ 202 467 6490, ⓦ ttembassy.org.

CANADA
High Commission 200 First Ave, Ottawa, Ontario K1S 2G6 ☎ 613 232 2418, ⓦ ttmissions.com.

HONORARY CONSULS
AUSTRALIA
Honorary Consul PO Box 109, Rose Bay, New South Wales 2029 ☎ 02 933 4391, ⓔ consgentt@aol.com.

NEW ZEALAND
Honorary Consul Level 26, IAG House, 151 Queen St, Auckland ☎ 09 379 9040, ⓔ wjfalcon@xtra.co.nz.

Gay and lesbian

Officially it is still illegal to practise anal sex in Trinidad and Tobago, and bizarrely, it's also against the law for homosexuals to enter the country (though quite how this would be enforced remains unclear). However, there is a creeping acceptance of the **gay community** and the government is under pressure to change the law. In relation to the rest of the Caribbean, T&T is noticeably less homophobic. There are gay bars in Port of Spain, but on the whole, the scene remains quite underground with events publicized by word of mouth. Gay and lesbian travellers are unlikely to suffer any direct prejudice but even so, be aware of your surroundings and always be discreet in your behaviour if you do not want to attract any negative attention: public displays of affection are best avoided.

Health

There are few health risks in Trinidad and Tobago: the islands are **nonmalarial**, and the chlorinated **tap water** is safe to drink (though it doesn't taste great, and most locals filter and/or boil it before drinking). There are no mandatory **immunizations**, though you should ensure that you're up to date with polio and tetanus vaccines, and if you intend to arrive by ferry from Venezuela (or by plane from South/Central America, Haiti, Dominican Republic, Asia and Africa), you'll need a yellow fever vaccination certificate.

The most likely hazards are overexposure to the sun, too much rum and the inevitable minor stomach upsets that come with unfamiliar food and water. Heat and humidity make **cuts and grazes** slower to heal, so apply iodine or antiseptic spray/powder (cream just keeps a cut wet) and try to keep the wound dry. **Heat rashes** are caused by blocked sweat ducts; to avoid them wear loose cotton clothes, and to treat a rash take frequent cool showers without soap, dust skin with medicated talcum powder, and don't use sunscreen or moisturizer. Always drink plenty of water (coconut water is especially rehydrating) and use a good-quality, high-factor sunscreen (plus, if possible, keep out of the sun between 11am and 3pm).

Trinidad and Tobago has the fourth highest incidence of **HIV & AIDS** in the Caribbean (around 1.5 percent prevalence), and cases of other sexually transmitted diseases like gonorrhoea and syphilis are also high. If you do have sex while away, always use a condom.

Animal and plant hazards

Mosquitoes and **sandflies** can be a real nuisance, particularly in the wet season (June–Dec). Sandflies in particular deliver an incredibly itchy and long-lasting bite and are at their most aggressive at sundown, especially around standing water. Cover your arms and legs at dusk and use plenty of strong insect repellent; Avon's Skin So Soft moisturizer is said to have miraculous anti-mosquito properties. Once you've been bitten, do not scratch or even touch the bites except to apply soothing creams – homeopathic pyrethrum is particularly good, as is a coating of fresh aloe vera gel, or more chemically loaded Benadryl cream. Note that mosquitoes here do carry **dengue fever**, an unpleasant viral infection that lasts for a couple of weeks and can be serious in the very young or old; and in 2014, there was an outbreak of another flu-like mosquito-borne virus, **chikungunya**, which also has the unpleasant side-effect of long-lasting joint pain. Neither has a vaccine, so best protection is to avoid getting bitten in the first place.

Another problem in the forests are **chiggers**, tiny mites whose bite leaves a very itchy and long-lasting red bump with a tendency to get infected; apply antiseptic regularly to keep the bite clean. Likewise, stings from hornet-like **wasps** (known as jackspaniards) are nasty but fairly harmless, though **African bees** are now common throughout Trinidad and are aggressive if disturbed; do not wear strong perfume in the bush and follow guides' directions. Never kill a bee after having been stung, as this will cause it to emit a pheromone which attracts even more bees.

ALOE VERA

The thick, spiky stems of **aloe vera** grow profusely throughout T&T. A staple of local healing and skin care, the plant is a veritable cure-all – drunk as a purgative, used as a conditioning rinse and applied to cuts, grazes and burns to draw out infection. It's an excellent remedy for sunburn, heat rash and insect bites, and is even distilled into aloes wine.

To extract fresh aloe gel from the stem, cut off a section and pare away the spiky edges. Slice in half and wipe the vaguely mauve gel onto the affected areas, scratching the surface to release more jelly as needed and being careful not to get it on clothing, since it leaves a stubborn purple stain.

Though there are no deadly snakes in Tobago, Trinidad's forests harbour four venomous varieties; the **fer-de-lance** and the **bushmaster** or **pit viper** (both known as *mapepire*, pronounced "mah-pee-pee"), and two species of brightly coloured **coral snake** (for more on snakes, see p.272). It's best to wear long trousers, shoes or boots and socks when walking in the bush, and to refrain from investigating rock crevices with your bare hands. If you do encounter a snake, simply move it gently out of the way with a long stick. In the event of a bite, keep calm; death from a snakebite is almost unheard of here, and your worst enemy is panic. Bandage the affected area tightly (if the bite is on a limb, tie a tourniquet above it), note down what the snake looked like, and seek medical help – all local hospitals have stocks of the relevant antidote.

Endowed with sharp teeth and a bit of an attitude if cornered, **barracuda** are best admired from a distance, as are moray eels. Don't stick your hand into rock crevices when diving or snorkelling, and never touch **coral**; quite apart from killing the organism with a caress, you'll probably come away with an unattractive, slow-healing rash. A far more likely encounter is with one of the many spiny **black sea urchins** that inhabit reefs and bays; if you tread on one, remove as much of the spine as possible, douse the area in vinegar (or urine) and see a doctor; washing with vinegar is also the best way to treat **jellyfish** stings. Take care to avoid the long trailing tendrils of the purple Portuguese man-of-war, fairly common in the waters around Trinidad. Seek medical help if you've been stung, and don't touch dead ones washed up on the beach, as they remain harmful.

Take care to avoid poisonous **manchineel trees**, easily identified with their wide, spreading crown of small, dark green leaves on long stalks and green flowers – the milky sap causes skin blisters. Though they've been removed from popular beaches and signs put up where they've been allowed to remain, some still grow in wilder coastal areas, and the incredibly poisonous fruit occasionally wash up on other stretches of sand.

Medical services

The main **hospitals** in Trinidad are Port of Spain General (169 Charlotte St ☎623 2951 or ☎623 2952) and Mount Hope in St Augustine (Eastern Main Rd ☎645 4673); there are also small hospitals in all the main towns, as well as the more efficient private establishment St Clair Medical Centre in Port of Spain (18 Elizabeth St ☎628 1451 or ☎628 8615). Tobago's new Scarborough General Hospital is at Signal Hill (☎660 4744), and has an A&E department. For an **ambulance**, call ☎811.

You won't have to pay for treatment at public hospitals, but will be charged a **fee** at Mount Hope and St Clair. Long waits and stretched facilities make it more sensible to plump for a private option, particularly as your insurance should cover costs. If you do find yourself in need of medical attention, remember that most insurance policies require you to pay up initially and retain the receipts.

Many pharmacies stock a modest range of herbal remedies and other **alternative medicines**, while some doctors can refer you to a reputable alternative health practitioner. Trinidad's best homeopath is Harry Ramnarine, an ex-surgeon turned alternative practitioner, based at 403 Rodney Rd, Chaguanas (☎665 8041). There's also an excellent osteopath, Rajesh Dharrie-Mahraj, 14 Murray St, Woodbrook, Port of Spain (☎624 2410).

Insurance

As Trinidad and Tobago's public health system is pretty basic, you'll want to seek private treatment should you fall ill, so it's therefore essential that you take out **travel insurance** before entering the country.

A typical travel insurance **policy** provides cover for the loss of baggage, tickets and – up to a

---

ROUGH GUIDES TRAVEL INSURANCE

Rough Guides has teamed up with WorldNomads.com to offer great **travel insurance deals**. Policies are available to residents of over 150 countries, with cover for a wide range of adventure sports, 24hr emergency assistance, high levels of medical and evacuation cover and a stream of travel safety information. Roughguides.com users can take advantage of their policies online 24/7, from anywhere in the world – even if you're already travelling. And since plans often change when you're on the road, you can extend your policy and even claim online. Roughguides.com users who buy travel insurance with WorldNomads.com can also leave a positive footprint and donate to a community development project. For more information, go to ⓦroughguides.com/travel-insurance.

certain limit – cash or cheques, as well as cancellation or curtailment of your journey. Most of them exclude so-called dangerous sports: in Trinidad and Tobago this can mean scuba diving, windsurfing and hiking, though probably not kayaking; read small print carefully as coverage can vary wildly for similar premiums. Many policies can also be chopped and changed to exclude coverage you don't need.

Internet

Almost all hotels and guesthouses in T&T have **wi-fi** these days (usually free), while the Rituals coffee-shop chain offers wireless hotspots, as do many cafés and bars. **Internet cafés** are also scattered around the islands.

Laundry

Most hotels provide a laundry service, albeit at extortionate rates in larger properties, while guesthouses often have a machine for guests' use. There is a coin-operated laundry in Crown Point, Tobago (see p.210).

Mail

The country's postal service, **TT Post** (Ⓦttpost .net), is inexpensive and reliable. Outgoing and incoming post travels reasonably quickly (one to two weeks to Europe and the US, three to Australia). The closer you are to the capital, the sooner your letters will be delivered. Send valuable items by registered mail, TT Post courier or by an international courier; FedEx and DHL both have local offices.

Most towns and villages have a post office; these are generally **open** Monday to Friday from 7am to 5pm and Saturday from 8am to noon; all post offices are detailed on the website above. Post-boxes on the street are small, red, quite rare and easily missed; many still bear the insignia of the British postal service, a remnant of the colonial era. Stamps are sold at post offices and letters and postcards cost under TT$5 to anywhere in the world.

Maps

The TDC and various private entities produce free maps of both Trinidad and Tobago, showing main roads, beaches and tourist attractions, which are adequate for mainstream exploration, and are available in hotel lobbies and at airport tourist booths. The Discover Trinidad & Tobago free booklet (see p.48) also carries decent island and city maps.

The most detailed of the few road maps available online is the Rough Guide Map of Trinidad and Tobago, though like its competitors, it hasn't been recently updated. T&T's Land and Surveys Division produce a 1:150,000 **road map** of Trinidad and the 1:50,000 map of Tobago, and a detailed map of Port of Spain, but again these are outdated, and impossible to find outside of T&T, where they're sometimes stocked in the islands' bookshops.

Money

The local currency is the **Trinidad and Tobago dollar**. This is usually abbreviated to TT$, and is divided into one hundred cents. Coins start at 1 cent and range up through 5, 10 and 25 cents. Notes start at one dollar and are in denominations of 5, 10, 20, 50 and 100. It's best to keep some of your cash in small denominations: supermarkets and bars can usually exchange TT$100, but taxis and street vendors often can't and should be paid with TT$20 or less.

At the time of writing, the **exchange rate** was US$1 to TT$6.3; £1 to TT$10.35 and €1 to TT$8. **Cambios** are few and far between (though see p.92 for details of the excellent FX Trader outlets in Trinidad), but you can change cash in all banks for a small commission. Though **travellers' cheques** are accepted by banks, they can be a bit problematic in T&T; some banks impose a limit (of US$250) on the amount you can cash, while others will accept only AmEx cheques, and most banks will make you hang around for hours while they phone through to check your cheques aren't stolen. Using a debit card in an **ATM** machine is a lot easier; ATMs are easy to find, and some dispense US dollars, which are also widely accepted locally. All major **credit cards** are widely accepted. Banking hours vary slightly depending on the bank, but are usually Monday to Thursday 8am to 3pm, Friday 8am to 1pm & 3 to 5pm. Most banks in Trinidad's larger malls open 10am to 6pm with no break.

Opening hours

Shop opening hours are Monday to Friday 8am to 5.30pm, and Saturday 8am to 5pm. Malls are open longer: Monday to Saturday 10am to 8 or 9pm.

Phones

Local operators bmobile (ⓌΙbmobile.co.tt) and Digicel (Ⓦdigiceltt.com) offer **pre-paid SIM cards** with credit, sold at their own outlets or at communications stores, both of which are ubiquitous islandwide. Bmobile also has a kiosk just past the immigration desks at Piarco, should you wish to get connected on arrival. You'll need photo ID to buy a SIM, and should carry the handset you'll be using so that you can ensure it's not locked; equally both companies usually have deals where you get a SIM and a basic phone for as little as TT$130. **Top-up credit** is widely available from shops, pharmacies and supermarkets, and from the odd machine. Calling rates are listed on the company websites, and are reasonable even for international calls.

The area code for Trinidad and Tobago is ☎868; local and international operator is ☎0, directory enquiries ☎6411, fire and ambulance ☎990, and police ☎999.

Photography

It's important to always ask permission before taking someone's picture – many visitors don't, much to the fury of the market trader or fisherman who doesn't appreciate being snapped while going about a day's work. Be sensitive, also, around temples and mosques, where photography may not be allowed.

Time

Trinidad and Tobago is four hours behind Greenwich Mean Time (five during the summer months), and one hour ahead of Eastern Standard Time.

CALLING HOME FROM ABROAD

To make an international call, dial the international access code (in Trinidad and Tobago it's 011), then the destination's country code, before the rest of the number. Note that the initial zero is omitted from the area code when dialling the UK, Ireland, Australia and New Zealand from abroad.

Australia + 61
New Zealand + 64
UK + 44
US and Canada + 1
Republic of Ireland + 353
South Africa + 27

Tourist information

Official **tourist information** in T&T is pretty poor, with no useful tourist offices other than booths at the airport. The websites of the Tourism Development Company or TDC (Ⓦgotrinidadand tobago.com), and the Tobago Division of Tourism (Ⓦvissittobago.gov.tt) are worth checking out, however, with accommodation and tour operator listings, and a calendar of events. See p.81 for Carnival websites. The radio and national press advertise upcoming events (especially during Carnival).

The fact-filled *Discover Trinidad and Tobago* (Ⓦdiscovertnt.com) includes features on Carnival and eco-tourism and hotel, restaurant and tour operator listings. The *Ins and Outs of Trinidad and Tobago* (Ⓦinsandoutstt.com) is a glossy annual publication which has sections on Carnival, shopping, art and craft, eco-tourism and business, along with accommodation, eating and nightlife listings for both islands, while *Créolé* (Ⓦwww .xn--crol-cpac.com) has detailed reviews of restaurants in both islands. These publications are available at hotels, tourist offices and other places frequented by foreigners.

Travellers with disabilities

There is little infrastructure for those with **disabilities** in T&T. However, a small but growing number of hotels, guesthouses and villas have been made accessible; these are mentioned in the text. If you want to make local contacts, try Disabled Peoples' Inter-national (☎624 6060, Ⓦdpi.org), at 13a Wrightson Rd, Port of Spain.

If you use a wheelchair, note that getting around Port of Spain and other large towns can be problematic. There are large gullies at the sides of most streets, and few of them have chair-accessible slopes or ramps.

Travelling with children

As most local people are fond of **children** and used to accommodating them, you'll find that travelling with youngsters is rarely a problem. Almost all local hotels are happy to accept families, and many provide babysitting services. Many beaches in Trinidad (and some in Tobago) can be risky for swimming, so it's best to keep a close eye on children when in the sea; even locals' favourite Maracas has a strong undertow. Tobago's Store Bay, Pigeon Point and Canoe Bay are the calmest, but

Macqueripe in Trinidad can be quite benign too. Check with locals, and if there's a risk stick to paddling.

Note also that attitudes towards children can be quite traditional, of the "seen and not heard" variety, so tantrums in public or backtalking adults will raise a few eyebrows, especially if these are not immediately quashed by the parent (spanking still remains a common disciplinary method in Trinidad and Tobago). As a mark of respect, Trinbagonian children often call adults "uncle" or "auntie"; encouraging your children to follow suit will be happily received.

Weddings

Couples can **marry** in Trinidad and Tobago as soon as three days after their arrival. Many hotels offer sumptuous honeymoon suites, and Tobago Weddings (☎639 4347, ⓦ tobagoweddings.com) will make necessary arrangements. You will need passports, airline tickets, and if either you or your soon-to-be spouse is divorced or widowed, the decree absolute or death certificate, along with proof of name change if it differs on the document. Under-18s must also have a documented consent form from a parent or legal guardian.

Port of Spain and the western tip

POUI TREES IN QUEEN'S PARK SAVANNAH

1 Port of Spain and the western tip

Spread over a peninsula extending towards Venezuela from the northern part of the island and dividing the Gulf of Paria and the Caribbean Sea, Trinidad's northwestern tip comprises the island's most urbanized area. The country's capital and its commercial and cultural centre, Port of Spain sits between the foothills of the forested Northern Range mountains and the choppy waters of the gulf. Home to nearly a third of Trinidad's population, as well as many immigrants from Venezuela and other islands in the region, this is a city that buzzes with metropolitan verve, a thriving place that serves as the hub of the southern Caribbean. Although exciting in any season, with a brilliant nightlife scene, the best time to be here is during the weeks leading up to Carnival, when there are nightly fetes and panyards to take in as well as the biggest Jouvert celebrations in Trinidad and, of course, the kaleidoscope of the Parade of the Bands.

Beyond the city's western suburbs, the landscape becomes increasingly less developed as the coastal road heads toward **Chaguaramas**, the playground of the capital. Protected as part of the Chaguaramas National Park, Tucker Valley is crisscrossed by a network of forest trails, and the sheltered cove of **Macqueripe** offers excellent swimming. The southern Chaguaramas coast is all business, however, its marinas and commercial boatyards interspersed with some appealing waterside bars and restaurants. The further west you go, the more wild and undeveloped the terrain becomes. Beyond Chaguaramas, the western tip crumbles into a series of rocky islands separated by rough, swirling channels known as the **Bocas del Dragon** – the Dragon's Mouth. Though the islands – the most accessible and developed of which is **Gaspar Grande**, the most isolated and atmospheric being **Chacachacare** – lie just a short distance offshore, they are completely free of motorized traffic. In the eighteenth century, they were a refuge for whalers, smugglers and pirates; today, they're the preserve of yachting enthusiasts, fishermen and anyone in search of tranquillity.

Port of Spain and its suburbs have a wide range of **accommodation** to suit all budgets. Whether you're visiting the city for Carnival or plan to explore other parts of Trinidad, you will almost certainly end up staying here at some point. Indeed, it's entirely feasible to base yourself in Port of Spain and visit the rest of Trinidad on day-trips, either by renting a car or using the public transport network that radiates out from the City Gate bus and maxi terminus.

CHACACHACARE

Highlights

① Queen's Park Savannah at dusk As the heat lifts, people gravitate here to walk, drink a coconut water or sample some street food. **See p.64**

② Carnival With panyards and fetes, Jouvert and the main parade, Port of Spain is the epicentre of Trini Carnival. **See pp.68–69 & pp.81–82**

③ Foodie Port of Spain From a roti to an *arepa* or a plate of fine Italian food, the capital's wonderful dining scene offers a wealth of variety. **See p.85**

④ Bar lime Start the rum and the conversation flowing along Ariapita Avenue and end your

night at the infamous *Smokey and Bunty* in St James. **See p.88**

⑤ Clubbing Port of Spain boasts a varied club scene and a party-hard crowd who keep going till dawn. **See p.88**

⑥ Chaguaramas Whether a walk in Tucker Valley, a swim at Macqueripe or a meal at a seaside restaurant, Chaguaramas is a lovely foil to the capital. **See pp.94–102**

⑦ Going "down the islands" Just a short boat ride from the mainland, the beautifully rugged Bocas offer sandy beaches, clear waters and plenty of peace. **See pp.102–105**

HIGHLIGHTS ARE MARKED ON THE MAP ON P.54

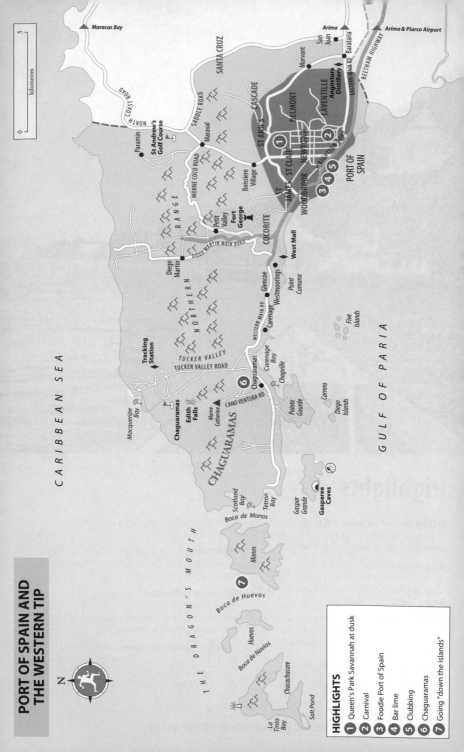

PORT OF SPAIN AND THE WESTERN TIP

CARIBBEAN SEA

GULF OF PARIA

THE DRAGON'S MOUTH

HIGHLIGHTS

1. Queen's Park Savannah at dusk
2. Carnival
3. Foodie Port of Spain
4. Bar lime
5. Clubbing
6. Chaguaramas
7. Going "down the islands"

Port of Spain

PORT OF SPAIN occupies a crucial place in T&T's national psyche. It's the hub of the republic's booming economy, the home of government and the media, and the crucible of Trinidad's rich **cultural life**, with legions of mas camps and panyards, art galleries and theatres. It was here that Carnival was first established in Trinidad, and – in the suburb of Laventille – that the steel pan was invented.

Spreading back from the Gulf of Paria and enclosed by crumpled green hills, Port of Spain has a dynamic, sophisticated feel that's markedly different from the rest of the country. Some 128,000 inhabitants jostle for space in and around its compact centre, which displays a rather schizophrenic mix of the old and the new, with street traders selling cinnamon sticks or mauby bark as well as sleek new shopping malls bursting with international chains, and glinting high-rises overlooking colonial-era squares. The mishmash of architectural styles makes for an ugly first impression, especially **downtown**, with its traffic-choked streets and dusty commercial buildings. But there are many fine nineteenth-century buildings here, from dignified churches and state offices to quaint "gingerbread" houses, named for their decorative wooden fretwork, while grandiose mansions of colonial planters overlook the large open space of the **Queen's Park Savannah**, which was created by enlightened town planners in the early nineteenth century and now affords the city some much-needed breathing room.

Stretching along the flat coastal plains to the west, the outlying districts of **Woodbrook** and **St James** are very much part of the city. Bars and restaurants line the after-dark hotspots of Ariapita Avenue and the Western Main Road, and costumes are created here at **mas camps** during the months preceding **Carnival**, when the city's volatile mix of style, hedonism, creativity and *joie de vivre* explodes onto the streets as bands of fantastically arrayed revellers wind their way through downtown Port of Spain and Woodbrook to cross the Savannah stage. Spreading north and east into the Northern Range foothills, **St Ann's**, **Cascade**, **Belmont** and **Laventille** are mostly residential, though the latter has a rather grim reputation for violent crime. North of the Savannah, leafy **Maraval** has some great places to eat, and is also the place to hop in a jeep taxi up to the friendly farming community of **Paramin** for heady city views and some welcome respite from the heat and bustle.

Brief history

Port of Spain became Trinidad's capital almost by accident. In 1757, a series of pirate attacks on the then capital St Joseph left the residence of the new **Spanish governor**, Don Pedro de la Moneda, uninhabitable, prompting him to move the seat of government to the more convenient location of Puerto de España (a port of Spain). Though the town consisted of no more than two streets with a few hundred residents and was built on swampy, flood-prone ground, it did have the great advantage of a fine natural **harbour**, and was quickly made the permanent capital.

The colonial era

As French Catholics flooded into Trinidad in the 1780s, Port of Spain's economy boomed and the city spread. Land was reclaimed from the sea, and streets were built over the surrounding mangrove swamps and woods. The last Spanish governor, Don Maria José Chacon, greatly facilitated this expansion when, in 1787, he diverted the St Ann's River to the outskirts of the town, along the foot of Laventille Hill, alleviating the floods that had often troubled central Port of Spain. Chacon was less effective, however, when it came to defending the city against the **British**, who invaded and took over the island in 1797. In 1808, a devastating fire led the British governor, Sir Ralph Woodford, to make a number of civic improvements, establishing the Queen's Park Savannah and developing Woodford Square. Learning from Spanish mistakes, the British also improved the city's defences by building Fort George and Fort Picton.

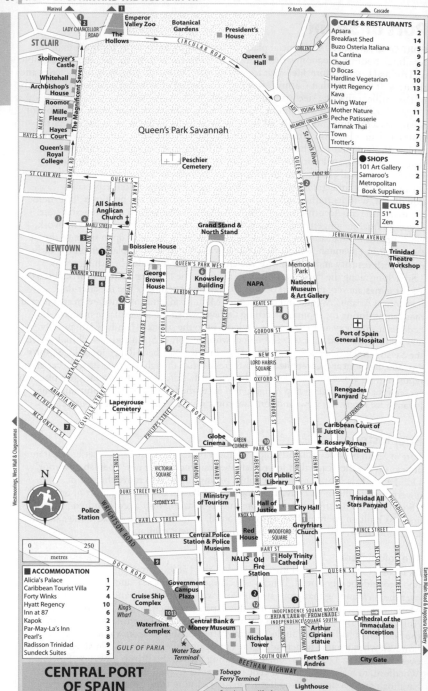

Maraval ▲▲   ▲▲ ▲1   St Ann's ▲▲   ▲ Cascade

St Clair
Stollmeyer's Castle
Whitehall
Archbishop's House
Roomor
Mille Fleurs
Hayes Court
Queen's Royal College
Newtown

Emperor Valley Zoo
Botanical Gardens
President's House
Queen's Hall
The Hollows
Lady Chancellor Road
Circular Road
Coblentz Ave
Lady Young Road
Belmont Circular Rd
Cadiz Rd

Queen's Park Savannah

Peschier Cemetery

All Saints Anglican Church
Grand Stand & North Stand
Boissiere House
George Brown House
Knowsley Building
NAPA
National Museum & Art Gallery
Memorial Park

Trinidad Theatre Workshop

Port of Spain General Hospital

Lapeyrouse Cemetery

Renegades Panyard
Caribbean Court of Justice
Rosary Roman Catholic Church

Globe Cinema
Green Corner
Victoria Square
Old Public Library

Ministry of Tourism
Hall of Justice
City Hall
Trinidad All Stars Panyard

Police Station
Central Police Station & Police Museum
Red House
Woodford Square
Greyfriars Church

NALIS Old Fire Station
Holy Trinity Cathedral

Government Campus Plaza
Cruise Ship Complex
King's Wharf
Waterfront Complex
Central Bank & Money Museum
Nicholas Tower
Independence Square North
Brian Lara Promenade
Independence Square South
Arthur Cipriani statue
Cathedral of the Immaculate Conception
City Gate

Water Taxi Terminal
Fort San Andrés
Lighthouse
Gulf of Paria
South Quay
Beetham Highway

Tobago Ferry Terminal
Queen's Wharf

N

0   250
metres

CENTRAL PORT OF SPAIN

Churchill Roosevelt & Uriah Butler highways & Piarco Airport

1

Emancipation and beyond

After **emancipation** in 1834, freed slaves left plantations to find work in the capital, settling in the hills to the east of the city where they established the suburbs of Laventille and Belmont. With a growing population of workers, traders and entrepreneurs, Port of Spain sprawled outwards into the old plantations of Maraval and St Ann's. Indian immigrants brought to Trinidad under indentured labour schemes settled in St James, while the population was further swelled by migrants from China, Portugal, Venezuela and Syria. The descendants of these groups, and those of the French and Spanish communities, compose the cosmopolitan mix of peoples and cultures that make Port of Spain unique today.

As the nation's capital, Port of Spain was naturally the focus for both the **political turmoil** and the **growing prosperity** that marked the country's history during the twentieth century. From the water riots of 1903, through the independence movement of the 1950s down to the bloody 1990 coup attempt, Woodford Square has been an arena of political strife. The dredging of the city's **deep-water harbour** in the 1930s made Port of Spain the leading port of the southern Caribbean, while the discovery of offshore oil in the 1970s funded the construction of the **financial district**, dominated by the imposing twin towers of the Central Bank.

Port of Spain today

Thanks to the expansionist dreams of former People's National Party Prime Minister Patrick Manning, Port of Spain's skyline now bristles with **high-rise blocks**, from sleek Nicholas Tower to the rash of new government buildings on Wrightson Road. The buoyant consumerism of the last twenty years or so has seen **lavish developments** springing up all over the city, from American-style luxury malls and exclusive gated communities to the futuristic National Academy for the Performing Arts on the Savannah and the slick new waterside promenade around the *Hyatt Regency* hotel. And though civic spending has contracted since the 2008 global economic collapse, with some of the high-rises still missing their interior finish and restoration of key public buildings such as the President's House at a standstill, Port of Spain has endured, with its prettiest public squares restored again to vibrant meeting places and its outlying districts electrified by a slew of new restaurants and bars.

Downtown Port of Spain

Dating back to the 1780s, **downtown** Port of Spain is the city's oldest district, and in places it still looks the part, though the colonial-era buildings on the backstreets are fast giving way to a rash of new development. Constantly reinventing itself in a frenzy of

---

PORT OF SPAIN ORIENTATION

Port of Spain's compact **downtown area** is based on a grid system, and is easy to explore on foot, with everything in walking distance of Independence Square/Brian Lara Promenade, one block north of City Gate, the main transport terminal. There are four main roads leading out of the central downtown area: **Wrightson Road** skirts the southern edge of the city, becoming the Audrey Jeffers Highway as it heads west past the suburbs of Diego Martin and Westmoorings, and out towards Chaguaramas. **Tragarete Road** and parallel **Ariapita Avenue** run from uptown Park Street through Woodbrook before joining, respectively, the **Western Main Road** into St James and the highway at the MovieTowne complex.

The green expanse of the Queen's Park Savannah serves as a boundary between downtown and the rest of the city. From its northwest corner, **Saddle Road** leads to Maraval and eventually Maracas Beach, and is the access point for Paramin. From the northeast corner of the Savannah, **St Ann's Road** takes you to St Ann's and Cascade, while minor roads on the Savannah's western edge thread into the businesslike districts of Newtown and St Clair.

1

modernization, this is the capital's shopping and financial centre. Within the compact grid of streets surrounding broad **Independence Square/Brian Lara Promenade** and bustling **Frederick Street**, shops jostle for space with old Spanish warehouses, coffee exporters' offices, finance houses and the paraphernalia of the **docks**, while the thoroughfares are jammed with traffic, pedestrians and pavement vendors.

Independence Square/Brian Lara Promenade

Set on two parallel streets, **Independence Square/Brian Lara Promenade** is divided by a shady paved area (the promenade) dotted with benches and concrete chess tables; it's a popular after-work liming spot, with street food vendors doing a brisk trade; the square is also home to what's said to be the most profitable *KFC* in the world, on the corner of Broadway. The throngs of people here inevitably attract a fair number of beggars (particularly around the cathedral), who patrol the promenade and tend to latch onto foreigners – keep your wits about you.

The cumbersome title is a result of frequent **name changes** in recent decades. Until independence in 1962, it was Marine Square, in honour of the fact that this land was reclaimed from the sea in 1816. It was rechristened Independence Square in 1962, and its central section was later renamed to honour Trinidad's most famous cricketer. The western end of the square is dominated by the sleek blue-and-silver **Nicholas Tower**, and the twin towers of the **Central Bank of Trinidad and Tobago**, completed in 1985 and brutally 1980s in style. The slew of high-rises overlooking the other side of the Promenade make up the new **Government Campus Plaza**, built to accommodate various government ministries from Legal Affairs to Customs and Excise. At its eastern end, Independence Square intersects with Nelson Street, which runs through one of Port of Spain's rougher areas and isn't a great place to wander, tempting as the crumbling colonial-era buildings may look.

Central Bank Money Museum

Eric Williams Plaza, Independence Square • Tues–Fri 10am–3pm • Free • ☎ 625 4843, ⑩ central-bank.org.tt

The **Central Bank** towers form the heart of Port of Spain's financial district and house the Central Bank and its **Money Museum**, which unsurprisingly concentrates on the history of cash, from cowrie shells to plastic money, as well as the slave trade oil and petrodollars. At the time of writing, the museum was undergoing restoration, and a new interactive exhibition is due to open in July 2015.

Arthur Cipriani statue

In the centre of Independence Square, at the junction with Frederick Street, the **Arthur Cipriani statue** commemorates a former Port of Spain mayor who campaigned energetically for compulsory education for all and self-government for the island – the only legislator of his day to defend workers' rights. He died in 1945 and is buried in the Lapeyrouse Cemetery in Woodbrook (see p.72).

Cathedral of the Immaculate Conception

Independence Square

At the eastern end of the square, the Promenade is taken up with the imposing Roman Catholic **Cathedral of the Immaculate Conception**, a legacy of Governor Woodford's post-fire reconstruction. Completed in 1836, the twin-towered Gothic construction took sixteen years to build; its ironwork frame was shipped from England, while the limestone wall blocks were quarried in Laventille. Restoration during the 1980s added sixteen **stained-glass windows** depicting T&T's many ethnic groups, the highlight of an otherwise rather drab interior.

The Promenade ends just east of the cathedral at diminutive **Columbus Square**, named after the colourful statue of the Spanish "discoverer" and today a very run-down spot that serves as a base for homeless people.

Charlotte Street

One block west of the Cathedral of the Immaculate Conception, **Charlotte Street** strikes north off Independence Square. Lined with fabric shops, general stores and umbrella-shaded street stalls selling everything from fruit and vegetables to leather sandals, sneakers and clothes, it's a vibrant place for a wander, thick with the aromas drifting out from the roti shops and the incense burned by stallholders, and ringing out with the reggae and soca played by music vendors and the parping of horns as cars squeeze through the narrow stretch of tarmac not taken up by commerce. It's also the best place to pick up a bargain in Port of Spain, whether you're on the lookout for souvenirs or spices – though do keep your wits about you.

King's Wharf

The city's southern edge is dominated by the gritty industrial area surrounding the docks, sliced through by Wrightson Road and overlooked by the chimneys of the Powergen electricity plant and the silos of the National Four Mills factory. With its vast warehouses and jagged skyline of cranes, gantries and mounds of containers, **King's Wharf** is the hub of Trinidad's booming import–export trade. Everything from cars to bananas passes through this hectic port, with most of the action taking place in the early hours when it's still relatively cool. Dredged in the 1930s, the deep-water harbour allowed Port of Spain to accommodate deep-draught ships, boosting Trinidad's economy and consolidating the city's position as the most important southern Caribbean port.

The Waterfront Complex

The only let-up in Wrightson Road's rows of warehouses and industrial buildings is at the western end of Independence Square, where the **Waterfront Complex** has opened up the Gulf of Paria to pedestrians. A promenade runs along the seafront past the *Hyatt* hotel and along to the cruise ship pier, and is a popular spot for an evening stroll, when its gushing fountains dance with coloured lights. The *Hyatt*'s oceanside restaurant and bar (see p.86) is a lovely spot for a drink or a meal; less expensive options are sold from a hole-in-the-wall bar at the *Breakfast Shed*.

South Quay

One block south of Independence Square, the parallel **South Quay** is a wide commercial street dominated by **City Gate**, a grand Victorian stone building that served as Port of Spain's train station until the line from here to Arima/San Fernando was shut down in 1968. It remains Trinidad's main transportation hub, with PTSC buses and maxi taxis arriving and departing to and from all parts of the country. It's also the site of the main downtown **judging point** during Carnival, when the rows of bleachers offer a great view of the bands as they pass.

Fort San Andrés

South Quay • Currently closed for restoration • ☎ 623 5861, Ⓦ nmag.gov.tt

The unassuming cream-painted building just west of City Gate, across Broadway, sits on the site of **Fort San Andrés**, built by the Spanish as the island's only defence against British invasion. The curved wall behind, embedded with rusting cannons, is all that survives of the original 5m-high perimeter, now mostly buried thanks to successive land reclamation projects. When the fort was constructed in 1787, the sea lapped against its ramparts; today it's a good couple of hundred metres inland. The British added a second storey to the original structure, and used it as a customs house and reading room, as well as a processing facility for some 65,000 African slaves and 30,000 Indian indentured workers entering Trinidad.

The building has suffered from neglect over the years, and both the structure and the formerly desultory **museum** inside, centred on the history of Port of Spain, are being

BEYOND THE LIGHTHOUSE

Past Port of Spain's lighthouse, the rusting corrugated-iron roofs and crumbling buildings that make up **Sea Lots** provide a stark contrast to the sleek glass and concrete of the waterfront high-rises. Condemned by many as a hotbed of crime, this impoverished community is hemmed in by the oily Gulf of Paria to one side and the highway to another; wall murals facing the highway commemorate the lives of Sea Lots resident Haydee Paul and her two children, tragically killed in a traffic accident in February 2013. Just beyond Sea Lots, the highway continues through **Beetham**, site of the country's main rubbish landfill and, on the inland side of the road, the notoriously rough residential community that has grown up around the dump, its boundaries marked by piles of scrap metal reclaimed by locals who make a living picking through the waste. Some 875 tonnes of rubbish find their way to the Beetham every day, and regular fires at the dump smother Sea Lots and Beetham in clouds of toxic smoke; residents here have some of the highest instances of respiratory disease in the country. Though the dump has reached its official capacity, plans to have it cleared and rehabilitated have yet to be realized, despite the continued efforts of local environmental campaigners who point out that the Beetham sits above the El Socorro aquifer, Trinidad's main source of groundwater, into which it's leaching a toxic chemical soup.

restored and upgraded, though it's unlikely to reopen any time soon; call or visit the website for an update. Through the perimeter fence on South Quay you can still see a locomotive that shunted along the tracks from Port of Spain to San Fernando, as well as the tarpaulin-swathed *Hummingbird II* sailboat, on which Harold and Kwailan La Borde circumnavigated the globe in 1965.

The lighthouse
Wrightson Rd

Presiding over Wrightson Road south of Fort San Andrés, Port of Spain's **lighthouse** was built in the 1880s at what was then the end of St Vincent Jetty. Some 19.5m high, the handsome hexagonal structure has since been marooned inland by reclamation, and is no longer operational. It stands in the middle of a traffic island, and the busy highway that thunders constantly past has skewed it five degrees from the vertical.

Frederick Street

Frederick Street is Port of Spain's main shopping drag, at its busiest between Independence Square and Park Street. Like much of the downtown area, Frederick Street has assumed a modern face in recent years, with many shops accommodated in multi-storeyed, air-conditioned malls complete with food courts; sadly, the mall hoardings obscure most of the intricate iron balconies that front the few remaining original buildings. The stalls on the corner of Frederick and Queen streets are all that's left of the **People's Mall** (or Drag Mall), which was razed to the ground in a 2005 fire; the maze of tiny shops selling hand-painted T-shirts, incense and Rasta craft are a good spot for a browse.

Greyfriars Church
50–52 Frederick St

Midway up Frederick Street, opposite Woodford Square, the angular white-painted **Greyfriars Church** is the oldest Presbyterian place of worship in Trinidad, built in 1837 thanks to the efforts of Scottish missionary Alexander Kennedy, who petitioned the then-Governor Woodford. The faithful have long since ceased to worship here, and the building has slowly lapsed into dereliction, its future even more uncertain following its purchase by private developer Alfred Galy in 2014, whose subsequent partial demolition of the church hall was halted only by a last-minute intervention by conservationists, who are campaigning for the building to be restored.

Woodford Square

Boundaried by Knox and Hart streets to the north and south, the pretty, tree-shaded **Woodford Square** (named after the British governor who had it built in the early nineteenth century) holds a picturesque colonial bandstand and an elegant cast-iron fountain supported by mermaids and mermen, which dates back to 1866. The square's main claim to fame, however, is as a centre of **political activism**. In 1903, it was the scene of a protest meeting against the introduction of new water rates, which quickly got out of hand – in the ensuing riots, the original Red House was burned to the ground. The square's reputation as a political cockpit really got going in 1956 with the establishment of the "**University of Woodford Square**". This was the brainchild of **Eric Williams** – historian, father of the national independence movement and first prime minister of the country – who delivered hugely popular weekly public lectures here on the issues of the day. In the 1970s, the square became a focal point for the Black Power movement, which renamed it the "people's parliament"; in April 1970, some 30,000 people converged here for the funeral of Basil Davis, a young activist shot dead by the police during a Black Power protest.

A Trinidadian version of Speaker's Corner, Woodford Square is still a centre of political discussion. On the eastern side of the square a blackboard lists the topic for discussion each day; these **debates** typically take place at a rather unsociable 7am and anyone can join in, provided that they can get a word in edgeways – it's not a platform for the fainthearted or soft-spoken.

Knox Street

The other public buildings around Woodford Square are a mishmash of architectural styles. On Knox Street, which forms the northeast border of the square, the oldest and most attractive building is the former **Public Library**, a large brick and stone structure built in 1901 and sporting a beautiful arcaded second storey. It's incongruously sandwiched between two brutally functional slabs of glass and concrete: to the east, on the corner of Frederick Street, is the plain **Hall of Justice**; built in 1979, it houses the Supreme Court of Trinidad and Tobago. The concrete pile on the corner of Abercromby Street is the 1961 **City Hall**, home to Port of Spain's council and the mayor's office.

The Red House

Abercromby St · Ⓦ ttparliament.org

Taking up half of a block between St Vincent and Abercromby streets, and bordered to the north and south by Knox and Hart streets, the imposing Neo-Renaissance **Red House** is actually more a faded, peeling terracotta; though you'll have to crane your neck to see any of it, as it's been under renovation since 1999, covered with a crude metal roof, swathed in scaffolding and enclosed by high construction-zone fences.

The Red House inherited its popular name from an earlier building on the site, which was painted bright red to celebrate Queen Victoria's diamond jubilee in 1897. The present structure, completed four years after its predecessor was burnt down in the 1903 water riots, was itself attacked in the **1990 coup** (see box, pp.62–63), and bullet holes still scar the stonework; outside the front entrance on Abercromby Street, an eternal flame commemorates the seven government and security personnel who died in the coup. Though the Red House has long served as the seat of Trinidad and Tobago's parliament, sessions have been shifted over to the International Waterfront Centre (one of the new high-rise buildings that make up the Waterfront Complex on Wrightson Road) during the current repair works.

Restoration of the building is ongoing, but the TT$5 billion works were put on temporary hold in early 2013 while archeologists investigated skeletal human remains and Amerindian artefacts, thought to date from between 430 AD and 1390 AD and found during excavations of the building's foundations. The somewhat optimistic estimate for the completion of the restoration is January 2016.

THE 1990 COUP

At 6.30pm on July 27, 1990, radical Islamic fundamentalist **Yasin Abu Bakr** interrupted programming of the state-run TTT TV company to announce that he had captured the station offices and overthrown the government of Trinidad and Tobago in a **coup d'état**. Thirty minutes earlier, members of his **Jamaat-al-Muslimeen** group had stormed the Red House and taken several government ministers hostage, including then-prime minister A.N.R. Robinson, while the old police headquarters around the corner on Sackville Street had been firebombed and all but destroyed. Looting took the capital by storm, and a **state of emergency** was called, requiring all citizens to remain indoors after dark; nonetheless, some 26 people were killed during the coup attempt, and millions of dollars' worth of damage were done to downtown Port of Spain.

THE AFTERMATH OF THE COUP

With little public support, and with food rations running low (the Muslimeen hadn't prepared for a drawn-out standoff), the rebels **surrendered** to the troops surrounding the Red House on August 1, after a six-day siege – though only after negotiating an **amnesty agreement** which guaranteed that perpetrators of the coup would not be arrested for their activities. Nonetheless, Bakr and 113 other Jamaat members were immediately taken into custody, and remained in jail for two years while the courts debated the validity of an amnesty which, it was argued, had been granted only as a means of preventing the hostages from being killed. The Jamaat members were eventually freed after a ruling by the UK Privy Council that the amnesty was invalid, but that it would be against due process to have them re-arrested and tried for the offences committed during the coup.

As well as relying on the army to support the revolt, the Jamaat had hoped to capitalize on public discontent with the harsh fiscal policies of the time (satirized by the calypsonian Sparrow in his song *Capitalism Gone Mad*). Yet however little love they may have had for the government, few Trinbagonians were willing to support its violent overthrow by an armed group of religious

Holy Trinity Cathedral

Hart St • No set hours

On the south side of Woodford Square, the Anglican **Holy Trinity Cathedral** was another of Governor Woodford's many initiatives to improve Port of Spain's public spaces. The original idea was to build it in the middle of the square itself, and work was already underway when the governor bowed to popular protest and moved it to its present site. Completed in 1818, the elegant stone structure is built along Gothic lines, with a large clock tower. The cool, shady interior boasts a mahogany hammer-beam roof, made in England and modelled on London's Westminster Hall. A life-size effigy of Governor Woodford lies on his tomb by the south wall; the plaques nearby commemorate various other colonial dignitaries. It's worth taking a stroll around the pretty gardens to see the stonework **labyrinth** at the side of the building.

NALIS

Cnr Hart & Abercromby streets • Mon–Fri 8.30am–6pm, Sat 8.30am–4pm • ☎ 623 6962, ⓦ nalis.gov.tt

On the southwest side of Woodford Square, the modern **NALIS**, Trinidad and Tobago's national library, was built to resemble a beached cruise ship – something that's particularly obvious when it's lit up at night. The main hall inside, with its *Rituals* coffeeshop and wi-fi, is a good place to take a break from the heat, and there are often small exhibitions centred on local history and culture. The **amphitheatre** outside is used to stage plays and workshops; check the website to see what's on.

Old Fire Station

Hart St

Next door to NALIS, and now part of the library complex, the **Old Fire Station** is a handsome cut-stone construction, built in 1896 and refurbished in 2000, when it got its crisp pink and grey paint job. Formerly home to the Trinidad Theatre Workshop

extremists. Many nonetheless found it hard to believe that such events could take place in their stable, democratic, party-loving country, and though reflections of the coup tend to be understandably sober today, many people also tell stories of wild **"curfew parties"** and imaginative explanations given to the police of the five TVs found in a neighbour's house.

THE JAMAAT TODAY

More than twenty years on, the coup remains a contentious and much-talked-about issue. The Jamaat-al-Muslimeen is still active in T&T: their **headquarters** at 1 Mucurapo Rd on the outskirts of Woodbrook hold a school and a mosque (there are also four other mosques dotted around the country), and membership – estimated at around 6800 nationally – continues to rise, despite allegations of links with shady dealings, from murders and drug smuggling to terrorism, as well as widespread assertions that Patrick Manning's PNM government provided covert financial backing for the Muslimeen in return for support (and strong-arming of votes in communities such as Laventille) during the 2002 election campaign. The Jamaat, meanwhile, remain unrepentant, and argue that the coup had its roots in state harassment of their group, which had been involved in many run-ins with the authorities prior to 1990 over a land dispute at Mucurapo and the killing of one of its members by the police.

THE COMMISSION OF ENQUIRY

In September 2010, Kamla Persad-Bissessar's People's Partnership government convened a **Commission of Enquiry** into the coup. Despite the fact that Abu Bakr refused to give evidence (and was taken to court as a result), some 100 witnesses did participate in the 17 hearings, including A.N.R. Robinson, former PM Basdeo Panday and one-time Jamaat activist Jamaal Shabazz, who participated in the takeover of the TTT offices. The Commission finally delivered its report in March 2014, citing numerous recommendations concerning national security, but for many the report was something of a damp squib, offering too little too late; and the issues surrounding the events of July 1990 remain shrouded in mystery and suspicion.

(see p.74), it's now used to stage talks, events and the odd temporary art exhibition (check boards put up outside or in NALIS), and serves as one of the main venues for the annual BOCAS literary festival.

Central Police Station

Cnr Sackville and St Vincent streets • Museum Tues–Fri 9am–3pm • Free • ☎ 624 6722, ⓦ nmag.gov.tt

Though it might look like a church, this elegant Gothic-style stone building, with its variegated brickwork and arched windows, is a renovated version of the **Central Police Station**, which was pretty much destroyed in the 1990 coup (see above). The upper floor holds a small **museum** centred around T&T's police service. Highlights include an old warrant book from 1941, in which the offences detailed include "fraudulent conversing" and "larceny of a fountain pen"; and a duty book from the same era which includes a complaint by one Monica Darlington of Delaford, who dropped into the station to report that "Mrs Blackman and her daughter Viva are always annoying her" – a far cry from the news that makes the headlines these days. Equally fascinating is a Criminal Register from 1882, with each page devoted to the crimes of the unhappy suspect in the photo at the top. The stairwell up to the gallery is bedecked with tributes to former Commissioners of Police alongside pictures of the Red House ablaze during the 1903 water riots.

Opposite the Central Police Station, on the other side of Sackville Street, is the **police administrative building**, which displays Trinidad and Tobago's police force emblem, a hummingbird and a police badge inside a Star of David, the latter the symbol not of a Jewish connection but of Governor Picton's patron saint.

Rosary Roman Catholic Church

Cnr Henry and Park streets

Built between 1892 and 1910, the dignified Gothic Revival **Rosary Roman Catholic Church** is the most impressive of the city's three main churches, though its imposing

1

towers and ornate stonework are hemmed in by buildings on all sides. You're in luck if you find it open, for the spacious interior is an oasis of peace in this hectic part of the city, and the old **stained glass**, with its finely detailed biblical scenes, is the most beautiful in Port of Spain. Unfortunately the effect is somewhat spoilt by the fluorescent lighting, peeling paint and general dilapidation.

Around the Savannah

Marking the division between downtown and the more upmarket surrounds of the city's upper reaches, the **Queen's Park Savannah** is Port of Spain's largest open space, and a great place to take a gentle walk and admire the capital's prettier side. Fringing the edge of the Savannah are Port of Spain's few concrete attractions: the **National Museum**, a passable **zoo** and the beautiful **Botanical Gardens**, while the palatial mansions of the **Magnificent Seven**, built by the colonial plantocracy, provide some architectural distraction.

Queen's Park Savannah

Despite the traffic that whizzes clockwise around the 3.7-km perimeter road, the **Queen's Park Savannah** is a surprisingly restful spot, crisscrossed by paths and shaded by the spreading branches of some lovely trees, from huge samaans and fragrant carobs to the pink and yellow pouis, which burst into spectacular bloom at the start of the rainy season.

Originally part of a sugar-cane estate, the Savannah was bought by Governor Woodford in 1817 and subsequently developed into a city park. The terms of the sale decreed that no permanent structures would be erected on the land, but though the Savannah has remained its original size, tarmac and Carnival-related buildings on the southern portion are slowly encroaching onto the grass. The largest of these are the semi-permanent Grand Stand and North Stand; each year, the stage constructed between these two spectator stands serves as the centrepiece for the **Carnival celebrations**, from the Panorama steel pan competition and Dimanche Gras show to the epicentre of the Parade of the Bands. The only other construction on the Savannah is the walled **Peschier Cemetery** right in the middle, the burial ground of the original French Creole owners and closed to the public. Otherwise, it's just wide-open spaces, though at the northwest corner, the dips and depressions of the **Hollows** sunken garden, with its fishponds and pathways, are popular with kids.

Pretty much deserted during the hot daylight hours, the Savannah comes to life in the cool of the afternoon, with football games and cricket matches on the grass, and walkers and joggers exercising along the boundary path, and the jelly-coconut vendors doing a roaring trade from the ornate vans parked up on the western boundary. During the windy months of March and April, the Savannah is also a favourite spot for flying **kites**; visit at this time and you'll usually be able to buy one of the brilliant home-made Mad Bulls, T&T's kite of choice, sold by a roving craftsman. Over on the southern paved area, meanwhile, stalls set up as the light fades and do a roaring trade in **street food** snacks such as pholouri, corn soup, roasted corn and barbecue chicken; if you're feeling adventurous, try the oysters doused in peppery tomato sauce, dispensed from a stall opposite the Knowsley Building on Queen's Park West.

National Academy for the Performing Arts

Queen's Park West • ☎ 625 4224

Occupying a block of Queen's Park West between Frederick Street and Chancery Lane, the futuristic **National Academy for the Performing Arts** glowers over the Savannah grass, its arcs of glass and steel looking somewhat incongruous against its colonial-era neighbours. Built at a cost of some TT$500 million by Patrick Manning's PNM government, and opened in 2009, the controversial centre has been lambasted as a white elephant thanks to its shoddy construction. Totally unsuitable as a performance space, it has numerous fundamental design flaws, from an analogue (rather than digital) sound and light system to a backstage loading area so small that even a steel drum can't fit through. To compound all of this, no maintenance programme was put in place after its construction, and by 2014, parts of the building were deemed unsafe and closed down by health and safety inspectors, who catalogued such faults as tiles falling off the exterior, crumbling stage supports and problems with the foundations. Whether there is any money – or political will – to commit to repairs remains to be seen, but for now, its neon-lit bulk certainly makes an interesting addition to the city skyline.

The National Museum and Art Gallery

Cnr Frederick and Keate streets • Tues–Sat 10am–6pm, Sun 2–6pm; **Cazabon gallery** Tues–Fri 10am–6pm • Free • ☎ 623 5941, ⓦ nmag.gov.tt

Just south of the Savannah, and now overshadowed by the NAPA building, the gabled Royal Victoria Institute was built in 1892 as part of the preparations for Queen Victoria's jubilee; today, however, it holds **The National Museum and Art Gallery**. The museum's collection is extensive, covering everything from early **Amerindian history** to the technology of the **oil industry**. Although some of the displays are very much twentieth-century in style, with plenty of yellowing typed labels rather than interactive verve, they provide an essential overview of Trinidad and Tobago's history and culture (though the section on Carnival had been taken down for restoration at the time of writing).

The ground floor

On the ground floor, you enter into a room taken up with the **geological history** of the islands, with racks of locally found specimens including some enormous quartz crystals. There's also plenty on the **colonial era** and beyond, including pictures of the long-defunct tram and trolley-bus networks, a re-creation of a 1940s **barrack yard** and yellowing photos of Port of Spain through the ages, including shots of the devastation wreaked by the 1808 fire. Local industry, from coconuts and cocoa to sugar, rum and oil, are also covered, and around the back, there's a nice little exhibit on the Shouter Baptist faith, with examples of items used for prayer, and a gallery detailing T&T's sporting achievements sponsored – with no hint of irony – by the local tobacco company, WITCO. There's also a room dedicated to Trinbago's music, from calypso to soca and rapso, with a nice montage of newspaper headings covering one wall, a calypso timeline and vintage tunes and footage playing on a video screen. To the rear of the building, across a courtyard with its battery of colonial-era cannons, another room is used to stage temporary exhibitions.

The upper level

The upper level of The National Museum and Art Gallery is mostly given over to **Trinbagonian art**, either pieces from the museum's collection or temporary exhibitions by local artists. The works change frequently, but you'll usually see pieces by big local names such as Leroy Clarke, Shastri Maharaj, Carlisle Chang and Boscoe Holder; on the stairwells, check out the Robert Fraser's wooden reliefs of the Savannah's Magnificent Seven buildings. Elsewhere, there's a room exploring T&T's **natural history**, with stuffed birds and animals, pickled snakes and desiccated spiders and insects, while the **Settlement Gallery** is dedicated to the islands' original Amerindian inhabitants, with heaps of pottery, a re-creation of a burial midden and a dugout canoe, as well as exhibitions on the Spanish, British and French eras. There's also a room filled with lithographs of old Port of Spain and bucolic scenes of rural Trinidad by nineteenth-century painter **Michel Cazabon**, a French Creole man who became Trinidad's first internationally known artist.

1

Queen's Park West

Travelling clockwise around the Savannah from Frederick Street on **Queen's Park West**, you'll come across numerous examples of the gingerbread buildings by Glaswegian architect George Brown, who mass-produced this distinctive fretted woodwork and used it extensively on his designs. Dating from 1904, the ornately decorated **Knowsley Building** at the corner of Chancery Lane resembles a child's fantasy doll's house; the black and white **George Brown House** at the corner of Victoria Avenue is somewhat plainer, though still graced by a great deal of refined fretwork. Just up from the junction with Cipriani Boulevard, **Boissiere House** is fondly called the "Gingerbread House" by locals, and you'd be hard pushed to find a better example of the style. Having been treated to a sensitive restoration, it's a splendidly whimsical concoction of fretted wooden finials and bargeboards, with stained glass depicting meandering strawberry vines and pagoda-like roofs.

The Magnificent Seven

Overlooking the northeast corner of the Savannah along **Maraval Road**, the magical-realist parade of buildings known as the **Magnificent Seven** are the result of the competing egos of rival plantation owners, each of whom tried to outdo his neighbours in the grandeur of their construction. Employing assorted European architectural styles infused with a tropical slant, the buildings were constructed in 1904 (except Hayes Court, which dates from 1910), but though three remain in regular use, some of the others have fallen into a sad state of disrepair. None are open to the public; they are best admired from the Savannah perimeter path.

Queen's Royal College

Working south to north along Maraval Road, the first of the Magnificent Seven is the handsomely restored **Queen's Royal College**, Trinidad's most prestigious school, whose former pupils include the authors V.S. and Shiva Naipaul and the country's first prime minister, Eric Williams. Built along Germanic Renaissance lines and topped with a clock tower, its arcaded balconies and cream-and-ochre stucco offset the blue limestone cornerstones.

Hayes Court

Across Hayes Street from QRC, **Hayes Court** is a grand mansion fusing French and British architectural influences, designed by George Brown and which his characteristic cast-iron pillars and railings along the lower veranda. It was built as the residence of Trinidad's Anglican bishop (and named after the second incumbent, Bishop Thomas Hayes), and is still in use by the Diocese today.

Mille Fleurs

Next to Hayes Court, **Mille Fleurs** is another of George Brown's elaborate gingerbread houses, originally built for Dr Henrique Prada, a well-to-do doctor who went on to serve as the city's mayor between 1914 and 1917. Now state-owned and unoccupied, it's in a terrible condition, much to the despair of conservationists, who lay wreaths of flowers at its gates each April to draw attention to its plight. Restoration is said to be underway, though progress has been slow so far.

Roomor

Commissioned by estate owner Lucien Ambard, **Roomor** is a florid exercise in French Baroque, slathered with Italian marble and tiles from France, its columns, galleries, towers and pinnacles decorated with elaborate ironwork. The only one of the Magnificent Seven that remains a private residence, its original name was the Ambard House; its current moniker is a combination of the surnames of Timothy

Roodal, who bought it in 1940, and that of his granddaughter Dr Yvette Morgan, the current owner.

Archbishop's House
Crossing Flood Street from Roomor, you'll come to the official home of Port of Spain's Roman Catholic archbishop, **Archbishop's House**. A weighty, Neo-Romanesque pile of Irish marble and red granite, capped by a copper roof, it's perhaps the least visually interesting of the Magnificent Seven.

Whitehall
The next house along is **Whitehall**, a Venetian-style palazzo whose gleaming white paintwork gives it the air of a freshly iced birthday cake. Originally the home of cocoa estate owner Joseph Leon Agostini, the building has had a somewhat chequered history. It was commandeered by the US military during World War II, after which it became a cultural centre, a library and then a broadcasting unit. In 1954 it was sold to the government and served as the Office of the Prime Minister until 2009; it's currently vacant.

Stollmeyer's Castle
The most outlandish structure of the seven, Killarney – more popularly known as **Stollmeyer's Castle** – stands at the northern end of Maraval Road just before it veers east into Circular Road. A fairy-tale castle of brick and limestone, bristling with turrets and spires, it was built for a German plantation owner named Stollmeyer by the Scottish architect Robert Giles, who modelled it on Queen Victoria's residence at Balmoral. Architectural historian John Newel Lewis perfectly captured Killarney's delicious absurdity when he wrote: "A German built a bit of an untypical Scottish castle in Trinidad and called it by an Irish name. He must have been by that time a Trinidadian, because only Trinidadians do these things". The Stollmeyer family sold the castle to the government in 1979, after which it entered rapid decline; however, it's in the process of undergoing restoration.

Lady Chancellor Road
The Savannah's northern edge is lined by Circular Road. Just past the Hollows, there's a signposted turn-off to **Lady Chancellor Road**, a precipitous meander of switchback turns that winds its way up the hillside past some palatial homes. A popular spot for afternoon walkers and joggers, Chancellor affords some lovely **views** over the Savannah and across the city skyline.

Emperor Valley Zoo
Circular Rd • Daily 9am–6pm, last tickets sold at 5.30pm • TT$30, children TT$15 • ⓦ zstt.org
First opened in 1952, the **Emperor Valley Zoo**'s original design wasn't particularly animal-friendly, with tiny cages predominating, but efforts are being made to move with the times by way of an ongoing enhancement programme, constrained somewhat by the small proportions of the complex. Though there are still many small cages that don't seem to offer much in terms of quality of life for their inhabitants, the new enclosures are much more animal-friendly. The zoo remains a magnet for local kids, with balloon- and novelty-sellers aplenty at the entrance; it also offers the chance to see local species that you're unlikely to spot in the wild. Close to the entrance is an **otter** enclosure with an underwater viewing area, while the upper reaches of the zoo hold enclosures for **giraffes** and **tigers**. Other residents include **brocket deer**, **quenk**, **capybara**, **lions** (fed daily at 2.30pm), a large selection of **monkeys** (including a cage of native howlers behind the reptile house), aquarium **fish** and **snakes**. There are also **tarantulas** and one of Trinidad's improbably large **giant centipedes**, as well as **ocelots**, **spectacled caiman** and numerous **birds**, including parrots, flamingos, toucans and scarlet ibis.

1

Botanical Gardens
Circular Rd • Daily 6am–6pm • Free

The lovely **Botanical Gardens** were established in 1818 by Governor Woodford and the botanist David Lockhart, and the collection of 700-odd trees is one of the oldest in the western hemisphere. Paths loop around the lawns and up the bamboo-smothered hillsides, and a small **cemetery** in the middle contains the crumbling gravestones of many of the island's governors, including Solomon Hochoy. It's a lovely spot for a wander, often deserted during the heat of the day but livelier in the late afternoon, when joggers, walkers and families take to the paths and lawns.

President's House

Behind the Botanical Gardens, in equally well-kept grounds, the austere, stately **President's House** was built in 1876 as the residence of the island's British governors, and the house and its attached Cottage were home to successive presidents until, in 2010, deterioration of the building following years of neglect saw most of the west wing collapse. It's now hunkered under a protective metal roof, pending restoration (slated to start in spring 2015); the grounds are closed to the public, but you can get a good view of what remains of the building from inside the Botanical Gardens. Hidden from sight behind the President's House, and likewise closed to the public, is the **Prime Minister's Residence**, treated to a lavish TT$244 million upgrade by PNM incumbent Patrick Manning; however, since the PNM lost the 2010 election, its night-lit moat and diplomatic centre have remained unused by People's Partnership PM Kamla Persad-Bissessar, who chose to build herself another house in South Trinidad and commute to Port of Spain by helicopter.

PLAYING MAS

The headquarters of Carnival costume bands (see p.81), **mas camps** are scattered throughout Port of Spain, with the majority in Woodbrook. Traditionally, these are the workshops in which Carnival costumes are made, with troops of mas-makers (many unpaid volunteers) labouring away to get the designs finished in time for the big day amid a sea of wire, sequins, feathers and glue-guns. Mas camps have long provided a focus for the Trinidadian arts community, with many a painter, actor, dancer or writer pitching in to make mas, but these days, with many costumes produced in the Far East and shipped over to be assembled here, fewer and fewer of the camps are places where costumes are actually made. Instead, they serve as a showroom for the designs, where potential masqueraders can get a close-up view of the various **sections** that make up a band; they're also the place where revellers **register to play mas** and, often, collect their costumes (though the larger bands often distribute at bigger venues such as the National Stadium or *Hilton Trinidad* hotel).

THEMES AND COSTUMES

Every year, each band chooses a **theme** to portray during Carnival, anything from the loosely whimsical – "Birds of a Feather" – to a historical period. The band is then divided into different named **sections**, each with its own costume linked to the theme, and with a designated position within the band during the street parades (note that it's fine for masqueraders to wander through the band when on the road, but you must stay with your section at judging points). Anyone with the inclination and the money to pay for the costume can register with a band to "play mas". In recent years, **costumes** have increasingly catered to the desire to wear as little as possible, including thongs and Brazil-style cage-bras for women; most female costumes, though, consist of a decorated bikini top and belt, plus bikini pants/boy shorts, a headpiece and accessories for the arms and legs; male costumes are less elaborate, usually board shorts, a small headpiece and some kind of sash around the chest. If skimpy "pretty mas" doesn't appeal, you could play with a steel band such as All Stars or Woodbrook Modernaires

1

Lady Young Road

Past the Botanical Gardens, a roundabout at the edge of the Savannah has exits for the residential districts of St Ann's and Cascade, and for **Lady Young Road**, a steep and twisting route up past the *Hilton* hotel and into the hills; a **viewing point** some ten minutes' drive from the Savannah affords excellent views over the city and of the container ships queuing up in the Gulf of Paria. Stalls sell Trini sweets, snacks and souvenirs.

Beyond the Lookout, Lady Young swings through **Morvant**, a close-knit but impoverished community that's sadly known for its high crime rate, much of it thanks to gang violence and drug wars.

Newtown

Spreading back southwest of the Savannah and bordered to the south by busy Tragarete Road lie the neighbouring districts of St Clair and Newtown, an upscale mix of commerce and residential streets. A network of narrow streets between Maraval Road and Queen's Park West, **NEWTOWN** holds some pretty colonial-era buildings, most housing offices these days, but no sights per se; however, with its decent accommodation options and burgeoning restaurant scene, it makes a good base from which to explore the city.

St Clair

West of Maraval Road, the leafy backstreets of **ST CLAIR** are home to the country's well-to-do as well as most of the country's diplomatic missions. An exclusive enclave of lavish houses protected by high walls, barking guard dogs and sophisticated security systems, St Clair holds some handsome and well-kept colonial-era mansions. The area

---

that produce simple costume bands, or opt for a smaller outfit such as Cat in Bag, which makes more individualistic and elaborate costumes.

It's usual not to wear your full costume on Carnival Monday, saving it for the main Tuesday parade. The all-inclusive bands used to give out T-shirts and shorts to their masqueraders, who'd add a few simple embellishments, but today, **Monday wear** is a whole industry, with revellers creating their own elaborate costumes or going to specialist Monday wear designers. You might also want to give a thought to **footwear**; while trainers are perfectly acceptable, most serious masqueraders play mas in decorated long boots. Again, there are a host of outfits that will decorate your footwear for you, though it's of course cheaper to buy some bling from a Carnival store (see p.92) and do it yourself.

REGISTERING WITH A BAND

To play mas, you must first **register** with a mas band; you can do this online at the band websites (see p.81) or, if you're in Trinidad ahead of Carnival, go directly to the mas camp and try your luck. All-inclusive packages with the big bands, including costume, and food and drink on both parade days, cost anything from TT$5000 for a basic "Backline" costume to TT$10,000 upwards for a "Frontline" or "Individual" extravaganza; however, smaller bands can be cheaper. Note also that if you wish to play in premium bands such as Tribe, Fantasy or Bliss, you'll need to check the Trinidad Carnival Diary website in early summer to find out when bands are launching and when registration begins; most sell out within a few days, while the hot costumes of the year are snapped up in a matter of hours. Bear in mind, though, that as the popular bands offer priority registration to previous masqueraders, you may not be able to get a costume however early you visit the website.

If you arrive in Trinidad late or decide you want to play mas at the last minute, you could try the costume classifieds at ⓦfineahban.com, though many sellers hike up prices to ridiculous levels if demand is high. Most bands also sell uncollected costumes on the Sunday before the main parade; contact the mas camps to check availability.

Note that contact details and more information on individual mas and Jouvert bands appears in our Carnival Listings section (see p.81).

is also home to the **Harts mas camp** at 5 Alcazar Street, run by the same family since 1959. Famous for their skimpy feathers-and-beads designs, Harts were the first to market themselves as a "fun" band and have been at the forefront of the development of bikini mas.

Queen's Park Oval

Tragarete Rd • **Grounds** Daily 8am–4pm; ask the security guard at the gate to let you in • **Museum** Appointment only ☎ 753 2775 • US$10 • **Matches** Seats in the stands cost TT$40–200 depending on the level of the match taking place, or you can pay TT$250–300 for an all-inclusive ticket to the Trini Posse stand (food and drink included) • Box office information ☎ 622 2295, ⓦ qpcc.com

On the southern border of St Clair stands the **Queen's Park Oval**, originally built in 1896 and still Trinidad's premier **cricket ground**, hosting national and international matches in season (Feb–April), as well as doubling as an occasional concert venue at Carnival time. Even if you're not a cricket fan, attending a match here is a unique and enjoyable experience; the game is a national obsession in Trinidad, and matches are followed with a passion. The atmosphere is rowdy but good-natured, with fans draped in the national flag and music blaring from sound systems after every over and wicket. Cricket fans might also want to check out the Oval's **Cricket Heritage Museum**; highlights include a bat signed by the 1950s West Indies team that won the region's first Test against England at Lord's, and a whole section dedicated to the legendary Brian Lara, including the bat he used to hit home his record-breaking 370, 400 and 501 Test runs.

Woodbrook

Immediately west of the downtown area, and demarked by Philipps Street to the east and the Maraval River to the west, the elegant old district of **WOODBROOK** was established in the early twentieth century on land that once formed part of a sugar estate owned by the Siegert family, creators of Trinidad's famous Angostura bitters (see p.77). Many of the streets here – such as Carlos, Luis and Siegert – bear their names, and you'll still see plenty of the houses built by the original middle-class inhabitants, with wonderful fretworked bargeboards and delicate balustrades and finials. Running straight through the centre of Woodbrook, the wide boulevard of **Ariapita Avenue**, the capital's primary liming and dining location, lined with bars and restaurants and a lively place to be most nights of the week. The Avenue is also one of the busiest parts of town during Carnival, with a main judging point at Adam Smith Square, and stalls and crowds lining the tarmac. Woodbrook's backstreets, meanwhile, hold a healthy sprinkling of mas camps, where the Carnival bands have their bases, as well as a host of inexpensive guesthouses.

JOUVERT

Carnival officially starts with **Jouvert** (see p.261), an anarchic and raunchy early-hours orgy of pure, unadulterated bacchanalia, with generous coatings of mud, chocolate, oil or body paint – and libations of local rum, of course – helping you lose all inhibitions and slide through the streets in an anonymous mass of dirty, drunken, happy humanity. You can just head out onto the streets of Woodbrook and St James and get stuck in, but given Jouvert's wild overtones it's a much better idea to join an organized **Jouvert band** and play "dirty mas". A fee of US$50–100 will get you a basic costume and all the mud, body paint or liquid chocolate you desire, as well as security (an excellent idea, as Jouvert can be wild). Many bands are all-inclusive, meaning you get drinks and snacks on the road, and breakfast afterwards. Some also offer a hose-down at the end of it all. New bands appear each year, so listen to radio adverts or check the press and ⓦ trinidadcarnivaldiary.com for details; our Carnival Listings section (see p.81) includes some of the most popular and long-standing bands.

1

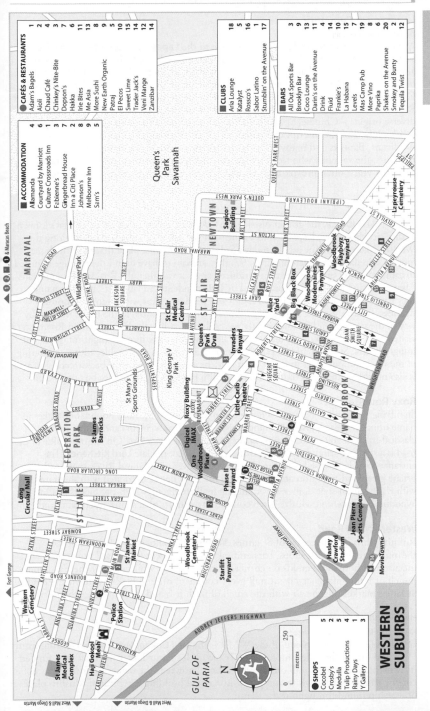

● CAFÉS & RESTAURANTS

Adam's Bagels	1
Aioli	2
Chaud Café	4
Chinkey's Nite-Bite	3
Dopson's	7
Hakka	6
Irie Bites	11
Me Asia	13
More Sushi	8
New Earth Organic	9
Patra	5
El Pecos	10
Sweet Lime	15
Trader Jack's	14
Veni Mangé	12
Zanzibar	14

■ CLUBS

Aria Lounge	18
Katalyst	5
Rossco's	16
Sabor Latino	1
Stumblin' on the Avenue	17

■ BARS

All Out Sports Bar	3
Brooklyn Bar	9
Coco Lounge	13
Darin's on the Avenue	11
Drink	4
Fluid	14
Frankie's	10
La Habana	15
Levels	7
Mas Camp Pub	19
More Vino	8
Paprika	6
Shakers on the Avenue	20
Smokey and Bunty	2
Tequila Twist	12

■ ACCOMMODATION

Alamanda	4
Courtyard by Marriott	6
Culture Crossroads Inn	1
Fabienne's	7
Gingerbread House	2
Inn a Citi Place	8
Johnson's	9
Melbourne Inn	3
Sam's	5

● SHOPS

Cocobel	5
Crosby's	2
Medulla	5
Tulip Productions	4
Rainy Days	1
Y Gallery	3

WESTERN SUBURBS

1

Lapeyrouse Cemetery

Philipps St • Daily 6am–6pm

At Woodbrook's eastern edge is the entrance to the **Lapeyrouse Cemetery**, a walled burial ground dating back to 1813. Victorian tombs adorned with Gothic spires and angels are eerily framed against the lush, tropical backdrop, while strands of ivy trail over the graves. The Siegert family are buried here, as are the labour leader Arthur Cipriani, the calypsonian Melody, and Charlie King, the policeman killed in the Butler Riots in the 1930s (see box, p.186). The names on the gravestones provide clues to the diverse origins – Chinese, Spanish, African, Indian and European – of Port of Spain's inhabitants, and the inscriptions reflect its varied religious affiliations: Catholics, Anglicans, Baptists and many other faiths are represented. The cemetery's newer residents, the vagrants who sleep in the more dilapidated tombs, have been a talking point for years, often provoking press articles about the problem of homelessness.

St James

West of Woodbrook, the grittier district of **ST JAMES** is a cosmopolitan place that's known as the "city that never sleeps" thanks to the string of bars and street-food stalls along the Western Main Road. The area of today's St James was the first place that the British set foot on Trinidadian soil; landing in 1797, they are said to have found the courage required to capture Port of Spain in the rum produced at what was then the Peru sugar-cane estate. After emancipation, the area was settled by **Indian** indentured labourers, and the names they gave to their streets – Calcutta, Delhi and Madras – bear witness to their home-sickness. Today, the estate is long-gone, but rum remains central to the life of the area by way of the street-front bars and slightly seedy clubs that line the Western Main Road, best visited after dark when music blares and stalls serve food late into the night for queues of hungry limers. St James' Indian population have also stayed very visible, with a smattering of mosques and puja flags in many front gardens along the residential backstreets. The area is also notable as the focus of the annual Muslim **Hosay** processions (see box opposite).

Roxy Roundabout

Signifying the division between Woodbrook and St James, the **Roxy Roundabout** takes its name from the adjacent **Roxy Building**, originally built as a cinema and with a ritzy classical-modern colonnade; it now houses a branch of *Pizza Hut*. On the other side of the road is a statue in tribute to the grandmaster of calypso, the late **Lord Kitchener**. The entrance to St James itself is marked by the bridge over the Maraval River, spanned by an ornate green-and-pink iron **archway** bearing the area's name, decorated with shells and with eight Hindu-style domes. Overhanging it all are the ugly high-rise blocks of One Woodbrook Place, an exclusive gated community with its own shops, restaurants and gym.

Western Main Road

Running through the centre of St James, **Western Main Road** (WMR) is a broad thoroughfare lined with shops, bars and takeaways. Street vendors sell vegetables, incense and household goods on corners during the day, while at night there's a food, punch or home-made ice-cream stall every couple of metres. Halfway down the road, **St James Market** fills the air with the smell of fresh fish and meat in the early mornings.

Haji Gokool Meah Masjid

Western Main Rd • Closed to non-worshippers

Overlooking the western end of the WMR is the **Haji Gokool Meah Masjid**, dating from 1927 and one of the oldest mosques in Trinidad. It's named after the man who funded its construction, a local millionaire who is best known as the owner of Trinidad's Globe cinema chain, and the white-and-green-minareted building is typical of Muslim places of worship found throughout the island.

HOSAY

The Islamic festival of **Hosay**, commemorating the martyrdom of Mohammad's grandsons Hussein and Hassan during the jihad (Holy War) in Persia, has been celebrated in Trinidad since the first Indian Muslims arrived in 1845. The festival's exposure to the island's other cultures has turned it into something resembling Carnival, with wining and loud music, but in recent years local Shi'a Muslims have taken great pains to restore the occasion's solemnity. This hasn't stopped St James' bars from making a mint on Hosay night, however – many locals watch the proceedings with a beer or rum in hand, much to the consternation of devout Muslims.

Hosay is celebrated in Curepe, Tunapuna, Couva and Cedros, but the best place to see it is undoubtedly St James. Trinis of all religions come here to view the festivities, which are held over four days (dates change according to the Islamic calendar; see ⓦ bestoftrinidad.com/culture .html). All of the night parades start at 11pm and continue into the early hours of the morning.

THE BUILD-UP

In the weeks leading up to Hosay, it's possible to watch craftsmen in St James building **tadjahs**, the ornate tombs made from bamboo and coloured paper that are carried in procession; the houses where they work have large flags planted in their yards. There are only five families who build the structures each year, four based in St James and one in Cocorite. Families have to be approved by a local committee, and strict rules apply – they must be the direct descendants of Indian immigrants with an ancestral tradition of *tadjah* building. The task involves great financial, physical and spiritual sacrifice; the materials can cost many thousands of dollars, and the builders have to fast during daylight hours and refrain from alcohol and sexual activity for the duration. Understandably, perhaps, not many of the younger generation find the prospect appealing, and as the years pass fewer and fewer *tadjahs* are being built.

THE FESTIVAL NIGHTS

The first procession is **flag night**, when hundreds of devotees walk through the streets with multicoloured flags representing the beginning of the battle of Kerbala, in which the brothers lost their lives.

On the **second night**, two small *tadjahs* are carried slowly through the streets to the throbbing beat of tassa drums; the shredded-paper fires at the side of the road are there to warm up the drums, which tightens the skins and produces a better sound.

The **third night** is the most spectacular. Large *tadjahs* more than 2m high are paraded through the streets, while dancers carry two large sickle moons representing the brothers. At midnight there is the ritual "kissing of the moons", as the dancers symbolically re-enact a brotherly embrace.

On the **fourth day**, after the moons have been paraded again through the streets, the exquisite *tadjahs* are traditionally thrown into the sea, a sacrifice to ensure that prayers for recovery from sickness and adversity will be answered. These days, however, most *tadjahs* are disposed of in more environmentally friendly ways. The celebrations usually finish at around 7pm.

Fort George

Fort George Rd • Daily 10am–6pm • Free

Perched on a hilltop above St James, ten minutes' drive north of the Western Main Road, **Fort George** affords some spectacular views of Port of Spain and beyond into Caroni and the Central Plains, as well as west along the coast to the Bocas. Taxis leave sporadically from the corner of Western Main Road and Bourne's Road; the route up passes through some slightly dodgy areas, so it's best not to walk. The fort was built in 1804 to defend the island against the French Caribbean fleet during the Napoleonic Wars, though it never saw any action; the original cannons still point out to sea.

Stone defensive walls surround the wooden **signal station** designed by an exiled West African prince, Kofi Nti, who came to Trinidad after becoming a Ward of the British courts following the Ashanti war of 1872; he's described on the information boards as a "quiet, unassuming man with a great interest in stamp collecting". The station itself was used to signal between here and the other post stations along the coast, and the bare interior displays an ornate, armoured wooden chest from Marseilles, thought to

1

have been brought here to store valuables. Though the fort's lock-up looks secure enough – check out the window bars made from rifle barrels – the only thing it ever guarded were the valuables of Port of Spain's merchants, who carted their treasures up here whenever the threat of insurrection loomed.

The **grounds** are dotted with picnic tables, and make a popular spot to come and get a little respite from the city, with a constant cooling breeze.

Belmont

A maze of narrow lanes flanking the eastern side of the Queen's Park Savannah, **BELMONT** is one of the most densely populated areas of Port of Spain. It was the city's first suburb, settled in the early nineteenth century by Africans who had escaped slavery on other Caribbean islands, and many original wooden houses survive from this era, proudly displaying their characteristically ornate gingerbread fretwork. After emancipation, freed slaves from Trinidad and a number of peoples from West Africa also settled here. In 1868, the tribal chieftain of the **Rada community** – a religious group from the French protectorate of Dahomey – bought land in the area to establish a settlement. Representatives from the Mandingo, Ibo, Yoruba and Krumen tribes also came to live here, and Belmont became an established African settlement. The community was well organized and close-knit, ensuring the survival of African traditions such as the Orisha religion (see p.253), whose feasts and festivities are still practised here – though you won't see much evidence of this as a casual visitor. Belmont was also the birthplace of **Stokely Carmichael** (1941–1998), founder of the **Black Power** movement and one of its vocal activists during the 1970s. Carmichael migrated to Harlem, New York, aged 11, and his civil rights work is today commemorated by a plaque outside his former home at 54 Oxford Street, now a community education centre.

At Carnival time, the community centre just off the Savannah on Jerningham Avenue is also worth a visit, as it hosts what's known as **Five Nights**, a brilliant reggae jam staged by the Twelve Tribes Rasta sect and a great antidote to the frenetic menu of soca, soca and soca.

Trinidad Theatre Workshop

23 Jerningham Ave • Open for performances only • ☎ 624 8502, ⓦ trinidadtheatreworkshop.com

Housed in a gorgeous little fretworked building, the **Trinidad Theatre Workshop** was founded in 1959 by poet, playwright and Nobel Laureate **Derek Walcott**. It established a theatrical tradition in Trinidad, made acting a recognized profession and launched the

---

VISITING PANYARDS

The best way to hear **steel pan** is live, in the open air – there is nothing as romantic as listening to its rich chiming harmonies drifting on the wind on a warm starry night. Throughout the year Port of Spain hosts events in which pan features prominently, but in the run-up to Carnival, it's well worth taking a tour around the city's panyards, where the musicians gather most nights to practise their compositions for the Panorama competition (see p.267). Visitors are welcome (crowds get quite sizeable as the big day approaches), and there's always a bar and somewhere to sit and take in the music – though bear in mind that you may hear a section of a song being practised over and over again rather than the whole thing. Panyards are also open at other times, though the scene isn't as animated.

If you don't have a car or want to get a better insight into pan, one of the best ways to visit the yards is to take an evening **tour** with Gunda Harewood of Island Experiences (☎621 0407 or ☎781 6235, ⓦislandexperiencestt.com; US$45). Details of Port of Spain's better-known **panyards** appear in our Carnival Listings section (see p.81); Phase II, Invaders, Silver Stars, Renegades and All Stars usually draw the biggest crowds. For full listings of the country's pan bands, visit ⓦpantrinbago.co.tt.

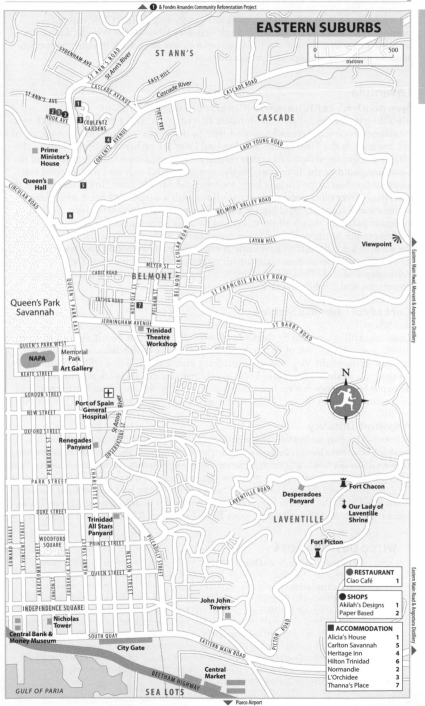

& Fondes Amandes Community Reforestation Project

EASTERN SUBURBS

1

0 — 500
metres

ST ANN'S

SYDENHAM AVE
ST ANN'S ROAD
St Ann's River
EAST HILL
CASCADE AVENUE
Cascade River
CASCADE ROAD

ST ANN'S AVE
NOOK AVE
COBLENTZ GARDENS
FIRST AVE
CASCADE

CORBLENTZ AVENUE
LADY YOUNG ROAD

Prime Minister's House

Queen's Hall

CIRCULAR ROAD

BELMONT VALLEY ROAD

LAYAN HILL
Viewpoint

MEYER ST
CADIZ ROAD
BELMONT
NORFOLK ST
PELHAM ST
BELMONT CIRCULAR ROAD
ST FRANCOIS VALLEY ROAD

Queen's Park Savannah

ERTHIG ROAD
JERNINGHAM AVENUE
ST BARBS ROAD

Trinidad Theatre Workshop

QUEEN'S PARK WEST
NAPA
Memorial Park
Art Gallery
KEATE STREET

QUEEN'S PARK EAST

GORDON STREET
NEW STREET
Port of Spain General Hospital
St Ann's River

OXFORD STREET
Renegades Panyard
OBSERVATORY ST

PEMBROKE ST
CHARLOTTE ST

PARK STREET
LAVENTILLE ROAD
Fort Chacon

DUKE STREET
Desperadoes Panyard
Our Lady of Laventille Shrine

EDWARD STREET
ST VINCENT STREET
Trinidad All Stars Panyard
WOODFORD SQUARE
PRINCE STREET
HENRY STREET
NELSON STREET
PICCADILLY STREET
LAVENTILLE
Fort Picton

ABERCROMBY ST
CHACON ST
FREDERICK STREET
QUEEN STREET

INDEPENDENCE SQUARE
John John Towers

Nicholas Tower

Central Bank & Money Museum
SOUTH QUAY
City Gate
EASTERN MAIN ROAD
PICTON ROAD

GULF OF PARIA
BEETHAM HIGHWAY
Central Market
SEA LOTS

Piarco Airport

N

Eastern Main Road, Morvant & Angostura Distillery

Eastern Main Road & Angostura Distillery

● RESTAURANT	
Ciao Café	1

● SHOPS	
Akilah's Designs	1
Paper Based	2

■ ACCOMMODATION	
Alicia's House	1
Carlton Savannah	5
Heritage Inn	4
Hilton Trinidad	6
Normandie	2
L'Orchidee	3
Thanna's Place	7

careers of many of the Caribbean's most famous thespians. The TTW enjoyed its heyday in the 1960s and 70s, and though Walcott's 1992 Nobel Prize for Literature inspired a regeneration of sorts, it's a quiet place these days, with its small performance space in use for workshops and productions.

Laventille

Elywyn Francis Tours 2–3hr, TT$125 per person, plus TT$150 for transport • ☎ 627 3377 or ☎ 356 5118

Tumbling down the hillside that borders Port of Spain to the east, **LAVENTILLE** was established by freed slaves who settled here in the 1840s – right "on the eyebrow of the enemy", as the Trinidadian novelist Earl Lovelace rather beautifully put it. The city's most impoverished and crime-ridden area, it remains a volatile place, said to be a stronghold of the Jamaat-al-Muslimeen (see pp.62–63) and forever used as a political football by politicians keen to swing the African vote. The birthplace of the steel pan, Laventille's winding lanes are lined with a dense mishmash of buildings – some made from salvaged boards topped with rusting galvanized iron, others veritable palaces – which sit on steep and twisting streets in defiance of gravity. However, due to the volatility of the area, it's not a place for a casual wander; if you do want to get a flavour of Laventille it's best to go on a **walking tour** with local Elwyn Francis who also works as a tour guide for the Chaguaramas Development Authority and is well placed to gauge if it's a good time to visit; violent flare-ups sometimes make it best avoided.

Our Lady of Laventille Shrine

Upper Picton Rd

Laventille Hill is crowned by **Our Lady of Laventille Shrine**, an imposing landmark that's visible from all over Port of Spain. Atop the 16m belfry of this white stone church stands a statue of the Virgin Mary, a gift from France in 1876 and still a pilgrimage site on the Feast of the Assumption. Look closely and you can also pick out the Martello Tower at **Fort Picton**, just up from the church, built by the notorious British governor of the same name in the late 1790s, and now an outpost of the Trinidad Defence Force.

Angostura Distillery

Cnr Eastern Main Rd & Trinity Ave • Tours Mon–Fri 9.30am and 1.30pm; 2hr 15min • US$10 • ☎ 623 1841, ⓦ angostura.com • To get there from downtown Port of Spain, it's a straight route along the Eastern Main Rd from South Quay; a more scenic alternative from the Savannah is to follow Lady Young Rd to the Morvant junction and turn right onto the Eastern Main Rd; the distillery entrance is on the left

Though Laventille proper isn't a place for sightseeing, it is worth making the trek out to its outskirts, where the rows of old warehouses between the highway and the Eastern Main Road hold the massive complex of the **Angostura Distillers**, producers of T&T's famous **bitters**, as well as its **rums**, from Black Label and White Oak to Forres Park

---

WITCO DESPERADOES

Celebrated by the Nobel laureate **Derek Walcott** in his poem *The Hills of Laventille*, many of the great calypsonians hail from Laventille, but as the birthplace of the steel pan and the home of the **Witco Desperadoes**, the area is more closely associated with Trinidad's national instrument. Established by Rudolph Charles in the 1940s and the oldest steel band in the country, Desperadoes (first known as the Dead End Kids) quickly notched up a deadly reputation, thanks both to the skill of their pannists and the quick fists of the "bad johns" that made up their numbers. With ten Panorama wins to their credit (the last in 2000), Despers attract a crowd of die-hard supporters who make performances an exciting prospect. However, the uneasy notion of venturing up to the panyard just off the main Laventille Road has led Despers to set up a temporary base overlooking the Savannah in the run-up to Carnival, on the corner of Queen's Park East and Cadiz Road.

THE ANGOSTURA SAGA

As T&T's sole producer of rum, **Angostura Distillers** hold a special place in the hearts of local limers. Trinbagonians stick by Angostura with a nationalistic zeal, declaring its rum the best in the world and adding a dash of its **aromatic bitters** to everything from drinks to marinades, soups and puddings, as well as swearing by the mixture as a cure for almost any ailment.

Angostura was founded by **J.G.B. Siegert**, a German surgeon who left his homeland to join Simón Bolívar in the fight for Venezuelan independence from Spain. Alarmed at the debilitating stomach ailments that plagued Bolívar's troops, Siegert began experimenting with South American herbs and spices to concoct a remedy. He succeeded in 1824, creating the secret blend of botanicals that still make up the **bitters** today, and named his tonic after the Venezuelan town where Bolívar's movement was based.

Popularized by sailors who brought wind of its curative powers to England, the mixture was first exported six years later, and demand increased rapidly. Production was shifted to the more economically and politically stable Trinidad, and the George Street plant soon dominated the small town of Port of Spain. After Siegert died in 1870, the company was taken over by his sons. The founder's great-grandson Robert Siegert, who took the helm in 1928, steered Angostura to loftier heights, establishing the Caribbean's most modern distillery in 1949 and exporting Trinidad's beloved product all over the world.

As the company became more valuable, so foreign investors began to make increasingly generous takeover bids. By now, however, Angostura had become so entrenched in the psyche (and the economy) of Trinidad that the government stepped in, taking control of the company in the mid-1950s and returning it to Siegert Holdings, who offered cut-price shares to employees and affirmed Angostura as the **"people's distiller"**. Despite its bitters being voted the world's worst-displayed product by the British Advertising Council in 1995 (the packaging has changed little since 1824), Angostura has gone from strength to strength, buying out other local distillers, establishing a shiny new factory on the outskirts of Laventille and winning scores of awards; no less than seven monarchs, including Britain's Queen Elizabeth, have given bitters the royal stamp.

The company continues to take its traditions seriously, and the **secret recipe** for bitters remains cloaked in mystery. No one knows the entire recipe for Angostura bitters; instead, five individuals memorize a specific section of some ingredients, and these five are not allowed to enter the blending room (or even travel) together. After mixing the ingredients, each sends their part of the blend down a chute to the same percolating container that's been used since the company began trading in Trinidad, where the herbs and spices are "shampooed" in alcohol for twenty hours before fermentation and bottling.

puncheon and the premium Single Barrel and 1919 brands. Tours of the rum factory cover the history of the company as well as a look around the bottling plant, distillery and bitters production area; you'll also see the 700-plus specimens of the Barcant Butterfly Collection, and get to sample the rums. Tours are only available to groups of ten or more; call to see if it's possible to fit in with existing bookings.

St Ann's and Cascade

From the northeast corner of the Queen's Park Savannah, St Ann's Road heads past the **Queen's Hall**, a favourite venue for pre-Carnival calypso revues, drama, dance and fashion shows. The leafy suburb of **ST ANN'S** melts almost seamlessly into the equally well-to-do **CASCADE** to the east, both residential districts that offer little in the way of sightseeing.

Fondes Amandes Community Reforestation Project

Fondes Amandes Rd • Daily, no set hours • Guided walks US$10–30 • ☎ 689 7794 or ☎ 750 1716, ⓦ facrp.org • From the Savannah, take St Ann's Rd, and then turn left and follow Fondes Amandes Rd to its end

It's well worth heading to the far reaches of St Ann's to seek out the brilliant **Fondes Amandes Community Reforestation Project**, which, as the name suggests, has been doing marvellous work replanting the denuded St Ann's hillsides and creating "fire paths" to stop seasonal bush fires in their tracks. Some 7000 trees have already been planted, and the project's land is laced with easy hiking trails that afford lovely views of the city. **Guided walks** are available, during which you can learn more about the project's work, and relax afterwards with a natural juice made with fruits from the trees which now flourish on the hillside.

Maraval

Some 5km north of central Port of Spain via Circular Road from the northwest corner of the Savannah, **MARAVAL** lies at the base of the Northern Range, surrounded by lush green hills. What was once a small village on the outskirts of the capital has now mushroomed into an upmarket residential suburb, with a sprinkling of hotels and guesthouses. Past the open-plan Ellerslie Plaza Shopping Centre, Maraval's main thoroughfare (and the route to Maracas Beach) **Saddle Road** is lined with shops and houses; just up from the junction with Long Circular Road, the Shoppes of Maraval and adjacent Royal Palm Plaza include a supermarket, pharmacy and several fast-food restaurants.

Our Lady of Lourdes
182 Saddle Rd

Directly opposite Morne Coco Road (a scenic and hilly route into Diego Martin valley), the cream-and-maroon Neo-Romanesque **Our Lady of Lourdes** Roman Catholic church dominates the hillside on the right-hand side of Saddle Road. Built in 1879 and enlarged in 1934, it's notable more for its picturesque exterior than a spectacular interior.

St Andrew's Golf Course
St Andrew's Wynd, Moka • Daily 6am–7pm • 9 holes TT$180–325, 18 holes TT$300–545 • ☎ 629 0066, Ⓦ golftrinidad.com • Follow Saddle Rd past Morne Coco Rd, and carry straight on along Perseverance Rd; turn right onto Moka Main Rd, and left onto St Andrew's Wynd

North of Saddle Road, you'll pass the turn-off for the expansive, well-kept **St Andrew's Golf Course** in Moka, its picturesque 18 holes nestled under the foothills of the Northern Range. Beyond St Andrew's, Saddle Road takes a scenic route over the hills, providing good views of the forested slopes of the Maraval Valley and eventually arriving – after many steep inclines and hairpin bends – at Maracas on the north coast.

ARRIVAL AND DEPARTURE
PORT OF SPAIN

BY PLANE

Domestic and international flights arrive and depart from Piarco International Airport (☎ 669 4866, Ⓦ piarcoairport .com), 24km east of Port of Spain via the Churchill Roosevelt Highway. The small tourist information office (daily 8am–midnight; ☎ 669 5196, Ⓦ gotrinidadandtobago.com) to the right of arrivals can provide you with maps and basic information. Just after you clear immigration there is a bureau de change (daily 24hr), and a bmobile outlet selling local SIM cards and mobile phones. The main concourse in between the arrivals and departure areas has ATMs and fast-food outlets; there's also a local food court adjacent to arrivals; turn left as you exit. There are several hotels nearby.

Airlines American Airlines ☎ 821 6000; British Airways ☎ 669 2630; Caribbean Airlines ☎ 625 7200; LIAT ☎ 1888 844 5428.

Airport taxis and transfers Official airport taxis, which wait outside the main entrance, will take you to Port of Spain for US$45 (30min, or 1–2hr during the 6–8am &

4–6pm rush hours). Prices to all destinations are listed in the arrivals hall where the car rental agencies are situated, and online at Ⓦ gotrinidadandtobago.com; drivers will accept US and local currency. Note that between 10pm and 6am fares to and from the airport increase by fifty percent. If you fancy a gentler introduction to Port of Spain than a taxi ride, with lots of local info thrown in to prime your trip, get in touch with Island Experiences (☎ 621 0407 or ☎ 781 6235), whose drivers charge around US$5 more than regular taxis.

Route taxis and maxis into town If you're travelling very light, a dirt-cheap option is to take a shared route taxi to Arouca Junction on the Eastern Main Rd, from where you can catch an eastbound red-band maxi taxi to downtown Port of Spain's City Gate (see opposite). However, route taxis don't come into the airport concourse – you'll have to walk for ten minutes to the main road, where taxis pass at regular intervals; and don't expect to be able to stow large cases.

Buses into town A PTSC bus runs between Piarco and Port of Spain's City Gate terminal fifteen times a day, departing from Piarco's main entrance (10min walk from arrivals) at 15min past the hour from 6.30am to 8.15pm; and City Gate at 5.45am, 6.30am and then at 5min past the hour until 7.05pm.

BY CAR

The only route into the city is the Churchill Roosevelt Hwy, which heads directly into Port of Spain, becoming Wrightson Rd as you pass Independence Square. The right-hand turn-off onto Colville St, next to the Powergen plant, is convenient for many of Port of Spain's accommodation options. For Woodbrook's Ariapita Ave, take the first left off Colville; to reach the Savannah and the turn-offs for Newtown, Maraval, St Ann's and Cascade, go straight across Tragarete Rd at the end of Colville, and onto Cipriani Blvd.

BY FERRY

Ferries from Tobago arrive and depart at the Port of Spain terminal on Wrightson Rd, opposite Independence Square (☎625 4906, ⓦhttps://ttitferry.com). There are usually two daily fast-ferry sailings, though schedules are increased at peak times (and are detailed on the website); sailing time is officially 2.5hr, but can take longer. Bear in mind that the journey between Trinidad and Tobago can be rough; take sea-sickness tablets, and try to find a seat in the middle of the ferry. There's no official private taxi rank, but you should be able to find a driver easily; alternatively head over to the rank on Independence Square (see p.80).

Tickets You can buy tickets for same-day sailings at the Ferry Terminal, but for all advance bookings (advisable well in advance in busy periods), you'll need to go in person to an authorized vendor; full details of these are on the website. Tickets cost TT$50/person (half-price for kids), plus $150 for a car.

BY BUS AND TAXI

Buses and maxi taxis All buses and maxi taxis arrive and depart at the busy City Gate terminal on South Quay, at the heart of downtown Port of Spain one block south of Independence Square, and in walking distance of the departure points for maxis and route taxis to elsewhere in the city (see p.80). City buses depart from City Gate; fares are TT$2.50 to anywhere in Port of Spain, and tickets need to be purchased before you board from outlets in the terminus.

Private taxis There's no official private taxi rank, but you should be able to find a driver easily, or head over to the rank on Independence Square (see p.80).

BY WATER TAXI

Water taxis arrive and depart from the Water Taxi Terminal (☎624 5137, ⓦnidco.co.tt) on Wrightson Rd, between the Ferry Terminal and the *Breakfast Shed*, adjacent to Independence Square. Taking a water taxi is an enjoyable way to beat the traffic, particularly if you're travelling at rush hour or are heading out to Chaguaramas for a Carnival fete.

Destinations Chaguaramas (15min; TT$10); San Fernando (45min; TT$15)

GETTING AROUND

During the day, Port of Spain and its environs are served by plenty of **buses**, **maxis** and **route taxis**, though traffic jams are terrible during the rush hours (roughly 7–9am & 4–6pm). Route taxis – and to a lesser extent maxis – also operate throughout the night on the more popular routes (including Maraval), albeit a lot less frequently than during the day. As they're subject to change and are always very small amounts, we haven't quoted exact fares for public transport. Most route or maxi taxi drivers are unlikely to try and rip you off, but the best plan is to ask around, watch what other passengers pay, or just offer up a 5- or 10-dollar note and hold out your hand for change (looking, of course, as though you know exactly what you should be getting back).

BY BUS

City buses PTSC (Public Transport Service Corporation ☎623 2262, ⓦptsc.co.tt) buses provide a fast, a/c means of travelling around the city, though services are not as frequent as you might hope. All buses start from City Gate, and fares are TT$2.50. The website carries detailed route maps and schedules, and lists fares. Routes start at around 6am, and end at 9 or 10pm.

USEFUL BUS ROUTES

To central Port of Spain (City Gate special): City Gate, Abercromby St, New St, Frederick St, Queen's Park Savannah, Belmont.

To Chaguaramas Same as Diego Martin route, but once on Audrey Jeffers Hwy the bus continues on through St James along the Western Main Rd, passing West Mall, West Moorings, Glencoe, Carenage and Chaguaramas, ending at the *Cove* hotel (5am–10pm).

To Diego Martin Wrightson Rd, Ariapita Ave, Mucurapo Rd, Audrey Jeffers Hwy, Diego Martin Hwy.

BY MAXI TAXI

Maxi taxis operating in Port of Spain and the western tip have yellow bands along the side of the vehicle. Routes are set although some drivers may be willing to make off-route drops, and if a maxi is empty, the driver may vary the route

1

in the hope of picking up some passengers. Note that many drivers now won't accept passengers not travelling the full (or most of) the route in what's called a "short drop"; if you need to go only partway, take a route taxi. For further information call the maxi rank on South Quay (☎ 625 4053). Port of Spain maxis depart from the fenced-off area between City Gate and Wrightson Rd, and from three main stops listed below.

MAXI RANKS

To Carenage and Chaguaramas (via Wrightson Rd) Departures from the junction of South Quay and St Vincent St.
To Maraval via St James Departures from the corner of Charlotte and Park streets, opposite the petrol station.
To Carenage and Chaguaramas (via Ariapita Ave in Woodbrook) Departures from Green Corner (cnr St Vincent and Park streets).

BY ROUTE TAXI

As in maxis, all off-route drops in route taxis depend on the driver's goodwill. Signposted starting points for city routes are dotted around downtown Port of Spain. Note that route taxis are the best option for heading downtown; the one-way system can be confusing and parking is a nightmare.

ROUTES AND TAXI STANDS

To Belmont Cnr of Charlotte St and Queen St.
To Chaguaramas Cnr of South Quay and Chacon St.
To Diego Martin/Petit Valley Cnr of Abercromby St and South Quay. Route ends at Diego Martin waterwheel via Four Roads and Diego Martin Main Rd. After 6pm Diego Martin taxis can be found near the Arthur Cipriani statue on Brian Lara Promenade.
To Laventille Cnr of Nelson St and Prince St.
To Maraval/Paramin Cnr of Duke St and Charlotte St. Route ends at Maraval village/beginning of Paramin.
To St Ann's Hart St, on the side adjacent to the Holy Trinity Anglican Cathedral. Route ends at Bishop Anstey School.
To St James/Tragarete Rd Hart St, on the side adjacent to Woodford Square. From around 7pm to 5am St James/Tragarete Rd taxis can be found on Independence Square,

at Henry St.
To Wrightson Rd/Long Circular Rd Cnr of Chacon St and South Quay. After 6pm Wrightson Rd/Long Circular Rd route starts from near the Arthur Cipriani statue on Brian Lara Promenade.

BY PRIVATE TAXI

Officially sporting "H" plates, and usually with a/c, private taxis are as expensive as cabs in New York or London. They're not hailed on the street, but ordered by phone or by going to their ranks, usually outside smart hotels such as the *Hilton* and *Kapok* or on Independence Square.
Taxi firms Reputable firms include Phone-a-Taxi (☎ 628 TAXI), a Maraval-based company with rates around half those of the competition. You can also try Ice House Taxi Service, Independence Square North (☎ 627 6984), or Independence Square Taxi Service, Independence Square, at Frederick St (☎ 625 3032).

BY CAR

Driving in Port of Spain As the downtown streets are choked with traffic and the one-way systems can seem confusing at first, cars are not the best way to explore the downtown area; it's better to park on the outskirts, or take a route taxi/maxi, and proceed on foot.
Parking If you do drive in Port of Spain, always use an official car park, as vehicles illegally parked are routinely "wrecked" as it's called here, and towed to either the lot between MovieTowne and the port, or across the road from the Central Market, just off the highway to the east of town. There's a multi-storey car park downtown on Richmond St, and a host of small, privately run car parks where you'll pay a small fee to leave your vehicle. It is possible to park on the streets, but seek local advice, pay attention to signs and road markings, and never park adjacent to a fire hydrant.
Car rental Alamo ☎ 826 689, ⊛ alamo.com; Avis ☎ 669 0905, ⊛ avistrinidad.com; Econo Cars ☎ 622 8072, ⊛ econocarrentals.com; Europcar ☎ 621 2159, ⊛ europe car.co.tt.com; Kalloo's ☎ 622 9073, ⊛ kalloos.com; Singh's ☎ 623 0150, ⊛ singhs.com.

INFORMATION

Tourist information Trinidad's tourist board, the TDC (☎ 675 7034, ⊛ gotrinidadandtobago.com), doesn't have an office in the city. You can pick up brochures and useful free magazines at the Ministry of Tourism office on the corner of Duke and St Vincent streets in downtown (Mon–Fri 8am–4.30pm; ☎ 624 1403, ⊛ tourism.gov.tt).

TOURS AND ACTIVITIES

City tours If you want to see Port of Spain from an insider's perspective, it's well worth joining one of the excellent city tours offered by Island Experiences (☎ 621 0407 or ☎ 781 6235, ⊛ islandexperiencestt.com), from daytime sight-seeing in Port of Spain, Chaguaramas and the Bocas islands to evening excursions taking in practice sessions at

panyards and live calypso (half-day and evening tours from US$45, full-day from US$80).
Activities Chaguaramas holds the bulk of the outdoor activities, from kayaking (see p.101) to zip lining (see p.100) and hiking (see p.95). Liquid Adrenaline, based at C3 Marina, 199 Western Main Rd, just past the Peake's service

station in Cocorite (☎ 779 6644, ⓦ liquid adrenalinett@gmail.com), offer a range of watersports in the Gulf waters just off Westmoorings, from waterskiing to wakeboarding, hydrosliding (aka knee-boarding), wakesurfing, and wakeskating; all cost TT$150 per session and include equipment and tuition.

CARNIVAL

Port of Spain is the epicentre of Trinidad's **Carnival**, home to the Panorama steel band competition (see p.267), the calypso tents (see p.265) and most of the mas camps (see p.68) of the bands that make up the main **costume parade** and the pre-festival **Jouvert** (see p.70).

CARNIVAL WEBSITES

Fineahban ⓦ fineahban.com. A lifesaver if you're scrabbling to find a costume and play mas last-minute, with a section advertising costumes for sale and swap, as well as Carnival accommodation and some fete info. The site ⓦ mycarnivalbands.com is an alternative for swaps and sales.

National Carnival Commission ⓦ ncctt.org. Somewhat clunky and slow to be updated, but does have an official calendar of Carnival events.

Trini Jungle Juice ⓦ trinijunglejuice.com. Fete pics and events info, and reviews of events.

Trini Scene ⓦ triniscene.com. Much visited for its shots of patrons at parties around T&T, but also good for listings and live streaming of fetes around Carnival time.

Trinidad Carnival Diary ⓦ trinidadcarnivaldiary.com. Run by a self-confessed "Carnival obsessive", this blog-turned-website has become *the* go-to place for Carnival information, from summer band launches and subsequent dissection of the costumes and on-the-road reviews to essential advice for "Carnival Virgins" and the lowdown on everything Carnival, from Monday wear, boots and tights to companies that buy fete tickets and deliver them to your hotel. Links to all the bands and relevant websites, too.

MAS BANDS

The list below represents a selection of the best-known large and medium mas bands in Port of Spain: for a full list, contact the National Carnival Bands Association (☎ 627 1422, ⓦ ncbatt.com); more reliably, consult the brilliant Trinidad Carnival Diary (see above); and note that new bands surface each year. The site ⓦ tntisland.com/mas .html lists lots of small and medium bands.

Bliss 18 Rosalino St, Woodbrook ☎ 625 6800, ⓦ blisscarnival.com. The "exclusive" offshoot of the mighty Tribe, and just as popular.

D Krewe Dundonald St, Port of Spain ☎ 624 8935, ⓦ dkrewecarnival.com. Bikini mas, but slightly less high-octane than Tribe or Fantasy (so you might even be able to get a costume).

Dream Team 76 Picton St, Newtown ☎ 627 4004, ⓦ dreamteamtnt.com. Solid mid-range band, with quality costumes and a fun vibe on the road.

Fantasy 3 Alfredo St, Woodbrook ☎ 221 4966, ⓦ mycarnivalfantasy.com. The preserve of the young and the beautiful, this is one of the apex "It" bands – so you're unlikely to get a costume unless you register as soon as the band launches or have an inside connection.

Harts 5 Alcazar St, St Clair ☎ 622 8038, ⓦ hartscarnival .com. The band of choice for Trinidad's white middle classes, young and old, and the originator of the feathers-and-beads style that predominates today. Sells out fast.

Island People 50 O'Connor St, Woodbrook ☎ 622 8145, ⓦ islandpeoplemas.com. Launched in the wake of Tribe and still one of the largest bands on the road, full of the young and the beautiful, and lots of fun.

Legacy 88 Roberts St, Woodbrook ☎ 622 7466, ⓦ legacycarnival.com. A little bit old-school, with no surprises in the feathers and bikinis on parade, but a bit more inclusive and forgiving of different body shapes and sizes; also good for more mature masqueraders.

Ronnie and Caro Cnr Anna & Warren streets, Woodbrook ☎ 628 4521, ⓦ ronnieandcaro.com. Great costumes and more of a family vibe than the large bikini bands; easier to get a costume, too.

Tribe 20 Rosalino St, Woodbrook ☎ 625 6800, ⓦ carnivaltribe.com. The naughty child of the once-mighty Poison, Tribe has long been the apex of bikini mas in Trinidad, though it's got some stiff competition from new bands these days. Get a costume early, or forget it.

Trini Revellers 35 Gallus St, Woodbrook ☎ 628 7275, ⓦ trinirevellersmas.com. Drawing a more mature crowd than Tribe or Fantasy, and with costumes that tend to display a bit less flesh, Revellers are a Carnival stalwart.

YUMA 12 Alcazar St, St Clair ☎ 628 1919, ⓦ yumavibe .com. Right up there with Tribe, Bliss and Fantasy, YUMA (Young Upwardly Mobile Adults) is a high-end band with suitably ornate costumes and emphasis on customer service. Hit the gym before you sign up (and do so in person, as there's no online registration).

JOUVERT BANDS

The list below covers bands that have stayed the course for several years; new ones pop up each year, so keep an eye on Trinidad Carnival Diary or listen to the radio once in T&T to keep abreast of what's new. We've given addresses for bands that have a fixed base.

3canal 33 Murray St, Woodbrook ☎ 622 1001, ⓦ 3canal.com. Since their first Jouvert band, Jocks-Tuh-Pose, in 1997, 3canal won a huge following, especially

1

CARNIVAL ACCOMMODATION

The run-up to **Carnival** is easily the busiest time of year in Port of Spain, and if you intend to stay anywhere in the city during this time it's essential to book well in advance. Regular Carnivalgoers reserve their accommodation for the following year on Ash Wednesday, and it's a good idea to book very early if you have your heart set on a particular place – or area, with downtown, Woodbrook, Newtown and St Clair being the most convenient for the parade route. As well as trying the places listed below, it's a good idea to check the classified sections of newspapers (also available online; see p.32), where rooms in private houses are advertised, sometimes at very reasonable rates, alongside last-minute vacancies in hotels and guesthouses. Sites such as Airbnb (see p.26) are also worth a look.

Carnival **prices**, which can be more than double normal rates, usually apply from the Wednesday or Friday preceding Carnival through to Ash Wednesday. The majority of hotels and guesthouses insist on five- to eight-night **minimum stays**, which you'll have to pay for even if you don't stay there the whole period. Note that the prices listed in this book are non-Carnival rates.

among Trinidad's arts intelligentsia. This is a simply brilliant Jouvert experience, for once not all-inclusive: you simply get a T-shirt, a bandana and endless joy.

Chocolate City 29 Stone St, Woodbrook ☎ 623 4727, ⓦ chocolatecitycarnival.com. A well-established and well-organized outfit whose USP is coating its patrons in liquid chocolate.

Dirty Dozen 2 Serpentine Place, St Clair ☎ 756 8829, ⓦ dirtydozenjouvert.com. Mud, paint and powder, plus all-inclusive food and drinks and tight security.

ILoveJouvert Mas Jumbies ☎ 472 5050, ⓦ ilove jouvert.com. A full Jouvert package, with a pre-party from 2am near the stadium, and all-inclusive on-the-road experience with paint and water, and an after-party cooldown.

Silver Mudders ☎ 721 7786, ✉ silvermudders@gmail .com. Silver mud (obviously), plus a pre-party, premium drinks and lots of snacks.

PANYARDS

Desperadoes Upper Laventille Rd, East Dry River, Laventille; and cnr Cadiz and Queen's Park East in Carnival season.

Invaders 147 Tragarete Rd, opposite the Queen's Park Oval, Woodbrook.

St James Tripolians 38c Western Main Rd, cnr Fort George Link Rd, St James.

Phase II Pan Groove 15 Hamilton St, off Damian St, Woodbrook.

Renegades 138 Charlotte St, Port of Spain.

Silver Stars 56 Tragarete Rd, Newtown.

Starlift Mucurapo Rd, St James.

Trinidad All Stars 46 Duke St, Port of Spain.

Woodbrook Modernaires 71 Tragarete Rd, cnr French St, Woodbrook.

Woodbrook Playboyz 37 Tragarete Rd, cnr Picton St, Woodbrook.

ACCOMMODATION

The **accommodation** options in Port of Spain are plentiful and varied, from inexpensive guesthouses to business-oriented chain hotels, with some nice boutique-type places in between. Staying **downtown** is convenient for shops, services and sightseeing, but it's quiet after dark here and there isn't much choice. **Woodbrook** is a better option, with the lion's share of the guesthouses, good public transport links and plenty of restaurants and bars – and if you stay at the eastern end of the suburb, the downtown area is only ten minutes' walk away. A short walk from the Savannah, **Newtown** and **St Clair** are less vibrant (though quieter), with a sprinkling of reasonably priced options, while there are a few lovely options on the outskirts of residential **St Ann's** and **Cascade**. Note that at the large business-oriented hotels – *Hyatt*, *Radisson*, *Marriot*, *Hilton* and *Carlton Savannah* – rates are reduced at weekends; we have quoted mid-week rates.

DOWNTOWN AND THE WATERFRONT

Hyatt Regency 1 Wrightson Rd ☎ 623 2222, ⓦ trinidad .hyatt.com; map p.56. This glinting tower on the waterfront is Trinidad's most upmarket hotel; facilities run from a gorgeous infinity pool overlooking the Gulf of Paria on the rooftop to a state-of-the art spa, gym, an excellent waterside restaurant/bar and a sushi bar (see p.86). The

rooms are anonymously chic, with bamboo floors, flat-screen TVs and handsome city views, and there's a huge private car park. US$195

Pearl's 3–4 Victoria Square East ☎ 625 2158, ✉ peterhenry@yahoo.com; map p.56. A rambling old colonial house with a veranda overlooking picturesque Victoria Square, this is the cheapest place in Port of Spain, and rates are reasonable for Carnival. The rooms are very basic, with standing fan and a sink; bathrooms are shared and there's a communal kitchen and TV room, but it's a great first stopoff with plenty of travellers passing through. Friendly, helpful hosts, and perfectly situated for Carnival and downtown sightseeing. **US$44**

Radisson Trinidad 1017 Wrightson Rd ☎ 625 3366, ⓦ radisson.com; map p.56. Glitzy, rather faceless corporate hotel, treated to a full refurb since it became part of the Radisson chain. Facilities are all you'd expect: pool, two restaurants, bar, gym, business centre, shops and a large car park. All rooms have excellent views of the city, and come well equipped. Wi-fi throughout. **US$139**

WOODBROOK AND ST JAMES

★**Allamanda** 61 Carlos St, Woodbrook ☎ 622 1480, ⓦ theallamanda.com; map p.71. Airy, professionally run place decked with plants and artwork, and with a small pool out back. The spotlessly clean en-suite rooms have a/c, cable TV, ceiling fan, tea- and coffee-making equipment and fridge, and there are also a couple of studios with the same facilities plus kitchenette. All guests are lent a mobile phone, and there's use of a kitchen (though breakfast is available for a little extra), plus free wi-fi. **US$80**

Caribbean Tourist Villa 7 Methuen St, Woodbrook ☎ 627 5423, ⓔ caribbeantouristvilla@gmail.com; map p.56. A great position on the downtown fringes of Woodbrook, though the rooms are dark and rather dated; all are clean and tidy, and have a/c, cable TV and fridge; there's also a small pool, though you pay extra to use this as well as the communal kitchen and laundry facilities. Free wi-fi. **US$65**

Courtyard by Marriott Invader's Bay, Audrey Jeffers Hwy, Woodbrook ☎ 627 5555, ⓦ marriott.com; map p.71. Within walking distance of MovieTowne and a favoured choice of business travellers, so rates are reduced on weekends. Rooms have all the amenities you'd expect of an international chain, including free wi-fi, and there's a pool, restaurant and bar. Neat, tidy and friendly if a little soulless. **US$194**

★**Culture Crossroads Inn** Cnr Bengal and Delhi streets, St James ☎ 622 8788, ⓦ culturecrossroadstt .com; map p.71. Great little boutique inn with the upmarket finish of a hotel, and supremely friendly and helpful staff/owners. Named after Trinidad's mas-men, calypsonians and steel pan bands, each of the attractive, modern rooms is finished with loving detail and equipped with all the necessary extras, as well as fridge, cable TV and a/c; some are equipped for people with disabilities. Security is super-tight and there's high-speed wi-fi. **US$100**

Fabienne's 15 Belle Smythe St, Woodbrook ☎ 622 2773, ⓔ fabiennes1961@hotmail.com; map p.71. Set in the owner's house, just steps from Ariapita Ave, and offering just two comfortable, plain en-suite rooms with fridge, fan and a/c. There's a communal lounge, laundry facilities, and breakfast is available. Free wi-fi. **US$65**

★**Gingerbread House** 8 Carlos St, Woodbrook ☎ 627 8170, ⓦ trinidadgingerbreadhouse.com; map p.71. Beautifully maintained gingerbread house with a wraparound veranda and quirky, chic modern touches courtesy of the architect owner. There are three lovely rooms in the main house, and another in a separate building with its own patio; all are en suite with a/c, fridge and cable TV, and there's a rather unique plunge pool out back. Full breakfast included. Fantastic value for the quality of accommodation; book well ahead. **US$70**

Inn a Citi Place 15 Gaston Johnson St, Woodbrook ☎ 622 0415, ⓦ inn-a-citi-place.com; map p.71. A great location just off Ariapita Ave, this is a friendly and very secure place offering clean, bright rooms, all with fan, a/c and cable TV, plus a communal kitchen and use of laundry facilities. Wi-fi throughout and breakfast included. **US$65**

Johnson's 16 Buller St, Woodbrook ☎ 628 7553, ⓔ johnsonsbandb@hotmail.com; map p.71. Friendly, helpful hosts and spotless, well-maintained rooms with fans and cable TV; a/c rooms with fridge cost a bit more, and the cheaper ones share bathrooms. Guests have use of a kitchen and lounge. Good value, and in walking distance of both Ariapita Ave and downtown Port of Spain; full breakfast is included in all rates. **US$55**

Melbourne Inn 7 French St, Woodbrook ☎ 623 4006, ⓔ melbourneinn@hotmail.com; map p.71. A slightly dilapidated air, but a great location for Carnival and perhaps the cheapest rooms in Woodbrook. All rooms are decent sized, with cable TV, ceiling and standing fans (US$48) or a/c (US$60), and private or shared bathrooms. There's wi-fi, a sundeck and a large communal veranda, and breakfast is available. **US$38**

Sam's 5 Alberto St, Woodbrook ☎ 627 4865, ⓦ sams guesthousett.com; map p.71. On the lower stretch of Alberto St, this is a supremely friendly place, with a homely lounge downstairs and rooms off a main corridor upstairs, where there's also a breezy communal balcony. Rooms are appealing, modern and clean, with a/c, fan, fridge and cable TV; the brightest overlook the balcony. Wi-fi available. **US$75**

THE SAVANNAH, ST ANN'S AND CASCADE

Alicia's House 7 Coblentz Gardens, St Ann's ☎ 623 2802, ⓦ aliciashouse.com; map p.75. Located on a quiet road close to the Savannah, all the rooms at this busy little hotel have wicker furniture, a/c, fridge, phone and cable TV; most are en suite, but a few share bathrooms, and there's a swimming pool, sundeck and jacuzzi. Meals are available, as is wi-fi, and breakfast is included. **US$65**

Alicia's Palace 1 ¾ Mile Post, Lady Chancellor Rd ☎ 624 8553, ⓦ aliciaspalace.com; map p.56. Gorgeous location on this scenic road, with cool breezes and a bird's-eye view of Port of Spain and down the coast to Caroni – rooms 98 and 105 have the best vistas (US$95). All rooms are en suite, with a/c, cable TV, fridge and phone, there's a pool and the veranda restaurant is beautifully situated overlooking the valley. Shuttle service down into town, wi-fi and breakfast included in the rates. US$73

Carlton Savannah Coblentz Ave, St Ann's ☎621 5000, ⓦ thecarltonsavannah.com; map p.75. The most upmarket place in the capital (even Britain's Queen Elizabeth stayed in 2009), this is an oasis of very un-Trinidadian designer style, with luxury stamped over everything from the gorgeous mosaic-tiled coffee tables in the lobby to the Molton Brown soap in the washrooms. Rooms have 300-thread-count Egyptian cotton sheets and every possible amenity, and there are two restaurants, three bars and a gym and lovely pool on site. US$155

★**Heritage Inn** 7 Coblentz Ave, Cascade ☎621 5663, ⓦ heritageinntrinidad.com, map p.75. Great location in an expansive old house, beautifully restored and with some of its original wooden floors, this is an excellent getaway from the city, with a large pool in flowered gardens and a range of appealing, spacious and tastefully decorated rooms, all with fridge, a/c and cable TV; the economy ones share bathrooms. Free wi-fi, and breakfast included. US$100

Hilton Trinidad Lady Young Rd, St Ann's ☎624 3211, ⓦ hiltoncaribbean.com; map p.75. "Upside down" hotel built down the side of a hill, with the reception at the top and the floors numbered downwards from 1 to 11. Each room has a balcony with excellent views over Port of Spain and the hotel's landscaped garden, plus all the usual *Hilton* amenities. Facilities include restaurants and bars, tennis courts, a sauna and fitness centre, and a large pool that serves as a popular venue for pre-Carnival fetes. US$168

Kapok 16–18 Cotton Hill ☎622 5765, ⓦ kapokhotel .com; map p.56. Elegant, stylish hotel decorated with handsome artwork, and in a great position for Carnival just off the Savannah. Rooms are spacious and with all the amenities you'd expect; studios and suites with kitchen facilities are also available, and there's free wi-fi. Good restaurant (see p.86), wine and coffee bar, swimming pool, gym and sundeck on site, and breakfast is included. Rooms & studios US$159; suites $214

L'Orchidee 3 Coblentz Gardens, St Ann's ☎621 0618, ⓦ trinidadhosthomes.com; map p.75. Tucked away on a side street off the Savannah, this is an inviting little hotel fitted out to a very high standard, with twelve bright, modern rooms themed around different orchids, plus a pretty outside terrace and excellent service from the very professional staff. Popular with business travellers, with free wi-fi and a full breakfast included. US$150

★**Normandie** 10 Nook Ave, St Ann's ☎624 1181, ⓦ normandiett.com; map p.75. On a quiet cul-de-sac just a five-minute walk from the Queen's Park Savannah, this is one of the city's more atmospheric large hotels, with a lively feel provided by the annual Carnival concerts and by the on-site boutiques, café and popular restaurant (see p.86). Most rooms have wooden floorboards (the refurbished ones are tiled), a/c, cable TV, phone, iron and board, hairdryer and en-suite bathroom, and there's a lovely pool and wi-fi throughout. Continental breakfast included. US$130

Thanna's Place 27 Erthig Rd, Belmont ☎225 6582, ⓦ thannas.com; map p.75. Tucked away off the Savannah in residential Belmont, but in walking distance of transport options and the Carnival parade, this is a businesslike place with bite, compact a/c rooms equipped with fridge and cable TV and a pretty little outdoor area. The rates are a little high considering the location, though single rooms are a bargain, and the hosts are extremely friendly and helpful. Wi-fi throughout; breakfast included. Doubles US$75; en suite US$80

NEWTON AND ST CLAIR

Forty Winks 24 Warner St, Newton ☎622 0484, ⓦ fortywinkstt.com; map p.56. Great little guesthouse aimed at the business traveller who doesn't want to stay at a typical business hotel. The en-suite rooms are on the smallish side, but all come with a/c, cable TV and phone. The house is brightly decorated and has an outdoor patio, a rooftop terrace and a kitchen for guests' use; there's wi-fi throughout. Breakfast included. US$105.50

Inn at 87 87 Woodford St, Newtown ☎621 0618, ⓦ innat87.com; map p.56. Set in a restored former printery dating from the 1930s, and boasting pretty exterior fretwork and beautiful high ceilings and original wooden floors in its communal lounge, this is an atmospheric place, very friendly and professionally run. With fresh, clean decor, rooms are comfortable and welcoming, with a/c, cable TV and fridge. Full breakfast included, as are tea and coffee all day. US$115

Par-May-La's Inn 53 Picton St, Newtown ☎628 2008, ⓦ parmaylas.com; map p.56. On a quiet street (though very convenient for downtown), this reliable Port of Spain stalwart boasts helpful hosts and a nice communal veranda where continental breakfast – included in the rates – is served. Very spacious a/c rooms with cable TV and fridge. Free wi-fi. US$65

Sundeck Suites 42–44 Picton St, Newtown ☎622 9560, ⓦ sundecktrinidad.com; map p.56. The self-catering version of sister establishment *Par-May-La's*, *Sundeck* has bright, tidy apartments, slightly dated but perfectly nice and with kitchenette, ceiling fans, a/c, and cable TV; some also have a small balcony. There's a sundeck on the roof, and facilities for the disabled. US$80

STREET FOOD AND TAKEAWAY

With its great tradition of street food, Port of Spain offers plenty of tantalizing alternatives to a sit-down meal. **Doubles** (see p.28) are sold from streetside carts from as early as 6am, and many of the most popular vendors run out by lunchtime. Everyone has their personal favourite, but you'll always see long queues at the George and George's X stalls on Carlos Street in Woodbrook (outside *Brooklyn Bar* and *Coco Lounge*, respectively); you can also find several vendors outside the main entrance to Long Circular Mall, and along Western Main Road in St James. The latter also holds the lion's share of the many stalls that set up in the city as the sun goes down, cooking up roti, aloo pies, corn soup, geera pork, pholouri and the like, as well as delicious home-made ice cream.

There is also a row of stalls on a paved area of the **Queen's Park Savannah** opposite the National Academy for the Performing Arts, and along **Independence Square**; at the latter, one not to miss is the brilliant ital (vegetarian) roti stall which sets up on the South Quay side of the square on Tuesdays, Thursdays and Fridays, and sells gorgeous rotis as well as macaroni/potato pie and accompanying veggie delights. Gyros (flatbread wraps filled with chicken, lamb, shrimp, fish or falafel) are also found at all the city's street food spots in ever-increasing numbers, while the adventurous might want to sample the local oysters slurped down with peppery tomato sauce from stalls around the Savannah on Queen's Mark West and Maraval Road.

FOOD COURTS AND TAKEAWAYS

For something more substantial, there are legions of hole-in-the-wall places offering inexpensive local lunches, while the **food courts** in all of the shopping malls are also good for a quick bite of something Chinese, Creole or Indian for around TT$35.

There are also **fast-food** outlets all over town, from excellent local fried-chicken outfits such as *Japs* (on Western Main Rd, St James) or the ubiquitous *Royal Castle* to KFC, McDonald's and *Pizza Hut*. There's a concentration of outlets along Independence Square, and you'll find *Dominos* pizza and *Subway* sandwiches along Ariapita Avenue, near the corner of Carlos Street. There are also a host of options in the MovieTowne complex, off the highway in Woodbrook opposite the Stadium, and in the Shoppes of Maraval complex at the start of Saddle Road in Maraval.

EATING

Port of Spain's **restaurant** scene has boomed in recent years, nowhere more so than along **Ariapita Avenue** in Woodbrook, which has everything from high-class establishments serving fancy nouvelle Caribbean cuisine to more casual places cooking up excellent local food and takeaway diners offering good budget eats. There is also a cluster of high-end places underneath the **One Woodbrook Place** complex between St James and Woodbrook, and in the residential streets of **Newtown**. Fiesta Plaza, in the **MovieTowne complex** opposite the stadium on Audrey Jeffers Highway, has a slew of places, from US chain *Ruby Tuesdays* to sushi and seafood restaurants, most of which have tables in the central courtyard as well as inside. If you have your own car, it's also well worth driving out to **Chaguaramas** (see p.94), which has a string of great places to dine right on the water. Note that many of the more fancy restaurants offer prix fixe lunch menus or buffets, which can work out to be surprisingly good deals for the quality and quantity of food. Many restaurants also double up as good places for a **drink**, and we've highlighted the best options in the reviews below.

DOWNTOWN

★**Breakfast Shed** Wrightson Rd, opposite Independence Square; map p.56. Established in 1936 to provide workers' meals, this breezy open-sided "shed" with communal tables overlooking the Gulf of Paria is filled with outlets selling excellent local food, from buljol or smoked herring breakfasts to fish broth, stewed chicken and all the usual Trini sides; you'll pay around TT$50 for a meal; head for the stall with the longest queue, as quality varies. There's also a stall selling fresh juice. Daily 6.30am–4pm.

D Bocas 68 Independence Square ☎627 3474; map p.56. Reliable, inexpensive Creole food; you pick what you want from the array of cooked dishes on display and pay by weight. Also a popular spot for a drink, with a lovely veranda overlooking the square, with regular drink promotions (though visitors are a definite rarity). Mon–Fri 9.30am–late.

Hardline Vegetarian 34 Park St ☎623 9560; map p.56. Adorned with piles of fresh fruit and vegetables, this justifiably popular lunchtime diner serves up delicious, healthy vegetarian meals – steamed veg, soya stew, marinated dumplings (from TT$40) – as well as fruit salads and refreshing blended fruit juices. A stall outside sells more snacky food, from pholouri to corn soup. Mon–Fri 6am–5.30pm.

1

Hyatt Regency 1 Wrightson Rd ☎ 821 6550; map p.56. *The Waterfront* restaurant combines a lovely setting by the Gulf of Paria with reliable food cooked with sustainable and local ingredients. Lunches run from soup and salad (TT$65–120) to burgers (TT$90–120), pastas and meat or fish mains (TT$135–210), while dinner highlights are the fantastic chilli-coconut marinated tuna starter with tomato choka and molasses dressing (TT$95), Aberdeen Angus steaks (TT$330) or seafood broth with Korean noodles (TT$250). The adjacent sushi bar serves some of the freshest sushi in town (rolls TT$60–75, sashimi TT$80–160), and the terrace bar is a cool spot for a cocktail. Waterfront daily 7am–10pm; sushi bar Mon–Sat 5–10pm.

Living Water 109 Frederick St ☎ 623 6570; map p.56. The a/c canteen of this Catholic charitable organization offers delicious, inexpensive meals, and channels profits into its good works. The menu changes daily: breakfasts range from buljol and bake to eggs, while lunches always include meat, fish and vegetarian options (including veggie gravy); you pay by weight, at TT$35 per lb. Trini-style cakes and pastries are also on offer. Mon–Fri 7–9am & 11am–2pm, Sat 9.30–11am.

★**Mother Nature** Cnr of St Vincent and Park streets ☎ 623 3300; map p.56. Inexpensive vegetarian meals and salads (from TT$35), plus wholewheat roti and Jamaican patties, smoothies and juices freshly made in front of you using a variety of fruits and energy supplements. The buffet-style a/c café is small with limited seating. Mon–Sat 6am–3pm.

AROUND THE SAVANNAH

Apsara 13 Queen's Park East ☎ 623 7659; map p.56. Traditional Northern Indian cuisine, from tandooris to tikka masala, served in very plush a/c surroundings; the lamb rogan jhosh (TT$150) is sublime. Lots of vegetarian choices and delicious desserts, but prices are high. Daily 11am–3pm & 6–11pm, closed Sun evening.

★**Chaud** 2 Queen's Park West ☎ 623 0375, ⓦ chaudkm .com; map p.56. Run by one of Trinidad's most celebrated chefs, this super-swanky place in a gorgeous old building offers Savannah views and seriously good cooking, with starters such as beef short-rib tortiglione or guava-barbecue scallops with crispy pork belly (both available as part of the TT$200 3-course fixed lunch); and dinner mains of tamarind-glazed pork with bacon-cassava hash and apple crema (TT$225) or lobster ravioli with scallops, melted leeks and sweetcorn milk (TT$150). Daily 11am–3pm & 6–10.30pm.

★**Ciao Café** Normandie Hotel, 10 Nook Ave, St Ann's ☎ 624 1181; map p.75. A great place for a quiet dinner, with tables outdoors on a fairy-lit terrace just a short way from the Savannah. Good wine, attentive service and a reliable menu of Caribbean and Italian food, from juicy

coconut shrimp to chicken with mushrooms and Marsala or almond-crusted snapper; mains are TT$79–185. There's also a good Venezuelan breakfast spread on Sundays (8–11.30am; TT$145). Daily 11.30am–3pm & 6–10.30pm.

Kava Kapok Hotel, 16–18 Cotton Hill ☎ 622 5283; map p.56. One of the better hotel restaurants, with a handsome minimalist decor and a menu centred around brick-oven pizzas topped with such things as goat's cheese, caramelized onions and capers, or prosciutto and fresh basil (TT$105–130); there's also burgers (TT$70–92) and more substantial mains such as herb-crusted red snapper (TT$128) or aubergine parmigiana (TT$90). A great spot for a drink, with free wi-fi, too. Mon–Sat 11am–11pm.

Tamnak Thai 13 Queen's Park East ☎ 625 0647, ⓦ tamnakthaitt.com; map p.56. Elegantly decorated in rich Thai style, this smart restaurant has indoor and outdoor sections, and the food is excellent and authentic, from starters of Tom Yum soup (TT$65) or satay chicken skewers (TT$55) to green curry (TT$135 with chicken), sautéed beef (TT$140) or steamed fish with salt plums, ginger and Chinese mushrooms (TT$175), plus the usual stir-fries and rice dishes. Good lunch deals and a lovely Sunday lunch buffet. Mon–Sat 11am–4pm & 6–10pm, Sun 10.30am–3pm & 6–10pm.

WOODBROOK

Chaud Café Damian St ☎ 628 9845, ⓦ chaudcafe.com; map p.71. Occupying the corner of the One Woodbrook Place development, this is a good spot for an upmarket sandwich, salad or pasta or lunch (TT$65–130), or more elaborate dinner dishes such as duck confit with lentils and spinach (TT$150). Enjoy a glass of wine on the terrace with the Woodbrook lights twinkling below; there are plenty of lovely small plates such as harissa-rubbed lamb ribs or ginger and garlic roasted aubergine (TT$60–150) to go with your drinks. Mon–Thurs 11am–11pm, Fri & Sat 11am–midnight.

El Pecos 84 Ariapita Ave ☎ 622 9713; map p.71. Basic, inexpensive Creole food: veg rice, lentil peas, macaroni pie, plus jerk and rotisserie chicken, fried fish and salads. You serve yourself and pay according to weight, and there are a few tables for dining in. Mon–Sat 11am–10pm.

Hakka 4 Taylor St ☎ 622 0004, ⓦ hakkarestaurant.com; map p.71. Chinese cuisine with an Indian flavour, served up in a handsome a/c dining room decked out in subtle shades of orange and brown. Menu highlights include starters of chilli paneer balls (TT$59) or pepper-and-salt calamari (TT$66), plus spicy Konjee crispy chicken, or Hong Kong pork with ginger and red chilli paste. Reasonable prices and reliable food. Mon–Thurs 11am–11pm, Fri & Sat 11am–midnight, Sun noon–10pm.

Irie Bites 71 Ariapita Ave ☎ 622 7364; map p.71. Jamaican jerk shack serving some of the tastiest and best-value meals in the city. Nicely seasoned and cooked over pimento wood, the generous portions of jerk chicken, pork and fish (from TT$50) are served with various side dishes such as plantain, fries or mixed vegetables and accompanied with a selection of excellent sauces. Ackee and saltfish available on Saturdays. Delivery available. Mon–Thurs 11am–9pm, Fri & Sat 11am–10pm.

Me Asia 48a Ariapita Ave ☎ 628 6888; map p.71. One of the best Chinese restaurants in town, offering reliable, reasonably priced Szechuan food – try the wonton soup or pepper shrimp (from TT$25) – and a pleasant a/c interior. It's also a popular spot among the local Chinese community for Sunday dim sum, while the late hours make it a good bet after a night out. Daily 11am–4am.

★**More Sushi** 23 O'Connor St ☎ 622 8466, ⓦ morevino .com; map p.71. This excellent wine bar offers great sushi and sashimi, reasonably priced and always super-fresh, and including rolls (TT$68–98) with a local twist such as the scorpion pepper and Maracas. The rest of the menu runs from Japanese katsu curries (TT$78–118), teriyaki risottos and pad Thai (both TT$68–128), to Italian pastas (from TT$68) plus a lovely crab dip starter (TT$88). Daily 11am–midnight.

New Earth Organic 80 Roberts St ☎ 381 3785; map p.71. Tiny little organic store and café offering fresh fruit and veg and reasonably priced vegetarian lunches, cooked with whatever fresh produce is in stock; look out also for baked goods such as banana muffins or spelt bread. Always delicious and a great place to meet people. Tues–Sat 8am–3pm.

Patraj 161 Tragarete Rd ☎ 221 9592; map p.71. Hailed by many Trinis as the capital's best roti shop, and now moved one building down from its original location. Consistently high-quality food, from the delicious morning sada roti with tomato choka to the usual array of skins and fillings for lunch and early dinner. Rotis from TT$25. Mon–Sat 8am–5pm.

Sweet Lime Ariapita Ave, cnr of French St ☎ 624 4048; map p.71. With outdoor tables positioned overlooking the Avenue, this is a great spot for people-watching over a meal from a varied, reasonably priced menu: good seafood and cutters, plus salads, ribs, pepper shrimp, steaks, burgers (including veggie) and several vegetarian options such as stuffed peppers and chow mein for mains. It's also a great liming spot, with occasional live music at weekends. Daily 11.30am–midnight.

Trader Jack's Fiesta Plaza, MovieTowne, Audrey Jeffers Hwy ☎ 625 5225, ⓦ traderjackstt.com; map p.71. Though its garish murals, plastic treehouse and centrepiece waterfalls lend it the air of an American theme park, this is a supremely upbeat place serving up grilled chicken, fish and meat (mahi-mahi TT$135, steak and mushrooms TT$165), alongside burgers (TT$55–75), pastas (TT$95–135) and colourful cocktails to an enthusiastic crowd.

Mon–Thurs 11am–midnight, Fri–Sun 11am–1am.

★**Veni Mange** 67 Ariapita Ave ☎ 624 4597, ⓦ venimange.com; map p.71. Set on the first floor of a greenery-swathed building and decorated with Caribbean artwork, *Veni* is a Port of Spain institution, as good a liming spot as it is a place to eat. The food is a happy blend of local staples with an international twist, such as fried grouper with almond and herb stuffing and a ginger sauce (TT$145) or oxtail strew with dumplings (TT$130). There's always a good veggie option, such as tofu cutlets with a coconut and tomato sauce (TT$1050), as well as hearty salads and excellent puddings. Mon–Fri 11.30am–3pm, plus Wed & Fri 7–10pm.

Zanzibar Fiesta Plaza, MovieTowne, Audrey Jeffers Hwy ☎ 627 0752, ⓦ zanzibartt.com; map p.71. This could be a chain restaurant in any American town, but it offers a decent and wide-ranging menu, including pastas such as champagne chicken farfalle (TT$150), plus burgers, burritos and pulled pork sandwiches (TT$58–135) and all manner of meaty variations from bourbon chicken (TT$99) to filet mignon (TT$198); fish and seafood are also well represented. The bar is a pleasant place for a drink, with big screens showing sports events. Mon–Thurs & Sun 11.30am–midnight, Fri & Sat 11.30am–1am.

ST JAMES, NEWTOWN AND ST CLAIR

★**Buzo Osteria Italiana** 6a Warner St, Newtown ☎ 222 2896; map p.56. Simply the best Italian food in T&T, served with style and humour in a very chic dining room within a lovely old cut-stone building. All the classics of Italian cuisine are on offer, from antipasti (TT$50–120) to perfect pizza (from TT$100). Other highlights include squid-ink tagiatelle with seafood (TT$110), pumpkin tortelli with sage (TT$100) and grouper with fresh tomato sauce, capers and olives (TT$145). The cocktails and wine list are fantastic, and there's a separate bar with an outdoor area for drinks and snacks. Book ahead. Mon–Sat 11.20am–11pm.

Chinkey's Nite-Bite Western Main Rd, St James; map p.71. Rasta-run food stall opposite *Smokey and Bunty* (see p.89) serving a loyal clientele with delicious veggie concoctions, fried fish, shark and bake, smoked herring and saltfish sandwiches, and fresh juices. A great pre- or post-clubbing option. Tues–Sun 7pm–late.

★**Dopson's** 28 Maraval Rd, Newtown ☎ 628 6141; map p.71. This brilliant takeaway sells some of the city's best roti: beautifully stretchy dhalpuri skins (or buss-up-shut) and excellent fillings, from shrimp to conch or goat, plus the usual veg, chicken or beef and a mean curry mango; rotis from TT$30. Expect queues. Mon–Fri 6.45am–5.30pm, Sat 8am–5.30pm.

La Cantina 12 Victoria Ave, Newtown ☎ 627 4992, ⓦ lacantinapizzeria.com; map p.56. The Trinidad branch of Tobago's best pizzeria, this is equally good, with a lovely setting in an airy colonial-era building. Baked in a wood-fired oven, the 40 thin-crust pizzas (TT$80–130) are reliably delicious, topped with all the classic combinations, while salads range from Greek to Caesar (TT$55–95). A great place for a glass of wine or a cocktail, with rather un-Italian platters of ribs, chicken and spicy calamari to soak up the booze. Tues–Thurs 11.30am–11pm, Fri & Sat 11.30am–12.30am, Sun 5–11pm.

Peche Patisserie 45 Picton St, Newtown; map p.56. 📞 222 8508. A great choice for lunch if you fancy something a little different to local cuisine, with several salads, from paneer to egg and smoked salmon to herbed crab (TT$100–135), and spectacular open sandwiches made with freshly baked bread and rolls. There are also more substantial mains, from lobster (TT$275) and shrimp (TT$153) with all the trimmings, and it's a very popular spot for weekend brunch. Great pastries and cakes too. Tues–Fri 7am–5.30pm, Sat & Sun 8.30am–5pm.

Town 51 Cipriani Blvd, Newtown 📞 627 8696, 🌐 town trinidad.com; map p.56. Tucked underneath *51°* nightclub, with tables out on a deck and inside, this classy place is popular with a moneyed set, who come to see and be seen. As well as pasta (lobster ravioli, sausage with penne; TT$75–150) there are grilled meats and fish mains, burgers and a long menu of Chinese dishes, from Szechuan beef to pork char sui (TT$100–150). It's also a popular place for a drink, with good cocktails. Mon–Sat 11am–late, kitchen closes 10pm.

Trotter's Cnr Maraval & Sweet Briar roads, St Clair 📞 627 8768, 🌐 trotters.net; map p.56. Cavernous sports bar and restaurant that's a popular place to watch big sporting events. The menu ranges from pork dumplings

(TT$63) to crab wonton (TT$58) starters to excellent burgers, tacos, salads and sandwiches (TT$69–119), American-style pizza (including a tandoori chicken version; TT$84), and mains such as spicy Bangkok chicken linguine (TT$97) or baby-back ribs (TT$189); they also do a "traditional British" pub menu on Sundays: bangers and mash, fish and chips and roast dinners (TT$99). Mon–Thurs & Sun 10am–midnight, Fri & Sat 10am–2am.

MARAVAL

★**Adam's Bagels** 15a Saddle Rd 📞 622 2435, 🌐 adamsbagels.com; map p.71. Busy deli selling all kinds of goodies, from fresh bread and cakes, savoury snacks (try the veg or beef kibbies) to baba ganoush and delicious pastelles in fish, chicken, beef and lentil varieties. There are also tables in the a/c rear section where you can order excellent bagels, sandwiches, soups, salads (try the limey pak choi with cucumber and onion), kebabs, burgers and a lovely Thai chicken wrap; breakfasts are great too, with plenty of local choices alongside the eggs and bacon. Mains around TT$60. Free wi-fi. Mon–Sat 7am–6pm.

★**Aioli** Ellerslie Plaza 📞 222 4654, 🌐 aiolitrinidad .com; map p.71. This is an absolute gem in the otherwise uninspiring surrounds of a small shopping plaza, with handsome modern decor and a mouthwatering Mediterranean/Fusion menu of beautifully presented food. Highlights include truffle lobster pasta (TT$295), cod fillet with endamame, snow peas and a soy mirin glaze (TT$230) or pork loin with sweet potato and apple purée and coffee anise sauce (TT$130). There's also a tapas menu (TT$55–85), a three-course lunch deal (TT$200), and great cocktails. Mon–Fri 11am–11.30pm, Sat 6.30–11.30pm.

DRINKING, NIGHTLIFE AND ENTERTAINMENT

Trinidadians wouldn't dream of restricting their **partying** to Carnival time – anything from a public holiday to the end of a workday is deemed a worthy cause to celebrate. Port of Spain is an excellent place to enjoy a night on the town at any time of the year, and you can find something going on every night of the week. Most bars and clubs come alive after 10pm and are busiest from Thursday to Saturday, with bars often deluged on a Friday for the customary "after-work lime". Published **opening hours** are often a bit hazy; if there's a crowd, places will stay open later; similarly, on a quiet night you may find doors closed early or not open at all. The daily newspapers have movie listings and details of upcoming parties, theatre productions and special events in their "**What's on**" sections, and special events are advertised on the radio.

BARS

Port of Spain's western suburbs are packed with bars, from intimate places with funky modernist decor and a good wine list to pumping outdoor spaces. Most host busy after-work limes on a Friday afternoon, with drinks promotions, and many have a happy hour and a DJ playing music, making them a more laidback option for a dance than a full-blown club. At the other end of the scale, there are rum shops on practically every corner in Port of Spain, especially in the market area east of Charlotte St. These tend to be small, basic joints frequented by middle-aged men, and are not particularly tourist-friendly; better to head for

places on Western Main Rd in St James. If you fancy a drink in more relaxed surroundings, head out to Chaguaramas (see p.94), where there are a string of lovely places by the sea.

WOODBROOK

★**Brooklyn Bar** Cnr Roberts and Carlos streets 📞 628 7904; map p.71. This casual, laidback place is a post-makeover rum bar, its traditional Woodbrook building having been painted over with murals. Beers are inexpensive and always "beastly" cold, and the good-natured crowd spills out onto the pavements for the busy

1

Friday night after-work lime. A great place to start your night. Daily 9am–1am.

Coco Lounge 35 Carlos St, cnr of Ariapita Ave ☎ 296 6210, ⓦ cocoloungett.com; map p.71. Popular with a well-dressed crown of pretty young (and not so young) things who come to lime on the raised balcony or dance in the indoor a/c lounge. Regular special events and drinks promotions, and always packed. Cover charge of TT$60 (often for men only) after 9pm. Fri 4pm–4am, Sat 9pm–5am.

Darin's on the Avenue Cnr Luis St and Ariapita Ave ☎ 622 2808; map p.71. Great little corner bar laid out over two floors with pool tables, a balcony overlooking the Avenue and a relaxed, laidback feel. Ice-cold beers, inexpensive drinks and regular DJs. Mon–Thurs & Sun 4pm–2am, Fri & Sat 4pm–4am.

★ **Drink** 63 Rosalino St, cnr Roberts and Warren streets ☎ 223 7243; map p.71. Cosy and friendly wine bar, popular with an arty crowd and offering a great wine list, excellent cocktails and good food, too. Nicely detached from the Avenue so offering a quieter place to drink and talk. Mon–Fri 11am–11.45pm, Sat 6pm–1am.

Fluid 63 Ariapita Ave ☎ 225 5001; map p.71. Cool little spot and a relative newcomer to the Avenue, popular with a young and upwardly mobile crowd and offering excellent sushi (try the Tuesday evening buffet; TT$195) as well as various drinks promotions throughout the week, from two-for-one Thurs and specials on rum each Friday, and a packed dancefloor at the weekends. Tues–Sat 6.30pm–late.

Frankie's 68 Ariapita Ave ☎ 622 6609; map p.71. Perpetually busy spot on the Avenue, with a fenced-off area outside that's always packed with crowds of drinkers enjoying inexpensive beers and cocktails, and simple barbecue and Indian food. Especially busy on Friday evenings. Daily 6am–late, kitchen closes 9pm.

★ **La Habana** 61 Ariapita Ave ☎ 625 7393; map p.71. This tiny little bar with a Latin flavour opens onto the street, and the friendly mixed crowd spills out over the pavement and onto the tarmac. DJs play Latin, soca and techno, and there's regular drinks promotions and special events. Mon–Sat 4pm–late.

Levels Cnr Taylor St & Ariapita Ave ☎ 622 5350, ⓦ levelsultrabar.com; map p.71. Upmarket bar and lounge, all leather sofas and wooden floors, divided into four cosy areas including a VIP zone, a sushi bar and an outdoor terrace. Specials each night, from a Tuesday sushi buffet (TT$220), to sangria and sushi platter on Thursdays (TT$275). Good cigars and regular drinks promotions, too. Tues–Thurs noon–midnight, Fri & Sat noon–1am, Sun 5–11pm.

★ **Mas Camp Pub** Cnr French St & Ariapita Ave, Woodbrook ☎ 627 4042; map p.71. Now renamed as the *Nu Pub*, but still universally known by its former moniker,

this long-standing Port of Spain favourite has pool tables and slot machines in a back room, and an a/c main area that's popular with an older local crowd, who come to dance to oldies on Sun. There's usually a calypso show on Wed evenings, and other themed nights, from Latin to karaoke, throughout the week – to see what's on, pick up a schedule of events at the entrance, or check the board outside. Cover charge varies. Daily 11am–late.

More Vino 23 O'Connor St, cnr of Ariapita Ave ☎ 622 8466, ⓦ morevino.com; map p.71. Popular with a mixed crowd of young and old, this is a lovely spot for a glass of wine or a cocktail, either on the decked area outside or the a/c indoor bar. Great service, excellent food (see p.87), regular drinks promotions and good music that's kept at a conversation-friendly level. Mon–Wed 11am–midnight, Thurs–Sat 11am–1am.

Shakers on the Avenue 43a Ariapita Ave ☎ 624 6612; map p.71. Set in a cute little gingerbread house, with tables in the garden area, on the veranda and in an a/c area inside, this is a busy, friendly and unpretentious place for a drink. Regular live music with a rock flavour, bar food to soak up the booze and daily drinks promotions. Mon 4pm–midnight, Tues–Thurs 4pm–2am, Fri & Sat 11am–2am.

Tequila Twist 58a Ariapita Ave (no phone); map p.71. Small but very loud, and perhaps a bit more rough around the edges than its neighbours, with raucous party nights, scantily clad "promo girls" strutting their stuff to keep the vibes going, and regular drinks promotions. Daily 11am–late.

ST JAMES, NEWTOWN & ST CLAIR

All Out Sports Bar and Grill 1st Floor, Queen's Park Oval, 94 Tragarete Rd, St Clair; map p.71. Rather macho hangout, popular for catching big games on the nine plasma screens and as a post-match haunt. English beers, and good food such as wings, calamari and the like, and an outdoor terrace. Free wi-fi. Mon–Thurs 11am–midnight, Fri 11am–1am, Sat & Sun 9am–midnight.

Paprika 15 Rust St, St Clair ☎ 622 5930; map p.71. With opulent decor that ranges between a Moroccan souk and a Parisian bordello, this is the spot *du jour* for Port of Spain's moneyed young things, who quaff champagne and premium cocktails and dance the night away to an eclectic playlist that might run from Machel Montano to Madonna. Tables inside and out, and a good wine list too. Tues–Sat 6pm–late.

★ **Smokey and Bunty** 97 Western Main Rd, St James ☎ 723 9679; map p.71. This Port of Spain institution is a popular late liming spot, drawing a very mixed crowd plus an ever-present coterie of St James' headcases who entertain the crowd with feats of bottle-balancing and other escapades. The clientele spills onto the pavement (where there are tables), the music is loud and a good-natured atmosphere prevails. Mon–Thurs 11pm–3am, Fri–Sun 10pm–6am.

1

CLUBS

As Port of Spain's bars offer good alternatives to full-blown clubs, often with DJs and dancefloors, there are surprisingly few dedicated club venues. All of them adhere to strict dress codes; although foreigners can usually get away with more than locals, bear in mind that men may be turned away if wearing sneakers, shorts or hats, while women should wear heels or strappy sandals (beach flip-flops are not deemed appropriate). Cover charges start at around TT$60, or up to TT$200 if drinks are included.

51° 51 Cipriani Blvd, Newtown ☎ 627 0051, ⊛ 51degrees .biz; map p.56. One of Trinidad's most popular clubs, attracting a mixed, uptownish party crowd and with a wide music policy, mostly dancehall, R&B and hip-hop, with some dance and "alternative" thrown in too. To be assured entry at weekends, arrive before 10pm, or call/email a guest list in advance. The main party nights are Friday and Saturday, but there's also karaoke on a Thursday. Thurs–Sat 9pm–late.

Aria Lounge Cnr Fitt St & Ariapita Ave, Woodbrook ☎ 225 2742; map p.71. Popular with a younger crowd but aiming

---

FETING CARNIVAL

With Christmas over and done with, the New Year in Trinidad means one thing for dedicated Carnivalists: **fetes**. Staged by everyone from the local water company to the T&T army, these huge outdoor parties get everyone in the Carnival mood and set you up for a great experience on the road. There are hundreds to choose from, all with a very different flavour and character, ranging from the more raw events such as WASA or Fire Fete to laidback, cooler parties where you bring your own drinks and top-end all-inclusive parties staged in gorgeous rural surroundings, with premium drinks and food. The roster of events changes each year, with new ones popping up and established parties fading away; check the web and listen to the radio (most local stations are available online; see p.32).

In recent years, **wet fetes** have become increasingly popular, with the crowd cooled down by jets of water from huge hoses. **Cooler fetes** mean most people arrive primed with a cooler stocked full of drinks and ice, but there's always a bar too. Note also that not all of the fetes are night-time affairs: many of the more upmarket events take place in the afternoon and run on into the evening (giving you time to hit a night-time fete too, if you have the stamina), while **breakfast fetes** (which start in the wee hours and end at lunchtime) are increasingly popular. Note that most evening fetes don't get going until around 11pm, and the best acts perform in the early hours, so don't arrive too early.

WHAT TO WEAR AND TAKE

As feting is a frenetic and extremely sweaty business, it pays to **dress appropriately**. For women, a pretty top (usually a vest – you'll get very hot when dancing) with shorts or jeans is de rigueur, while a rag to wave and wipe your brow with is also essential – you'll often find promotional rags stamped with logos given away on the night. High-end all-inclusive fetes, however, are a very different kettle of fish, with patrons dressing to impress and heels aplenty for the women.

In terms of **security**, pickpocketing is fairly common at the more hardcore events and at shows such as Soca Monarch – thieves often work in teams, with one person dancing with the unsuspecting victim while another slides a hand into a pocket to remove cash or valuables. Be aware of this, and don't carry much cash with you; expensive jewellery or watches, and a wallet full of credit cards, are also best left at your hotel.

TICKETS AND PRICES

Many of Carnival websites (see p.81) carry fete schedules, with details of dates, prices and ticket outlets. You can buy **tickets** from music stores such as Cleves and Crosby's (see p.92) as well as selected outlets in Port of Spain's malls; listen to the radio or check online for details. If you don't buy ahead, you can invariably get a ticket outside the venue from a tout (or scalper, as they're known here); most ask a lot more than face value, but you can usually negotiate a deal, especially if you're buying a few tickets. Ticket Federation (⊛ ticketfederation.com) is a useful service that will secure fete tickets for you. Fete prices range enormously, and seem to rise alarmingly each year; the average for the large, more hardcore fetes is TT$200, while the high-end all-inclusives cost up to TT$900 and average at around TT$700. Many of the mid-range fetes sell both general admission and VIP tickets; the latter usually include some drinks and allow you to get close to the stage without mixing in the melee of the main crowd – worth considering if you're new to feting or want slightly superior facilities.

for an upmarket, sophisticated vibe, this is the Avenue's newest club, with the obligatory VIP area downstairs and both indoor and outdoor sections for the masses below. Music tends toward EDM, hip-hop and soca, and the cover charge is TT$100. Dress code in effect. Wed, Fri & Sat 10pm–4.30am.

Katalyst 1 Gray St, cnr of Rust St, St Clair ☎ 222 3632; map p.71. Mixed-age, fairly well-heeled crowd and a lovely venue, with all sorts of nooks and crannies and an open-air section. The busiest night is the Saturday free drinks night (TT$150). Fri & Sat 6pm–late.

Rossco's 32 Fitt St, Woodbrook ☎ 225 7275; map p.71. Popular spot for a young crowd, with regular drinks promotions such as Lime Light Wednesdays, with cheap rum, beer and vodka on a Friday after-work lime and Bottle Up on a Saturday (entry includes a bottle of spirits). Music ranges from hip-hop, soca and R&B to EDM and dubstep. Cover charge varies. Wed–Fri 4am–4am, Sat 6pm–4am.

Sabor Latino Shoppes of Maraval, Saddle Rd, Maraval ☎ 628 0927, ☜ saborlatinolive.com; map p.71. Perhaps past its glory days, but this diminutive place (still known by its old name, *Attic*) remains friendly and unpretentious, with lots of dark corners in which to dance – though it can be a bit of a pick-up joint. Latin nights on Thurs and Sat (with salsa classes 5.30–7.45pm) draw a twirling Venezuelan-dominated salsa crowd; other nights see the playlist widened to include soca and reggae. Tues–Sun 10pm–5am.

★Stumblin' on the Avenue 42 Ariapita Ave, Woodbrook ☎ 223 5017; map p.71. This unpretentious club-bar, with its dancefloor opening out onto a streetside terrace, is one of the liveliest places in town, with great music (soca, reggae, hip-hop etc) and a friendly, laidback crowd of all ages packing out the place till the wee hours. Drinks are reasonably priced and entry is often free. Tues–Sat 6pm–late.

Zen 9–11 Keate St, Port of Spain ☎ 351 4642; map p.56. Set over three floors in a redecorated former cinema, with a rooftop lounge, a "VIP" area and a main dancefloor for the masses, this is Port of Spain's biggest club, but perhaps isn't the hotspot it once was. Nonetheless, its Wednesday student night remains enduringly popular, as does the Saturday party night; both include free drinks with entry. Women sometimes get in free before 11.30pm. Cover charge TT$100–150. Wed & Sat 9pm–late.

GALLERIES

101 Art Gallery 84 Woodford St, Newtown ☎ 628 4081, ☜ 101artgallery.com; map p.56. Regular exhibitions by well-known local artists including Peter Sheppard, Martin Superville and Geoffrey Holder.

Medulla 37 Fitt St, Woodbrook ☎ 622 1196, ☜ cocobel chocolate.com; map p.71. Thought-provoking exhibitions by upcoming and established artists from Edward Bowen and Bunty O'Conner to Justin de Verteuil and Richard Mark Rawlins.

Y Gallery 26 Taylor St, Woodbrook ☎ 628 4186, ☜ yartgallery.com; map p.71. Swish gallery that represents some prestigious local artists, from Christopher Cozier to Jackie Hinkson, LeRoy Clarke and Peter Shim.

THEATRE AND THE ARTS

When Port of Spain is not preoccupied with the continuous live entertainment of Carnival season, theatre becomes a popular diversion, with a hugely varied set of productions staged at Queen's Hall, alongside the odd play at the Trinidad Theatre Workshop or Little Carib Theatre. As well as staging their brilliant annual Carnival show, rapso band 3canal (☜ 3canal.com) sometimes produce a summer show; check their website for details.

★Alice Yard 80 Roberts St, Woodbrook (no phone) ☜ aliceyard.blogspot.com. The backyard of the former family home of a local architect, Alice Yard is an eclectic arts space curated by artists and writers which stages a wonderful range of events, from visual arts to poetry readings and workshops.

Big Black Box 33 Murray St ☎ 623 7411, ☜ 3canal .com. A new performance space created by Rapso group 3canal, with regular performances from them as well as productions featuring a wealth of local talent, and regular BackYard Jam parties in the run up to Carnival season.

Central Bank Auditorium Twin Towers financial complex, Independence Square South ☎ 623 0845, ☜ central-bank.org.tt. Entrance through Eric Williams Plaza. The most comfortable and high-tech theatre in Port of Spain features productions by well-known Trinidad theatre companies – usually comedies.

Little Carib Theatre White St, cnr Roberts, Woodbrook ☎ 622 4644. Opened in 1948 and recently refurbished, this intimate and historic theatre concentrates on plays and shows highlighting local talent and culture.

Queen's Hall 1–3 St Ann's Rd, St Ann's ☎ 624 1284, ☜ queenshalltt.com. Opposite the *Hilton Trinidad*, this is the largest theatre in Trinidad, featuring drama, dance, music and fashion shows, as well as calypso concerts in Carnival season; it's also the regular venue for 3canal's renowned pre-Carnival show, definitely one to look out for.

Trinidad Theatre Workshop 23 Jerningham Ave ☎ 624 8502, ☜ trinidadtheatreworkshop.com. A tiny and intimate performance space, with an eclectic programme of productions.

Under the Trees Normandie Hotel, 10 Nook Ave, St Ann's ☎ 624 1181, ☜ normandiett.com. Atmospheric evening performances under the stars in the grounds of the *Normandie* hotel, showcasing local artists doing everything from calypso to stand-up comedy and choral concerts.

CINEMA

MovieTowne is by far the most popular place to see a film; less mainstream cinema is showcased during the Trinidad &

Tobago Film Festival and the European Film Festival, staged in September and May (see p.35) respectively.

Digicel IMAX One Woodbrook Place, Damian St, Woodbrook ☎ 299 4629, ⓦ imax.tt. The only IMAX cinema in the Caribbean, newly constructed and with a single screen showing 3D movies for adults and children.

Globe Cnr St Vincent and Park streets ☎ 623 1063. The only old-timer remaining of Port of Spain's cinemas, in the heart of the downtown area, screening double bills of the latest American blockbusters; be ready for loud and often witty commentary from the audience.

MovieTowne Audrey Jeffers Hwy ☎ 627 8277, ⓦ movietowne.com. Port of Spain's cinema scene hinges around the ten screens at the fiercely a/c complex opposite the Hasley Crawford Stadium; expect all the latest blockbusters.

SHOPPING

Downtown Port of Spain's main shopping area is around **Frederick Street** and **Charlotte Street**, where you can buy everything from make-up to market goods. More upmarket shopping (though less local colour) is to be had at the air-conditioned **West Mall** in Westmoorings and **Long Circular** in St James, both of which have international clothing store chains as well as local retailers. There are **supermarkets** at West Mall, Long Circular Mall, Saddle Road in Maraval, just off St Ann's Road in Cascade and French Street in Woodbrook.

CARNIVAL SUPPLIES

Samaroo's 11–13 Abercromby St, Port of Spain ☎ 624 8431; and First Floor, Fiesta Plaza, MovieTowne, ⓦ samaroosgroup.com; map p.56. The original purveyor of feathers, sequins, glue-guns and the like, with everything you need to make your own costume or adapt the one you buy. Downtown Mon–Fri 8.30am–5pm, Sat 8.20am–2pm, MovieTowne Mon–Thurs 11am–7pm, Fri & Sat 10am–7pm.

Tulip Productions 76 Ariapita Ave, Woodbrook ☎ 627 2230, ⓦ tulipproduction.com; map p.71. As well as a great range of Carnival paraphernalia including ready-decorated bras, Tulip have party supplies and fancy-dress costumes. Mon–Fri 8am–4.30pm, Sat 9am–1pm.

BOOKSHOPS

Metropolitan Book Suppliers Capital Plaza (formerly Colsort Mall), 11–13 Frederick St; map p.56. In the basement of this little mall, Metropolitan has an excellent range of books on T&T's history and culture as well as Caribbean fiction. Mon–Fri 8.30am–4pm, Sat 9am–1pm.

★**Paper Based** Normandie Hotel, Nook Ave, St Ann's ☎ 625 3197, ⓦ paperbased.org; map p.75. Fantastic little bookshop, conveniently located just off the Savannah and with a great array of carefully chosen fiction and non-fiction from the Caribbean and beyond. Regular readings and book launches, and a great website with discussion of the titles on sale. Mon–Fri 10am–6pm, Sat 10am–4pm.

CHOCOLATE

★**Cocobel** 37 Fitt St ☎ 622 1196, ⓦ cocobelchocolate .com; map p.71. Cocobel's handmade chocolates are as beautiful as they are delicious, each a little work of art courtesy of architect-turned-chocolatier Isabel Brash, who also designed the building in which Cocobel is based. Trinidad fine-flavour cocoa is combined with local ingredients to create such delights as Mermaid's Kiss (pineapple and chadon beni under dark chocolate, with salt crystals) or Basil Wild (dark ganache with Paramin mint); there are also chocolate-covered cocoa and coffee beans, bars and flavoured chocolate sticks. Call ahead to arrange a tasting session. Mon–Fri 10.30am–6pm, Sat by appt only.

CRAFTS

Rainy Days 60 Ellerslie Plaza, Maraval ☎ 622 5597; map p.71. The best place in town for locally made crafts and souvenirs, with everything from miniature wooden rum shops to hand-painted postcard-sized watercolours, batiks, DVDs and CDs. Daily 10am–5pm.

Akilah's Designs Fondes Amandes Community Reforestation Project, Fondes Amandes Rd, St Ann's ☎ 689 7794 or ☎ 750 1716, ⓦ facrp.org; map p.75. Made by the woman behind this fantastic community project (see p.77), this beautiful natural jewellery is crafted from local seeds, pods and nuts, and is completely unique. Daily, no set hours.

MUSIC

Crosby's 54 Western Main Rd, St James ☎ 622 7644; map p.71. All you could ask for in the way of soca, plus reggae and other Caribbean music. Mon–Sat 9am–5pm.

DIRECTORY

Banks Numerous branches (all with ATMs) on Independence Square downtown; Republic Bank also has branches in West Mall and Long Circular Mall, and Ariapita Ave (cnr of Murray St) in Woodbrook. Scotiabank is at Ellerslie Plaza in Maraval and Western Main Rd (cnr of Bengal St) in St James. You'll get a better rate of exchange at FX Trader, with locations at Excellent Stores, on the corner of Frederick St and Independence Square (Mon–Thurs 8.30am–5pm, Fri 9am–6pm, Sat 8.30am–2.30pm); Excellent Stores on the corner of Frederick and Park streets (Mon–Thurs 8am–5pm,

Fri 8am–5.30pm, Sat 9am–2pm); next to Mario's in City Gate bus station (Mon–Fri 8am–5pm, Sat 8am–2pm).

Embassies and high commissions British High Commission, 19 St Clair Ave, St Clair (Mon–Fri 7.30–11.30am; ☎350 0444, ⓦ ukintt.fco.gov.uk/en); Canadian High Commission, 3–3a Sweet Briar Rd, St Clair (Mon–Thurs 7.30am–noon & 12.30–4pm, Fri 7.30am–1pm; ☎622 6232, ⓦ trinidadandtobago.gc.ca); US Embassy, 15 Queen's Park West (Mon–Fri 7.30–11am; ☎622 6371, ⓦ trinidad.usembassy.gov).

Hospital The main public hospital is Port of Spain General, 169 Charlotte St (☎623 2951–52); waiting times can be long and facilities basic. The private St Clair Medical Centre, 18 Elizabeth St, St Clair (☎628 1451 or ☎8615, ⓦ medcorpltd.com) is a good private hospital with an A&E

department. For an ambulance, dial ☎811 or ☎624 4343.

Pharmacies SuperPharm, 1 Columbus Circle, West Mall complex, Westmoorings (☎633 1663), and Royal Palm Plaza, Maraval (☎622 6025), both open Mon–Sat 7.30am–11pm, Sun 8.30am–11pm.

Police Report crimes at the Central Police Station, St Vincent St, at Hart ☎625 1261 or ☎625 2684. In an emergency, dial ☎999.

Post office TT Post has several branches, including: 23 Chacon St (Mon–Fri 7am–5pm, Sat 9am–2pm); City Gate, South Quay (Mon–Fri 7am–6pm, Sat 8am–1pm); 177 Tragarete Rd, next to Roxy roundabout, Woodbrook (Mon–Fri 7am–5pm, Sat 8am–noon).

Swimming pool The *Hilton Trinidad* (see p.84) now allows non-guests to swim for a daily fee of around TT$80.

Paramin

Occupying the rolling hills above Port of Spain's Maraval district and spreading back towards the north coast, the charming hillside community of **PARAMIN** seems a million miles from the hustle of the city streets laid out below. The area is known as the "herb basket of Trinidad" thanks to its many farmers, who have carved terraced plots into the precipitous peaks to grow the French and Spanish thyme, mint, celery and spring onions (here known as chives), used to make up the tied bundles sold in shops and markets throughout T&T, and blended into bottles of the green seasoning which flavours Trinbago cooking. The local population are descended from French Creoles who came to Trinidad in the colonial era, as well as Venezuelans who arrived in the nineteenth century to plant cocoa, and the close-knit but friendly community maintains many of its traditions, most famously in its **parang** bands, who travel from house to house during the Christmas season, singing nativity songs in a mix of French and Spanish. The Monday before Christmas, Paramin hosts a **parang festival** at the soccer field at the lower end of town, while on the afternoon of Carnival Monday, the town is overtaken by troupes of **blue devils**: traditional Carnival characters impersonating imps from hell, who dance through the streets demanding money from onlookers and daubing them with a little of their trademark blue – it's the most anarchic display of Blue Devil mas you'll see anywhere in the country.

Paramin has few specific sights, but the neatly tended hillsides of seasoning plants and the green-swathed mountains are superbly scenic and often swathed in mist; on clear days, there are many lovely views down to the sea, while the clear, clean air is fragrant and noticeably cooler than down on the flats. For the best of the **views**, head up to the mobile phone masts on Saut D'Eau Road.

Our Lady of Guadalupe Church

Morne Cyril, Paramin

At the lower end of Paramin, on a terrace overlooking the Maraval Valley, the beautiful **Our Lady of Guadalupe Church** looks more like a conservatory than a place of worship, with its green roof and plant-lined windows; each year on the Sunday before Carnival, a Mass is conducted here entirely in the French Creole patois that's still spoken by Paramin elders.

ARRIVAL AND DEPARTURE   **PARAMIN**

By jeep Paramin's insanely steep, switchbacking roads are out of the question for those that don't know the area and are driving a regular car. The most sensible way to get to the

area is to take one of the jeeps which run between Paramin and the base of Morne Coco Rd; to get to the departure point, take the turn-off onto Morne Coco Rd from Saddle Rd in Maraval opposite the church and next to the petrol station; after some 200m, the road forks; jeeps depart from the start of the right-hand fork. Fares depend upon how far you're going, but won't be more than TT$10 for short drops. **By organized tour** Caribbean Discovery Tours (☎ 624 7281) offers 4WD tours of Paramin, which include a visit to a seasoning farm and a stopoff at the gorgeous North Deck, a viewing platform overlooking Saut D'Eau island on the north coast. For a more local flavour, Portia Brown (☎ 629 0441 or ☎ 779 629 4848), driver of the Paramin jeep "General" and a resident of the area, conducts informal excursions; prices are negotiable.

EATING AND DRINKING

Kool Breeze Bar Saut D'Eau Rd, Paramin (no phone). This is a rum shop with a view. Friendly and a fantastic place to drink a cold beer or a glass of rum and enjoy the breeze. Daily no set hours.

The western tip

From Port of Spain, the Audrey Jeffers Highway heads east along the coast, past the turn-off to the residential suburbs of Diego Martin, Petit Valley and Westmoorings, the latter home to the plush **West Mall** shopping centre. Just past here, the road narrows and swings through upscale **Glencoe**, where there's a mini shopping mall with a supermarket, fast-food outlets and an RBTT bank. Beyond here, things get more ramshackle, with the rum shop and rickety wooden stalls at **Carenage** selling fruit and vegetables, and some lovely vistas out over the Gulf of Paria to the so-called Five Islands, of which the largest, Nelson, was used as a processing point and quarantine for Indian indentured workers and later as a prison. Past Carenage, the coast road trundles along parallel to the sea, its twists and turns revealing lovely vistas out to the Bocas and back to Port of Spain, before entering **Chaguaramas**, Port of Spain's playground, with its waterside restaurants, hiking trails and string of marinas where yachts hole up during the hurricane season or dry-dock to do maintenance work. The area still has a very military flavour, with training camps for the army and coastguard in Chaguaramas town; the final section of the coast road is blocked to civilian traffic and the peninsula is the exclusive preserve of the military, with the Trinidad and Tobago Regiment headquarters at Teteron Bay and the Coast Guard at nearby Staubles Bay.

Carenage

Spreading inland of the coast, run-down **Carenage** takes its name from the time when ships were taken here to be careened by Spanish colonists. After the British took the island in 1797, Carenage reverted to a fishing village and sank into a century-and-a-half-long torpor, but its character changed drastically with the arrival of the Americans in 1941, when Chaguaramas was turned into a US military base and all the western tip's residents were forcibly relocated to this spot. The village soon acquired a seedy reputation as a place where American soldiers went to have fun and find local women, and there are still a couple of flophouses around advertising rooms for rent by the hour. Today, it retains a somewhat salty air and a dodgy reputation.

Chaguaramas

A few hundred metres west from Carenage, past the large white bauxite loading plant that juts into the sea, the Western Main Road enters **CHAGUARAMAS** (pronounced "sha-ger-*rah*-mus"). Home to red howler and capuchin monkeys, armadillos, ocelots and anteaters, much of this land here has remained virtually untouched, with shallow beaches around the coast and miles of virgin rainforest in its mountainous interior, much of which is now a protected **national park**. Along the coast, however, the hulking hangars left by the Americans aren't particularly pretty, and the string of marinas obscures most of the southern waterline. The area's administrators, the Chaguaramas

Development Company (CDA), have made efforts in recent years to beautify the coast, lining Williams Bay with a lovely boardwalk and, at the time of writing, constructing an adjacent leisure development slated to include a children's playground and climbing walls. More ambitious plans yet to come to fruition include an upgrade of the golf course at Chagville Beach and construction of a new resort hotel.

The open stretches of coast that remain are popular spots for locals to swim or go fishing; come to Chaguaramas on a weekend and you'll see people liming on the beaches, paddling Williams Bay in kayaks or splashing in the shallows and, in Tucker Valley, cycling and jogging along the quiet roads and hiking in the forests. Many also make a beeline for **Macqueripe Beach**, a delightful north coast cove at the far end of the valley and the best beach in the Port of Spain environs, with cool green waters and some handsome landscaping. Chaguaramas is also well worth a visit at night, when a glamorous crowd comes in from the capital to frequent the restaurants or attend one of the regular parties staged in the area's open-air venues.

Brief history

The name Chaguaramas, derived from the Amerindian word for the palms that once lined this coast, is the only remnant of the area's indigenous population. The protected natural harbours here provided the **Spanish** with a hiding place for their ships when the **British** invaded in 1797, though when it became clear that defeat was inevitable, the ships were scuttled. The harbour at Williams Bay was also the reason the **US military** wanted Chaguaramas as its Caribbean base during World War II, and they leased the peninsula from the British in 1940 in return for fifty used destroyers.

Though initially greeted with a warm welcome, the American soldiers quickly became unpopular. Many Trinidadians resented the US occupation of the beaches and countryside that were most easily accessible from the capital, not to mention the social effect of having so many young American men living in the region. The GIs outnumbered the local men, who couldn't compete with the Americans' ostentatious wealth, and the resentment this generated was immortalized by Lord Invader in his famous calypso *Rum and Coca Cola*:

Rum and Coca-Cola,
Go down to Point Cumana,
Both mother and daughter,
Working for the Yankee Dollar

CHAGUARAMAS DEVELOPMENT AUTHORITY (CDA)

Based in the orange-painted building behind the Chaguaramas Hotel and Convention Centre on Airways Road, the **Chaguaramas Development Authority** (Mon–Fri 8am–4pm; ☎634 4227 or ☎634 4312, ⓦchagdev.com) offer excellent and educational **tours**, led by experienced and knowledgeable guides, into the Chaguaramas National Park, most of which pass through the lush vegetation, rivers and cultivated forest of the Tucker Valley. All tours are detailed on the CDA website, and though they specify a minimum group size of ten, this is sometimes waived; equally, you may be able to join with existing bookings, many of which are with local schools. Perhaps the best hike is to **Covigne River** (TT$85), a moderately challenging four-hour hike along a riverbed, which includes a beautiful section of twisting gorge and a rope-aided climb up a waterfall to an emerald bathing pool surrounded by rainforest. On the way back, you can pick your own nutmeg at an abandoned plantation and bathe in a spring. The CDA also provide guides for the **Golf Course to Macqueripe** trail (3hr; TT$85), a fairly strenuous hike that affords lovely views over Tucker Valley, the north coast and over to Venezuela, as well as trips to the Bocas (see p.105); as well as the two-hour walk to the top of **Morne Catherine** (TT$50) and the **Edith Falls** trail (2hr; TT$40). The rates above cover transport from the CDA office to the start of the hike and back, though not to and from Chaguaramas; if you're going "down the islands" with the CDA, you'll need to get yourself to the Island Property Owners marina (see p.104). You should bring your own water and snacks on all trips.

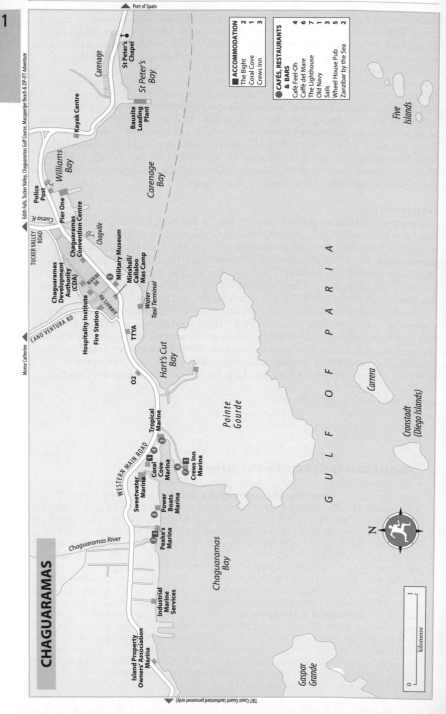

CHAGUARAMAS

ACCOMMODATION

The Bight	2
Coral Cove	1
Crews Inn	3

CAFÉS, RESTAURANTS & BARS

Café Feel-Oh	4
Caffé del Mare	6
The Lighthouse	7
Old Navy	1
Sails	3
Wheel House Pub	5
Zanzibar by the Sea	2

(Ironically, a bastardized version of the song saw The Andrews Sisters spend ten weeks at the top of the US billboard charts in 1945, much to the disgust of Invader, who successfully sued for copyright infringement.) The situation in Chaguaramas was not improved by the Americans' attitude towards **race**. A 1945 edition of *Life* magazine reported that "US soldiers confused by the mix of colour lines would keep a brown paper bag at the doorway to their parties. Anyone whose skin was lighter than the bag was considered white (and allowed entry)." With the growth of the **independence movement**, Chaguaramas became a focus of conflict between the British colonial government and the local population, and in April 1960, thousands of local residents marched through the rain to campaign for the return of Chaguaramas. Their goal was achieved the following February, when the area was returned to Trinidad and the Americans departed.

Chaguaramas today

Chaguaramas has long been a place of recreation for Trinidadians, and with this in mind the government declared the region a **national park** in 1961, also granting protected status to the area's wildlife and rainforest. The built-up part of Chaguaramas, which contains many buildings abandoned by the Americans, was promoted as the seat of the future Caribbean parliament, but these plans were thwarted by the collapse of the West Indian Federation in 1962. Subsequently, the **Chaguaramas Development Authority** (CDA) was established to maintain the nature reserve and encourage leisure-oriented businesses. In 1999, Chaguaramas served as the venue for the **Miss Universe** competition, and the resulting beautification saw an upgrade in the CDA's hotel and cavernous conference facilities. These days, though, the long-floundering hotel serves as a police training centre and there's a bit of a ghost-town feel to Chaguaramas away from the marinas – though this may well change as a result of ambitious development plans for the area, most of which were unconfirmed at the time of writing.

Williams Bay

A wide cove enclosed by a forested outcrop to the west, **Williams Bay** has a narrow beach overhung by a paved boardwalk, popular with beachgoers by day and strolling families in the evenings. Local bathers descend en masse at weekends, bringing coolers packed with food and drink and making a day of it, but the water isn't particularly inviting, its brownish waves tinted with petrol rainbows from the heavy traffic of container ships in the Gulf of Paria. Better to rent a **kayak** from the Kayak Centre (see p.101), in a signposted building in the concrete lot on the eastern side of the bay.

Phase II of the Wiliams Bay boardwalk opened in late 2014, with a circle of vendors booths forming an outdoor food court, a performance space and a water feature that local wits immediately christened "Lake Chikungunya" in honour of the disease that swept through the island and the rest of the Caribbean in 2014. (Though as the water is treated and filtered, it's not in fact a breeding ground for the mosquitoes that spread the virus.)

Chaguaramas town

Beyond Williams Bay, the Western Main Road straightens out to become the main drag of **Chaguaramas town**, flanked on either side by the ugly concrete structures that were constructed in 1940 by the US military. Nowadays most of the aircraft hangars, warehouses and official buildings have been converted for use by businesses or government departments – you'll often see trainee coastguards or soldiers on parade – while the incongruously grand flagpole-lined driveway of the former Chaguaramas Hotel and Convention Centre looks out of place amid its no-nonsense neighbours.

Chagville Beach

An unremarkable strip of pebbly sand lapped by muddy water, **Chagville Beach** stretches along Carenage Bay for about half the length of Chaguaramas town. It's

1

fringed by grass and almond trees and separated from the Western Main Road by a car park. Although swimming is not recommended during the wet season due to downstream pollution, the water still gets packed with bathers at weekends and public holidays. There are toilets and showers, a bar and a handful of kiosks selling snack foods, basic meals and cold drinks.

Chaguaramas Military History and Aerospace Museum

Tues–Sun 9am–5pm • TT$50, children TT$30 • ☎ 634 3491 or ☎ 634 2992

Next to the Coast Guard's training ground and heliport, the **Chaguaramas Military History and Aerospace Museum** is hard to miss thanks to the collection of military hardware on the forecourt, including a monumental 88-ton, US Army LARC (lighter amphibious resupply cargo) vessel, a rusting tank and a battered ex-BWIA jet, which had to be dismantled into nineteen pieces to transport it along the winding route from Piarco. Inside the main building, wedged between some smaller pieces of military equipment, the exhibits chronicle the military history of T&T from 1498 to the present, as well as touching on wider world militaria and history. Although the presentation can be somewhat haphazard, it's an absorbing and occasionally touching array, worth a glimpse if only because it so sharply counteracts the usual beaches-and-palms image of the Caribbean. Tours are usually available, and there's a restaurant and bar on site. **Exhibits** include a re-creation of a World War II trench and a German machine-gun bunker, complete with flashing lights simulating explosions and battle

---

PETER MINSHALL AND THE CALLALOO COMPANY

Awarded an Emmy for costume design for his work on the 2002 Winter Olympics opening ceremony, and the Chaconia Medal (the country's second-highest honour) in 1987 for his services to the nation, **Peter Minshall** is the most controversial and admired of T&T's Carnival designers, whose unique combination of traditional Carnival characters and innovative techniques are known for being presented with a strong sense of theatre.

Born and raised in Trinidad, Minshall studied theatre design at the Central School of Art and Design in London. He designed his first Carnival band for London's Notting Hill Carnival in 1975, and returned to Trinidad soon afterwards to bring out **Paradise Lost**, the first of his many acclaimed presentations. Minshall's **Callaloo Company**, formed in 1991, featured many of Trinidad's best actors, dancers and artists, and functioned as a production company, mas factory and performance group. This close-knit and loyal crew took its name from Trinidad's national dish, whose various ingredients reflect the country's ethnic mix: "all ah we is one" was the company's philosophy.

Unlike many Carnival costumes, which are thrown away on Ash Wednesday, dusty Minshall creations still decorate houses throughout Trinidad. While most contemporary mas presentations tend to concentrate on escapist, fantasy themes with minimal costumes, Minshall's lavish and detailed works tended to deal with spiritual and political issues: the environment, the interconnectedness of humanity, the transience of life. Many of his pieces are more like kinetic sculptures than costumes in the traditional sense, where puppets have moving limbs and butterflies fluttering wings. In emphasizing the aspect of Carnival that allows people to escape their own identity by playing a role, Minshall has continued the tradition of Carnival as theatre for all: "In most countries," he has often remarked, "people pay to see others perform. However in Trinidad, people pay to perform".

Sadly, however, Minshall's dissatisfaction with the bikinis and good-time carelessness that make "pretty mas", alongside the general lack of regard for the creative traditions of Carnival, have seen him take a step back from mas in Trinidad in recent years. He produced his last large-scale mas, Picoplat, in 2002, but continues to work overseas. In 2006 he brought out an AIDS-themed band, the Sacred Heart, which saw the return of some of his most popular King and Queen costumes in the form of Son of Saga Boy and Miss Universe, a tribute to the seminal Tan Tan and Saga Boy designs from his 1990 mas, Tantana. In 2014, he designed a small Monday-only band, Miss Miles (A Band on Corruption); whether any of his fabulous designs will again cross the Savannah stage on Carnival Tuesday remains to be seen; check ⓦ callaloo.co.tt for an update.

sounds, as well as a series of photos and explanatory panels highlighting the extensive (and often overlooked) role of local soldiers in international warfare. Pirates, the Trinidadian police and local battles are also covered, with detailed drawings of the Battle of Scarborough Bay in Tobago and the British takeover of Trinidad, while newspaper photographs from the 1990 coup provide a glimpse of the turmoil in Trinidad during the six-day siege. A shop sells military prints, pamphlets and a good selection of greeting cards.

Callaloo Mas Camp
Western Main Rd • Call to arrange a visit ☏ 634 4491

Opposite the old heliport, a hulking hangar surrounded by wire fencing houses the workshop of Trinidad's most famous mas band, Callaloo, led by designer **Peter Minshall** (see box opposite). Known for the innovative techniques and high quality of his immensely detailed mas presentations, Minshall and his crew used everything from leaves to bottle tops or lengths of fibreglass to manufacture the amazing costumes that won them many a **Band of the Year title** during their glory years in the late 1980s and 90s, as well as creating costumes and pieces for the opening ceremonies of the **Olympics** and **World Cup**. Visitors are welcome, though given that Minshall last brought out a large-scale Carnival band in 2006, there may not be much going on, though other artists do work at the mas camp year-round.

Tucker Valley

Immediately north of Chaguaramas town via a signposted road just past the police post on Williams Bay, **Tucker Valley** is the highlight of Chaguaramas, a gorgeous swathe of thick forest, most of which is undeveloped and laced with hiking trails and gentle natural attractions, all of which are heralded by signs courtesy of the **Chaguaramas Development Authority** (see p.95), which promotes and maintains the lush countryside of the Chaguaramas National Park. You'll need your own transport to travel the length of the Tucker Valley Road to Macqueripe, or up to the golf course – truly beautiful drives, with pastures and fields dotted with enormous, bromeliad-smothered samaan trees to each side, gently rising to meet forested peaks. If you want to stop, the most convenient spot is **Samaan Park**, a grassy area shaded by huge trees to the right of the road.

Mount St Pleasant village

Driving north along the main Tucker Valley Road, the haphazard group of gravestones and the dilapidated St Chad's church on the right are pretty much all that's left of **Mount St Pleasant** village. During the colonial era, when this fertile valley was planted with citrus, cocoa and coffee as part of the Tucker Estate, Mount St Pleasant was a thriving settlement, home to many estate workers and their families; today, the remaining buildings are derelict and barely standing. Among the plain gravestones you can pick out the rather grand tomb of Amelia Tripp, daughter of the estate's English owner, William Sanger Tucker.

Edith Falls

Back on Tucker Valley Road, the well-signposted left turn to **Edith Falls** takes you onto Bellerande Road, from where the beginning of the trail to the falls is clearly marked – on the left of the road just before the practice range of the Chaguaramas Golf Course. It's an easy forty-minute (1.5km) walk past stands of towering bamboo interspersed with fishtail palms and rubber trees seeping black sap; blue emperor butterflies are common, and if you're lucky, you'll hear the distinctive roar of the valley's troops of howler monkeys. At the end of the trail, you scramble up a few boulders to reach the waterfall itself. Water seeps through the steep craggy rockface, sending showers tumbling 180m into the shallow pool below (not deep enough for swimming). The falls slow to a trickle in dry season (Nov–June).

1

Bellerand Park

No set hours • Free

Beyond the falls trail, Bellerande Road passes **Bellerand Park** on the left, a children's playground with a jungle gym, a "human sized" chequers board, toilets and picnic tables. It's also the start of the so-called "**Chag 10**", an exercise trail around the valley with ten designated points where signboards detail various different exercises.

Chaguaramas Golf Course

Bellerand Rd • Daily 6am–6pm • TT$95 for nine holes, TT$190 for eighteen holes, lessons and gear rental also available • ☎ 634 4227, ⓦ chagdev.com

Bellerande Road ends at the **Chaguaramas Golf Course**, built on a former tonka-bean plantation by American servicemen during World War II. There's a breezy bar in the **clubhouse**, the only place to get a drink or a meal in the vicinity. From the golf course, you can follow a 2.5km-long **hiking trail** up through the forest to Macqueripe Beach, with gorgeous views of the north coast at several points.

Macqueripe Beach

Lifeguards daily 10am–6pm • Car park daily 9am–6pm • Cars TT$20, pedestrians free • Changing facilities TT$1

Beyond the golf course turn-off, Tucker Valley Road ends at the small, picturesque cove of **Macqueripe Beach**, given an upgrade and some handsome landscaping following the laying of new fibre-optic cables in 2009. From the car park, where there's a snack bar selling soft drinks and, at the weekends, corn soup and snacks, wooden-fenced steps switchback down the neatly landscaped hillside to a concrete deck. The slip of beach below is pretty small, and the deck's wall detracts somewhat from the beauty of the surrounding wooded hillside, but it's a gorgeous spot, with stunning sunsets and a distant view of Venezuela's Paria Peninsula. The sea on this side of the peninsula is unpolluted and wonderful for swimming (and even a spot of snorkelling if you have your own gear), and though the beach can get crowded at weekends, you'll often find it deserted in the week. Keep in mind that strong currents make it unwise to swim out too far.

Just before the car park, there are picnic gazebos on a grassy verge and, on the right, a lovely **children's playground**.

ZIP-ITT Adventure

Tues–Fri 10am–4pm, Sat & Sun 10am–4.30pm • TT$140 • ☎ 381 8543, ⓦ chagdev.com • Shoes with covered toes are required

Just above Macqueripe, accessed from the platform just behind the path down to the beach, **ZIPP-ITT Adventure** offers seven zip lines and five net bridges which allow you to get up into the forest canopy and swoop across the Macqueripe Bay, getting some fantastic views of the Chaguaramas coastline and a bit of an adrenaline rush.

Bamboo Cathedral

Just before the entrance road to Macqueripe Beach, a signposted right turn-off from Tucker Valley Road leads to the **Bamboo Cathedral**, a whimsical but apt name for the tunnel of bamboo that encloses a section of the tarmac, the thick foliage allowing shafts of green-tinged sunlight to filter through. It's a scene that inspired renowned Trinidadian artist and national hero **Michel Cazabon**, who included the cathedral in the many paintings he did of the Tucker Valley in the nineteenth century.

The tracking station

Past the Bamboo Cathedral, off Tucker Valley Road, the path into the interior snakes upwards towards the rusting bulk of the **tracking station** at the top of the ridge. This huge dish was erected by the US military in the 1950s to track nuclear missiles, though its main claim to fame is less sinister. The dish's technology soon became redundant, and the radar scanner was converted into a radio transmitter in 1960; on August 12 of the same year it was used to transmit the first radio signal to be bounced off a satellite

1

– the signal was received at Floyd Air Force Base in New York. The station was used to develop the technique until 1972, when it was abandoned. The tracking station stands on a nine-acre plateau with gorgeous views of Tucker Valley, the north coast and of Venezuela. On the way down, keep an eye (or an ear) out for the wide variety of **birds** and troops of **howler monkeys** that inhabit the area. The road up is often barred; contact the CDA if you want to drive up.

Morne Catherine

Opposite the military museum, Cano Ventura Road snakes northwards from the Western Main Road into the hills, arriving after a steep and beautiful climb along a road overhung with trees and bamboo at the **Morne Catherine**, the highest peak in the Chaguaramas National Park. As with the tracking station, you'll need to get in touch with the CDA if you want to drive up; walkers and cyclists have free access. A fork off to the right leads to a radar dish, but there's nothing much to see there; instead, stop anywhere along the road to appreciate the abundant birdlife, from toucans to oropendolas and hummingbirds.

ARRIVAL AND GETTING AROUND   THE WESTERN TIP

By car A rental car is by far the most convenient way to get to and around Chaguaramas, particularly Tucker Valley (where there's no public transport); there are numerous rental outfits in Port of Spain (see p.80).

By bus and maxi taxi There is regular public transport along the Western Main Rd, with PTSC buses and maxis linking Port of Spain and the Island Property Owners' Marina in Chaguaramas stopping at all points in between.

By water taxi Water taxis (15min; TT$10; ☎ 624 5137, ⓦ nidco.co.tt) from the Wrightson Rd terminal in Port of Spain (see p.79) arrive and depart from La Soufriere,

behind a blue wall just past the heliport on Western Main Rd. The journey offers some lovely views of the Port of Spain coastline, but sailings are limited (Port of Spain–Chaguaramas Mon–Fri 7.30am, Sat 10.30am; Chaguaramas–Port of Spain Mon–Fri 4.15pm, Sat 4pm).

By ferry The Wednesday ferry service between Pier One in Williams Bay and the Venezuelan town of Guiria had been suspended at the time of writing, though may be reinstated; for an update, call ☎ 634 4472 or visit ⓦ pier1tt.com.

TOURS AND ACTIVITIES

Kayaking In a signposted building in the concrete lot on the eastern side of Williams Bay, the Kayak Centre (daily 6am–6pm; ☎ 633 7871 or ☎ 680 6244, ⓔ trinikayak @gmail.com) offers an hour's paddling for TT$30 for a single kayak and TT$50 for a double, and stand-up paddleboarding for TT$30/hr; all prices raise by TT$10/hr at

weekends. You can also contact Courtenay Rooks at Paria Springs Tours (☎ 620 8240, ⓦ pariasprings.com) for more adventurous guided kayak tours around the Bocas islands.

Mountain biking Courtenay Rooks also offers excellent guided rides along off-road trails in Tucker Valley; US$55–105 depending upon route and duration, bike included.

ACCOMMODATION

CHAGUARAMAS BAY

The Bight Peake's Marina, Western Main Rd ☎ 634 4427, ⓦ peakeyachts.com. Ten smart rooms in Peake's marina west of town, used mainly by visiting yachties. In a lovely position overlooking the water right by the sea's edge, rooms are tastefully furnished and have a/c, cable TV and en-suite bathrooms. **US$75**

Coral Cove Coral Cove Marina, Western Main Rd ☎ 634 2040, ⓦ coralcovemarina.com. Rather uninspired but efficient and friendly hotel. Rooms are on the expensive

side but clean and modern, with a/c, cable TV, phone and kitchenette, and there's a pool on site. Free wi-fi. **US$89**

Crews Inn Point Gourde ☎ 634 4000, ⓦ crewsinn.com. Overlooking the busy marina, this is the smartest place to stay in Chaguaramas, and the only resort-like place among them, with high-end prices to match. Recently refurbished in a clean, minimalist style, the rooms have all the amenities you'd expect, as well as kitchenette and balconies overlooking the sea, and there's a restaurant, bar, gym and a lovely pool. Rates include continental breakfast and wi-fi. **US$275**

EATING, DRINKING AND NIGHTLIFE

Port of Spain's lack of waterside eating and drinking is more than made up for in Chaguaramas. The marinas along the Western Main Road hold plenty of open-air **restaurants**, some quite low-key, others quite upmarket, and most doubling up as a good place for a **drink**. The vendors' booths at the Williams Bay boardwalk are also a good option, selling everything

1

from Trini-Indian delights to soup. The club scene that once had Chaguaramas buzzing every weekend has slowed down, but venues such as the *02* and *Pier One* still host fetes throughout the year, particularly at Carnival time. The restaurant formerly known as the *Lure*, in a lovely waterside setting at Sweetwater marina, was undergoing transformation into a more informal diner and sports bar at the time of writing; call ☎ 681 8011 for an update.

CHAGUARAMAS BAY

Café Feel-Oh Coral Cove Marina, Western Main Rd ☎ 634 2323. Facing the road, with a cool, dark a/c interior and a couple of tables outside, this is a convenient stopoff right in the middle of Chaguaramas, with inexpensive breakfasts of sada roti or eggs (TT$20–40) plus fish sandwiches, fresh fish and pasta dishes (around TT$50) during the rest of the day. Mon–Sat 7.30am–11pm, Sun 10am–10pm.

Caffè del Mare Crews Inn Marina, Point Gourde Rd ☎ 634 3484. Swish coffee shop, shifted slightly to pole position at the front of the marina, with tables inside and on the deck overlooking the water. Italian coffees, pastries and ice cream, plus panini, soup and quiche with salad. Sandwiches from TT$40, mains from TT$65. Mon–Fri & Sun 7am–8pm, Sat & Sun 7am–9pm.

The Lighthouse Crews Inn Marina, Point Gourde Rd ☎ 634 4384, ⓦ crewsinn.com. Attractive open-air restaurant and bar overlooking the marina, underneath a red-and-white-striped lighthouse. Aimed mainly at a yachting clientele, it serves tasty international-style food, from great burgers to fish and chips, alongside frothy cocktails and good desserts. During the week there are lunch specials (TT$40 or two courses TT$99), plus a three-course set dinner (TT$199); Sunday brunch (6.30–10am) is TT$199. Daily 7am–11pm.

Old Navy Chaguaramas Military Museum, Western Main Rd ☎ 734 3435. Good choice for a beer or inexpensive Creole lunch (TT$30–40), with a blackboard menu posted outside detailing the dishes of the day, from steamed fish to chicken tenders and the odd Venezuelan dish. Popular spot with soldiers from the military training camp, just opposite. Takeaway available. Daily 9am–midnight.

Sails Power Boats Marina, Western Main Rd ☎ 634 1712, ⓦ sailsrestpub.com. Great little bar and restaurant patronized by a casual crowd of yachties and locals, with tables by the water and in an indoor bar area with a pool table. Local-style lunches are TT$45, though prices do go up after dark for such things as lasagne (TT$125), meat, fish and seafood kebabs or baby-back ribs (TT$170), kingfish with garlic butter and herbs (TT$210) or lamb chops (TT$240). There's usually a genial drinking crowd to lime with after you eat. Mon–Fri 11am–midnight, Fri & Sat 8am–midnight; kitchen closes 10pm.

Wheel House Pub Tropical Marine, Western Main Rd ☎ 634 2339. Tucked behind the tiny marina just past Crews Inn, this is a cool little spot for drink or a local meal, with shaded waterside tables overlooking the bobbing boats and a pool table in the a/c interior. The restaurant cooks up simple, tasty plates of grilled lamb or tuna, fried shrimp, lasagne and salad and catch of the day. Lunch TT$40–55, dinner TT$100–140. Daily 10am–11pm.

Zanzibar by the Sea Peake's Marina, Western Main Rd ☎ 634 3346, ⓦ zanzibartt.com. Similarly buzzy offshoot of the MovieTown original, *Zanzibar*, serving a massively varied menu that runs from burritos to burgers, grilled meat and fish, pasta and seafood (TT$100–200). Good lunchtime specials (TT$60–70) from Cuban pork with cassava and black beans to parmesan-crusted fish, plus a long list of cocktails. Breakfast (around TT$30) includes saltfish and scrambled eggs, pancakes and arepas. Mon–Thurs & Sun 7am–11pm, Fri & Sat 8am–midnight.

The Bocas

When Trinidadians refer to **THE BOCAS**, they talk of "down the islands" in tones of wistful longing. These rocky islets are separated from the mainland, and from one another, by the **Bocas del Dragon (Dragon's Mouth)**, a series of channels connecting the Gulf of Paria with the Caribbean. The name is appropriate, for the coastlines here are jagged and rocky, and the sea hides treacherous currents and undertows that can make even the short journey to the nearest island, **Gaspar Grande**, a rough ride. Dolphins frequent the waters here, so keep your eyes peeled; if you're lucky, you may see a leatherback turtle or a pilot whale.

The islands had a thriving **whaling industry** in the eighteenth century, with whaling stations on Gaspar Grande, **Monos** and **Chacachacare**. Today the Bocas are sparsely inhabited, lacking any roads and with dense forest covering the interiors and holiday homes, accessible only by boat, scattered along the coasts. For Trinis the islands have always been a popular weekend getaway from the mainland, when yachts drop anchor in the bays for an afternoon of eating, drinking and swimming, and there are several operators offering boat trips to the islands as well as to the **Gasparee Caves** at Gaspar Grande. Apart from one intermittently functioning resort on Gaspar Grande, there are no hotels, guesthouses, restaurants or bars, and away from popular mooring points such as Scotland Bay (actually on the mainland), the atmosphere is so still that it can verge on the uncanny – especially on deserted Chacachacare, with its abandoned leper colony and accompanying ghostly legends.

Carrera

The first island you pass when heading down the Bocas chain from Chaguaramas marinas is the small and rocky **Carrera**, Trinidad's equivalent of Alcatraz. Its only buildings form the prison complex, established in 1876, where convicts still do hard labour. It's said that seven individuals have braved the strong currents and shark-infested waters to swim to the mainland, but only three made it, and were all recaptured within a couple of weeks.

Gaspar Grande and Gasparee Caves

CDA Gasparee Cave tours, including the boat from the mainland, cost TT$100; most tour operators (see p.104) also include the caves in their itineraries

Just fifteen minutes by boat from the mainland, **GASPAR GRANDE** (also known as **Gasparee**) is the most accessible of the islands. The eerie **Gasparee Caves** at Point Baleine – "Whale Point", named after its former role as a whaling station – were once used by pirates to hide their booty; these days, the only thing that glitters are the walls and the huge, green-tinged stalactites and stalagmites. It's also an excellent place to observe the **fruit bats**, which inhabit the caves and the many local species of bird, which congregate outside them. If you want to **visit**, you'll first need to contact the CDA (see p.95); turn up unannounced, and you're likely to find the entrance locked up.

The caves

To get to Gasparee Caves, follow the signposted concrete path from the jetty through the forest; look out for unusual tan-coloured trees, whose rather politically incorrect nickname, "naked Indian", derives from the colour of their peeling bark. If you've prearranged your trip, you'll meet your **CDA tour guide** by the wooden house just before the mouth of the cave. An impressive, cathedral-like cavern some 35m deep, it's a weirdly beautiful place, silent but for the chirping fruit bats and dripping water. Reflected sunlight causes calcium crystals in the rocks to sparkle, and a deep, clear, marvellously turquoise tidal pool reflects the colours and shapes of the stalactites and stalagmites. The water changes daily with the tides, and offers lovely swimming. Past the pool, there's a short path to the back of the cave, where you can gaze up at roosting bats and pick out the rock formations that have been given apt nicknames such as "the Lovers", "Buddha" and the "Virgin Mary".

Scotland Bay

Though actually part of the mainland, **Scotland Bay** is always considered as being "down the islands", since it can only be reached by boat. Right at the end of the peninsula, it's an idyllic small cove blessed with soft sand and calm waters that offer opportunities for snorkelling. Spreading back from the shore is some gorgeous primary rainforest that provides a habitat for howler monkeys and a rich array of birds and plants.

Monos

Scotland Bay looks out across the swirling waters of the Boca de Monos to the island of **Monos**, whose densely wooded interior once supported a large colony of howler monkeys – the island's name is Spanish for apes – but these are now confined to the mainland. There's a passable stretch of **beach** here, reminiscent of Macqueripe; follow the path from the main marina. Beyond the sheer western ramparts of Monos and another fierce *boca* lies the privately owned and seldom-visited island of **Huevos**.

Chacachacare

The CDA offers guided walks to the lighthouse or the salt pond for TT$135 including boat transport; you can also go with private tour companies (see p.105)

Utterly peaceful **Chacachacare** (*shak*-a-shak-*are*-eee) is the largest island of the Bocas and, at an hour's boat ride from the mainland, also the farthest-flung. It has none of the well-to-do holiday homes found on the other islands, and the mountainous interior is covered in dense forest. There is just one useable road, leading from the jetty to the lighthouse; the others, which serviced the now-abandoned **leper colony**, have long been overgrown, and only tracks remain.

Brief history

Chacachacare's name may derive from *chac-chac*, the Amerindian word for cotton, which grows profusely here, or might also have something to do with the chattering of the monkeys once found in droves on the island. According to discovered remains dated from around 100–400 AD, Chacachacare was once inhabited by Amerindians. Under Spanish rule it became a cotton plantation, and subsequently a whaling station was established. It developed into a popular health and holiday resort with Trinis from the mainland until, to their consternation, a **leper colony** was established in 1887. The Dominican nuns ran the colony like a prison, and conditions provoked strikes among the patients to gain such rights as male–female fraternization. The last thirty patients left in 1984, and all that remains are the decaying wooden houses, the infirmary, the nuns' quarters and the chapel, all poking through the foliage to the right as you approach the island from the mainland.

The island

You're free to explore the structures of Chacachacare's former leper colony, but as they're all derelict, you should watch your step. Also on this stretch are a string of lovely **beaches**, with pale sand and shallow, calm, crystal-clear water; these see some traffic at weekends, but are often deserted during the week.

Chacachacare is now uninhabited except for its wildlife (look out for unusually large iguanas) and the two men who work the small, white **lighthouse**, built in 1885. On the southwest of the island is **La Tinta Bay**; the name, meaning "ink" in Spanish, alludes to the black sand of its beaches. Once a favourite place for smugglers, today this coarse-grained beach is deserted save for the refuse washed up by the tide, and the odd iguana and scavenging hawk. Nearby is the **Salt Pond**, a marsh-fringed sulphurous lake that provides the perfect habitat for unusual trees such as the campecho, known locally as the **bread and cheese tree** on account of its textured fruit with a cheesy taste. Its bathwater-warm waters offer some interesting swimming, with the high salt content allowing you to float with ease.

Note that the odd **manchineel** tree also grows on the island's beaches. Its beautiful yellow flowers hide the fact that it produces a toxic fruit, used by the Amerindians to make poisoned arrows. Avoid contact with any part of this tree: its sap causes painful blisters (see p.46).

ARRIVAL AND DEPARTURE

By water taxi The Island Property Owners' Association marina, on the Western Main Rd just before the *Cove* hotel, is the base for boats that serve as unofficial water taxis to the islands; it also has a small grocery where you can stock up with food and drink before you go. Local boatman Spider (☎ 681 8167 or ☎ 769 2469) offers transport to and from the island, as does Santie (T 335 7495); you can also call the main guard booth to arrange a boat (T 634 4331). Fares For two people, per-person return fares are as follows: TT$200 to Gaspar Grande, TT$230 to Monos and TT$1000 to Chacachacare.

TOURS

The CDA trips to the Gasparee Caves and Chacachacare can be a little dry; for a more leisure-oriented trip, opt for a private tour company.

★**Dolphin Adventures** T 706 6004, W dolphinadventures.weebly.com. This small-scale company offers excellent boat trips, going "down the islands" in true Trini style, without the feel of being on a "tour"; groups are small and Captain Nevie Boos offers informed and humorous commentary on all the sights. You can bring your own food and drink (4hr US$150/person 1–2 people, 6hr US$125/person 3–4 people or US$85 5–8 people), or pay a little more to have snacks and drinks or a full picnic lunch with bar.

In-Joy tours T 633 4733 or T 753 2775, W injoytours.com. Excellent trips covering all the islands and taking in Scotland Bay, Gasparee Cave and swimming and relaxation at beaches on Monos or Chacachacare, all accompanied by entertaining and thoughtful commentary on the islands' history. Tours from US$45.

Island Experiences T 621 0407 or T 781 6235, W islandexperiencestt.com. Great tours for groups of four-plus people aboard a comfortable yacht, taking in all the islands plus Gasparee Caves, and with enthusiastic and charming guides. Half-day tour from US$45, full-day from US$80, meals and drinks not included.

ACCOMMODATION AND EATING

Staying on one of the Bocas offers a lovely getaway from Port of Spain, with great swimming and snorkelling on your doorstep. Most houses are privately owned, but a few are let out to visitors (look in the Classifieds section of the local papers), and there's one hotel on Gaspar Grande, which also has a restaurant. If you do stay here, you'll need to arrange a boat over from the Island Property Owners Marina, and bring all **groceries** and **supplies** with you; stock up in Glencoe.

Bombshell Bay Villas Gaspar Grande T 672 6549, W bombshellbayvillas.com. Recently refurbished, these smart a/c studios and one-bedroom villas built on a hillside overlooking the waters of Bombshell Bay have a lounge and a kitchenette. There's a restaurant, bar, swimming pool and tennis court on the property, and a good sandy beach just below. Studio **TT$1000**, villa **TT$1800**

The Island Villa Gaspar Grande T 625 6841, W trinidadgingerbreadhouse.com. Owned by the family behind the lovely *Gingerbread House* in Woodbrook (see p.83), this is a gorgeous villa, with four bedrooms (sleeping 14 altogether), two recreation rooms, full kitchen and a veranda overlooking the sea. Steps lead down to the water, which offers safe swimming. Two-night minimum stay. **TT$1800**

Northern Trinidad

LEATHERBACK TURTLE, GRANDE RIVIERE BEACH

Northern Trinidad

The north of Trinidad is dominated by the rainforested mountains of the Northern Range, which form a rugged spine, rising up dramatically from the coastline to over 900m at the peaks of El Cerro del Aripo and El Tucuche. The region is also lined with Trinidad's most stunning beaches, of which Maracas Bay and Las Cuevas are the most popular. Beyond is the glorious, laidback seashore of Blanchisseuse, where the road dissolves into undeveloped coastline. A narrow pass winds through the mountains south of the village, providing an opportunity to see some of the island's prolific birdlife at Asa Wright Nature Centre and the idyllic village of Brasso Seco.

Occupying the stretch of land south of the jungle-smothered mountains is one of Trinidad's most **densely populated** areas, a string of traffic-choked urban communities known collectively as the **East–West Corridor**, spreading back from each side of the Eastern Main Road and bordered to the south by the Churchill Roosevelt Highway. Though you'll see plenty of temples, mosques and Hindu prayer flags around **Tunapuna**, Indian culture is far less visible here than in the south: Creole cooking reigns supreme and the soundtrack that blares from shops, bars and maxis is **soca** and Jamaican **dancehall** rather than chutney. Of the individual communities, **St Joseph** is the most absorbing, named by the Spanish as the island's first capital, with a historic church and barracks. Slightly further east, **St Augustine** is dominated from the hills above by the stunning **Mount St Benedict Monastery**, home to a lovely guesthouse that's one of the most attractive of the low-key and little-used **accommodation** options across the region. The East–West Corridor also offers access to a host of interior mountain attractions: numerous spectacular waterfalls and opportunities for river swimming are to be found at **Maracas Valley**, **Caura**, **Lopinot** and, especially, from the **Heights of Guanapo Road**, the starting point of several fantastic Northern Range **hikes**.

From **Arima** – home to Trinidad's only Amerindian parade – shops and houses are replaced by the winding minor roads that span the weather-beaten **northeastern tip**. A wild and rugged peninsula, this **Toco coast** juts some 20km into the Atlantic Ocean, and is one of Trinidad's best-kept secrets. Between March and August **leatherback turtles** clamber up onto wave-battered sandy beaches like **Matura** and **Grande Riviere** to lay their eggs, backed by spectacular scenery.

Many of the places along the East–West Corridor, as well as Maracas and Las Cuevas beaches, are best seen by way of day-trips from Port of Spain; however, Blanchisseuse has a smattering of **accommodation** options, and if you plan on making the long drive up to Grande Riviere, you'll almost certainly want to stay a night or two before heading back.

GETTING AROUND   NORTHERN TRINIDAD

By car As is the case everywhere in Trinidad, a car is the most convenient way to see the sights in the north, particularly far-flung spots such as Blanchisseuse, Asa Wright, Toco and Grande Riviere. There are plenty of rental

NORTHERN RANGE WATERFALL

Highlights

❶ **North Coast Road** Switchback through the lush Northern Range jungle and enjoy the rugged coastline between Maracas and Blanchisseuse. **See pp.112–118**

❷ **Paria Bay** A pristine swathe of sand with a waterfall just inland, Paria is the ultimate deserted island beach. **See p.119**

❸ **Brasso Seco** A low-key ecotourism destination in the heart of the mountains, Brasso is a must for hikers, birdwatchers and relaxation seekers. **See p.121**

❹ **Yerette** Sit in a flowered garden bedecked with feeders as iridescent hummingbirds whir

through the air all around you. **See p.127**

❺ **Mount St Benedict Monastery** Stunning views over the central plains and a historic guesthouse provide soothing respite from the East–West Corridor below. **See p.128**

❻ **Café Mariposa, Lopinot** Eat a wonderful Creole-Latin meal in this verdant and beguiling mountain valley. **See p.131**

❼ **Grande Riviere** With rainforest hikes, river swims, great places to stay and a rugged golden-sand beach where hundreds of turtles lay eggs each night during the spring, Grande Riviere is simply unique. **See pp.141–144**

HIGHLIGHTS ARE MARKED ON THE MAP ON PP.110–111

companies in Port of Spain (see p.80).

By public transport The north is fairly well served by public transport – taxis and maxis travel along the East–West Corridor 24 hours a day via the fast-track Priority Bus Route and the Eastern Main Rd, and also serve the communities inland of the EMR, while most rural areas are also covered, but long waits are common. As with everywhere in Trinidad, relying on public transport can be a little time-consuming; to get to places off the EMR such as Lopinot, for example, you'd need to take a maxi or route taxi from Port of Spain, change into a Lopinot route taxi at the junction of the valley road on the EMR, and then do the same on the way back, probably with a wait at each of the stages.

By organized tour Most tour companies (see p.38) include the top northern sights – the north coast, Asa Wright/Brasso Seco, Mt St Benedict, Yerette – in their itineraries.

Santa Cruz Valley

Beyond the grand residences of Maraval at the northern fringe of Port of Spain, buildings give way to abundant rainforest and the road climbs through a succession of hairpin bends to where a **junction** is marked by two 4m-high stone pillars. To the left is the **North Coast Road** (see p.112); continuing straight ahead, **Saddle Road** squeezes through a narrow gorge of solid rock before meandering downhill through pastoral

NORTHERN TRINIDAD

Santa Cruz valley, a very scenic half-hour jaunt past cattle pastures and farmland south towards the urban bedlam of San Juan (see p.125).

The valley's neat cocoa groves, flower gardens with orchids, crumbling mud-walled **tapia** houses and dilapidated gingerbread mansions are punctuated by towering samaan trees and impressive clumps of bamboo, mango, sapodilla and banana, though a thriving nearby **quarry** has gouged messy yellow scars into the hillsides. Cricket legend **Brian Lara** spent his childhood in **Cantaro Village**, about 3km along the road. The place has a friendly, suburban feel, its lively main street lined with roti restaurants and rum bars. At the back of the village is a cricket stadium built in Lara's honour, with a placard outlining his remarkable world Test records.

2

La Sagesse trail

The northern end of San Juan is the starting point for a hilly but popular **hike** to Maracas Bay along the **La Sagesse trail**; it's pretty easy to follow on your own but it's sensible to hike in a group and a guide is recommended (see p.135). It's a pleasant 8km hill walk through secondary forest with great views; to get to the start, turn off the Saddle Road at Gasparillo Road (marked by a signpost for a quarry) and

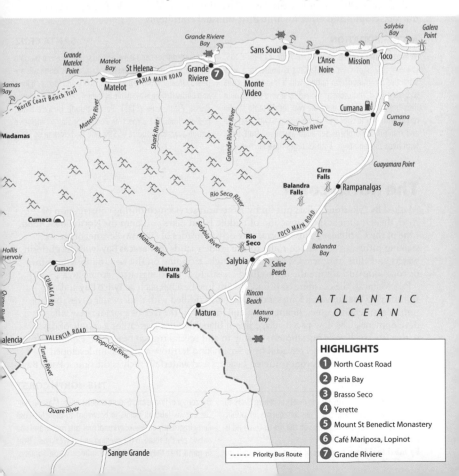

HIGHLIGHTS

1. North Coast Road
2. Paria Bay
3. Brasso Seco
4. Yerette
5. Mount St Benedict Monastery
6. Café Mariposa, Lopinot
7. Grande Riviere

------ Priority Bus Route

carry straight on, passing the quarry on the right. The hike begins where the houses end; ask for directions.

San Antonio Green Market

Pole 213, Saddle Rd, nr Cutucapano Rd, Upper Santa Cruz • Sat 6am–2pm, Sun 8am–2pm • Car park TT$20 • ☎ 221 9116, ⓦ sanantoniogreenmarket.com

Hunkered under the valley's green, jungle-clad hills, the **San Antonio Green Market** is a fantastic initiative, offering the chance to buy local craft and sample quality food and drink. The market's beautiful setting is reason to visit in itself, with naturalistic landscaping, bird feeders busy with hummingbirds, plenty of tables and benches and a kids' playground. Locals flock to the stalls heaped with fresh produce (much of it organic), from dasheen bush and ground provisions to tropical fruit and North Coast fish, while up on the top level, open-sided thatch-roof booths house vendors selling traditional cocoa tea (just the thing if you arrive in the early morning), as well as local breakfast delicacies such as smoked herring or saltfish buljol with coconut bake, plus cakes, pastries, Venezuelan street food, home-made wine and fantastic unsweetened juices (try the tamarind or *pomme cythere*). You can also explore a recreated cocoa house and nature trails, and peruse displays of handmade wooden bowls, soaps, jewellery, mirrors, clothes and other high-quality, unusual craft items.

ACCOMMODATION   SANTA CRUZ

★**Waterville Estate** ☎ 676 7057 or ☎ 396 6165, ⓦ watervilleestate.com. Santa Cruz is home to a very attractive accommodation option, which is ideal for visits to both capital and country. Owned by a very welcoming Irish-Trinidadian family, there are two comfortable studio rooms with verandas, as well as two cottages with a private and tranquil atmosphere, set amid abundant fruit trees with birds flitting about. Both cottages have kitchenette, stone-tiled floors and large veranda, and one is a bargain for four, with both twin and double rooms. Hiking trails are nearby (Maracas Bay is under 2hr walk), and further hiking and birdwatching is available at their sister property *Mount Brasso Estate* (see p.123). Rates include breakfast and pick-up from the airport or Port of Spain; all-inclusive option available. Studios <u>US$90</u>, one-bed cottage <u>US$150</u>

The north coast

Marked by two stone pillars put up by American servicemen during construction of the road, the left turn at the Y-junction of Saddle Road takes you onto the **North Coast Road**. One of the Caribbean's most spectacular drives, hordes of city-dwellers negotiate its snaking turns at weekends en route to the golden sands of **Maracas Bay**, with its glittering waters and cliffs smothered with tangled jungle, stopping on the way to buy salt prunes or corn soup and admire the unravelling coastline at the designated "scenic area".

Past Maracas, the coastline is sprinkled with fine beaches such as **Tyrico Bay** and shimmering **Las Cuevas**, a long sandy beach also riddled with underwater **caves**, but the north coast remains quiet, maintaining equanimity in the face of sporadic new villa developments. The slow-paced village life of **Blanchisseuse** is great for a couple of days, with a few small-scale **guesthouses** to stay in and several rugged beaches to explore. After this the coastal road ends, replaced by prime **hiking** territory along the undeveloped coastline, with perfect coconut-littered beaches and **waterfalls** such as the one at **Paria Bay**.

GETTING AROUND   THE NORTH COAST

By car As ever, a car is by far the most convenient way to explore the north coast, given the infrequency of public transport. The only petrol station on the North Coast Rd is at Maracas.

By maxi taxi Maxis from Port of Spain (departing from the corner of Prince and George streets) run to Maracas Bay, Las Cuevas (and all points in between) to Blanchisseuse fairly frequently on weekdays until mid-afternoon, and one or two ply the route in the evening and at weekends. Bear in mind that they are extremely infrequent on Sundays.

Maxis leave Port of Spain for Blanchisseuse at 5.30am, 6.30am and 7.30am, then intermittently throughout the rest of the day, and stop at all the villages, settlements and beaches along the way. Note that there is no service from Blanchisseuse onwards to Arima.

By bus Slightly slower but marginally cheaper PTSC buses run Mon–Sat from City Gate at 4.30am, 9am and 1.30pm and 5pm, returning roughly two and a half hours later from Blanchisseuse, and stopping at all points in between.

The North Coast Road

The **North Coast Road** offers one of Trinidad's most dramatic drives, teetering along 300m-high cliffs and tunnelling past precipices of rainforest with occasional views of faraway peaks. Bois cano trees drop claw-like leaves onto the tarmac and mineral springs pour down into roadside gullies; the water is chilled, delicious and safe to drink. Despite its spiralling course, this is also one of the island's smoothest roads, built by the US Army in 1944 as a recompense for their use of the Chaguaramas peninsula, which deprived residents of sea bathing at Macqueripe and other bays; it's still sometimes called the "American Road". Be warned that at weekends it becomes heavily congested, and is prone to frequent landslides during the rainy season.

The first of many spectacular panoramas stretches over the Maraval valley to the tiny spice and parang centre of Paramin and down into the outskirts of Port of Spain. Cliffs and jungle close in beyond here (with glimpses of Santa Cruz to the right), and a few kilometres further reveals a gorgeous coastal prospect, the ocean far below dotted with rocky islets. The largest of these is **Saut D'Eau**, a 100,000-square-metre breeding colony for brown pelicans, chestnut-collared swift and the rufous-necked wood rail.

La Vache Scenic Area

The North Coast Road is punctuated by fruit stalls and refreshment huts with dramatic sea views, the air noticeably cooling as you climb to **La Vache Scenic Area**, the highest point on the North Coast Road. The coastal views are marvellous from here, and vendors sell souvenirs, cold drinks and East Indian sweets to the weekend hordes on their way to Maracas Beach, while a talented **busker** improvises calypsos and will expect a few dollars if he makes you laugh.

Maracas Bay

Lifeguards on duty daily 10am–6pm • Car park TT$10 per entry • Changing rooms/toilets daily 10am–6pm, TT$2

Some 45 minutes' drive from Port of Spain, the North Coast Road plunges down to **MARACAS BAY**, a ravishing generous curve of fine, off-white sand bordered by groves of skinny-stemmed palm trees and with a stunning mountainous backdrop. Easily the most popular beach on the island, Maracas is an institution: thousands make the traditional Sunday pilgrimage to show off their newest swimwear, frolic in the water, sunbathe and network. During the week, it's a much quieter scene, and perhaps all the more enjoyable for it.

THE MAGNETIC ROAD TO MARACAS BAY

A small stretch of apparently ordinary tarmac between La Vache and Maracas Bay has a unique claim to fame. According to local folklore, this is the "**magnetic road**", where vehicles roll up an incline in defiance of gravity – and it's easily experienced. Stop just before the North Coast Road begins its descent to Maracas Bay. As the cliffs to the right recede, revealing the Northern Range, the road ahead appears to have a definite upward incline. On stopping your vehicle, putting the gears in neutral and releasing the handbrake, you'd assume that the car would obey gravity and roll backwards; in fact you move forward in what feels like the "wrong" direction. Although this marvel is nothing more than an optical illusion, more romantic locals insist that it's the work of God, *obeah*, or a bizarre magnetic field.

2

A concrete pillar with silver lettering and silver waves stands in the centre of a roundabout, heralding your arrival. Continuing on the main road, you'll find a huge **car park** (you'll get a ticket if you park elsewhere at weekends) and beach **facilities** such as showers, changing rooms and toilets, plus a flurry of food stalls selling the famed Maracas bake and shark sandwiches (see p.29). On the other side of the coast road is the wide swathe of **beach**. Licked into a fury by passing currents and the wind tunnel effect of surrounding headlands, the waves often reach a metre or two high and make for an exhilarating swim, and the water is usually emerald green. Be wary of tides and undercurrents, however, as they're often dangerously strong; stick to the areas between red and yellow flags where **lifeguards** stand by, whistling furiously at anyone who goes too far out.

Maracas Bay Village

The left-hand turn-off from the North Coast Road at the western end of Maracas Bay leads across a small river and down to **Maracas Bay Village**, a fishing hamlet whose catch – fresh carite, cavalli and shark – is in demand throughout the north. Here you'll find a couple of rum bars, a grocery and post office, alongside lots of beached pirogues and drying nets and a very pretty cream-and-blue church next door to the *Maracas Bay* hotel. The village is also home to a profusion of scavenging dogs and few bathers; most people stick to the main beach to avoid the odd fishy entrail.

ACCOMMODATION AND EATING   MARACAS BAY

Accommodation in the area is fairly limited. The odd budget room is available to rent elsewhere in the village. Alternatively, *Waterville Estate* in Santa Cruz (see p.112) is a great option if you have your own car or like the idea of hiking over the hill to reach Maracas Bay. When it comes to **eating**, bake and shark (see p.29) is the Maracas Bay mainstay: two fried breads (the bake) with seasoned fried shark, topped at a buffet with all manner of condiments from tamarind, chadon beni, garlic and pepper sauces to coleslaw, salad and fresh pineapple. You'll find it for around TT$30 from multiple takeaway outlets, some of which also serve the more sustainable kingfish and bake (from TT$50), as well as aloo, beef and fish pies (from TT$12), pholouri and roti. Cold **beers** and **soft drinks** are available at all the stalls.

Asha's Maracas Bay car park (no phone). Tucked behind *Richard's* and offering more variety, from fried chicken, burgers (including veggie versions) and hot-dogs to fried bake with shrimp, salmon, kingfish and flying fish (TT$40–60), plus fries and pies, ice cream and coffee. Daily 8am–7pm.
Maracas Bay Hotel ☎ 669 1914, ⊛ maracasbay.com. Bland yet reliable place at the west end of the bay, this is the only place to stay on Maracas, offering decent if plain rooms with en-suite bathroom, a/c, and sea-facing porches; ask for one in the refurbished east wing. The hotel's *Bandanya* restaurant serves breakfast, lunch and dinner, and the food is basic but good: fish sandwich and fries at TT$75, grilled fish or chicken with sides at TT$140/110. There's a small bar on site. Wi-fi and breakfast

included. TT$550
Richard's Maracas Bay car park (no phone). The eternally popular *Richard's* always has the longest lines of all the Maracas bake and shark vendors, and the quick turnover means the sandwiches, dressings and condiments are always super-fresh. If you're concerned about sustainability, plump for kingfish, carite or cheese instead of shark meat. Daily 8am–7pm.
Uncle Sam's Maracas Bay (no phone). This bar and grocery store at the eastern end of the bay is the most popular drinking location on the beach – sound systems pump reggae and soca and draw large, spirited, crowds, and the bake and shark is eternally popular, too. Tues–Sun 8am–late.

Tyrico Bay

Lifeguards on duty daily 10am–6pm

Hidden from Maracas Bay by a steep headland, **Tyrico Bay** is about a kilometre east, past two hairpin bends and marked by a black-and-white pole. Popular with the Indian community who flock here for weekend picnics and family beach-cricket tournaments, the bay is roughly half the size of Maracas with slightly less in the way of wave action, making it a better choice if you are travelling with children. There's also a small lagoon on the west side of the beach for very safe paddling. Luxuriant, fine yellow sand and a gentle shelf add to the feeling of calm, and there are no food and drink vendors. The only buildings are the lifeguard towers and portable toilets, and you can drive right down to the sand.

Diamier Bay

Diamier Bay is a quiet, isolated beach with a sheltered stretch of sand on its far side, overlooked by houses perched high on the hill; the sea in front of you is calm and practically windless. Bring your own food and drink as there are no facilities. The track to the beach is marked by a sign for *Nanan's Retreat*; park at the piece of high ground just off the main road, and take the steep track to the right down to the bay (don't drive down as there's no room to turn around).

2

Las Cuevas

Lifeguards on duty daily 10am–6pm • Changing rooms/toilets daily 10am–6pm, TT$2 • Las Cuevas is a 10min drive from Maracas Bay, and an easy day-trip from Port of Spain

After an inland curve that provides impressive views of the jagged double apex of Mount El Tucuche, Trinidad's second highest mountain, the North Coast Road turns back to the sea at **Las Cuevas**, the north coast's longest beach. Named by the Spanish after the caves that riddle both the seabed and the rocks to the west end of the bay, Las Cuevas boasts a wide, clean and unadorned swathe of whitish sand, fringed by coconut palms and invitingly calm emerald waters that provide better swimming than Maracas. It's also a great place for beachcombing, especially along the seldom-visited western reaches, littered with shells and stones. The beach is surrounded by headlands, which enclose the bay in a tight horseshoe and provide protection from the wind and a relatively gentle surf. During the week it's often deserted, although the fishing community is still very active, but weekends see the sand dotted with family groups who make a day of it, bringing coolers packed with food and drink and beach umbrellas to provide much-needed shade. Keep in mind, though, that the legendary **sandfly** population, a particular problem in the late afternoon or after rain, can make for unpleasant sunbathing – take repellent and cover up as the day wears on.

There's a large (free) car park above the bay, as well as changing rooms, showers, toilets and a first aid room. Lifeguards patrol and put out yellow and red flags to mark safe bathing spots, and it's not a good idea to swim outside of these areas. The calmest waters are to the eastern side of the bay.

ACCOMMODATION AND EATING   LAS CUEVAS

Las Cuevas Beach Lodge ☎ 669 6945. Precariously balanced on a ridge above the beach, this is the only place to stay in Las Cuevas. Recently redecorated, the rooms range quite a bit in size, and only the larger studio apartments get the full benefit of the view, but all are clean and bright, with a/c, plus fridge and microwave in the apartments. The wooden terrace bar and restaurant (daily 8am–10pm) offers fantastic view, and serves simple lunches and dinners

such as local fish (TT$95), grilled chicken and shrimp (TT$70/110), steaks (TT$90–285) and baby-back ribs (TT$125). Doubles TT$400, apartments TT$700

McLean's (no phone). This bar at the western edge of the Las Cuevas car park is a favourite with local fishermen, serving budget-priced Creole breakfasts and fish-and-chip lunches (around TT$60) alongside soft drinks, beer and rum. Daily 6am–5pm.

One Hundred Steps Beach

Mitchell Trace, North Coast Rd

A fifteen-minute drive east of Las Cuevas along the North Coast Road, just before the village of La Filette is the secluded **One Hundred Steps Beach**, so called because of the seemingly endless concrete steps that wind down the cliffs – though be warned that landslides have made navigating them a little dangerous. To find it, turn down

Mitchell's Trace, a dirt track opposite the larger Rincon Trace, which strikes inland from the North Coast Road a couple of kilometres east of Las Cuevas. Ideal for a secluded swim and popular with local fishermen, this curve of soft, greyish sand is backed by almond trees and a few **manchineels**, which should be treated with caution (see p.46). Be careful of strong tides here, even on apparently calm days, as there's no one to help if you encounter problems. It's also quite lonely, and best visited in a group.

Rincon waterfall

Hike Seekers ☎ 784 3296 or ☎ 399 1135, ⓦ hikeseekers.com

Inland of One Hundred Steps Beach, Rincon Trace is also the route to spectacular **Rincon**, the largest waterfall in Trinidad, a good two-and-a-half-hour uphill trek through the bush. Nestled on the side of El Tucuche, the falls tumble over 30m of rocks before cascading into a large pool safe for bathing. You'll need a guide to find it; Laurence "Snakeman" Pierre at Hike Seekers knows the area intimately.

La Filette

As you take the North Coast Road past Chupara Point, with its improbably suburban row of bright yellow holiday villas, it narrows and becomes increasingly potholed before entering the fishing village of **LA FILETTE**, a pretty cluster of neat houses and blooming front gardens straddled over two hillocks about 5km from Las Cuevas. A rum bar and cookshop on the western outskirts is good for watching the world go by with a "beastly" cold beer, or for gossiping with the fishermen about the rumoured contraband landing spots on this part of the coast.

Yarra

A few kilometres east of La Filette, a series of narrow bridges force traffic to slow down before the road passes through a teak plantation, after which you enter **YARRA**, a rather quiet hamlet. Look out for a grassy turn-off towards the sea, the only one not leading to a house; this goes to **Yarra Beach**, another perfect, wide and deserted seashore. A Yarra River tributary runs down to the sea here, and is sometimes deep enough for you to whitewater bodysurf right into the ocean. As always on this coast, be sensible if you enter the water, as the beach is known for dangerous riptides and strong currents.

Blanchisseuse

A five-minute drive east of Yarra and the last village before the North Coast Road trails off into the bush, **BLANCHISSEUSE** (pronounced "blaan-she-shers"), is a popular holiday retreat for Trinidadians. Local folklore suggests the name comes from a white woman – probably a French Creole plantation owner – who was seen washing here in the Marianne River.

With a population of around three thousand and spanning over 3km of road, Blanchisseuse isn't exactly a hamlet, and its clutch of flashy holiday homes – some garish, some tasteful – are testament to its popularity. Even so it's still pretty quiet; the atmosphere is relaxed and friendly, and most visitors are weekend day-trippers from Port of Spain. The few overseas tourists that do visit this Caribbean gem divide their time between the four marvellous sandy **beaches**, make the hike to gorgeous **Paria Bay** and Falls, or walk through the rainforest for river swimming at nearby **Three Pools**, or **Avocat Falls** on the Arima–Blanchisseuse Road.

Like most on this coastline, the beaches at **Blanchisseuse** are ruggedly beautiful, though they do have a reputation for **treacherous waters**, particularly between October and February when breakers crash onto the sand and surfers come into their element; ask local advice before taking the plunge.

Lower Blanchisseuse

Lower Blanchisseuse to the west is the older portion of the village, a lengthy and attractive assortment of weather-beaten board houses and crumbling tapia buildings wreathed by rambling bougainvillea and neat croton hedges. Steep cliffs plunge down to the ocean, while breaks in the palms or almond trees reveal white-tipped waves below. The small village atmosphere is reinforced by a couple of rum bars, a fishermen's cooperative, the attractive arched windows and blue porticoes of the Georgian-style **police station**, and a boxy, single-spired Catholic **church** overlooking the sea, complete with three bells housed in an outdoor tower.

Lower Blanchisseuse beaches

Opposite the police station, and marked by a broken sign, an easy flight of stone steps lead down to a marvellous and secluded bathing **beach**, with 100m of soft greyish sand, headlands offering protection, and almonds and sea grapes tangling down the cliffs. The fishermen's beach – 50m back down the road next to the cooperative – is a better place to lime than swim, as it has a measly pebble shore.

There's another beach just off the Paria Main Road to the west of the lower village, right before the old stone bridge, where a track leads down to the sea and a swath of wide sand, surrounded by cliffs at both ends. There's a tiny parking area but the beach is usually deserted, save for the odd surfer.

L'Anse Martin

Popular with sun-bronzed surfers, **L'Anse Martin** has been locally renamed in their honour as Surfer's Beach; its true name is seldom used, though it is marked as such on the sign. There is an almost imperceptible shelf here that makes for excellent waves, while craggy rocks border each end and the forest drips down onto the sand. The beach is accessed via a walkway opposite the dilapidated sign for the long-gone *Surf's Country Inn*.

Upper Blanchisseuse

Upper Blanchisseuse begins after the Paria Main Road loops inland to meet the improbably large intersection with the Arima–Blanchisseuse Road. This is the main residential area, with a couple of tiny general stores and pastel-painted homes clustered by the roadside, and streets trailing uphill into the area known as "Paradise". Towards the eastern end of the village are the community centre and sports field, while past here the road goes down to sea level and runs parallel to **Marianne Beach**.

Marianne Beach

Car park TT$15; beach facilities TT$10; kayak rental TT$30 per 30min, contact Eric Blackman on ☎ 669 3995

The town's longest and most popular beach, **Marianne** is a breathtaking seashore, its yellow sand battered by crashing waves – the perfect place to watch the moon rising over the headlands from the east, ideally on an evening when **leatherback turtles** are to be found laying their eggs (March–Aug).

At the eastern end the clear water of the Marianne River is partially dammed by the ever-shifting sands into a **lagoon** – an inviting place to swim when the water is flowing out to the sea. Locals tend to congregate here for an after-work bathe or cricket match, and fishermen paddle rough canoes in search of freshwater salmon. There are rudimentary showers and toilets at the sandy car park and house ambitiously named the *Marianne Beach Resort*, which occasionally has a bar selling drinks; otherwise the *Cocos Hut* restaurant (see p.118) lies just above the beach (separated from it by a grove of trees).

2

Marianne River and Three Pools

Three Pools tours TT$150/person, contact Eric Blackman on ☎ 669 3995

East of Marianne beach, the North Coast Road runs alongside the **Marianne River** and terminates at the water's edge, adjacent to a rusting suspension bridge and its ugly modern replacement. Over the bridge, the road continues past more luxury villas before becoming a rutted bench trail eastwards to Paria Bay (see opposite). Originating at Brasso Seco (see p.121), the river tumbles downhill, carving deep swimming pools and waterfalls along the way, and offers good **birdwatching** – green woodpeckers, yellow orioles and silvered antbirds are commonly seen – as well as a lovely watery trek south along the riverbed to **Three Pools**, forty minutes or so from the mouth of the Marianne. Most people hire a guide in the village to lead the way, but it's a fairly straightforward route you can follow independently; the easiest way is to follow the riverbed, splashing through sometimes deep water and swimming, though a path does lead along the river's western bank, crossing to the east about halfway (any "No Entry" signs are universally ignored). Overhung by vines, ferns and huge buttress-rooted trees, it's a gorgeous and easy wade, and the stunning Three Pools easily surpass any of the other swimming spots along the way.

The first of the three, 12m across, is the least impressive, with a natural **water-slide** of sorts, through a narrow channel in the rock. Passing over the grey rock, you'll find the second pool, so deep that it's difficult to touch the bottom, with another gushing channel creating a **natural jacuzzi**. The third pool is the smallest but also the most impressive, overhung by tall cliffs, with rock carved into bizarre folds and small caves you can swim into and climb up to see the waterfall above. To go beyond this point to the spectacular **Avocat Falls**, you'll need a guide; best option is the jovial Eric Blackman, owner of *Northern Sea View Villa*.

ARRIVAL AND DEPARTURE BLANCHISSEUSE

By public transport Maxis and route taxis can drop you in either Lower or Upper Blanchisseuse; go for upper if you want to head for the beach or the Marianne River.

ACCOMMODATION AND EATING

Blanchisseuse is a lovely place to really get away from it all for a few days, staying in one of the three local **guesthouses**, but you may find eating something of a challenge unless you cook for yourself. There are a couple of cookshops in the village, though these open only sporadically; ask at your guesthouse if you want to arrange regular meals from one of them. If you plan to **self-cater** you'll need to stock up before arriving here; there's very little in the way of groceries on offer in Blanchisseuse itself, other than a tiny bar and general store in the lower village, and a smaller roadside store on the main road in Upper Blanchisseuse.

Cocos Hut ☎ 628 3731. The only proper restaurant in Blanchisseuse, set in a converted cocoa-drying house at the roadside opposite *Laguna Mar* hotel, and often the only place in town selling hot food. The moderately priced lunches and dinners (TT$100–150) consist of decent fish, tasty chicken, beef or pork, and vegetarians are catered for. The bar is great for a drink, its end-of-the-road location and regular clientele providing a sense of cosy isolation. Daily 8am–9pm.

Laguna Mar ☎ 669 2963 or ☎ 628 3731, ⊛ lagunamar .com. The most established hotel in the village is located just above Marianne Beach. Rooms are on the inland side of the road in blocks of six with a lovely communal balcony. Each has two double beds, fan and bathroom and upstairs rooms are noticeably breezier. There's a restaurant, *Cocos Hut*, across the road. US$70

Northern Sea View Villa ☎ 669 3995 or ☎ 759 9514. These spotlessly clean apartments offer few luxuries, but a great location opposite Marianne Beach and an extremely friendly owner, Eric Blackman. Each has two bedrooms (though you can have just one room rather than a whole apartment) with fans, full kitchen, spacious veranda and living room, and there's a homely feel with crafts dotted around. US$50

★ **Second Spring** Lamp Post 191, Paria Main Rd ☎ 669 3909 or ☎ 638 4739, ⊛ secondspringtnt.com. Small guesthouse near the beach at the western end of the lower village, with three attractive studios and a smart private two-room cottage right on the clifftop (not suitable for small children). Each has fans, mosquito nets, a veranda and a kitchenette, and walls hung with lovely local art. Offering coastal views, the grounds are lovingly tended by the friendly French/Trini owners, and there's a splendid deck overlooking the water, with steps down to the sea. Studios US$75, cottage US$120

The north coast bench trail

East of Blanchisseuse, the North Coast Road gives way to undeveloped coastline. The next piece of tarmac is some 30km to the east at Matelot (see p.144); in between, you'll find some impressive **hiking** along a beautiful **bench trail** – the local name for the old donkey tracks cut in the late nineteenth century to transport goods and service the then thriving cocoa estates. Well-trodden, the trail dips and climbs through the remnants of abandoned estates and secondary forest, with the sea swinging spectacularly in and out of view. Despite periodic government proposals to construct a road along this stretch of the coast, the area remains a sanctuary for bird and animal life. Many of the beaches are prime laying spots for the giant **leatherback turtle** during the March–August season (see p.142), and the birdwatching is superb; together with fine fishing for pampano, tarpin, jackfish and ancho, the area offers rich pickings for nature lovers.

Though few attempt it, you can hike the bench trail all the way from Blanchisseuse to Matelot, but only the fittest can hope to complete the journey in a day. Most make the trip in two stages, camping on a beach along the way. Though it is easy to follow, it's not a good idea to walk the trail alone past Paria Bay; there have been reports of drug-smuggler landings at deserted bays. Saturdays, Sundays and public holidays are prime times for local hiking groups to take to the bush. Make sure you start your hike with a full bottle of **water**, and you can fill up from streams along the way.

GETTING AROUND · THE NORTH COAST BENCH TRAIL

By organized tour Caribbean Discovery Tours (☎620 1989 or ☎339 1989, ⓦcaribbeandiscoverytours.com) organize excellent packages in this area, hiking or by boat, and overnighting at Petit Tacaribe. Guides Carl "Wang" Fitzjames (☎669 6054, ⓔcarlfitzjames @hotmail.com), who lives in Brasso Seco, or Cristo Adonis

from Arima (☎664 5976 or ☎488 8539), will organize overnight trips.

By boat Local fishermen in Blanchisseuse will take you along the coastline parallel to the bench trail by boat. Ask around or at your hotel; it costs around TT$200/person each way to/from Paria Bay.

Marianne to Paria Bay

The moderately challenging round-trip trek to **Paria Bay** is the most common hike from Blanchisseuse. You can do each way in two hours at a good pace, though most take a picnic and make a day of it, stopping to eat and swim at Paria. Past the Blanchisseuse bridge over the Marianne River, the track passes beach homes for the first couple of kilometres, before dipping down to a stream and entering the forest. The trail can get a little muddy in the rainy season, but nothing can detract from the marvellous scenery: look out for massive termite nests and a splendid specimen of the weird **cannonball tree**, with its heavily perfumed rotund pink flowers, twisted branches and trunk supporting 15cm-wide "cannonballs". There is a constant accompaniment of birdsong, though the soothing calls are often shattered by the raucous shriek of passing parrots.

Passing a number of stunning coves along the way, you finally emerge onto the beach at **Paria Bay** – an idyllic 1.5km of fine, coconut-littered golden sand with a backdrop of thick jungle. Other than a couple of fishermen's shacks above its eastern end, the sands are completely undisturbed, with craggy grey rocks out to sea; the high headland above is **Paria Point**. Swimming is fairly safe, with the exception of October to January/February when currents become more intense. Leatherback turtles come here in good numbers to lay their eggs in springtime, the eggs hatching from July to September.

Paria waterfall

If you've walked as far as Paria Bay, it's well worth pressing on for another fifteen minutes to the secluded **waterfall** for a freshwater bathe. Three-quarters of the way up Paria beach, the track to the waterfall heads inland, passing through anthurium lilies and forest before reaching a fork. The right fork heads up to the point and eventually to Brasso Seco village (see p.121), while the left one meets the Paria River a few

2

PETIT TACARIBE

Petit Tacaribe is the most unusual place to stay in Trinidad, a magical and secluded spot comprised of three cedar-framed bamboo *cabañas* and a cooking shed overlooking the bay (c/o Stephen Broadbridge ☎ 620 1989 or ☎ 339 1989, ⓦ caribbeandiscoverytours.com; US$150). Rates are per person, per night and cover transport to Blanchisseuse, boat trip to Petit Tacaribe and great meals made with fresh produce (though you should bring any extras – beer, rum, chocolate and so on), plus excursions into the forest. The boat from Blanchisseuse takes about half an hour; six people and their baggage can cram in, but you can always hike if you're feeling hardy, with the boat bringing just your bags.

---

minutes later. Head upstream for five minutes to arrive at the waterfall, where cold spring water crashes down the 5m cascade into a deep grotto 10m across, perfect for a dip. Blue emperor butterflies flit about for the first few months of the year, and you're unlikely to see another soul for the entire route.

Paria Bay to Matelot

Past Paria Bay, the bench trail is less well travelled and a little more overgrown. After ten minutes' walk, you pass through attractive **Murphy Bay**, and it takes around an hour and a half to reach **Petit Tacaribe bay**, with **Grande Tacaribe** over the headland (inexplicably named Trou Bouilli-Riz Point) a further half an hour. Both have marvellous sandy beaches and plentiful fruit trees such as mammee apple and mango. From here, it's a five- to six-hour jungle walk onward to civilization at Matelot. Gorgeous **Madamas Bay** is reached after around an hour and a half: it's a curve of deserted off-white sand with a river **lagoon** at one end, almost rivalling Paria in beauty. Half an hour inland from the beach is another splendid cataract, **Madamas waterfall**, though you'll need a guide to find it, as well as the **Madamas Gorge** even further into the interior.

The Arima–Blanchisseuse Road

The **Arima–Blanchisseuse Road** cuts through the middle of the steamy Northern Range forest, climbing high into misty, breeze-cooled peaks, between which **Brasso Seco** village is an excellent starting point for exploring the **waterfalls** that course through the mountains. A little closer to civilization you descend to the **Asa Wright Nature Centre**, one of the Caribbean's finest birdwatching sites. The sharply winding, potholed and generally ill-kept road is not for the faint of heart (especially as parts of it had been rendered surfaceless by ongoing drainage work at the time of writing), but the payoff is tremendous. Light filtering through the overhanging canopies of mahogany, teak, poui, cedar and immortelle colours the tunnel-like road green, and every available surface is smothered in plant life: mosses, ferns and lichens cover rocks and tree trunks already laden with massive wild pine bromeliads, and vines and monkey's ladder lianas trail down to the tarmac.

Closer to **Arima**, the road dips downhill, rounding spectacular corners and passing hillsides cleared for christophene cultivation supported on rough trellises (the fruits, which resemble avocado pears, are commonly used in Chinese cooking), and former cocoa estates left to grow wild. As the jungle thins out and a few sporadic buildings appear, look out for the numerous Hindu prayer flags fluttering in the breeze and tiny do-it-yourself temples on the eastern side of the road.

GETTING AROUND   THE ARIMA–BLANCHISSEUSE ROAD

By car Though the odd route taxi plies between Brasso Seco and Arima, services are so infrequent that there is no feasible public transport along the Arima–Blanchisseuse Rd; the only sensible way to travel is in your own car.

By organized tour If you don't fancy driving yourself through the mountains, an organized tour (see p.38) can be a great way to see the area.

Avocat Falls

Wet and humid, the first portion of road up into the Northern Range from Blanchisseuse is a succession of leaf-covered hairpin bends, climbing gently up from the coast, with quarter-miles marked by roadside posts (though many have crumbled). Just before the twenty-and-a-quarter-mile marker (around 5km from Blanchisseuse), look out for a neat grove of pommerac trees to the left; here, a track leads past a few dwellings towards **Avocat Falls**. After a ten-minute walk, you turn left along the banks of a shallow riverbed for fifteen minutes until you reach a watery junction. Wade upstream a few minutes until you arrive at a steep bank, haul yourself up with the aid of tree roots and straight in front of you is a stunning 12m cascade with a deep swimming pool. Many local guides offer tours here, and Eric Blackman in Blanchisseuse (see p.118) is usually available too.

Morne La Croix

A short way south of Avocat, the mountain road climbs a steep hill before entering picturesque hamlet **MORNE LA CROIX**, where most of the inhabitants still speak French Creole as well as Trini English. A tiny general store and bar is the only place for limited **food and drink** here, but the main attractions are the impressive views and superb **birdlife** wherever you stop. Just beyond the town, look for a hedge of purple-flowered vervain, a favourite haunt of yellow-breasted ruby-topaz **hummingbirds** and the red-crested tufted coquette, and also for the metre-long, teardrop-shaped nests of the crested oropendola, whose manic calls can be heard echoing across the peaks. As the road climbs ever higher, a lookout point adjacent to the dirt track Andrew's Trace – at 600m – provides chilly breezes and sweeping views through a break in the forest, with the sea just visible; above you can often see hawks coasting on thermal updraughts.

Brasso Seco

Tucked away at the end of a well-signposted turn-off from the Arima–Blanchisseuse Road, a good up-and-down 7km from Morne La Croix or Asa Wright, **BRASSO SECO** is a naturalists' dream. Translating as "dry branch" in reference to an arm of the Paria River which only ever gets wet in heavy rainy seasons, the village is populated by people of mixed Amerindian, Spanish and African descent (and clearly recognizable as such; some of the elders still speak Spanish); known as "**cocoa panyols**", many are descended from people who moved to Trinidad from Venezuela in the nineteenth century to work on the burgeoning cocoa and coffee estates.

Today, the village is probably the best base for **hiking** in Trinidad (see box, p.122), owing to its proximity to both mountains and coastline, at least five **waterfalls** and numerous river pools, as well as its variety of **accommodation** options. Though few serious **birdwatchers** come to the area, the diversity they find here often exceeds that of the island's well-known birdwatching centres; scientists from a variety of universities have made this their base for studying rarely seen species and leking sites (communal display sites where males show off their prowess to potential mates). Red-legged honeycreepers, bearded bellbirds, tufted coquette hummingbirds, all types of parrot, green and red macaws, the black-faced ant-thrush and the endangered piping guan are all to be found, among innumerable others.

Hunkered under the dramatic 941m peak of El Cerro del Aripo to the south, the community is charming, languorous and picturesque, consisting of converted cocoa sheds and still-occupied tapia houses, alongside a rum shop-cum-parlour, church, school and community centre. Children play cricket in the middle of the road, young men lime outside the rec club and everyone has time to greet each other.

If you're in Trinidad in mid-October, try to get up to Brasso Seco for their annual village festival, which celebrates local culture, indigenous and otherwise, by way of dancing, parang and plenty of amazing local food and drink, from wine and cocoa to pastelles and smoked meat.

Brasso Seco Visitor Facility
Madamas Rd • Open on request only • ☎ 718 8605, ⓦ brassosecoparia.com

Signs on the outskirts of the village alert you to the **Brasso Seco Visitor Facility**, a small building run by the local community association, the Brasso Seco Tourism Action Committee, and which should be your first stop on arrival in Brasso (call in advance if possible). As well as connecting with members and learning a little more about the local area, you can arrange a meal or accommodation, set up guided hikes in the surrounding area and buy a range of fantastic local produce, from wine and ice cream made with organic coffee and cocoa to jewellery, pepper sauce, coffee beans and cocoa powder. An information display details a recent camera-trap project, which photographed wild animals in the Northern Range forests.

Manchuria Estate
Tailor-made tours by request, from US$100 for a full-day visit with a small group • ☎ 718 8605, ⓦ brassosecoparia.com

Reachable via a bumpy forest track just off the main road through the village, **Manchuria Estate** is a new agro-tourism project run by the Brasso Seco Tourism Action Committee, and is well worth a visit if you'd like to learn a little more about

---

HIKES AND TOURS FROM BRASSO SECO

Hiking possibilities here range in difficulty from medium half-day treks to hard overnighters – a few routes are summarized below. You will need a **guide** for almost all the walks, not only to keep you from getting lost, but to clear pathways and provide assistance in the highly unlikely event you're confronted by a snake. More likely is that you'll come across an unlicensed hunter, when it's also advisable to be accompanied by a local person. For general information on hiking around Brasso Seco, contact the Visitor Centre on ☎ 718 8605, or visit their website (ⓦ brassosecoparia.com). The best local guide is **Carl "Wang" Fitzjames**, who lives right in Brasso on Madamas Road (wooden house at last light pole on left; ☎ 669 6054 or ☎ 486 6059, ✉ carlfitzjames@hotmail.com; US$20–100), who has good knowledge of birds, leking sites and medicinal plants, organizes cooked meals and barbecues, and likes to share his personal philosophies. He has also established a campsite halfway to Tacaribe on the north coast for overnight stays. Many of Trinidad's tour companies (see box, p.135) also offer hiking in the area.

MODERATE HIKES
Double River Falls (3–4hr round trip) follows a track through cocoa and coffee plantations, with wonderful views, good birding and a brief ascent through lush jungle to the 8m falls and swimming pool, also easy by mountain-bike. **Madamas Falls** (6–7hr round trip) is a further 90min on the same trail to a slightly larger falls; it's good for butterflies and birds. **Sobo Falls** (4hr round trip) is an impressive three-tier waterfall deep in the forest, while **Paria Bay and waterfall** (7–8hr round trip) follows a relatively well-worn path along the Paria River to the most stunning beach in Trinidad and equally pretty waterfall.

DIFFICULT HIKES
El Cerro del Aripo (7–9hr round trip) is the most challenging on the island, involving steep and rocky stretches, thick elfin forest, sights of golden tree frogs, but limited views. **Morne Bleu** peak is reached en route, ideal for serious birders, with regular sightings of blue-capped tanagers and the minute bumble bee-like woodchaf. **Petit and Grand Tacaribe Bays** (8–9hr one way, or overnight with a bush or beach camp) is a forest ridge and river walk, arriving at two spectacular deserted bays; from here you could hike onwards along the coast or back to Brasso Seco, or else organize a boat to Blanchisseuse or Matelot. **Madamas Gorge** (3-day round trip) is a stunning cliff-lined river with rock pools and falls you swim/walk through; this could also be extended to finish at the coast. **Macajuel Pond** (6hr round trip) is a dense-forest hike with steep climbs to a deep pond and waterfall for swimming.

traditional ways of life in the mountains, or just soak up the scenery and take a swim in a crystal-clear river. Planted with cocoa and coffee, the estate's fifteen acres are being slowly rehabilitated as an organic plantation, and in a newly constructed **cocoa house** by the side of the river, you can see (season permitting) the whole cacao production process, from fermenting the beans to drying, roasting, shelling and grinding; coffee processing is a similar business, though without the fermentation stage.

ARRIVAL AND DEPARTURE   BRASSO SECO   2

By car Transport to Brasso Seco can be something of a problem without your own vehicle. Hitchhiking is possible from Blanchisseuse or Calvary Hill in Arima, though lifts can be few and far between.

By bus While there is now an early-morning PTSC bus (Ⓦptsc.com) from Arima, it's hardly a convenient way to get there, leaving Arima daily at 5am and 8am.

By organized tour or transfer Some accommodation options (like *Mount Brasso Estate*) organize airport transfers or transport from elsewhere, or you can hire a driver; ask around or contact one of the tour guides (see p.135).

ACCOMMODATION

It's worth staying a few days in Brasso Seco to fully appreciate the tranquillity of the valley. From **host homes** to **dormitories** or **private cottages**, there is some really attractive accommodation here, all offering wonderful views. If you choose to rent a house, check in advance whom you can hire to **cook** for you, or stock up well from supermarkets in advance (you may be able to buy chicken, fruit and vegetables locally).

★**Mount Brasso Estate** C/o O'Farrell, Maraval ☎222 6071, Ⓦwatervilleestate.com. The sister property of an estate in Santa Cruz (see p.112), this is the highest driveable point in Trinidad, on the lower slopes of El Cerro del Aripo. Only accessed from the village by Land Rover or on foot (pick-up available), the 17-acre grounds contain a converted cocoa-drying shed equipped with eight bunks and a full kitchen; you cook your own meals or arrange for someone to cater for you via the Brasso Visitor Facility. There's also a walkway down to a natural swimming pool, and a wonderful thatched outdoor kitchen/dining area. Cocoa, coffee, citrus, soursop, orchids and bois cano trees are scattered throughout, and the rich forest surrounds are a birder's paradise. Bunks U̲S̲$̲4̲0̲

★**Pacheco's Host Home** ☎669 6139 or ☎669 3781. In the heart of the village, the Pacheco family is a Brasso institution, running both shop and village school. Supremely friendly and of mixed Amerindian and Spanish descent, Mrs Pacheco makes her own pink grapefruit candy and hot cocoa

tea made from locally grown beans – stop by even if you're not staying here. The rooms in one of the two beautiful old houses are simple but sparklingly clean, with fans, mosquito nets and a lovely porch with mountain views. Rates include dinner and a big breakfast; packed lunches available if you're off hiking. Singles T̲T̲$̲3̲5̲0̲, doubles T̲T̲$̲7̲0̲0̲

Paria Falls Nature Resort ☎701 8669 or ☎790 1382. A grand name for two cottages for rent, but this is a fantastic location on the hillside ten minutes' walk from the village centre, with a small swimming pool and a bounty of breadfruit, cashew, pois doux, citrus and banana trees. Both cottages are private and comfortable with hot and cold water, kitchen, lounge and veranda with French windows; one has two bedrooms with a/c, satellite TV and stunning view, though the other (three-bedroom) is much more airy and rents for the same price – a bargain for four or more people. There's also a camping area, and you can take just a double room if necessary. Doubles T̲T̲$̲4̲5̲0̲, three-bed cottage T̲T̲$̲6̲5̲0̲

EATING AND DRINKING

For local **food**, there's only really one place to eat if you're not staying in the village, though the Visitor Facility can arrange for meals to be cooked for you locally. If you're here for a few nights, however, it's worth calling local guide and chef Pepe (☎669 6144 or ☎779 3504) and arranging for him to cook you some delicious "Buccaneer" style (often wild) meat, a local speciality which is slowly smoked over a fire. There are two small stores in Brasso Seco, one right at the start of the village (also a bar) and the other on the hill above the Pacheco home.

★**Pacheco's** ☎669 6139 or ☎669 3781. Home-cooked lunch (from TT$75) at the Pacheco's dining table is a highlight of a visit to Brasso Seco, and might consist of deliciously seasoned chicken with rice, ground provisions and salad, perhaps with pastelles thrown in at Christmas

time, and always washed down with fresh fruit juice from the garden. Finish off with a cup of cocoa-tea on the veranda, overlooking the garden and the hills beyond as the hummingbirds flit between the flowers. No set hours; call a day in advance to book.

2

Asa Wright Nature Centre

90-minute tours daily 10.30am & 1.30pm • US$10 • ☎ 667 4655, ⓦ asawright.org

Internationally famous for its birdwatching, the 1500-acre **Asa Wright Nature Centre** was originally a coffee, citrus and cocoa plantation. In 1947 it was bought by Dr Newcome Wright and his Icelandic wife, Asa. Both were keen naturalists and birdwatchers, and when the New York Zoological Society set up the Simla Tropical Research Station on neighbouring land, the couple began to accommodate visiting researchers. After her husband died, Mrs Wright sold the land on the condition it remained a **conservation area**. A non-profit-making trust was set up in 1967, which established a nature centre for naturalists and birdwatchers, a first in the Caribbean. Simla donated its land and research station to the centre in 1970, and though tropical research is still undertaken here, Asa Wright is mainly visited these days as one of the most popular **birdwatching retreats** in the Caribbean. Resident guests tend to be middle-aged to retired North American or British bird fanatics, enthusiastically compiling checklists of the day's sightings over sunset rum punches, single malts and reminiscences of the good old days. You can also visit as a half-day trip, watching birds from the veranda, taking a tour of the grounds and having lunch or afternoon tea. Between January and April (Mon–Fri), tours from docked **cruise ships** often crowd the centre from mid-morning to mid-afternoon; if you're not staying here but still wish to do some birdwatching during these times, arrive before 10am to avoid the rush.

The great house and veranda

Asa Wright revolves around a tapia **great house**, a maze of polished mahogany floors, stately heirlooms and antique furniture. At 360m above sea level, the views of the Arima valley rainforest are spectacular, and since Mrs Wright began feeding birds here in the 1950s, the **veranda** now attracts up to forty species per day, including dazzlingly colourful, thumb-sized hummingbirds, green- and red-legged honeycreepers, blue-grey tanagers, white-bearded or golden-headed manakins and many precocious bananaquits. Matte lizards and agoutis clear up the scraps below, three species of tarantula are easily seen at night around the drive, and the surrounding trees glitter with the bright feathers of nesting and roosting birds: rufous-tailed jacamars, toucans, mot-mots, woodpeckers, trogons, yellow orioles and the yellow-tailed crested oropendola. The multitude of creatures attracts daily crowds of birdwatchers, the low murmur of voices broken by the excited squeals of an unusual sighting (noted in a log book), or by the click of paparazzi-style cameras.

The grounds

A network of well-marked **trails** thread through the grounds, which non-resident visitors can only access on one of the expertly conducted 90-minute introductory **tours**, which take in manakin leks and allow you to see some of the more reclusive forest birds which don't frequent the veranda. Residents of more than three nights get a tour of **Dunston Cave**, which houses the world's most accessible colony of **oilbirds**; but everyone can take a dip in the centre's lovely **natural swimming pool**. Coffee is still grown and processed on site in the traditional method; you can see the production process and purchase bags of fresh beans in the small on-site shop.

ARRIVAL AND INFORMATION	ASA WRIGHT NATURE CENTRE
By car As ever, given the paucity of public transport along the Arima–Blanchisseuse Rd, renting a vehicle is the most convenient way to get to Asa Wright.	**By organized tour** Most people visit Asa Wright as part of an organized tour; all the operators run trips in the area (see p.38).

ACCOMMODATION AND EATING	
Asa Wright Lodge ☎ 667 4655, ⓦ asawright.org. Asa Wright has 24 comfortable (though not luxurious) rooms in	a number of lodges. All have large screened verandas, private bathroom and two double beds; rates include all

meals, afternoon tea, and tours of the grounds conducted in early mornings before day visitors arrive. Staying up here, right in the middle of the rainforest, is a unique experience, and the lodge offers a pleasant old-world charm. You can also book birding tours to all of Trinidad (and Tobago's) top sites. If you don't stay, it's well worth

coinciding your visit to enjoy the excellent buffet lunch (TT$140 Mon–Sat, TT$200 Sun); sandwiches are available on the veranda for a little less. Wi-fi available; also room rates are much reduced in the summer. Lunch daily noon–1pm, sandwich menu daily 11am–4pm. <u>US$215</u>

The East–West Corridor

2

Spreading south from the flanks of the Northern Range, the **East–West Corridor** is a sprawling conurbation between Trinidad's east and west coasts, its numerous communities so close together it's hard to tell where one tails off and another begins. Its whole length is traversed by three separate roads running parallel: the first, the traffic-clogged **Eastern Main Road** (EMR) is lined with shops, businesses, restaurants and rum bars for almost its entire distance; people partially avoid the rush by taking the second road, the **Priority Bus Route** – a fast-track thoroughfare for public transport just south of the EMR, built where the now-obsolete train tracks were once in service; the third is the multi-lane **Churchill Roosevelt Highway** a kilometre or so to the south. The highway has encouraged major development in the form of three large **shopping malls**, signposted along its route, while it's also the access point for Piarco International Airport.

Frenetic, hot and dusty as it is, the East–West Corridor does have sights worth seeing. The EMR is the gateway to the old Spanish capital of **St Joseph**, where elegant colonial edifices sit incongruously with a more recent rash of concrete. The **Mount St Benedict Monastery** dominates the hillside eastwards, providing panoramic views of the Caroni Plains, superlative **birdwatching**, and a restful spot for afternoon tea. Heading north into the mountains, a series of access roads to **Maracas**, **Caura**, **Lopinot** and **Guanapo** all lead to off-the-beaten-path waterfalls, river swimming and hiking. And the grinding pace of traffic along the EMR itself at least allows you to absorb the commercial chaos outside of the capital. The road buzzes with life – shoppers dodging delivery trucks throng the pavements and vendors fill the air with the sweet aroma of street food.

In terms of **accommodation**, much of the area can be visited on day-trips from the capital, though there is a stand-out guesthouse at Mount St Benedict and a couple of options in **Arima** that are conveniently close to the airport and other sights such as the Asa Wright Nature Centre and mountain waterfalls.

GETTING AROUND   **THE EAST–WEST CORRIDOR**

By car As waiting times for public transport can be very long – maxis and route taxis are seriously over-subscribed at rush hours – a car is by far the most convenient way to get around. However, bear in mind that as traffic on the EMR can be pretty bad, it's often quicker to take the highway for most of the way, and then just turn off onto the EMR when you near your destination. Make sure that you do not, under any circumstances, drive onto the Priority Bus Route when crossing between the EMR and the highway. This is reserved for buses, maxis and licensed taxis

only, but it's not always signposted; however, the lack of regular traffic and the constant procession of whizzing maxis make it easy to pick out.

By route taxi and maxi The EMR is well served by both maxis and route taxis, and services into mountain communities arrive and depart from the EMR at the appropriate junction; just ask locals where to catch one. From Port of Spain, some maxis use the Priority Bus Route for express journeys between the capital and their destination.

San Juan

East of Port of Spain and its unsightly suburb, **Barataria**, commercial **SAN JUAN** (pronounced "sah-wah") is focused around the "**croisee**" (pronounced "kway-zay"), a bustling junction marked by the Scotiabank clock tower, which was named when

French Creole was the main local vernacular. It's a scene of agreeable, organized pandemonium; doubles vendors, fruit stalls and racks of sportswear line the streets while fleets of taxis honk endlessly. The croisee is equally lively after dark, when the flambeaux of oyster salesmen throw up whiffs of pitch oil and "power punch" milkshake vendors provide party-goers with sustenance. North from the croisee, the Saddle Road to Santa Cruz and the north coast begins. South of San Juan, between the EMR and the highway, are the **El Socorro** and **Aranguez** districts, the latter dominated by the **Aranguez Savannah**, a main venue for the annual **Phagwah** celebrations in March.

EATING AND DRINKING   **SAN JUAN**

Sylvie's 4 Back Chain St, San Juan (no phone). If you're hungry, forgo the host of eateries on the EMR and head for San Juan's Back Chain St (behind the bus route), where *Sylvie's* is considered by many to serve the finest roti in the East–West Corridor (though some bestow this honour to *Patraj* or *Ali's*, on the same street). The curry shrimp here is simply delicious. Mon–Sat 6am–6pm.

St Joseph

Old meets new as you follow the EMR east across the bridge into **ST JOSEPH**, Trinidad's oldest European town and first official **capital**. On the right is the elaborate **Mohammed Al Jinnah Memorial Mosque**, resplendent with a crescent- and star-topped main dome flanked by two minarets (there's not much to see inside, but drop by the caretaker's house behind the mosque if you want to take a look). The main streets, however, are on St Joseph Hill just to the north, lined with genteel colonial French and Spanish architecture jostling with newer concrete structures.

Brief history

In 1592, Lieutenant Domingo de Vera founded a town on the site of an Amerindian settlement. Christening it **San José de Oruna**, de Vera built a church, a prison-cum-police barracks (the rebuilt remains of which are to be found directly opposite the mosque), a governor's residence and a *cabildo* (town hall). In 1595 **Sir Walter Raleigh** attacked San José, burning down the church and the barracks, though by 1606 both were rebuilt, only to be destroyed by the **Dutch** in 1637 and ransacked by **Caribs** in 1640. During the eighteenth century, San José prospered as a **plantation town**, but in 1766 was hit by a devastating **earthquake**. It never really recovered, and eighteen years later the last Spanish governor relocated the capital to Port of Spain. The town's troubles weren't over yet, however; in 1837, a detachment of the British West Indian Regiment stationed here **mutinied**. Led by a Yoruba ex-slave known as Daaga, the soldiers were protesting against the apprenticeship system that kept freed Africans in a state of semi-slavery. They set fire to the barracks and fought for several days before being overwhelmed. In the aftermath, forty Africans lay dead, and Daaga and two of his comrades were **executed** by firing squad.

Abercromby Street

From St Joseph's mosque and police station on the EMR, **Abercromby Street** strikes uphill, meeting **St Joseph's Catholic Church** after a couple of hundred metres. Sacked three times, the structure has undergone many changes since it was first consecrated in 1593, and today's Gothic stone and red-brick style dates back to 1815. Impressed by the religious devotion of the townspeople who clubbed together to fund the first stages of construction, British Governor Sir Ralph Woodford donated £2000 and laid the foundation stone. Inside, beautiful **stained-glass** windows depict the Holy Family, St John and St Andrew; the ornate Italian marble **high altar** was imported from Dublin in 1912. The graveyard behind contains headstones with inscriptions in French, English and Spanish; the oldest tombstone in the island, a weathered slab known as the **tombstone of the pirate**, is marked with a skull and crossbones and the date 1682, but no one knows the identity of the buccaneer interred beneath. Further up Abercromby Street and framed by elegantly fretworked colonial houses, **George Earl Park** was the old Spanish town square, used for evening promenades, military parades and as a burial ground.

Maracas–St Joseph Valley

Cutting inland from the EMR at St Joseph, Abercromby Street becomes **Maracas Royal Road** less than a kilometre from the EMR, crossing the grand First River Bridge and winding north into the lush **MARACAS–ST JOSEPH VALLEY. Maracas** itself is a tiny place with a post office and the steepled church of St Michael, the houses separated by clumps of fluffy bamboo and neat provision grounds. A few kilometres further on, the Maracas Royal Road ends at **Loango Village**, at a T-junction with the bumpy tarmac of San Pedro Road. There is easy access to **bathing pools** along the Maracas River here, the deepest usually filled with swimmers from the village. The riverbed is scattered with sparkling bronze sedimentary rocks, which fed rumours of **gold** deposits in the early twentieth century.

Yerette

88 Valley View, Maracas–St Joseph • Tours by appointment only, at 8am, 11.30am & 3pm • US$25 with light breakfast, light lunch or afternoon tea, TT$35 with full breakfast, TT$45 with full lunch • ☎ 663 2623, 🌐 yerette.com • Most tour companies include Yerette in their itineraries, but if you're driving yourself, the owners will send comprehensive directions to get there from Maracas Royal Rd; Valley View is about 5km into the valley from the EMR

Set in a private home overlooking the Maracas valley, **Yerette** is one of the island's prime visitor attractions, allowing you to get a magical, close-up view of the many **hummingbirds** found in Trinidad. Some thirteen species are regular visitors, drinking delicately from the hundreds of sugar-water feeders dotted around the terrace and flowered gardens, and making acrobatic dives and swoops through the air as they perform complicated courtship rituals or defend their territory with surprising aggression. Most common are the metallic emerald-and-magenta-tailed copper-rumped hummingbirds, but (depending upon the season) you may also see the spectacular flame-tailed ruby-topaz and the equally colourful tufted coquette, the second-smallest bird in the world. Visits are chaperoned by Yerette's charismatic owner, Theo Ferguson, who provides some background on these fascinating little birds as well as taking you through a slide show that details each of the seventeen hummingbird species found in Trinidad. You're also able to browse a gallery of exquisitely detailed photographs (all of which are available to buy) as well as hummingbird-themed craft items, and the visit includes a delicious breakfast, lunch or afternoon tea.

HIKES FROM MARACAS–ST JOSEPH

The Maracas–St Joseph Valley is the starting point for a couple of adventurous **hikes**. From the Maracas River bathing pools you can hike over the mountains to **Maracas Bay**, a stiff three-hour trek along an old fisherman's trail, or – if you've got the stamina – climb the 936m **El Tucuche** (variously pronounced "*tuh-cutchee*" or "*too-koosh*"), Trinidad's second-highest mountain. It's an eight-hour round trip, and a section of the trail is bordered by a tree-covered, 300m cliff, but you'll be rewarded by epiphyte-laden montane as well as high-altitude, mist-drenched elfin forests. If you're lucky, you'll see **red howler monkeys**, though you're unlikely to catch a glimpse of the **golden tree frog**, Trinidad's only endemic animal which lives in the waterlogged leaves of wild pine bromeliads.

A **guide** is essential for both of these walks – try Paria Springs, Caribbean Discovery Tours or Ieri Nature Tours (see p.135).

Note that all visits must be booked in advance, usually a week ahead at least, as Yerette is very oversubscribed and does not operate regular hours.

Maracas Valley Waterfall

No set hours • Free • Turn right from the Maracas Royal Rd onto the signposted Waterfall Rd; the turn is about 8km from the EMR. Route taxis run from Curepe junction between 7am and 6pm; most drivers will go off-route to Waterfall Rd for an extra fee

It's well worth heading deep into Maracas–St Joseph Valley to see the **Maracas Valley Waterfall**, which crashes magnificently down 90m of sheer rock. At the end of Waterfall Road you can park and, if needed, locate a guide at the neighbouring house; the route is simple and easy to follow independently, but guides can impart some interesting background on the trees and flowers en route. After twenty minutes of uphill walking along a wide track lined by groves of tall balata trees, a path strikes off right to three tiers of mini-waterfalls with two swimmable, ice-cold **pools**. Signs warning "no candles" are puzzling until you near the **main falls** twenty minutes further; here you'll see clusters of candles or pools of wax on the rocks, left by followers of the Hindu, Spiritual Baptist and Orisha religions, who regard the waterfall as a sacred place.

Curepe and St Augustine

CUREPE is a hub for **transport** all over the island: route taxis and maxis go from here to Port of Spain, east along the EMR as well as south to San Fernando and into the mountains of the Northern Range – though if you're heading to Lopinot, you should change at Arouca further east. There's little to stimulate the imagination in Curepe, save for locally famous doubles vendor *Sauce*, south of the bus terminus; people drive all the way from Port of Spain just for a Curepe doubles fix.

Curepe merges imperceptibly into **St Augustine**, a wealthier residential area north of the EMR, while just south the Priority Bus Route mounts a cut-stone flyover under which a road takes you to the **University of the West Indies St Augustine Campus**. Usually referred to by its acronym, UWI ("yoo-wee") also has branches in Jamaica and Barbados. The campus was formerly a sugar plantation, and the great house now serves as the principal's home. The students are a cosmopolitan mix from across the Caribbean, and the campus offers numerous **fast-food** outlets and the especially comfy *Rituals* coffee shop.

Mount St Benedict

Towering over St Augustine with phenomenal views of the south of Trinidad coast to coast is the **Mount St Benedict Monastery**. An eye-catching network of white-walled, red-roofed buildings dominating the hillside, the monastery was established in 1912 by Benedictine monks fleeing religious persecution in Brazil. The first of its kind in the Caribbean, the monastery initially consisted of nothing more than a mud-walled, thatch-roofed *ajoupa* at the peak of Mount Tabor; additional buildings were added over the years, including in 1918 a gorgeous burnt-orange central tapia house, now slowly crumbling. With a boxy steeple tower forming the tallest portion of the complex, at 243m above sea level, the imposing **church** was consecrated as an **abbey** in 1947. In keeping with their motto "ora et labora" (prayers and work), the ten (now ageing) resident monks maintain an estate of coffee, cocoa, citrus and planted forest, as well as producing delicious yoghurt for domestic use and commercial sale. Mount St Benedict houses the Caribbean's main regional training college for priests, the **St John Vianney and the Uganda Martyrs Seminary**, which is also UWI's theology faculty. Nearby **St Bede's Vocational School** is also run by the monks, who teach local youngsters practical skills such as machining, welding, plumbing and carpentry. Though firmly a centre of Catholic study and worship, the site nonetheless remains inclusively Trinidadian, with Spiritual Baptists and Hindus undertaking pilgrimages here at different times of the year.

For a **panoramic view** of Trinidad that surpasses even the vistas at the monastery, take the Alben Ride trail just before the final monastery buildings and climb the fire tower, built to give warning of blazes in the plantations below.

Pax Guest House

☎ 662 4084, 🖥 paxguesthouse.com

Constructed in 1916 to fulfil the Benedictine tradition of welcoming travellers, and sitting pretty just below the Mount St Benedict Monastery complex, **Pax** is the oldest guesthouse in Trinidad and remains a popular place for Trinidadians to celebrate a special occasion. A favourite haunt of American soldiers based in Trinidad during World War II, today the guesthouse caters for birders, nature lovers and anyone in need of tranquillity, and is well worth a visit for a meal or a drink even if you're not staying here. At 800 feet above sea level, it's cooled by mountain breezes and offers lovely views of the plains below, and its creaking wooden floors and antique furniture offer a glimpse into a Trinidad long ago replaced by concrete and commercialism.

Pax has a long reputation as a specialist **birdwatching centre**. Manager Gerard Ramsawak organizes **tours** through the grounds, home to a huge array of birds; the elevation means that raptors – hawks, vultures, kites and falcons – are common, as are woodpeckers, parrots and thirteen of the island's sixteen species of hummingbird (you can hand-feed a hummingbird from the terrace). Five **trails** (30min–2hr) weave through jungle and secondary forest of Caribbean pine: a beautifully illustrated trail guide is available from the guesthouse. Gerard is also an expert on the monastery and its history, and can conduct tours of some parts of the building, such as the small **observatory**.

ARRIVAL AND DEPARTURE   MOUNT ST BENEDICT

By car Mount St Benedict is located at the top of crucifix-lined St John's Rd, which leads north off the EMR between the communities of St Augustine and Tunapuna.

By public transport Route taxis leave from opposite the Scotiabank on the corner every few minutes; alternatively,

there's an unreliable bus service from Curepe which plies the route every half an hour from 6am to 6pm; you could also join the evening power walkers who hike up the hill to keep fit.

ACCOMMODATION, EATING AND ENTERTAINMENT

★**Pax Guest House** Mount St Benedict Rd ☎ 662 4084, 🖥 paxguesthouse.com. An atmospheric and serenely peaceful place to stay, *Pax* exudes a feeling of calm and serenity that many find addictive; you'll even come across business visitors in search of a homely, friendly atmosphere. In keeping with their monastic history, the rooms are simple and fitted with solid furniture, some of which was made by the monks; all are cooled by a/c and fans, and some share bathrooms. Rates include breakfast and a complimentary glass of rum punch, while after the dinner gong echoes through the corridors at 7.30pm a superb three-course Caribbean meal is served, on the

candlelit avian terrace facing the rainforests of the Northern Range. If you don't stay here, it's well worth booking in for afternoon tea (daily 3–6pm; TT$35), served in the new Japanese gardens; lunch and dinner (TT$125–150) are also available by reservation. Wi-fi throughout. U̲S̲$̲5̲5̲, en suite U̲S̲$̲8̲5̲

Trevor's Edge St John's Rd ☎ 685 1001. Vaguely alternative bar just off the EMR on the road to *Pax*, popular with UWI students and hosting a wide variety of events, from arthouse film screenings to poetry and spoken-word nights, karaoke and live music, including parang in the run-up to Christmas. Daily 10am–late.

Caura Valley

There's no public transport to Caura, so you'll need a car to get here

Towards the eastern end of **Tunapuna**, itself a bustling conurbation with a lively fruit and veg market, the Caura Royal Road turns north to the **Caura Valley** – one of the most popular **picnic spots** on the East–West Corridor. Carved by the serpentine

Tacarigua River, the valley was nearly turned into a reservoir in the 1940s: the inhabitants – many mixed Amerindian and Spanish – were relocated to Lopinot and even Brasso Seco, but the proposed **dam** was thwarted by the sandy soil and never built.

About 6km up the Caura Royal Road from the EMR is a right turn that will take you to a well-used **swimming spot**. Picnic tables line the bamboo-fringed riverbanks, and at weekends cooking fires smoulder and the shallow water is crowded with families enjoying a dip – though it does often look murky in the dry season.

Past the picnic spots, high walls of bamboo form an intermittent tunnel over the road, opening up to reveal small-scale farms and homes at **La Veronica** hamlet. As the Caura Royal Road emerges onto the Tacarigua riverbanks, the water deepens and picnicking is more secluded – the road is eventually terminated by a river tributary. The drive back to the EMR affords some spectacular views of the central plains that are easily missed on the way up.

Tacarigua Forest Reserve

There are several walking and mountain biking dirt tracks of varying lengths into the **Tacarigua Forest Reserve**, an attractive patchwork of abandoned plantations and lower montane woodlands. Hikes range from ten-minute jaunts to whole-day adventures to the peak of El Tucuche; tour guides Courtenay Rooks and Ivan Charles (see box, p.135) both organize excellent, if challenging, **mountain bike tours** to a point halfway up the mountain. It's an exhilarating ride, but make sure you bring cycling shorts and at least two litres of liquid.

Lopinot

Ten kilometres from the EMR, via a winding road lined with lush jungle and Caribbean pines, **LOPINOT** is a pretty hamlet with a remote feel, clustered around a sports field and the neat flowerbeds of a former cocoa estate that has been transformed into a beautiful recreation spot.

The valley was first settled by one Charles Josef, **Compte de Lopinot**, a planter who fled Haiti following Toussaint L'Ouverture's 1791 revolution. He arrived in 1800 with his wife and a hundred slaves, and it's not difficult to see why he chose to settle in this absurdly abundant alluvial valley surrounded by high, protective mountains. Lopinot's cocoa thrived, allowing him to build a tapia estate house, a prison and slave quarters and to amass a small fortune before his death in 1819. The Compte is buried alongside his wife by the Arouca River, which runs through the valley, and local legend has it that on stormy full moon nights his ghost rides through the estate on a white horse. A photograph taken in 1981, now on display in the great house, claims to show exactly that.

Today, Lopinot is a great place to **picnic** or to take a gentle **hike** into the surrounding forest. The community's annual **Fiesta de Lopinot**, a festival of parang, food and drink, takes place in late November, and is well worth checking out, as is the **Cocoa Innovations** festival, staged at *Café Mariposa* on the Saturday after Carnival, a fantastic celebration of cooking with cocoa with lots of samples of savoury and sweet delights.

The great house and picnic ground
Daily 6am–6pm • Free

The modest restored **great house** now has a glassed-over section showing the original mud walls, and the surrounding gardens are meticulously maintained, linked to the road by a quaint wooden bridge with a roof smothered with wild pine bromeliads. The grounds contain a cocoa-drying house and a dirt oven, while picnic tables shaded by several enormous samaan trees make an ideal spot for relaxation and a bit of birdwatching; look out for the white-shouldered tanager, bare-eyed thrush and violaceous euphonia. The beauty of the valley somewhat belies its rather violent history of enslavement – something that is not addressed at all in the saccharine info-boards dotted around the place, or in the small **museum** inside the house, dedicated to the culture of the local community. Of Spanish, African and Amerindian descent, they were relocated here when the Caura dam was proposed, and Lopinot has since spawned some of Trinidad's finest parang players. Each Christmas, a band of roving players still serenades each household, and a number of parang bars in the valley hold regular events from September to Christmas.

2

The rest of the valley

The boxy, cut-stone **La Veronica Roman Catholic church** near the playing field was originally built in Caura in 1897, but was taken piece by piece from the neighbouring valley during the Caura evacuation and reassembled here. Beyond, lichen-smothered cocoa trees line the road, and a downhill turn-off leads to the **La Pastora** chapel and shrine, one of many on the island with the title. This dedication to the Virgin of Shepherds stems from Capuchin monks who established several missions on the island during the late seventeenth century, instilling devotion to La Pastora in their Amerindian converts. Carved in the 1940s, the plain white shrine inside the chapel depicts the Virgin Mary, and is said to have been chipped directly from the mountain. Buildings thin out heading north, and the road eventually forks; a left down San Francisco Road brings you to a series of deep, swimmable **pools** on the river.

ARRIVAL AND ACTIVITIES   LOPINOT

By car There's a clearly signposted junction to get onto Lopinot Rd at Arouca on the EMR; the road forks at one point, and the sign pointing to the right-hand turn is partially obscured by a tree, so keep your eyes peeled.

By public transport Route taxis and PTSC buses run up to Lopinot from the EMR, but waits can be long, especially on Sundays; it's best to have your own transport.

Hiking Lopinot has some good hiking in the surrounding mountains, offering gorgeous views and the chance to explore bat-filled caves; guides can be arranged via the caretakers at the great house. The staff at *Café Mariposa* conduct guided walks of their organic gardens, planted with medicinal plants and herbs, as well as walks up the Mariposa mountain to see panoramic views and interesting rock formations (US$30–60 depending on duration).

Fishing *Mariposa* also offer fishing in their tilapia pond; you can have your catch cooked up for you in the café.

ACCOMMODATION AND EATING

★Café Mariposa 58 Village Settlement, Lopinot ☎669 8647 or ☎684 9358, ⓦmariposalopinot.com. Signposted opposite the village school, and with tables on a veranda overlooking the gardens, this is a fantastic place to sample Spanish Creole cooking, from tortillas to pastelles, plus fish, chicken and vegetarian dishes, all cooked lovingly and with imagination using organic herbs and vegetables from the garden. Cocoa is employed in a variety of delicious ways, from seasoned rice to cocoa-crusted lamb and sublime cocoa-avocado ice cream, and all the chutneys and sauces are made from scratch; the fresh juices are truly memorable, too. Handmade chocolate is also available to buy, and gluten- or dairy-free meals are on the menu. Mains TT$200–250; book ahead for all meals. Two appealing wood-panelled rooms are available for rent, with balconies looking out over the hillside; rates include breakfast. TT$480

Arima

Named "Naparima" by its original indigenous inhabitants, **ARIMA** is situated 6.5km from the Lopinot turn-off of the EMR, or about 7km from Piarco airport along the highway. The third largest town in Trinidad, it's also one of the most confusing places for drivers as the EMR departs from its ruler-straight course and gets swiftly swallowed up in a complicated one-way system through the urban clamour of shops, banks and wandering pedestrians; it's far easier to soak up the hustle, bustle and blaring soca and reggae on foot if you wish to explore. The attractions of Arima are decidedly limited: the main landmark is the **Arima Dial**, featuring a four-faced timepiece presented to the townspeople by then-mayor John Francis Wallen in 1898, while on **Hollis Avenue** the line of local street vendors stops at a small park with a statue of venerated calypsonian **Lord Kitchener**. There's an open-air **market** (liveliest on Sat), while the adjacent Arima Velodrome is the setting for many a wild Carnival fete.

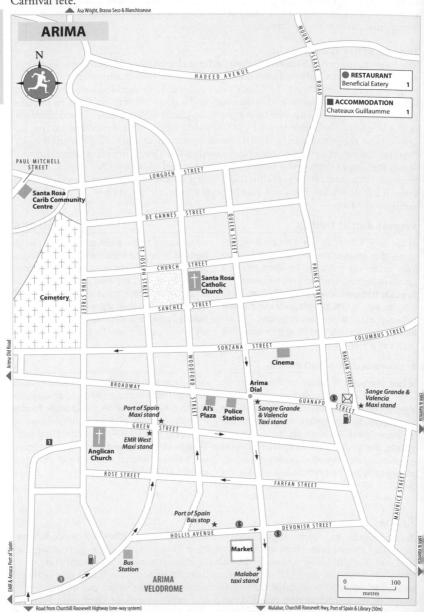

ARIMA

▲ Asa Wright, Brasso Seco & Blanchisseuse

HADEED AVENUE

MOUNT PLEASE ROAD

● **RESTAURANT**
Beneficial Eatery 1

■ **ACCOMMODATION**
Chateaux Guillaumme 1

PAUL MITCHELL STREET

LONGDEN STREET

Santa Rosa Carib Community Centre

DE GANNES STREET

QUEEN STREET

ST JOSEPH STREET

CHURCH STREET

Santa Rosa Catholic Church

PRINCE STREET

Cemetery

KING STREET

SANCHEZ STREET

COLUMBUS STREET

SORZANA STREET

Arima Old Road ◄

WOODFORD STREET

Cinema

Arima Dial

RAGLAN STREET

BROADWAY

Port of Spain Maxi stand

Al's Plaza

Police Station

Sangre Grande & Valencia Taxi stand

GUANAPO STREET

Sange Grande & Valencia Maxi stand

EMR & Valencia ►

GREEN STREET

EMR West Maxi stand

Anglican Church

ROSE STREET

FARFAN STREET

MAURICE STREET

EMR & Valencia ►

Port of Spain Bus stop

DEVONISH STREET

HOLLIS AVENUE

Market

EMR & Arouca Port of Spain ◄

Bus Station

ARIMA VELODROME

Malabar taxi stand

0   100
metres

▼ Road from Churchill Roosevelt Highway (one-way system)

▼ Malabar, Churchill Roosevelt Hwy, Port of Spain & Library (50m)

2

THE CARIBS OF ARIMA

Arima has a far deeper history than its commercial facade would suggest, as it's home to what's left of Trinidad's **Amerindian** (Carib) community, most of whom live around the crucifix-strewn **Calvary Hill**, a precipitous thoroughfare that overlooks the town from the north and connects to the Arima–Blanchisseuse Road. Many are distant relatives of the Carinepogoto tribe who once inhabited the Northern Range, and family names such as Boneo, Campo, Calderon, Castillo, Hernandez, Martinez and Peña are common. Though the community has dwindled over the years, there have been efforts of late to preserve Carib traditions and heritage. The **Santa Rosa Carib Community Association** (☎664 1897, ⓦsantarosafirstpeoples.org) was formed in 1974 to look after the interests of people with Amerindian ancestry, and is the only organized Amerindian group in the country. It's led by a President (currently Ricardo Bharath Hernandez), alongside prominent members such as the community's Shaman (Cristo Adonis) and its Queen (currently Medina Valentina), and is based in the Carib Community Centre at 7 Paul Mitchell St, behind the cemetery, some three blocks west of the Santa Rosa RC church – a good first stopoff to learn about local Amerindian culture or purchase good-quality crafts such as baskets and calabashes. The only remaining **ajoupa** (the traditional Carib thatched hut) in Arima sits on Calvary Hill in the front yard of shaman Cristo Adonis (☎664 5976 or ☎488 8539), ⓔcristo_adonis@hotmail.com), a local Carib shaman and vociferous defender of his people; he welcomes visitors if he's at home, and is a mine of information on Amerindian medicine and all things pertaining to the Caribs. There are also displays on Carib heritage at the Cleaver Woods museum, just outside Arima (see below).

CARIB FESTIVALS

The main festival in the local Carib calendar is the **Feast of Santa Rosa de Lima**, held over the last weekend of August. The oldest continuously celebrated event in Trinidad, having been inaugurated in 1786, it's also the only one in the island that honours the first canonized Roman Catholic saint of the "New World". Following a morning of church services, the year's Carib King and Queen are crowned, and a white-gowned statue of Santa Rosa is paraded through the streets, the procession bedecked with white, yellow, pink and red roses. Rum flows, and traditional Amerindian foods such as pastelles and cassava bread are eaten. The origins of the festival are somewhat murky, but in true fairy-tale style, Carib elders relate that three hunters chanced upon a young girl lying in the woods, and brought her back to Calvary Hill. She disappeared three times, only to be returned to the community. A local priest told the Caribs that this was no normal child but the spirit of Santa Rosa, and that they should make an image of her while she was still with them, for if she vanished again, her physical body would never be seen again. They made the statue, and the girl duly disappeared, leaving only a crown of roses where she had first been discovered. Ever since, Santa Rosa has been the patron saint of Arima's Carib community.

Cleaver Woods Amerindian Museum

Eastern Main Rd, D'Abadie • Daily 6am–6pm • Free • ☎ 645 1203

Just east of Arima, as you enter the fringes of Arima at the diminutive village of **D'Abadie**, the EMR runs through the pines and cocorite palms of **Cleaver Woods**, home to the signposted **Amerindian Museum**. Housed in a thatch-roof *ajoupa* hut, the displays are interesting, if slightly neglected, and include a model Carib village, pottery, hunting traps, bows and arrows and equipment used to process cassava, which was farmed by Amerindians and formed a major part of their diet. There's also a few yellowing pictures of local Carib elders dressed up for the Santa Rosa Festival.

You can also walk **trails** that weave through the 32 acres of forest that spread back from each side of the EMR around the museum, made up of poui, bois cano, jereton, silk cotton, balata and crappo trees as well as many cocorite palms.

ARRIVAL
ARIMA

By route taxi Route taxis to Sangre Grande and Valencia leave from the Dial, and taxis to Port of Spain can be caught on Broadway.

By maxi taxi Maxis are the most constant service for Port

2

of Spain, arriving and departing from the junction of St Joseph and Green streets, though bear in mind there are separate lines for the express bus route and the much slower EMR journey. Maxis for Sangre Grande, Manzanilla, Toco and Mayaro leave from the corner of Raglan St and Broadway.

ACCOMMODATION AND EATING

Though Arima doesn't have much to offer for tourists, it's a strategic base for trips into the mountains, or as more characterful alternative to the airport hotels if you want to stay close to Piarco. As for places to eat, there are many low-key self-service Trini stalls clustered around the central streets offering great breakfasts, Chinese food, roti and pelau at rock-bottom prices.

Beneficial Eatery 25 Hollis Ave ☎664 3850. Good breakfasts (from TT$25), from sada roti and tomato/aubergine choka to fried bake and saltfish, plus a range of scrumptious and inexpensive salads, sandwiches, stir-fries and Caribbean Indian meals (TT$40 and up), all served up on an attractive outdoor terrace. Daily 6am–8pm.

Chateaux Guillaumme 3 Rawle Circular ☎667 6670, ⓦcaribsurf.net/cguillaumme. Close to the town centre, and set in a large building with an attractive garden, the four rooms here have tiled floors and either double or twin beds, each with a/c, private bathroom and TV. Owners Joan and Matthew are extremely welcoming, offer island-wide tours, a full Carnival package, and also arrange discount car rental. Rates include wi-fi, a good Trini breakfast and airport pick-up if staying three nights. US$65

Heights of Guanapo Road

The Churchill Roosevelt Highway comes to an abrupt end east of Arima, with barely signposted turns north to the EMR, which itself switches abruptly from commercial thoroughfare to rural road, dominated by farmland and an impenetrable wall of rainforest pierced by a few country lanes leading to some marvellous natural attractions. Just after the EMR meets a road heading northwards to join the Arima–Blanchisseuse Road, a turn-off marked "WASA Guanapo Waterworks" brings you to the **Heights of Guanapo Road**, which runs along the Guanapo River for 3km before petering out into a country lane, often churned up by logging vehicles and best accessed by four-wheel-drive. The logging activity in the area is kept pretty low-key and the area remains a peaceful and beautiful hikers' paradise, for which you'll need the help of a knowledgeable **guide**. Though you can drive further uphill for the lovely views at **La Laja Heights**, it's a good idea to park in the large clearing below where logging workers have built a hut, and then walk, as the road is heavily potholed. The main attractions of the area are the breathtaking **Guanapo Gorge**, and the **La Laja** and **Sombasson waterfalls**, two of the most impressive on the island. With effort, you can see both the falls and the gorge in a day, but you'll need to be pretty fit.

Guanapo Gorge

About an hour's walk from the Heights of Guanapo Road, **Guanapo Gorge** is a narrow deep-water channel whose vine-wreathed walls of smooth grey rock tower 15–30m above the water. Dark and cool even on a hot sunny day, the gorge runs for some 400m; exploring it – wading and swimming all the way – can be quite hard work. Though you can start the trek from the southern (downstream) end, it is more exciting to begin upstream, where a large boulder blocking the river has created a small waterfall. From here, you enter the gorge by simply jumping into the deep pool and swimming a few metres before your feet meet the riverbed. Water levels vary according to the time of year – there is a risk of flash floods in rainy season (making the gorge best avoided if it's raining), but you shouldn't have to swim further than 25m for most of the year. The tiny **Tumbason River** threads through rocks to meet the Guanapo at the southern end of the gorge; a 45-minute walk upstream meets another small **waterfall** with a deep **pool**.

La Laja and Sombasson waterfalls

The La Laja and Sombasson **waterfalls** are hidden deep in the folds of the Northern Range – a long, difficult, though exciting hike through abandoned cocoa plantations and forests of bois cano, sandbuck, nutmeg, balata and silk cotton. The trail dips and climbs constantly, but frequent use by wild meat hunters has kept the majority of the trails passable, though your guide will no doubt need to blaze a path in the last stages. The first of the falls, **La Laja** is the smaller at about 20m high, with a couple of good pools below; the water is kept icy cold by the overhanging cliffs and dense foliage. Above La Laja you're in virgin forest, and the trek to **Sombasson Falls** is harder, but the three-tiered 50m cascade with deep pools is well worth the effort.

2

Aripo Road and around

Lonely fields line the EMR for a couple of kilometres east of Heights of Guanapo Road before it meets the nondescript-looking **Aripo Road**, which meanders northwards uphill for 14km into the mountains, following a valley cut by the Aripo River. As the road is rough and potholed, you'll need a car with high clearance. The road's upper reaches are pretty and pass through some quiet rural communities. If you're in the mood for a **river swim**, look out for a metal arch with the inscription "Jai Guru Data"; take the steps down the hill to a deep **pool**.

Aripo Caves

Even though they're weather-beaten and battered, you can still make out the Forestry Division signs along the road which point the way to the **Aripo Caves**, Trinidad's largest

---

NORTHERN RANGE HIKING GUIDES

Having a **good guide** is essential if you intend to go hiking in the Northern Range; trails are not well marked and are impossible to follow without local knowledge, and apart from being able to tell the difference between a harmless rainbow boa and a venomous mapipire snake, a guide will also be able to enrich your hike with background on the fauna and flora of the forests. Full listings of tour companies in Trinidad are given in Basics (see p.38); most will be able to drive you up to Asa Wright and Brasso Seco, but the companies listed below specialize in Northern Range hiking. Another option is to join up on one of the weekend outings of the Port of Spain Hash House Harriers (ⓦposh3.wordpress.com), a hiking outfit that describe themselves as a "drinking club with a running problem", and which organize regular trips to various far-flung parts of Trinidad; walkers are as welcome as those that want to run.

TOUR COMPANIES AND GUIDES

Caribbean Discovery Tours ⓣ620 1989 or ⓣ339 1989, ⓦcaribbeandiscoverytours.com. Owner Stephen Broadbridge works closely with guides and accommodations in Brasso Seco, and can organize packages that include food, transport and accommodation as well as hikes and trips along the undeveloped northern coastline to Petit Tacaribe. He's also a good contact for birding and local transport; his Land Rover is perfectly suited to the Northern Range terrain, and tour options take in far-flung mountain spots.
Cristo Adonis ⓣ664 5976 or ⓣ488 8539. An individual guide rather than a tour company, Cristo Adonis is a shaman of Arima's Carib community and has a good knowledge of trails in the area, as well as being a fount of information on all things Amerindian and a companionable tour guide.

Hikeseekers ⓣ784 3296 or ⓣ399 1135, ⓦhike seekers.com. This hiking club has a set itinerary of hikes throughout Trinidad that take place a couple of times a month; many are in the Northern Range, and are an inexpensive way to get out into the forests. Be aware, though, that group sizes can be large, so you may not see much wildlife.
Ieri Nature Tours ⓣ667 5636 or ⓣ685 6206, ⓔierinatureadventures@hotmail.com). Based in Arima, and owned and operated by former pro cyclist Ivan Charles, this is a good option for mountain biking as well as hiking tours.
Paria Springs ⓣ620 8240, ⓦpariasprings.com. Led by the so-called "Bushman" Courtenay Rooks, tours run from adrenaline-fuelled hiking such as to the summit of El Cerro del Aripo, as well as more moderate walks, climbing, river-walks, rappelling, birdwatching, mountain biking at all levels and north coast kayaking.

2

system of caverns; note that a guide (see p.135) is essential if you plan on exploring them, as they will take care of the permissions required to enter the area, a scientific reserve. After a cocoa grove – which sports fruits that turn purple when ripe rather than the usual orange – there's a clearing where you can park, and a sign for the trail. The fairly taxing two- to three-hour trek through undisturbed forest, with plenty of hills and gullies to navigate, is best undertaken in the dry season (Jan–March), when the three rivers that cross the path usually slow to a trickle; if it's been raining, you'll have to wade them. In the rainy season, you'll also have to get wet to enter the caves, as a river courses straight into the mouth – the going can be slippery. Nearing the entrance to the caves, you get the occasional view of the Central Plains below, and you'll start to hear the unearthly rasping shriek of one of the island's few colonies of **oilbirds** (see p.273). The **mouth** is large and dramatic, with a rather fusty mist rising constantly. Water drips from the limestone roof, and every surface is covered with fruit stones and guano. With a good torch you can navigate the rocks and go fairly deep inside, but the oilbirds' cries near an ear-splitting pitch; the Amerindians named them "Guacharo", meaning "the one who wails and mourns". If you want to go deeper, you'll need rope, a compass and caving experience.

El Cerro del Aripo

The Aripo forests are richly populated by Trinidad's **mammals**, and hunters make regular forays after agouti, armadillo, wild pig and manicou. If you're really lucky, you might catch sight of an ocelot on the flanks of the 941m **El Cerro del Aripo**, the island's highest mountain. The peak is covered with prehistoric-looking elfin (cloud) forest: short, scrubby and smothered with lichen, mosses and epiphytic growth. It's a tough full-day hike from the top of the Aripo Road, but as the temperature at the peak is ten degrees lower than in the Lowlands, you don't have to worry about the heat. Note that this hike can also be undertaken from Brasso Seco (see p.122).

The northeast tip

The wild and rugged coastline of Trinidad's **northeast tip** feels more remote than anywhere else in the region; it takes close to four hours to drive from Port of Spain to **Matelot**, where the paved road ends. Cut off from most of the island by the dense rainforest of the Northern Range, the region seems suspended in a time warp; people and houses are few and far between and an air of hypnotic quiet pervades. The villages strung along the coast are close-knit and spirited communities, making their own entertainment at **rum shops**, country parties and fishermen's fetes. **Farming** and **fishing** are the mainstays of the economy, with tiny roadside stalls offering fruit and vegetables, plus shark oil, saltfish, honey and sea moss.

The Toco Main Road (also known as Matura or Paria Road) loops northeast from Sangre Grande to Matelot, beyond which untamed bush and unreachable rocky coves entice you to scramble down the cliffs. While a number of fantastic **waterfalls** lie inland, the region's coastline is most famous for the **leatherback turtles**, which lumber up onto the sand here to lay eggs between February and August, their eggs hatching tiny shuffling babies between June and September. **Matura** and **Grande Riviere** are the most well-known places for guided night-time turtle-watching. Grande Riviere has the advantage of a good choice of **accommodation**, though its distance from Port of Spain means some visitors opt for Matura, enabling them to do some turtle-watching and return home the same night. Most people take a few days to visit this region, however, in order to fully appreciate its awe-inspiring coastline of weather-beaten cliffs and golden beaches, with **surfers** riding the breakers.

GETTING AROUND   **THE NORTHEAST TIP**

By car If you're driving from Port of Spain, take the Churchill Roosevelt Hwy until its end, turn left and then right onto the quiet portion of the Eastern Main Rd to Valencia. Follow the road straight through the town, keeping straight at a Y-junction on the main commercial street onto the Valencia Rd. After another 20min or so, you reach a T-junction; turning right takes you to Sangre Grande, left to Matura, Toco and, ultimately, Grande Riviere and Matelot. The northeast tip's only petrol station is in Cumana (Mon–Sat 8.30am–6pm, Sun 8.30am–noon).

By transfer Given the long and winding journey, you might prefer to arrange a transfer with your hotel if heading for Grande Riviere; you'll pay around US$130 for up to four people.

By public transport Sangre Grande, in central Trinidad, is the region's main transport hub; most public transport to Toco starts here, though you may be able to pick up a route taxi in Arima or Valencia. PTSC buses (ⓦptsc.com) and maxis leave from central Sangre Grande and run all along the north coast, from Matura to Matelot twice a day, in the early morning and evening; route taxis run with the same frequency, though are marginally more expensive.

Valencia

The small town of **VALENCIA** sits about 8km down the EMR from Arima, a bustling centre with shops, bars, restaurants, the last petrol station until Cumana, and plenty of street vendors selling everything from jelly coconuts to doubles and pholouri. At the eastern end of the main drag, the EMR swings right toward Sangre Grande; driving straight takes you onto the **Valencia Road**. A short way northeast of Valencia, via the Quare Road, the **Hollis Reservoir** lies like a sea in the middle of the forest, and is a serene spot for birdwatching if you visit early in the morning; as you need a permit, it's best to go with an established tour company (see p.135), which will be able to secure one for you. Slightly further east along Valencia Road is the well-signposted North Oropouche River recreational facility – a rather grand name for picnic tables by the river. There's a good **hike** 6km upriver from here, though you'll need a guide – the North Oropouche gouges its way through the rock and jungle, opening up a series of deep pools suitable for diving, the route finishing at the **Cumaca caves**, where colonies of **oilbirds** and bats are easily viewed – though you'll need a guide (see p.135) to do so.

Matura

Some 19km east along the Toco Main Road from Valencia, the elongated town of **MATURA** consists of a police station, school, health centre, a handful of grocery stores and residential houses slung along a mile of tarmac. Other than stopping for a drink, the only reasons to spend any time in the area are the **beach** – a windswept,

---

NATURE SEEKERS AND MATURA'S LEATHERBACK TURTLES

With a well-signed headquarters on the main road in the centre of Matura, **Nature Seekers** (☎668 7337, ⓦnatureseekers.org) was established in 1990, and is run by a team of dedicated volunteers who patrol the beach and educate locals and visitors on the importance of conserving this endangered species. Most volunteers come from the local community, whose indiscriminate poaching was once the main cause of concern for turtle numbers here. Now, they earn a living as guides, patrol the beach day and night, and move nests from at-risk areas, which saves hundreds of turtles every year. During the nesting season (March–Aug), Nature Seekers arrange turtle-watching tours (US$20) that allow you to view the amazing laying process and provide the opportunity to get involved in tagging and recording; you can also become a conservation volunteer here for a longer period. The institution also offers accommodation in the village at *Suzan's Guest House* (☎398 3038; TT$400), where rooms have a/c and private bathroom; and arranges **hiking** and **river kayaking** trips. They also make and sell attractive jewellery, imaginatively fashioned from oddments found on the beach with gold or silver chains.

4km stretch of fine yellow sand strewn with coconut husks and flotsam and jetsam washed up by the fearsome waves – and a wide **waterfall** and river pool, a good three-hour hike up the Matura River led by guides at Nature Seekers (see box, p.137). There are two entrances to the beach, both marked by Forestry Division signs; the first a potholed tarmac and gravel road from the centre of Matura, and the other reached from the far side of town down a dirt track, and signposted **Rincon Beach**. Though local people often take a dip, it's not a place for the uninitiated to swim, as the currents are extremely powerful. The beach is a protected area and a permit and guide are required at all times to enter, due to the presence of Matura's real attraction: the **leatherback turtles** which haul themselves onto the sand to lay eggs.

Salybia

Past Matura, the Toco Road meets the east coast for the first time. The view is often obscured by a thick cover of bush, though you do catch sight of some stunning small, wave-battered coves. On the other side of the road the bush conceals recent quarries that scar the landscape for a short stretch, before you arrive in the tiny village of **SALYBIA** 4km further on, with its roadside vendors selling home-made ice cream and pholouri. Across the road, the grand *Playa del Este* and adjacent *Salybia Nature Resort* (see opposite) hotels seem incongruously upmarket in this otherwise quiet area; both offer day passes if you want to stop by to swim and have lunch.

Saline Beach
Lifeguard on duty Sat & Sun 10.30am–3.30pm

The small rugged beach in front of the *Salybia Resort* is not safe for swimming, though a great option nearby is **Saline Beach**, a short downhill stretch just to the west, across a large concrete bridge over the Rio Seco. Just before the bridge a turn-off leads down to the sands, a popular chill-out spot at weekends when families come to bathe and picnic. For less crowded swimming, a small lagoon at the point where the river meets the sea is ideal for children. For **food**, try the stall in the beach car park, which sells great roti and pholouri at weekends.

Rio Seco waterfall

On the main road opposite the Saline Beach turn-off is the clearly signposted trail to the **Rio Seco waterfall**, one of the country's most spectacular falls (known locally as Salybia Waterfall). You can drive up a paved road for ten minutes and park by the caretaker's house on the left, just before the tarmac ends – the house is marked by a couple of green-painted benches and a sign giving information on the Matura Forest. Past the house, the path is easy to follow, with signposts at the few junctions. After twenty minutes' walk, the path reaches the river, and you can scramble down to the water to bathe in one of the many deep swimming pools. After crossing a river tributary and meandering through some gorgeous mature forest, the trail enters its final steep stretch, and you get a good prospect of the waterfall and its wide pool of turquoise water. The waterfall itself tumbles some 8m down the rocks, with plenty of handholds and a rope for an easy climb up and a dive from the top, while the break in the canopy above the pool means that it's bathed in sunshine most of the day.

From the road, the walk takes about an hour, and the falls make a great picnic spot. If you prefer to tackle the trail with a **guide** (see p.135), though it's easily followed without one, a particularly good option is with Arima-based Ivan Charles, who combines Rio Seco with a visit to the impressive Tamana bat caves in Central Trinidad, while Paria Springs walk up to the waterfall along the rivercourse rather than the trail, and also offer hikes to the sublime Mermaid's Pool.

Playa del Este ☎ 691 2632, ⓦ playadelesteresort.com. With a higher pool quotient than its neighbour Salybia (there's a waterfall pool and a plunge pool), this offers much of the same, plus a huge oceanfront terrace that's often employed for host weddings. The spacious rooms come with all amenities, and there's a restaurant, bar and full spa. Rates include breakfast, lunch and dinner. Day passes are TT$199 with a buffet lunch. Wi-fi throughout. $\overline{TT$1350}$
Salybia Nature Resort ☎ 691 3210, ⓦ salybiaresort

.com. Panoramic views, a fantastic oceanfront pool with waterfall, hidden caves and swim-up bar, and clean, bright rooms and more expensive suites have the added bonus of a sea-facing jacuzzi. Suite rates include breakfast and dinner, rooms breakfast only. The on-site restaurant offers good-quality cuisine: main course options (TT$200–300) vary from shrimp in pepper sauce to stuffed aubergine. Day passes, including lunch and use of the pool, are TT$160. Wi-fi available. Doubles $\overline{TT$825}$, suites $\overline{TT$1900}$

Balandra and Rampanalgas

After cutting inland across some wild and undeveloped bush, the Toco Road rejoins the coast at **BALANDRA**, a pretty fishing village with a popular **beach**, the entrance to which is at the western end of the village, marked by a small sign. You should be able to find a space in the car park unless you visit at a weekend, when cars line the path to the road. Backed by the fishing village and fringed by palm trees and Indian almonds, the beach is wide and inviting, with clean yellow sand and moderate waves. Most of the weekend crowds swim by the sheltered walled area past the car park, though swimming is safe along the whole length of the beach.

Balandra flows imperceptibly into **Rampanalgas**, which trails into the hills on the landward side of the road. It's a friendly sort of place – the local hot spot is *Arthur's*, which boasts a hotel) grocery and internet café.

Balandra Pools and Cirra Falls

A short trek inland of Balandra brings you to some lovely deep swimming spots known as **Balandra Pools** and **Cirra Falls**. From a backroad, which strikes off the Toco Road just past the sign announcing the village, a trail leads inland, crossing a stream and winding uphill. You pass a rather grand wooden house on the right and after a ten-minute walk come to a river, where crazy paving leads to the cascade. The waterfall is small but attractive, with a deep, greenery-wreathed pool and a tree stump as a diving board. You can climb up the bank to the top of the falls, where there's another, smaller cascade. If you're interested in exploring contact **tour guide** Ivan Charles (see p.135).

Arthur's ☎ 670 4384 or ☎ 727 3585, ⓦ darthurshotel .com. A great little ten-room hotel, with smart, bright rooms of varying sized, plus a huge suite, all with a/c and satellite TV; there's also a communal area with kitchenette and supremely friendly staff. Wi-fi and breakfast included. Doubles $\overline{TT$540}$, suite $\overline{TT$840}$
★**Jenny's Country Kitchen/Kay's Pot** ☎ 351 0234. Run from the same building by separate members of the

same family, this is a fantastic place to try proper Trini country cooking, from bowls of rich, thick cowheel soup to curry crab and dumplin', pelau or fish with macaroni pie, callaloo and provisions at lunchtime (TT$40–70), or traditional breakfasts of sada roti and tomato choka or coconut bake with saltfish buljol. Grab a drink from the bar at the back of the building and go early as food runs out by around 1pm. Daily 6am–2pm.

Cumana

Three kilometres past Rampanalgas the Toco Road goes uphill to **Guayamara Point**, a jut in the headland whose wooden benches are perfect for a picnic or to admire fantastic views stretching south to Matura and Manzanilla. Just beyond, there's a lively stretch of open shoreline that invites a stop to drink in the sea breezes and sink your toes in the sand; the rough waters make swimming inadvisable. The next village, another 4km north, is **CUMANA**, once the focal point for missionary work in the area, and still one of the larger communities in the north, with constant traffic at its petrol station, bars and cookshop. Cumana Depot Road leads off from the main road to a short swathe of **beach** protected by offshore reefs.

ACCOMMODATION AND EATING CUMANA

Though much of the beachfront land has been bought up for villa development by Trinidad's elite, foreign tourists are still few and far between, most preferring to continue on to Grand Riviere. **Accommodation** here is therefore still low-key, with good opportunities to get to know local people. There are a couple of noisy but friendly **bars** on the main road.

Agro-Tourism Centre Anglais Rd, Cumana ☎366 1687 or ☎322 1518, ⓦtocoagrotourismcenter.org. A community project run by the Toco Foundation, offering training for locals in anything from hospitality to tour-guiding and aquaculture, this is a popular stopoff for church and school groups on retreats, and is a great place to get a flavour of Toco country living. Rooms upstairs have a/c, satellite TV and pretty views over the countryside; meals are available. To find the centre, turn off the main road just before the petrol station onto Anglais Rd, continue through the village for about 1.5km, and turn right just before the football ground – the centre is on the left. TT$250

Sweet Hand (no phone). Adjacent to the petrol station at the start of Anglais Rd, this is a simple cookshop dishing up no-nonsense Creole lunches: stewed chicken or fresh fish with rice, macaroni pie or provisions, for around TT$50. Mon–Sat 9am–2pm.

Toco

A few kilometres north of Cumana sits the largest community along this stretch of coast. **TOCO** is an attractive, quiet fishing village with a distinctly antiquated air. This proud, close-knit community has one of the largest concentrations of Baptists in the Caribbean, which helped inspire one of its sons, the great Trinidadian writer Earl Lovelace, to write *The Wine of Astonishment*, a novel about Baptist persecution under colonial rule (see "Books", p.277). Most of the buildings are dilapidated gingerbreads made of weather-beaten wood. Though most residents make their money from fishing or farming, much family land has been sold off to developers, tempted by high real-estate prices for the proposed (but never delivered) **ferry terminal** here to serve Tobago, a mere 20km away and easily visible on clear days.

Toco enjoyed a brief spell in the (local) limelight in 2012, when the whopping 84.58m throw by local lad **Keshorn Walcott** earned him the gold medal for javelin at the London Olympics – the first black male athlete to do so. Just 19 when he competed in London, Walcott was also the youngest ever Olympic javelin champion. A placard on the Toco Main Road, just past the turn-off from the Valencia Road, celebrates his achievement.

Toco Folk Museum

Daily 8am–3.30pm or ring to make appointment • TT$5 adults, TT$3 children • ☎670 2554 • To get here, take Galera Rd (the right-hand turn from the main road as you enter town); the museum is housed in the Toco Secondary School

Started as a school project, the small **Toco Folk Museum** houses Amerindian artefacts, local shells, snakeskins, butterflies and insects, and household items, including a gramophone and some rare 78rpm calypso records, which can be played if requested. The curators, mainly schoolteachers, are an excellent source of local history.

Toco beach

Past Toco Secondary School, Galera Road continues to a good **beach**, a double horseshoe of brown and yellow sand, its calm waters protected by an offshore reef. It's a popular weekend spot for a cook-out among locals, who drive pick-ups loaded with food and drink right up to the shoreline. Fried fish, soft drinks and local sweets are sold from a couple of stalls; bear in mind, though, that the portable toilets are often closed due to lack of water.

Galera Point

Galera Road meanders onward past Toco beach to **Galera Point**, Trinidad's extreme eastern tip and site of the Galera **lighthouse**. A stocky tower built in 1897, the lighthouse flashes its red beacon over a treacherous stretch of sea known to fishermen as the "graveyard". Below the lighthouse is a windblown, rocky bluff – known as Fishing Rock – pounded by crashing waves that send up mists of salty spray; a blowhole under the rocks gives off occasional moans, and the point where the royal blue Caribbean Sea meets the murky, pastel blue Atlantic Ocean is easily visible far out to sea. Local people maintain that the point is haunted, with tales of car doors slamming when there is no car, and ghostly wails in the still of the night. The tales spring from an incident that occurred during a 1699 **rebellion** at a Spanish *encomienda* in San Rafael, in which Amerindians killed three Capuchin monks. Incensed, Spanish forces pursued the culprits to Galera, where they leapt off the cliffs to their deaths rather than be killed by the slave-masters.

2

ACCOMMODATION AND EATING   TOCO

Toco doesn't have any dedicated **restaurants**, though there are a couple of bars on the main road that occasionally do a barbecue and serve basic food, and a sometimes open cookshop at the start of the Galera Rd. If you're planning to **stay** here, it's best to bring groceries with you, as little is available locally.

★**Almond Park Estate** Hambug Crown Trace, Toco ☎ 670 2580 or ☎ 681 2037, ⊛ jammevbeachresorts.com. Owned by Soca superstar Machel Montano and managed by his charming father Monty, who lives on site, this is a lovely retreat, just a 10min walk from Toco's beach in its own valley planted with hundreds of fruit trees. Rooms in a low-lying block are spacious and modern, with kitchenette and satellite TV; there's also a larger apartment which sleeps 5–6, with a full kitchen, as well as two self-contained two-bedroom cabins, one with a jacuzzi on its deck, the other (on the other side of the valley) with a lovely outdoor shower and plenty of privacy; all units have a/c. There's a large pool overlooking the valley, outdoor cooking facilities and a hammock-strewn veranda. Fantastic meals cooked by Monty are available on request. Wi-fi available. Cabins T̲T̲$̲5̲0̲0̲, doubles T̲T̲$̲6̲0̲0̲, apartment T̲T̲$̲8̲0̲0̲

Mission and L'Anse Noir

The Toco Main Road becomes **Paria Main Road** as it turns west onto the north coast, running close to the cliffs and making for a beautiful – if occasionally heart-stopping – drive. You quickly enter the community of **Mission**, where Mervyn Dillon Street honours the locally born West Indies cricketer – and no doubt inspires the village's children who play cricket in the road. Further west is the tiny village of **L'Anse Noire**, with a small but safe beach. Beach house rentals are advertised by weatherworn signs along this stretch of road.

Sans Souci

There are several relatively safe beaches at the next village, **Sans Souci**, all boasting waves large enough to make this the island's **surfing** capital and a regular venue for competitions – as well as for egg-laying leatherbacks in season. From here you can see Tobago on a clear day (or its lights at night). Past the bay, Paria Main Road winds inland through impossibly lush rainforest, which lets up only at tiny **Monte Video** village, notable for the cold beers on sale at its lone bar.

Grande Riviere

With a spectacularly rugged curve of wave-whipped beach, capped by jungle-covered hills to each side and with a wide, clear river offering calm freshwater swimming, **GRANDE RIVIERE** is a truly beguiling place, far enough from Port of Spain to feel deliciously remote, but with a sprinkling of appealing places to stay and eat and a

2

LEATHERBACK TURTLES

Weighing up to 700kg and measuring up to a metre across, **leatherback turtles** have undergone few evolutionary alterations in their 150-million-year history. Named for the soft, leathery texture of their ridged, blue-grey carapace (more like a skin than a shell, which bleeds if cut), leatherbacks spend most of the year in cool temperate waters gorging on jellyfish. During the egg-laying season (March–Aug), females swim thousands of miles, returning to the beach of their birth to lay their own eggs in the sand, a fascinating and moving process that usually takes place under the cover of night.

Leatherbacks can return to the same beach up to ten times per season – a necessary repetition, as only sixty percent of all eggs laid will mature into hatchlings. Many are dug up by dogs or poachers, and only one or two eggs from each clutch will become fully-grown turtles. **Hatchlings** emerge from the sand about sixty days later and make a moon-guided dash for the sea; if they're lucky, they'll escape being eaten by predators.

TURTLE-WATCHING

The best spots for **turtle-watching** are Grande Riviere and Matura in Trinidad (see opposite & p.137), and Stonehaven and Turtle beaches in Tobago (see p.216 & p.217). Turtles also nest on many other beaches in both islands, from Las Cuevas and Paria to Pirate's Bay, but only the places listed above offer organized trips with trained guides. If you do want to go turtle-watching (or if you happen upon a laying turtle by chance), it's important to ensure that your presence doesn't disturb the laying process. Guides use infra-red lights when close to turtles, and it's best to avoid using torches anywhere on laying beaches; flash photography is a no-no, though bear in mind that in places such as Grande Riviere, many turtles lay in the early morning or even in full sunshine, allowing to photograph the event non-invasively. On laying beaches it's best to walk close to the shoreline so as to avoid compacting the sand and damaging nests, and of course never discard plastic bags on the beach, as many turtles die after eating them, mistaking them for jellyfish. Though they're rarely seen these days, souvenirs made from turtle-shells are illegal and are obviously not something you should consider buying.

welcoming community-based approach to visitors, as many of whom are Trinidadians as foreign. Nicknamed "beyond God's back", this close-knit village owes much of its popularity with visitors to the **leatherback turtles** (see above) which lay their eggs in the coarse sand here; with some 500 females lumbering up on to the beach each night at the peak of the season, Grande Riviere is one of the most important nesting sites in the world, and certainly the one with the highest density of turtles visiting to lay. After the beautiful *Mt Plaisir Estate* hotel (see p.144) opened up right on the beach in the 1990s, a host of local residents and international entrepreneurs established other **guesthouses** and places to eat, but the end-of-the-road location has kept development low-key and the village remains unspoilt and idyllic. Interaction between visitors and local people has little of the money-oriented duplicity of resorts elsewhere, and local people tend to be genuinely welcoming to visitors.

There's plenty to do in Grande Riviere even if you don't visit during turtle season. Most people divide their time between the beach and river and the interior, where there are hosts of **waterfalls** and **river walks** as well as excellent **birdwatching** – the rare **piping guan** or pawi, a kind of wild turkey that has died out in more developed areas, is quite common here.

Grande Riviere beach

To get to the beach, take the side road off the main road through the village, signposted for the *Mt Plaisir* hotel

Named after the wide, fast-flowing river that originates deep in the Northern Range and runs down to the sea at the eastern end of town, Grande Riviere also boasts a superlative **beach**, a gentle curve of coarse sand with a few unobtrusive buildings. Tall headlands border the sand to the east, where you can take a freshwater bath in the river, while a good kilometre away the western end is sealed by rocky outcrops. Strong waves provide an invigorating swim (and can make swimming inadvisable between Nov and Jan), and give **leatherback turtles** the extra push they need to haul themselves up the sand at laying time; hawksbill and Olive Ridley turtles also nest here. As in Matura, note that the beach is a protected area in the March–August laying season, and you'll need a permit to enter (see below). During this time, the sand is littered with the shells of empty eggs, some discarded by recent hatchlings, others dug up by turtles themselves as they create their own nests – the high density of turtles that visit Grande Riviere means that it's almost impossible for the leatherbacks to find a virgin space as the season wears on. If you're here late in the season, you'll also be able to see **hatchlings** emerging from nests and making a break for the sea. Those that emerge during the day are placed in boxes and released en masse around sunset, a beautiful and touching sight. Behind the beach, towards the centre, the GRNTGA have also set up sandboxes into which they transfer eggs from nests made too close to the waterline, (and thus liable to flood) or by less common visitors such as hawksbills.

The liveliest part of the beach centres around the *Mt Plaisir* and *Grande Almandier* hotels, where their **bars** are favourite liming spots and a lovely stall on the beach sells fine calabash art and locally made jewellery.

ACCOMMODATION   GRANDE RIVIERE

Acajou Hotel Paria Main Rd ☎ 670 3771, ☷ acajou trinidad.com. Six luxurious and well-ventilated hardwood *cabañas* are located in a lush garden on the river, 50m from the beach. Each comes with ceiling fan, mosquito net, sundeck with hammock and a four-poster bed; two are family cabins with a ceiling platform for children. Rates include continental breakfast, but increase by about US$50/night during turtle season. Wi-fi throughout. US$138, family cabin US$185

Le Grande Almandier Grand Riviere beach ☎ 670 2294, ⌖ legrandealmandier.com. The comfortable, pleasant rooms of this attractive and friendly hotel, situated off a large sea-facing sundeck right on the beach, can sleep from two to six people, have a fan, a/c, en-suite bathroom and small veranda, and rates include

full breakfast. The lovely beachfront bar/restaurant downstairs (see p.144) is usually lively too. Rates are reduced by fifteen percent outside of turtle season. US$151

McHaven Bristol and Thomas sts ☎ 670 1014 or ☎ 291 9811, ☷ mchaventt@gmail.com. This yellow guesthouse perched on the hillside (take the road uphill opposite the beach turn-off) provides clean, homely rooms sleeping up to five, with a/c, fans, mosquito nets, satellite TV and en-suite bathroom. Fantastically friendly owner Ingrid is a font of local information, her husband Eric is "Roots" of the local band Roots and Branches, which started the careers of many famous local musicians, and their children are all tour guides. Guests can use the open-air kitchen, and meals are available. TT$450

GRANDE RIVIERE GUIDES AND TOURS

Most guides in the village work through the **Grande Riviere Nature Tour Guide Association** (GRNTGA), housed in a **Visitor Information Centre** (turtle season daily 7pm–2am, rest of the year 8am–1pm; ☎ 469 1288, ⌖ grntga@gmail.com), set back from the road to the beach adjacent to *Mt Plaisir Estate* hotel. During the turtle-nesting season (March 1–August 31), the GRNTGA offer excellent **turtle-watching tours** (US$16 including permit); you go to the Information Centre on the evening you want to tour, pay your fee and collect your permit, and a guide will come and get you at your hotel when there are turtles on the beach; if you're not staying in town you can wait at the centre. Group sizes vary, but are always kept pretty small, and guides provide an informed commentary on both the laying process and on the turtles themselves, as well as explaining the tagging programme being conducted in Grande Riviere. You can also ask for a personalized individual tour if you prefer; costs depend on group size. A tip for your guide at the end of any tour is appreciated.

GRNTGA also offer other trips, such as **hikes** (TT$200–300) into the forest with river swimming, up a gorge near Monte Video village through abandoned cocoa and coffee plantations, as well as along the bench trail from Matelot to Blanchisseuse. **Boat trips** (from TT$600/day) are also a fantastic way to explore the local coastline, head out to Tacaribe or Paria beach and waterfall, or do a little fishing; you're in an open pirogue, so wear a hat and plenty of sunscreen. Lifejackets are available.

2

★ **Mt Plaisir Estate** Grande Riviere beach ☎ 670 1868 or ☎ 670 2217, ⓦ mtplaisir.com. Easy-going, ecofriendly and located right on the beach, this hotel oozes rustic class rather than straightforward luxury; en-suite rooms are fitted with locally made furniture, much of it refurbished antique pieces, while beautiful paintings hang on the walls and surfaces are decorated with driftwood oddities; those upstairs are more luxurious, with a lovely veranda overlooking the beach, while downstairs rooms are right on the sand. All have a/c, fans and mosquito nets, and the on-site restaurant (see p.144) is the best in town. Wi-fi in some areas only. **US$175**

Tenbrin Cottage Paria Main Rd, Grande Riviere ☎ 775 8851 or ☎ 360 8737. In a bright pink bungalow on the main road in the centre of the village, this is a clean and pleasant little budget option, with simple, bright double rooms with a/c, satellite TV, kitchenette and en-suite bathroom. **TT$500**

EATING AND DRINKING

For evening **dining**, you're restricted to the hotels along the beach, though in the daytime, the three cookshops on Paria Main Rd provide an inexpensive alternative (though opening hours are sporadic). **Nightlife** is nonexistent here save for the odd party at *McHaven* hotel's bar area. Aside from the beach hotel bars, you can have a rum or a beer with the locals at the rum shop on the main road, perhaps with background music courtesy of a practice session by Roots and Branches, the local band, who rehearse in a hall just above. The annual **fishermen's fete**, on the last weekend of June, is a raucous affair, with much music, dancing and drinking.

Le Grande Almandier Grand Riviere Beach ☎ 670 2294, ⓦ legrandealmandier.com. A reliable place to eat, dishing up burgers, chicken and fish with fries (TT$65–125) plus sandwiches (TT$45) and more elaborate meat and fish mains (from TT$150). Dinner options (TT$160–250) include chicken in a white wine and mushroom sauce, braised lamb in a red wine sauce and fish in tamarind sauce. The bar is usually a lively spot for a drink. Daily 7.30am–9pm.

Lime Inn Acajou Hotel, Paria Main Rd ☎ 670 3771, ⓦ acajoutrinidad.com. A lovely setting on an open wooden terrace by the river's edge, though not perhaps as busy as the beachside places and sometimes with limited choices. Good light lunches of Greek salad, gazpacho or crab bisque and chicken with fries (TT$45–80), as well as dinner mains from brioche hamburgers to linguine with pesto and coconut-curried fish (TT$105–185); good desserts, too. Daily 7.30am–9pm.

★ **Ylang Ylang** Mt Plaisir Estate Grande Riviere beach ☎ 670 8381 or ☎ 670 2217, ⓦ mtplaisir.com. A lovely beachside setting, and delicious food made with fresh, often organic ingredients and cheese produced in the owner's dairy. Try the smooth Greek-style yoghurt with fruit for breakfast, or the coconut bake with tomato/aubergine choka (eggs, bacon and pancakes also available; all around TT$50); lunch might be tomato and mozzarella salad, calamari or a fish/chicken sandwich (TT$60–75), while dinner might be home-made spaghetti bolognese, coconut shrimp or delicately cooked fish (TT$140–180). Daily 8am–10pm.

DIRECTORY

Shopping Basic groceries are available from the rum shop on the main street and a small supermarket opposite.

Petrol There's no petrol station in town, but staff at the rum shop can usually sell you petrol should you be caught short.

Shark River

Of the many plank-lined bridges that pepper the Paria Main Road past Grande Riviere, the one crossing **Shark River** is the largest. A popular swimming spot, the river has a couple of deep **pools** from the sea all the way upstream; during holiday weekends, campers pitch tents along its banks. Walking upriver makes a great excursion, though you have to clamber over some mighty rocks to reach the best pools. You'll probably need a guide, perhaps from the GRNTGA (see p.143), to negotiate several tributaries and the occasional swing off into the bush.

Matelot

There's not much to keep you in the hamlet of **Matelot**, the last settlement on the Paria Main Road. A track leads down to the fishermen's beach, houses meander up the hillsides, while swimming is possible in the **Matelot River** – follow the main road to the left and bear right. The adjacent football field sees plenty of action at dusk, and in one corner a large TDC sign points the way to the Madamas River Nature Walk, the start of a wild and undeveloped coast bench trail to Paria and ultimately Blanchisseuse, 19km to the west. Locals have formed the Pawi Sports Culture & Eco Club (see below), a group of licensed **tour guides** who can take you along the coast and into the forest inland of Matelot, which is riddled with hunters' trails; one of the best treks is the half-day hike to 3m **Matelot Waterfall**, with its wide, deep pool. Like their counterparts in Matura, Pawi members are part of the monitoring and protection programme for leatherback turtles.

2

ACTIVITIES   MATELOT

Hiking guides Contact Renwick "Pawi Boy" Roberts (☎702 0789), or ask for him around in the village, to arrange guided walks into the surrounding forest (from TT$300).

Central Trinidad

SCARLET IBIS AT CARONI SWAMP

Central Trinidad

Central Trinidad encompasses a fantastic variety of landscapes. Alongside the brash commercial centre of Chaguanas, the gritty, industrialized west coast holds unexpected natural oases such as the Caroni Swamp, home of the scarlet ibis, while the peaceful pools of Point-a-Pierre Wildfowl Trust to the south boast an unlikely location within a huge oil refinery. In the centre of the island, the flatlands of the Caroni Plains are dotted with the somnolent villages that characterize Trinidad's centre, an overwhelmingly rural area where many still make their living from the land. The plains rise gently to the wooded Central Range and Montserrat Hills to the south, and are bordered to the east by the remarkable Aripo Savannahs, a beautiful protected area and prime birdwatching spot. There's more excellent birdwatching along the banks of the Caroni Arena reservoir and the Navet Dam, while the Tamana caves make for an awesome spectacle at dusk, when millions of bats fly out to feed.

To the northeast of the region, the chaotic market centre of **Sangre Grande** is the gateway to the east coast, where the road runs parallel to the sea for some 46km and offers a spectacular drive past the stunning **Manzanilla Beach**, where the **Cocal** avenue of palms forms a coastal barrier that protects the starkly beautiful **Nariva Swamp**, and on to drowsy **Mayaro**, a popular local getaway with another spectacular undeveloped beach. Central Trinidad's population is mostly descended from the Indian indentured labourers who arrived in Trinidad during the 1840s following the abolition of slavery, and today this heritage is very much in evidence. Hindu shrines and prayer flags adorn front gardens, and ornate temples are ten-a-penny, but the **Waterloo Temple**, sitting on the brown waters of the Gulf of Paria south of Chaguanas, is particularly stunning, as is the towering **Hanuman Murti** statue nearby. Both are given some context by the nearby **Indian Caribbean Museum** at Carapaichima, which provides a fascinating insight into Indo-Trinidadian history and culture.

Accommodation in untouristy "Central" is minimal; there are a few options on the west coast geared towards business travellers, but this isn't a particularly enticing place to stay, and it's far better to base yourself in Port of Spain or San Fernando and see the area on day-trips. The only exception is Mayaro on the east coast, where a string of beach houses and hotels offer the opportunity of some Trini-style beach time. As for **eating**, there are innumerable hole-in-the wall places selling delicious roti and Creole food, while doubles and other Indian snacks are also easy to find, as are fast-food joints, Chinese takeaways and, of course, **rum shops**.

CARVED DOOR AT SRI DATTAREYA YOGA CENTRE, CARAPICHAIMA

Highlights

❶ Caroni Swamp Take a lazy boat trip through this maze of mangroves to see the flocks of scarlet ibis that swoop in en masse to roost each evening. **See p.152**

❷ Carapichaima Waterloo Temple in the Sea, the gigantic statue of monkey-god Hanuman and the Indian Caribbean Museum provide an impressive insight into Trinidad's Indian culture **See p.155**

❸ Sunrise at Aripo Savannahs Take in a dramatic light show through moriche palm trees and a fantastic range of birdlife at this most atmospheric of Trinidadian landscapes. **See p.162**

❹ Tamana caves Walk up through cocoa groves to witness the awesome exodus of over

a million bats as they leave their daytime roost by twilight to search for food. **See p.163**

❺ The Cocal Where else in the touristy Caribbean could you find twenty-four unbroken kilometres of sand flanked by nothing more obtrusive than coconut trees swaying in the breeze? **See p.166**

❻ Nariva Swamp A kayak is the ideal way to explore this important wetland area, where a freshwater ecosystem supports a vast array of wildlife. **See p.167**

❼ Mayaro A world away from the sanitized Caribbean seashore, Mayaro offers beachtime Trini-style: football on the sand, cookouts and endless swathes of golden sand. **See p.168**

HIGHLIGHTS ARE MARKED ON THE MAP ON PP.150–151

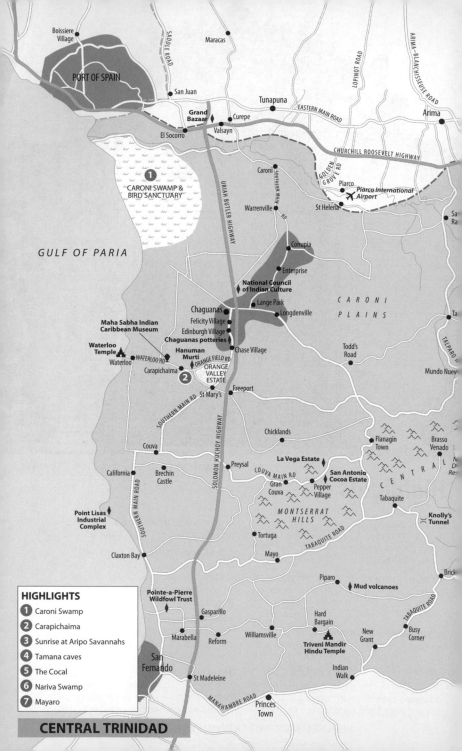

HIGHLIGHTS

1. Caroni Swamp
2. Carapichaima
3. Sunrise at Aripo Savannahs
4. Tamana caves
5. The Cocal
6. Nariva Swamp
7. Mayaro

CENTRAL TRINIDAD

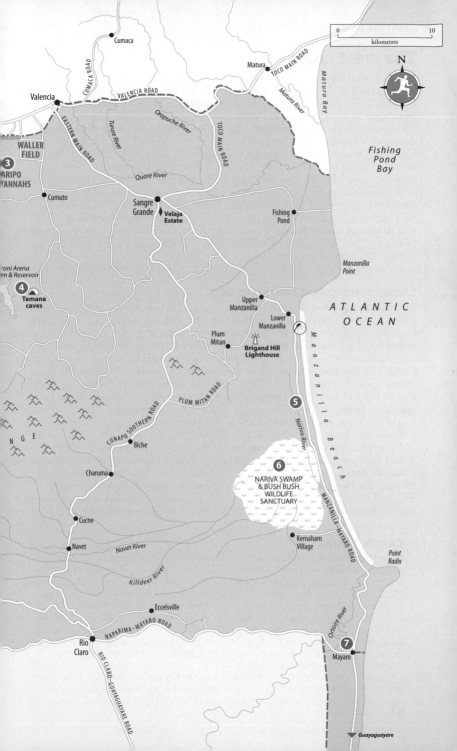

The west coast

Trinidad's **west coast** is as far as many visitors venture into the centre of the island, heading down to the **Caroni Swamp** for a boat tour in search of scarlet ibis, and perhaps stopping off for a look at the remarkable **Waterloo Temple in the Sea** and **Hanuman Murti** statue at Carapichaima. But there are some interesting lesser-known attractions, from the family-run **Chaguanas potteries** at Chase Village, which produce industrial quantities of the deya lights used in Diwali festivities, to the busy and vibrant Chaguanas market, perhaps the most visitor-friendly place on the island to check out all matter of tropical fruit and veg. The area is also pretty easy-access in terms of **transport**, with turn-offs from the Uriah Butler and Solomon Hochoy highways to all of the small villages and settlements, and plenty of maxis from Port of Spain to Chaguanas, from where route taxis depart for all points in the area. The precursor to the highway, and a slower if more interesting route, the **Southern Main Road** (SMR) runs parallel to (but quite a way east of) the Uriah Butler Highway from Curepe, but crosses over onto the western side of the highway at Chaguanas and continues south through **Couva** and **Point-a-Pierre**.

Caroni Swamp and Bird Sanctuary

Caroni Swamp and Bird Sanctuary is one of Trinidad's most popular attractions, situated a few kilometres south of the East–West Corridor, and accessed via the Uriah Butler Highway. As well as serving as a roosting spot for flocks of elegant and spectacularly red **scarlet ibis**, T&T's national bird, these forty square kilometres of tidal lagoons, marshland and mangrove forest bordering the Gulf of Paria between the mouths of the Caroni and Madame Espagnole rivers are home to 157 species of birds, while caimans, snakes, opossums, racoons and silky anteaters live in the water and mangrove canopy. Rich in fish and oysters, the swamp is also a spawning ground for massive tarpon and groupers (the largest caught here weighed 250lb). It was designated a protected wildlife area in 1953, but poaching still occurs, and industrial waste pollution remains a problem. Nonetheless, it's a beguiling and beautiful place, and is well worth a visit.

Most people visit Caroni for a **boat tour** of the swamp; two companies offer trips aboard open pirogues that chug slowly through a maze of channels into the mangroves, which themselves have an otherworldly appearance: some have twisted aerial roots growing downwards into the water, while others have roots that grow upwards, emerging from the murky depths like stalagmites. Guides point out birds, plants and animals of interest – you'll usually see snakes and common wetland birds such as egrets

---

CARONI TOURS

Caroni boat tours leave daily at 4pm from the assembly point in the car park and last two and half hours; advance booking advisable (though not essential), and you should get there by 3.40pm. Of the two operators, **Nanan's** (☏645 1305 or ☏861 8274, ⓦnananecotours.com; tour TT$60, with taxi to and from Port of Spain TT$400) is the larger, a professional outfit whose numerous boats often carry up to thirty people; **Madoo's** tours (☏663 0458 or ☏737 2069; TT$90) are more personalized, with smaller groups, and better for serious birders. Whichever operator you choose, try to sit at the front of the boat to avoid engine noise and fumes, and always douse yourself in plenty of repellent as mosquitoes here are rapacious. It's also a good idea to bring binoculars or a powerful zoom lens, as it's not possible to get close to the roosting spots without disturbing the ibis.

An excellent alternative to standard boat trips are the **kayak tours** offered by Paria Springs (☏620 8240, ⓦpariasprings.com), which start from the southern side of the swamp and paddle through a narrow channel to the roosting site; the lack of engines allows for much better wildlife viewing.

and blue herons – but the main attraction are the **scarlet ibis**, which roost on mangrove islands in the middle of open lagoons far into the swamp. Once the boat engines shudder to a halt, a spectacular scene unfolds as thousands of birds flock in, gradually turning their preferred clump of trees a vibrant red. This intense plumage owes its pigment to carotene, derived from the bird's main prey – shrimp, worms and fiddler and tree-climbing crabs. In April and May, breeding pairs construct flat, open nests in the mangroves; once laid, their eggs incubate for just under a month before all-black hatchlings emerge – it takes up to three years for their diet to replace the dark feathers with a brilliant crimson.

ARRIVAL AND DEPARTURE

CARONI SWAMP

By car Driving to the swamp from Port of Spain, it's best to leave at around 2.30pm to catch the 4pm tour, as rush-hour traffic can be terrible. From the Churchill Roosevelt Hwy, you turn off to the south via the flyover onto the Uriah Butler Hwy, and then take the first exit with a bridge over the highway (there was no signpost at the time of writing); cross the highway and follow the signs to the large car park.
By taxi and organized tour A taxi to and from Port of

Spain will cost around TT$400 including waiting time. All Trinidad's tour operators (see p.38) can take you to Caroni, often as the final stop on a day-long tour.
By maxi and route taxi Maxis and route taxis from Port of Spain to Chaguanas can drop you at the side of the Uriah Butler Hwy at the Caroni exit (a five-minute walk to the start of the tour), but you must arrange for a taxi pick-up as it's unsafe to wait on the highway after dark.

Chaguanas

The sprawling settlement of **CHAGUANAS** is one of the island's oldest and largest towns. Ranged around the junction of Chaguanas Main Road and the old Southern Main Road (which runs parallel to the highway), **central Chaguanas** is a busy amalgam of shops and streetside stalls ranged around three large malls: Mid Centre, the slightly dilapidated Centre Pointe and Centre City. All are great places to find bargains in shoes and clothes, including imports direct from India.

Brief history

Taking its name from its original inhabitants (the Chaguanes Amerindian tribe), Chaguanas was pretty much a one-horse town until Indian indentured labourers came in the 1840s to work on nearby sugar and cocoa estates. By the 1880s Chaguanas had become the most important **market town** in central Trinidad, connected to Port of Spain by rail lines and steamer ships. As the sugar industry declined in the early twentieth century, many Indians moved into professions such as journalism and law, creating the middle-class intelligentsia from which **V.S. Naipaul** emerged and which served as the milieu for some of his early novels. Though the trains and steamer are long gone, the construction of the Uriah Butler and Solomon Hochoy highways has ensured that the town remains well connected to the rest of the island, while the 1970s **oil boom** gave Chaguanas a new lease of life; conveniently located near the oil-rich south, it developed into a shopping centre for those who prefer not to travel all the way into Port of Spain. The swanky Lange Park suburb, alongside out-of-town shopping mall Price Plaza, attests to the area's continuing prosperity.

The markets

Occupying the narrow alleys stretching back from the southern end of Chaguanas Main Road, the big, old-fashioned **market** is equally absorbing: the pavements are chock-a-block with wooden stalls selling dirt-cheap clothes, ornaments and accessories, while the giant **produce market**, in an industrial-style hangar bedecked with bright red wrought-iron arches, is a feast for the eyes, with wizened stallholders presiding over stands groaning under the weight of plantain, dasheen, peppers, ground provisions and artfully arranged piles of fruit. Main trading days are Friday to Sunday, when the markets and the entire central area buzz with activity.

Lion House

West along Chaguanas Main Rd from the market • Closed to the public • ⓦ thelionhouse.com

The stocky, arch-fronted **Lion House** was the birthplace and childhood home of Trinidad's most celebrated writer, **V.S. Naipaul**, who was awarded the Nobel Prize for Literature in 2002. A fine, glaringly white-painted example of classic North Indian architecture, with the eponymous lions adorning stout columns supporting its grand arcade, it was built in 1926 by the Pundit Capildeo, and became the residence of the Naipaul family when the writer's father Seepersad married Capildeo's daughter. Naipaul's 1961 novel *A House for Mr Biswas* describes growing up here surrounded by his stepmother's wealthy, religious and domineering family. Still a private residence, the Lion House is not open to the public, though if you're lucky you'll be able to poke your head around the door to see the ornate interior, its walls decorated with carvings of Hindu deities.

ARRIVAL AND DEPARTURE

CHAGUANAS

By public transport From Port of Spain, Chaguanas maxis depart from City Gate and drop off next to the Mid Centre Mall, as do route taxis, which depart from Broadway, Port of Spain, while PTSC buses stop next to *KFC* near the Uriah Butler Hwy. Maxis and route taxis to the rest of the west coast depart from the transportation stands at the Mid Centre Mall.

PHAGWAH

A joyous celebration of the new year and the arrival of spring, the Hindu Holi festival – known in the Caribbean as **Phagwah** (pronounced "pag-wah") – is held around the first full moon in March to mark the end of the Hindu calendar's twelfth month (Phagun). Upbeat and lighthearted – to the horror of more traditional Hindus, who consider this attitude *adharamic* (anti-religious) – Phagwah celebrations are massive outdoor parties that represent a symbolic triumph of light over darkness and happiness over suffering. In Indian religious mythology, the festival commemorates the death of Holika, the sister of evil king Hiranyakashyapu, who repeatedly tried to murder his son Prahalad because of the latter's insistence on worshipping Vishnu as the only God. Immune to flames, Holika carried Prahalad into a fire, but the gods ensured that she burned to death; her brother was later slain by Vishnu. Holika's conflagration is re-enacted the night before the main festivities, when sins amassed in the previous year are ceremonially consumed by the flames of large bonfires.

The main festivities revolve around traditions such as the singing of devotional folk songs called **chowtals**, sung in a mix of English and Hindi and composed specifically for Phagwah to tell the story of the festival, normally accompanied by goatskin *dholak* drums and brass cymbals called *ghanj*. Local businesses sponsor *chowtal* competitions in the weeks preceding Phagwah, and the winners perform on the day itself. The principal focus of the festival, though, are intense dyes of various colours including the fuchsia-pink *abir*, which is strewn about as powder or mixed with water and squirted from a plastic bottle renamed a *pichakaaree*; participants wear white to make the most of the ensuing glorious mess. As the festivities wear on, classical Indian dancers display their movements and chutney soca fuels the more risqué dancing. Games add to the fun; adults participate in **makhan chor**, where teams form a human pyramid in order to grab a suspended flag; and children compete in roti-eating contests in which skins are strung through the middle and tied in a line to be eaten with no hands allowed.

PHAGWA PRACTICALITIES

Celebrations tend to begin around 1pm and are held all over Trinidad; foreigners should expect to get very dirty as they're extra special targets for dye throwing. In the north, Aranguez Savannah in San Juan is particularly lively, whereas Tunapuna Hindu School close to the Churchill Roosevelt Highway holds a slightly more restrained event. At Chaguanas, the car park of the National Council of Indian Culture is a popular location, as is the **Kendra Phagwah Festival** in an open space on Ragoonan Road, off Longdenville Old Road. Bear in mind none are widely publicized – to find the exact date, you'll have to scan the community events listings in the newspapers, contact a tour guide, or ask around.

EATING AND ENTERTAINMENT

There's no real reason to stay in Chaguanas but there is plenty of fantastic Indian food available from the legions of **roti shops** and **doubles stalls** all over town; the malls also have air-conditioned restaurants serving Creole and Chinese food. The upmarket **Price Plaza** shopping mall, just off the highway a little way out of town, has international chain stores alongside American-style restaurants and fast-food joints, and a MovieTowne cinema (☎ 627 8277, ⓦ movietowne.com).

Felicity Village

A couple of kilometres south of Chaguanas centre, on the western side of the highway, the Southern Main Road (known here as the Felicity Main Road) is bordered to the left by acre upon acre of arable fields, some still used for the cultivation of sugar cane. To the right, backstreets lead into **FELICITY VILLAGE**, a thoroughly Indian community where you'll see a mini-temple outside most homes. Come **Diwali**, Felicity residents are particularly lavish with their decorations, and this is one of the best places in Trinidad to take in the celebrations, usually held just off the main road, on Pierre Road and Cancadee Road. Complicated bamboo structures are fashioned to hold some 100,000 deyas (pottery bowls filled with oil and a wick to light), and fairy lights are strung up above the streets, which give off an incredible glow in the evening. There's also tassa drummers, Indian dancers, fireworks and loads of delicious food to sample. Since traffic slows to a standstill during Diwali, it's best to park closer to Chaguanas and walk to Felicity (about fifteen minutes).

3

Edinburgh Temple

Southern Main Rd, Edinburgh Village • Service Sun • ⓦ ehtemplett.com

The SMR winds through a string of indistinguishable Indian communities; as you pass through the otherwise unremarkable Edinburgh Village, look out for the ornate, white-painted **Edinburgh Temple** on the right, its walls, arches and turrets richly embellished with plaster reliefs and with a colourful shrine to Kali outside. Interfaith services are conducted each Sunday in the richly decorated **interior**, with its brightly painted plaster statues of the Hindu deities.

Chaguanas potteries

Benny's Pottery Works & Radika's Pottery Shop Mon–Sat 8am–5pm, Sun 8am–1pm • ☎ 665 4267

The string of ceramics stalls lining the road at Chase Village are known collectively as the **Chaguanas potteries**, the oldest and most famous of which is **Benny's Pottery Works**, at the back of Radika's Pottery Shop. The thousands of beautiful wind chimes, wall plaques, pots and ornaments on sale in Radika's are all produced in Benny's workshop using traditional methods passed down from the present owner's grandfather, who learnt his craft in India. The clay is kneaded by foot to remove stones and lumps, then hand-rolled or shaped on a wheel before being fired in the open wood-fuelled kiln at the centre of the workshop.

Carapichaima

The collective name for the cluster of villages on and around the SMR south of Edinburgh, **CARAPICHAIMA**, like its neighbours, is home to a predominantly Indian population, whose forefathers settled here to work on the vast sugar estates that once covered the area. For the moment, at least, this is still prime **sugar territory**: fields of cane undulate in the wind and graceful royal palms tower over the road as they have done since the early plantation days, when the land was owned by the Tate and Lyle sugar producers. Present-day Carapichaima is wholeheartedly Trinidadian, however:

3

INDO-TRINIDADIAN RELIGIONS

T&T's largest religious denomination after Catholicism, **Hinduism** was brought to Trinidad in the nineteenth century by indentured Indian workers, whose wide-ranging geographical and social origins reflected the huge differences in religious practice and status in India. As they settled into their new life in the Caribbean, Indo-Trinidadians created a hybrid Hinduism that's unique to the island. One of the main differences to India is the lack of a **caste system** in T&T. The strong friendships forged during the passage over – which gave rise to the term *jihaji bhai* ("ship brother") – transcended differences in social status, and many new-found friends chose to settle together and work the same plantations. Slowly, the caste system was eroded; only the priestly Brahmin caste, whose pundits officiate at religious rites, has survived in Trinidad.

Rituals have also been modified. Prayers for blessing – **pujas** – are lengthy processes in India, each with a specific meaning and directed towards a particular deity, but in Trinidad, several *pujas* are often combined, with multiple deities involved. At sacred places such as Waterloo, you'll often see the scattered remains of articles required for *pujas* – incense, flowers, pictures (*murtis*) of the deity to be honoured, while the smell of the oils, herbs, spices and ghee offered to the gods hang heavy in the air; bamboo poles topped with a **jhandi** (prayer flag) in the colours of the relevant deity are also essential to *pujas*, and you'll see clusters of them at *puja* sites island-wide as well as fluttering in the gardens of Hindu households.

Though you'd hardly believe it judging by the proliferation of grandiose mosques, **Islam** actually has a much smaller worship base, with just six percent of the population practising Muslims. For the most part, Islamic religious practice has changed little since arriving in T&T, save for the festival of **Hosay**, which has grown from a rather sombre ceremony to a Carnival-esque affair, much to the distress of the devout.

---

along the central **Waterloo Main Road**, the Church of Zion and Presbyterian school sit side by side with a healthy quota of rum shops, while Hindu prayer flags flutter next to trees strung with blue plastic bottles that traditionally ward off *maljo*, or bad luck. Nowhere else is the creative potential of Trinidad's cosmopolitan cultural mix more clearly visible than at Carapichaima's **Carnival** celebrations, where the length of the main road is lit up with lanterns each night, and a masquerade of traditional carnival characters such as robbers, jab jabs and jamettes (see p.262), combined with Indian drumming and costume, draws hundreds of visitors – this and other aspects of Indian culture are covered at the also excellent **Indian Caribbean Museum**.

As well as the museum, Carapichaima is home to two of Trinidad's most spectacular Hindu sites, the towering **Hanuman statue** and the unique **Temple in the Sea**, while the coastline here offers excellent **birdwatching**, with both Waterloo and nearby Brick Field good places to see skimmers, wattled jacanas, long-winged harriers, ospreys, neotropic cormorants, plovers, ruddy turnstones and the striking red-breasted blackbird. Courtenay Rooks of Paria Springs (see p.38) organizes regular birding tours in the area.

Hanuman Murti and the Sri Dattareya Yoga Centre

Orange Field Rd • Temple Mon–Fri 6am–noon & 5–8pm, Sat & Sun 6am–noon & 4–8pm • To book tours call President of the Temple, Ramesh Persad Maharaj on ☎ 689 6581 • Sri Dattatreya Yoga Centre ☎ 673 5328 • Donation accepted for photography • The centre is at Orange Field, 200m up from the junction of the Orange Field and Waterloo roads

Surrounded by a cluster of neat 1920s bungalows built for sugar estate managers, the majestic **Hanuman Murti** is the largest representation of the Hindu monkey god outside of India, its 26 metres towering over the attached temple. Consecrated in June 2003, the statue was a gift from Ganapati Sachchidananda, a Swami (spiritual teacher) from Mysore in southern India. Its workmanship rivals anything to be found in Asia, with beautifully detailed and colourful relief work courtesy of twenty expert craftsmen sent over from India by the Swami.

In Hindu teaching, Hanuman is an immortal guru who observes your actions and offers protection from wrongdoing; interestingly, literature available at the temple informs that Hanuman came to the rescue against kidnappings in ancient India, a reference to the recent spate of abductions of prominent East Indian business people here in Trinidad. The complex's bright pink **temple** is both the largest in Trinidad and the only one in the ornate and long, single-storey South Indian style, its entrance flanked by two elegant concrete elephants and its interior awash with superb and brightly coloured bas-reliefs of Hindu deities. The temple is home to the **Sri Dattatreya Yoga Centre**, a very active yoga and meditation centre.

Maha Sabha Indian Caribbean Museum

Waterloo Main Rd • Wed–Sun 10am–5pm • Free • ☎ 673 7007

Waterloo village is home to the **Maha Sabha Indian Caribbean Museum**, the only permanent exhibition of its kind in the region. Put together with extensive research from both local and expatriate sources, it's a thoughtful and absorbing collection that documents the Indian experience in Trinidad across Hindu, Muslim and Christian religions, something that often gets overlooked in a society whose culture can be dominated by the calypso, soca and steel pan of the Afro-Trinidadian population. Exhibits include letters and photographs of early **Indian arrivals** on the island and models of the ships that brought the first immigrants, while sugar is a running theme throughout, with agricultural tools and photos documenting rural life and indentureship, and information on the phasing out of **sugar cane** attesting to the psychological importance of the crop to Indo-Trinidadians. Traditional clothing, paintings and musical instruments are all well represented, as are marijuana pipes – cannabis was originally brought to the Caribbean by Indians, and according to many Hindus it was only outlawed when rum factories were built, so as to promote consumption of the new drug of choice.

Religious festivals and icons form a sizeable part of the collection, from displays on Diwali and Phagwah to tassa drums and photos of early Tadjas from the Muslim Hosay commemoration, as well as a translation of the Bible into Hindi by nineteenth-century Presbyterian missionaries. The construction of Hindu schools from the 1950s holds particular significance, as this is seen as the point at which Hindus began to be accepted into Trinidadian society. The museum's knowledgeable curator is on hand to answer any questions about the exhibits or wider issues.

Waterloo Temple in the Sea

Waterloo Main Rd • Tues, Wed, Sat & Sun 8am–3pm, though these times depend on when the caretaker arrives • Donation accepted

Waterloo Main Road meanders towards the sea, with some pretty wooden buildings intermingled with the concrete; on the right hand side, look out for the former train station, once a stop on the Port of Spain–San Fernando line. Just before you meet the sea, the old Anglican cemetery on the right includes a plot reserved for Muslim burials, and just beyond this, a car park and information board (and, through a hedge, traditional Hindu cremation pyres at the water's edge) mark the site of the unfailingly impressive **Waterloo Temple**. A gleaming white onion-shaped dome, it sits at the end of a concrete causeway surrounded by the Gulf of Paria at high tide, and at low tide by extensive mud flats. It's a stunning setting, inordinately peaceful and spiritual, with the shore littered with broken coconut shells and fruits left by Hindus during *puja* ceremonies, and legions of flags (*jhande*) – representing prayers and offerings – flapping in the breeze.

The octagonal temple – used by the local Hindu community for weddings and *puja* ceremonies – covers an area of over 100 square metres, with coloured-glass windows that enable you to see the brightly painted stone and marble gods inside. Anyone can enter the temple, provided they remove their shoes first. The causeway, meanwhile, is a good vantage point from which to view the **birds**, including terns, gulls, whimbrels and skimmers, which feed in the mud flats throughout the year.

Back at the car park, there's also a life-size statue of **Sewdass Sadhu**, an Indian labourer whose zeal and persistence enabled the temple to be built. Sadhu constructed a temple on the shore here in 1947, on land owned by the state sugar monopoly Caroni, but the government bulldozed the structure five years later, and sent him to jail for fourteen days. He then decided to rebuild his temple in the sea, where no permission was required, and struggled single-handedly for the next 25 years, using a bicycle to carry the foundation rocks out into the water and placing barrels full of concrete on the sea floor at low tide. Help finally came in 1995, when the 150th anniversary of the arrival of Indians in Trinidad inspired the government to declare the temple an Unemployment Relief Project. With labourers paid by the state to rebuild the structure, the causeway was added and the temple swiftly completed.

ARRIVAL AND DEPARTURE
CARAPICHAIMA

By car Carapichaima is most easily accessed from the Freeport exit of the Solomon Hochoy Hwy: head west crossing the Southern Main Rd at St Mary's village (look for the *KFC*); at the next junction, turn right onto Orange Field Rd for Hanuman Murti and left for the museum and Waterloo Temple.

By public transport You can take a route taxi from the Mid Centre Mall in Chaguanas to St Mary's Junction on the Southern Main Rd just beyond the Orange Field Rd turn-off, where you pick up another taxi to the junction of Orange Field and Waterloo Main roads. Route taxis ply the lengthy Waterloo Main Rd from Orange Field to Waterloo Temple.

Point Lisas

South of Carapichaima, the SMR enters Trinidad's industrial heartland, with the west coast lined by a series of smoggy towns interspersed with oil refineries and petrochemical plants. The liveliest settlement in the area is **Couva**, with a few lovely gingerbread houses surviving among the concrete, and several places to eat and drink lined up along the road. Just south of Couva, a roundabout marks the turn-off to the massive **Point Lisas Industrial Complex**, whose belching chimneys are visible from miles around. The complex was built during the oil boom years of the 1970s to produce liquefied natural gas, steel and fertilizers (it has the unfortunate distinction of being the largest exporter of fertilizer in the world), but, industrial as it is, Point Lisas still has its wildlife. Every year between December and June, thousands of **blue crabs** make the hazardous journey across the main road from the swampland beside the complex to lay eggs in the sea; given the road traffic here, many don't make it, leaving a crunchy trail of broken shells on the tarmac. Just by the turn-off for Point Lisas, **Atlantic Plaza** offers air-conditioned respite from the heat in the form of a *Rituals* coffee shop and food court.

Point-a-Pierre Wildfowl Trust

Petrotrin Oil Refinery, Point-a-Pierre • Mon–Fri 9am–5pm, Sat & Sun 10am–5pm; tours 9.30am & 1.30pm • TT$15 • ☎ 658 4200 ext 2512, ⊕ papwildfowltrust.org

Perhaps the most unlikely bird sanctuary in Trinidad, the remarkable **Point-a-Pierre Wildfowl Trust** is a series of greenery-swathed pools right in the midst of the huge Petrotrin Oil Refinery at Point-a-Pierre, just north of San Fernando. The reserve came into being in 1966, when a hunter who worked at the refinery realized that wildfowl stocks were diminishing, and set aside an area within the complex to breed the birds. In time it became an established reserve, supported financially by the Canadian and British governments as well as by Shell – though barely at all by Petrotrin itself. Today, the reserve's attractively landscaped grounds surround two lakes filled with lotus and water lilies and bordered by wooden walkways. Many **rare bird species** can be seen here, including the wild Muscovy duck, the red-billed whistling duck, the white-cheeked pintail and red-capped cardinal. Notwithstanding the fact that some of the rarer birds, including scarlet ibis, are caged within an aviary to allow breeding programmes to continue, the reserve doesn't feel at all like a zoo. Indeed, the ibis breeding programme has been something of a landmark project, particularly as some of the released birds have chosen to stay on the site, allowing you the only chance you'll get in Trinidad to see wild scarlet ibis up close; at Caroni Swamp, home of the scarlet ibis (see p.152), you're usually some distance from the ibis roosting trees.

The **learning centre** at the entrance has good photographic displays of the reserve's flora and fauna, plus a small collection of shells and insect specimens alongside Amerindian artefacts, with a very informative account of the culture and belief systems of Trinidad's original inhabitants. The trust's guides are vastly knowledgeable not only about the birdlife, but also the medicinal qualities of Trinidad's indigenous plants, and though you can explore the reserve independently, you'll get a lot more from your visit if you arrange for a tour. The best time to visit is before 11am or after 3pm, as many birds hide in the shade during the hottest part of the day; spend the midday hours enjoying lunch on the veranda of the *Petrea Place* restaurant (see below).

ARRIVAL AND DEPARTURE

POINT-A-PIERRE WILDFOWL TRUST

By car To drive to Point-a-Pierre from Port of Spain or San Fernando, leave the Solomon Hochoy Hwy at the Gasparillo–Point-a-Pierre exit and follow the signs west through the Petrotrin Oil Refinery; otherwise the turning is signposted from the SMR.

By public transport The Chaguanas–Couva–San Fernando maxi route passes in front of the refinery. Of the multiple entrances to the refinery, the one closest to the reserve is between oil drums 84 and 85, on the left-hand side of the SMR if coming from the north. Once inside, turn left on Regent Rd; it's a twenty-minute walk or five-minute drive to the Trust entrance.

ACCOMMODATION AND EATING

★**Petrea Place** Petrotrin Oil Refinery ⊕658 5322, ⓦpetreaplace.com. Adjacent to the Wildfowl Trust inside the Petrotrin plant, this is a lovely little guesthouse, much beloved of birdwatchers. The large, homely bedrooms (one of which is equipped for people with disabilities) have rug-covered wood floors, a/c and TV, while the restaurant (advance booking only), offers high-quality, reasonably priced Caribbean cuisine alongside afternoon tea with a range of sweets and savouries, served on a veranda surrounded by climbing creepers and petrea flowers. Wi-fi included; rates include breakfast. **TT$500**

The interior

Despite the beauty of its rolling countryside, **the interior** holds few specific draws for visitors; in fact, perhaps the best way to get a feel for the area is simply to get happily lost in its maze of rural roads, stopping off for a drink or an Indian snack at one of the innumerable small bars and food stalls in the villages. As **maxis** and **taxis** take long, circular routes to the villages, this is a difficult area to explore without your own vehicle, though the absence of road signs can be frustrating; asking for directions is usually your best bet for finding the right road.

The Montserrat Hills

East of the Solomon Hochoy Highway, the **Montserrat Hills** are the most picturesque part of the Central Range, a rolling landscape which shelters huge cocoa estates and the **Navet Dam and Reservoir**, as well as some of Trinidad's sleepiest villages, accessed via winding roads with rickety wooden bridges. The nineteenth-century English novelist Charles Kingsley, who visited in 1870, described the panorama from the top of Montserrat as "the most vast and most lovely which I have ever seen". Most of the villages have little specific to recommend them apart from the odd picturesque colonial house and a great deal of rural charm, though there are a few gentle attractions on which to hinge a visit.

La Vega Estate

Couva Main Rd • Daily 9am–5pm; free if you've come to shop, TT$25 to picnic and walk the signposted nature trail • Fishing TT$30 • Paddleboating TT$40 for 30min • Mountain biking TT$50 for 30min • ⊕679 9522, ⓦlavegaestate.com

A thriving commercial plant nursery with a few recreational activities for visitors as well, the **La Vega Estate** is nestled in the hills about 10km east of the Solomon Hochoy

Highway, between Gran Couva and Flanagin Town. A large swathe of the estate is devoted to exquisitely **landscaped gardens**, which you can explore independently or on a guided tour; there are also ponds for fishing and paddleboating (public holidays only), as well as picnic tables in sheltered bamboo groves, bromeliad and Japanese gardens, a meditation space and a children's play area. At weekends, you can usually buy delicious ice cream made with estate fruits, in flavours such as silk fig, barbadine and carambola.

San Antonio Cocoa Estate

619 Couva Main Rd, a few kilometres west of La Vega · Guided tours only, must be arranged in advance · TT$50 · 📞 679 9515 or 📞 377 7780, ✉ m_deverteuil@hotmail.com · Take the Gran Couva exit from the Solomon Hochoy Hwy and follow the road past Gran Couva for about 20min

The 250-acre **San Antonio Cocoa Estate** is a working **cocoa plantation**, owned and managed by Richard de Verteuil. His family has operated the estate in the traditional manner for hundreds of years, and an hour's tour offers a fascinating glimpse into the workings of this end of the cocoa industry, from the planting and picking of the pods through to the drying process in sheds with sliding roofs, and the storing of the beans for export. It's best to go between November and June, when the bulk of the crop is processed. Trinidad produces "fine flavour" cocoa beans, some of the best in the world, and much of the crop ends up in expensive Belgian chocolate. However, local producers are leading a resurgence in Trini-made chocolate (see p.238); San Antonio is the main collection point for cocoa grown by members of the Montserrat Cocoa Farmers Co-Operative Society, who bring their beans here for processing and whose members make delectable chocolate bars (containing 70 percent cocoa) as well as other cocoa products available to buy on site.

Knolly's Tunnel

John William Trace

East of the Montserrat Hills, past the tiny village of Tabaquite, there are lovely views of the central range from the main Tabaquite Road. It's worth turning off along John William Trace to peer into the abandoned **Knolly's Tunnel**, an abandoned railway tunnel named after the colonial Governor who opened it in 1898. You can walk or drive right through the 180m tunnel, home to a sizeable colony of bats, and the surrounding area has been prettily landscaped, with a couple of shady picnic areas.

Navet Dam and Reservoir

Tabaquite Rd · Daily 8am–6pm · Take the Gasparillo exit from Solomon Hochoy Hwy and follow Tabaquite Rd, which runs along the southern slopes of the Montserrat Hills to the dam

With only the minuscule hamlet of Brasso Venado nearby, the towering **Navet Dam** is an isolated place, excellent for quiet picnics and birdwatching, with plenty of waterfowl scooting around on the reservoir's intricate network of inlets and coves. As with visits to Caroni Arena, you need a **permit** to enter the area, best arranged via a company such as Caribbean Discovery Tours or Paria Springs (see p.38).

Piparo

Piparo is a 20min drive from the Solomon Hochoy Hwy (take the Gasparillo exit, follow the main road and take a left turn at Williamsville)

Set in beautiful low-lying hills south of Montserrat, about 10km from both Tortuga and Tabaquite, **PIPARO** has the dubious distinction of having suffered one of the Trinidad's largest **mud volcano** eruptions in 1997, which saw mud spewed 60m into the air, covering 2.5 square kilometres and displacing 31 families. Half of the village cemetery remains buried under the (now solidified) mud "lake", which has two small oozing mounds at its centre that occasionally spatter out small eruptions of mud. Piparo is also infamous as the former home of notorious drug lord, **Dole Chadee** (see box below), whose 1994 arrest drew attention both to the significance of cocaine as part of the island's economy, and to the extent of his Piparo estate, close to the volcano site, where an extensive mansion and Hindu temple behind 4.5m razor-wired walls attest to the extravagance of the cocaine don's lifestyle. The rest of his land, just north of the village, was seized by the government and now houses a rehabilitation centre for drug users and the homeless.

Triveni Mandir

Tours by arrangement only • Donation expected • ☎ 656 0526 or ☎ 784 9808, ⓦ trivenimandir.com • Turn off the Solomon Hochoy Hwy at the Gasparillo exit

Set among the canefields of south-central Trinidad, in the fantastically named community of Hard Bargain, the remarkably large **Triveni Mandir** owes its existence to the vision and devotion of local furniture-seller-cum-Hindu teacher Shri Ramoonsingh, who spent his entire life savings on the temple's construction. It's

THE RISE AND FALL OF DOLE CHADEE

Widely claimed to have been Trinidad's most influential and successful drug lord, **Dole Chadee's** story reads something like an illicit Colombian rags-to-riches tale. Born Nankissoon Boodram to a poor Indo-Trinidadian family in Curepe, Chadee went from mason to cocaine empire-builder, and was a charitable community godfather who skillfully avoided arrest until his eventual downfall, which was shrouded in unanswered questions and political intrigue.

At the peak of his reign, Chadee owned a large estate guarded by gun-wielding henchmen at the village of **Piparo**; he had his own ornate no-expense-spared Hindu temple, owned racehorses, a fleet of flashy cars (despite not having a driving licence), as well as shopping centres and petrol stations as far afield as Princes Town and San Fernando. Chadee employed a large contingent of the Piparo community and was intent on looking after the village's welfare, offering money for food and electricity at difficult times, as well as funds for sporting events and other community activities. His group remained seemingly untouchable (he's even said to have bought a car from former prime minister, Patrick Manning), despite showing a ruthless side which saw witnesses to alleged crimes poisoned, killed or their jaws shot off, and families intimidated or murdered.

Chadee was never tried as a narco-trafficker, however. Despite US authorities' suspicions that he, along with partner "Shortman" Beharry, were heading the eastern Caribbean's leading cocaine cartel, in league with Cali of Colombia, it was for a dual **murder charge** that he and eight accomplices were eventually arrested in 1994. They were found guilty and sentenced to death by hanging in 1996, and a lengthy appeal process ensued; Chadee and the other accused maintained they had no involvement in the murder and were the victims of a witch-hunt for drug traffickers by a range of conspirators. The authorities disagreed, and in 1999, all nine went to the gallows. Though Chadee and his cohorts were certainly no angels, there are inconsistencies over their ultimate demise: regardless of their guilt in the murder charge, the group apparently leapfrogged a long line of murderers waiting on death row; jurors on the case were said to have been cobbled together without due process; and Amnesty International points to the failure of political officials to disclose evidence. Chadee certainly served a purpose as a media tool: the war on drugs was seen to be visibly waged, despite the fact that Trinidad continued to be flooded with cocaine. Chadee's downfall is also alleged to have been orchestrated by rival Syrian operators with political clout in both T&T's main parties, who didn't like the fact that Chadee's gang were "independent players" operating at the risk side of the business rather than in the cartel they were purported to be part of; certainly, the moneyed side of cocaine trading in Trinidad remains wholeheartedly intertwined with legitimate businesses.

wonderfully detailed, with huge elephant sculptures outside and solid marble figurines of Shiva, Ganesh and Laksmi set in recesses in the walls both inside and out, while stained-glass windows and ornate paintings on the inside walls add to the atmosphere. Shri Ramoonsingh died before the temple was completed, but a small plaque at the front of the building dedicates the mandir to him.

The Caroni Plains

Running roughly parallel to the Uriah Butler Highway, the old **Southern Main Road** south from Curepe on the Churchill Roosevelt Highway is little more than a parochial thoroughfare these days as it potters through one small community after another surrounded on all sides by the **Caroni Plains**, Trinidad's original sugar heartland and a region dominated by the East Indian community, whose ancestors settled here as indentured workers (see p.251). The complete restructuring of the sugar industry during the 1990s and the eventual closure of the state-owned Caroni Sugar Company in 2004 has forced farmers to diversify, however, planting rice, pigeon peas and cassava in the former canefields. Some 5km south of Curepe, **Caroni village** was founded around the old Caroni Sugar Factory, though this and the rum distillery closed in 2003; you can still sample local rum in any number of rum shops along the road, however. Set in a former train station, the *Railway Bar* is especially distinctive.

South of Caroni, the SMR becomes increasingly urban as you pass through **Warrenville**, home of a particularly attractive mosque, which merges imperceptibly into **Conupia**, itself morphing into a suburb of Chaguanas. The route displays a fascinating combination of old and new Trinidad, with mandirs and mosques interspersed with evangelical churches, while extravagant signboards shout out the wares of the small shops and mom-and-pop restaurants that line the road, many of the latter selling excellent **Indian fast food**.

Aripo Savannahs

Northeast of the Caroni Plains and right at the end of the Churchill Roosevelt Highway, stone pillars at the edge of the tarmac mark the entrance to the former American airbase at **Waller Field**. The hangars, barrack blocks and control rooms are long gone, though the old runway is used for regular drag racing meets. The main draw in the area, however, are the 18 square kilometres of the **Aripo Savannah Scientific Reserve**, Trinidad's last remaining portion of savannah land, which was given protected status in 1934. In 1871, author Charles Kingsley wrote that the area "filled me with more admiration than anything I have seen in the island", and it's still a startlingly beautiful place, vast, eerie and empty despite its proximity to the Northern Range and the clamour of the East–West Corridor. The emptiness is deceiving, however; the area's sensitive ecosystem provides a home to 260 species of **birds** and 243 documented species of **flora**, many of which are rarely (if ever) seen elsewhere on the island. Among the plants are parasitic vines, wild calabash, ground orchids and the endemic carnivorous sundew plant, while savannah hawks, red-bellied macaws and fork-tailed palm swifts (among innumerable others) are more easily spotted here than elsewhere on Trinidad. Each savannah is divided by impressive galba-palm forests and palm marshes including abundant moriche palm trees, while the disused bunkers and wells are a legacy of World War II, when the Americans leased 1600 acres here to use for training exercises.

The signposted entrance to the Aripo Savannah Scientific Reserve is at **Cumuto**, about 5km south of Waller Field. The best time to visit is at dawn, when you will be rewarded with a spectacular aspect of the palms glowing in the light, along with the birds' enchanting early morning chorus.

INFORMATION | **ARIPO SAVANNAHS**

Permits As the Savannahs are a protected area, you need a permit from the Parks Section of the Forestry Division based in St Joseph (☎645 1203). Getting a permit is a complicated process; it's easiest to ask a tour company to secure one for you.

Guides and tours Visiting with a guide is essential, both to prevent you getting lost and to point out the flora and fauna. Paria Springs and Caribbean Discovery Tours (see p.38) offer trips to the area, as does locally based guide Thomas Gill (☎643 4911).

Talparo Road

Signposted from the Churchill Roosevelt Highway, **Talparo Road** runs south through serene rainforest where you'll rarely meet another car. As you pass the tiny settlements of Brazil and Talparo, the foothills of the Central Range appear, cloaked in luxuriant vegetation: thickets of bamboo jostle with papaya, mango, banana, cashew and breadfruit trees. The blooms of the golden poui dominate in April, while from December to March magnificent immortelle trees blaze a fiery red.

3

The Caroni Arena Dam and Reservoir

Daily 8am–6pm • For tours call Paria Springs ☎ 622 8826 • 1km due east of Talparo Rd on the signposted Caroni Arena Rd

Reaching 40.85m at its highest elevation, the **Caroni Arena Dam** is Trinidad and Tobago's largest, while the **Reservoir** covers 6.8 square kilometres. Caroni is a haven for **birds** and **animals**. Parrots, hawks and white egrets are frequent visitors to the area while blue emperor butterflies flutter among the reeds by the water's edge, caimans lurk in the swamps bordering the reservoir and red howler and capuchin monkeys, toucans and tree porcupines inhabit the surrounding forest. There's no public transport to the dam, though Paria Springs offer a marvellous birding tour here, and will be able to arrange the necessary permits for entering the area.

ACCOMMODATION | **THE CARONI ARENA DAM AND RESERVOIR**

Hacienda Jacana Talparo ☎498 7597, ⓦhacienda jacana.com. A tranquil and charming place to stay, a short drive southwest of the Caroni Arena Dam and Reservoir nestled amid trees on a riverbank. The smart wood-panelled cottages contain locally made teak furniture, and there is a pool, a lake for fishing and canoeing, and excellent birdwatching. Meals (breakfast US$15, lunch and dinner US$30) are available. One-bedroom cottage U̲S̲$̲1̲7̲5̲

Mount Tamana bat caves

The distinctive, flat-topped **Mount Tamana** is the highest in the Central Range at 308m, and its porous limestone core holds a series of lengthy **cave systems** which provide the perfect home for huge colonies of **bats**. The gentle thirty-minute walk up Tamana's slopes is pleasant enough, threading through shady groves of lichen-covered cocoa trees and under giant silk cotton trees, with the occasional eye-popping view over the Caroni Plains. However, the real draw here are the bats, which make a spectacular exit en masse at **dusk** to feed. It's best to arrive around 3pm, in order to have enough time to walk up to the top of the hill and admire the spectacular views over the forested slopes of the Central Range, and descend to the caves before the sun goes down. It's easy to go inside the first of the caves to peek at the ceiling – almost every inch is covered with roosting bats (though be warned that the bat droppings are copious). As dusk approaches, the first stragglers make their way out, and as the darkness thickens, the trickle becomes a stream as about a million and a half bats shoot past like furry, flapping balls, their sonars clicking away as they avoid flying into you.

By organized tour Bang in the centre of Trinidad, Tamana is most easily reached from Sangre Grande (see below) via the Cunapo Rd. From there, it's a winding journey along heavily potholed minor roads, but as most of the route isn't signposted, and there's no easy way to find the path to the caves unless you know it, it's nigh-on impossible to visit Tamana independently. Caribbean Discovery Tours, Paria Springs, Limeland and Ieri Nature Tours (see p.38) all offer trips.

The east coast

South of **Sangre Grande**, the largest town on this side of the island and a transportation hub of considerable commercial vigour, Trinidad's **east coast** is dominated by the **Cocal**, 24km of unbroken sand lined by swaying coconut palms, that begins at **Manzanilla** and stretches south to Point Radix. Beyond here the beach continues at **Mayaro**, long a popular holiday resort with Trinidadians but almost entirely undiscovered by foreign visitors. The Manzanilla–Mayaro Road runs the length of the east coast down to Galeota Point and **Guayaguayare**, fringed inland by the pristine rainforest and mangrove-smothered wetlands of **Nariva Swamp**, a primary breeding ground and habitat for all manner of rare animals and birds, including manatees and monkeys.

By car As taxis between Sangre Grande and Manzanilla are fairly infrequent, the only practical way to explore the east coast is by car.

By public transport Manzanilla taxis leave from the Republic Bank in Sangre Grande; if you're headed on to Mayaro, you need to wait by *Hotel Carries on the Bay* in Manzanilla. Taxis are few and far between and waits can be long. There is also a rather scanty bus service between Sangre Grande and Manzanilla/Mayaro.

Sangre Grande

A thriving little market town slung along the Eastern Main Road, **SANGRE GRANDE** ("big blood", after a long-forgotten battle between Amerindians and the incoming Spanish) – pronounced "sandy grandy" but usually just called "grandy" – is a bustling transportation hub for the whole east coast from Toco to Mayaro, and the only place in the region with a bank or ATM. Residents of surrounding villages crowd the pavements every Friday to deposit wage cheques, shop at the market stalls, take a fast-food fix and drink the night away at the many **rum shops**. Most visitors pass through en route to somewhere else, or stop off to change taxis and maxis, but it's well worth diverting just south of town to check out the excellent **Velaja** cocoa estate.

Velaja Estate

Cunapo Southern Main Rd · 1hr tours Mon–Sat 9am–2pm; book in advance · US$20/person for groups of six or more, call for prices for smaller groups · ☎ 683 2203, ⓦ grandeagrotourism.com · To get there, turn right from the EMR onto Paul St (first right after ScotiaBank) as you enter town, then take another right onto Cunapo Southern Main Rd by the mosque; the estate is on the left by the 2 1/4 mile marker

This ten-acre working estate **Velaja Estate** offers a fantastic insight into traditional **cacao production**. Trinidad Select Hybrid cocoa is grown and processed on site using age-old methods, and the estate has been opened up to visitors by way of a couple of excellent tours. The "Love of Cocoa" trip takes you through the shady cocoa groves, with guides explaining how the trees are maintained and the cocoa pods harvested, and into the processing house, where the raw beans are fermented, "danced" to remove the sweet outer pulp, and then dried ready to be ground into cocoa powder; the tour also includes tasting of raw beans, cocoa nibs and a cup of hot chocolate tea. There's also a "Secrets of the Forest" tour, a moderately challenging hike up into the high reaches of the estate to learn about the trees which make up the woodlands here, and how they've been used in traditional agriculture and husbandry. Workshops on organic and hydroponic gardening are also regularly staged, as are special activities for kids; and custom-designed tours are available: call ahead to find out what's on.

ARRIVAL AND DEPARTURE
SANGRE GRANDE

By bus Buses arrive and depart from the square behind *Royal Castle* in the middle of the main drag; ask around to find the correct queue. There are early morning services to Manzanilla (5am, 6.30am, 8am & 9.30am) and to Mayaro (4.30am &

8.30am), returning straight back to Sangre Grande.
By route taxi Manzanilla Beach taxis leave from the main street, just past the police station next to the Republic Bank on the eastern side of town.

Brigand Hill Lighthouse
Daily 8am–5pm • Free

Sitting pretty on a hilltop above Manzanilla is **Brigand Hill Lighthouse**, whose sweeping views down the east coast offer a great perspective over the whole area. Built in 1958, this stubby white-painted lighthouse is one of only three in Trinidad. You can't enter the building itself, but you can climb the steep twenty-odd iron stairs that run up the outside for a magnificent **view** stretching from Toco in the north to Galeota Point in the south, taking in the Caroni Plains and the flatlands of Nariva Swamp. Red **howler monkeys** inhabit the trees around the lighthouse, and the troop passes close by each evening at around 5.30pm.

About 5km inland of Manzanilla Beach by road, the lighthouse is signposted off Plum Mitan Road, the right-hand turn at the T-junction where the main road heads down to the sea. Follow the road through Plum Mitan village, and take the signposted turn-off to the left, from where the road climbs steeply uphill. A word with the security guard should gain you entry at the gate.

Manzanilla
Lifeguards daily 10am–6pm • Changing facilities TT$1 • There's a free car park at the northern end of the beach

South of Sangre Grande, the Eastern Main Road cuts a picturesque and winding 8km route towards the Atlantic coast; underground waterflows regularly cause subsidence, so if you're driving, take things slowly. A quiet and attractive village of gingerbread houses, **MANZANILLA** village straggles along roadside and down to the sea from the T-junction at the end of the Eastern Main Road (turn left at the end of the EMR at the signpost for "Manzanilla Beach"). Windswept and exposed, the wide expanse of fine, brownish sand is usually deserted during the week but becomes a popular swimming spot at the weekends (though the murky water isn't particularly enticing), when locals descend with car boots full of food and drink. Take care while swimming, as the undercurrents can be dangerous; look out also for the jellyfish-like Portuguese man-of-war occasionally found in the waters here.

THE MANZANILLA FLOODS

In November 2014, eastern Trinidad was inundated with the highest rainfall in thirty years. Already saturated by prolonged rainy season downpours, the Nariva Swamp **flooded**, its waters overrunning the Mayaro–Manzanilla Road and completely destroying some 3km of tarmac as well as several beachside houses, and carving out brand-new watercourses into the sea.

Given the **environmental sensitivity** of the freshwater swamp, which needs to be protected from tidal salt water flowing up the channels caused by flooding, local NGOs lobbied for environmental studies on the viability of the roadway here before reconstruction began, arguing that it might be necessary to rethink rather than rebuild like-for-like. Nonetheless, construction crews moved in as soon as the waters receded, and reopened the Manzanilla–Mayaro Road by December 2014. It seems likely, though, that it will only be a matter of time before the floods return.

Manzanilla beach makes a good base from which to explore the Nariva Swamp, but though the setting is glorious, the area can feel a bit forlorn; if you're after sun and sand, head down to Mayaro. **Eating** options are few and far between; the café-bar at the beach facility often inexpensive local lunches, though opening hours are sporadic, and there are a couple of small bars and snack shops just up from the beach in Manzanilla village.

Coconut Cove 33–36 Calypso Rd, Manzanilla Beach ☎691 5939 or ☎374 8220, ⊛dcoconutcove.com. Located at the end of the dirt track past *Hotel Carries* (turn left as the coast road meets the sea at the northern end of the beach) this is Manzanilla's only "proper" hotel, right on the beach and sheltered by the Manzanilla Point headland. The smart double rooms have a/c, TV, DVD, microwave, fridge and a balcony overlooking the swimming pool and sea, and there's a restaurant on site. Limited wi-fi. TT$500

D'Hammerhead Beach Bar Manzanilla–Mayaro Rd ☎691 0034. On the main road as it meets the sea just as you enter Manzanilla, this is a basic beer joint offering cold

Carib and Stag; simple meals such as barbecue chicken and pork with fries and salad (from TT$30) are occasionally available. Daily 10am–late.

Limeland House Old Plum Rd, Manzanilla ☎668 1356 or ☎798 5750, ⊛limeland-tours.com. Located a few hundred metres along a bumpy road inland from *Dougie's* bar, just up from the beach, these two smart self-contained apartments offer a good alternative to the beachside options. Each has two bedrooms with double and twin beds and a/c, plus kitchen and bathroom. Friendly English-Trini host Kayman Sagar is a knowledgeable tour guide and mine of local information. US$100

The Cocal

Source of most of the **coconuts** sold in Trinidad, the waving groves of coconut palms that line the Manzanilla–Mayaro Road, known collectively as the **Cocal**, make for an awe-inspiring drive: 24km of graceful, leaning coconut trees dancing in the wind, with unspoilt, wave-pounded beach to one side and the wetlands of Nariva Swamp to the other. There are no hotels or restaurants anywhere along the road (the only buildings are private holidays homes), but roadside stalls sell the shellfish known as chip-chip, freshly caught crabs, black conch, fish and, in season, watermelon. Note, however, that the Manzanilla–Mayaro Road through the Cocal was impassable at the time of writing due to severe flooding of Nariva Swamp (see box, p.165).

Three-quarters of the way along, the road crosses the **Nariva River**, worth a stop for a lovely view of the mangroves along the banks; the waters are a popular swimming spot come the weekends, when cars line the roadside and chutney music blares out over the smooth sands. Nearing Mayaro (see p.168), the road runs past a coconut processing plant, surrounded by huge mounds of discarded husks. Between 5.30 and 6pm every night the air around here is raucous with the calls of the **red-chested macaws** that come to roost in the trees (binocular-toting birdwatchers often mark the spot), while the surrounding swampland is a good place to see southern lapwings and the rare red-breasted tanager. The ponds in this area are full of **cascadura**, a small brown fresh-water fish, properly known as an armoured catfish, with a tough skeletal covering.

COCONUTS

Grown on estates throughout eastern Trinidad and the southwest peninsula, **coconuts** are in constant demand on account of their sheer versatility. Depending on when they are harvested, they can be a source of drink, food, oil, soap or animal feed, while their fibrous husk makes an alternative to peat for potting plants. Green nuts are full of sweet **water**, a popular drink sold fresh from the fruit from many an old Bedford van around the country. As the nut matures, much of the liquid is replaced by an equally delicious edible white **jelly**. A few weeks later, the jelly solidifies into firm white flesh, which can be grated, dried and roasted in cooking. Later still, a bread-like substance grows in the centre of the fruit; if caught at the right time, it makes a tasty snack. Soon afterwards it develops into a sprout, from which a new tree will grow. Depending on the type, a tree will take five to ten years to mature and live for many years after that, producing nuts all year round.

NARIVA'S WILDLIFE AND ECOLOGY

Nariva is the only place in Trinidad where you can see the impossibly endearing **manatee**, or sea-cow, an elephantine mammal whose peculiar appearance once fuelled rumours of mermaids lurking in the brackish depths. Seldom seen, manatees grow up to 3m in length, weigh over 900kg, and feed on water hyacinth, moss and water lilies. They're currently in danger of extinction: in the 1970s hundreds inhabited Nariva's swampland, but their numbers are now down to around forty as a result of increased human activity in the area, notably fishermen's nets. Equally hard to spot are **freshwater turtles**, though the swamp is an excellent place to view **caimans**, **red howler monkeys** (whose rather alarming, otherworldly roars reverberate around the forest), white-fronted **capuchin monkeys** (which have been known to shower human intruders with a hail of twigs), **opossums**, **porcupines** and three-toed and silky **anteaters**. Snakes include **macajuel boa constrictors** and non-venomous, greenish-brown, black-spotted **anacondas**, which can grow up to 9m long and are the heaviest reptiles in the world. Reputedly washed here from South America on the current of the Orinoco River, they're rarely seen despite their impressive size, and there have been no known attacks on humans in Trinidad.

The swamp has many impressive **trees**, including the island's largest sandbox, with its vicious-looking spiked trunk, and plenty of cannonball trees (locally known as jumbie calabash), whose heavy fruits grow directly from the trunk. The canopies and the flatlands also harbour a wide variety of birds, from **savannah hawks** to **dicksissels**, **orange-winged** and **yellow-capped Amazon parrots**, and blue-gold and red-bellied **macaws**.

3

It's said that if you eat their chewy brown meat (invariably served curried), you'll return to end your days in Trinidad, but picking and sucking the flesh from beneath the armour is a messy business.

Nariva Swamp

One of Trinidad's most significant wildlife areas, the **Nariva Swamp** covers fifteen square kilometres behind the coconut estates along the coast south of Manzanilla. The area is made up of agricultural land (rice and watermelons are the main crops), as well as reed-fringed marshes and, between the Mayaro–Manzanilla Road and the swamp itself, mangrove thickets. Deep in the southwestern corner lies the 16 square kilometres of **Bush Bush Wildlife Sanctuary** (often referred to as an island but actually a peninsula standing around 3m higher than the surrounding land), bordered by palmiste and moriche palms and covered in hardwood forest and silk cotton trees, and designated a protected sanctuary in 1968. A unique freshwater ecosystem, Nariva harbours large concentrations of rare **wildlife**, with some 58 species of mammals, 37 species of reptiles and 171 species of birds. It's also home to 92 species of mosquito, so remember to bring your insect repellent.

The 1996 **Ramsar Convention** – to which Trinidad and Tobago is a signatory – designated the swamp a "Wetland of International Importance", placing a legal obligation on the government to protect and maintain the area. Reconciling human needs with the demands of conservation hasn't been easy, however. Many locals still hunt for both sport and sale, while illegal rice farming has destroyed much of the swamp's northern end. The government has expelled the major rice farmers, but small-scale cultivation continues. In addition, **bush fires**, often deliberately set to clear land, have ravaged almost half the territory; as a result, access is often prohibited during the dry season.

Nariva is hard to explore in any real depth independently, but if you're just passing by, it's worth taking a stroll along the signposted Kernaham Trace, which swings in from the Manzanilla–Mayaro Road to **Kernaham Village**, a widely dispersed collection of picturesque board houses, mostly on stilts, that are home to a friendly, overwhelmingly Indian community of farmers and fishermen. It's a beautiful scene, with the flatlands opening up huge expanses of open sky. Kernaham has a bar which occasionally serves food, as well as a building for worship that accommodates the community's Hindus, Muslims and Christians; it's marked with a moon and stars design on the outside, and a peek through the wall reveals icons (in picture form) of all three religions, illustrating Trinidad's strong tradition of cultural and religious acceptance.

INFORMATION AND TOURS

Organized tours If you want to visit Bush Bush and Nariva, a guide is essential; prices vary. Both Paria Springs and Caribbean Discovery Tours (see p.38) offer a marvellous walk through Bush Bush, with a kayaking/dinghy trip if water levels permit and an Indian lunch cooked by

NARIVA SWAMP

residents of Kernaham Village. Kayman Sagar of Limeland Tours (☎ 668 1356, ⓦ limeland-tours.com) is based in Manzanilla and visits the swamp regularly; his half-day tours include kayaking and a Bush Bush walk, and he's an expert on Nariva's flora and fauna.

3 Mayaro and around

Some 24km south of Manzanilla, the coast road heads inland at Point Radix, crossing over the Ortoire River and passing the local market, where stalls sell fresh fish, lobsters and strings of wriggling crabs. **MAYARO** itself has grown out of two old French villages, Pierreville and Plaisance, and is still marked as such on some maps. **Pierreville**, on the Mayaro–Guayaguayare Road, is the business end of town, a neat nexus of fast-food outlets, shops and small businesses. A side road cuts east to the village's seaside quarter, **Plaisance**, a lovely place with a thoroughly relaxing atmosphere whose greatest attraction is its **beach**, a gentle, coconut-tree-lined curve of clean, soft brown sand that's one of the most popular bathing spots on Mayaro Bay, along with **Queen's Beach** a couple of kilometres further south (signboards for the oceanside hotels here mark the turn-off from the Mayaro–Guayaguayare Road); both spots only see crowds at the weekends, however. Lifeguards keep a watch on bathers, but there are no public changing rooms, toilets or other facilities on this or any other part of the bay. The Queen's Beach resorts all have restaurants and non-guests can usually use the swimming pool at the *Radix Beach Resort* for a small charge. Note that the sea in this area has **strong currents**, so exercise caution.

Past Queen's Beach, the road swings past pasturelands and, with increasing frequency, luxurious houses built by the oil companies for their managers and workers; BP even have an entire compound, a fenced-off affair reminiscent of a 1950s holiday camp.

ACCOMMODATION, EATING AND DRINKING

MAYARO AND AROUND

As well as the places listed below, Mayaro holds a number of private houses rented out as **holiday homes**, which are advertised in the classified sections of the local papers and are great if you're travelling in a group and want to make a weekend of it. Trini holidaymakers tend to do their own cooking, often barbecuing on the beach, and most hotels have rooms with kitchens; stock up on supplies before you arrive, as the supermarkets along the Mayaro–Guayagayare Rd and in Mayaro Village aren't up to much. In terms of **restaurants**, there are several fast-food outlets, from *Subway* to *KFC* in the village centre, as well as rum shops and places selling Creole food and roti in the centre and down by Plaisance Beach.

Queen's Beach Hotel & Holiday Resort Church Rd, Radix Village ☎ 630 5532, ⓦ queensbeachresort.com. One of the largest beachside properties, and one of the few that feels like a proper resort hotel, this is a friendly place with a personal touch. The large rooms have a/c, TV, fridge and en-suite bathrooms, plus there's a lovely pool, beachside decks, two restaurants (*Chip Chip* for casual dining, *Three Palms* for more elaborate meals) and a lively bar with a pool table on site. Rates include breakfast. <u>TT$1035</u>

The Ranch Mayaro–Guayaguayare Rd ☎ 223 6798. Professionally run place with a cool a/c interior and some seating outside, great for ice-cold beers and for a spot of lunch and dinner (from TT$50), from bake and shark to fish broth and crab and dumplings, or burgers, shrimp and fish dishes. Sports games on the plasma TV and pool tables, too. Daily 10.30am–midnight, lunch Wed–Sun only.

R.A.S.H. Beachfront Resort Church Rd, Radix Village ☎ 630 7274 or ☎ 386 5803. A collection of brightly painted 1- to 4-bedroom self-contained apartments with a/c, full kitchens, cable TV, balcony and ocean views; linen is provided, but towels are not. There's a covered, hammock-slung gazebo for barbecues and chilling out, recliners for relaxing on the beach, and a pool, jacuzzi and sauna on site. TT$500

Galeota Point and Guayaguayare

The southeastern tip of Trinidad, **Galeota Point** is strictly the domain of American oil companies, with oil storage tanks dotted along the roadside and several rigs offshore. The point itself is the private reserve of Amoco. Two kilometres past Galeota Point, the road swings onto the south coast at **GUAYAGUAYARE**, a quiet fishing village with a flotilla of pirogues bobbing in the bay, which holds the distinction of having been the place where oil was first discovered on the island in 1819; the village blossomed in the early twentieth century when the petroleum industry really got going. Unless you are here in connection with the oil business, however, it's a quiet and uneventful place, with the action centred around the roadside *Sea Wall Beach and Boat Club* bar.

3

San Fernando and the south

FISHING BOAT ON COLUMBUS BAY, CEDROS

San Fernando and the south

Geographically, Trinidad's south presents a mirror image of the north: a long littoral extending beyond the main body of the island, with the low ridge of the forested Southern Range as its spine. In the Gulf of Paria, where the southwest peninsula crooks a finger towards Venezuela, Trinidad's second city, precipitous San Fernando, sits at the base of its oddly shaped landmark hill, while to the south, the vast reserves of asphalt at the Pitch Lake represents the only organized attraction in these parts.

That's as far as the comparison goes, however. San Fernando is a booming business town, but beyond its city limits lies Trinidad's most sparsely populated region. Although many southerners still earn a living from agriculture and fishing, the economy here is hinged around **oil**, pumped both from offshore rigs and the 1600-odd pumping jacks scattered all over the countryside, many in large expanses of forest which, aside from the pumps, remain largely undeveloped. The coast, meanwhile, is similarly untouched, with picturesque **Cedros** and **Icacos**, and the remote fishing village of **Moruga**, seeing few visitors, despite offering gorgeous scenery and lovely yellow-sand **beaches**, best visited during the dry season (December to May) when the sea and sand are clear; during the rainy months, rivers wash mud and a fair bit of rubbish into the sea.

Though the south isn't traditional tourist territory, you'll find that hospitality is second to none here, with locals keen to show visitors what Trini life is like away from the capital. The lack of tourism is a mixed blessing, though: there are no crowds but also few facilities for visitors. Outside of San Fernando, **accommodation** is practically nonexistent, but given the somnolent nature of the south, and its relatively compact area, you're best off staying in San Fernando anyway, exploring by way of day-trips and returning in the evenings to take advantage of the city's bars and restaurants. Given that Port of Spain is only an hour's drive from San Fernando, it's also more than possible to see the south from there.

GETTING AROUND

THE SOUTH

By car A car is easily the most convenient way to get around the south. In and around the Pitch Lake, roads can often be quite rough thanks to the bitumen seeping up to the surface; drive slowly and defensively.

By public transport San Fernando is the transport hub for south and central Trinidad, with buses, maxis and route taxis going direct to the major towns, as well as some farther flung destinations such as Erin and Cedros. As ever, waiting times can be long and public transport isn't a practical way to explore the region.

San Fernando

Nestled against the base of its eponymous flat-top hill, **SAN FERNANDO** boasts a striking setting, and despite its status as T&T's industrial capital, the city has a surprisingly old-fashioned and laidback charm. With sloping streets that are reminiscent of a miniature, low-key San Francisco, its warren of steep, winding lanes

The Brian Lara Stadium saga p.176
The highway debate p.180
Pitch perfect p.182
The Festival of La Divina Pastora p.185

Uriah Butler p.186
Columbus in Trinidad p.188
Mud volcanoes p.189

PITCH LAKE, LA BREA

Highlights

① San Fernando Trinidad's second city boasts a host of handsome gingerbread buildings and some great restaurants, bars and clubs in which to dine and lime. See pp.172–179

② Kayaking the Oropuche Lagoon An easily accessible kayak tour through rarely visited but pristine mangrove, with a variety of birdlife. See p.181

③ Pitch Lake This fascinating geological wonder is the largest natural deposit of pitch in the world. See p.181

④ Icacos and the far southwest One of the island's most stunning landscapes: quiet, undulating roads bordered by coconut plantations and wetlands, and some wild, undeveloped beaches. See p.183

⑤ Indian food at Debe Arrive in the village at dusk for the best street food on the island, from great doubles to *saheena* and super-sweet traditional sweets. See p.184

⑥ Moruga Isolated, but still accessible and with a lovely beach, this quiet and deeply religious fishing village has a unique atmosphere all its own. See p.187

HIGHLIGHTS ARE MARKED ON THE MAP ON PP.174–175

offer pretty sea views, while many weather-beaten gingerbread buildings have survived the rapid industrial development of recent years.

San Fernando – known as just "Sando" to locals – has always maintained an independent spirit. An oil city first and foremost, it sees many business visitors but few sightseers, and tourists are basically left to figure it out independently – though the friendly and hospitable residents make it a pleasurable place to get a flavour of Trini life. And in recent years, the burgeoning wealth from the natural gas and oil industries have helped to push up demand for quality entertainment, from the annual **Jazz Festival** on San Fernando Hill to a slew of high-class **bars**, **restaurants** and **clubs** alongside the many more grass-roots options for dining, drinking and partying.

Bordered by the Gulf of Paria on one side and the rocky, wooded outcrop of **San Fernando Hill** on the other, the city's compact centre is easily negotiated on foot, with most of the historical sights, shops and transport stands located on and around **Harris Promenade**, a broad, elegant boulevard running west from the main junction and focal point, **Library Corner**.

Brief history

Having served as a sacred spot for Amerindian tribes, San Fernando's first European arrival was **Sir Walter Raleigh**, who put to shore here during a voyage in 1595 – he was unimpressed and sailed on. **Capuchin priests** established a mission in 1687, but the settlement only began to flourish after 1784, when French plantation owners attracted by the *cedula* (see p.250) were allocated land here and established the first estates; in the same year, Spanish governor José Maria Chacon named the settlement San Fernando de Naparima in honour of King Carlos III's new son. By 1797, when the British captured the island, San Fernando had more than a thousand inhabitants, twenty sugar mills and eight rum distilleries. Surrounded by fertile agricultural land, the town continued to grow, and by 1811 the population had

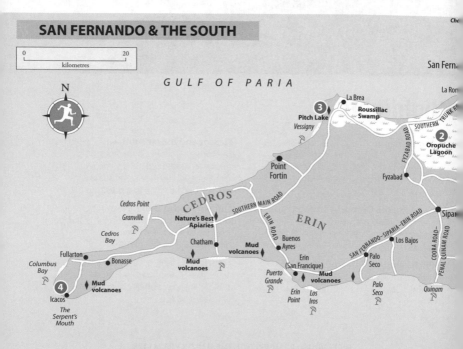

SAN FERNANDO & THE SOUTH

trebled; by the middle of the century, it was the hub of the entire south, a busy trading centre for the region's planters, with a regular coastal steamer to Port of Spain – the overland route took three days of rough riding through forests and swamps. The arrival of the **railway** in 1882 led to another population increase, and by the late 1880s San Fernando had been thoroughly modernized. Suburbs grew as the plantations disappeared – the result of falling sugar prices in the 1920s – and the town was soon dominated by the expanding **oil industry**. Designated a city in 1988, San Fernando continued to expand through the early 1990s, bringing the northern city limits up to the oil refinery at Point-a-Pierre and increasing its population by around 10,000 (it's a little over 60,000 today), with many inhabitants moving out to the chocolate-box housing developments on the eastern outskirts of town.

San Fernando Hill

Circular Courts Rd • Daily 9am–6pm • Free • The clearly signposted road to the summit is off Circular Rd next to *Soong's Great Wall* restaurant

At 200m high, **San Fernando Hill** overshadows the town centre, and has long been a sacred place for **Amerindian** tribes from the South American mainland, who made annual pilgrimages to the site from 6500 BC up to the early 1900s. According to legend, the hill is the final resting place of Haburi the Hero and his mother, who were fleeing from the Frog Woman in the Orinoco Delta in Venezuela; on reaching Trinidad, however, they were turned into "Anaparima", the original Amerindian name for the hill. Half flattened, with steep protruding points, it owes its modern-day profile to years of gravel mining, which lopped off a third of its original height. Protests by locals saw quarrying put to a stop and the hill declared a national park in 1980.

The summit has been landscaped, with shaded picnic tables, a children's playground, café, public toilets and several lookouts from which to enjoy the **views**; there's a telescope mounted on the open balcony of the new visitor centre. The panorama

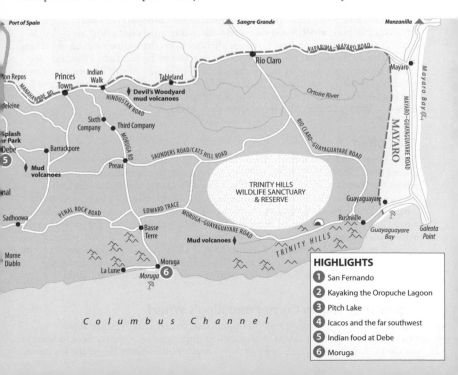

HIGHLIGHTS

1. San Fernando
2. Kayaking the Oropuche Lagoon
3. Pitch Lake
4. Icacos and the far southwest
5. Indian food at Debe
6. Moruga

THE BRIAN LARA STADIUM SAGA

Adjacent to the ice-cream colours of the new housing developments east of San Fernando are the floodlights of the controversial **Brian Lara Stadium**, adjacent to the highway at Tarouba. Supposed to have been completed in 2007 for the Cricket World Cup, the still unfinished complex has become a huge white elephant, shrouded in accusations of corruption that led to an investigation by a Commission of Enquiry into UDeCOTT, the state company responsible for its construction. To date, the project has eaten up more than TT$850 million of public funds, and may need another TT$200 million to complete – though some experts assert that the geological fragility of the site means that it could never support a cricket pitch.

---

includes the city and the exclusive St Joseph Village suburb, the Gulf of Paria and the flaming chimneys at Point-a-Pierre and Point Lisas, and the ever-growing suburbs and agricultural plains of the interior.

Harris Promenade

The centre of San Fernando's civic life and the location of several attractive colonial-era buildings, **Harris Promenade** stretches from the long 1950s-style facade of **San Fernando General Hospital** to Library Corner in the east, its shady paved centre dotted with benches and tables, an ornate Victorian bandstand and **statues** of Mahatma Gandhi and Jamaican black rights activist Marcus Garvey. On the southwestern end, the distinctive yellow-stone building with its curving arched windows is the city's **police station**; half of it remains roofless after a fire in 2009. Across the road, the grand Neoclassical **City Hall** from 1930 dominates the western end of the promenade, though it faces stiff competition from the Catholic **Church of Our Lady of Perpetual Help** one block to the east, a huge white modern building with a tall clock tower that can be seen from most places in the city.

The promenade's two roads converge in front of the **Carnegie Free Library**, an ornate terracotta pile built in 1919 and financed – like many others the world over – by the Scottish philanthropist Andrew Carnegie. Behind it, on the promenade, an old **steam locomotive** recalls the last run from Port of Spain to San Fernando in 1968. People packed the carriages, hanging out of the windows to be part of this historic occasion, which was subsequently immortalized by the late Lord Kitchener's famous calypso *Last Train to San Fernando*. The chaotic junction of seven roads just east of the library is known as **Library Corner**, with its modern clock tower.

The Coffee

Coffee Street, south of Carib Street, takes its name from the coffee plantations that once thrived here. "The Coffee", as it's familiarly known, was the original home of many of the south's **steel bands**, including the highly acclaimed **Fonclaire**, now located on Dottin Street, one block south of Coffee Street. A brightly painted statue of a pan player at the junction of Coffee and Cipero streets celebrates the area's musical heritage. A little further down Coffee Street opposite the Southern Food Basket supermarket is the panyard of the **Skiffle Bunch**, a regular participant in the Panorama Finals at Carnival time. Just past the panyard, on the corner of Cipero Street, a statue of a lone pannist attests to the importance of T&T's national instrument to the area. The Coffee is particularly lively during the run-up to Carnival, when Skiffle Bunch practice sessions ring out into the street.

High Street, Happy Corner and King's Wharf

High Street is San Fernando's main shopping drag, where street vendors hawk everything from plastic trinkets to leopardskin underwear on the pavement in front of the stores. At its western end, as High Street doglegs into Queen Street, the sea comes into view. This area, ironically known as **Happy Corner**, is the most run-down in the city, but a few colonial buildings, including *Hotel Happy Corner* (a flophouse) with its pretty balcony overlooking the junction of Queen and King streets, provide some architectural interest, while the patrons of the local rum shops add a touch of raffish zest. Happy Corner gives onto **King's Wharf**, a scruffy tarmac dock fronting a small harbour where fishing boats bob up and down on the swell; the adjacent **fish market** stands next to the **Water Taxi Terminal**.

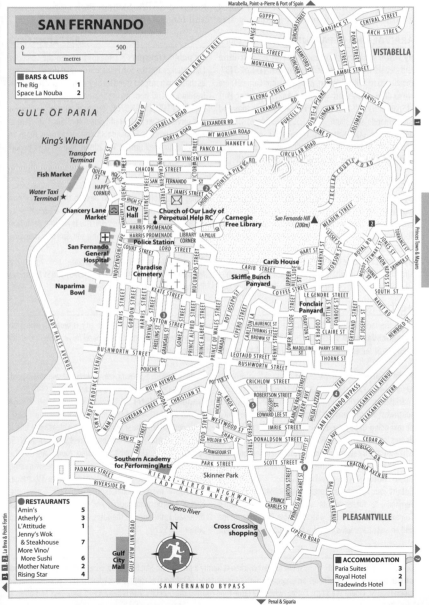

SAN FERNANDO

Marabella, Point-a-Pierre & Port of Spain

0   500
metres

BARS & CLUBS
The Rig   1
Space La Nouba   2

GULF OF PARIA

VISTABELLA

King's Wharf

Transport Terminal

Fish Market

Water Taxi Terminal

Chancery Lane Market

City Hall

Church of Our Lady of Perpetual Help RC

Carnegie Free Library

San Fernando Hill (200m)

San Fernando General Hospital

Police Station

Paradise Cemetery

Naparima Bowl

Carib House

Skiffle Bunch Panyard

Fonclair Panyard

Southern Academy for Performing Arts

Skinner Park

Cipero River

Cross Crossing shopping

Gulf City Mall

PLEASANTVILLE

RESTAURANTS
Amin's   5
Atherly's   3
L'Attitude   1
Jenny's Wok
  & Steakhouse   7
More Vino/
  More Sushi   6
Mother Nature   2
Rising Star   4

ACCOMMODATION
Paria Suites   3
Royal Hotel   2
Tradewinds Hotel   1

SAN FERNANDO BYPASS

Penal & Siparia

Lady Hales Avenue

Lady Hales Avenues skirts the coast then veers east through the southern part of the city (where it runs parallel with the Rienzi-Kirton Highway), close to San Fernando's two major **shopping malls**, the enormous Gulf City and Cross Crossing, with their food courts and scores of International shops, and the **Southern Academy for Performing Arts** (SAPA), the sister building to the one on the Queen's Park Savannah in Port of Spain, and without its northern counterpart's infrastructural problems; it's regularly used for concerts and other events. Just past SAPA, **Skinner Park** cricket ground serves as a venue for regular concerts and fetes as well as sporting events.

ARRIVAL AND DEPARTURE   SAN FERNANDO

By water taxi Services to and from Port of Spain arrive and depart from the Water Taxi Terminal (☏ 624 5137, ⓦ nidco.co.tt) at King's Wharf, just past Happy Corner. There are six daily services each way on weekdays, departing Port of Spain every half-hour from 5–8am and then at 3pm, and San Fernando at 6.30am, 7am, 1.30pm, 3.30pm, 4.30pm and 5.30pm. On Saturdays there's just one service, departing San Fernando at 9.30am, and Port of Spain at 4.45pm. Journey time is 45min and tickets cost TT$15.

By public transport A large lot between the Chancery Lane Market and the San Fernando General Hospital serves as the main transport stand for buses, maxis and route taxis heading to and from all destinations in the south of the country. PTSC (☏ 652 3705, ⓦ ptsc.co.tt) runs an express bus service between Port of Spain (Mon–Sat from 5am to 8.20pm) and San Fernando (Mon–Sat from 4.30am to 7.40pm); journey time is 1hr 20min, and services depart every 15–20min.

GETTING AROUND

By car Given the city's sprawling layout and its numerous hills, you'll need a car or public transport to get around if heading away from the centre. Car rental is available from Southern (☏ 657 8541, ⓦ southernsalestt.com) or Alamo (☏ 826 6893, ⓦ alamo.com).

By route taxi Route taxis ply the streets around the clock; almost all routes originate at – or at least pass through – Library Corner, but be sure to ask the driver where he's

going before getting in. From next to the *KFC* in Library Corner, "round the road" taxis follow a loop around the city centre, circling San Fernando Hill; this is also the departure point for taxis to the Cross Crossing and Gulf City shopping malls.

By private taxi Two local private taxi firms are Mattadeen's Taxicab Service (☏ 658 4973) and St Anthony's Taxicab Co-Operative (☏ 648 3941).

ACCOMMODATION

Given the lack of tourist infrastructure and the expense accounts of business travellers, the city is woefully short on **accommodation** at the cheaper end of the spectrum. Be aware that the disarmingly named *Hotel Tokyo*, right in the city centre on St James St, and *Villa Capri* in Marabella just north of San Fernando, are both brothels.

Paria Suites Southern Main Rd, La Romaine ☏ 697 1442, ⓦ pariasuites.com ⓦ techadmi9.wix.com /pariasuites. Overlooking the Gulf of Paria a few kilometres southwest of San Fernando, but easily reached on any maxi or taxi going to La Brea, Point Fortin, Fyzabad or Siparia. Rooms come with a/c, private bathrooms and cable TV, while an on-site swimming pool, restaurant and busy bar provide welcome entertainment. Wi-fi available. US$125
Royal Hotel 46–54 Royal Rd ☏ 652 4881, ⓦ royal hoteltt.com. As central a location as you're going to get in San Fernando, a fifteen-minute walk from Library Corner. Comfortable, bright rooms with a/c, cable TV, phone, fridge and en-suite bathrooms. There's a breezy open-air restaurant

on site, as well as a pleasant, reasonably large swimming pool. Rates include continental breakfast and wi-fi. US$148.50
Tradewinds Hotel 38 London St, St Joseph Village ☏ 652 9463, ⓦ tradewindshotel.com. The best-equipped hotel in the south, occupying a pleasant – albeit not very central – location on a breezy hill in quiet St Joseph Village. The most appealing rooms are in the renovated and ultramodern building next to the swimming pool, bar and restaurant, all with a/c, cable TV, fridge, microwave oven, minibar, kettle and nice bathrooms. There's a large gym, jacuzzi and free wi-fi; good buffet breakfast is included in the rates, as is a shuttle to Piarco airport. US$170

EATING

Grabbing a quick fix of roti, chow mein or fried chicken is hardly a problem in San Fernando, where numerous **fast-food outlets** line the streets. There's an especially high concentration of informal places for weekday lunches or early dinners along High St, Cipero St and the Coffee, while the large food court at the Gulf City Mall is heaving on Saturdays and offers a variety of food for most tastes. If you're after some evening **street food**, check the stalls that set up on Lady Hales Ave opposite Skinner Park, serving corn soup, doubles and the like.

Amin's 10 Cipero St ☎ 652 5108. Reckoned by many to be the best roti shop in town, with all the usual fillings and long queues forming at lunchtime. Food tends to run out by 2 or 3pm, so go early. Rotis from TT$25. Mon–Sat 7am–5pm.

Atherly's 34 Sutton St ☎ 652 7373. Relocated to a more central spot, *Atherly's* offers inexpensive, reliable Creole and Indian dishes (from TT$60), principally at lunchtime, when there's a buffet on Wednesdays. Good for a drink in the evenings, when a DJ plays a nice selection of calypso, reggae and old hits Tues–Sun, and there's a happy hour on Friday evenings. Daily 10am–2am.

★ **L'Attitude** 18–24 Quenca St ☎ 657 8033. Upmarket place with an innovative international menu; starters (from TT$50) include mussels in tequila or scallops with mushrooms and cream; mains (TT$100 upwards) range from duck or lamb in almond butter to lobster thermidore, pepper T-bone steaks, and signature Chicken L'Attitude with shrimp, white wine and lime. There's a good cocktail menu, and the upstairs terrace adds to the cosy ambience. Good lunch deals during the week. Mon–Fri 11am–2.30pm, Tues–Sat 6–10pm.

Jenny's Wok & Steakhouse 175 Cipero Rd, Victoria Village ☎ 652 1807. Located some distance from the town centre in a warehouse-dominated industrial area, but a popular after-work liming spot all the same with its large, three-sided American-style bar and decent, though somewhat pricey, Chinese food, steaks and seafood (mains from TT$70). Delivery available. Mon–Thurs 11am–10pm, Fri & Sat 11am–11pm.

★ **More Vino/More Sushi** 33 Scott St ☎ 223 8466, ⓦ morevino.com. The sister establishment of the enduringly popular Ariapita Ave sushi restaurant-cum-wine bar, the southern version is just as good, with a wide variety of rolls and sashimi (from TT$88) to katsu curry (from TT$78) to pad Thai (TT$68) to Italian pastas. Great wine list and cocktails, and a lively liming spot. Mon–Wed 11am–midnight, Thurs–Sat 11am–1am.

Mother Nature 58 St James St ☎ 313 0777. This shop and café is known for its good range of inexpensive natural juices and vegetarian snacks, alongside "miracle" vitamin supplements. Provides a good break from the downtown Sando mayhem. Lunch is around TT$40. Mon–Sat 6am–3pm.

Rising Star M. Rampersad Building, Hilda Lazzari Terrace ☎ 685 9539. Busy place, serving a huge menu of reasonably priced Chinese food (around TT$50 per half-portion) including good veggie options, as well as steaks and grilled chicken and fish (TT$90–120), while the bar area makes a good liming spot, with regular live music. You can puff away on hookah pipes, too. Daily 10am–late.

DRINKING, NIGHTLIFE AND ENTERTAINMENT

The city's numerous friendly **rum shops** remain the evening of choice for the majority of locals – the ideal place to sink a few beers and partake in some drunken conversation. There are also some lively bars, and several of the restaurants listed above are good for a drink. San Fernando also has several **cinemas**, each catering to distinctly different tastes. Many of the restaurants listed below are also a good bet for a drink

BARS AND CLUBS

The Rig Southern Trunk Rd, La Romaine ☎ 653 9129. Just on the outskirts of town, this is a busy, popular bar with regular live music and a buzzing atmosphere. Food also available, and there are regular drinks promotions. Daily 10am–late.

Space La Nouba Southern Trunk Rd, La Romaine ☎ 697 1165, ⓦ spacetrinidad.com. Purpose-built circular building with a Star Trek-style interior, this is an ever-busy spot, with regular drinks-inclusive nights and a changing music selection each week. Cover around TT$100. Wed, Fri & Sat 10pm–4am.

LIVE MUSIC VENUES

Naparima Bowl 19 Paradise Pasture ☎ 657 8770. A worthy venue year-round.

Skinner Park Rienzi-Kirton Hwy ☎ 657 7168. At the southern edge of the city, hosts Carnival fetes and concerts; entrance tickets vary.

Southern Academy for the Performing Arts Cnr Rienzi-Kirton Hwy & Todd St ☎ 657 4380, ext 1245. Two large theatres used for concerts and plays.

DIRECTORY

Banks and exchange facilities First Citizens, High St, at Penitence ☎ 652 2757; Republic, 92–94 Cipero St ☎ 652 3736; Scotiabank, Cipero St, at Rushworth ☎ 657 7109. All have ATMs. FX Trader at Tropical Trends, La Pique Plaza, High St, or Ground Floor, Gulf City Mall (☎ 657 1812), has the best rates on currency exchange.

Hospital San Fernando General, Independence Ave (☎ 652 3581).

Pharmacy SuperPharm, Gulf City Mall, Southern Trunk Rd, La Romaine ☎ 653 9934. Mon–Sat 9am–10.30pm, Sun 9am–9pm.

Police The main police station is at the western end of Harris Promenade ☎ 652 3206.

Post office Carlton Centre, St James St. Mon–Fri 7am–5pm, Sat 8am–2pm.

The southwest peninsula

Often referred to as the "deep south", Trinidad's **southwest peninsula** offers a mix of gritty industrial development around oil towns such as **Point Fortin**, **Siparia** and **Fyzabad** as well as some marvellous drives to sleepy backwaters such as **Erin** and down through teak plantations to gorgeous beaches like **Quinam**, where the soft brown sand is backed by red-earth cliffs and lapped by calm seas – an escapist's fantasy and usually deserted apart from the odd fisherman. Heading along the Southern Main Road down to Trinidad's extreme southwest tip takes you though seaside **Cedros** and down through the vast coconut plantations around Columbus Bay to **Icacos Point**, with its rugged fishing beach and pretty wetlands. The atmosphere in this part of Trinidad is irresistibly low-key – and this tranquillity, along with the scenery, is its main draw.

Despite its proximity to industrial San Fernando, and its threatened status thanks to the construction of the new highway between San Fernando and Point Fortin (see below) the mangrove swampland of the **Oropuche Lagoon** remains a wildlife haven, teeming with tropical birds and seldom visited. The area's most important tourist site, though, is the unique **Pitch Lake** at **La Brea**, an interesting and worthwhile excursion if you are in the area. As to culinary exploration, look no further than the delicious roti shops and street-food stalls of **Debe**, one of Trinidad's most wholeheartedly Indian settlements.

4

THE HIGHWAY DEBATE

For those living in southern Trinidad, commuting from outlying centres such as Point Fortin and Debe to San Fernando and beyond has long been a wretched experience, with gridlocked traffic stretching for miles along the single-lane main roads at peak hours. To alleviate the congestion, the government has begun a huge **road building programme**, extending the Solomon Hochoy Highway south of San Fernando to Point Fortin, and constructing a second highway, between Debe and Mon Desir, to link the old and new portions of the Solomon Hochoy.

Though many have greeted the prospect of a quicker commute with open arms, there has also been plenty of opposition, principally from the **Highway Re-Route Movement** (HRM), a lobby group led by environmentalist and academic **Dr Wayne Kublalsingh**. The HRM argued that the route of the Debe–Mon Desir road was going straight through the ecologically sensitive Oropuche Lagoon, as well as several small communities, necessitating the demolition of some 300 homes; they also questioned the immense estimated costs (TT$5.5 billion) of constructing the link road. In 2012, Kublalsingh embarked on a **hunger strike** as a protest against the plans, which ended after 21 days when the government agreed to hold an independent review of the highway plans. Published in late 2013 and known as the **Armstrong Report**, the review recommended that the highway construction be halted to enable a re-assesment of the project's social and economic impacts, and identified several problems regarding the fulfilling of conditions contained in the Certificate of Environmental Clearance (CEC) issued for the highway by the Environmental Management Authority.

Despite having agreed in principle to abide by the conclusions of the Armstrong Report, the government did not cease construction and continued with the project as per its original plans; and on September 17th 2014, Kublalsingh began a **second hunger strike**, vowing only to begin eating if the government abide by the Armstrong recommendations, and open up negotiations with the HRM to discuss alternatives to the link route. Despite the vocal public support of many local luminaries, from mas maker Peter Minshall to Roman Catholic priest Clive Harvey, alongside protest marches and a 40-day fast by HRM supporters, PM Kamla Persad-Bissessar has so far remained steadfast in her refusal to negotiate.

It's difficult to predict what the final outcome of the HRM's protests will be, but for the time being, any journey into southern Trinidad involves negotiating the various roadworks of the highway construction.

Oropuche Lagoon

Eco Sense tours Sat & Sun only, US$50 • ☎ 766 4035 or ☎ 625 5472, ⊚ trinikayak.tripod.com

Spreading back from the Southern Main Road some 6km south of San Fernando, the little-visited tidal mangrove swamps of the **Oropuche Lagoon** have been left relatively undisturbed, and are an excellent place to view **butterflies** as well as **birds** such as egrets, black-bellied whistling duck, American bittern, ringed kingfish, white-headed marsh tyrant, pygmy kingfisher, spotted toddy flycatcher and a variety of herons. The best way to explore is by **kayak**: Sham at Eco Sense Nature Tours organizes a superb half-day trip for both novice and advanced kayakers, beginning at 7am at the mouth of the river and returning at lunchtime. Paria Springs (see p.38) also includes the Oropuche Lagoon on its excellent West Coast Wetlands and Icacos **birding tours**, tending to go to the inland areas of the swamp at dusk.

Rousillac

Just south of Oropuche, **ROUSILLAC** is best known for the landmark **roadside pepper sauce** stall at the community's southwestern end. Run by the Thomas family for the past 25 years, the stacks of brightly coloured fine pepper, tamarind and chadon beni sauces, alongside lime pepper, the fiery "mother-in-law" and mango chutneys, is impossible to miss and makes a great photo opportunity as well as a chance to take home a truly authentic taste of Trinidad.

La Brea

Taking its name from the Spanish word for "pitch", the community of **LA BREA** (also called Union village) is usually bypassed by those en route to the **Pitch Lake**. One of the first two oil wells in the world was drilled here in 1857 by the American Merrimac Oil Company, but even with the omnipresent pumping jacks and the fact that the lake has been commercially exploited since the early twentieth century, it's one of Trinidad's more impoverished communities today. Spreading back from the main road towards the sea, La Brea's many colonial-era buildings are well worth a look: the grand old police station and courthouse right at the water's edge are particularly impressive, as is the old rum shop at the village's centre (if it hasn't been pulled down by the time you visit like so many old buildings in Trinidad), which makes for an atmospheric stopoff for a quick drink.

Vessigny Beach

3km south of La Brea • Lifeguards daily 10am–6pm • Changing rooms TT$1

The wide brown sands and shallow waters of **Vessigny Beach** are popular with Trinis at weekends. There are changing rooms, a snack bar and kayaks for rent, but it's not especially appealing for swimming as a river discharges muddy water into the bay here.

Pitch Lake

Southern Main Rd, 1.5km south of La Brea • Daily 9am–5pm • Tours TT$50 • ☎ 651 1232

Just south of La Brea, the **Pitch Lake** is touted by some Trinis as the eighth wonder of the world. It may not look particularly impressive from a distance, bearing a remarkable resemblance to a flooded car park (albeit one ringed with cashew trees and Bird of Paradise flowers), but this 40,000-square-metre site is the largest deposit of pitch in the world, and it's well worth taking a guided tour of the lake to learn more about its intriguing complexities.

PITCH PERFECT

La Brea's **Pitch Lake** was formed some five to six million years ago, when asphaltic oil flowed into a huge mud volcano here and slowly developed into pitch. Some 180 tonnes are now extracted each day, to be refined into asphalt and used to pave roads the world over. The depth of the lake is estimated at 75m and the level of pitch rises naturally after each excavation – calculations suggest that there's enough to last four or five centuries, but nonetheless the surface is several metres lower than it was when excavation began in 1867.

Amerindians believed that the lake was created to punish a Carib tribe that killed and ate the sacred hummingbird, and were swallowed up in its depths. **Sir Walter Raleigh** was the first European "discoverer", happening upon the lake in 1595, and using the pitch to caulk his ships, while colonial governor Sir Ralph Woodford used it to pave over the capital's dirt roads in 1815, making Port of Spain the first city in the world with asphalt streets. Control of pitch excavation remained in British hands until 1978, when it was taken over by the T&T government.

The pitch lake is not the only place hereabouts that asphalt swells from the earth: local **roads** are often excruciatingly bumpy thanks to upward pressure from the underground volcanic eruptions that replenish the lake, while many a front garden or driveway hereabouts is paved with lumpy local pitch.

Although there's nothing stopping you from exploring the lake on your own, it's pretty much essential to take a **guided tour**; some parts of the lake are unsafe to walk on, and a guide will provide some illuminating commentary as well as ensuring that you stay safe (and don't leave with your shoes covered in tar). Official guides (identifiable by their orange T&T-monogrammed shirts) are available via the museum, the complex on your left as you enter the lake. On arrival you'll probably be approached by unofficial guides, too, who will usually negotiate on tour prices and who are based at the yellow snack shop on the left as you enter the lake; they charge a little less but may not offer as full a tour.

Taking up some 25 percent of the total surface, the gooey, tar-like "**mother of the lake**" is not firm enough to walk on and virtually impossible to remove if caught on clothing – soft patches are difficult for the uninitiated to recognize, and guides will guide you through safely. They'll also explain the lake's history and its various geological features, and use a stick to scoop up some of the soft tar, which feeds the pitch, but is in itself useless for making asphalt. Dotted with reeds and water lilies and frequented by wading birds, the pretty pools around the edges of the lake are popular spots for locals to take an evening dip, as their sulphur-rich waters are said to be good for mosquito bites and skin conditions. Lake tours also include a look around the **museum**, which covers the lake's history, from the Amerindian legends to commercial pitch extraction.

Point Fortin

The south's industrial flavour continues at the oil town of **POINT FORTIN**. The tennis courts, golf course and old country club were built for expat managers by Shell (former owners of the refinery here), while the suburbs are characterized by sprawling houses with high walls and barking dogs. Point Fortin offers very little to visitors unless you happen to have a personal interest in the oil industry, and only comes to life after 4pm, when workers come out to lime in the **bars** and hang around the main junction. By far the best time to visit Point Fortin is for the annual **Borough Day** celebrations at the beginning of May: two weeks of Carnival revelry and music and dance competitions, including its own raucous Jouvert morning and a two-day procession: see ⓦpointalive.com for more information.

South Western Court 16 Cap-de-Ville Main Rd ☎ 648 0075, ⓦ swc-hotel.com. Useful for Borough Day or as an alternative southern base to Sando, this is a fifteen-room business-oriented place with large dining and conference facilities, wi-fi and bright a/c rooms with cable TV, some with balconies. It's obliquely opposite the market. In the unlikely event that the rooms here are full, ask about the nearby sister property, *Clifton Hill Manor*. <u>US$143</u>

Cedros

The catch-all name for the extreme tip of the southwest peninsula, **CEDROS** was first settled by Spaniards, whose influence lingered longer in this isolated region than in the rest of the island; despite an influx of Indian indentured labourers, Spanish was still widely spoken until the 1880s, almost a century after the British had captured Trinidad. During the nineteenth-century heyday of the sugar estates, Cedros was a bustling place, with twice the population of today and no less than seven rum distilleries. These are long-gone, however, and Cedros village is a fairly sleepy place today, its network of residential streets spreading back from a seafront promenade. In the middle of the bay is a concrete jetty, kept busy by local fishermen and the many Venezuelans who make the nine-mile pirogue journey from the mainland to Trinidad to shop, checking in at the village's tiny customs post before heading in to San Fernando's malls

Nature's Best

Off the Southern Main Rd, just outside Cedros • No set hours • Call to arrange a visit ☎ 690 2061 or ☎ 330 5462

Nature's Best is one of three apiaries in the area, and manufactures beeswax, royal jelly and a couple of skin- and hair-care products. You can view the production process and buy some products at source at the home of apiary owner Chunilal Roopnarine, a font of information on bee-keeping in Trinidad.

Cedros beaches

Every bay in Cedros seems to have a picture-postcard **beach**, where the idyllic setting more than compensates for the total lack of facilities. At **Chatham**, a left turn runs about 6km to the south coast, where there's a picturesque and deserted beach of sand and red rocks. The beach at **Granville** is so far off the beaten track – 5.5km from the Southern Main Road through the village of the same name, about halfway between Point Fortin and Icacos Point – that it's often completely deserted.

Columbus Bay

Some 2km from the roadside village of **Fullarton** is the lovely **Columbus Bay**, a long stretch of beach lined with the coconut palms of the huge San Rafael Estate, one of the most extensive in Trinidad. The eye-popping views extend down to the South American mainland, and looking southwest it's difficult to tell where Trinidad ends and Venezuela begins. It's a view that's changed little from the one that greeted the eponymous explorer when he stopped here after landing at Moruga in 1498 (see box, p.188); just offshore lie the three **Sisters Rocks**, while the eastern end of the bay is capped by the brown sandstone Los Gallos Point, its cliffs eroded into intricate formations by the tides. Columbus Bay attracts small crowds of bathers at weekends, and there are basic facilities available, including a bathroom/changing room and a snack shop.

Icacos Point

Southwest of Columbus Bay, the views become ever more spectacular as the road winds through the coconut plantation and along a causeway through some beautiful

4

wetlands, with acres of marsh and limpid pools home to a huge variety of birds – look out for **scarlet ibis**, which roost here at dusk. Past the wetlands, the road winds down to the sleepy little village of **Icacos** ("eye-*car*-cus"), a tiny place that nonetheless has a mosque, church and Hindu temple. Turn right when you arrive at the village and walk for about twenty minutes along a track bordered by coconut trees to reach **Icacos Point**, Trinidad's extreme southwest tip. It's a faraway spot, with the vague outline of the Venezuelan coast 11km away across the **Serpent's Mouth**, whose swirling waters don't deter the drug smugglers who use the area's beaches to bring in Colombian cocaine via Venezuela, eventually destined for the American mainland. Nine kilometres west out to sea, the craggy silhouette of **Soldado Rock** marks the division between Venezuelan and Trinidadian territorial waters, and is a major breeding site for frigate birds, grey-breasted martins and brown pelicans, and a nesting site of sooty and noddy terns.

Erin

Blessed with many pretty villages and little-visited beaches, the area east of Cedros and south of Point Fortin and La Brea is known as **ERIN**. Driving from the Cedros side, tiny **Buenos Ayres** is especially attractive, with beautifully dilapidated colonial houses and a couple of good rum shops. **Erin village** (San Francique on many maps) is equally easy on the eye, with old board houses set in flowering gardens and fishing boats bobbing in the bay – this is one of Trinidad's most important fishing villages. During the fishing season (June–Dec), **Puerto Grande** beach buzzes with activity, as fishermen land their catch and weigh it on large old-fashioned scales at the shoreline, discussing prices in discreet tones, while nets are mended or laid out to dry on the sand. It's a fascinating scene, though things are a lot quieter out of season, when the boats move to Moruga to follow the fish.

Erin's beaches

The Erin area has some attractive secluded bathing spots off the San Fernando–Siparia–Erin Road. Some 2km east of Puerto Grande via a signposted turn-off, the pretty cove of **Los Iros** offers calm, clean waters and a small snack parlour and bar; at weekends, whole families descend with Sunday lunch loaded into pots, containers and coolers. Eight kilometres east of Erin village, there's another marvellous beach at **Palo Seco Bay**; turn onto Beach Road by the YKC & Son supermarket in Palo Seco village. Park at the Petrotrin beach club, and walk for fifteen minutes along a dirt road to reach the driftwood-scattered 4km beach.

Debe

On the southern outskirts of San Fernando at **La Romaine**, a left turn by *Paria Suites* hotel brings you onto the San Fernando–Siparia–Erin Road (usually shortened to the SS–Erin Road), which threads through the wholeheartedly Indian communities of the island's oil belt. Note, however, that at the time of writing the junction was being worked on as part of the new highway extension (see box, p.180), and the road layout may well change once the highway link road is constructed. Heralded by the riot of clashing shop signs that wouldn't look out of place in the Delhi of Kolkata, the first town of any size is **DEBE**, credited for the invention of doubles, Trinidad's most popular street food (see p.28). Doubles are sold at the roadside daily from 6am, and as the afternoon cools down, vendors also set up stalls selling a huge variety of fantastic **Indian snacks**, from pholouri to the less widely available *baigani* (sliced aubergine in batter), *saheena* (split-pea and dasheen-leaf fritters) and *katchourie*, fried fingers of ground channa and spices; sweets include *kurma* doughballs, milk and ginger *barfi*, and *jalebi*, a sticky neon orange curl of fried

---

THE FESTIVAL OF LA DIVINA PASTORA

Held on the second Sunday after Easter since the early twentieth century, Siparia's **Festival of La Divina Pastora** holds a special place in Trinidad's religious calendar as the only day of the year on which Hindus worship at a Catholic church. The celebrations are centred around the Black Virgin statue, who is decked out in new clothes and carried in procession through the streets to the beat of *tassa* drums, and showered with offerings of gold bracelets, flowers, sweets, fruit, oil and money. The festival is one big street party, with the whole town coming out to celebrate, and culminates in a blow-out feast. Though the statue's origins are hazy, she's said to have been responsible for many miracles, while Spiritual Baptists accredit her with mystical powers. Hindus associate her with the goddess Kali, the destroyer of sorrow, and call her **Siparee Mai** or Mother of Siparia. Before the festival, special barbers set up along the main street to give Hindu children their first haircut, with the locks then being presented as offerings to the statue in the hope of ensuring good luck in the year ahead.

---

batter. Debe and its neighbour, **PENAL**, are both known for their lively **Diwali celebrations**, when the streets are lit up at nights and Indian dancers and *tassa* drummers provide the entertainment.

Fun Splash Water Park

M2 Ring Rd, north of Debe • Daily 10am–6pm • Adults TT$70, children TT$30 • ☎ 647 0350, ⓦ funsplashtnt.com

The excellent **Fun Splash Water Park** offers a welcome chance to cool off, with pools (one is for adults only) and eleven water-slides for adults and kids, plus kayaking and pedal boats; there are picnic areas and snack shops on site, plus a sizeable car park, and you can bring your own coolers. Ample parking, too.

Siparia

Penal slides imperceptibly into **SIPARIA**, though the main street here retains a few attractive **colonial houses** alongside the concrete storefronts. As well as poking around the central produce market, it's worth peeking into the **La Divina Pastora Catholic church** (follow the road that branches off the Southern Main Road opposite Republic Bank) to see the **Black Virgin**, a small statue of the Virgin Mary which is carried through the streets as the centrepiece of the annual La Divina Pastora festival.

Quinam Beach

Lifeguards daily 10am–6pm

South of Siparia, the Coora Road/Penal–Quinam Road (turn off the SS–Erin Road just before *KFC* and follow the signs) swings past pumping jacks and through teak plantations to **Quinam Beach**, the south coast's most popular swimming spot, with a wide swathe of sand at low tide overlooked by crumbling cliffs studded with Baptist, Muslim and Hindu prayer flags and devotional figurines. There are several thatch-roofed barbecue pits close to the car park, but unless you're here at the weekend, when vendors sell snacks and drinks, you'll need to bring your own refreshment.

Fyzabad

North of Siparia, the Siparia–Fyzabad Road strikes north towards the coast; some 5km along, the rather raggle-taggle **FYZABAD** was named by Indian indentured workers after the Uttar Pradesh district where most of them hailed from. After oil was discovered here in 1917, the town became the centre of the emergent labour movement, while the original Indo-Trinidadian Presbyterian community were quickly outnumbered by migrants from Grenada and St Vincent who came to work on the oilfields, and whose descendants make up the majority of the town's population today.

URIAH BUTLER

Trinidad's foremost trade union activist, **Tubal Uriah "Buzz" Butler** was a Grenadian who came to work in Trinidad's oilfields in 1921. After an industrial accident in 1929 left him unfit for oil work, he joined the Moravian Baptist church and became a preacher, developing the rousing oratorical skills that characterized his political career. Disillusioned with Cipriani's Trinidad Workingmen's Association (see p.254) after it failed to support an oilworkers' strike in 1935, he established the **British Empire Workers** (BEW) to further the "heroic struggle for British justice for British Blacks in a British colony".

The BEW campaigned for better pay and working conditions in the oilfields, where many of the managers were white South Africans who had instituted an apartheid-type regime. Among the workers' many grievances were low wages, long working hours and the frequency of industrial accidents, for which there was no compensation. Workers were liable to be dismissed on the spot and, once sacked, a blackballing system made it impossible for them to find work elsewhere.

DISSENT AND PROTEST

In June 1937 strikers started a **sit-in** at the Forest Reserve oilfield. The police broke up the protest, and in response the strikers set fire to two wells in the Apex oilfield. When the police arrived at Fyzabad to arrest Butler on a charge of agitation, they found him addressing a large crowd; as they attempted to serve the warrant, a **riot** broke out. One plain-clothes officer, the deeply unpopular **Charlie King**, fled into a nearby shop, found himself trapped, and jumped from an upstairs window, breaking his leg; the furious crowd burned him alive, and when his colleagues tried to retrieve his body, a British police officer was shot dead. A 1938 calypso caught the popular mood: "Everybody's rejoicing, How they burned Charlie King, Everybody was glad, Nobody was sad, When they beat him and they burned him, In Fyzabad."

Strikes spread like wildfire, and became increasingly violent, with a mounting death toll on both sides. Butler, in hiding after the riot, was soon discovered and sentenced to two years in prison. Nonetheless, the strikes won important concessions: public workers were granted an eight-hour day and a higher minimum wage, while trade unions were given official recognition (though the police continued to harass union officials). On his release in 1939, Butler was given a hero's welcome, but during his imprisonment the BEW had changed, adopting a more mainstream position, and he was soon expelled. In September 1939 Butler was once again incarcerated for sedition, and remained behind bars till the end of World War II.

BUTLER'S LATER YEARS

Butler continued to be politically active after his release in 1945, campaigning in the national elections, but though his party won the largest block of seats in 1950, he was outflanked by the rise of Eric Williams's nationalist politics (see p.255), and his star faded. In remembrance of his role in defending workers' rights, the Princess Margaret Highway linking north and south Trinidad was renamed in his honour in the 1960s. In 1971 the government awarded him the **Trinity Cross** – the highest honour in the land, and June 19, the day of the riots, was declared a public holiday, celebrated in Fyzabad with a parade through the streets. Butler died in February 1977, and is buried in Fyzabad's cemetery.

The compact commercial centre clusters around Charlie King Junction, overlooked by the Oil Workers' Trade Union Hall (OWTU) and a statue of the workers' leader **Uriah Butler** (see box above) in his black suit and bowler hat. Come **Labour Day** (June 19), the street here is blocked to traffic to make way for a street party with a political undercurrent, with fiery speeches and the inevitable calypso and soca blasting from speakers.

The southern central region

South-central Trinidad is one of the most impenetrable parts of the island. Running from the west to the east coast through rolling plains of sugar cane, and linking the region's two main towns, **Princes Town** and **Rio Claro**, the Manahambre/Naparima–Mayaro Road is the only transport artery. South of the tarmac, wild forest predominates. There are few passable roads, signs are almost nonexistent and trying to follow a map is a lesson in frustration – you'll need to ask for directions if driving yourself. Moruga Road is the only decent thoroughfare through this wilderness, running down to the isolated fishing village of **Moruga**.

GETTING AROUND

By car Though south-central Trinidad is covered by maxis and route taxis, renting a car is the best way to get around, unless you're happy to endure long waits and lots of changes. **By maxi and route taxi** Maxis and taxis are frequent along the Naparima–Mayaro Rd from Princes Town to Rio Claro. To go to Devil's Woodyard mud volcano – roughly halfway between the two – take a maxi from San Fernando to Princes Town, change here and get another from the main stand direct to Devil's Woodyard. You can also get a maxi or taxi to Moruga from Princes Town. The maxi stand in Princes Town is in the Nipdec Car Park on the main drag just east of the market.

Princes Town

East of San Fernando, beyond the blackened chimneys of the old **St Madeleine Sugar Factory** – now closed but still a rather incongruous sight in the midst of rolling fields and lines of palm trees – **PRINCES TOWN** is a mishmash of new buildings in every imaginable style (check out the colourful murals and reliefs of Hindu gods and the Statue of Liberty on the walls of the **Tyre Warehouse** store), alongside more sober structures such as the grand mosque on the east side of the centre, with its copper dome and steel-plated minarets.

4

The Company Villages

On the outskirts of Princes Town, the tiny villages of **First**, **Third**, **Fourth**, **Fifth** and **Sixth Company** are a legacy of black American soldiers (and former slaves) who fought for the British in the War of 1812 in return for the promise of land; after the British defeat, they were allocated lots in Trinidad, and became known as **Merikins**. Landing here in 1816, the soldiers managed to establish successful plantations in what had been uncharted jungle, earning themselves the reputation of pioneers, but their complaints about the condition of the land went unheard; British governor Ralph Woodford not only wanted to open up the southern interior, but had a vested interest in keeping radical black soldiers isolated from potentially rebellious slaves elsewhere on the island. There is no village called Second Company – this unit was lost at sea on the voyage to Trinidad.

Devil's Woodyard

To drive to Devil's Woodyard, turn down the signposted Hindustan Rd, 4.5km past Indian Walk off the Naparima–Mayaro Rd

Devil's Woodyard sees a regular procession of Trinidadian visitors, but the rather underwhelming series of grey mud hillocks bubbling lazily to the surface don't really live up to their ominous name, bestowed after an 1852 eruption scattered the planks of surrounding houses like matchsticks. Amerindians believed that mud volcanoes were passages between this world and the one below, and that the explosions were the Devil coming out to shake the earth. Even now, local children are pacified by a corrupted version of the tale: at midnight the smartly dressed devil is said to dance on the volcano, and if you're awake to see it you vanish forever. The reality is less dramatic, but if you're curious to see a mud volcano this is the most accessible site, with a children's playground, picnic tables, toilets and competing sound systems on Sundays, when the area is a popular liming spot.

Moruga

South of Princes Town, the Moruga Road threads through untamed forest for 21km before meeting the sea at **MORUGA**, a pretty and very remote village that seems to have

COLUMBUS IN TRINIDAD

Christopher Columbus had nearly run out of drinking water when, on July 31, 1498, he sighted the three peaks of the Trinity Hills, which are said to have inspired him to name the island Trinidad. He landed near present-day **Moruga**, where he gathered fresh water from the river. His crew reported seeing fishing implements that had clearly been abandoned in haste, and realized that they had arrived in a region that was already well populated. In fact, there were some 35,000 **Amerindians** (from the Arawak, Shebaio, Nepoio, Carinepagoto and Yao peoples) then living on the island that they called "Ieri", the land of the hummingbird.

Columbus sailed west and encountered the island's residents the next day while anchored off Icacos Point. Twenty-four Amerindians armed with bows and arrows set off in a large canoe to investigate the foreign ship; upon sighting them, Columbus ordered a drum to be played and the sailors to dance, believing the indigenous population would be entertained by this spectacle. However, the Amerindians mistook it for a war dance and rained arrows on the Spaniards; as the latter returned fire, the Amerindians fled. That night, Columbus had little sleep as strong currents here tossed the ship, rocking it so violently that the anchor broke. Bewildered and fearful, Columbus swiftly sailed on, though not before bestowing the name "Serpent's Mouth" for the treacherous waters between Trinidad and Venezuela.

changed little since it was settled by black American soldiers after the War of 1812 (see p.252). The bright colours of the old board houses have weathered to pastel shades, but colourful fishing boats still lie on the seashore and fishermen while away their spare hours playing cricket or liming outside the shops-cum-bars on the main road. The seafront Catholic church dominates both the physical surroundings and the life of the villagers. This is a place of strong but heterodox beliefs: Morugans may avow allegiance to Catholicism, to the Spiritual Baptist faith or to Rastafari, but many believe in aspects of all (alongside a sprinkling of obeah; see p.251) and, perhaps thanks to the area's isolation, a palpably religious, well-nigh superstitious, atmosphere pervades.

Columbus Beach

Moruga's yellow-sand **Columbus Beach** is a gorgeous swathe of sand backed with impressive rocky outcrops, and is named after Christopher Columbus, who briefly landed nearby in 1498 (see box above). This is celebrated in the annual **Columbus Festival**, held on August 1, a holiday replaced elsewhere in Trinidad by Emancipation Day, which commemorates the abolition of slavery; controversially, the festival organizers hold the view that without Columbus, the majority of Trinidadians would not have the benefit of living on the island, or of the Catholic faith. Whatever the motivation, the yearly festival brings in plenty of visitors and provides an excuse for a good party and street bazaar. The festivities take place on the beach, where three boats are decorated as fifteenth-century galleons and locals play the part of Columbus and the Amerindians who greet the explorer armed with bows and arrows – not exactly an accurate account, but an entertaining spectacle nonetheless. Also on the beach is a 4.5m-high statue of **St Peter**, erected by the St Vincent Ferrer Society, a Catholic community group which has revitalized Moruga's St Peter's Day celebrations in July and opened a new **museum**.

Moruga Museum

40 Grand Chemin, Moruga • Mon–Sat 9am–4pm • TT$20 • ☎ 320 3108, Ⓦ morugamuseum1.wordpress.com

Opened in late 2014, the **Moruga Museum** holds some 800 artefacts, from fossils to housewares, clothing, bottles, shells and Amerindian ceramics, as well as displays centred on Catholicism in Trinidad and the Merikin peoples who settled in the Company villages (see p.187). Its energetic founder Eric Lewis is also the man behind the local St Vincent Ferrer Society, and the collection he has amassed was honoured in December 2014 by the presentation of a silver medal of Pope Francis from the Vatican's

Caribbean representative, Archbishop Nicola Girasoli. Guided tours of the museum are usually available, as are trips into the surrounding area.

Rio Claro

Located on the Naparima–Mayaro Road some 24km east of Princes Town, **RIO CLARO** is the region's administrative hub, and a busy place compared with its surroundings – though that's not saying much in this somnolent corner of the island. The town enjoyed a period of prosperity between 1914 and 1965, when it was connected to Trinidad's major cities by the railway, but has been in a long decline ever since the trains stopped running, as young people abandon agricultural work for more profitable jobs in the oilfields and the cities. Rio Claro's connections with its Spanish heritage emerges towards Christmas, as the town's famous **parang** singers (see p.264) come out to entertain the clientele of the local bars and clubs. There's little to occupy you at other times, though on the western outskirts, the grand wedding-cake-pink and ice-blue **Catholic church** and **Hindu temple** with a stepped dome and gold and blue trimmings are worth a look.

Trinity Hills Wildlife Sanctuary

Some 65 square kilometres of evergreen forest running down to the sea east of the Rio Claro–Guayaguayare Road, the **Trinity Hills Wildlife Sanctuary** encompasses the Trinity Hills and Mount Derrick, the tallest peak in the south at 314m. The hills form a watershed that's vital to the nation's water supply, and was declared a protected reserve in 1900. The many **rivers**, **streams** and **waterfalls** are excellent for bathing, while the lush forests of carat, redwood, cooperhoop and bois pois trees shelter animals such as lappe, agouti, quenk, tatoo and red howler monkeys, as well as rarely seen ocelots, capuchin monkeys, buck deer, armadillos and opossums. The wide variety of birdlife includes the mountain quail dove, while deep caves harbour many species of bats. A 45-minute hike from the road is a **mud volcano** and lake known as **Lagoon Bouffe**, at 100m wide one of Trinidad's largest.

If you don't visit via an organized tour, you could drive or mountain-bike along the Moruga–Guayaguayare Road (also known as Edward Trace), an exceptionally pretty route which loops through thick virgin forest; you'll rarely see another soul the entire 35km. To avoid any problems at the oilfield gateposts, it's wise to get a free permit from Petrotrin, who have a number of pipelines running through the reserve.

INFORMATION AND TOURS / TRINITY HILLS WILDLIFE SANCTUARY

Organized tours Information on the reserve is hard to find due to its remoteness and the paucity of visitors. Caribbean Discovery Tours (see p.38) offer full-day excursions, while tour guide Jalaludin Khan (see p.38) can also advise on trips there and set you up with a local guide.

Permits Call Petrotrin on ☎ 649 5539 or ☎ 658 4200 Mon–Sat, on Sun and public hols call ☎ 649 5500 or ☎ 5501.

MUD VOLCANOES

Though marked on many maps and promoted as something of a tourist attraction, South Trinidad's many **mud volcanoes** are largely inaccessible – unless you like chopping through dense forest – and in most cases it's not worth the effort. The volcanoes are small mounds mostly less than a metre high that seep grey sulphuric mud, which is believed to be good for skin conditions.

The volcanoes can appear anywhere: in the middle of the bush, in people's back gardens and by the road. They are usually ignored, though those who live near them do so at their peril, for they have a tendency to explode every few years. The most recent and damaging explosion was in **Piparo** in central Trinidad in 1997 (see p.160).

Tobago

HORSERIDING ON TURTLE BEACH

5

Tobago

An elongated oval just 41km by 14km, Tobago manages a surprising diversity within her craggy coastal fringes. Rich in natural allure, from deserted palm-lined beaches and lively coral reefs to a wealth of lush rainforest, and with plenty of tourist infrastructure in its southwest corner, the island offers something for every taste. Tobago's greatest appeal, however, is its relatively unspoilt feel. Although tourism has definitely taken root here, development has so far been fairly low-key when compared with many other Caribbean islands. There are few all-inclusive resorts and none of the high-rise hotels that have blighted many other tropical paradises – and the hustler mentality that exists on more touristy islands is less intense here.

A place where locals and tourists tend to co-exist in an easy equilibrium, with everyone frequenting the same beaches, bars and nightclubs, Tobago's overall vibe is overwhelmingly laidback and relaxing. Moreover, celebrations such as the Easter **goat races** are attended by more Tobagonians than tourists, and local culture is honoured at the annual **Heritage Festival** each August. The uniquely friendly mentality here is best expressed at the year-round **Harvest Festivals**, where entire villages open their doors to passing revellers.

Tobago is breathtakingly beautiful; heavy industry is confined to Trinidad, so the beaches here are clean and the landscape left largely to its own devices. The flat coral and limestone plateau of the **southwest tip** is the island's most heavily developed region, with the majority of hotels, bars and restaurants as well as the best – albeit most commercialized – beaches such as **Pigeon Point** and **Store Bay**. There are also quieter stretches of sand along the area's smart hotel coast, where glass-bottom boats head for **Buccoo Reef**, palms sway over the **Mount Irvine** golf course, and hotels around **Plymouth** run night excursions to watch giant **turtles** laying eggs on the beach. Strong currents in this area provide some excellent **surfing** possibilities, with the rough seas between November and February (the height of the tourist season) producing big breakers at Mount Irvine Beach.

But Tobago isn't just sun, sand, surf and the tourist dollar. The commercial clamour of the southwest tip is kept in check by the capital, **Scarborough**, a lively, picturesque port town tumbling down a fort-topped hillside. Pummelled by the dark-green, wave-whipped Atlantic, the island's rugged **windward** (south) **coast** is lined with appealing fishing villages; **Speyside** and **Charlotteville** in the remote eastern reaches have **coral reefs** as ornate as you'll find anywhere in the Caribbean and **scuba diving** is a burgeoning industry. Tobago is an excellent and inexpensive place to learn to dive, and

Miss Trim's
CRAB + DUMPLING
LONCH + DUMPLING

VEGI RICE
MACARONI PIE
STEA VEG
PEAS or
CALLALLOO

STEWS
CHICKEN
PORK
CURRY FISH
CURRY GOAT

ROTI

MENU AT *MISS TRIM'S*, STORE BAY

Highlights

❶ Get active Take a horseback ride through Buccoo Bay, a stand-up paddle in Bon Accord Lagoon, a bike ride across the interior or a round of golf at either of Tobago's two beautiful courses. **See pp.202–203 & p.205**

❷ Coastal cruise Hop onto a boat and cruise along Tobago's ravishing Caribbean coast, with stops for snorkelling at some of the island's best reefs and a barbecue lunch on a deserted beach. **See p.203**

❸ Creole lunch at Store Bay Fresh fish, "blue food" and curry crab and dumplin', the delectable staples of Tobagonian cooking are served up at a row of booths by the sea. **See p.208**

❹ Sunday School Dance your cares away every Sunday at this big, brash open-air party in Buccoo. **See p.211**

❺ Castara This picturesque fishing village has embraced tourism without being consumed by it, and boasts two fantastic beaches. **See p.228**

❻ Tobago's rainforest The oldest protected rainforest in the western hemisphere makes a sublime location for hiking or birdwatching. **See p.234**

❼ Pirate's Bay This secluded Charlotteville beach offers excellent swimming and snorkelling in an idyllic setting. **See p.244**

HIGHLIGHTS ARE MARKED ON THE MAP ON PP.194–195

5

there's plenty of challenging drift diving for the more experienced, while the many fringing reefs within swimming distance of the beaches make for fantastic **snorkelling**. Coral sands and glassy Caribbean waters along the **leeward** (north) **coast** provide some of Tobago's finest beaches; some, like **Englishman's Bay**, are regularly deserted, while at **Parlatuvier** and **Bloody Bay**, you'll share the sand with local fishermen. **Castara**, meanwhile, holds the only real tourist infrastructure along Tobago's Caribbean coast, with a host of guesthouses and places to enjoy the excellent fresh fish meals.

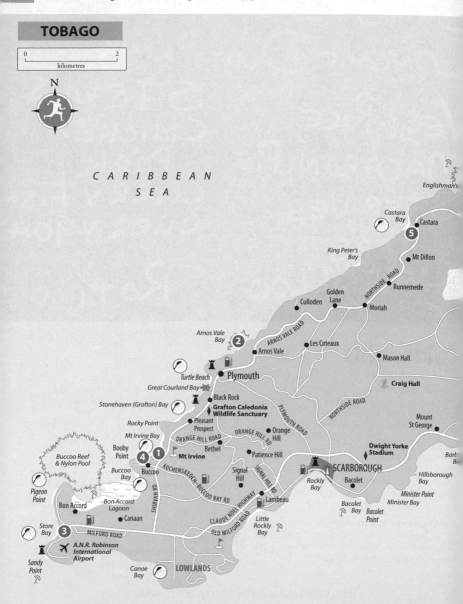

TOBAGO

0   2
kilometres

N

CARIBBEAN
SEA

Englishman's

Castara
Bay   Castara
5

King Peter's
Bay   Mt Dillon

NORTHSIDE ROAD

Runnemede

Golden
Culloden   Lane   Moriah

Arnos Vale
Bay
2   ARNOS VALE ROAD   Les Coteaux
   Arnos Vale   Mason Hall

Turtle Beach   **Plymouth**   **Craig Hall**

Great Courland Bay   Black Rock
Stonehaven (Grafton) Bay   **Grafton Caledonia**
       Wildlife Sanctuary   NORTHSIDE ROAD
Rocky Point   Pleasant   Orange
      Prospect   ORANGE HILL RD   Hill   Mount
Mt Irvine Bay   ORANGE HILL ROAD   St George
Booby   Bethel   **Dwight Yorke**
Buccoo Reef   Point   **4 1 Mt Irvine**   Patience Hill   **Stadium**   Barb
& Nylon Pool   Signal   Ba
  Buccoo   Buccoo   Hill   **SCARBOROUGH**
Pigeon   Bay   AUCHENSKEOCH-BUCCOO BAY RD   Rockly   Bacolet   Hillsborough
Point   Bay   Bay
Bon Accord   Bon Accord   SHIRVAN ROAD   Lambeau   Minister Point
Store   Lagoon   Canaan   CLAUDE NOEL HIGHWAY   Bacolet   Minister Bay
Bay   **3**   OLD MILFORD ROAD   Little   Bay   Bacolet
      MILFORD ROAD   Rockly   Point
Sandy   **A.N.R. Robinson**   Bay
Point   **International**
    Airport
      Canoe   **LOWLANDS**
      Bay

5

The landscape of the eastern interior rises steeply into the hillocks and rolling bluffs which make up the central **Main Ridge**. These mountains shelter the **Forest Reserve** – the oldest protected rainforest in the western hemisphere – an abundant tangle of mist-shrouded greenery dripping down to fabulous coastlines, often with neither building nor road to interrupt the flow. Ornithologists and naturalists flock in for the **bird**– and **animal** life that flourishes here; David Attenborough filmed parts of his celebrated *Trials of Life* series at **Little Tobago**, a solitary sea-bird sanctuary off the coast

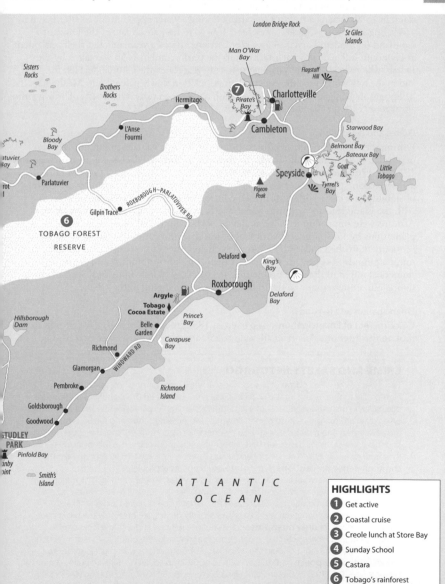

London Bridge Rock

St Giles Islands

Man O'War Bay

Flagstaff Hill

Sisters Rocks

Brothers Rocks

Hermitage

7 Pirate's Bay

Charlotteville

Cambleton

L'Anse Fourmi

Bloody Bay

...tuvier ...ay

Parlatuvier

...rot ...l

Gilpin Trace

ROXBOROUGH–PARLATUVIER RD

6 TOBAGO FOREST RESERVE

Starwood Bay

Belmont Bay

Bateaux Bay

Speyside

Goat Is.

Little Tobago

Tyrrel's Bay

Pigeon Peak

Delaford

King's Bay

Roxborough

Delaford Bay

Argyle
Tobago Cocoa Estate

Prince's Bay

Hillsborough Dam

Belle Garden

Carapuse Bay

Richmond

WINDWARD RD

Glamorgan

Richmond Island

Pembroke

Goldsborough

Goodwood

STUDLEY PARK

Pinfold Bay

...anby ...oint

Smith's Island

ATLANTIC OCEAN

HIGHLIGHTS

1 Get active

2 Coastal cruise

3 Creole lunch at Store Bay

4 Sunday School

5 Castara

6 Tobago's rainforest

7 Pirate's Bay

5

of Speyside. For slightly less committed nature-lovers, the island's forested interior offers plenty of opportunities for birdwatching or a splash in the icy **waterfalls**.

Brief history

Tobago has long been a hotly contested property. The original **Carib** population fiercely defended the paradisiacal island that they called Tavaco (the name is derived from the Indian word for tobacco) against other Amerindian tribes, and thwarted European colonization throughout the late 1500s and early 1600s. English sailors staked Britain's claim in 1580, tacking a flag to a tree trunk during a water stop en route to Brazil; and in 1641, England's King Charles I presented Tobago to his godson James, the Duke of Courland (in modern Latvia). A group of **Latvians** arrived a year later, but their settlement at Plymouth suffered constant attacks from the Caribs, and in 1658 was taken by the Dutch, who called it Nieuw Vlissingen. Twenty years later, the Courlanders left for good, and in the following years, the Amerindian population slowly petered out. Meanwhile, the belligerent shenanigans of the Dutch, English and French turned the coasts of Tobago into a **war zone**, with the island changing hands 31 times before 1814.

Pirates and plantations

During the eighteenth century, forts sprang up at every vantage point, and Tobago descended into turmoil, plundered by **pirates** and officially declared a no-man's-land in 1702. In 1762, however, the British took decisive action and sent a powerful fleet to Tobago, taking possession of the island with swift precision. Sustained by the promise of stability that came with firm British control, **plantation culture** began in earnest, with the island transformed into a highly efficient sugar, cotton and indigo factory. Africans were shipped in to work as **slaves**, with around 3000 toiling on the plantations by 1772, under the control of less than three hundred Europeans. The economy flourished and, by 1777, the island's eighty or so estates had exported 1.5 million pounds of cotton, as well as vast quantities of rum, indigo and sugar. The numerical might of the slave population led to many bloody **uprisings**, with planters doling out amputations and death by burning and hanging to the rebels.

Emancipation and beyond

Once the **Act of Emancipation** was passed in 1834, most of Tobago's African population took to the interior to plant small-scale farms, and also established coastal fishing

---

CRIME AND SAFETY IN TOBAGO

There was a time when **crime** of any sort was virtually unheard of in Tobago, but several high-profile robberies and attacks in recent years have tarnished the island's reputation as a safe haven in the Caribbean. Most of the victims have been expat residents rather than people on holiday, and many put these crimes down to disputes and simmering tensions between the newcomers and their local neighbours rather than opportunism. Nonetheless, it has to be said that crime statistics have risen here in recent years, and while some Tobagonians still leave their front doors unlocked and their parked cars open, visitors are well advised to take the **common-sense precautions** (see p.41) to avoid potential problems.

Another main concern of late has been break-ins at **villas**, whose often-idyllic locations – in the middle of nowhere with only the birds for company – are irresistible to tourists and criminals alike. If you do stay in a villa, bear in mind that those clustered together in a resort-style complex, complete with gates and security guards, are obviously the safest choice. Always ask about **security measures** such as outside lighting and window locks or grilles before renting, and make sure that you lock doors and windows securely before going out and when retiring for the night. Should the worst happen, don't offer any kind of resistance to thieves; and call the **police** on ☎ 999 as soon as possible; in addition, there are police stations at Scarborough (☎ 639 2512), Crown Point (☎ 639 0042 or ☎ 639 9872), Old Grange (☎ 639 8888), Moriah (☎ 660 0029 or ☎ 660 0100), Roxborough (☎ 660 4333) and Charlotteville (☎ 660 4388).

communities. Some continued to work the estates as free men and women, but when Britain removed its protective tariffs on sugar sales, Tobago's unmechanized industry was unable to compete with other, more efficient producers. A severe hurricane in 1847, along with the collapse of the West India Bank (which underwrote the plantations), marked the beginning of the end for the island's sugar estates.

In the aftermath of the **Belmanna Riots** (see p.239), Tobago's Legislative Council relinquished its tenuous rule, and the island became a Crown Colony in 1879. Having reaped all it could from the island and its sugar industry, England had little further need for this troublesome, ailing dependency. In 1899, Tobago was made a ward of Trinidad, effectively becoming the bigger island's poor relation with little control over her own destiny. With the **collapse of the sugar industry**, the islanders fell back upon other crops, planting the acres of limes, coconuts and cocoa that still remain in patches today. Boosted by the arrival of **free Africans** in the mid-1800s, the black population clubbed together to farm the land, tending their food crops in the efficient "**Len-Hand**" **system** of shared labour that is still celebrated during Harvest Festivals. By the early 1900s Tobago was exporting fruit and vegetables to Trinidad, and was granted a single seat on the legislative council in 1927.

Tobago today

In 1963, **Hurricane Flora** (see p.236) razed whole villages and laid waste to most of the island's crops; the ensuing restructuring programme saw the first tentative steps towards developing a tourist industry. By 1980, the island had her sovereignty partially restored when the **Tobago House of Assembly** (THA) was reconvened, but it had authority only over the island's more mundane affairs while the main decisions were still made in Trinidad. Although Tobago now has a stronger profile in the republic's affairs, the island is still perceived to be looked down on by bigger Trinidad, much to the resentment of the local populace.

In terms of economy, **tourism** remains the island's main earner, and development projects abound, many slated for some of the island's most pristine and lovely stretches of coast. It remains to be seen whether all this construction will erode the very things that attract tourists to Tobago in the first place.

ARRIVAL AND DEPARTURE
TOBAGO

BY PLANE

A.N.R Robinson International Airport Both international and domestic flights (see p.25) land at A.N.R Robinson International Airport, an airy complex that's small enough to feel overwhelmed by the arrival of a single jet. The little row of shops opposite the terminal building holds a newsagent selling mobile phone top-ups and Companion phonecards; a b-mobile shop selling local SIM cards; and two restaurants.

Airport taxis The hotels in Crown Point are all within walking distance of the airport, though it's of course easier to take a taxi than lug your case in the tropical heat. There is a taxi price list on the wall of the arrivals lounge; rates are used by all the licensed taxi drivers who meet each flight, and are high, but not wildly so; note that fares increase by ten percent after 10pm. If you're on a budget, you can cross the street and haggle with the sometimes-cheaper unlicensed drivers or catch a route taxi (see p.198) or bus (see p.198) going to Scarborough.

Destinations London (5–9 weekly; 10hr) New York (3 weekly; 5hr).

BY FERRY

Some visitors arrive on the fast ferry (see p.224) from Port of Spain, which docks at Scarborough twice a day; a cheaper if less pleasant way to make the journey over.

GETTING AROUND

Given Tobago's small size, public transport can be a useful option for short journeys, particularly in the southwest, with plenty of route taxis, maxis (with blue bands in Tobago) and buses plying the main roads. In remote corners of Tobago, and on Sundays throughout the island, waiting times can be long. All public transport to outlying spots such as Castara, Charlotteville or Speyside departs from Scarborough (see p.224); bear in mind that it's best to get an early start, since many of the services to outlying towns and villages leave early in the morning, with a significant lull during the middle part of the day. Renting a car is by far the easiest way to explore the island, even if you just rent one for a day for a round-Tobago whirlwind trip.

5

BY BUS

Services and information The cheapest way to get around the island is on Tobago's public bus system, run by the Public Transport Service Company (PTSC; ☎ 639 2293, ⓦ ptsc.co.tt). Information on specific bus routes has been given under the relevant headings in this chapter.

Tickets and fares Fares range between TT$2 and TT$8; all tickets must be pre-purchased as drivers will not accept cash; they are available from the shops opposite the airport complex, the bus station in Scarborough or from bars and mini-marts throughout the island.

BY ROUTE TAXI

Legions of route taxis ply the western portion of the island; travelling between Crown Point, Buccoo, Mount Irvine or Plymouth simply involves standing on the correct side of the road for your destination, sticking out your hand and asking the taxi driver where they're heading. Traffic is lighter along the windward and leeward sides of the island, but even here you should find something going in your direction if you're patient.

BY TAXI

As well as using taxis for short journeys, you can also hire one for a full or half-day (around US$25/hr) to explore the island; you can concentrate on the scenery not the road, and you'll get a commentary on the island along the way. Taxi drivers congregate at the airport; you can also call the Tobago Owner Drivers' Association (☎ 639 2692) or Tobago Taxi Cab Co-Operative (☎ 639 2659). Of individual drivers, try Vernon Abraham (☎ 639 4475) or Liz Lezama (☎ 639 2309).

BY CAR AND BIKE

There are petrol stations along Milford Rd in Bon Accord, in Scarborough, the Claude Noel Hwy on the junction with Orange Hill Rd, Plymouth, Carnbee (take the first right from Shirvan Rd or the turn-off from the highway marked for Auchenskeoch), Roxborough and Charlotteville. Opening hours are generally Mon–Sat 7am–8pm and Sun 7am–noon; the Milford Rd station opens 24hr. The speed limit is 30mph/50kmph throughout the island, even on the highway.

Car rental Most of the international car rental firms – as well as the local operators with two or three vehicles to rent – are clustered around the airport. You'll pay US$40–50/day for a car or jeep. Local operators tend to be cheaper than their international counterparts, but the smaller the company, the less likely you are to be offered 24-hour assistance and adequate coverage in case of an accident: some of the most reliable local firms include KCNN (☎ 682 2888, ⓦ tobago carhire.com), Sherman's (☎ 639 2292, ⓦ shermansrental.com) and 4A (☎ 688 5498, ✉ rich4arentals@hotmail.com); while Yes Tourism (☎ 357 0064, ⓦ yes-tourism.com) acts as a broker for several operators and has online booking.

Bike and scooter rental Car rental firms occasionally rent motorbikes and scooters for around US$30/day. Be especially careful to check the condition of your bike and helmet before you ride away, as some are less than perfect. Bicycles are good for short hops, though the daytime heat is intense and riding on the roads can feel a bit precarious. Mountain biking tour companies can rent bikes, as can **Easy Goers**, on Airport Rd in Crown Point (☎ 681 8025 or ☎ 787 0685, ⓦ easygoersbikes.com).

Crown Point and around

Tobago's flat, low-lying southwest tip is the island's most heavily developed, accessible and populated region, with the **Crown Point** area around the airport home to the vast majority of its hotels, restaurants and nightclubs, as well as its most popular beaches – **Store Bay** is just a couple of minutes on foot from the airport, and **Pigeon Point** ten minutes further. The terrain between the two is jam-packed with all the familiar tourist trappings – craft stalls, restaurants, bars and endless hotels – and many people never make it any further into the island. This highly commercialized hotchpotch sometimes lacks aesthetic charm, but the concentration of facilities and activities offers practical convenience as well as Tobago's most energetic vibe.

DRIVING TIMES

While the roads around Scarborough can be busy during peak times, approximate **driving times** are:

Crown Point to Scarborough – 15min	Plymouth to Bloody Bay – 1hr
Roxborough to Speyside – 30min	Scarborough to Castara – 45min
Speyside to Charlotteville – 10min	Bloody Bay to Roxborough – 45min
Scarborough to Plymouth – 20min	Crown Point to Castara – 1hr

5

BUCCOO REEF AND NYLON POOL

Covering around 12sq km of Caribbean seabed between Pigeon Point and Buccoo Bay, **Buccoo Reef** is Tobago's largest and most heavily visited collection of corals, from hard stag and elkhorn varieties to waving purple sea fans and peach-coloured fire coral, patrolled by the brilliantly coloured trigger, butterfly, surgeon and parrot fish which thrive here. To the south of the reef is **Nylon Pool**, a gleaming coralline sandbar forming an appealing metre-deep swimming pool smack in the middle of the sea. It's said to have been named by Princess Margaret during her stay in the 1950s; she supposedly remarked that the water was as clear as her nylon stockings – nylon had just been invented.

Sadly, however, human interference has taken a devastating toll. Carelessly placed anchors and thoughtless removal of coral souvenirs – not to mention the inevitable pollution – mean that many parts have been terribly **damaged**, and bear more resemblance to a coral graveyard than a living reef. Buccoo also took a pounding during the years when boat operators handed out plastic shoes to allow visitors to walk on the reef as a part of the glass-bottom boat tour. Large sections have died off completely, leaving white skeletons in their wake, while overfishing has reduced the fish and crustacean populations, and poorly aimed spear guns have ripped chunks from the coral. The situation became so bad that Buccoo was declared a **protected national park** in 1973, but with scant resources to enforce the law the legal status meant little and the damage continued practically unabated. Today, glass-bottom boat operators are more conscientious, no longer promoting reef walks and anchoring at designated buoys, as well as warning visitors that touching or removing reef matter and shells is illegal. The **Buccoo Reef Trust** (☎635 2000, ⓦbuccooreeftrust.org), meanwhile, is a local NGO working to help preserve the reef and educate boat operators and fishermen about sustainable practices. You can do your bit by standing on the seabed only and refusing to buy any coral trinkets.

Despite the damage, there's still plenty to see at Buccoo, particularly at outlying areas such as Coral Gardens. You'll have no difficulty in finding a **glass-bottom boat** to take you; most leave from Store Bay (see below) and, to a lesser degree, Buccoo and Pigeon Point. Two- to three-hour trips cost around US$25, and usually leave at about 11am and 2pm; touts prowl all the main beaches. The tours are often fairly raucous, accompanied by loud music on the way home, but offer a good glimpse of the coral as well as a pretty perspective back over Tobago's southwest coastline and hilly interior.

Directly east of Crown Point, Airport Road serves as a rough boundary line between Crown Point and **Bon Accord**, directly east and distinguishable only by its preponderance of residential streets threading towards the lovely Bon Accord wetlands. Airport Road leads into ruler-straight **Milford Road**, bisecting the southwest tip, and the main thoroughfare through the southwest. Trucks, cars and route taxis fly past a roadside lined with shops, fruit stalls and houses, and the whole stretch is the busiest you'll find away from Scarborough. Milford merges into the Claude Noel Highway just before the sign for the pretty **Canoe Bay beach**. Running parallel to Milford Road, **Store Bay Local Road** is a quieter affair but still home to a fair few accommodation and eating options.

Store Bay Beach

Lifeguards on duty daily 10am–6pm • Changing facilities daily 10am–5.45pm, TT$5/entry; lockers TT$10/day

A two-minute walk from the airport brings you to Crown Point's best place to swim, **Store Bay Beach**. Named after early Dutch settler Jan Stoer, this is some of the most popular sand in Tobago, and deservedly so; it's close to the main hotels, has tasty and inexpensive local food and is a great place to buy crafts from the many huts behind the beach. Store Bay offers up a lively scene: holidaymakers (many of them from Trinidad) consume vast quantities of curry crab and dumplin' and keep the beach-chair operators busy, while glass-bottom boats load and offload groups of visitors in the bay.

Though fairly small and hemmed in by the *Coco Reef* hotel (see p.207) and the rocks, the beach is excellent: tides govern the extent of the fine, off-white sand, and lifeguards patrol the area flagged off for safe bathing. With a gentle shelf and crystal-clear water, a calm Store

5

Bay is a good choice for adults and children – though be careful on rougher days, when waves get pretty big. Store Bay is the finishing point for the Great Race powerboat contest each August (see p.35), as well as a venue for open-air parties around Easter weekend, and the bars opposite are a popular liming spot, particularly during and after sunset.

Opposite the beach there are a couple of bars blasting reggae and soca, an ice-cream kiosk and the row of shacks housing the irresistible cookshops where most people purchase their lunch (see box, p.208).

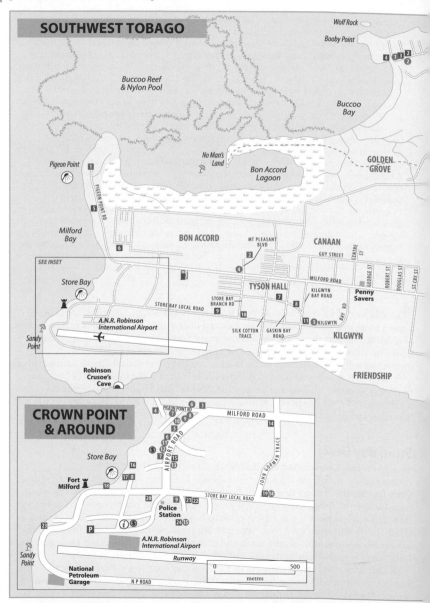

Fort Milford

Store Bay Local Rd • No set hours • Free

From Airport Road, Store Bay Local Road runs west, past the small dead-end road that leads to Store Bay Beach, and threads around the headland to hotel-filled Sandy Point and the **Fort Milford** stockade. The ruins of gun-slitted coral stone were built by the British in 1777, and briefly appropriated by the French during their 1781–93 occupation of Tobago. Of the six cannons that remain, five are British and one French.

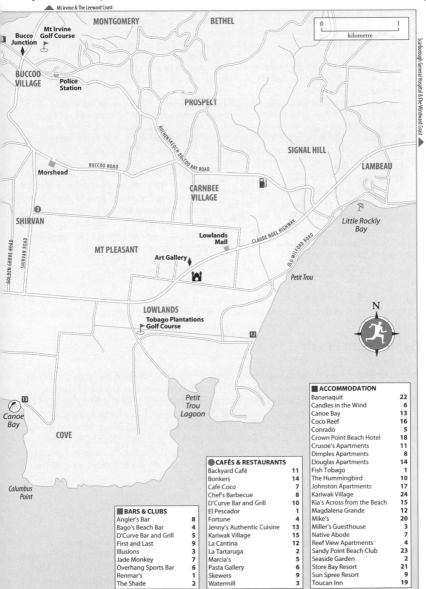

Mt Irvine & The Leeward Coast

MONTGOMERY   BETHEL

Mt Irvine
Bucco   Golf Course
Junction

BUCCOO
VILLAGE   Police
Station

PROSPECT

SIGNAL HILL

AUCHENSKEOCH BUCCOO BAY ROAD

BUCCOO ROAD   LAMBEAU

Morshead

CARNBEE
VILLAGE

SHIRVAN   Little Rockly
Bay

Lowlands
Mall   CLAUDE NOEL HIGHWAY

GOLDEN GROVE ROAD

SHIRVAN ROAD

MT PLEASANT   OLD MILFORD ROAD

Art Gallery

Petit Trou

LOWLANDS
Tobago Plantations
Golf Course

N

Petit
Trou
Lagoon

Canoe
Bay   COVE

Columbus
Point

Scarborough General Hospital & The Windward Coast

CAFÉS & RESTAURANTS

Backyard Café	11
Bonkers	14
Café Coco	7
Chef's Barbecue	8
D'Curve Bar and Grill	10
El Pescador	1
Fortune	4
Jenny's Authentic Cuisine	13
Kariwak Village	15
La Cantina	12
La Tartaruga	2
Marcia's	5
Pasta Gallery	6
Skewers	9
Watermill	3

BARS & CLUBS

Angler's Bar	8
Bago's Beach Bar	4
D'Curve Bar and Grill	5
First and Last	9
Illusions	3
Jade Monkey	7
Overhang Sports Bar	6
Renmar's	1
The Shade	2

ACCOMMODATION

Bananaquit	22
Candles in the Wind	6
Canoe Bay	13
Coco Reef	16
Conrado	5
Crown Point Beach Hotel	18
Crusoe's Apartments	11
Dimples Apartments	8
Douglas Apartments	14
Fish Tobago	1
The Hummingbird	10
Johnston Apartments	17
Kariwak Village	24
Kia's Across from the Beach	15
Magdalena Grande	12
Mike's	20
Miller's Guesthouse	3
Native Abode	7
Reef View Apartments	4
Sandy Point Beach Club	23
Seaside Garden	2
Store Bay Resort	21
Sun Spree Resort	9
Toucan Inn	19

5

ORGANIZED TOURS

Tobago has a bewildering number of **tour companies and guides**, with options ranging from the highly qualified and experienced to the downright charlatan (note that certified guides have an ID badge issued by the Tobago House of Assembly). It's worth spending time considering the options before parting with your cash. Several established companies offer standard island tours covering Tobago's main sights, which are great if you want a hassle-free overview of the island. A **boat ride** is one of the best ways to appreciate Tobago's gorgeous coastline and get some excellent snorkelling. Several operators work the waters, and trips usually include lunch, snorkelling at Englishman's Bay or other similarly deserted coves, and an open bar; half-day, or sunset and moonlight dinner trips are also on the roster of most operators.

Full-day tours (land or sea) of eight hours or so almost always include lunch and cost US$70–90 per person; half-day tours hover at around US$50 for four to five hours. Most people book through reps who visit the main hotels or trawl the beaches, but you can sign up independently as well. Note that the prices given below are for adults; all companies offer reduced rates for children.

There are also several guides (see box, p.234) who specialize in the **Forest Reserve**, and who are usually to be found at the main entrance, Gilpin Trace. **Glass-bottom boats to Buccoo Reef** (see box, p.199) are one of the most popular tour options on Tobago; all leave from Store Bay. Other more active tour options include **fishing** (see p.205), **mountain biking** (see p.205), **golf** (see p.205), **horseriding** (see p.205) and **scuba diving** (see p.205).

ISLAND TOURS

Alibaba Tours ☎ 635 1017 or ☎ 686 7957, ⊛ alibaba -tours.com. One of the best all-round operators, based in Castara and offering the standard rainforest and island trips, which can be arranged to include whatever you want to see, plus boat trips with snorkelling, fun fishing and beach barbecues, and island sightseeing tours – (half day US$60, full day including lunch US$80).

Harris' Jungle Tours ☎ 639 0513 or ☎ 759 0170, ⊛ harris-jungle-tours.com. Genial former lifeguard Harris McDonald is a lovely guide for all the Tobago sights, plus conducts full- and half-day rainforest and birdwatching walks, including breakfast, and an exciting night-time rainforest walk. Also offers Sunday School trips.

Surrounded by well-kept gardens that make a quiet, shady chill-out spot, the fort gives a panoramic perspective over Store Bay Beach and Milford Bay right up to Pigeon Point.

Sandy Point Beach

Store Bay Local Rd

South of Fort Milford, Store Bay Local Road swings left before meeting the fences of the airport runway, encircled by narrow NP Road. Obscured by trees and shrubs, pretty and often deserted **Sandy Point Beach** is easy to miss; take the first dirt road off NP into the bush (just opposite the end of the tarmac) and you'll emerge onto a picturesque and completely undeveloped strip of fine white sand and translucent sea bordered by sea grapes and palms. Swimming is safe if you stick to the left of the beach; currents get strong around the headland to the right. Sandy Point is a popular lunch spot and a great place to watch the **sunset**, with cars parked up at a small paved area next to the sea wall.

Pigeon Point

Daily 8am–5.30pm • TT$20/entry, shower blocks, beach loungers TT$18

Some 200m north of the Store Bay turn-off, where Airport Road swings right to become Milford Road, the left-hand turn-off onto **Pigeon Point Road** leads to the spot where the Atlantic Ocean meets the Caribbean Sea. The shoreline here – unlike the majority of Tobago's rugged beaches – is definitively Caribbean: powdery white sand with calm turquoise sea on one side and the ubiquitous swaying palms on the other.

S. McLetchie Tours ☎639 0265, ⓦtobago
-adventure.com. A reliable and enthusiastic operator,
based in the Crown Point area, and good for
birdwatching as well as island tours.

Tobago Now ☎639 1476, ⓦtobagonow.com.
Island tours and trips focused on local art and culture,
but best for its full- or half-day jeep safaris in open-
topped vehicles that take you off-road and into
abandoned plantations and to a little-visited waterfall,
where you can take a swim.

Yes Tourism ☎357 0064, ⓦyes-tourism.com.
Reliable, professional outfit offering all the standard
island trips, plus snorkelling and fishing at decent rates.
Excursions to Trinidad, too.

BIRDING AND WILDLIFE TOURS

NG Nature Tours ☎660 5463 or ☎754 7881,
ⓦnewtongeorge.com. One of the best birding guides in
Tobago, Newton George works with many visiting groups
and is excellent for serious birders and novices alike, his
light-pen (sensitively) employed to help you pick out
even the most reclusive species. Trips cover the Forest
Reserve, Little Tobago, Bon Accord Lagoon, Grafton bird
sanctuary and the Magdalena Grande wetlands.

Peter Cox Wildlife Tours ☎751 5822 or ☎294
3086, ⓦtobagonaturetours.com. A great birding
guide, and also good for turtle-watching (see p.216)
during the laying season, plus night-time rainforest

walks (perfect for seeing nocturnal creatures such as
armadillos and owls) and trips tailored for children in
which you explore forest rivers and pools home to
wabeen and crayfish.

BOAT TRIPS AND PADDLEBOAT TOURS

Frankie's Tours ☎681 3717 or ☎394 4553,
ⓦfrankietours.com. Perhaps the largest of the boat-
tour operators, with a base at Mount Irvine Beach car
park and a varied selection of cruises aboard small boats
with a covered area, plus fishing, hiking and sightseeing
tours.

Island Girl ☎639 7245, ⓦsailtobago.com. An
alternative to the usual boat tours, this bright yellow
catamaran is the only vessel offering sailing (wind
permitting) rather than just motor-power. It's also a
great bet for families, with plenty of space to relax on
board.

Radical Watersports ☎631 5150 or ☎728 5483,
ⓦradicalsportstobago.com. Watersports specialists
offering stand-up paddleboarding (1hr lesson US$60)
and a range of paddleboarding tours from a Petit Trou
lagoon and around the southwest coast; you can also
drive along the Caribbean coast to explore little-visited
rivers and beaches by board. The best option, though, is
the fantastic night-time tour through the Bon Accord
Lagoon to see bioluminescence caused by blooming
phytoplankton (6.30–9pm; US$60).

Lauded as the island's best beach, **Pigeon Point** has shady picnic gazebos, shower blocks
and a weathered wooden pier topped with a thatch-roofed hut that's easily Tobago's
most photographed spot. The gentle shelf and tame currents make swimming benign,
and there's ample space on the sand to stake out your niche without feeling cramped
– though it can get busy on a cruise-ship day. East around the headland, the wind
whips over the Bon Accord Lagoon, providing a welcome respite from the steamy heat
of the beach as well as ideal conditions for kite-boarding and windsurfing – there's an
outlet offering lessons and equipment rental (see above). Close to the entrance, shops
sell beachwear, clothes and souvenirs, while the two **bars** at each end of the beach are
popular liming spots at sundown; like Sandy Point, the sunset views here are
magnificent. A handful of **food outlets** sell inexpensive roti and other snacks, and a
branch of *Rituals/Pizza Boys* dishes out iced coffees and pepperoni slices. If you want
something more substantial, there's a restaurant at the Bon Accord end of the beach
selling Creole lunches.

Picturesque as it is, Pigeon Point is not without **controversy**. It was the first beach on
Tobago (and still the only one) to charge an entry fee, much to the consternation of
locals and the fishermen whose right to walk and fish freely from the beach has been
curtailed. Equally, many bemoan the water quality, thanks to runoff from the area's
many hotels, and lack of water circulation following constriction of groynes.

Bon Accord Lagoon

Milford Road becomes ruler-straight as it Crown Point slips imperceptibly into the
BON ACCORD district, a mostly residential area whose main point of interest is the **Bon

5

Accord Lagoon, a sweeping oval of mangrove swamp and reef-sheltered, shallow water which forms one of the most important fish nurseries on the island. Though the marine life has been adversely affected by runoff from a nearby sewage treatment plant, the lagoon's sea-grass beds remain a sanctuary for conch, snails, shrimp, oysters, crab, urchins and sponges.

Most of the land skirting the swamp is **privately owned.** You can get pretty close by turning down Golden Grove Road, the turn-off for which lies a couple of kilometres east along Milford Road, and taking the first dirt track you come to – passing the crumbling remains of a windmill and cocoa drying house, once part of the Bon Accord sugar estate (note that the road becomes extremely bumpy after the small bridge, and is best attempted with 4WD in the wet season). You can drive right down to the water by taking Gaskin Bay Road, a wide paved turn-off to the left from Milford just before the housing scheme. A better way to see the lagoon is on a Buccoo Reef boat tour (see p.199) that includes a barbecue at a deserted sandy spit on the lagoon's north side known as **No Man's Land,** an idyllic place to swim.

Canaan

Bon Accord merges into **CANAAN,** another residential district, given its rather odd name by Moravian missionaries. The area was once carved up into individual sugar plantations, and away from the main road there are still large tracts of undeveloped land where cattle graze or coconut trees sway heavy with nuts. These days, though, Canaan is a place to stock up on provisions, with the island's largest supermarket, Penny Savers, right on Milford Road, and a host of excellent fruit and veg stores as well as plenty of small-scale rum shops and cookshops in which to sink a few beers or pick up a local-style meal.

Canoe Bay

Daily 9am–5pm • TT$20, includes use of showers and bathroom

Milford Road's commercial activity tails off past the junction with Shirvan Road, the route to Buccoo (see p.211); just beyond here, a turn-off to the right is signposted for **Canoe Bay,** a pretty and quiet **beach** that was once the site of a large Amerindian settlement; the English named it after the Indian pirogues moored here. Today, the fifteen acres around the bay are beautifully landscaped and an appealingly peaceful place to spend the day. The main area boasts lawns, thatched

---

WATERSPORTS IN SOUTHWEST TOBAGO

The southwest is the best place to indulge in watersports, with a large variety of outlets and operators. **Jet-skis** have gained in popularity, and you can rent them from operators working the sands at Store Bay Beach and Pigeon Point for around US$40 per half-hour. Many also rent snorkel equipment for around US$10 per day (though if you plan on **snorkelling** a lot, it's best to bring or buy your own). For **kite-boarding** (1hr private lesson US$90), **windsurfing** (equipment rental US$45/hr or US$83/day, 1hr lesson US$70), **kayaking** (US$20/hr) and **sailing** on a hobie cat (1hr rental US$45, 1hr lesson US$65; 2 people TT$300 per flight), check Radical Watersports (☏631 5150 or ☏728 5483, ⊛radicalsportstobago.com) on the Bon Accord side of Pigeon Point beach, which is also the best place for the above sports. Radical also offer **stand-up paddleboarding** (see p.203) and an array of paddleboard tours.

During the season (Oct–March), there's excellent **surfing** at Mount Irvine Beach – early morning often sees twenty to thirty surfers riding the waves (see p.214). The southwest is also ideal for **scuba diving**, with a host of operators (see p.205), many of whom rent snorkelling gear. **Fishing** is also lots of fun, whether you opt for deep-sea sport fishing (see p.205) or throwing a line from a pirogue, which you can do with several of the island's tour operators (see p.203).

gazebos, picnic tables and a secluded beach of clean yellow sand and calm waters (slightly marred by some sea-grass beds) – the view stretches right down to Crown Point. This is an excellent place to come if you're travelling with children, since the sheltered water makes for safe swimming and the large grassy areas are perfect for ball games, and a bar serves drinks.

ARRIVAL AND INFORMATION

CROWN POINT AND AROUND

By bus An hourly shuttle service operates between Crown Point (there's a stop just outside the airport complex) and the island's main depot on Sangster Hill Rd in Scarborough; buses leave at roughly half past the hour from Crown Point and on the hour from Scarborough between 5am and 9pm.

Tourist information The tourist office is housed in the last shop on the left of the row opposite the airport arrivals (daily 6am–10pm; ☎639 0509). Staff can provide basic advice on accommodation, transport and activities, and have free maps of Tobago and copies of tourist-oriented magazines.

ACTIVITIES

SCUBA DIVING

Though the best dive sites (see p.241) in Tobago are outside the Crown Point area, many of the island's diver operators are located here. We've listed some of the reliable operators below, all of which are members of the Association of Tobago Dive Operators (ⓦtobagoscubadiving.com), also a good source of general information on diving the island's waters.

Blue Waters Dive'N Blue Waters Inn, Batteaux Bay, Speyside ☎660 5445, ⓦbluewatersinn.com.

Extra Divers Stonehaven Bay ☎639 7424; and Speyside Inn, Speyside ☎660 4852, ⓦextradiverstobago.eu.

Frontier Divers Sandy Point Beach Club, Crown Point ☎631 8138, ⓦtobagofrontierdivers.com.

R & Sea Diving Company Toucan Inn, Store Bay Local Rd, Bon Accord ☎639 8120, ⓦrseadivers.com.

Undersea Tobago Coco Reef, Crown Point ☎631 2626, ⓦunderseatobago.com.

FISHING

Chartering a sport fishing boat is exciting but expensive; rich pickings of marlin, sailfish, tuna and dolphin are caught year-round. A speedy boat accommodating up to six and equipped with rods, tackle and bait will cost in excess of US$450/half-day, US$900 for a full day; some also offer inshore spinning and fly-fishing from a small boat (around US470/hr or US$200 half-day). Reliable operators are listed below.

Grand Slam ☎639 9961 or ☎683 1958, ⓦgrandslamtobago.com.

Hardplay ☎639 7108 or ☎682 3474, ⓦhardplay.net.

MOUNTAIN BIKE TOURS

Mountain Biking Tobago ☎639 9709 or ☎681 5695, ⓦmountainbikingtobago.com. A wide roster of tours for both beginners and serious riders. Tours from US$40.

Slow Leak ☎332 5872, ⓦtobagomountainbike.com. Offers everything from an easy no-hills cycle around the Bon Accord lagoon to an extreme downhill ride from Moriah. Tours from US$45.

HORSERIDING

★ Being with Horses Buccoo ☎639 0953, ⓦbeing-with-horses.com. This wonderful, small-scale operation takes a refreshingly alternative attitude to riding, using bitless bridles and bareback pads rather than saddles. Rides include a trip around the Buccoo headland with a chance to swim your mount across the bay (US$85); there's also a sensory garden back at the stables, great for children and specially designed for those with disabilities.

Friendship Riding Stables Caanan ☎660 8563, ⓦfriendshipridingstables.com. 1.5hr beach rides through mangroves and onto the beach (TT$350), as well as lessons and gentle rides for small children.

GOLF

Mount Irvine ☎639 8871, ⓦmtirvine.com. The oldest course on Tobago, and very pretty, with its par-72, 18 holes (18 holes US$55, club rental US$30, lessons US$40/hr) set on undulating greens, lined with palm trees and overlooked by luxury villas.

Tobago Plantations Golf Club ☎387 0288, ⓦmagdalenagrand.com. Refurbished in 2013, this is a par-72, 18-hole course overlooking the ocean (18 holes US$90, plus US$62.50 for club rental; lessons US$90/hr).

THERAPIES, TREATMENTS AND YOGA

Kariwak Village, Crown Point ☎639 8442, ⓦkariwak.com. Yoga and t'ai chi (TT$70) in a gorgeous thatch-roofed open-sided ajoupa, surrounded by tinkling waterfalls and flowering plants, plus a wide range of alternative therapies and treatments, including Ayurvedic and Thai massages, shiatsu, acupuncture and a therapeutic ozone bath (from TT$360/hr) in the Holistic Treatment Centre.

5

ACCOMMODATION

The sheer amount of **accommodation** in the Crown Point area makes choosing a place to stay mind-boggling. Space is at a premium here, with many hotels and guesthouses built back-to-back with little individuality and scant regard for aesthetics. On the other hand, the high competition keeps prices fairly low, and the absence of ugly high-rise developments makes things feel much less crowded than they actually are. You're also in walking distance of the busiest beaches, restaurants and bars, and can often stroll straight from the airport tarmac to your room. Hotels bordering the runway get some aircraft noise, though there are too few flights for this to be a problem. Bon Accord, meanwhile, holds a few quieter options, as does Store Bay Local Rd.

GUESTHOUSES AND APARTMENTS

Bananaquit Store Bay Local Rd, Bon Accord ☎ 639 9733 or ☎ 368 3539, ⓦ bananaquit.com. Set around a shaded grassy courtyard, these eclectic studios and apartments have plenty of character, with rattan furnishings and kitchenettes or full kitchen. All have a/c, fan and cable TV, and there's free access to the pool at the adjacent *Store Bay Resort*. Wi-fi throughout. TT$450

Candles in the Wind 145 Anthony Charles Crescent, Bon Accord ☎ 631 5335, ⓦ candlesinthewind.8k.com. This very friendly hotel in a quiet, mainly residential part of Bon Accord contains eight en-suite rooms with cable TV and a/c; there's also an attic dorm with bunk beds (US$25) for those on a budget. There are two fully equipped shared kitchens and laundry facilities on site, and wi-fi available. US$65

Canoe Bay Cove Estate ☎ 631 0367, ⓦ canoett.com. Right on the beach and in spacious grounds, this beautifully secluded place has lovely apartments with a/c, TV, balcony and kitchenette; there's also a bar and a heart-shaped pool, and it's an ideal spot for families. Wi-fi available. TT$440

Crusoe's Apartments Store Bay Local Rd, Bon Accord ☎ 639 7789, ⓦ crusoes.net. Spacious self-contained one- and two-bedroom apartments, tastefully decorated in blue and orange with a/c, cable TV, fully equipped kitchen and pool; wi-fi also available. Friendly and very good value. One-bedroom TT$450

★**Dimples Apartments** Store Bay Branch Rd, Bon Accord ☎ 660 8156 or ☎ 786 8134, ⓦ dimples -apartments.com. Just back from Store Bay Local Rd, and run by a friendly English/Tobagonian couple, this is a real bargain, with spotless, comfortable one-bedroom a/c apartments with a full kitchen/living room and a porch. Wi-fi throughout. TT$300

Douglas Apartments John Gorman Trace, at Milford Rd, Bon Accord ☎ 639 7723, ⓦ douglastobago.com. Sparkling clean, spacious one- and two-bedroom apartments, each with a lounge, full kitchen, patio, a/c and TV – the three loft rooms sleeping five are especially nice. Pool and a friendly family atmosphere. Car rental is available on site. US$85

Johnston Apartments Store Bay Rd, Crown Point ☎ 639 8915, ⓦ johnstonapartments.com. Right above Store Bay and sharing the pool and restaurant of its larger neighbour, *Crown Point Beach Hotel*, these studios and one- and three-bedroom apartments are huge (one sleeps eight) and come with fully equipped kitchen, living room, a/c, cable TV and phone – and immediate access to the sand and sea (as reflected in the price). Wi-fi throughout. US$115

Kia's Across from the Beach Airport Rd, Crown Point ☎ 475 6344, ⓦ kiasacrossfromthebeach.com. Opposite the entrance to the Store Bay car park rather than the sand, but right in the middle of the Crown Point action and with brightly painted a/c rooms of varying sizes; the cheapest (TT$250) have a shared bathroom. TT$390

Mike's Store Bay Rd, Crown Point ☎ 639 8050. Excellent value and a two-minute walk from the airport, this busy, locally owned place has spacious, clean and inviting one-, two- and three-bedroom apartments with a/c, ceiling fan, cable TV and full kitchen. There's a mini-mart on site. TT$300

Native Abode 13 Fourth St ☎ 631 1285, ⓦ native abode.com, Bon Accord. Just off Gaskin Bay Rd (itself off Store Bay Local Rd), and boasting a quiet location in the middle of residential streets. The owner's garden has plenty of fruit trees which guests can pick from, and the a/c rooms with kitchenette are attractively decorated in a modern, swish style. Rates include breakfast. US$120

Sandy Point Beach Club Store Bay Local Rd, Crown Point ☎ 639 0820, ⓦ sandypointbeachclub.com. Overlooking the sea at the western extreme of Store Bay Local Rd, this is a well-run place with studios and one-bedroom apartments with a/c, kitchen and TV; facilities include a pool, outdoor hot tubs, tennis court, kids' playground and a beach bar. Daily shuttle to local beaches, and wi-fi available. Studio US$130, one-bedroom apartments US$170

Store Bay Resort Store Bay Local Rd, Crown Point ☎ 639 8810, ⓦ storebayholidays.com. Friendly place in a excellent location close to Store Bay, with friendly staff, a pool and modern, appealing studios and suites with a/c, TV and fully equipped kitchenettes. TT$540

Sun Spree Resort Store Bay Local Rd, Bon Accord ☎ 631 5195, ⓦ sunspreeresortltd.com. Great little place spreading back from the road with a pool, restaurant and bar and spacious, modern rooms with a/c, cable TV, fridge and safe. Excellent value, close to the beaches and restaurants but still nice and quiet, and very friendly staff. TT$530

5

SUPERMARKETS IN TOBAGO

If you're staying in self-catering accommodation and plan cooking for yourself, bear in mind that supermarkets outside of southwest Tobago sell only the most basic items. Even if you're staying in Castara or further afield, it's best to stock up here on your way from the airport. The best all-round **supermarket** is Penny Savers (Mon–Sat 8am–8.30pm, Sun 8am–1pm), on Milford Road at the Canaan end; it's competitively priced, relatively well stocked and has lots of imported foods. There's another branch in Carnbee, on the Auchenskeoch–Buccoo Bay Road, and one on Wilson Road in Scarborough. Also in the capital, Cost Cutters on the Plymouth side of Wilson Road, is well stocked and inexpensive. Morshead Delicatessen on Buccoo Road, off Shirvan Road (Mon–Fri 8am–6pm, Sat 8am–7pm, Sun 8am–noon) sells a wealth of imported goods, including cold meats and cheeses, plus some local delights such as Tobago Cocoa Estate Chocolate, though prices are high. For fruit and veg, head to the Canaan Food Basket on Milford Rd (usually daily 9am–8pm).

HOTELS

Coco Reef Airport Rd, Crown Point ☎ 639 8571, in US and Canada ☎ 800 221 1294, ⓦ cocoreef.com. This peach-painted enclave is Crown Point's largest hotel and the most resort-like on the island, with high perimeter walls enclosing the grounds and a man-made white sand beach. Two restaurants, two bars, health spa, tennis courts, pool, watersports and rooms with every associated frippery offer opulence at the expense of atmosphere. Rates include breakfast and all-inclusive plans available. US$326

★**Conrado** Pigeon Point Rd, Crown Point ☎ 639 0145, ⓦ conradobeachresort.com. The closest you can stay to Pigeon Point and one of the relatively few hotels in Tobago next to the beach – indeed, you can almost feel the ocean spray from the expansive balconies that come with the sea-view rooms. The rooms are modestly proportioned, but come with en-suite bathrooms, a/c and cable TV. Good breakfasts (included) and an on-site restaurant/bar right by the sand. US$105

Crown Point Beach Hotel Store Bay Local Rd, Crown Point ☎ 639 8781, ⓦ crownpointbeachhotel.com. Expansive hotel on the westerly side of Store Bay Beach. The modern, comfortable rooms all have sea-facing views, as do the more private *cabanas* dotting the garden. Both have kitchenette, a/c, phone, cable TV and small patio/balcony, and there's a pool, restaurant and tennis courts on site. Usually busy with a Trinidadian/European crowd. Rooms US$115, *cabanas* US$130

The Hummingbird 128 Store Bay Local Rd, Bon Accord ☎ 635 0241, ⓦ hummingbirdtobago.com. This intimate, family-run hotel has a pool, restaurant and bar and ten spotless en-suite rooms named after tropical

flowers – all have a/c, fridge and cable TV, and suites have a kitchenette, too. The likeable Anglo-Trinidadian owners are a useful source of information. Rooms US$60, suites US$90

★**Kariwak Village** Store Bay Local Rd, Crown Point ☎ 639 8442, ⓦ kariwak.com. A jewel in the middle of this bustling area: yoga classes in the lush gardens, excellent, friendly staff and peaceful atmosphere give a real feeling of holistic retreat. The thatch-roofed *cabanas* are split in two and furnished using local wood crafted on the premises; each has a/c and phone. There's also the option of larger and more luxurious garden rooms, and facilities include an ozonated pool, outdoor waterfall-fed jacuzzi, and a fabulous restaurant/bar (see p.208). Rates include excellent breakfast. US$205

Magdalena Grande Tobago Plantations, Lowlands ☎ 660 8503, ⓦ magdalenagrand.com. Overhanging the ocean behind the Tobago Plantations Golf Course, which it now maintains, this is the largest hotel on the island, with extensive facilities that include three pools, sauna, spa, fitness centre tennis courts and kids' playground, plus several restaurants and bars. The private beach isn't Tobago's best, though you do get constant breezes via the Atlantic winds that blast the coastline here. US$235

Toucan Inn Store Bay Local Rd, Crown Point ☎ 639 7173, ⓦ toucan-inn.com. This welcoming hotel is a little removed from the area's bustle, but still within easy walking distance of the action. Decked out with wooden fittings, the garden rooms or cabanas around the pool all have a/c, tea- and coffee-making equipment and a porch area. *Bonkers* – the on-site restaurant – is a local institution (see p.208). US$120

EATING

Crown Point has **eating** options for all tastes and budgets, mostly within easy walking distance of the area's hotels and guesthouses. For inexpensive barbecue, look for stalls set up by the roadside at lunchtime and on weekend evenings; close to *Mike's* resort on Store Bay Rd, there's also a van selling rotis and a cream-painted little wooden building dishing up good local lunches.

5

STORE BAY DINING

An essential part of any visit to Tobago is a plate of crab and dumplin', macaroni pie with callaloo, or fresh fish with provisions from one of the row of **food huts** facing Store Bay Beach. This strip of cookshops (from right to left there's *Miss Jean's*, *Miss Trim's*, *Miss Joycie's*, *Alma's*, *Sylvia's* and *Miss Esmie's*) offer tasty, inexpensive local cuisine, and the covered sea-facing gazebo with seating and tables is an attractive place to sit, eat and watch the world go by. Prices and food vary little from stall to stall: bake with fish or eggs, buljol and smoked herring for **breakfast**; while for **lunch**, there's goat, beef, chicken or vegetable roti, stewed beef or chicken, conch or crab and dumplin', pelau, vegetable rice, stewed lentils, macaroni pie, callaloo and ground provisions. Most stalls also make **juices** such as mauby or grapefruit, and perhaps peanut or sea-moss punch. All are open daily from around 8.30am to 8.30pm, but the flow of custom dictates business hours.

The Backyard Café Airport Rd, Crown Point ☎639 7264. Affordable and easy-going café by day, serving excellent baguette sandwiches such as salami and brie (around TT$55) as well as salads (around TT$69), homemade cakes, fresh juices and decent coffee. In the evenings, dinner options run from chicken escalope (TT$99) to fish in coconut sauce (TT$129). Mon–Fri 11am–3pm, Wed–Fri 6–9pm.

Bonkers Toucan Inn, Store Bay Local Rd, Crown Point ☎639 7173. This excellent and popular restaurant serves tasty, mid-priced Tobagonian food under a shady pavilion or at poolside tables. Breakfast is local- or European-style, while lunch usually includes sandwiches and soup. Dinner highlights (TT$70–200) include "voodoo" shrimp, "lambaabaa" curry, lobster and steak tenderloin. There's a varied wine list and regular live music in high season. Daily 7.30–10.30am, 11.30am–2.30pm & 7–10pm.

Café Coco Just off Pigeon Point Rd, Crown Point ☎639 0996. Ornate gardens decorated with waterfalls, fountains and ponds provide attractive surroundings, although the mid-priced food – which draws on influences from around the Caribbean and includes dishes such as Cuban-style stewed beef or chargrilled lamb with aubergine choka – is rather hit and miss. Mains TT$75–175. Daily 5.30–9.30pm.

Chef's Barbecue Airport Rd, Crown Point ☎631 3000. This is a great option for a cheap takeaway (though there are a couple of tables out front), selling barbecued chicken and pigtail or grilled fish, plus local staples such as pigeon peas, macaroni pie, callaloo and salads. You pay by weight; a meal should cost about TT$50. Saltfish and bake breakfasts are also well executed. Daily 8am–10pm.

D'Curve Bar and Grill Pigeon Point Rd, Crown Point ☎741 7768. Good service and tasty mains (TT$80–130) such as coconut curry shrimp with basmati rice or whole grilled snapper, plus inexpensive burgers and bar snacks such as wings, flying fish, geera port and jerk chicken. Mon–Tues & Thurs–Sat 11am–late.

Fortune Milford Rd, Bon Accord ☎639 8818. Decent Chinese restaurant with an excellent range of well-priced dishes, as well as a varied vegetarian selection, to eat in or take away. Mains TT$50–150. Daily 11am–11pm.

Jenny's Authentic Cuisine Airport Rd, Crown Point ☎778 6663. In a prime position on a shaded veranda in the middle of Crown Point's busiest stretch, this is a pleasant spot for local breakfasts such as sada roti with tomato choka, and smoked herring or buljol with coconut bake (TT$20–25), though eggs, bacon and the like are also available, as well as roti lunches (from TT$40). Daily 8am–3.30pm.

★**Kariwak Village** Store Bay Local Rd, Crown Point ☎639 8442. Homegrown vegetables and herbs, inventive slants on local staples and a relaxing setting make this hotel restaurant one of the best places to eat in Tobago. Breakfast (from TT$30) might be saltfish buljol with coconut bake or a herb omelette, while at lunch you can get sandwiches and salads, from shrimp to Tobagonian goat's cheese (TT$80–90). Dinner menus are set (three courses around TT$185–230), usually with a meat, fish or vegetarian option, and everything is supremely fresh, succulently cooked and completely delicious. Accompanied by live music, the Friday and Saturday night buffet (TT$230) is particularly worth checking out. Great service and vegan food available. Daily 7am–10pm.

★**La Cantina** RBTT compound, Airport Rd, Crown Point ☎639 8242, ⓦlacantinapizzeria.com. Bustling little place serving truly excellent pizzas (TT$60–100) baked in a wood-fired oven. The forty different toppings range from capricciosa (tomato, mozzarella, prosciutto, mushroom, artichokes and anchovies) to Greca (mozzarella, feta, tomato), and there are also artful salads and specials, plus excellent cocktails and wines (including prosecco). No bookings so you may have to wait for a table, but takeaway available. Tues & Wed noon–2.45pm, Mon & Thurs–Sat noon–9.45pm, Sun 6–9.45pm.

Marcia's Store Bay Local Rd, Bon Accord ☎639 0359. The genial owners make this one of the most welcoming small restaurants in the area, offering great, affordable local food (mains from TT$80): anything from red snapper Creole, lobster in coconut garlic sauce, stewed or curried conch and Sunday-style stewed chicken with macaroni pie and callaloo, all served with rice and ground provisions. Gorgeous cassava pudding for dessert. Daily 11am–2pm & 7–10pm.

★ **Pasta Gallery** Pigeon Point Rd, Crown Point ☎ 727 8200, ⓦ pastagallery.net. Great little pasta joint, with tables outside on the patio and in the indoor art-bedecked dining room, serving reliable pasta dishes (TT$75–95) such as fettucine with shrimp, spaghetti with mixed seafood, pesto linguine, beef lasagne and spaghetti carbonara. Great service and decent wine.

Gluten-free pasta available, as is takeaway. Mon & Tues 6.30–10pm, Thurs & Fri noon–2pm & 6–10pm, Sat 6.30–10pm.

Skewers Airport Rd, Crown Point ☎ 631 8964. Permanently busy (and tiny) Middle Eastern place with a couple of tables, serving mostly takeaway orders of grilled chicken, shrimp or fish, plus steak, usually served as a combo with one side order (TT$40–75), plus gyros with beef, chicken or fish (TT$30) and home-made, well-spiced falafel, tabbouleh, baba ghanoush, fatoush and hummus (TT$25). Daily 10am–10pm.

DRINKING, NIGHTLIFE AND ENTERTAINMENT

Crown Point is the centre of Tobago's **nightlife** scene, which is concentrated along the stretch of Airport Rd between the Store Bay and Pigeon Point turn-offs; the paved area at the corner of Pigeon Point and Milford roads is something of a hub after dark, with ice-cream stalls doing a roaring trade and plenty of people milling around and enjoying the cool evening air. Of other entertainment possibilities, the Lowlands Mall holds Tobago's only **cinema**.

BARS AND CLUBS

Angler's Bar Store Bay Beach, Crown Point (no phone). Facing the sea at Store Bay, this is a good spot to sink a few beers as the sun sets, accompanied by blasting dancehall and soca. Daily 9am–10pm.

★ **Bago's Beach Bar** Pigeon Point Rd, Crown Point ☎ 384 2460. Popular beach bar in a quiet spot next to a pretty stretch of sand on the way to Pigeon Point. Cold beers, cocktails and occasional karaoke – there's no better place to have a few drinks while watching the sun set than here. Happy hour 5.30–7pm. Daily 6pm–midnight.

D'Curve Bar and Grill Pigeon Point Rd, Crown Point ☎ 741 7768. Cheap beers (often TT$10) and decent cocktails, too, served on a spacious porch just back from the Crown Point melee. DJ on Friday and Saturday nights, too.

Mon–Tues & Thurs–Sat 11am–late.

First and Last Store Bay Local Rd, Crown Point (no phone). Just off Airport Rd, on the first stretch of Store Bay Local Rd, this classic Tobago rum shop puts out the speakers on weekend evenings to pump gentle reggae into the streets – and the beers are truly "beastly" cold. Daily 11am–late.

Illusions Pigeon Point Rd, Crown Point ☎ 639 7876. With an outdoor bar area pumping high-octane soca into the street, and an a/c indoor section with pool tables and room to dance, this is usually a lively spot, with occasional live entertainment. Daily 10am–6am.

Jade Monkey Airport Rd, Crown Point ☎ 631 0500. Open-air bar (with an attached casino), with lots of booths under thatch-roofed gazebos, which attracts a mixed clientele.

TOBAGO FESTIVALS

Though Carnival in Trinidad tends to take precedence in the T&T festival calendar, Tobago more than holds its own in terms of celebrations, and even if your visit doesn't coincide with some of the bigger events, there's almost always a beach party or fete to liven things up. Of the annual festivals, August means **Great Race** (see p.35), when a flotilla of high-powered speedboats compete to be the first to cross the waters between the two islands. This being T&T, there's more concentration on partying than maritime action: the whole shebang kicks off with the massive Great Fete outdoor party and stageshow at Pigeon Point, and on race day itself, huge crowds gather at the Store Bay finish line, all the while entertained by blaring soca, rhythm sections, pan bands and copious quantities of rum and beer. A similar scene unravels at the annual round of **fishermen's festivals**, which celebrate patron of the trade St Peter by way of friendly beach parties at Castara and Charlotteville: vats of pacro water (shellfish soup) simmer and stacks of speakers get everyone in the mood for dancing. For something gentler, you might check out the **Harvest Festivals** (see pp.33–35) held in the island's villages throughout the year, which feature folk singing and dancing, heaps of "blue food" such as dasheen and tannia, and a friendly, community vibe. But the most hyped event on the island these days is the **Tobago Jazz Festival** (see p.35), held between April and June by the sea at Plymouth and featuring international acts alongside the best of local talent – past performers include Diana Ross, Elton John, Sting, Emile Sandé, Erykah Badu, John Legend and, of course, T&T's own Machel Montano. .

5

Music from DJs in the evenings, this is one of the liveliest spots in the area for a few drinks. Live music on Thursdays and special events throughout the year. Daily 11am–late.

Overhang Sports Bar Airport Rd, Crown Point ☎639 8929. With a raised veranda that's great for people-watching and a chilly a/c interior with a dancefloor, this genial place offers karaoke, sports games on the big-screen TVs and lots of drinks specials throughout the week. DJ Fri & Sat evening, plus a menu of burgers and bar snacks. Tues–Sun 6pm–late.

Renmar's Pigeon Point Beach, Crown Point ☎631 8768. Right on the famed sands of Pigeon Point – the drinks are a little overpriced but the sunsets are magical and the setting lovely. Daily 9am–8pm.

★**The Shade** Mt Pleasant Blvd, Bon Accord ☎639 9651. Just off Milford Rd, this is Tobago's biggest and best nightclub, with a dancefloor under a large, open-air thatched cabana a few minutes' walk from Crown Point. Invariably packed with both locals and tourists, but only from around midnight onwards. Cover charge Fri & Sat. Wed–Sat 8pm–late.

CINEMAS

MovieTowne Claude Noel Hwy, Lowlands ☎631 1843, ⓦmovietowne.com. Past the Tobago Plantations golf course, the Lowlands Mall holds this modern cinema screening Hollywood hits. Icy a/c, so bring something warm.

SHOPPING

Shopping is not one of the southwest's – or Tobago's – strong points. You can pick up souvenirs from the craft market at Store Bay Beach, though the selection at **Shore Things** (see p.226) is better quality. The concrete conglomeration of the **Lowlands Mall** on Claude Noel Hwy has a book store, toyshop, various clothing stores and a shop selling cigars. Adjacent to the mall, just off the highway, the signposted **Art Gallery** (☎631 1424, ⓦtobagoartgallery.com; Mon, Tues, Thurs & Fri 9am–5pm) has a decent collection of high-quality local art for sale, from sculpture to painting.

DIRECTORY

Banks and exchange There's a bureau de change upstairs in the airport terminal, and a branch of Republic Bank (Mon–Thurs 8am–3pm, Fri 8am–1pm & 3–5pm) with an ATM in the shops opposite the arrivals area. Other ATMs in the area are located at the RBTT bank on Airport Rd, just past the turn-off to Store Bay, and at Penny Savers supermarket on Milford Rd and in Canaan. There are also several banks in Scarborough.

Hospitals and medical care The new Scarborough General Hospital (☎660 4744) is just off the Claude Noel Hwy at Signal Hill, and has an A&E department. For an ambulance, call ☎990. If you need a doctor, try Dr Sonia Telfer (☎772 5770).

Laundry The Clothes Wash Café, in the RBC Bank compound on Airport Rd (daily 8am–8pm; ☎639 0007), have self-service machines, and will also wash and fold for you.

Pharmacies Late-opening pharmacies include Dove Drugs, in the Real Value Plaza on Auchenskeoch–Buccoo Bay Rd, Carnbee, which runs from Claude Noel Hwy to Shirvan Rd (Mon–Sat 8am–7pm, Sun and public holidays 9am–noon; ☎639 2976). In Scarborough, there's Scarborough Drugs, opposite *KFC* on the corner of Carrington St and Wilson Rd (Mon–Sat 8am–8pm, Sun and public holidays 8am–noon; ☎639 4161).

The northwest coast

Just before Milford Road widens into the highway, the left-hand turn-off of **Shirvan Road** is the route to Tobago's **northwest coast**, home to **Buccoo Bay** and its famous **reef**, the golf course and surfing beach at **Mount Irvine** and, ultimately, **Stonehaven Bay**, **Turtle Beach** and the neat town of **Plymouth**, from which the Northside Road threads along the Caribbean coastline through **Arnos Vale** and the pretty hilltop villages of **Golden Lane** and **Les Coteaux**. In easy driving distance from the beaches, restaurants and nightlife of Crown Point, but with a much more laidback and sometimes upmarket feel, this is a great area in which to base yourself, with plenty of lovely, less high-octane beaches and a smattering of great places to eat and drink.

Shirvan Road

North of the new shopping plaza at the corner of Milford Road, the first stretch of **Shirvan Road** is bordered to the left by a plantation of towering coconut palms and to the right by thick hedges masking what was once Shirvan Park **horse racing track**. A fire in 1985 put a

5

> **SUNDAY SCHOOL**
>
> A Tobago institution, **Sunday School** is most definitely not for the pious. This outdoor party is the highlight of the week's nightlife, with swarms of people, food stalls and cars taking over Buccoo village. The action begins at around 8pm, when the **Buccooneers Steel Orchestra** play pan (sometimes at the beach facility, or otherwise at the Captain's Sand Bar just up the hill on the main road) for a couple of hours while the crowds sample food or browse the craft stalls; there's also traditional dancing and drumming at *Hendrix* bar, opposite the beach facility, which also plays more sedate "back in times" music as the night wears on. The crowd begins to thicken at around 10pm, when the **sound system** starts up in the beach facility; music policy is Jamaican dancehall with the most popular soca, hip-hop and R&B tunes thrown in, and the dancefloor is invariably jumping as experienced winers (see "Glossary," p.282) display their skills, foreigners let loose or take a wining lesson, and the gigolos (and tourists) scout for a partner – Sunday School is well known as a kind of pick-up joint, so it's the ideal place to watch the intricate mating dance of thrill-seeking foreigners and hard-working local lotharios. Sunday School is not just for the young – locals and tourists of all ages come here to chill out and many tour guides offer Sunday School trips for about US$20. Note that parking can be difficult as the night wears on, so try to arrive early.
>
> It hardly needs saying that Sunday School is a place where you should be more mindful than usual of the risk of **theft**. Leave valuables and other items you can't afford to lose at the hotel, avoid getting so drunk that you become a sitting duck for opportunistic robbers and, if driving, try to park in busy, well-lit places, since muggings have been known to take place as revellers return to their cars at the end of the evening.

permanent stop to horse racing in Tobago and today part of the site has been slated for development. Continuing north, Shirvan Road passes turn-offs to quietly residential **Mount Pleasant** and **Carnbee** (the latter has a couple of supermarkets; see p.207), while several smart restaurants overlook the road. A cluster of tourist-oriented signposts mark the next crossroads, **Buccoo Junction**. Here, route taxis running between Scarborough and the north coast pick up and drop off passengers, so you'll often see beckoning hands if you're driving. The right turn at the crossroads is Auchenskeoch (pronounced "or-kins-styor") Buccoo Bay Road – take the first left from this road and you'll climb into the residential portion of **Mount Irvine**, with its lavish villas and fantastic views down over Buccoo Reef; carry straight on and you head through residential Carnbee to meet the highway.

A little further up Shirvan Road and you're at the outskirts of tiny **Bethel**, a precipitously situated and completely charming rural village that affords more wonderful views of Lowlands and the Buccoo coast. From Bethel, Orange Hill Road eventually meets Claude Noel Highway a couple of kilometres west of Scarborough.

Buccoo

The seaward turn-off from Shirvan Road at Buccoo Junction runs past a small supermarket and into **BUCCOO** village, haphazardly built around the calm and beautiful bay that shares its name. Fishing remains a major industry here – the day's catch is cleaned and sold next to the beach when the boats return in the late afternoon – but this close-knit community is best known for the weekly **Sunday School** (see box above) shenanigans and for the annual Easter **goat races**, now held at a smart purpose-built track and pavilion behind the new **Buccoo Integrated Facility**, a rather incongruously large concrete complex just back from the beach which encompasses a dancefloor used for Sunday School, an upstairs seafood restaurant, craft vendors' booths, a rather desultory tourist information kiosk and a big car park.

The **beachfront** immediately in front is primarily the preserve of fishermen and not really a place to swim, but the undeveloped, palm-lined western fringe of the bay is gorgeous, with clean water and plenty of shells and coral fragments to collect. Trees and mangroves separate the beach from the Bon Accord Wetland, and if you walk right to the end of the

5

GOAT RACES

Easter weekend is to Tobago what Carnival is to Trinidad: an unofficial national holiday when hotels are filled to the brim and the island erupts with festivities. A succession of huge open-air parties and well-attended harvest feasts culminate on Easter Tuesday at the **Buccoo goat races**, a tradition since 1925. Though attempting to race one of the world's most belligerent animals may seem a little ridiculous to the uninitiated, these tournaments are taken very seriously by aficionados, who study the form (and character) of the sleekly groomed animals and place bets on their favourites. Raised separately from the run-of-the-mill roadside grazer, racing goats undergo a rigorous training routine and return to the tracks year after year. Prize specimens live out their days as stud goats to breed more potential champions.

The preliminary round at the Mount Pleasant Family Fun Day on Easter Monday gives everyone a chance to see which goat is running best, but the main event is at Buccoo on the Tuesday. Food vendors and craft stalls line the streets and a carnival atmosphere builds as fast as the crowds, who are kept entertained by dancing and drumming in between stakes. Smartly attired in white shorts and coloured vests, the jockeys limber up by the side of the tracks, a necessary exercise, as their ability to keep up with their goat (and keep hold of it) over the 150m race has more influence on their success or failure than the capabilities of the goat itself: animals are raced at the end of a rope, and kept on course via taps from a long switch. Once the jockeys manage to manoeuvre their malignant charges into starting position, the actual races are a joy to watch. With wild-eyed stares, the goats tear haphazardly down the track, often taking a diagonal course that trips up competitors and runners alike, to the delight of the spectators. The best of the bunch battle for supremacy in the final "Champ of Champs" race, while "Champion Jockey", "Champion Trainer" and "Most Outstanding Goat" prizes are also presented.

Once all the races are over on Tuesday, the final all-night party swings into action, and the dancing continues until dawn.

---

sands and clamber into the bush, you can explore the remains of the house that Britain's Princess Margaret stayed in during a Tobago sojourn in the late 1950s. Note that many of the coastal trees here are toxic manchineels (see p.271); offenders have a white strip painted around the trunk.

ACCOMMODATION

BUCCOO

Buccoo holds a few inexpensive places to **stay**, as well as a couple of good **restaurants**, and there are a couple of alternatives on Old Grange Rd, above the golf course. There are also several inexpensive cookshops selling local food on Buccoo's main road. If you're self-catering, note there are a couple of supermarkets in the area (see p.207).

HOTELS AND GUESTHOUSES

Fish Tobago 26a Buccoo Point ☎ 309 0062, ⓦ fish tobago.com. Set back from the main street as you enter Buccoo, this is a popular little guesthouse, well run and a good place to meet fellow visitors. The brightly painted rooms are all well appointed with kitchenette/living area and a separate a/c bedroom with en-suite bathroom; some are larger than others, and there are also two-bedroom apartments and a dorm (beds US$30) with shared kitchen. All units have TV/DVD player and wi-fi. Rooms US$35

★ **Miller's Guesthouse** Miller St ☎ 660 8371 or ☎ 772 5609, ⓦ millersguesthouse.com. Pleasant guesthouse in a nice spot overlooking Buccoo Bay. The rooms (sleeping two or three) are basic yet comfortable, with private bathroom, sink and fan. Dorm beds (US$27.50) are available for budget travellers, and there's also a one-bedroom apartment with kitchen and great views. All rooms have a/c, cable TV and wi-fi. Doubles US$54, apartment US$72

Reef View Apartments Miller St ☎ 660 7264 or ☎ 373 0904, ⓦ reefviewapts.com. In a fantastic hilltop position overlooking Buccoo Bay, this locally run place is a great option. One-bed apartments have two double beds, living room and a kitchen, as well as lovely sea views from the private porch; there are also two-bedroom apartments downstairs. All have a/c, cable TV and wi-fi. TT$400

★ **Seaside Garden** 29 Buccoo Point ☎ 639 0682, ⓦ tobago-guesthouse.com. A great bargain, within walking distance of the action in the centre of Buccoo, and offering clean, simple and inviting rooms, some smaller than others, with a/c or ceiling fans and en-suite bathrooms; those downstairs have gorgeous antique beds, and there's a shared kitchen and sundeck. The upstairs apartment with living area and fully equipped kitchen has lovely bay views. Bike rental available, and wi-fi throughout. Rooms US$42, apartment US$100

EATING, DRINKING AND ENTERTAINMENT

Buccoo is a great place for a **drink** overlooking the bay as the sun sinks behind Pigeon Point, and the town and surrounding area are home to some of the best restaurants in the southwest. On Sundays, vendors set up elaborate **food stalls** around the beach facility to cater to Sunday School patrons, serving anything from barbecued fish or chicken with all the trimmings to lobster; ask about pricing in advance, as they can be surprisingly expensive. There are also a host of little cookshops along the main road offering inexpensive fish, chicken and roti lunches.

★**El Pescador** Buccoo Point, Buccoo ☎ 631 1266, 🌐 leos-pescador.com. In a fantastic setting on a terrace overlooking the sea and reachable via Miller St or by walking along the seafront, the location is as enjoyable as the food, with sea breezes and a perfect sunset view best enjoyed with a rum punch in hand. The menu is dominated by seafood (mains TT$125–320) and includes shrimp salad and calamari at lunchtime, and nicely cooked fish, lobster and seafood for dinner, alongside great pizzas, steaks and lamb chops. Breakfast is also available; try the huevos rancheros: eggs with red beans, ham, fried plantain and garlic bread. Tues–Sun 8am–10pm.

★**La Tartaruga** Buccoo Village ☎ 639 0940. Owned and run by a mercurial Italian émigré, with tables indoors or on an open-air patio. It features top-class Italian cuisine: lovely starters (TT$25–95) include fish carpaccio, parmesan eggplant or antipasti; there's also a range of home-made pasta (gnocchi in gorgonzola sauce, sage ravioli, beef and

mushroom cannelloni; TT$75–145) or specialities such as grilled lobster, shrimp and fish (TT$85–185). Desserts – Drambuie crème caramel, home-made Italian ice cream – are equally memorable. The food is reasonably priced given the quality, but the extensive wine selection can increase your bill considerably. Mon–Sat 6.30–10pm.

★**Watermill** Shirvan Rd ☎ 639 0000. In a lovely setting under the cut-stone roof of a former mill, this long-standing restaurant has been revitalized by its new operators, who cook up excellent Caribbean/international cuisine. The daily offerings are written up on a board; lunch (TT$45–70) runs from well-executed sandwiches (try the coronation chicken or grilled aubergine with goat's cheese) to salads and burgers, while for dinner (TT$140–175) you might start with a Creole saltfish gratin and go on to rack of lamb with chilli and mint or mahi-mahi in a dill beurre blanc. Wonderful desserts, too. Mon–Sat noon–3pm & 6–10pm.

Mount Irvine

The swaying palms and shaven greens of Tobago's first **golf course** herald the outskirts of **MOUNT IRVINE**, the next coastal village north from Buccoo, a scattered community of luxury villas around the golf course that's centred around its gorgeous main beach, home to Tobago's surfing scene and one of the nicest spots in the southwest to spend a day by the sea. Beyond the golf course, the hitherto hidden Caribbean Sea coast swings spectacularly back into view; yachts bob on the waves and craggy volcanic rock formations bordering Booby Point make an arresting backdrop to the west. There's a lovely section of undeveloped beach known as **Grange** or Mount Irvine Wall behind a low concrete bulwark just past the golf course; it's very popular with locals who often sit chatting in the emerald-green water.

Mount Irvine Beach

Lifeguards daily 10am–6pm • Changing facilities TT$1

North of Grange Beach and around the next bend of Shirvan Road is **Mount Irvine Beach**, a busy slip of fine yellow sand surrounded by covered gazebos for picnicking and the ubiquitous palms and sea grape trees. The showers and changing facilities are adequate, and there's a bar/restaurant doling out cold drinks and simple fish-and-chips lunches. During the summer months, the sea here is calm enough to make exploration of the ornate offshore **reef** a joy, and the clear, greenish waters offer excellent swimming year-round. However, Mount Irvine is at its liveliest between December and March, when it becomes one of the island's best **surfing** beaches, with huge breakers crashing in and a cool surfers' scene on the sand, a world away from the packaged postcard-Caribbean feel of Pigeon Point and known to its devotees as the "Office". Note that the water here is initially shallow and there's a reef directly offshore, so surf fins can be badly damaged and no protective footwear is allowed (this is done to protect the reef from over-eager surfers jumping in and damaging the coral).

5

Mount Irvine hotel beach

Just to the south of the public area, past where fishermen sell their daily catch, the semi-private section of beach maintained by the *Mount Irvine Bay Hotel* offers even better swimming and excellent snorkelling, though it's perhaps less atmospheric, and parking is limited. Non-guests are welcome to swim; recliners are available to rent, and there's a restaurant serving lunch and drinks.

Back Bay

Around the headland that caps the eastern end of Mount Irvine Beach, **Back Bay** is a much quieter swathe of sand. To get there, take the dirt track toward the sea off from the main road opposite Gleneagles Drive; you have to scramble down a bank to get to the sand. A gorgeous and completely undeveloped swathe of sand with several very photogenic rocky outcrops, Back Bay is a secluded spot. As currents can be dangerous, however, it's best to stick to paddling or bodysurfing in the shallows – and as the beach is quite remote and robberies have occurred, you're well advised to visit in a group.

ACTIVITIES   MOUNT IRVINE

Surfing Boards (around US$25/hr) can usually be rented at Mount Irvine Beach; ask around. George Charles (☎ 294 6509, ⊛ surf-tobago.com/george) has been offering surfing classes here for some years, and is one of the best choices should you want to learn to surf. Another good option is Jason Apparicio (☎ 367 1744, ✉ appas_j@hotmail.com). Both charge around US$50/lesson.

ACCOMMODATION AND EATING

★**Bijou des Caraibes** 3 Jacamar Drive, Mount Irvine ☎ 639 9604 or ☎ 734 7303, ⊛ bijou-des-caraibe.com. In a quiet residential setting above Mount Irvine golf course, this is a peaceful little hideaway, with a row of studios and one- or two-bedroom apartments, with a/c bedrooms and kitchenette set in flower-filled gardens with a good-sized pool. All are clean and functional, but not luxurious, and are ideal if you want a degree of independence. The helpful owner is a mine of information on Tobago. Studios US$65, one-bedroom apartment US$80

★**Jackie's Roti** Mount Irvine Beach ☎ 767 9385. Based in a blue-painted kiosk at the roadside above the beach car park, Jackie makes some of the best roti in Tobago, freshly cooked each day and dressed with home-made curry mango or *pomme cythere*; rotis come in chicken, veg or flying fish versions (from TT$30), but call ahead or go early as food is often sold out by midday. Mon–Fri & Sun 10am–2pm.

Mount Irvine Bay Hotel and Golf Club ☎ 639 8871, ⊛ mtirvine.com. The grand old lady of Tobago hotels, this sprawling property adjacent to the golf course and above Mount Irvine Beach has tennis courts, sauna, huge pool, three restaurants and five bars. Rooms are spacious and equipped with a/c, phone, satellite TV and patio, though they're a little dated and perhaps overpriced. US$150

Kimme Museum

Kimme Drive • Sun 10am–2pm, appointments taken for other days • TT$20 • ☎ 639 0257, ⊛ luisekimme.com • Take the right turn just past the Mount Irvine golf course then follow the signposts

Nestled in the hills behind the beach along Orange Hill Road is the **Kimme Museum**, the private gallery of German sculptor Luise Kimme, who settled in Tobago in 1979, and who died here in 2013. Her eerily beguiling wood sculptures are still dotted around the surrounds of her quirky, mural-decorated turreted home, the "Fairyhaus". Though much of the collection was shipped to Germany for an exhibition in early 2013, what remains is stunning: 3m-high figures carved from whole trunks of oak depict the subtlest nuances of Tobagonian dancing, while Kimme's interpretations of local folklore characters such as the Soucouyant are powerful. In her latter years, Kimme spent long periods in Cuba learning the art of lost wax casting; you can admire the results of these studies in a room full of her intricate bronze sculptures. There's also a room downstairs full of the more abstract but equally beautiful work of Kimme's Cuban mentor **Dunieski Lora Pileta**, whose pieces combine found objects with more classical sculpture.

Stonehaven Bay

5

Past Mount Irvine, Shirvan Road becomes Grafton Road. Its narrower forefather, Old Stonehaven Road (marked by a flurry of signs advertising villas and hotels) turns off to the left and runs along almost the whole length of **Stonehaven Bay** (also known as Grafton Beach). A glorious, wide swathe with coarse sand that attracts the turtles that lay their eggs here in the March–August season, the beach offers some great swimming, and is deliciously uncommercialized. The presence of two large hotels overlooking the sand detract little from the beauty of the scene, particularly pretty at late afternoon as the sun sinks behind the black volcanic rocks that punctuate the seashore.

ACCOMMODATION   STONEHAVEN BAY

Grafton Beach Resort/Le Grand Courlan Stonehaven Bay Rd ☎639 9667, ⓦlegrandtobago.com and ⓦgraftontobago.com. Side by side and overlooking Stonehaven Bay, these garishly painted twin hotels limp along despite years of under-occupation, seemingly kept going by great package deals organized in conjunction with airlines from the UK. The *Courlan* side is adults-only, while the *Grafton* is family-friendly, both share restaurant and pool, and have loungers down on the beach. There's a tennis court, spa and gym on site, and rooms have all the usual amenities. US$160

★**Plantation Beach Villas** Stonehaven Bay Rd ☎639 9377, ⓦplantationbeachvillas.com. Gorgeous three-bedroom villas set in lush gardens, beautifully designed and with gingerbread fretwork and wraparound verandas overlooking the sea. Four-poster beds, rocking chairs and all mod cons – including wi-fi – as well as washing machine, dryer and well-equipped kitchen and spacious living room complete the perfection. There's a bar/restaurant and pool, the sea is a minute away and the staff are efficient and supremely friendly. US$313

Seahorse Inn Stonehaven Bay Rd ☎639 0686, ⓦseahorseinntobago.com. Small hotel right on a turtle-nesting beach offering four comfortable rooms with appealing quirks like arched windows and teak floors. Rooms come with a/c, ceiling fan, en-suite bathroom, cable TV and patios with great sea views. There's a good restaurant on site (rates include continental breakfast) and evening entertainment during high season. US$140

The Villas at Stonehaven Grafton Estate, Black Rock ☎639 0361, ⓦstonehavenvillas.com. Fourteen huge and very expensive three- and four-bedroom villas fitted with mahogany, marble and granite and every conceivable luxury: four-poster beds, private infinity pool and stunning views over Stonehaven Bay. The secure complex includes a clubhouse with bar and open-air restaurant. US$468

EATING AND DRINKING

Buccaneer Beach Bar Stonehaven Bay Rd ☎639 0191. The beachside restaurant of the *Grafton/Grand Courlan* hotels, this is a lively little spot, set on a deck overlooking the water and serving up salads, burgers and fries and fresh fish (TT$40–80), as well as cold beers, cocktails and soft drinks. Daily 10am–6pm.

★**Seahorse Inn** Stonehaven Bay Rd ☎639 0686. The perfect place for a romantic dinner with the sound of the waves crashing below, with an imaginative and deservedly expensive menu featuring well-executed appetizers such Creole crab cakes or seared scallop risotto (TT$65–85), and excellent mains (TT$145–355), from curried shrimp to blackened grouper and lobster thermidore plus steaks, rack of lamb or pan-roasted duck in a pineapple glaze. Good desserts, one of the best wine lists in Tobago, and English beers, too. Happy hour 5.30–6.30pm. Daily noon–3.30pm & 6.30–10pm.

Pleasant Prospect

Opposite the southern end of Old Stonehaven Road, and looping off the main road in a crescent, the main street of **Pleasant Prospect** offers a smattering of restaurants and bars kept busy by Mount Irvine surfers, as well as people using the ATM, supermarket, fruit and veg stall and the *Rituals* coffee shop. The area comes into its own after dark, when music wafts from the bars, limers hang out in the street and diners drift in and out of the restaurants.

EATING AND DRINKING   PLEASANT PROSPECT

Pleasant Prospect has some excellent **restaurants** for all budgets. It's also well worth checking out the takeaway kiosk next to the supermarket (daily 6.30–9pm), which sells inexpensive boxes of fresh local food, from fish to stewed chicken or beef, with all the trimmings.

5

★**The Fish Pot** Pleasant Prospect Main St ☎ 635 1728. Brilliant restaurant/bar with a blackboard menu dominated by super-fresh seafood. Starters (TT$40–45) might range from crab cakes to rum liver pâté, jerk fish with plantain or goat's cheese salad, while mains (TT$70–180) are determined by whatever the fishermen bring in that day, grilled or pan-fried in clever combinations of spices and fresh herbs; you can also get steaks and home-made burgers. The raised deck overlooking Pleasant Prospect is great for watching the world go by, and there's live music on Fri. Mon–Sat 11am–3pm, & 7–10pm.

Legger's Bar Grafton Rd (no phone). Across the road from *Pizza Boys*, and still universally known by its old name, *Ocean View*, this unpretentious rum shop is perched on a cliff top overlooking Stonehaven Bay and is a picturesque spot for a drink, especially during the sunset hours when the view over the ocean comes into it's own. Daily 9am–late.

Moon Over Water Pleasant Prospect Main St ☎ 709 9896. This cool little bar, pumping mellow reggae out over the lower end of the crescent, makes a nice place to chill out over a beer or shoot some pool. Regular special events and drinks promotions. Daily noon–late.

★**Pleasant Prospect Café** Pleasant Prospect Main St ☎ 639 4409. Set above the supermarket, with a balcony providing great sunset views and Pleasant Prospect people-watching, this is an excellent spot for dinner, with a Caribbean fusion menu of anything from fish salad, Trini bruschetta (buljol on coconut bake) or seafood crêpes (TT$55–75) to mains (TT$130–185) of grilled chicken in a lime-ginger butter, catch of the day in Creole coconut sauce or Asian-style pork loin in guava sauce. Tues–Sun 4.30–10pm.

Grafton Caledonia Bird Sanctuary

Grafton Rd · Daylight hours · Free, but donation welcome · ⓦ graftonhouse-tobago.com

North of Pleasant Prospect, a sun-bleached sign on the right of Grafton Road marks the entrance to the **Grafton Caledonia Bird Sanctuary**. Now somewhat run-down, the sanctuary was founded by the late owner of the surrounding estate, Eleanor Alefounder, who began feeding hungry local birds following the devastation wreaked by Hurricane Flora in 1963 (see p.236). Today, 8am and 4pm are feeding time for mot-mots, cocricos, bananaquits and practically every other feathered specimen found on the island, many of which will peck right out of your hand. There are extensive trails through the property which make for excellent, easy and scenic **hiking**.

Black Rock

Northeast of Pleasant Prospect, the main road narrows as it swings through **Black Rock**, a busy, friendly village with a couple of nice rum bars and a sprinkling of grocery stores. On the western outskirts of town, where Old Stonehaven Road loops back up from the sea, is a signpost for **Fort Bennet**, a still-intact stockade built by English mercenary Lieutenant Robert Bennet in 1680. During the plantation era, the fort was expanded by British troops, who built a brick oven to heat up the metal used to make cannonballs and placed two cannons here to defend the bay against US privateers during the American War of Independence. There are benches and a couple of gazebos, and the views – over Stonehaven Bay and down to the Pigeon Point headland to the west, and over Turtle Beach to Plymouth to the east – are spectacular, particularly at sunset.

TURTLE-WATCHING IN TOBAGO

Turtle Beach acquired its colloquial title on account of the **leatherback turtles** (see p.142) that still lay eggs here in the dark of night. The main laying season runs between March and August, and six weeks after the eggs are laid, hatchlings make a dash for the sea; both equally moving sights. All of the hotels along this stretch organize a turtle watch during the laying and hatching seasons, but if you're not staying in the area, contact one of the tour companies listed on pp.202–203. Save Our Sea Turtles Tobago (☎ 328 7351, ⓦ sos-tobago.org), a locally run charity, often do free lectures on turtle nesting during the season, and their website has plenty of more detailed information.

VILLAS

Though **villas** are conventionally seen as luxury accommodation, they can work out to be quite cost-effective if you're travelling in a large group. Most of the newer villas are aimed at the wealthier traveller, and there are a particular concentration of properties around the Mount Irvine golf course, and east along the coast toward Plymouth. Unfortunately, due to their sometimes isolated locations and the lack of round-the-clock security, villas have been targeted by burglars in recent years, so it's wise to check security before you book (see p.196) and ensure you lock up at night.

When renting, you'll often have to deal with an agency: Villas of Tobago (☎639 9600, ⓦvillasoftobago.com) is a well-established and professional operation with an excellent range of properties for all budgets. The My Tobago website also lists a good selection of villas at ⓦmytobago.info/tobago-villas1.htm. Of individual properties here, *Tobago Villas on the Green*, Jacamar Drive (☎718 4306, ⓦtobagovillasonthegreen.com), has five three-bedroom villas in fenced-off grounds with 24-hour security. Each has a small pool, jacuzzi, and every imaginable amenity, and there's also a large communal pool. *Birdsong* (☎639 7737, ⓦvrbo.com/187521), just above Mount Irvine at Grange, is another gorgeous option, with three bedrooms, a pool and really reasonable rates.

Turtle Beach

North of Black Rock, the road swings around a blind bend before entering a straight stretch. Trees mask lovely **Turtle Beach** (officially Great Courland Bay), a picturesque kilometre of coarse yellow sand flecked with the occasional swathe of volcanic grey; there are several dirt tracks from which to enter the bay from the road. The water shelves steeply from the beach and the waves are large, making for exhilarating swimming, while a river at the western end can sometimes be nice for a freshwater dip, but it's often dammed up and stagnant in the dry season. Jealously guarding pole position in the centre of the bay (only guests are allowed to use the thatched sunshades), the two-storey all-inclusive *Turtle Beach* hotel dominates the sand, and the constant presence of its guests has generated an ideal captive market for vendors selling sarongs and crafts or touting an aloe massage.

Plymouth

Roughly a kilometre past Turtle Beach, Grafton Road meets a junction: going straight will put you on Wilson Road to Scarborough, while to the left, a narrow bridge over the Courland River brings you to the outskirts of **PLYMOUTH**. Tobago's first European community, Plymouth was settled by a group of roving Latvians, usually referred to as Courlanders, then by the Dutch and finally by the British. Today, it's an attractive little town, predominantly residential, with neat board houses lining the grid-patterned streets and a handful of very low-key historical sights. Life in Plymouth centres around *TJ's Grocery & Bar* at the junction of Shelbourne and Halifax streets; it's also the only place on the Caribbean coast with a petrol station.

The mystery tombstone

Turning left at *TJ's* and continuing down Shelbourne Street will take you to Plymouth's main attractions, the first of which is the so-called **mystery tombstone**. Well signposted and sitting alone on a concrete platform close to the sea, about 200m down Shelbourne Street from *TJ's*, the eighteenth-century tombstone is an enigmatic, if rather depressing, reminder of Tobago's history of slavery. The double grave of a child and her 23-year-old mother, Betty Stiven, the "mystery" is the inscription on the stone slab: "What was remarkable of her; she was a mother without knowing it, and a wife without letting her husband know it, except by her kind indulgences to him." Betty is said to have been an African slave and lover of Dutch planter Alex Stiven, and the general hypothesis has two

5

strands: either she gave birth to Stiven's child and he took charge of it, raising it as his but not acknowledging Betty as the mother, giving her "freedom" to carry on as his lover and making her a "mother without knowing it"; or that the affair between Alex and Betty was illicit and scandalous but passionate, carried out in secret to save the face of a white man. When she died giving birth to his child, he was overcome with grief and left this cryptic message in commemoration of their love.

Great Courland Bay Monument

A few metres before the mystery tombstone, a road opposite leads down to the stark concrete blocks of the **Great Courland Bay Monument**, put up in 1976 (and very much a product of its era) in testament to the "bold, enterprising and industrious" Latvians who colonized the area and lent their name to the bay.

Fort James

Carrying straight on past the mystery tombstone (head through the gates to the sports ground and follow the road around the headland) brings you to **Fort James**, the oldest stockade in Tobago, dating from 1650 and named after the Duke of Courland (in modern Latvia), godson of England's King Charles I and the former ruler of the island. The solid coral-stone structure and four cannons that remain today are a British legacy, added in 1811, and there's an excellent view of Turtle Beach from the lawns in front.

Adventure Farm and Nature Reserve

Mon–Fri 9am–6pm, Sat 9am–1pm • US$10 • ☎ 639 2839, ⓦ adventure-ecovillas.com

On the eastern outskirts of Plymouth, on the Arnos Vale Road, a sign directs you to the turn-off for the **Adventure Farm and Nature Reserve**, a twelve-acre working organic estate planted with grapefruit, oranges, mangoes, bananas, papaya and guavas, as well as a huge range of mature tropical trees including towering samaans bedecked with epiphytic bromeliads and orchids. The woodlands attract an array of animals and birds, from matte lizards and agouti to mot-mots to green herons and cocricos, and there are a couple of marked trails down from the main house through the estate, past a man-made waterfall that splashes down into a fishpond. Up at the main house, sugar-water feeders on the covered porch attract a multitude of **hummingbirds**, from the common copper-rumped variety to the gorgeous little ruby-topaz, and you can sit and watch the antics of these surprisingly aggressive little birds at close quarters. A host of other birds regularly appear to feed in the late afternoon to the sound of an antique ship's bell.

ACCOMMODATION   **PLYMOUTH**

★**Adventure Eco Villas** Arnos Vale Rd, Plymouth ☎ 639 2839, ⓦ adventure-ecovillas.com. An oasis for bird-watchers, and for anyone seeking a little nature and serenity, these two lovely villas are built out of Guyanese greenheart wood and perched over a tree-filled valley in the Adventure Farm and Nature Reserve, with a large shared deck area. Both have a kitchen, a/c, cable TV and screened windows, and a living room with floor-to-ceiling louvres on one side that can open onto the trees. A cheaper apartment in the main house is also available. Apartment U̲S̲$̲8̲5̲, villas U̲S̲$̲1̲4̲0̲

Changrela Cocrico Inn North St, at Commissioner,

Plymouth ☎ 639 2961, ⓦ changrela.com. This comfortable and friendly place has a restaurant, pool and quiet location in residential backstreets. Eclectic accommodation ranges from clean, simple rooms with fan to larger units with a/c, fridge, cable TV and kitchen. Wi-fi available. U̲S̲$̲4̲0̲

Tropical Pleasure River Rd, Plymouth ☎ 660 2222, ⓦ tropicalpleasure.net. Incongruously large, orange-painted block on your left as you enter Plymouth, where the well-maintained rooms have a/c, cable TV, kitchenette and patio. Not very atmospheric but reasonably priced and a good base from which to explore the area. U̲S̲$̲8̲5̲

DIRECTORY

Petrol station If you're driving up the coast, it's wise to fill your tank at Plymouth's petrol station, located next to TJ's, as it's the only one for miles (Mon–Sat 7am–9pm, Sun 7am–noon).

Supermarkets Plymouth has a couple of small-scale supermarkets and fruit and veg stalls, all on the main street through town.

Arnos Vale

Arnos Vale Road meanders through the greenery towards **Arnos Vale**, one of the few former sugar plantations to keep its land, part of which is taken up with a resort hotel, which has long been in decline and has now closed to the public, as has the adjacent waterwheel and museum, which you can just see through the trees from the main road. **Arnos Vale Beach** is very pretty, though the crumbling hotel buildings behind add a very *Marie Celeste* air, and the snorkelling just offshore is some of the island's best; however, its secluded nature and lack of security mean that robberies have occurred here, so unless you're in a big group it's best visited as part of a boat trip; many day-cruises stop here for snorkelling.

ACCOMMODATION   **ARNOS VALE**

★**Top O' Tobago** Arnos Vale Estate ✆ 639 3166 or ✆ 687 0121, ⓦ topotobago.com. Perched above Arnos Vale Bay and cooled by constant breezes, this is a unique and beguiling place with great hill and sea views and plenty of birdlife. Stylishly decorated with great attention to detail, the main two-bedroom house sleeps up to six and has a large sitting room, two bathrooms, fully equipped kitchen, patio, flat-screen TV, stereo, and washer and dryer. Smaller *cabanas* are equally appealing, with a king-size bed and two sofabeds, kitchen and private patio; and all have use of the pool. Free airport pick-up, and wonderful personalized service. *Cabana* <u>US$150</u>, house <u>US$300</u>

Golden Lane and Les Coteaux

Beyond Arnos Vale, the main road heads into the hills and through **Golden Lane** and **Les Coteaux**, tiny but attractive villages that have some associations with local superstitions. Rumours of witchery and potions abound, and Golden Lane is said to hold the grave of a witch known as Gang Gang Sara, who flew here from Africa and married a local man – the community hosts spooky story sessions during the Heritage Festival celebrations. Beyond Les Coteaux, the Arnos Vale Road meets the Northside Road (see p.227) in a T-junction; turn left to reach Scarborough, and right to carry on up the leeward coast toward Castara.

ACCOMMODATION   **GOLDEN LANE AND LES COTEAUX**

Footprints Culloden Bay Rd, Golden Lane ✆ 660 0416, ⓦ footprintsecoresort.com. Overlooking Culloden Bay, this remote, 62-acre self-styled "eco resort" (it uses lots of recycled or recyclable materials) has its own nature trails, saltwater pools, excellent snorkelling just steps from the rooms and plenty of peace and quiet, though it also has a somewhat forsaken air and feels very remote. Accommodation ranges from standard suites to self-contained villas with jacuzzi and pool, and there's a restaurant on site. Doubles <u>TT$700</u>, garden studios <u>TT$850</u>, villas <u>TT$1050</u>

Scarborough

Tobago's raucous, hot and dusty capital, precipitous **SCARBOROUGH** is a surprisingly appealing place, its houses and roads spilling higgledy-piggledy down a hillside, with the Atlantic providing a magnificent backdrop for **Fort King George**, perched at the top of the hill. The island's administrative centre and its main **port**, Scarborough is a flourishing town, brimming with a brisk vibrancy. Devoid of any touristy pretensions, its street corners buzz with liming locals, while pavement stalls are perused by shoppers and the bars spill out onto the streets. Away from the bustle, the shady suburb of **Bacolet** is home to some of Tobago's most upmarket hotels and the secluded Bacolet Bay Beach – in former times the playground of many a rich and famous visitor to Tobago.

Though the largest town on the island, Scarborough is still pretty tiny, with most of the commercial action spreading back up from the port and along the precipitous Main Street. The heat, traffic and steep climbs can make it a bit tiring to explore, but the cool breezes and views from the port and the elevated parts of town offer respite.

5

Brief history

The **Dutch** were the first Europeans to settle what became one of Tobago's most hotly contested pieces of land. They navigated the treacherous harbour rocks in 1654, and constructed a fort and a few buildings, naming it **Lampsinsburgh**. Around the same time, a group of Courlanders (Latvians) were building up their stronghold on the opposite coast at Plymouth (see p.217). In 1658, the Dutch captured Plymouth – an act that led to the destruction of their own settlement when, in 1666, a British fleet came to the aid of the Latvians and blew Lampsinsburgh to smithereens.

The **British** officially won the island in 1672, but didn't maintain a presence, allowing the Dutch to return and build Lampsinsburgh into a more substantial settlement, with houses, a single street and a church, as well as warehouses and wharves at the harbour and a new fort. However, during the French assault of 1677, the newly improved **fortifications** proved to be the undoing of the Dutch; a French cannonball hit the fort's ammunition dump, and the resulting fireball destroyed the structure and killed all 250 occupants. Though still commemorated in the current name Dutch Fort Road, there's nothing left today of that original settlement.

The British bestowed the name **Scarborough** when they regained control of Tobago in 1762, establishing the House of Assembly here and constructing Fort King George. The **French** returned to take control, after a bloody and prolonged fight, in 1781. Scarborough was renamed Port Louis, while Fort King George – with finishing touches added by French soldiers – became **Fort Castries**. The town ricocheted between the British and French until Tobago was finally ceded to the British in 1814.

Central Scarborough

Central Scarborough constitutes the area around the market and the port and is where you'll find most of the action, with shoppers, office workers, taxi drivers and street vendors giving the place a hectic feel. Entering via car-choked Wilson Road, a left on Darrel Spring Road and then a right down Gardenside Street will take you past the back of **NIB Mall** to the right, and the Botanical Gardens (and a car park) to the left. Behind the mall is the capital's **market**. Main trading days are Friday and Saturday, but throughout the week vendors sell every tropical fruit and vegetable imaginable. The indoor meat section is an odoriferous melange of goat, beef, lamb, mutton and chicken,

SCARBOROUGH

Plymouth & the Leeward Coast
Mason Hall, Moriah & the Leeward Coast

CLAUDE NOEL HIGHWAY

Crown Point &

0 — 250 metres

Jubilee Park

WILSON ROAD
DARREL SPRING ROAD
GARDENSIDE STREET
POST OFFICE St
DUTCH FORT STREET
SANGSTER HILL ROAD
NORTHSIDE ROAD
SARGEANT CAIN ROAD
BACOLET EXTENSION ROAD
CALDER HALL ROAD
BATEAU ST

Botanical Gardens

MARKET SQUARE
Scarborough Public Library
Scarborough Public Market
NIB Mall
James Shopping Mall

Temporary Bus Station

SMITHFIELD ROAD
MT MARIE ROAD
Old Milford Road

CARRINGTON STREET

King's Well
James Park
Courthouse
HAMILTON STREET
PICCOTS STREET
ROSE HILL
PIGGOT STREET
CUFF ST
KEEN ST
PARK STREET
CALDER HALL ROAD
BAGATELLE TRACE

Cruise Ship & Ferry Terminal
Taxi Rank

ROCKLY BAY

BURNETT STREET
CASTRIES STREET
BACOLET STREET
MAIN STREET
FORT STREET
YOUNG STREET
MILL ST
BURROUGHS STREET
Fire Station
KEEN ST
MCKAY HILL
TERRINGTON

Police Station
St Andrew's Anglican Church

Fort King George, Tobago Museum & Tobago County Hospital

Bacolet, The Windward Coast, **5**, **6**, **7**, **8**, **9** & **6**

■ ACCOMMODATION

Ade's Domicil	5
Bacolet Beach Club	6
Bacolet Inn	7
Blue Haven	8
Half Moon Blue	9
Hope Cottage	1
Mill's Guesthouse	4
Sandy's Guesthouse	3
Shingle Cottage	2

● CAFÉS & RESTAURANTS

Blue Crab	5
Café Havana	6
Ciao Café	3
Rena's Chattack Roti Shop	2
Salsa Kitchen	1
Shore Things	4

■ BAR

Bar Code	1

while fish on ice gleam at the back section, where stallholders attract customers by blowing on a **conch shell**. It's a friendly and absorbing scene, great for bargains and a chat with the stallholders, who can explain how to cook any unfamiliar produce. If you're after souvenirs such as knitted Rasta hats, sandals and woodcarvings, or cheap CDs and DVDs, check out the stalls lining busy Wilson Road and the western side of NIB Mall.

Botanical Gardens

Greenside St • Daily, daylight hours • Free • There are entrances on Gardenside St, Northside Rd (south of the highway) and from a signposted layby on the Claude Noel Hwy

A soothing oasis after the heat-retaining concrete and traffic fumes of downtown Scarborough, the **Botanical Gardens** are laid over eighteen acres of what was once the Dal Fair and Rockly Vale sugar plantations; the land was requisitioned by the British in the late nineteenth century with the intention of creating a public botanical garden. Today, the broad sweeps of lawn interspersed with planted beds and shade trees could pass for an English park, were it not for the garish crimson of towering African tulips, flamboyant trees and the yellow and pink cascades of the poui trees. The gardens remain a firm favourite for wedding photos, but generally they're pretty much deserted. There are no guided **tours** as such, but the gardeners are usually on site to answer questions.

The waterfront

Though some older buildings remain in Scarborough's steep heights, most of the **waterfront** is relatively new. Souped up in 1990 by the addition of a deep-water cruise-ship pier (the deep-water harbour was built in 1953), the harbour area is dominated by the modern **ferry terminal**. As well as the ticket office, the complex holds a few shops and Scarborough's main **post office**. The circular wooden buildings on Milford Road's seafront **esplanade** sell snacks, ice cream, cold beers and souvenirs, and the main open-air gazebo is often used to host concerts and special events; otherwise, it's a nice shady spot in which to enjoy the sea breeze.

Old Milford Road

Old Milford Rd doesn't run directly into Milford Rd, as there's a short section of unpaved coastline between the two; to get onto Old Milford Rd from Scarborough, follow Milford Rd, which becomes Orange Hill Rd as it swings away from the sea and uphill, take the first left onto Milford Rd Extension and carry straight on past the Shaw Park Cultural Complex

West of Scarborough, **Old Milford Road** was the main thoroughfare through the southwest before the construction of the highway, which it connects to opposite the Lowlands shopping mall. Now little more than a backroad, Old Milford cuts a winding and scenic route along the coast, with lovely views of the wind-whipped Atlantic peeking between the palms and houses, and salt spray crashing onto the tarmac thanks to the constant ocean breeze. Around halfway along, the venerable *Shore Things* (see p.226) offers meals and drinks, and some of the best craft available in Tobago.

There's an "official" beach facility by the side of the road at **Little Rockly Bay**, which was used as a site for horse racing before the construction of Shirvan racetrack, but the ruggedness of the coastline, the strong undercurrents and murky waters mean it's not a great place to swim. At low tide, the wide swathe of compacted yellow-brown sand makes for a fabulous beach walk, while the constant wind makes this one of Tobago's top spots for kitesurfing and windsurfing (see p.204). The most scenic part of the beach is adjacent to the **Petit Trou** car park, with its grove of swaying palm trees. Locals often park up here to eat lunch or just enjoy the breeze.

Upper Scarborough

Comprising the hilly streets on the eastern side of the town, **Upper Scarborough** is a busy area with plenty of shops and banks, but gets steadily quieter the higher you climb.

5

Proceeding east from the ferry terminal along Carrington Street, you soon reach a junction known as **King's Well**, originally the site of the town's main watercourse, but now home to an excellent Italian café (see p.226). A sharp left here takes you out of town along Northside Road and the edge of the Botanical Gardens, while the sharp right is Castries Street, the route to **Main Street**. Between the two, steeply inclining **Burnett Street** is one of Scarborough's best places for knick-knack **shopping** – anything from T-shirts to lingerie.

James Park and the Courthouse

As Burnett Street reaches a plateau, you enter **James Park**, a small walled square decorated with Luise Kimme's bronze of A.P.T. James, a former Minister of Tobago Affairs. The park is bordered to the north by the imposing old **courthouse**, which has housed the administrative offices of the Tobago House of Assembly since the judiciary were shifted to their current Bacolet Street base in the late 1980s. Built between 1821 and 1825, the cut-stone structure was considered one of the finest examples of Georgian architecture in the Caribbean on completion. Subsequent alterations have, unfortunately, smothered the original brickwork with white paint and removed the pillars, rendering it a shadow of its former glory.

Bacolet Street

One block northeast of James Park, on the other side of the bustling shop-and-office-lined Main Street, **Bacolet Street** is the route to the fire station, the main police station (and only jail) and the short **Gun Bridge**, sporting railings made from rifle barrels and stone walls embellished with four cannons, two at either end, taken from Fort George – a commemoration of the town's historical discord. A few metres past the bridge is **St Andrew's Anglican Church**, originally built in 1819 but razed by Hurricane Flora in 1963 and reconstructed a year later. The fire and police stations are opposite and behind the church respectively. Further south down Bacolet Street, the buildings thin out as you enter the quiet and attractive Bacolet suburbs (see p.223).

Fort King George

Forking off Main Street, Fort Street twists its way up a steep hill past the imposing Methodist Church and some attractive but dishevelled colonial architecture on its way to one of the most prominent sights in town, **Fort King George**. If the precipitous fifteen-minute walk looks too much and you decide to **drive**, you can almost always find a parking space in the car park adjacent to the museum and main fort. The complex is the largest fortification in Tobago, built by the British in 1777 and initially composed of some thirty buildings, but reduced to around ten by an 1847 hurricane. It was occupied by French troops between 1781 and 1793, who built the solid stone perimeter walls. Inspired by the French Revolution, the soldiers **mutinied** in 1790, imprisoning their officers and razing the town below. There are several signs dotted around the complex giving some background to the buildings, and you can also get a guided tour from one of the THA personnel in the Tourism division, to the left of the car park at the top of the fort area.

As you approach, the first of the fort's buildings is a ruined red-brick **prison**; it hasn't undergone the restoration of the main buildings, and time and the elements have opened its tiny, dingy cells to shafts of sunlight. Around the next bend, past the closed-up **Tobago County Hospital**, its 1930s buildings slowly crumbling since the opening of the Signal Hill complex in 2012, is the start of the fort complex proper. The first building on the left is the dome-shaped cover of an old **well**, built in 1926 to service the hospital. Over the road from the well, a path leads below the main complex to a landscaped **park**, lush with poui trees and colourful planted beds. Benches are perfectly placed for soaking up marvellous views of Scarborough and the Orange Hill district. In the shade of a massive, buttressed silk cotton tree is the (usually locked) **powder magazine**, a sturdy structure built to house stocks of ammunition and gunpowder.

ROBINSON CRUSOE'S ISLE

5

"The Life and Strange Surprising Adventures of Robinson Crusoe of York, Mariner
Who lived eight and twenty Years all alone, on an uninhabited Island on the coast of America, near the
mouth of the Great River of Oroonoque
Having been Cast on Shore by shipwreck, wherein all the Men perished but himself."
Thus reads the introductory blurb to the first edition of Daniel Defoe's **Robinson Crusoe**,
dated April 25, 1719 and the oft-cited rationale behind the claim that Tobago was the setting
for Defoe's story. In the book, the fabled island was situated, like Tobago, off the coast of
(South) America near the mouth of the Orinoco River.

In the late seventeenth century, the then sovereign Duke of Courland commissioned an
Englishman, John Poyntz, to develop the island. Poyntz wrote a pamphlet praising Tobago's
beauty and natural riches as well as giving a physical description of the island. Believers argue
that Defoe got hold of the document and used it as the basis for his novel.

However, this clashes with the accepted notion that Defoe based the book on the
experience of Alexander Selkirk, a crew member on the ship of English explorer and pirate
William Dampier. During a voyage in the Pacific Ocean, Selkirk quarrelled with another crew
member and, rather than continue in his company, volunteered to be put ashore at the tiny
island of Juan Fernandez, off the coast of Chile. He spent four years alone there before Dampier
rescued him. After Selkirk's return to England in 1711, his story became well known through
various pamphlets, on which Defoe's novel was almost certainly based.

At the top level of the complex, some 140m above sea level, the **Officer's Mess** is
the fort's largest building, now housing the Tobago Museum. Beyond the Mess, a
series of cannons point through cut-stone walls and out to sea; the walls afford
spectacular views of Bacolet Bay, Minister Point and the rugged interior to the east,
and Rockly Bay and the north coast of Trinidad to the west. Behind the Mess is the
lighthouse, a squat structure transferred from Galera Point in Trinidad in 1958;
the Fresnel lens beams 50km out to sea and sweeps spectacularly over the
Scarborough suburbs.

Tobago Museum

Mon–Fri 9am–4.30pm, closed public holidays • TT$10 • ☎ 639 3970

Laid out in the cool confines of the refurbished Officer's Mess, the **Tobago Museum** has
a small but fascinating collection of idiosyncratic artefacts, with displays on everything
from Amerindian society to life in the nineteenth century (as well as, rather
incongruously, many pieces of Nigerian sculpture). There's an extensive collection of
pre-Columbian axe-heads, chisels, cooking ware and talismans, known as *adornos*,
found at Amerindian sites across the island, as well as three skeletons unearthed at
Amerindian burial sites. Racks of shells and fossils give way to relics from the colonial
era, from military ephemera to coins and notes and some rather chilling logs detailing
names and "condition" of the slaves sold to the island's various estates. Look out also
for satirical prints depicting the exploits of "Johnny Newcome in Love in the West
Indies", and a copy of the second edition of the *Pleasant Prospect of the Famous and
Fertile Island of Tobago* by John Poyntz, the pamphlet which local legend claims Daniel
Defoe used as the inspiration for the setting of *Robinson Crusoe*. Bric-a-brac from the
early twentieth century includes a plate commemorating the inauguration of Eric
Williams as Trinidad and Tobago's first prime minister.

Bacolet

As Bacolet Street eases east out of Scarborough along the coast past Sandy Hall and
Fairfield Complex – the main administrative base of the Tobago House of Assembly as
well as the Tobago Hall of Justice court and the island's main cemetery – the roadside

5

homes become noticeably grander. Though **Bacolet** suffered a lull when its eponymous street was replaced by Claude Noel Highway as the main route to the windward coast, this is still a suburb of choice for Tobago's elite.

The area enjoyed a heady prestige during the late 1960s and early 70s, boasting a couple of luxury hotels, the *Bacolet* and *Blue Haven*. Rita Hayworth and Robert Mitchum stayed here while filming *Fire Down Below*, and the **Beatles** frolicked on Bacolet Bay Beach, which also provided the setting for Walt Disney's *Swiss Family Robinson*. The *Blue Haven* (see p.225) was once part of Tobago's battlements: a cannon still stands on the hotel's grounds, the base of the hotel is surrounded by stone walls dating back to 1770 and the bay itself was the site of many sea battles. The hotels tried to cordon off the sand in the 1960s but Dr Eric Williams – the premier who once declared that he had no intention of ruling "a nation of waiters and bellhops" – intervened to keep the beach public. South of the beach, the houses thin out as Bacolet Street swings left to meet with the highway and the traffic on its way along the windward coast (see p.235).

Bacolet Bay Beach

The best reason to linger here is the crescent-shaped **Bacolet Bay Beach**, a tranquil spot mostly visited by guests from the nearby hotels, with its yellow sand shaded by palms and Indian almond trees. A protective coral reef ensures good swimming despite the location on the Atlantic side of the island – but be aware of the occasional dangerous undercurrents and rough seas in winter. From the road, concrete steps lead down the cliff side to the sand, where a beach bar serves up drinks and snacks.

ARRIVAL AND DEPARTURE   SCARBOROUGH

By car Most people enter Scarborough via the Wilson Rd turn-off from Claude Noel Hwy and follow the one-way system towards the wharves bordering Carrington St; you can also turn down Orange Hill Rd (turn by the large petrol station) from the highway and, on the other side of town, via Northside Rd. Free parking is available at the wharf car park on the corner of Carrington and Castries streets, in the NIB Mall car park off Gardenside St (strictly speaking for shoppers only) and in the huge lot off Gardenside St.

By ferry Ferries between Trinidad and Tobago arrive and depart from the main waterfront opposite Independence Square (☎639 2417 or ☎639 4906, ⊛https://ttitferry .com). There are usually two daily fast-ferry sailings, though schedules are increased at peak times (and are detailed on the website); sailing time is officially 2.5hr, but can take longer. You can buy tickets for same-day sailings at the ferry terminal, but for all advance bookings (advisable well in advance in busy periods), you'll need to go in person to an authorized vendor; full details of these are on the website. Tickets cost TT$50/person (half-price for kids), plus $150 for a car. Bear in mind that the journey between Trinidad and Tobago can be rough; take sea-sickness tablets, and try to find a seat in the middle of the ferry. Taxis line up at the rank directly outside the terminal building.

By bus The PTSC bus depot (☎639 2293, ⊛ptsc.co.tt) is located five minutes from the centre on Sangster Hill Rd. Buses to all corners of the island run daily between roughly 4.30am and 8pm; remember to purchase your tickets before boarding.

Destinations Black Rock (Mon–Sat 15 daily); Buccoo (Mon–Sat 5 daily); Charlotteville (Mon–Sat 4 daily); Crown Point (Mon–Sat 15 daily); L'Anse Fourmi via Castara (Mon–Sat 4 daily); Mason Hall (Mon–Sat 5 daily); Plymouth via Arnos Vale (Mon–Sat 15 daily); Roxborough (Mon–Sat 4 daily).

By route taxi Scarborough is the departure point for route taxis serving the whole of the island, though finding where to catch your ride can be confusing. For Crown Point, Bon Accord, Mount Irvine, Buccoo, Carnbee, Bethel, Mount Pleasant, Plymouth, Black Rock and Lambeau go to the "west end" taxi stand directly outside the ferry terminal. There are two lanes: the one nearest the terminal is for Crown Point and places along Milford Rd; the outside lane is for all other destinations. An alternative departure point for Plymouth, Black Rock and Mount Pleasant is on Wilson Rd opposite *KFC*, at the junction with Carrington St. This is also where you'll find taxis running the Northside Rd to Castara and Parlatuvier. If you have no luck here, walk 50m or so up Wilson Rd to Penny Savers supermarket, where you can find transport to Mason Hall, from where it's easier to get taxis going further up Northside Rd. Taxis to Speyside and Charlotteville leave from Republic Bank on Main St and sometimes from next to St James Park.

By maxi taxi Maxis to Charlotteville leave a few times a day from next to James Park on Ross St. With all of these taxi stands it can be confusing to know exactly where to wait – but if you're not sure just ask around.

ACCOMMODATION

Though Scarborough and the Bacolet suburbs were popular in the 1960s and 1970s during the early years of Tobagonian tourism, they've now been eclipsed by Crown Point. Some excellent **hotels** remain in Bacolet, while Scarborough has some inexpensive options, especially convenient if you're catching an early ferry. Staying in a **host home** or B&B (see Basics, p.27) is another viable budget option.

SCARBOROUGH

Hope Cottage Calder Hall Rd ☎ 639 2179, ✉ hcghtobago@hotmail.com. Once the residence of Tobago's British governor of Tobago (who was buried in the back garden in 1876), this is one of Tobago's oldest guesthouses, having opened its doors in 1940. Showing its age a bit nowadays, but a great bargain nonetheless. Rooms are plain, some with shared bathroom, and there's a large communal kitchen. Genial hosts and a peaceful location in a hilly part of town close to Fort King George. Wi-fi. TT$220

Mill's Guesthouse Young St ☎ 639 2193, ✉ cristalj @hotmail.com. The spotless rooms of this pretty blue guesthouse set high on a hillside are pleasant and well maintained – all have a/c and TV, one affords panoramic views over Scarborough, and another with bunk beds is good for groups or families. Wi-fi, a well-equipped communal kitchen and reasonable rates. TT$300

Sandy's Guesthouse 5 Robinson St ☎ 639 2737, ✉ tobagobluecrab.com. Run by Auntie Alison, the hospitable owner of the *Blue Crab* restaurant (see below), this inviting guesthouse has four pretty, spotless and large rooms with a/c, private bathroom, TV and fridge; rates include breakfast. US$80

Shingle Cottage Calder Hall Rd, Scarborough ☎ 625 4994 or ☎ 639 7737, ✉ joegoddard@gmail.com. Beautifully restored colonial-era house in upper Scarborough, with wooden floors, high ceilings and lovely views down over town. Two a/c bedrooms, and a daybed on the porch, and bags of atmosphere. Discounts available for just two guests or for longer stays. US$100

BACOLET

Ade's Domicil 19 Old Lighthouse Rd, Bacolet Point ☎ 639 4306, ✉ adesdomicil.de. This lovely spacious white plantation-style house is 250m from the beach. Both the studio and one-bedroom apartment have en-suite bathroom, a/c and ceiling fan, cable TV, wi-fi, fully equipped kitchen and a sea view. Good value. Studio US$60, apartment US$75

Bacolet Beach Club Bacolet Bay ☎ 639 2357, ✉ bacoletbeachclub.com. Chic boutique hotel, with a fabulous infinity pool and a small, effectively private, beach. Rooms and suites are decked out in a quirky vintage-meets-modern style, and all have a/c, flat-screen TV/CD/DVD player and balcony. A cute little bridge leads to the excellent on-site restaurant. US$220

Bacolet Inn 36 Bacolet St ☎ 639 2531 or ☎ 313 3507, ✉ tobagobeachhotel.com. Set in a pretty old house on the cliffside, with lovely sea views and a large pool overlooking the ocean. The simple rooms with bathroom, cable TV and a/c are clean and good value, and there's a shared kitchen and TV area. It's a ten-minute walk to Scarborough. TT$275

Blue Haven Bacolet Bay ☎ 660 7400, ✉ blue havenhotel.com. This historic hotel was originally an outpost of Fort King George and retains its stunning panoramic views of the bay it once protected. The stylish rooms have four-poster or sleigh beds, gorgeous wooden floors, a/c, TV, minibar, phone, spacious bathrooms and a balcony overlooking stunning Bacolet Bay. There's a swimming pool with ornamental waterfall, mini-gym, spa and tennis court, and an excellent restaurant on site as well as a small bar on the adjacent Bacolet Beach. Scarborough is a twenty-minute walk away. US$238

Half Moon Blue 73 Bacolet St ☎ 639 3551, ✉ halfmoonblue.com. Comfortable en-suite rooms decorated in an unusual mixture of traditional and modern styles, with a/c, fan, fridge, TV, phone, hairdryer and great views of Bacolet Bay from private balconies; there's also access to a "private" beach. The open-plan penthouse suite is gorgeous, if you've got the money. There's also a spacious garden and a dreamy infinity pool; rates include breakfast. US$160

EATING, DRINKING AND NIGHTLIFE

Scarborough's **dining scene** offers everything from the excellent low-cost meals found all over town to Bacolet's exclusive eateries; in between, there are some excellent and unusual options, too. Fast-food outlets such as *KFC* on the corner of Wilson Rd and Carrington St, *Royal Castle* on Wilson Rd and *Chef's* on Carrington St all enjoy a strong local following. For drinks, there are plenty of **rum shops** along Carrington St and Wilson Rd, very much a locals' preserve but worth checking out, especially on Friday evenings when everybody celebrates the end of the working week.

CAFÉS AND RESTAURANTS

★ **Blue Crab** Cnr Robinson and Main sts, Scarborough ☎ 639 2737. Popular with an office crowd, this busy, friendly restaurant is a great place to sample traditional Creole cuisine, with tables in an a/c dining room and on a shady terrace with sea views. The lunch menu (mains

5

TT$65) changes according to whatever's fresh in the market that day, but always includes fresh fish with sides such as cassava salad, bhaji (spinach) rice and fried plantain; great unsweetened juices too. Dinner (soup, salad, main and coffee from TT$200) is by reservation only. Tues–Fri 11am–3pm.

Café Havana Bacolet Bay, Bacolet ☎ 639 2357, ⓦ cafehavana.org. Set in an airy split-level building, all white paint and wooden floors, with a menu that ranges from Cuban to Asian and Creole food: fish sandwiches, salads, and burgers at lunchtime (TT$57–107), and a dinner menu that includes chicken satay (TT$63), scallops in beurre blanc (TT$157), curry shrimp (TT$139) or Cajun-style pork chops (TT$151). It's also good for a drink, with excellent cocktails including proper mojitos; happy "hour" is 3–7pm. Daily 7.30–10am, noon–3pm & 6pm–late.

★ **Ciao Café** King's Well, Scarborough ☎ 639 3001. This fantastic Italian café and bar with an outside terrace serves authentic cappuccino, panini, over twenty different flavours of delicious home-made gelato, fine Italian wine, good beer and colourful cocktails along with inexpensive parmigiana (TT$40), antipasti (TT$128) and mains (from TT$90) such as pesto pasta, shrimp risotto or seared tuna. The attached pizza restaurant is similarly excellent (pizzas TT$75–90). Mon, Wed & Thurs 9am–11pm, Fri & Sat 9am–midnight, Sun 5–11pm.

Rena's Chattack Roti Shop TLH Mall, Milford Rd, Scarborough ☎ 635 7684. Some of Tobago's best rotis are cooked up in the nondescript little building just off the waterfront. Standard fillings such as channa, chicken or goat are always available, while more exotic ingredients like liver or conch are offered on Fridays. Rotis from TT$25. Mon–Sat 8am–4pm.

★ **Salsa Kitchen** 8 Pump Mill Rd, Scarborough ☎ 639 1522. A lovely setting on a plant-wreathed veranda, best after dark when the fairy lights twinkle but also nice and shady at lunchtime. The fabulous Venezuelan-style tapas dishes (from TT$80) are cooked to order and might include lamb with tamarind and tomato choka, chadon beni marinated fish, minted pork, kebab skewers with tamarind or peanut sauce and goat's cheese and mozzarella with onion and olive confit – perfect for sharing. Reasonably priced and very popular; reservations essential. Tues–Sun 6–11pm.

★ **Shore Things** Old Milford Rd, Lowlands ☎ 635 1072. Beautifully situated among the greenery right on the cliffside, and cooled with delightful Atlantic winds, this is a lovely little café offering a menu of home-made pizza, burgers, salads, quiche and daily lunch specials from baked chicken with all the trimmings to soup or pelau (from TT$65), served on the veranda or the waterside terrace. Juices, coffee, cakes and pastries are also excellent. Mon–Fri 11am–6pm.

BARS

Bar Code Milford Rd, Scarborough ☎ 635 2633. Scarborough's liveliest bar, complete with big-screen TV for watching sports and pool tables; the breezy outside deck has lovely sea views, too. Regular party nights at weekends, and karaoke on a Thursday. Daily 11am–2am.

DIRECTORY

Banks Scarborough has several banks: there's the Republic Bank and Scotiabank on Carrington St opposite the wharf, Royal and Republic on Main St and First Citizens in the NIB Mall. All have ATMs; there is also one at the ferry terminal.

Petrol stations There are two petrol stations on Milford Rd.

Post office The post office (Mon–Fri 7.30am–6pm, Sat 9am–1pm) is at the waterfront next to the ferry terminal.

Tourist information For information, head to the offices of the Tobago House of Assembly Division of Tourism, close to the bus station at 12 Sangster Hill (Mon–Fri 8am–4pm; ☎ 639 2125, ⓦ visittobago.gov.tt).

The leeward coast

Northeast of Plymouth, the dramatic and sparsely populated **leeward coast** feels more wonderfully remote than any other part of the island; here, the claim that Tobago is not just paradise, but the capital of paradise, begins to ring true, lapped by the Caribbean Sea and drenched in tropical greenery. Apart from at the lovely coastal village of **Castara**, tourist development is very understated, with the ravishing beaches at **Englishman's Bay**, **Parlatuvier** and **Bloody Bay** much the same as they were decades ago. Locals still make a living off the land and sea: clusters of bobbing pirogues in every bay and seine nets drying in the sun reveal the importance of **fishing** to this area, and you'll often see machete-wielding fellows trudging the route to small-scale plantations or meandering along with a pack of hunting dogs.

Although you might assume the most direct way to the leeward coast would be the coastal Arnos Vale Road from Plymouth, this is actually the slowest route, due to its twists and turns; a better (if less scenic) bet is to take the **Northside Road** up from Scarborough, which meets the coast just before Moriah.

| GETTING AROUND | THE LEEWARD COAST |

By car The vast majority of visitors explore the leeward coast by car, and the Arnos Vale Rd and Northside Rd, though narrow and winding, are in fairly good condition. Keep your eyes peeled for loose cattle left to graze by the roadside, and sound your horn at blind corners.

By public transport This part of the island is among the least travelled by public transport. Buses from Scarborough run to L'Anse Fourmi a few times a day (see p.224), but maxis and route taxis often only go as far as Mason Hall or Moriah, so be prepared for vehicle changes and longer waits than elsewhere.

The Northside Road from Scarborough

Less than a kilometre east of Scarborough on the Claude Noel Highway, the well-signposted **Northside Road** strikes right across the middle of Tobago and connects the windward with the leeward coast. Barely 50m along it, the right-hand turn by the bridge takes you up a narrow, near-perpendicular road to **French Fort**, the site of a Gallic garrison in the 1780s. It's now home to several towering radio transmitters and satellite pylons and the only hint of its history is a plaque nestled in the trees. The journey up to the fort is definitely worthwhile, though, for its panoramic **views** of Scarborough, Fort King George, Rockly Bay and Lowlands, the northern coast around Plymouth and Arnos Vale, and the southeast as far as Granby Point. Past French Fort turn-off, the Northside Road swings past the armed guards and clipped hedges flanking the **President's House** (closed to the public), and continues its snaking climb uphill, passing through the quiet village of **Cinnamon Hill**.

Mason Hall

About halfway between the coasts lies the residential community of **Mason Hall**. The village itself contains little to detain you, but the marvellous **waterfall** hidden on its outskirts is worth seeking out. To find it, look for the roadside WASA sign for the Craig Hall water intake. Half an hour's walk from the road along the Sandy River will bring you to **Craig Hall Falls**, one of the island's tallest at about 50m. Taking the Craig Hall route leads you to the top of the main cascade, where there's another, smaller waterfall with a pool deep enough to jump into without touching the bottom. Several of the island's tour operators (see pp.202–203) offer guided walks to the falls.

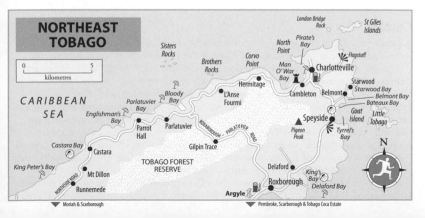

5

Moriah

Reachable both from the Northside Road and the Arnos Vale Road (take a left at the only T-junction), the village of **Moriah** is a picturesque settlement teetering at the top of steep hills, which plummet straight into a valley from the road. The views from here are superlative, with terraces on the surrounding hills supporting crops of pigeon peas and ground provisions, and Baptist prayer flags fluttering in the breeze. Moriah is best known for the **"Old Time" wedding procession** during the summer Heritage Festival, which sees the narrow main road lined with crowds to see the "grooms" adorned in formal black suits and top hats escort their elaborately costumed brides along the street to "walk the wedding" and perform the traditional brush-back dance.

King Peter's Bay

A downhill turn-off to the left just north of Moriah leads to **King Peter's Bay**, a seldom-visited but beautiful yellow-sand beach named after a Carib cacique. If you strike west from the beach into the bush over the next bluff you'll find an even more beautiful strip, with a good reef to boot. Check on the **security** situation before visiting King Peter's Bay, as robberies have occurred; equally, as the access road gets rough, you're best off walking the last stretch.

Runnemede and Mount Dillon

Past the King Peter's Bay turn-off, Northside Road heads for the coast, providing breathtaking views as you pass through the tiny community of **Runnemede**. Look out for a truly monumental **silk cotton** tree at the roadside; its buttressed roots are said to be haunted by jumbies (ghosts). For one of the best vistas around, turn right at the signposted fork just after Runnemede to **Mount Dillon**, where benches are set up to admire the unravelling coastline and, on a clear day, the island of Grenada. There's also a small takeaway snack shop and a souvenir stall.

ACCOMMODATION AND EATING   **RUNNEMEDE**

★**Cuffie River Nature Retreat** Runnemede ☎ 660 0505, ⓦ cuffie-river.com. Very popular with British birding groups, this is a peaceful family-run hideaway where the large, airy and comfortable en-suite rooms are nestled into the forest on the site of an old sugar plantation; tours and hikes of the surrounding forest are offered to guests and non-guests. The swimming pool, elevated a metre above the forest floor, is the perfect place from which to enjoy the surrounds. Cuffie River is also the best place to eat in the area, its atmospheric restaurant serving delicious, nutritious lunches (three courses US$35; book ahead), freshly prepared with local ingredients as you look out over the forest from the veranda. US$135

Castara

A picturesque fishing village, with terrific beaches and a laidback vibe that have made it increasingly popular with visitors, **CASTARA** is the busiest "resort" on this coastline – though don't expect anything as packaged and touristy as Crown Point. Although the number of guesthouses has grown exponentially in recent years, Castara's remote location has so far saved it from being eaten up by resort hotels, and there's an appealingly harmonious balance between visitors and locals. Fishing remains the main earner, and the beach is one of the best places to participate in the pulling of a **seine net**, still in constant use by the posse of Rasta fishermen. The village abandons its languid air each August, when the beach is packed with revellers attending the **Castara Fishermen's Fete**, one of Tobago's biggest; the drinking, dancing, eating and swimming start at about midday and continue until well after dark.

To get your bearings before you enter the village proper from the west, pull up in the layby to the left just before the Northside Road makes its final steep descent – there's a postcard-perfect **view** of the village and the main **Big Bay** beach, separated from the smaller **Little Bay** (also known as Heavenly Bay) by a rocky outcrop, and all framed by the lush green tips of the rainforest.

Castara village

Straddling the Northside Road, the main body of the village consists of a post office and a few weather-beaten rum shops interspersed with homes. A bridge on the western side of town crosses the **Castara River**; a ten-minute walk southeast along the riverbed brings you to a small **waterfall** with a fairly deep swimming pool below. Crossing the playing field behind the bridge cuts the walking time, and the pool is popular among local lads cooling off after a game of football; these frenetic, foul-filled tournaments take place in the late afternoon, and often attract a small crowd of spectators.

Big Bay

Lifeguards daily 10am–6pm • Changing facilities 10am–6pm, TT$1 • Lounger rentals available at the western end for TT$20

Castara's main beach, **Big Bay**, is a generous swathe of coarse shell- and pebble-strewn yellow sand divided by the Castara River. If there hasn't been rain (which can turn the ocean a little murky), the water is a joy – crystal clear and relatively calm owing to the protection of the surrounding forested headlands, and patrolled most days by a couple of rays that drift up and down close to the shore. Flotillas of seagull-infested pirogues bob out to sea, birds swoop overhead and there's always activity around the Fishermen's Co-Op building, where the day's catch is weighed, scaled and sold. The beach is also one of the best places in Tobago to watch (and lend a hand) as fishermen pull in their

CASTARA

●CAFÉS & RESTAURANTS	
D'Almond Tree	2
The Boat House	1
Cascreole	3
Castara Retreats	
Scenic Restaurant	6
Cheno's	5
Marguerite's	4

■ACCOMMODATION	
Alibaba's Sea Breeze	2
Angel Apartments	4
The Beach House	5
Blue Mango	9
Boatview Apartments	3
Carpe Diem	8
Castara Bliss	12
Castara Cottage	7
Castara Retreats	13
Lillibets	1
The Naturalist	11
Sea Level	10
Sea Scape	6

Waterfall

5

seine nets. Just behind the beach, by the bridge over the river, delicious bread, cake and pastries are baked in a traditional **clay oven** each Wednesday and Saturday; go in the morning to order and come back after lunch to collect.

Little Bay

To get here from Big Bay, head northeast out of the village, passing the turn-off for *Castara Cottage* and taking the next left, Depot Rd; if you're walking, look for the small track linking Second Bay and Depot roads just before *Blue Mango*.

Separated from Big Bay by an outcrop of rocks, the smaller beach to the east of Big Bay is **Little Bay**, also known as Heavenly Bay, and a quiet spot despite the profusion of guesthouses that now overlook the sand. The waters are often calmer than at Big Bay, and there's excellent **snorkelling** to be had on the reef that stretches around the headland from here; expect to see stingrays and perhaps the odd turtle. There are no changing facilities at Little Bay, although there is a lively beach bar/restaurant (see opposite).

ARRIVAL

By car You can drive right on to Big Bay via Castara Bay Rd in the middle of the village, signposted for Castara Bay; there's a car park of sorts at the end of the road, and more space to park on the other side of the bridge over the Castara River. There's also the dead-end Second Bay Rd down to the eastern end of the beach (best not attempted in a car), and the steep but driveable Depot Rd just past this

CASTARA

turn-off, which heads down to Little Bay. Many accommodation options offer pick-ups from the airport, sometimes included in the accommodation rate.

Car rental Porridge (see p.232) is a reliable option for car rental, as is Taylor's in Little Bay (☎354 5743, ⓦ taylorstobagoautorental.com).

ACCOMMODATION

Castara is the only village along this section of coast where you'll find a choice of **places to stay**, many of them ranged around Big or Little bays and set in charming wooden cottages with lovely views. All places have wi-fi, though reception can be patchy. The majority of rooms here include some kind of cooking facilities, and if you plan on making a lot of meals yourself, you'd be well advised to stock up on provisions in Crown Point, as the shops here sell only the most basic of items.

BIG BAY AND CASTARA VILLAGE

Blue Mango Second Bay Rd ☎635 1570 or ☎768 0007, ⓦ blue-mango.com. Castara old-timer; the three Sweet Point apartments have great bay views, cool breezes, kitchens, fans, mosquito nets and plenty of privacy, while "Sea Steps" cottage has indoor and outdoor showers and a sundeck overhanging your own private cove, from where you can watch dolphins; all are showing their age a little, however. There are also a couple of less appealing options set back from the sea. Apartments US$70, cottage US$150

Carpe Diem Castara Village ☎639 3135, in UK ☎01932 848831, ⓦ castara.net. Two fresh and airy apartments below the owner's gorgeous wood-built home, set on the hill and affording lovely views over both the bays. Equipped with netted bed, fan, full kitchen and large bathrooms, the spotless studios downstairs are nicely styled and very inviting, while the self-contained two-bedroom apartment upstairs, with its huge veranda, is rented when the owners aren't in residence. Studios US$70, apartment US$150

Castara Bliss Castara Village ☎352 5727, ⓦ castarabliss.moonfruit.com. Set back from the main road in a lofty position overlooking the football field and the sea, these neat, appealing self-contained studio apartments have standing fans, kitchenettes, nets over the

beds, hot and cold water and cool sea breezes on the veranda. Friendly, helpful owner, too. TT$360

★ **Castara Retreats** Northside Rd ☎766 3656, in UK ☎07841 645238, ⓦ castararetreats.com. Ranged across the hill on the southwest side of the village, and with gorgeous views over the beaches, bay and village, these airy wooden studios, and one- or two-bedroom apartments with private porches and sundecks, are thoughtfully designed, with spacious modern kitchens equipped with quality wares that make cooking a pleasure, and bedrooms that allow you to see the sea from between the sheets. The lovely gardens attract plenty of birdlife, the staff are welcoming and efficient and the owners go to great lengths to promote sustainable tourism in the village. Great restaurant and bar, and easily one of the most appealing places to stay in the whole island. Studios US$115, one-bed apartments US$220

The Naturalist Castara Village ☎639 5901, ⓦ naturalist-tobago.com. Right on the beach, tucked into the corner of Big Bay at the bottom of the road between the two bays, with some lovely all-wood rooms upstairs with full kitchen, a/c, fan and TV; the standard rooms downstairs are a little older. US$55

Sea Level Second Bay Rd ☎660 7311 or ☎369 7165,

5

Ⓦ tobago.de. Just up the hill from the *Naturalist*, but still close to the beach, this guesthouse is a good budget choice. Rooms are comfortable and offer good value; all have kitchen, balcony, mosquito nets and fan, and some have sea views. US$45

LITTLE BAY
★**Alibaba's Sea Breeze** Little Bay Ⓣ 686 7957, Ⓦ alibaba-tours.com. Four en-suite apartments occupying the best location in Little Bay: close to the beach and with immaculate views of Castara Bay. All suites have private balconies, well-equipped kitchens, fans and mosquito nets over the bamboo four-poster beds. The friendly owners are a great source of information and also run one of Tobago's most professional tour operators. US$85

Angel Apartments Little Bay Ⓣ 639 5291 or Ⓣ 363 0374, in UK Ⓣ 01787 282671, Ⓦ angel-apartments .com. This concrete block a few metres from the beach is a bit of an eyesore, but the en-suite apartments with a/c, living area, kitchen and TV are very spacious, and there's a swimming pool (the only one in the village). Second- and third-floor apartments have verandas with sea views (and cost a little more). US$65

The Beach House Little Bay Ⓣ 660 7702, Ⓦ tobago beachhouse.com. Cute little wood-built house with a one-bedroom apartment upstairs and two studios downstairs (which can interconnect), set almost on the sands of Little Bay. All have appealing decor, nets over the beds, full kitchens, hammocks and a balcony overlooking the water, and the rates are very reasonable. Studios US$65, one-bed apartment US$105

Boatview Apartments Ⓣ 483 0964, Ⓔ sha13taylor @gmx.com. In a lovely location overlooking the waters of Little Bay, these are basic but decent apartments, with kitchen and a balcony overlooking the bay. Bathrooms have cold water only, but the rates are pretty reasonable. US$60

★**Castara Cottage** Second Bay Rd Ⓣ 757 1044, in UK Ⓣ 07525 724 201, Ⓦ castaracottage.com. Beautiful wooden house split into three separate self-contained apartments, two with two bedrooms, one a studio (US$70). All are lovingly decorated and with many personal touches courtesy of the owners, and each has a kitchen, mosquito nets, safe and private patio. Plants and trees surround the property, giving it a secluded feel despite being only a two-minute walk from the beach, and the Tamarind cottage in particular is great for kids. US$90

Lillibets Little Bay Ⓣ 760 6357, Ⓦ lillibets.com. Built into the hillside above Little Bay and accessible via a steep wooden staircase behind *Angel Apartments* (so not suitable if you have mobility issues), these four suites come with a separate living area, cable TV, a/c, full kitchen, mosquito nets and private bathroom. The views from this elevated spot are excellent, enjoyed from a communal balcony with hanging chairs and bird feeders. US$80

★**Sea Scape** Little Bay Ⓣ 1 559 287 9270 (in US), Ⓦ seascapetobago.com. Gorgeous wooden building perched high above Little Bay and reachable via steep steps, with two luxurious apartments that offer fabulous views from the balconies and bedrooms. Both are beautifully appointed with high-spec kitchen, netted beds and safe; the larger apartment is split-level, with one of its two en-suite bedrooms upstairs. US$195

EATING AND DRINKING

There may not be a huge amount of choice when it comes to **eating** in Castara, but there are several places offering excellent and inexpensive local cooking often featuring supremely fresh local fish. Note, however, that with a couple of exceptions (*Cheno's* and *Castara Retreats*), **opening hours** are more of a guide than a given; many places simply shut up shop if things are quiet. As for entertainment, the rum shop on the main road is a great place for a **drink** and a chat with the locals, and you'll see the odd party night or beach bonfire advertised on posters around town. For visitors, the main event is the Wednesday night jam at *The Boat House*.

CAFÉS AND RESTAURANTS

D'Almond Tree Big Bay Ⓣ 683 3593. Set back from the sea but right on Big Bay beach, with tables on an open-sided deck, this is a nice little spot for Creole cooking (curry shrimp, catch of the day, baked chicken etc; from TT$60) as well as rotis with all the usual curry fillings. Opening times can be erratic and service a little slow; no alcohol but you can bring your own. Mon–Sat 11am–3pm & 6–10pm.

The Boat House Little Bay Ⓣ 483 0964. English-run restaurant whose daily changing lunch and dinner menu usually includes local dishes such as a bowl of coconut curried shrimp (from TT$70) plus burgers, chicken and fish, and good home-made pizzas on Sundays. It's a lovely spot

for a drink overlooking the water, and becomes the focal point of the village on Wednesday nights, with African drumming and dancing. Mon, Wed & Fri 9.30am–10pm, Tues & Thurs 9.30am–5pm, Sun 10am–5pm.

★**Cascreole** Big Bay Ⓣ 721 5700. Right on the beach with tables set on a wooden deck built above the sand, this is one of the nicest locations in town. The cooking is great, too, with mains (TT$50–100) such as fish in coconut sauce or chicken with pineapple served with tasty sides from aubergine gratin to stewed pigeon peas. Mon–Tues & Thurs–Sat 11am–4pm & 6–10pm.

★**Castara Retreats Scenic Restaurant** Northside Rd Ⓣ 766 1010, Ⓦ castararetreats.com. This eponymous

5

restaurant really does live up to its name, with gorgeous bay views that are especially lovely if enjoyed at sunset with one of their seriously good cocktails in hand. With a mission to offer something different to the usual fare that's done so well down in the village, the cooking here is a blend of Italian and Venezuelan, with home-made pasta (try the carrot and ricotta ravioli) and super-fresh fish, succulently grilled and served with green, tomato or mango salsa; chicken Provencal with potatoes or aubergine involtini are also delicious, as are desserts such as a silky mousse made with Tobago chocolate or home-made ice cream. Mains from TT$105. Mon, Sat & Sun noon–10pm, Tues–Fri 5–10pm.

Cheno's Northside Rd ☎704 7819. This friendly diner,

with tables in a little courtyard off the main road as you enter Castara from the south, is the village's best breakfast spot. Saltfish or eggs and bacon with coconut bake are excellent (around TT$50); they also serve coffee, cakes, home-made ice cream and reasonably priced local dinners (around TT$100) of fish, chicken and crab, and have the odd party night. Daily 8.15am–1pm.

Marguerite's Northside Rd ☎710 6645. Across the street from *Cheno's*, with tables in an open-sided dining room, and offering local cooking with a bit of a twist (the chef worked overseas for a while); expect shrimp, fish, goat and chicken cooked with unusual veg combinations (mains from TT$80). No alcohol licence, but you can bring your own. Mon–Sat 11am–3pm & 6–9pm.

DIRECTORY

Banks There's an ATM at the First Citizens Bank on a ridge above the main road as you exit the village to the north; however, bear in mind that it runs out of cash fairly frequently.

Shops Castara's few general-purpose shops are on the main street through town; all sell basic food provisions. For fruit and veg, check out Bingi's stall at the corner of Depot Rd. Alcohol is available from Codrington's rum shop just by the Second Bay Rd turn-off.

Tours One of Tobago's best tour operators, Alibaba Tours (see p.202), is based in Castara, and runs excellent boat and

land tours from the village. Of the other enterprising locals who offer trips, best is the ever-pleasant and very professional Derrick Lopez, aka Porridge (☎766 3656 or ☎787 0992), a one-man whirlwind who does pretty much any island tour (full-day tours US$100/couple). Porridge's son also offers boat tours aboard the well-equipped *Sonarise*, with fishing, snorkelling, drinks and a beach barbecue (TT$450/person), and a sunset cruise (TT$150), as does the affable Loady from Country Wave Tours (☎363 7678), whose trips are a little cheaper.

Englishman's Bay

East of Castara, houses, shops and most of the traffic melt away, and the Northside Road is flanked by enormous tufts of whispering, creaking bamboo, broken occasionally to reveal marvellous jungle-clad hilly prospects. The next worthy beach, about 3km along the Northside Road, is **Englishman's Bay**, hidden from the road by a thick cover of bush; look out for the blue and white sign, opposite a WASA building, marking a left-hand turn and the gravel track which leads to the beach's small car park. Utterly ravishing and virtually undeveloped, the bay offers a perfect crescent of pure yellow sand, deep blue water and offshore reef – from the sea, the forested hillside appears completely untouched, as the bush drips right down to the sand. The bay remains delightfully remote, the quintessential "deserted beach" destination of many a pleasure boat cruise. For this reason, there have unfortunately been a few thefts from tourists at Englishman's Bay; the crime and safety box (see p.196), for some general advice when visiting Tobago's more isolated beaches. There are no lifeguards here, but beach chairs can be rented from *Eula's*.

EATING

ENGLISHMAN'S BAY

Eula's Café by the Sea Englishman's Bay ☎639 6408. Adjacent to the car park and right on the beach, *Eula's* serves rather overpriced hot meals including roti, chicken,

fish and lobster (mains around TT$100), as well as cold drinks, ice cream and a nice selection of crafts. Daily 10am–6pm.

Parlatuvier

The coast road climbs upward and inland east of Englishman's Bay, passing through the diminutive community of **Parrot Hall** after about 3km before descending to reveal one of the most arresting views on the island: **Parlatuvier** is another crescent of pearly sand flanked by an absurdly pretty hillside scattered with palms, terraced provision grounds and ice-cream-coloured houses; you can get a great view over the village from the car park adjacent to the *Glasgow Bar* (see below). The pier in the middle of the bay is testament to Parlatuvier's dedication to fishing, as are the gulls that roost on the rocks at either side of the bay, patiently awaiting the return of the boats. **Swimming** here is a vigorous experience as waves are usually quite strong and the water deepens sharply from the sand; be careful as there is no lifeguard on duty, and what with the fishing paraphernalia, it's not really a place to lay down a towel and sunbathe.

Top River Falls

Daily 9am–6pm • TT$20 • The signposted entrance to the falls is right on the Northside Rd at Parlatuvier, and there's a huge grassy car park

Set up by enterprising locals, **Top River Falls** offers an easy-access cooldown. From the car park, a path winds down through frothy stands of bamboo to the river, from where it's a five-minute walk along the bank to the waterfall, a three-tiered affair with two deep pools of clear, cold water. There are basic changing rooms at the bottom, and a couple of barbecue pits popular with local families who come and cook by the water. Soft drinks are available from the ticket booth at the entrance.

ACCOMMODATION, EATING AND DRINKING | PARLATUVIER

Culture Foods Parlatuvuer Village ☎ 298 8870. Adjacent to the parking area by the community centre in the western side of the village, this bar/restaurant offers cold beers and simple lunches such as fish broth or catch of the day for around TT$60. Daily 11am–5pm.

★ **Glasgow Bar** Northside Rd ☎ 380 8900. In pole position overlooking Parlatuvier, this two-storey bar offers spectacular views down over the bay, and is a great place to chat to locals over a few drinks. The adjacent cookshop also offers chips and chicken lunches (TT$25–45). Daily 10am–late.

★ **Gloucester Place** Northside Rd ☎ 639 5476, in US ☎ 252 571 0224, ⓦ gloucesterplace.com. Set high above the sea on the main road just east of Parlatuvier, this is fantastically peaceful place with precipitous gardens lush with fruit trees and an infinity pool overlooking the ocean. Decorated with Caribbean artworks, the spacious main house operates as a B&B (Nov–April only), and has three a/c en-suite double rooms and access to the lounge and kitchen; there's also a separate self-contained two-bedroom cottage (open year-round), hanging over the cliff and with great views from the balcony. Guesthouse US$130, cottage US$140

Parlatuvier Tourist Resort Parlatuvier village ☎ 639 5629, ⓦ parlatuviertouristresort.com. Close to the sea and right down in the village, these brightly painted, breezy apartments have fan and a/c, kitchen and a balcony overlooking the beach. Great value and a nice alternative to the leeward resorts. US$45

Bloody Bay

Lifeguards daily 10am–5pm • Changing facilities TT$1 • Turn left at the T-junction signposted for the Forest Reserve and Roxborough

The last accessible beach on the leeward coast before Charlotteville is **Bloody Bay**, roughly 2km beyond Parlatuvier and named after a battle between English soldiers and African slaves in 1771 that was fierce enough to turn the sea crimson with blood; Dead Bay River, which runs across the sand and into the sea, is named for the same event. The beach itself is fine brown sand, strewn with pebbles and driftwood and frequented by no one except the odd fisherman. From here, directly opposite the bay and clearly visible 5km out to sea, the **Sisters Rocks** form an attractive cluster of tiny, verdant islands; it's also fun to explore the river which flows into the sea at the north end of the bay. The Tobago House of Assembly have constructed a string of luridly painted buildings on the beach which house changing facilities and a restaurant, but do detract a bit from the formerly unspoilt beauty of the place.

EATING AND DRINKING | BLOODY BAY

★ **Sunshine** Northside Rd ☎ 337 4160 or ☎ 289 5710. This locally run restaurant and bar is a great place to stop off for a meal, with succulent Creole-style fish, chicken pork and goat with all the trimmings – rice, coo-coo, callaloo, stewed peas and salad – for around TT$65; shrimp and lobster (TT$100–150) are also available. Staff are supremely friendly and the little gazebos overlooking the valley and sea make a great spot for a few drinks. Daily 7am–10pm.

5

L'Anse Fourmi

East of Bloody Bay, the road continues to the lofty village of **L'Anse Fourmi**, a one-street town that's remote enough to make the sight of a tourist a talking point; there are a couple of **bars** in which to refresh yourself. The only point of interest is the roadside **gallery** of Jason Nedd (intermittent hours), whose vivid paintings of local scenes are well worth a look should you be lucky enough to find it open. Beyond the village, it's trees rather than houses that line the smooth new coast road to Charlotteville (see p.243), though this pacific scene may soon be set to change if a buyer is found for the 300-acre estate adjacent to the village, put up for sale in late 2014 for development as a luxury resort.

Tobago Forest Reserve

Swinging inland from the Northside Road at Bloody Bay, the Roxborough–Parlatuvier Road connects the leeward and windward coasts, running straight through the **Tobago Forest Reserve** and the central mountain range. Construction of the road began in 1958, prior to which the two sides of the island were only linked by small trails. However, Hurricane Flora (see box, p.236) ravaged it mercilessly five years later, and the road was not repaired until the mid-1990s. Now it's a beautifully quiet half-hour drive through the rainforest; lined with pioneer ferns and parrot-apple trees, the tarmac is in generally good shape (though watch out for a few water-damaged spots) and traffic is rare.

The reserve itself acquired its status as the oldest protected rainforest in the western hemisphere during the plantation era, when British scientist Stephen Hales began researching the relationship between rainfall and trees and communicated his findings to Soame Jenyns, a British MP responsible for the development of Tobago. At the time, plantations were concentrated in low-lying parts of the island, but the estates began encroaching on the more precipitous forest areas, felling trees for fuel or clearing land to make way for yet more sugar cane. It took Jenyns ten years to convince Tobago's planters that if they continued to cut down the forest, the island would soon be incapable of supporting the smallest of shrubs, let alone a massive sugar plantation. Ultimately, he was successful, and on April 13, 1776, 14,000 acres of central Tobago were designated a protected Crown Reserve.

RAINFOREST GUIDES

Tempting as it may be to walk through the Forest Reserve alone, it's far better to hire a **guide**: you won't lose your way, guides can point out things you may otherwise miss, such as bachac ants carrying their leaf shreds back to the nest, and you'll learn a lot more about forest dynamics. If you do decide to walk alone, remember that the sun sets quickly on the island, resulting in a rapid drop in temperature and the increased possibility of getting lost. Since this is an isolated spot, you should also be mindful of the security risks of walking alone in the forest. During daylight hours, **registered guides** (usually ex-foresters) wait at the entrance to Gilpin Trace (registered individuals all have an ID badge), and you can also visit as part of a longer tour (see box, pp.202-203). Most forest guides are from nearby villages such as Parlatuvier and Roxborough, and all of them are far cheaper than the hotel-arranged guides, charging about TT$160 for a 1.5hr trip, or TT$240 for 2.5hr, or TT$300 for the 3hr hike down to Bloody Bay. Reliable, certified guides include Dexter James (☎660 7852 or ☎757 0761), who lives in the second house after the Northside Road/Parlatuvier–Roxborough Road junction; Fitzroy Quamina (☎660 7836 or ☎344 1895), Junior Thomas (☎660 7847), Darlington Chance (☎660 7828 or ☎660 7823) and the only female guide, Shurland James (☎660 7883 or ☎294 3470). All guides also offer walks to local waterfalls, and night walks into the Reserve (prices negotiable).

In addition to the local guides mentioned above, there are several other reputable guides who offer rainforest tours (see box, pp.202-203).

5

Gilpin Trace

The main point of access into the Forest Reserve is the **Gilpin Trace**, marked by a painted sign 3km along the Roxborough–Parlatuvier Road. The 5km trail which strikes straight into the forest from here is well marked and maintained, though often very muddy regardless of the weather – the forest gets around 380cm of rain each year. You'll be offered rubber boots to rent for TT$20 on the approach to Gilpin Trace, and it's a good idea to take a pair (bring your own socks). The trail takes about two and a half hours to walk at a leisurely pace, taking you through some spectacular forest dotted with huge termite nests, with lianas and vines blocking out most of the light. The birdlife in the forest is most active early in the morning, so birdwatchers should aim to be on the trail by about 6am. Later in the day, you might see the odd hummingbird, mot-mot or woodpecker, if you're lucky. Typically, tour guides will take you past three small waterfalls – none are suitable for swimming – before turning back. If you follow the trail to its end, you'll come out of the forest just after the reserve boundary, towards the windward side, approximately 3km north of Roxborough – remember that it is a steep uphill walk along the road back to the start of the trail if you've parked there.

EATING AND DRINKING   **TOBAGO FOREST RESERVE**

There are no restaurants or bars in the Reserve, but two of the forest guides offer refreshments at their small restaurants by reservation only, which makes a nice finale to a rainforest walk; don't expect to find anything ready if you turn up on spec.

Rainforest Café ☎ 660 7836 or ☎ 680 0349. This roadside stopoff is run by Mrs Malder-Taylor, aunt of guide Fitzroy Quamina and a specialist with dasheen, who cooks up everything from punch to ice cream from this venerable tuber, as well as lunches of crab and dumplings, stewed chicken, fish in a curry coconut sauce (TT$45–55). Give at least a day's notice. By reservation only.

Shirland's Nature Park and Coffee Shop ☎ 660 7883 or ☎ 294 3470. Just at the roadside as you approach the Reserve from the leeward coast, this is run by forest guide Shirland James, who offers light refreshments from fresh natural juices and chocolate tea to home-made dasheen ice cream, plus coffee, tea and, if desired, full Creole lunches (from around TT$50). By reservation only.

The windward coast

Rugged and continually breathtaking, Tobago's southern shoreline is usually referred to as the **windward coast**. It's spanned by the narrow, winding Windward Road, which sticks close to the sea and provides fantastic views of choppy Atlantic waters and tiny spray-shrouded islands. The parade of languid coastal villages here is a complete contrast to the more developed southwest, and though there is the odd guesthouse on or around the main road, this isn't the most enticing area to stay – tides and strong undercurrents make some of the most attractive-looking **beaches** unsuitable for swimming, and where they're not, the often muddied water can be a bit off-putting. Nonetheless, the coastline between Scarborough and the King's Bay, where the road swings inland on its way to Speyside does make for a fantastically scenic drive, with plenty of roadside bars and diners in which to stop off and have a beer or some lunch and one or two diverting attractions, the most popular of which is a tour and a taste of local chocolate at the gorgeous **Tobago Cocoa Estate**, followed by a refreshing dip at **Argyle Waterfall**, one of the prettiest in the island. Beyond **Roxborough**, the largest settlement on the windward coast, the road swings inland and upwards, swooping spectacularly down to the sea again at **Speyside**, best known for its fantastic snorkelling and scuba diving, and the only place on the coast with any kind of tourist development.

Mount St George

A couple of kilometres east of Scarborough, the Claude Noel Highway ends abruptly just after the Dwight Yorke Stadium, named after the Tobago-born soccer

5

hero who made his name playing with Manchester United. The last fast and straight section of road then sweeps past the glorious **Hillsborough Bay** (also known as **Hope Bay**) about 2km later; although the long stretch of windswept sand looks inviting, stick to paddling and enjoying the breeze – the riptides are dangerous. Past the beach and over a narrow bridge, the road swings round a sharp corner and into tiny **Mount St George**, on the eastern side of this large bay, its roadside houses fronted with attractive flowered gardens. There's no discernible sign that this was once Georgetown, the island's first British **capital**, named in honour of King George III. The British began to develop Georgetown after they captured the island in 1762, building houses and a base (now destroyed) for the House of Assembly, which held its inaugural meeting here in April 1768. British occupation was short-lived, however; by 1769, they shifted the capital to Scarborough. There's still one tenuous connection to sovereignty in the town, though – set at the top of a breezy hillock overlooking the village below is the official residence of the prime minister, a seldom-used, whitewashed structure that's closed to the public.

Granby Point

Just beyond Mount St George, you'll pass Studley Park Quarry on your left, a busy commercial enterprise that's steadily eating into the surrounding hillsides. Beyond the unassuming village of **Studley Park**, home to Tobago's municipal dump, a right-hand turn onto a short gravel track leads to the sea at **Granby Point**. The track ends at a car park where you'll find a small children's **playground**. A flight of concrete steps leads off the car park and through some rather fly-infested bush to **Fort Granby**, originally built on Granby Point by the British in around 1765 to protect Georgetown and briefly occupied by the French between 1781 and 1787. Nothing remains of the original fortification; the cannons are long gone, replaced by pretty gazebos, mown lawns and picnic tables. The views of the sea and nearby **Smith's Island** are fantastic, and there is good swimming to be had on either of the **beaches** which flank the point. **Barbados Bay** to the right is the more populated; the fishermen's shacks on the sand make it a good spot to hang out, while the more deserted **Pinfold Bay** on the other side is a better bet if you fancy sunbathing; neither has any facilities, however, and both are only accessible from Granby Point. There's a small bar in the car park at the base of the steps, serving drinks and basic meals.

HURRICANE FLORA

On September 30, 1963, **Hurricane Flora** swept over Tobago and completely devastated the island. Most of the banana, coconut and cocoa plantations were wiped out, and large tracts of the forest reserve laid to waste, with 30-metre-high trees toppling like matchsticks. The catastrophic Flora killed thirty people, injured hundreds and razed to the ground sixty percent of the island's fragile board houses. Moriah, Concordia, Argyle and Richmond were completely demolished, roads were impassable and there was no mains water or electricity outside Scarborough for more than six weeks.

A **relief fund** helped to repair the worst of the damage, and the United Nations provided foodstuffs that fed the population for nearly a year, while other Caribbean islands pitched in, too. You can still see the effect of the hurricane in the forest reserve today, as there are few of the really huge trees that formerly made up the forest – much of those you see today are relatively small specimens that grew after Flora (or were saplings at the time). The hurricane also had a profound influence on Tobago's future; a tentative agricultural economy was abandoned, and the island began to devote its energy to tourism. Tobagonians still remember Flora with a shudder, but thankfully hurricanes are very rare this far south, and a similar event has not occurred since.

Goodwood

5

As the Windward Road swings into the tiny village of **GOODWOOD**, with its appealing gingerbread houses and neat playing field, you'll begin to see the views for which the windward coast is famous – starting with a spectacular panorama of the unravelling coast and distant **Richmond Island**. There's a track leading from the centre of Goodwood down to the **beach**; the palm trees and greyish sand are nothing to shout about, but it's nevertheless a pleasant place for a stroll, and a popular swimming spot with locals.

Genesis Nature Park & Art Gallery

Windward Rd, Goodwood • Mon–Sat 9.30am–5pm • TT$60 • ☎ 660 4668

The **Genesis Nature Park & Art Gallery** is home to a variety of animals, including capuchin monkeys, a boa constrictor, cocricos – the national bird of Tobago – a cayman and wild hogs (in small cages), housed on the pretty landscaped grounds. The entrance fee includes a tour of the menagerie and the not-as-interesting art gallery, which exhibits sculptures and paintings by the owner.

Pembroke

A Lilliputian-sized village which spreads down to the sea from the road, **Pembroke** is a friendly place with a smattering of rum bars and a pretty clapboard Anglican church set on cliffs overlooking the Atlantic. As the road dips down again, there's a right-hand turn to the **beach**, which is mostly dedicated to fishing, but nice enough for a swim. Pembroke is the venue for the annual **Salaka Feast** celebrations, now an important part of the Heritage Festival (see pp.33–35), and staged in the purpose-built **Pembroke Heritage Park**. A kind of African thanksgiving to the ancestors, the feast commemorates the community's founding by the first slaves brought to the area, and honours obeah spirits through dancing, singing, storytelling, drumming and offerings of fruit and other foods, followed by plenty of eating and drinking.

Argyle Waterfall

Daily 9am–4.30pm, last tour at 4pm • TT$60 adults, TT$30 children • ☎ 660 4154, ⓦ argylewaterfall.org

East of neat Glamorgan village, the Windward Road passes the Richmond waterworks on the right before returning to the coast at the tiny village of **Belle Garden**. Another few kilometres further along Carapuse Bay will take you to the entrance road to the much-visited **Argyle Waterfall**, the island's highest waterfall, tumbling 54m out of the greenery into a deep pool.

Just past the entrance, you pay the entrance fee at the Roxborough Estate Visitor Service Co-Operative booth; there's also a café selling soft drinks and snack. To **access the falls**, you follow the easily passable cocoa-tree-lined path to a grassy car park. Official guides wearing blue, green or yellow Argyle Waterfall shirts will be waiting here to walk with you to the falls (the guide's services are included in the entrance fee, although a tip is expected), giving a brief history of the Roxborough Estate and pointing out birds and flowers on the way.

The falls themselves are a pleasant fifteen-minute walk from the car park, and you can hear the water long before you reach it. Argyle is one of Tobago's most accessible cascades, but to see the best parts you'll have to exert yourself a little and climb up the right-hand side along steep and sometimes bushy paths. There are **three main waterfalls**; the second is particularly strong – increased flow during the rainy season (June–Nov) creates a constant fine mist that soon soaks you to the skin. The second tier is great for a dip in a natural jacuzzi, as there are plenty of rocky seats on which to perch and get a pounding shoulder massage. If you're feeling energetic, climb up even further to the deepest swimming pool – and the smallest section of waterfall – where you can dive or swing in Tarzan-style on a vine. If the climb doesn't appeal, drive right up to the highest swimming spot.

Tobago Cocoa Estate

1hr tours Mon, Wed & Fri 11am, TT$60 • Culinary tours by reservation only, from US$85 • ☎ 390 2021, ⓦ tobagococoa.com • From the Windward Rd, the access road to Argyle Waterfall meets a T-junction; right is to the falls, while the left-hand turning winds a pretty but potholed route up into the hills and to the estate gates

A working cocoa plantation overlooking a gorgeous valley with views down to the Atlantic, the **Tobago Cocoa Estate** is a low-key but beguiling visitor attraction. Lasting an hour or so, tours of the estate offer a offer a gentle and fun introduction to cocoa production, taking you along the edges of the groves of Trinidad Select Hybrid or "fine flavour" cocoa grown here, the fermentation and drying process of the cocoa beans, as well as covering the history of cocoa production in Tobago via some historical displays. In 2009, the estate produced its own chocolate bars, a first for Tobago, and the owners take their product seriously – made in France in small batches, the bars contain only single-estate cocoa grown here, and have won numerous prestigious awards; you get a taste at the end of the tour. Between December and May, you can combine the regular tour with afternoon tea or dinner, both with chocolate- and/or rum-tasting sessions. Bars of the estate's chocolate are, of course, available to buy at the end of all tours.

Roxborough

ROXBOROUGH is the largest town along the windward coast. Its main drag runs parallel to the sea, although – unlike almost everywhere else on the windward parade – there are also a few residential streets stretching inland. The few small shops are interspersed with plenty of dilapidated and abandoned buildings, giving the town a rather

---

COCOA MOTION

The Roxborough environs are **cocoa** country; just west of town on the main road, 100m past the Argyle Waterfall turn-off, a left fork cuts straight through the old Roxborough Estate, one of Tobago's largest cocoa plantations and home of a colonial-era cocoa house that's still used to dry local beans. Once a huge industry here, with French and British settlers establishing cocoa plantations throughout Trinidad and Tobago from the mid-eighteenth century onwards, cocoa began a slow decline in the twentieth century, as local youth turned away from agriculture and its associations with colonial-era labour exploitation, rife in a country still reeling from the effects of slavery. However, in recent years, the **cocoa industry** has undergone something of a renaissance; in Tobago, this is thanks mostly to the international success of the chocolate made from beans grown on the nearby Tobago Cocoa Estate, while over in Trinidad, there's a growing buzz surrounding the many local operators who have revived cocoa and chocolate production, promoting an ethical, sustainable business model based on fair trade as well as making some superb products. Cocoa growers in Lopinot (see p.130) and Brasso Seco (see p.121) are producing fantastic **dark chocolate** from their very own beans, while chocolatiers such as Cocobel (see p.92) operate chocolate tasting sessions and have earned huge local kudos for their delicious handmade chocolates, and small-scale outfits such as Soular and Sun Eaters Organics (see p.43) have pioneered the production of 60 and 70 percent cocoa bars as well as cocoa powder, cocoa nibs and brownie mix. Working **cocoa estates** such as Velaja (see p.164), San Antonio (see p.160) and Manchuria in Brasso Seco (see p.122) have also been opened up to visitors, allowing you to get an insight into traditional cocoa production from bean to bar. The majority of cocoa plantations in Trinidad and Tobago produce **Trinitario "fine flavour" cocoa**, widely acknowledged to be some of the best in the world, and it's this high quality that has helped to revive local cocoa production, and which makes local chocolate so utterly delicious.

5

THE BELMANNA UPRISING

Disgusted with the low pay and abysmal working conditions which dogged the ailing sugar industry after emancipation, African plantation workers from the Roxborough Estate **rebelled** in 1876, burning down the estate manager's home and rioting in the streets; in the ensuing melee, one of their comrades, a female labourer called Ti Piggy, was killed by police. Enraged, the workers surrounded the police station and demanded that the chief officer, **Constable Belmanna** – whom they held responsible for the death – should come out and confront them. Unwisely, he did; the mob descended, mutilating his body and beating him to death. As the unrest continued, the workers' ranks swelled with sympathizers from surrounding villages. Hopelessly outnumbered, the police could do little but retreat and call for external assistance; it came a week later in the form of a British warship, which transported hundreds of the dissenters to Scarborough, where they were slammed into jail and put on trial, most receiving a life sentence or banishment from the island.

The riot left self-governed Tobago in turmoil. Feeling they had completely lost control of the island and its predominantly black population, and fearing total chaos, the Legislative Council swiftly washed their hands of the whole affair and handed the running of Tobago back to the British. On January 1, 1877, Tobago became a **crown colony**, but the Belmanna repercussions were not to be quelled so easily. Continual unrest that followed throughout the island contributed to the final collapse of the sugar industry and the overall economic decline which led to the official coupling of Trinidad and Tobago in 1879.

run-down appearance. It's a laidback and peaceful place, although that hasn't always been the case. In the hard times that followed emancipation, Roxborough was the scene of the infamous and bloody **Belmanna Riots** (see box above), a rebellion that was to have a far-reaching effect on Tobago's system of governance. Apart from filling up your petrol tank or picking up a takeaway lunch, there's no real reason to linger; the rubbish-strewn **beach** is nothing special.

DIRECTORY ROXBOROUGH

Roxborough has the only **petrol station** on the Windward Coast; a huge affair just west of town, close to the turn-off for the Roxborough–Parlatuvier Rd. There's also an **ATM**, on the sea side of the road about midway through the village, and several small **cookshops** on the main drag offering basic local lunches.

King's Bay

Daily, daylight hours • Changing facilities TT$1

Turning inland east of Roxborough, the Windward Road swings through the hilltop village of **Delaford**, making one almighty bend at the outskirts to reveal a breathtaking view of the spiky coconut plantation surrounding the beautiful, deep blue **King's Bay** below. The **beach** here is one of the few along the windward coast to provide changing facilities, and offers gentle waters, reefs and fine dark sand; nonetheless, it's almost always deserted save for the lifeguards. There are also six attractive gazebos on a strip of grass next to the beach which make good spots for picnicking, and a small café selling snacks and drinks. The profusion of Carib Indian artefacts found here (on display at the Tobago Museum – see p.223) indicate that King's Bay was once the site of a large settlement; some suggest that the bay is named after Carib cacique (chief) King Peter, though it's more likely that that honour goes to King Peter's Bay on the Caribbean coast (see p.228).

EATING AND DRINKING KING'S BAY

★**King's Bay Café** Delaford ☎771 2716 or ☎392 8585. Overlooking the bay on the main Windward Rd, with tables on a tiny breeze-cooled veranda that affords gorgeous views over the water, this friendly place has long been the windward coast's favourite lunch stopoff. The original menu of succulent home-made burgers and grilled fish has been extended a little to cover breakfast (local specialities plus muffins, eggs and the like; from TT$20) as

5

well as Creole-style lunch and dinner (from TT$50), from sandwiches to chicken with chips. Great bread and cakes, plus tea and coffee, too. Book ahead to be sure of a table. Mon–Sat 7am–9pm.

Speyside

The last sizeable village on the windward coast, **SPEYSIDE** is not as pretty as nearby Charlotteville, with just a thin slip of grey-sand beach, but then most people come here to explore the fantastic offshore reefs rather than to admire the scenery. Despite its emergence as a **scuba-diving** paradise and the easy accessibility of nearby reefs for some of the best **snorkelling** on the island, Speyside is a soporific kind of a place with a very end-of-the-road feel. The smattering of hotels seem to only ever have a couple of guests, with most of the activity confined to the dive shops and the tour buses that stop off at lunchtime to disgorge visitors at ever-popular *Jemma's* restaurant.

Speyside lookout

Though Speyside itself isn't particularly scenic, it's hard not to be blown away by the amazing view from the **lookout** point on its western outskirts, just before the Windward Road descends into the village proper. This lofty spot affords a marvellous panorama of the village, the turquoise reef-studded waters of **Tyrrel's Bay** and the emerald-green hillocks of **Little Tobago** and **Goat Island**, the former a renowned birdwatching spot. There's good forest hiking to be had along Murchiston Trace, a tiny road that strikes off to the right from the Windward Road just before the Speyside lookout; ask in Speyside for a local guide.

Speyside village

The Windward Road hits the coast in the centre of Speyside; turn right past the playing field to the **beach** facilities, though the skinny slip of sand isn't particularly inviting; turning left takes you into what could loosely be termed the tourist strip, containing several shops, hotels and restaurants, including the famous *Jemma's* – built around a tree overlooking the sea. Just past *Manta Lodge* hotel, the road forks; left takes you across the island's interior and on to Charlotteville, while the right turn to Batteaux Bay runs past the ruins of a coral-stone building and colonial-era **waterwheel** both being slowly overtaken by the foliage. There are a couple of benches under the almond trees at the sea's edge here, and following the rocky path up the small hillock opposite the ruins brings you to a nice lookout point with a couple more benches.

Batteaux Bay and the northeast

Site of the luxurious *Blue Waters Inn* (see p.242), and the departure point for glass-bottom boat tours to Little Tobago and the Speyside reefs (see p.242), the deliciously blue waters, white sands and rich reefs of **Bateaux Bay** are a much more inviting prospect for a swim than Speyside's main beach. Though the hotel is built right on the sand, the beach itself is public, and you can use the hotel's bathrooms if having lunch or drinks at the restaurant and bar; they're also happy for diners to have a dip in the lovely waterside swimming pool.

Beyond Bateaux, the road to picturesque **Belmont** and **Starwood** bays is often impassable by car; you can walk it, but bear in mind that swimming at both is dangerous because of strong currents.

Goat Island

Of the two misshapen islets sitting 5km or so out from Speyside in Tyrrel's Bay, **Goat Island** is the closer. The white house nestled in its centre was built as the Tobagonian holiday home of Caribbean devotee Ian Fleming, author of the James Bond novels, who once owned the island. Both house and island are government owned and closed to the public. However, birdwatchers and hikers flock to the larger Little Tobago, a kilometre further out to sea.

Little Tobago

The most easterly point of the T&T republic, the two-square-kilometre outcrop of **Little Tobago** has been known as "Bird of Paradise Island" since the beginning of the twentieth century, when it was bought by keen ornithologist Sir William Ingram, who in 1909 transported 24 **greater birds of paradise** (*Paradisaea apoda*) from Aru island in New Guinea and installed them in the island, though they slowly died out thanks to hurricanes and hunters. When Sir William died in 1924, his heirs gave Little Tobago back to the government on the condition that it receive protected status. It has remained a **bird sanctuary** ever since, uninhabited except for one of the Caribbean's largest **sea-bird colonies**, which includes impressive flocks of frigate birds, boobies, terns and the spectacular red-billed tropic bird. You'll also hear the crows and clucks of feral cocks and chickens brought here by the now-departed resident caretaker, who was unable to round up his private flock before leaving the island. Most people visit the island as part of a glass-bottom boat tour (see p.242), but birdwatchers can also arrange specialist tours with the island's eco-oriented tour companies (see pp.202–203). There are no facilities on Little Tobago, so bring water and snacks with you.

All the boats dock at a small beach facing the mainland, from where you get beautiful views of Speyside and Pigeon Peak above, one of Tobago's highest points at 576m. Just

SCUBA DIVING

Tobago is one of the best **scuba-diving** spots in the southeastern Caribbean, yet it has relatively few divers visiting its dazzling coral reefs, volcanic formations and marine wrecks. The island is internationally recognized for the exciting and challenging **drift dives** caused by the Guyana current, which results from the confluence of the Caribbean Sea and the Atlantic Ocean. The seas around Tobago are home to 300 species of South Atlantic **coral** and a variety of spectacular multicoloured **fish**, not to mention larger species such as **stingrays, manta rays, sharks, dolphins, turtles** and **squid**. Rarer species such as toadfish and shortnose batfish are also occasionally spotted. Adding a touch of history to underwater encounters are the sunken ships that litter the sea floor.

There are many dive shops in Crown Point thanks to the sheer volume of visitors in the southwest, but Speyside is the island's premier diving destination, with a variety of spectacular sites surrounding the offshore islands: Goat Island is popular for drift dives; St Giles for its rocky pinnacles and underwater canyon; and there's a reasonable chance of seeing manta rays on dives around Little Tobago. Popular dive sites in the area include London Bridge, Bookends, Angel Reef, The Cathedral and Kelliston Drain – the site of the single largest brain coral in the Caribbean, and possibly the largest in the world. For more advanced divers, Sisters Rocks, offshore of Bloody Bay – with the sea shelf falling to 667m – is especially popular for larger species of fish including hammerhead sharks.

Tobago's **diving industry** was only established in the 1980s but since then scuba-diving operations have multiplied with many hotels, beaches and guesthouses sporting their own centres. Prices vary slightly between operators; in general one to three dives cost about US$50 each, half-day resort courses US$65, five-day PADI open water certification courses US$480 and advanced open water from US$385. When deciding who to dive with it's worth contacting the Association of Tobago Dive Operators (☎660 5445, ⦿tobagoscubadiving.com); they can provide a list of certified scuba-diving operators. Always check for the prominent display of a dive affiliation, such as NAUI, PADI, SSI or BSAC. A good operator will always ask you to fill in paperwork and present a diving certification card. The rental equipment should be well rinsed; if you see sand or salt crystals this may indicate careless equipment care. Inspect all equipment thoroughly, check hoses for wear, see that mouthpieces are secure and ensure they give you a depth gauge and air-pressure gauge. Listen for air leaks when you gear up and smell the air, which should be odourless. If you smell oil or anything else, search for a different operator. In case of accidents, Tobago has a recompression chamber in Roxborough (☎660 4000).

5

up from the dock, the THA have built a handsome wooden structure slated to hold a museum at some distant point in the future. Beyond here, several **trails** cut during the island's brief spell as a cotton plantation thread into interior and up to a gazebo offering gorgeous views of the island's rocky coastline and the nesting grounds of the red-billed tropic bird.

ACTIVITIES
SPEYSIDE

Scuba diving and snorkelling Speyside's dive shops (see p.205) rent snorkel equipment for around US$10/day; however, the best snorkelling is on the far-off reefs visited by the glass-bottom boats.

Glass-bottom boat tours Run by Frank's (☎ 660 5438) and *Top Ranking* (☎ 660 4904), glass-bottom boats are a good way to see the reefs if you don't want to get wet, but also take you closer to the best snorkelling as well. Trips cost US$25 and include a walk around Little Tobago and a stop for snorkelling (equipment provided); you can also get shorter glass-bottom tours of the reef for a little less, and longer cruises around St Giles Island (US$60).

ACCOMMODATION

With three **hotels** and a number of **guesthouses**, finding accommodation in Speyside shouldn't be a problem, even in high season. However, unless you're here for the diving or ensconce yourself at *Blue Waters Inn*, Charlotteville (just ten minutes' drive away on the Caribbean coast) makes a much more pleasant base.

★**Blue Waters Inn** Bateaux Bay ☎ 660 4341, ⓦ bluewatersinn.com. Speyside's largest and grandest hotel, set around stunning Bateaux Bay and separated from the village by a steep road. Recently refurbished, rooms are spacious and luxurious, with sleek modern furnishings a/c, porch/balcony and a sea view; there are also one- and two-bedroom self-catering rooms and bungalows. There's a pool, restaurant, bar, games room, dive shop and tennis court as well as 46 acres of lush tropical grounds with two nature trails. US$170

Davis Atlantic View Main Rd ☎ 660 4231. Diagonally opposite *Jemma's* and a good budget option within walking distance of the town's restaurants and dive shops, this guesthouse has four basic and clean rooms in two separate units, with each unit sharing a kitchen and TV area. Rooms have a/c and hot water in the private bathrooms. TT$300

Manta Lodge Main Rd ☎ 660 5268, ⓦ mantalodge .com. The rooms here are decent, with a/c and coffeemakers, but the place has a rather forsaken air and the service can be indifferent. Pool and restaurant and a dive shop on site. The rates include breakfast, but wi-fi costs an astounding US$10/day. US$110

Speyside Inn Main Rd ☎ 660 4852, ⓦ speysideinn .com. Simple and nicely styled with great bay views, this is much the better of the two hotels on the main road, with cabins and bungalows overlooking the pool (itself on a deck set back from the road), plus a new block of rooms facing the bay; all have balcony, fridge, safe and a/c or fan. There's a good restaurant on site (rates include breakfast) and the obligatory dive shop. Wi-fi. US$144

Top Ranking Hill View Guesthouse Top Hill St, off Main Rd ☎ 660 4904 or ☎ 682 3622, ⓦ topranking tobago.com. Set in a huge pink house on the hillside above town, this is a great little place, with friendly owners who also operate one of the Speyside glass-bottom boats. The spotless and appealing rooms have kitchenette, fan, porch or balcony and en-suite bathroom with hot and cold water and a/c, too. Reasonable rates, free one-way beach shuttle, wi-fi, and car rental available. US$55

EATING AND DRINKING

Speyside isn't exactly a metropolis, even during the high season, and in the low season, you'll find the town pretty much deserted as some of the cafés and dive operators close up shop. Nonetheless, there are a couple of good local **restaurants**, as well as some more upmarket choices in the hotels.

Birdwatcher's Speyside Main Rd ☎ 660 5438. Brightly painted café at the sea's edge, next door to *Jemma's*, with an indoor dining room and a more pleasant outdoor eating area overlooking the water. Friendly staff serve all the usual staples of Creole chicken and fish with tasty sides, (from TT$70, dinner from TT$90), although there are usually only one or two choices on any given day. Daily 10am–9pm.

★**Blue Waters Inn** ☎ 660 4341. Recently overhauled, with refreshed decor and a new chef, this in-hotel restaurant and bar is a lovely place for a frosty cocktail or a meal, with tables set on an open-sided deck overlooking Batteaux Bay. The lunch menu (mains around TT$75) runs from wraps, salads and burgers with fries to Creole-style fish or chicken – no surprises but well done and reasonably priced. Dinner is often a buffet (around TT$250), with mains such as chicken with passion fruit. Daily 7.30am–1 0pm.

★**Jemma's Seaview Kitchen** Main Rd ☎ 660 4066.

Popular with every island tour bus, with dining areas on several levels built around the boughs of a tree, and offering fantastic sea views and ocean breezes. The Creole food is reliably tasty and pretty reasonably priced: breakfast (from TT$25) is eggs, bacon or local fish dishes, while lunch and dinner menus (mains from TT$70) include grilled, curried or stewed fish, baked chicken in a mushroom or barbecue sauce, plus shrimp and lobster and lovely sides of breadfruit pie, tannia fritters or aubergine casserole. Mon–Thurs & Sun 8am–8pm, Fri 8am–4pm.

Redman's Main Rd (no phone). This basic restaurant in the pink building next door to *Jemma's* has a lovely sea-facing terrace decorated with conch shells, and serves tasty and simple local dishes – think chicken and rice or fish with pigeon peas, macaroni pie and veg – from TT$50. Opening

can be sporadic. Daily 10am–3pm.

Speyside Inn Main Rd ☎ 660 4852. With tables on a covered patio overlooking the sea, this in-hotel restaurant is worth a try, and is often the busiest spot in Speyside after dark (though that's not saying much). The reasonably priced daily changing menu might feature mains of pasta with Bolognese sauce, mahi-mahi with tamarind sauce or kingfish cooked with coconut (TT$80–170), and breakfast is also available. Daily 7.30–9.30am, noon–3pm & 6.30–9pm.

Speyside Lookout Windward Rd ☎ 686 6365. In a fantastic position with the panoramic views of the bay unfolding below, this is a scenic spot in which to drink a beer or a natural juice or have an ice cream, or enjoy local fish or chicken dishes (TT$50–60). Daily noon–10pm.

Flagstaff Hill

The Windward Road strikes inland from Speyside's eastern outskirts on its way from the Atlantic to the Caribbean coast, climbing steeply upwards through the island's central spike before plummeting down to the opposite shoreline. Tobago's most easterly portion of tarmac marks the last sign of "civilization"; northeast of here, the land is completely undeveloped, with no electricity or piped water for the hardy handful of small-scale farmers, bush hunters and fishermen who live here. Just before the descent to the Caribbean, there's a signposted turn-off for **Flagstaff Hill**, with the road sweeping past some very fancy homes. At the crest of the hill, the road opens up to reveal a wide grassy area dotted with benches and overlooked by a lofty communications tower and mobile phone mast. The wind whistles through the metal and the **views** are absolutely superlative: Tyrel's Bay, with Little Tobago and Goat Island to one side, and to the other, Man O' War Bay, Booby Island, Cambleton Battery and, much further out, Sisters Rocks. This excellent vantage point was once used by British and French soldiers, who used mirrors to warn their colleagues stationed at Cambleton Battery below of an approaching ship.

Charlotteville

Tumbling willy-nilly down a hillside to a horseshoe bay of calm Caribbean waters, where frigate birds swoop over the fishing boats, the absurdly pretty **CHARLOTTEVILLE** looks its very best as you approach the village on the Windward Road. Snugly situated under the protective cover of **Man O' War Bay**, Charlotteville is one of Tobago's foremost fishing communities – more than sixty percent of the island's total catch is brought in by local fishermen. Bordered on each side by steep forested hills, the village has an isolated feel, although this is in fact one of Tobago's biggest communities with around 5000 inhabitants. It is also one of its oldest, first settled by Caribs and then by the Dutch in 1633 – for many years the bay was known as Jan De Moor Bay after an early Frisian occupant. During the plantation era, the area was divided into two successful estates, Pirate's Bay and Charlotteville; sugar shipments made regular departures from the bay, and the village prospered. In 1865, both estates were purchased by the Turpin family, who still own much of the surrounding land. Today, tourism plays its part – albeit as second fiddle to fishing – in sustaining the local economy, and the village is increasingly popular with independent types who come for the quiet beaches and

5

laidback charm. If you're seeking peace, quiet and great beaches, it's hard not to become utterly besotted with Charlotteville.

The hole-in-the-wall shops and sprinkling of restaurants that make up Charlotteville's centre line the road along the beach, while the streets that stretch inland and uphill, spreading back from a central playing field, are mostly residential. Slap in the centre of the village is the **Fishermen's Co-Operative**, where the day's catch is weighed, scaled and sold (and in the midst of an upgrade at the time of writing); adjacent to it is the proposed site for the controversial new **Charlotteville Beachfront Mall**. Beyond the site, the bay view opens up, the sea wall dotted with benches and the beach mostly taken up with fishing boats and nets drying on the sand. The long concrete **pier** offers a lovely perspective back over the village, and is a great spot from which to watch the sun set.

Charlotteville Beachfront Mall

Slated to be similar to the bulky concrete complex and Buccoo, the two-storey **Charlotteville Beachfront Mall** has been vigorously opposed by many local residents, several of whom had their businessplaces torn down when the site was cleared in early 2014, and who argue that the planned complex is completely out of place in this small village of low-rise buildings. Legal proceedings instituted by the Charlotteville Beachfront Movement pressure group saw construction halted when it was discovered that the THA had cleared the land without obtaining planning permission or the correct Certificate of Environmental Clearance for the complex. At the time of writing, the cleared land had been left abandoned and fenced off with boards, awaiting a decision as to what will be built – and no one is clear as to when or what that might be.

Man O' War Bay Beach

Changing facilities daylight hours, TT$1

There's little to actually do in Charlotteville but enjoy the sea, whether you arrange a **fishing** trip aboard the many pirogues which moor up in the bay, or just while away the hours on the fine yellow sand of **Man O' War Bay Beach** – site of Tobago's most popular fisherman's fete, held to celebrate St Peter's Day. The best stretch of sand in Man O' War Bay is five minutes' walk west of the town centre, where you'll find changing/ shower facilities as well as a beach bar and restaurant (see p.247). The bay itself is clean, calm and inviting, with good snorkelling.

Pirate's Bay

Charlotteville's main street veers away from the coast at the eastern end of the village, but a dirt track continues along the shoreline to the town's – and, for many, Tobago's – most attractive beach, **Pirate's Bay**. After walking for about fifteen minutes along the

---

BUSTIN' THE BAMBOO

In Charlotteville and other rural Tobago communities, music at open-air celebrations and Christmas/Old Year's festivities is often given an ear-splitting percussive accompaniment. Loved by small boys for the incredibly loud, cannon-like explosion that's produced, the tradition of **"bustin' the bamboo"** remains a popular – if rather dangerous – sport. To achieve the desired earth-shaking report, the prospective buster must have the know-how to first select a piece of bamboo of the correct age and durability with at least four or five internal joints, and then cut the section so that joints seal each end. A hole is pierced at one end, and the bamboo is filled with pitch oil (kerosene) from a slit at the opposite end. The fuel is lit and fanned until it heats up sufficiently to blow out the remaining joints, which creates the resounding boom and often results in the loss of eyelashes and moustaches.

steep track you'll come to a long concrete stairway, at the bottom of which you're rewarded with a stunning horseshoe of calm emerald-green water and fine yellow sand, with a backdrop of trees, ferns and foliage. A tumbledown fisherman's hut is the only building in sight, and there's even a freshwater rinse, courtesy of a stream trickling down from the hills. The bay's translucent waters offer fantastic **snorkelling**, especially on the left-hand side. The seventeenth-century buccaneers after whom it was named may have gone, but the bay still has its freebooters, a large colony of **frigate birds**, which feed by snatching recently caught fish from the beaks of smaller sea birds. These, and other birds such as terns and pelicans can be found at St Giles Island a few kilometres to the north, but strong currents make it difficult for small boats – and thus birdwatchers – to get there. If the walk (or the stairs) are too much for you, you can usually arrange for one of the village's fishermen to drop you at the beach and pick you up. Though the track is partially driveable, it's best to leave your car in town – the only place to park is also the only turning spot, so leaving your vehicle there means anyone else will have to reverse back down the hill.

Cambleton Battery

No set hours • Free

Reached via a steep and potholed lane striking off from the main road at the western outskirts of Charlotteville, **Cambleton Battery** was built by the British in 1777, who placed two cannons here to defend against attack from marauding American warships; the sweeping views of Charlotteville, Booby Island and Pirate's Bay explain why they chose this site. It's now a popular cooling-off spot for locals, who lime away under the shade of the gazebo.

ARRIVAL AND INFORMATION   CHARLOTTEVILLE

By bus Buses from Scarborough (see p.224) stop opposite the Fishermen's Co-Operative; ask around to get details of departure times of buses back to Scarborough.
Tourist information On the bayfront, at the back of the

car park adjacent to the pavilion, there's a small tourist office (Mon–Fri 8am–4.15pm) where you can get basic information on the town and its surrounds.

ACTIVITIES

Scuba diving and snorkelling Right on the beach in Man O' War Bay, Blue Caribbean Environmental Conservation (☎ 355 8616, ⍓ bluecaribbeanconservation .org) is a non-profit research outfit working to promote environmental awareness in Charlotteville and conduct research into the health of the area's reefs and waters; they also offer diving courses and volunteer programmes, as do the Environmental Research Institute Tobago (ERIC; ☎ 788

3550, ⍓ eric-tobago.org), a little further west around the bay.
Land and sea tours Locally run Workshop Sea Tours, opposite *Sharon and Pheb's* restaurant (☎ 660 6281 or ☎ 727 3989, ⍓ workshopseatours.com), offer half-day fishing trips (US$250) as well as offshore island tours and bird- and dolphin-watching expeditions (prices negotiable) and island tours such as to Argyle Waterfall (from US$45).

ACCOMMODATION

The generous quota of **guesthouses** in Charlotteville is usually enough to cope with demand, but the period from December to April can get quite busy, so book ahead if visiting at this time.

Belle Aire Belle Aire St ☎ 660 5984. Just before the Pirate's Bay track, these four basic, white-painted rooms have fan, mosquito nets, en-suite bathroom and fridge. All except one have porches and there is a shared kitchen and dining room. The small garden has a barbecue pit and a gazebo for picnics. TT$300
Big Fish Man O' War Bay ☎ 660 5717 or ☎ 683 9723. Upstairs from *Sharon and Pheb's* restaurant, with good

views over the village and bay from the private porches out front. Apartments are well maintained and have a/c, cable TV and kitchenette, and you're just steps from the beach facility. Wi-fi. TT$400
Charlottevilla Northside Rd, Cambleton ☎ 639 6331 or ☎ 304 6542, ⍓ charlottevilla.com. A handsome two-storey building opposite the road to the beach facilities on the outskirts of town, with two one-bedroom apartments

5

on the ground floor and a two-bedroom unit taking up the top floor, with its wraparound veranda. All have fans, kitchen, lovely wooden furnishings and en-suite bathrooms. Wi-fi. TT$300

★**Cholson Chalets** Man O' War Bay ☎639 8553, ⓦcholsonchalets.com. The most atmospheric option in town, set in beautifully maintained old green and white houses overlooking the beach at the Pirate's Bay end of town. The six simple apartments have a deliciously antiquated feel with their muslin curtains, wooden floors and furniture passed down through the owner's family; those on the top floor (US$88) are the nicest. All have fans, private bathroom, kitchenette and cable TV. US$66

Green Corner Villa 82 Bay St ☎776 5326 or ☎313 4667. Opposite the Pirate's Bay Track (and painted orange rather than green), this basic but friendly place is a great budget option. The two small, clean and cosy rooms, one en suite, one overlooking the sea, with mosquito nets and fans. Shared kitchen. US$60

★**Man-O-War Bay Cottages** Man O' War Bay ☎660 4327, ⓦman-o-warbaycottages.com. With easily the best location in town, in a shady grove of trees right on the beach, these basic wooden one- to three-bedroom cottages may not have many modern conveniences, and could do with a bit of sprucing up, but you get lulled to sleep by the sound of the waves and the breeze swishing through the trees above. All are spacious with ceiling and standing fans, hot water and kitchen. US$65

Moore's Guesthouse Belle Aire St ☎639 1078 or ☎470 7612, ⓔmvionecia@yahoo.com. Opposite *Belle Aire* and accessed via a steep staircase, the clean and well kept *Moore's* has the best views of all the guesthouses located in this part of town. Of the four large, basic rooms, two are en suite with a fridge, double bed and fan, and there's a shared kitchen, small lounge and simple bathroom. US$40

Nicoville Spring St ☎639 8553, ⓦcholsonchalets.com. In a good location just behind *Cholson Chalets* and managed by the same owners, the studio and one- and two-bedroom apartments here are decently priced. All have standing fans, hot and cold water and kitchenette, and those at the top overlook the playing field. Studio US$40, one-bedroom US$55

Ocean View 11 Mission Rd ☎660 4891, ⓦoceanview -tobago.com. These small, spotless apartments done in typical Tobagonian decor are perched on Charlotteville's hillside, with wonderful views over Man O' War Bay from the balcony. Each has a/c, cable TV, en-suite bathroom, fully equipped kitchen and a shared balcony from which to gaze out over the town and bay. US$60

Rosa's ☎660 5984. At the start of the track to Pirate's Bay and in a lovely spot right on the water, these two basic apartments have kitchen, netted beds and hot and cold water, as well as a decent-sized porch. TT$400

★**Top River Pearl** 32–34 Spring St ☎660 6011 or ☎354 7427, ⓦtopriver.com. Set away from Charlotteville's main seafront area, these airy, well maintained en-suite apartments have kitchenettes, balconies and ceiling fans, and a large communal sundeck complete with hammocks and views of the bay; meals are available. Wi-fi. US$60

EATING AND DRINKING

Charlotteville's supermarkets stock only basic provisions, but you can buy fresh fish daily from the Fishermen's Co-Operative. The village isn't blessed with swanky **restaurants**, but there are plenty of places cooking up inexpensive and delicious local food; bear in mind that the opening hours below are merely a guideline; many places shut up shop if things are quiet, so it's well worth calling ahead to arrange dinner.

★**G's** Bay St (no phone). Right on the roadside opposite *Sharon and Pheb's*, and with a covered terrace behind, overlooking the beach that makes a nice spot for a sunset rum and coke or beer from the adjoining bar. The Creole food – baked chicken, fish with all the trimmings, fish and chips – is delicious and fresh, with a fish lunch at around TT$50. Daily 10am–10pm.

★**Gail's** Bay St ☎688 5492. Prepared by the charming Gail herself, this is a lovely little spot for dinner, with tables on a terrace just across from the water and close to the Pirate's Bay track. The Creole food is well seasoned and nicely presented, with fish and chicken starting at around TT$60 including a soup starter. Breakfast and lunch are also available with prior notice. Mon–Sat 7pm–late.

Naturalness Bay St (no phone). Little shack by the proposed new mall, serving early-morning potato and fish pies (TT$5), plus rotis from 11am (veg TT$15, chicken TT$25), plus soup on Saturdays and a Sunday fish lunch (TT$40). Simple dishes such as roti are served alongside the beers and spirits at this hole-in-the-wall rum shop on the main street. Mon–Fri 7am–5pm, Sat & Sun 11am–5pm.

Sharon and Pheb's Bay St ☎660 5717. This local institution is the most polished outfit in Charlotteville, always reliable and with good service. For breakfast, there's saltfish or fried with coconut bakes and cocoa tea, plus eggs, bacon and the like, while lunch and dinner rests on staples such as barbecue chicken and Creole fish, served with tasty sides (scallop potatoes, mixed veg and the like) on an attractive veranda raised a little above street level. Mains TT$40–80. Mon–Sat 8am–10pm.

★**Suckhole** Man O'War Bay beach facility (no phone). Perfect little beach bar overlooking the swimming area at Man O'War Bay, decorated with fishing nets and maritime paraphernalia, and a great place for a lunch (from TT$40) of fish or shrimp in coconut curry sauce, Creole-style chicken or just a burger and fries, all served up a range of sides (steamed veg, macaroni pie, coleslaw etc). Good rum punch and ice-cold beers, too. Daily 10am–6pm.

DIRECTORY

Charlotteville has a police station, health centre and branch of **First Citizens bank** (with an ATM) on the inland side of the playing field in the town centre, opposite the library. There are a couple of small supermarkets (usually Mon–Sat 8am–9pm, Sun 8am–3pm) on the main street, and fruit and veg are sold in the bandstand opposite the pier on Saturday mornings. **Workshop Sea Tours** (see p.245) offer a laundry service (TT$40/load). The petrol station (Mon–Sat 6am–8pm) is next to the Fishermen's Co-Op.

FORT GEORGE, PORT OF SPAIN

Contexts

History

Trinidad was the first Caribbean island with a human population, having been settled by Amerindians from South America as early as 5000 BC. The early incomers were Arawaks – peaceful farmers and fishers – who called their new home "Ieri", the land of the hummingbird and were joined after 1000 AD by more warlike Carib tribes.

The Amerindians and European conquest

When **Christopher Columbus** "discovered" Trinidad in 1498, the Amerindian population of some 35,000 had created a structured society, with organized villages along the coastline presided over by chiefs and a self-sufficient economy that exploited the abundant natural resources and extensive trade with the South American mainland. Sighting the three peaks of the Trinity Hills, Columbus named the island **Trinidad**, landing at Moruga on the south coast. Despite an initial skirmish with the local tribes, Columbus's sailors considered them the friendliest in the Caribbean islands. This didn't suit the Spanish **slave traders** who followed hot on Columbus's heels; despite protests from Spanish priests such as Bartolomeo de las Casas, they exaggerated the Caribs' occasional ritual **cannibalism** to justify enslaving them.

The first permanent **Spanish settlers** came to Trinidad in 1592, establishing the small town of San José – present-day St Joseph – complete with governor's residence, *cabildo* (council chamber) and church. Although this fledgling capital was sacked in 1595 by **Sir Walter Raleigh** as he headed for South America in search of El Dorado, it was quickly rebuilt, and the colony survived, despite its vulnerability to foreign attacks and pirate raids, growing tobacco and cocoa for export to Europe. In 1687, Capuchin monks arrived from Spain, setting up several **missions** around the island. Alongside the proselytizing, the missions were also a means to control the Amerindians through the *encomienda* labour system, a kind of semi-slavery in which they were forced to work on plantations and build more churches.

To evade this threat to their way of life, some Amerindians moved to the interior, while others fought back – in 1699, Amerindians in San Rafael rebelled against Spanish missionaries attempting to forcibly convert them and subject them to *encomienda*. Three priests and then-governor José de León y Echales were killed, and the reprisals were savage: Spanish troops slaughtered the region's entire Amerindian population in what's now known as the **Arena Massacre**. Amerindians were further threatened by European diseases to which they had no resistance, and by the end of the eighteenth century, some three centuries after Columbus's arrival, the indigenous population had been all but wiped out.

Spanish Trinidad

Despite all the depredations they visited upon the Amerindians, the Spanish had neither the desire nor the resources to develop Trinidad, treating it as little more than a convenient

5000 BC	1498	1592
Amerindian peoples cross over from the South American mainland and establish settlements on Trinidad and Tobago.	Christopher Columbus makes a brief stop on Trinidad, naming the island after three hills in its southeast corner.	Spanish settlers establish a capital at present-day St Joseph, and claim Trinidad as a colony of Spain.

watering-hole en route to the riches of South America. Their governors were left to do as they pleased – illegal trading of goods and slaves was commonplace – and due to its poor defences, the island suffered repeated attacks from French, Dutch and English **pirates**. When Don Pedro de la Moneda arrived from Spain to take up the governorship in 1757, he found his St Joseph residence practically in ruins, and decamped to Port of Spain.

Eventually, though, the Spanish realized that if they didn't develop this neglected colony, somebody else would. Issued in 1783, the **Cedula of Population** was designed to encourage fellow Catholics – **French planters** suffering Protestant discrimination in British Grenada and Martinique – to settle in Trinidad; the amount of land they were allocated depended on the number of slaves they brought with them. Immigrants of mixed European/African race (termed "**Free Coloured**" by the Spanish) who brought slaves could also receive land (though only half as much as their white counterparts), thus opening the way for the development of a property-owning middle class of non-whites, whose ancestors still run much of Trinidad's big business today.

To implement the Cedula, Spain despatched a new governor, **José Maria Chacon**, in 1784. The economy flourished under his energetic administration, and people of French and African descent came to dominate the population. The island's culture also became increasingly French: it was during this period that **Carnival** was introduced, the French language created a local patois, and a society based on aristocratic principles of birth and connections developed.

As the repercussions of the **French Revolution** gave rise to civil and inter-national wars throughout the West Indies, many more French – both republicans and royalists, white and mixed-race – sought refuge in neutral Trinidad, but to Chacon's alarm, they brought their ideological conflicts with them. Increasingly anxious, the governor reported to Madrid that some of the newcomers' radical ideas were encouraging the slaves to "dream of liberty and equality".

The British conquest

Keen to augment their sizeable list of Caribbean colonies, the British seized upon the idea that Trinidad had become a nest of republicans and "bad people of all descriptions", despatching an invasion fleet under **Sir Ralph Abercromby** in 1797. The island had few defences: just five ships compared to the British force of eighteen, and only two thousand soldiers – many of whom had deserted – against seven thousand. The Spanish surrendered with hardly a shot fired, scuttling their own ships in Chaguaramas harbour, and Chacon was recalled to Spain in disgrace.

Abercromby's terms of defeat were lenient – residents could retain their property and Spanish law would remain in force – but his choice of governor, **Thomas Picton**, was less fortunate. Left in charge with near absolute powers, Picton instituted a reign of terror, deporting and executing suspected subversives (mostly slaves and "Free Coloureds") on the flimsiest evidence, with confessions frequently obtained under torture. Followers of African religious traditions were persecuted especially harshly; those suspected of practising **obeah** (see box opposite) were hauled before a tribunal, and whipped, hanged, mutilated or burned to death if found guilty. By 1802, Picton's activities had become an embarrassment to the British government, then facing an influential anti-slavery lobby at home, and he was demoted.

1580–1841	1783
Tobago changes hands 31 times as Dutch, Latvian, British and French colonists fight for ownership. The British establish plantations and bring in African slaves.	The incentives of Spain's Cedula of Population see mixed-race "Free Coloured" and French white immigrants establish a plantation culture in Trinidad.

Trinidad presented a unique administrative conundrum for the British, however. Their other Caribbean possessions were governed by colonial assemblies, but this wasn't an option for Trinidad – any such body would inevitably be dominated by planters, who would never agree to share power with "Free Coloureds", despite the fact that many of the latter were substantial property owners and thus difficult to exclude from government under British law. The island therefore remained a **crown colony**, governed by French and Spanish law, with directions issued straight from the colonial office in London.

Emancipation and beyond

Though life for the **slaves** on Trinidad and Tobago's estates was no less brutal than in any of the British colonies, the islands never developed into the full-blown plantation societies of Jamaica or Barbados. Rather than the massive estates established elsewhere, plantations in T&T were relatively small-scale, and the British touted Trinidad as a "model" colony thanks to the introduction of a few tentative measures that attempted to curb the worst of the planters' abuses. Nonetheless, it was a miserable life for the Africans, who resisted by organizing secret societies with their own militias and carrying out several **rebellions**.

Indentureship begins

The British abolished the slave trade in 1807, though this meant nothing to the slaves still working T&T's estates; and even after the **Act of Emancipation** in 1834, freed slaves were required to serve as apprentices for a further six years. When the

---

OBEAH

A retention of African animist traditions, **obeah** (from the Ashanti *obayfoi*, meaning witchcraft or magic) is the belief in a spiritual power that can influence events in the temporal world, curing disease, providing good fortune or wreaking revenge. Though dismissed by most as mumbo-jumbo, obeah still lingers on in Trinidad and Tobago via common superstitions and practices passed down over the generations. In rural areas, you'll often see **blue bottles** placed over front doors or in gardens to ward off the evil spirits known as jumbies (see p.278) or protect against the evil eye or **maljo** (*mal yeux*), and there are still those who enlist the services of an **obeah man** (or woman), also known as an **ojhaman** or **seer-man** in the Indian community, usually a respected figure dispensing herbal medicines rather than a sinister character cooking up bubbling potions under a full moon. During the plantation era, every slave community had a herbalist who doled out concoctions for all kinds of ailments, and elements of these traditions remain strong in Trinbagonian attitudes to health. As spiritual and physical problems are seen as being connected, practitioners might prescribe plants, herbs, roots and barks alongside shop-bought substances such as red lavender to be infused into the skin through a bush bath, said to get rid of "blight" or maljo or turn around a run of bad luck; or advise an internal cleanse and purge by way of a dose of cooling herbs such as wild senna, caraili, mauby or pawpaw bark, followed by a cleansing dose of aloes or castor oil. Less commonly (as such practices are illegal in Trinidad and Tobago), special circumstances such as a case of unrequited love or a feud, may see an obeah practitioner paid to invoke or dispel a curse, which is done through a ritual to bring on the desired effect – called "**working obeah**" – that is reversible only by a more powerful practitioner.

1797	1802	1834
Britain captures Trinidad from Spain; heavy-handed governor Thomas Picton is demoted in 1802 and Trinidad is designated a Crown Colony.	Spain formally cedes Trinidad to Britain under the Treaty of Amiens; Tobago follows suit in 1814.	Slavery is abolished between 1845 and 1917, some 145,000 indentured workers arrive from India to fill the labour gap.

apprenticeship system was abolished in 1838, many former slaves moved to urban areas, leaving the planters desperately short of labour, and the British government sanctioned the immigration of **indentured labourers** from India as a means of easing the situation on the estates. In May 1845, the first 225 workers arrived aboard the *Fatel Rozack*; by 1917, when the indenture system ended, some 145,000 Indians, mainly from Calcutta, had come to T&T. Fleeing poverty and the increasingly harsh British rule, the immigrants were signed up to work for five years in return for their passage home. (In 1854 the indenture was extended to ten years, and after 1895 the immigrants had to pay a proportion of their return passage.)

Post-emancipation life

Though indentureship was better regulated and monitored than slavery, the working and living conditions of labourers and slaves were practically indistinguishable. The Indians lived in unsanitary single-room barrack houses where disease was rife, and plantation owners failed to honour pledges on wages and working conditions. Nonetheless, many stayed on at the end of their indentureship, accepting land in lieu of a passage home. Known then and today as "**East Indians**" to differentiate them from the "West Indians", they formed the lowest rung of society, working in the agricultural sector scorned by ex-slaves and establishing tight-knit communities that maintained the religious and cultural traditions of their homeland (much to the resentment of the African population, whose ancestors had been afforded no such indulgence). The white ruling class, however, painted the Indians as heathens and barbarians – in 1884, 22 Indians were shot dead by police and hundreds wounded as they tried to enter San Fernando during the annual Hosay festival parade, while East Indian children were considered illegitimate until 1945, as Muslim and Hindu marriages were not recognized. Despite their persecution, Indian immigrants contributed greatly to Trinidad's developing national identity. Just as the Europeans had brought Carnival, which was taken up and enriched by former slaves, Indians introduced their own festivities and culture. The Muslims introduced **Hosay** (see box, p.73), the Hindus brought the festival of light, **Diwali**, while Indian foods such as roti and curry became staples for all Trinbagonians.

Immigrants arrive

Trinidad and Tobago's ethnic mix was further enriched by immigrants arriving from other parts of the world. Several companies of **black American soldiers** who fought for Britain in its 1812 war against the US were given grants of land in southern Trinidad, where they founded villages named after the units in which they had served while, after emancipation, freed slaves from other **Caribbean islands** were attracted to Trinidad by the relatively high wages for field labourers. **Africans** liberated by the British Navy on anti-slave patrols settled in urban areas, becoming craftsmen and construction workers and establishing strong communities that maintained their own cultural institutions and heritage. The first **Chinese immigrants** arrived in 1853 as part of another attempt by the government to meet the continuing labour shortage on the plantations. The plan failed on account of the high transport costs and an appalling mortality rate among the immigrants; those who survived tended to become shopkeepers, and their descendants constitute a small but visible minority today. **Portuguese** labourers were also brought to

1899	1903	1941
Economic woes see Tobago made a ward of Trinidad.	The Red House burns during the Water Riots in Port of Spain; Arthur Cipriani and Uriah Butler lead a newly politicized labour movement.	The American government lease Chaguaramas, the Bocas Islands and Waller Field to use as military bases.

AFRICAN RELIGIONS

Centred upon the acceptance of a synthesis between the spiritual and temporal worlds, and the belief in spirits or gods which organize and animate the material world, T&T's **African-based religions** combine Christianity with elements of traditional West African belief systems brought to the island by slaves. The most visible sect is the **Spiritual Baptist** faith, which was established in the late nineteenth century by American ex-slaves who had fought for the British in the War of 1812. Then known as **Shouter Baptists** thanks to their propensity for loud and demonstrative worship, the sect was frowned upon by the British, who banned membership through the Shouters Prohibition Ordinance of 1917. Years of campaigning finally saw the law repealed in 1951, an act that's commemorated in the **Shouter Baptist Liberation** national holiday on March 30.

A well-organized faith, Spiritual Baptists have **churches** throughout Trinidad and Tobago which, as well as the usual pews and altar, feature a **centre pole** decorated with flowers, jugs of water and candles to harness and attract the spirits. Services usually involve purification rituals designed to cast out jumbies (evil spirits) that might be lurking in the church: lighted candles are placed in front of doors and windows, incense is lit, brass bells are rung and perfumed water strewn about. Bible readings precede chants and handclapping, which intensify as a kind of hyperventilation known as **adoption** brings about **spirit possession**, accompanied by bell-ringing and chanting called trumpeting the spirit, the origin of the "shouter" tag. Those who "catch the power" may grunt, gesticulate, speak in tongues or relay the spirit's message in English or even Hindi. The characteristic white robes and colourful headwraps worn by followers (which signify their dedication to a particular saint or spirit) are a notable part of the Trinbago Sunday scenery, you may also see outdoor **baptisms**, where white-clad converts are ritually dipped into rivers or the sea.

A Yoruba religion driven underground during British rule, **Orisha** (also Orisa or Shango) remains a somewhat clandestine cult. The faith centres upon worship of several deities – orishas – who are seen to have a distinct influence upon the living and must therefore be (depending on the situation) respected, pacified, praised, worshipped or feared through ritual dances, chants, drumbeats, offerings and prayer. Each orisha's personality is described in stories that reveal their activities on earth, with each assigned an individual drumbeat, colour, day of the week, favourite food and liquor, sacrificial animal (usually a chicken or goat) and an association with a Christian saint; this last tradition allowed Orisha to be syncretized with Christian festivals when the faith was outlawed. Orisha worship takes place in a **palais**, usually an open-roofed structure decorated with the symbols of individual orishas – daggers, cutlasses, hammers, jugs of water and ritual items such as olive oil for anointing, and offerings of flowers, fruit and foods. Known as **feasts**, most ceremonies take place over several days, and begin with the specialized drum patterns that summon Ogun. Drumming, dancing, chanting and hyperventilation encourage possession of devotees by various orishas, while sacrifices may be performed to honour the spirits that descend.

the country in the mid-1800s, but the practice was short-lived as the employment of Europeans in manual work was seen as a threat to the established racial hierarchy.

Except for a handful of **Jews** who arrived during World War II, the last group of immigrants to join Trinidad's melting pot were the **Syrians** who came in 1913, seeking refuge from religious persecution in the Lebanon. Though they only account for 0.1 percent of the country's population (around 1000 people in total), their business acumen has given them a high profile, and they remain a tight-knit and influential community today.

1945	1956	1958
Universal suffrage is granted, though the islands' legislative council is afforded only limited powers by the British.	Dr Eric Williams founds the People's National Movement (PNM); his election victory marks the start of a thirty-year reign for the PNM.	Trinidad and Tobago joins the West Indies Federation, inaugurated in Chaguaramas but dissolved in 1962 after Jamaica leaves.

Into the twentieth century

Trinidadian society remained deeply stratified along race and class lines for most of the nineteenth century, with white planters firmly at the top of the heap, but in the 1880s and 1890s, reform movements began to challenge the status quo. An improved national education system and an enlarged franchise inspired the formation of **political pressure groups** linked to the international labour movement, from the Trinidad Workingmen's Association (TWA) and East Indian National Association to the Pan African Association, which lobbied the British Colonial Office for an elected governing body for the island.

In 1899, Britain made ailing **Tobago** a ward of Trinidad, though the latter still had no effective form of self-government (for more on the history of Tobago, see p.196). Resentment came to a head over the introduction of new water rates, and in 1903 a protest meeting in Port of Spain's Woodford Square erupted into a **riot**. Eighteen people were shot dead by the police, and the Red House – seat of the colonial government – was burned to the ground. Although Britain finally agreed to an **elected assembly** for Trinidad and Tobago in 1913 (albeit one with very limited powers), it was still more than ten years before the first Legislative Council convened in the rebuilt Red House.

Trinidad's burgeoning **oil industry** and the aftermath of **World War I** further politicized the populace. High inflation led to strikes, resulting in increased cooperation between Africans and Indians, while fuel was added to the fire by Trinidadian soldiers who returned from the Great War with stories of discrimination at the hands of the British. The tide had finally turned, with socialism, national independence and the concept of black consciousness, as promoted by Jamaica's Marcus Garvey, now firmly planted in the public mind. In 1925, TWA president **Arthur Cipriani** was elected to the new legislative council, campaigning hard for workers' rights and securing some important concessions, including compensation for industrial injuries. His reformist politics had little effect on the underlying balance of power, however; wages were actually falling, malnutrition was widespread, living conditions grim and industrial accidents appallingly common. As the world economy nosedived into the **Great Depression** of the 1930s, Cipriani found himself outflanked by a new generation of radicals such as the charismatic **Uriah Butler** (see box, p.186), who formed the **British Empire Workers** trade union in 1935.

The road to independence

During World War II, Trinidad's socioeconomic character was altered radically by the presence of the **US military**, who leased Chaguaramas, the Bocas Islands and Waller Field in 1941 to provide a strategic base for their Caribbean fleet. The Americans improved Trinidad's infrastructure and exposed the population to high-level technology for the first time, while the **high wages** they were paid for the construction of buildings and roads lured workers from the agricultural sector and led to the decline of many estates. The Americans' racial attitudes, cruder than the more subtle prejudice of the British, and the aura of easy money that attracted many Trinidadian women, caused plenty of resentment, however, and further increased the desire for independence.

1962	1970	1974
Trinidad and Tobago is granted its independence, with Eric Williams as the country's first prime minister.	The Black Power movement gains widespread support, and a state of emergency is declared after a brief army mutiny in support of the protests.	Vast oil reserves are discovered just off Trinidad's east coast.

The rise of the PNM
Universal suffrage was granted in 1945, and the 1946 and 1950 elections were won by political parties linked to the trade unions, but Britain was not prepared to hand over total control while radical labour politics dominated the political arena. In January 1956, a group of black intellectuals formed the **People's National Movement** (PNM) under the leadership of Oxford-educated historian **Dr Eric Williams**. The party's black nationalist policies and the charismatic leadership and immense intellectual authority of "the Doctor" gained widespread support among a population tired of colonial government and the divisions within the labour movement; their only serious opposition was from the **People's Democratic Party** (PDP), later the **Democratic Labour Party** (DLP) supported primarily by rural Hindus. After a controversial campaign that raised racial tension by portraying the DLP as reactionary Hindus, the PNM won a tentative victory in the 1956 election; they were to remain in power for the next thirty years, with Williams as prime minister until his death in 1981.

Caribbean unity and racial division
Many Caribbean leaders saw West Indian confederacy as the way forward for the region's tiny territories, and initially Williams was an enthusiastic proponent of the idea. In 1958, the **West Indies Federation** was launched at Chaguaramas, but political rivalries and the reluctance of larger islands to subsidize smaller ones resulted in a watered-down Federation with no tax-raising powers. When Jamaica voted to leave in September 1961, Williams announced that "one from ten leaves nought"; Trinidad followed suit, and the Federation was swiftly dissolved.

The early 1960s saw the PNM adopting a radical stance, booting out the US military in 1961 and campaigning vigorously for independence, while politics split further along racial lines, with government the preserve of Afro-Caribbeans, and opposition that of East Indians. After **Independence** was finally granted in 1962, things further degenerated when the PNM created a new constitution without consulting the DLP. Autonomy from the "motherland" had done little to change the colonial structure of T&T's society, and the electorate became increasingly disenchanted with their new-found "freedom".

The Black Power years
The late 1960s were marked by repeated unrest. The American **Black Power** movement caught the imagination of many disaffected young men and women, and in 1970 its supporters launched a wave of marches, protests and **wildcat strikes** that shook Trinidad to the core. Businesses and banks were bombed, and when the police shot dead a protester named **Basil Davis** in April 1970, 30,000 people took to the streets for his funeral. Facing a possible general strike, Eric Williams declared a state of emergency and arrested several Black Power leaders, only to be faced by an **army mutiny** at the Teteron base in Chaguaramas, staged by officers outraged at government heavy-handedness. It was only quashed when coastguard vessels prevented the soldiers from marching on Port of Spain by shelling the main road; rumours abounded that a bloody coup had been averted and plans had been discovered for mass executions of "enemies of the people".

1976	**1981**
Trinidad and Tobago become a republic, with new President, Ellis Clark, replacing Britain's Queen Elizabeth as head of state.	Falling oil prices trigger a recession, and George Chambers becomes prime minister following the death of Eric Williams.

Black gold

The Black Power crisis proved cathartic. Many whites had fled the country; those who remained could no longer expect the deference to which they had been accustomed, while the government encouraged locals to be trained for jobs previously occupied by expatriates. The country was teetering on the edge of **bankruptcy**, with the PNM remaining in office primarily thanks to divisions in the opposition. "We are winning by default," PNM minister Hector McLean observed dryly. But salvation was ahead in the form of **oil**. Just as the world was sliding into the oil crisis of 1974, vast reserves were discovered off Trinidad's east coast, and T&T found itself swimming in money overnight. Ambitious public projects were undertaken and the country settled back to enjoy the boom years. But this sudden wealth had its downside. People got used to the easy life – productivity fell and agriculture dwindled, but **corruption** thrived.

Recession and radicalism

When oil prices fell in the 1980s, the economy went into **recession**, unemployment rose sharply and inflation soared. In 1981, Williams died a disillusioned man with his policies in ruins; his former finance minister George Chambers took over the reins. As the population became increasingly dissatisfied, the opposition parties started to unify. In 1986, the PNM was ousted by the **National Alliance for Reconstruction** (NAR), led by A.N.R. Robinson, who had resigned from Williams' government in 1970 following the Basil Davis debacle. The NAR tried to resolve some of the more pressing problems facing the country, but within a year the government was breaking up into factions. Harsh economic measures, including **devaluation** of the TT dollar and a stringent IMF-inspired recovery programme, were widely seen as undemocratic and beneficial only to the rich. In 1990, the radical Muslim group **Jamaat-al-Muslimeen** (see pp.62–63) attempted to overthrow the government, holding Robinson and several of his cabinet hostage. Though the coup was crushed after a six-day siege, the government's authority was irreparably undermined, and the following year the PNM returned to power under **Patrick Manning**.

The UNC and the return of the PNM

In the early 90s increased oil revenues during the Gulf War helped the PNM stabilize the economy and pay off the IMF, but the 1995 election split the country down the middle, with the PNM and the Indo-Trinidadian **United National Congress** (UNC) both winning seventeen seats. The two NAR representatives held the balance of power, and used it to support the UNC, making lawyer and former union leader **Basdeo Panday** the country's first East Indian prime minister. Although the 2000 election returned the UNC to power with nineteen seats, Panday's government lasted just ten months; in October 2001, three UNC MPs defected to the opposition, and with their majority removed, the UNC were forced to call an election. Another hung parliament ensued, with both the PNM and UNC returning 18 of the 36 total seats each. Though the UNC won more votes, President A.N.R. Robinson appointed Patrick Manning as leader, but with no clear mandate to govern Manning called another election; in October 2002, he returned to office with a decisive majority.

1986	1990	1991
A.N.R. Robinson's National Alliance for Reconstruction (NAR) win the general election. Economic woes see the dollar devalued.	The Jamaat-al-Muslimeen stage a short-lived coup, holding Robinson and several of his cabinet hostage for six days before surrendering.	The PNM return to power under Patrick Manning.

Politricks and corruption

In 2006, the political waters were muddied by the formation of a new party, the **Congress of the People** (COP). Fronted by former UNC leader **Winston Dookeran**, COP represented the first credible alternative to the two-party dominance of the UNC and PNM since the ill-fated NAR, and despite Dookeran's somewhat lacklustre leadership style, they took 22.72 percent of the vote in the 2007 elections – to the chagrin of the UNC, which copped 29.84 and asserted that as the PNM had managed only 46 percent of the total vote, COP had effectively split the opposition and allowed Patrick Manning another term in office. Though their share of the 2007 vote didn't translate to any seats in parliament, COP soldiered on nonetheless, scoring many points among Trinbagonians for its efforts to distance the party from the race-based voting of the past, where Indians traditionally sided with the UNC and Africans with the PNM. The UNC, meanwhile, was struggling under the increasingly erratic reins of Basdeo Panday, and internal elections in early 2010 saw **Kamla Persad-Bissessar** replace him as UNC leader, marking the end both of Panday's 33-year political career and of an era in Trinidadian politics. Patrick Manning, too, was coming under fire both for his increasingly dictatorial style of leadership and for the PNM's culpability in the scandal surrounding Urban Development Company of Trinidad and Tobago (**UDeCOTT**), a state-owned company established in 2004. The PNM pumped millions of dollars into ever-more lavish UDeCOTT projects, including Port of Spain's waterfront complex and the National Academy of the Performing Arts, but in March 2010 executive Chairman **Calder Hart** resigned after it was revealed that lucrative contracts had been given to a company owned by his wife's family. The entire board were fired the following month in the wake of a Commission of Enquiry report that pointed to irregularities in numerous projects, from the TT$700 million Brian Lara stadium in Tarouba to the TT$368 million Ministry of Legal Affairs tower in Port of Spain, built by CH Construction, a company with alleged links to Hart. Reeling from the effects of the scandal, Manning called an early election in May 2010, with detractors arguing that he was going to the polls only to avoid an imminent vote of no confidence. The opposition were finally able to unite under the banner of the **People's Partnership**, with Persad-Bissessar as their candidate for Prime Minister.

A **landslide victory** at the polls ensued, with the People's Partnership taking 29 seats and the PNM just twelve. Kamla Persad-Bissessar became the republic's first female Prime Minister and immediately distanced the new coalition administration from the somewhat despotic ruling style of Manning's PNM, creating a Ministry of the People to allow public grievances to be aired and announcing a raft of policies that included an assault on poor environmental practices and a rethink of water resource management. However, despite an election campaign that championed zero tolerance on corruption, the People's Partnership came under fire early on thanks to a perceived conflict of interests concerning **Austin "Jack" Warner**, appointed by Persad-Bissessar as Minster of Works and Transport despite holding the post of Vice-President of FIFA. By 2011, allegations of ongoing corruption saw Warner resign from his FIFA position, and by 2013 he had also fallen foul of the People's Partnership, leaving the PP to form his own political party, the Independent Liberals, and retaking the Chaguanas West constituency in a July by-election.

The PNM, meanwhile, were left in disarray by the People's Partnership victory. Vilified by his party for having lost the election thanks to controversial multi-million

1994	1995	2000–2002
Brian Lara takes the record for the highest individual score in Test cricket with his 501 not out for Warwickshire.	The NAR throw in their lot with the United National Congress (UNC) to form a coalition government.	The UNC win the 2002 election, but political shenanigans and a hung parliament leads to elections in 2001 and 2002, when Manning's PNM manage a decisive victory.

dollar projects as well as his links to the UdeCOTT scandal and alleged involvement in the construction of a TT$30 million church at Heights of Guanapo near Arima, Patrick Manning resigned as PNM leader and was replaced by his arch-rival, **Keith Rowley**, a controversial figure whose parliamentary questions led to the official probe into UDeCOTT.

Current issues

One of the most pressing problems in modern Trinidad and Tobago has been rising **crime**, particularly the kidnapping of high-profile businesspeople and the violent fallout from Trinidad's uneasy status as one of the Caribbean's main transhipment points for South American cocaine. Until the 1970s, T&T was virtually crime-free; today, it's a rather different picture. In 2000, 119 **murders** were reported; by 2009, the figure had shot up to 509, and now averages at around 400 per year, slightly down on the previous year's 550. The PNM government unleashed various initiatives, including a series of cripplingly expensive airships equipped with state-of-the-art surveillance gear that patrol the skies above (and waters around) Trinidad, and crime remains one of the main challenges facing the People's Partnership administration. In August 2011, they imposed a three-month state of emergency to try and tackle the problem, but though the murder rate for that year was 354, the initiative seems to have had little long-term effect.

Another matter of pressing concern for Persad-Bissessar is **corruption**, with a series of court cases against politicians regularly hitting the headlines; even former UNC prime minister Basdeo Panday spent time behind bars in 2007, having been found guilty of not declaring a foreign bank account (a charge that was later quashed on appeal). The People's Partnership were inevitably tainted by the scandal surrounding Jack Warner's fall from FIFA grace, and the administration itself has been continually dogged with allegations of corruption, with several ministers leaving office in controversial circumstances. Perhaps the most high-profile resignation was the 2014 departure of Minister for Sport Anil Roberts in the wake of allegations of fraud, theft and financial discrepancies concerning the **Sport Life** programme that he administered.

On a more positive note, Trinidad and Tobago continue to enjoy the status of having the most **stable economy** in the Caribbean thanks to the republic's reserves of oil and natural gas, which account for around forty percent of GDP and eighty percent of exports, and which have provided something of a buffer from the global economic downturn; equally, T&T's external debt is relatively insignificant compared to other Caribbean nations. The income generated from oil and gas is increasingly being used to develop other sectors, including manufacturing, finance, services and tourism, though as reserves are being fast depleted – it's widely agreed that they'll be exhausted within twenty years – there is a real need to diversify the economy. And despite its natural riches, T&T remains a very polarized nation, where high-tech malls co-exist with board shacks where inhabitants live without electricity or running water. Such inequality has created an uneasy tension in this country of extremes.

2010	2012	2013
Reeling from various corruption scandals, Patrick Manning calls a snap election; Kamla Persad-Bissessar becomes the republic's first female prime minister.	Keshorn Walcott, a 19-year old from Toco, becomes the first black man to win an Olympic gold for javelin.	George Maxwell Richards is succeeded as President of T&T by Anthony Carmona.

Carnival

Trinidad's fabulous Carnival has its origins in the Roman feast of Saturnalia, a midwinter celebration of birth, renewal and inversion of the norm. During the Middle Ages, it developed into the Feast of Fools, in which the pretensions of the Catholic Church were scabrously mocked and which the Church did its best to suppress. In the long run, however, assimilation proved more effective, and Carnival was incorporated into the Catholic faith as a final binge (carne vale or "farewell to flesh") before the fasting period of Lent.

Carnival through the years

Introduced by **French planters** in the late eighteenth century, Trinidad's Carnival was initially the preserve of the white Creole establishment. A comparatively decorous affair, it consisted of masked balls that allowed the gentry a brief fictive escape from the "cares" of power and respectability: the men would dress as "negres jardins" (field labourers), the women as "mulatresses", representing their slaves or their husbands' mulatto mistresses.

African mas

Carnival was also celebrated in semi-secret by slaves on the plantations; after **emancipation** in 1834, free Africans took their own Carnival procession onto the streets in bands, protected by groups of *batonniers* or stick men. Continuing the tradition of inversion, some costumes satirized the affectations and eccentricities of the French Creoles, with men dressing as **Dame Lorraines**: caricatured planters' wives with fancy gowns and exaggerated breasts and buttocks. Other characters – the little demon known as **jab jab** and the stilt-walking **moko jumbie** – drew on West African traditions and folklore. The parade was enlivened by the use of percussion instruments and the introduction of **canboulay**, which celebrated the end of the difficult and dangerous task of saving burning cane fields by parading through the streets with flaming flambeaux – the name is derived from the French *cannes brûlées*, or burning cane.

Inversion and prohibition

Disapproving of what they saw as the "desecration" of the Sabbath by the first day of Carnival, the British authorities decreed in 1843 that the festivities could not begin until Monday morning. Since no time was specified, carnivalgoers started celebrating on the stroke of midnight, and today's anarchic **Jouvert** parade was born. Many of the masquerades acted out in the street processions took the form of trenchant **satires** of the colonial government, and in 1846 the authorities attempted to prohibit the wearing of masks. Carnival found defenders in unexpected quarters, however: the French planters, keen to defend their own traditions in the face of increasing Anglicization; and the "Free Coloured" middle class, whose desire for respectability kept them aloof from Carnival itself but who saw attempts to control it as an assertion of white domination.

Carnival continued to provide an outlet for irreverence and satire through the nineteenth century, with outrageous parodies of British **sailors** stationed on the island, as well as characters representing underworld archetypes: **jamettes** (prostitutes) and transvestite **pissenlets** (literally "wet-the-bed"). Bands organized **drumming** and **kalenda** (**stickfighting**), and none of it went down too well with the colonial administrators from Victorian Britain. In 1877, police chief **Captain Arthur Baker** began a campaign to tame Carnival, but when he attempted to ban the canboulay outright in 1881, the so-called **Canboulay Riots** broke out (commemorated today in a dawn re-enactment on the Friday before Carnival). Undeterred, the authorities went on to prohibit what had become known as "jamette Carnival" on the grounds of its lewdness. African-style drumming was banned in 1884, while canboulay and stickfighting – seen respectively as a fire hazard and an incitement to violence – were outlawed a year later under the **Peace Preservation Act**.

Structure and competition

Carnival was not so easily quashed, and continued in an albeit more sedate manner. Social protest was channelled into the emerging labour movement (see p.254), and Carnival became an officially tolerated safety valve for social pressures, with the black middle class joining in. During the 1890s, the festival became increasingly organized and socially acceptable with the introduction of a **competition** for best band, and in 1921, the calypsonian Chieftain Douglas opened the first organized **calypso tent** to preview the songs that would be heard in the forthcoming Carnival.

During **World War II**, Carnival was suspended by the colonial government as a possible threat to public order, and when it returned on VE Day 1945, it marched to the sound of a different beat – the **steel pan**, fashioned from oil drums brought to the island by the US military. As the national independence movement gained momentum, Carnival flourished alongside. Recognizing its importance to Trinidad's cultural identity and sense of nationhood, Eric Williams established the National Carnival Commission in 1957 to organize and promote the festivities, and set up the Calypso King competition.

Bikinis and beads

Though parades during the 1970s saw masquerade bands exploring topics such as racism and white control of the economy, and **Peter Minshall**'s fabulous presentations in the 1980s and 1990s took mas to a new creative level, Carnival today is more about fun than politics, satire or social inversion. "**Pretty mas**" bands of revellers decked out in identikit costumes of feathers and beads are now the order of the day, and given the high price tag and exclusive aura of the prevailing all-inclusive mas bands, many now argue that Carnival has turned full circle, with the parades the sole preserve of the rich.

ESSENTIAL CARNIVAL VOCABULARY

Bands These are not musical bands, but an organized group of costumed masqueraders that parade trough the streets on Carnival Monday and Tuesday.

Chipping Slow, shuffling dance-cum-walk with a rhythm dictated by the music from trucks and steel bands.

Fete A large open-air party or concert held during the run-up to Carnival.

Jump up To dance in the parade.

Mas Short for masquerade.

Mas camp The headquarters of Carnival bands, where costumes are made and displayed, and where you can register to play mas. See pp.68–69.

Ole' mas Traditional Carnival characters such as jab jabs, imps and sailors; ole' mas also refers to placard-carrying characters with a mission to lambast the politicians of the day.

Play mas To join a Carnival band and take part in the costumed parade.

Road march The soca song played the most at the judging points along the Carnival route – the winner gets the coveted road march title for that year.

Rhythm section The classic accompaniment of Jouvert, as well as the "engine room" that drives a steel band, this is a percussion group who "beat iron"– scrapped brake drums from cars or vans played with metal rods alongside cowbells, shakers and anything that can make a rhythm.

Wining The classic hip-wiggling, gyrating Trini dance, which comes in many variations: be prepared to wine, and be wined on, at any point during Carnival.

Equally, though costume construction has traditionally been highly specialized and skilled, the drive to cut costs means that most bikini mas isn't even made in T&T these days, instead being imported from the Far East. Nonetheless, designers such as **Brian MacFarlane** have brought out contemporary bands with a creative edge, and smaller outfits continue to create gorgeous sailor and fancy Indians mas, while the establishment of a Mas Academy in Woodbrook in 2009 should help to ensure that the unique skills of Trinidad's mas-makers are continued into future generations.

Carnival today

To the eye of an uneducated onlooker, the two explosive days of the main Carnival parades might appear a chaotic spectacle, but underpinning the whole event is an order and structure that is the culmination of exhaustive preparations. The countdown begins in late summer, when the large mas bands (see p.81) hold **launches** for their Carnival designs. Once Christmas is out of the way, things get serious. The big steel bands (see p.82) open up their yards for visitors to watch practice sessions, calypsonians perform their Carnival compositions in the "tents" in Port of Spain and around the country, and each week features a bewildering choice of pre-Carnival **fetes** (see p.90), from raucous affairs featuring foam and powder paint to seriously classy all-inclusives where tickets average at TT$900.

Kiddies' Carnival to Dimanche Gras

On the Saturday before Carnival weekend, the parades kick off with the **Red Cross Children's Carnival**, with kids displaying their costumes at the Savannah; the following day, there's a children's parade along Western Main Road in St James. The Sunday sees the popular Panorama semi-final at the Savannah. Come the next weekend, "Fantastic Friday" sees a re-creation of the **Canboulay Riots** at 5am in downtown Port of Spain, and the **Soca Monarch** competition in the evening, while on Saturday there's another **Children's Carnival** parade from South Quay to the Savannah, which makes way for the **Panorama** finals later that day. On Sunday evening, the **Dimanche Gras** competition includes the crowning of the **King and Queen of the Bands** and the all-important **Calypso Monarch**.

Jouvert

Carnival officially starts at 4am on the Monday morning with **Jouvert** (see p.70) or dirty mas, when participants dress in macabre or satirical home-made costumes, or join a mud band and smear themselves with mud, grease, body paint or liquid chocolate before taking to the streets in an anarchical expression of Carnival's darker side. This wild party lasts into the daylight hours of Monday, and even if you're not playing with a Jouvert band, it's still a good idea to wear old clothes, as revellers delight in getting everyone as dirty as possible. Certainly, it's a time to leave your inhibitions (and your valuables) at home.

The main parades

Once the bacchanal of Jouvert has dispersed, the **Carnival Monday** parade begins by 11am, when the mas bands take to the streets, with masqueraders wearing either parts of their costume, a hotpants/shorts and T-shirt combo or more elaborate "Monday Wear" (these days local designers offer special Monday Wear collections each year), and dancing along to the accompaniment of steel pan bands or monstrous trucks bearing columns of speakers. **Tuesday** is Carnival's big day, with masqueraders dressing in full costume and parading through the streets as loudly and proudly as they can. Most of the bands competing for the much coveted **Band of the Year** title, but some of the huge pretty mas bands no longer compete, citing long waits to cross the stage as a disincentive, and establishing an alternative stage at the "Socadrome" in the Jean Pierre

TEN COMMANDMENTS OF PLAYING MAS

• Get to Trinidad in time to **collect your costume early** and make any necessary adjustments; you can buy supplies at several shops in Port of Spain (see p.92). Listen to the radio, tap into the year's soca on YouTube and go to some fetes so you know all the year's big tunes before you hit the road.

• **Cut your toenails** very short to minimize damage from the pummelling they'll take, and wear quality, well-fitting, worn-in footwear and absorbent sports socks.

• If you're going to wear **tights** with your costume, get them early before shades and sizes run out. Buy two pairs in case of snags, and cut the toes off to avoid damaging your nails. Micles in West Mall and Samaroos (see p.92) have a good selection.

• No matter what your skin colour, start Carnival Monday and Tuesday by dousing yourself in factor 50 **sunblock**. Take some with you, and re-apply it regularly. Aerosol sunblock is easier than cream.

• Build up stamina with some **exercise** before the main event; some of the larger mas bands organize pre-Carnival walks and runs.

• Bring a **disposable camera** rather than anything expensive, and get a cheap pair of sunglasses, too. Take souvenir selfies before you leave home when everything's looking fresh.

• Eat a good breakfast before setting out, don't skip lunch, and **drink water** throughout the day. Alternate alcoholic drinks with something soft.

• Prearrange how you'll be **getting home** on Carnival Monday and Tuesday – book a cab, or designate a driver. Try to find out where your band will be finishing to simplify pick-ups.

• Everyone loosens up a bit come Carnival, but don't lose sight of your **common sense**. Stick with your friends, don't accept drinks from strangers, and if you can't find a toilet en route, don't head off alone down dark alleys.

• **Smile** for the cameras, wine, wave, chip and jump – it's Carnival!

Complex. All bands follow set routes, however, with judging points along the way where panels of experts (and crowds of spectators) wait to mark those competing for Band of the Year. The main "stage" and judging point, where each band struts as much of its stuff as possible, is the Queen's Park Savannah in Port of Spain (and Scarborough's Market Square in Tobago). Some of the large bikini bands forego the Savannah and instead cross the stage at the "**Socadrome**", established in 2014 as an alternative display space for the more upmarket bands that do not compete for the "Band of the Year" title. As well as the bikini bands, Carnival also features smaller outfits portraying **traditional mas** characters from blue devils to Dame Lorraines, jab jabs and midnight robbers; to really get a flavour of old mas, take in one of the separate parades from South Quay to Adam Smith Square on the two Sundays preceding Carnival; check the press for details. Another brilliant option is to head up to Paramin (see p.93), where a wild parade of **blue devils** takes to the streets on Carnival Monday afternoon and continues well into the night.

Carnival's **las' lap** kicks in at dusk on Carnival Tuesday when everything becomes just a bit more frantic as the last hours of the event are made the most of, with large bands such as Harts and Tribe continuing the party at the Socadrome in the Jean Pierre Complex. Once midnight strikes, Carnival officially ends and the countdown to next year's begins.

Music

Trinidad and Tobago's music scene is one of the most exciting and influential in the Caribbean, inextricably linked to the annual Carnival celebrations which give the islands' homegrown genres a stage in which to shine. Downtempo, lyrically based calypso (more traditionally known as kaiso) is very much alive thanks largely to the festival's performance "tents" and Calypso Monarch competition, while the fetes – and the parades of Caribbean carnivals throughout the region and the world – reverberate to the faster, more contemporary-sounding soca. And since it was invented by industrious Trinidadians in the early twentieth century, the lilting tinkle of the steel pan has become synonymous with the region.

However, T&T's musical spectrum is a broad church: at Christmas, you'll hear the Spanish guitars and nasal crooning of **parang**, while East Indian festivals such as Hosay and Phagwah take place to the sound of frenetic **tassa** drumming. Jamaican-style dancehall reggae is extremely popular here, with a host of local artists offering their take on the genre, while **rapso** fuses calypso-style political lyrics, hip-hop beats and distinctly Caribbean basslines. There's also a healthy "alternative" scene, with a slew of great local **rock** bands such as Orange Sky and Jointpop, which blend classic guitar riffs with calypso and reggae.

Calypso to soca

The heart of T&T's music scene and one of its greatest cultural exports, **calypso** represents far more than catchy melodies and witty lyrics for older Trinbagonians, most of whom are expert scholars of the genre, using the most obscure quote to illustrate an argument and singing along to classic compositions without skipping a single nuance. Though calypso is less of a national obsession these days, each crop of compositions is still closely analysed and discussed until the messages become ingrained in the national consciousness. While foreigners often equate the genre with the glib Caribbean clichés of Harry Belafonte's *Banana Boat Song* or *Island in the Sun*, Trinbagonians see calypso as their most accessible form of **social commentary**. Calypsonians use double entendre and allegory to make points that would get a politician arrested for libel or a pop singer for lewdness, and over the years, their lyrics have addressed every phase of T&T's development, commenting on shifts in society and attitudes towards love, sex, marriage, masculinity, race and religion – not to mention politics.

Calypso has its roots in the songs of praise and derision performed in Africa by travelling troubadours known as **griots**. Slaves on the sugar plantations used song as a means of covert communication as well as a rhythmic accompaniment to their back-breaking work, and their **cariso** or **kaiso** was also a form of entertainment for the planters; notorious Diego Martin estate owner Pierre Begorrat could be tempered only by the sweet verses of **Gros Jean**, his personal **chantuelle**, as these nascent calypsonians were known. After emancipation, when the chantuelles were finally able to express themselves as free men, they entertained Carnival revellers with insurgent and satirical lyrics. However, the British found their uninhibited displays unsettling and associated calypso with vulgarity and **civil disobedience**, a stigma that remained for many years. Clashes between revellers and colonial officers, as well as objections from the upper classes to "obscenity" in lyrics, led to the prohibition of African drumming in 1884. In

PARANG

Created by the combined influences of Spanish missionaries and Venezuelan cocoa workers, the Christmas-time sound of **parang** is one of the last vestiges of Spanish influence in Trinidad. During the season, which starts in October and ends with Epiphany (Jan 6), *parranderos* perform *aguinaldos*, sentimental Spanish songs accompanied by rapid, Mediterranean-style strums on four-stringed instruments, usually guitar, mandolin and cuatros, with violin, box bass, tambourines, maracas and other percussion instruments providing backup. Traditionally, *parranderos* went from house to house during the festive season, but these days most performances take place in bars and clubs.

Parang's Spanish lyrics can be romantic or humorous, though many are devoted to religious themes such as the exploits of saints and the birth of Jesus. Whatever the lyric, the music is always infused with a sense of joyous celebration, and the festivities are enhanced by the consumption of Spanish-derived dishes such as pastelles, arepas and strong draughts of rum or poncha creme, a rum-laced eggnog.

Though the parang tradition has waned a little in recent years, it still remains strong in communities dominated by people of Spanish and Amerindian ancestry, such as Paramin, Lopinot, Santa Cruz, San Raphael and St Joseph; and if you visit T&T around Christmas, you'll hear plenty of parang and the more contemporary soca-parang on the radio.

the absence of drums, musicians were forced to be inventive, and created the **tamboo bamboo** – tuned sticks of bamboo beaten on the ground to give a variety of percussive notes – to provide a legal rhythm for their mas and calypso.

Calypso's golden era

Calypso evolved rapidly in the early twentieth century: English replaced French patois, and brass and string instruments took over from the basic rhythms of the tamboo bamboo. Armed with suitably boastful sobriquets, calypsonians such as **Atilla the Hun**, **Growling Tiger**, **Lord Invader**, **Lord Melody** and **Chieftain Douglas** refined their art and turned professional, performing for paying audiences at makeshift venues in downtown Port of Spain known as **tents**. Though veiled in metaphor and double entendre, much of the early material was as risqué and **controversial** as it is today; sex, religion, race and satirical portrayals of public figures were the meat of calypsos that usually included the patois disclaimer "**sans humanité**" – "without mercy".

During the 1930s, calypso also found an overseas audience, largely through the efforts of white appropriators such as Paul Whiteman, whose *Sly Mongoose* became a huge US hit in the 1920s. Calypso gradually gained a level of social acceptance, but the colonial government still had a vested interest in controlling what they perceived to be subversive lyrics, and the 1934 **Theatre and Dance Halls Ordinance** enabled the censorship of so-called "offensive" compositions and the outright prohibition of pieces deemed particularly seditious; in reality, any calypso seen to undermine British rule (or champion black culture) was swiftly banned. Calypsonians were required to submit their compositions for government inspection before public performance, and officers stationed in the tents ensured that songs met with British approval. Unsurprisingly, calypsos from this time (which you'll still hear today) are often anti-colonial and anti-European.

The Yankee dollar

During World War II, calypso got another boost through the support of **American troops** stationed at Chaguaramas. Entertainment-hungry soldiers responded enthusiastically to calypso-based nightclub floorshows and the tents were packed to the rafters, the lyrics now accompanied by sophisticated **brass bands**. Calypso's success overseas undermined British suppression, and the genre flourished, though the soldiers' preference for comedy and frivolity over politics or picong (private jokes that went over the head of a foreign audience) led to a trivialization of the lyrics. The brawling, fornicating habits of the soldiers didn't go unnoticed, however, and calypsonians adeptly documented the morally bereft Port of Spain society during American occupation. An infamously cynical take on the American presence, Lord Invader's *Rum and Coca Cola* (see p.95) was one of the best of these biting commentaries; ironically, a cover version by the Andrews Sisters sold five million copies in the US, though Maxine Andrews later commented that none of the sisters gave a moment's thought to the lyrics, which just "went over our heads". Denied a share of the profits, Invader successfully sued.

Dominated by **Mighty Sparrow** and the inimitable late **Lord Kitchener**, calypso grew in popularity throughout the 1950s and 1960s. Tourists descended on T&T to experience this latest craze first-hand and the tents went from strength to strength, with new venues springing up each year. In 1956, Dr Eric Williams' newly elected PNM government created the **Calypso King** competition, and Sparrow swept to victory with the classic *Jean and Dinah*, which gloried in the fact that local women would have to fall back on Trini men now that US soldiers had departed. Crowned monarch so many times that he was eventually barred from competition and given the special title of "Calypso King of the World", Sparrow continued to overshadow his competitors, and calypso lyrics settled into two strands: political praise or picong, and salacious references to love and sex.

Soca on the rise

Though Independence in 1962 prompted a slew of calypsos infused with optimism, the late 1960s saw militant lyricists such as **Valentino**, **Black Stalin** and **Mighty Chalkdust** delivering incisive commentaries on post-colonial society. But despite some innovations – **Calypso Rose** became the first female "king" in 1978, and the competition was renamed **Calypso Monarch** – the 1970s turned out to be a decade of stagnation for calypso. As the anti-establishment, pro-black themes of Jamaican roots reggae held sway over Caribbean musical tastes and sensibilities, calypso lyrics sank to an all-time low of banality. From the early 1980s onwards, **soca** (see p.266) began to overshadow its parent during Carnival season, its more danceable style proving irresistible to revellers, but calypso returned to its roots in the middle of the decade via the sensitive, thoughtful work of **David Rudder**, who in 1986 secured an unheard-of triple victory in the Young King, Calypso Monarch and Road March competitions with his beautiful *Bahia Girl*.

Calypso today

Calypso chugged on through the 1990s and into the new millennium, with the Dimanche Gras performances of artists such as **Shadow**, **Singing Sandra**, **Sugar Aloes** and **Gypsy** becoming increasingly extravagant, with props and costumes that make each delivery into a piece of mini theatre – in 2010, **Kurt Allen** caused a sensation by singing his winning composition *Too Bright* while dressed as a vagrant and surrounded by a full set that re-created Woodford Square; his lyrics, meanwhile – a scathing criticism of the incumbent PNM government and the opposition – marked a return to the glory days of the genre. Female calypsonians such as **Karen Ashe**, who took the monarch title 2011, are also making their mark; while judging from the fantastic performances of the kids who compete for the title of Junior Calypso Monarch, the future of calypso seems a lot brighter these days.

The adult monarch competition is still underpinned by the **tents** (see p.34), where an older crowd of enthusiasts disentangle the metaphors and squeal at jokes that are often unintelligible without a good knowledge of Trinbago affairs and gossip. Most calypsonians concentrate on two numbers during the season, usually one with a political slant and another with a more light-hearted theme, be it picong or sex; whether they get to perform them both is up to the audience – after the first few verses, each artist leaves the stage, returning only if the claps and catcalls are deemed loud enough to bring them back on. These days, the most established tents have a permanent location and a roster of well-known artists supplemented by the year's crop of promising newcomers; line-ups change annually.

Soca

Most attribute the birth of **soca** to the great calypsonian **Lord Shorty** (later known as Ras Shorty I after he converted to Rastafarianism), who died in 2000. Distressed at the moribund state of 1970s calypso, he made a conscious decision to breathe new life into the genre. The Indian instrumentation and souped-up rhythmic structure of what he called **sokah** was an infinitely more danceable form that fitted right in with the disco craze, and when he unveiled his song *Indrani* in 1973, it took T&T by storm.

Since Blue Boy's *Soca Baptist* became the Road March (the most heavily played tune as mas bands pass judging points on the Carnival route) of 1980, soca has dominated Carnival and become the music of choice among a nation of professional feters, sustained by more than 400 new releases per year. From November or December onwards, soca artists release their new material; by the time they perform them at the Carnival fetes, everyone knows the year's crop of music well, waving their rags when commanded or launching into the dances that accompany some of the most popular songs. In 1993, the soca/calypso dichotomy was officially recognized when a separate **Soca Monarch** competition was set up. The climax of the soca madness that envelops pre-Carnival Trinidad, Soca Monarch on Fantastic Friday easily surpasses Calypso Monarch in terms of crowd numbers, with pyrotechnics and ever more extravagant performances serving as an explosive opener to Carnival weekend. The early years of the competition were dominated by **Super Blue**, who returned to take the title in 2013 with *Fantastic Friday*; his daughter, **Fay-Ann Lyons**, has won twice, in 2003 and 2009. Other recent winners include Lyons' husband, **Bunji Garlin**, as well as **Shurwayne Winchester** and **Iwer George**, but recent years have been dominated by soca superstar **Machel Montano**, Soca Monarch in 2011, 2012, 2013 (shared with Super Blue) and 2014, and also a frequent winner of the **Groovy Soca Monarch**, a slightly slower and more mellow category. Montano has also claimed most of the **Road March** titles in recent years. Having shot to fame in 1986 with *Too Young to Soca* while still in primary school, he went on to form the band **Xtatic**, a conglomeration of artists within which Machel was always the most prominent. Today, his Machel Montano HD "family" of Machel, **Patrice Roberts**, **Farmer Nappy** and others are easily the most popular soca act around. Other artists to look out for include **Destra Garcia**, one of the genre's few enduring female artists; ladies' favourites **Kes the Band** and **Benjai**, sweet-singing **Olajunji** and **Kerwin Du Bois**, and the ever-raunchy **Denise Belfon**. Soca's big names also include a strong contingent from other Caribbean islands, such as Skinny Fabulous from **St Vincent**, or Mr Killa and Talpree from **Grenada**; **Barbados** has produced soca legends Rupee and Alison Hinds. Arrow, the man behind the world's most overplayed soca hit *Hot, Hot, Hot*, actually hails from Montserrat.

Chutney soca

Sparse, fast soca-style beats mixed with sitars, thumping *dholak* drums and vocals that lean heavily on traditional Indian singing styles, **chutney** is a contemporary take on classical Indian music and *filmi* movie songs. Sung in a mixture of Hindi and English, lyrics tend towards the light-hearted (often with a good dollop of sentimentality), while chutney fetes have become a showcase for sensual dance steps that combine athletic wining with the delicate arm and hand movements of classical Indian dance. However, many older Hindus dislike chutney, finding the overtly sexual dancing and sometimes risqué lyrics distasteful.

Established in 1996, the **National Chutney Soca Monarch** competition is the annual focus for chutney artists, and the finals (usually held at Skinner Park in San Fernando) now attract up to 20,000 enthusiasts. Classic chutney performers include the wonderful **Drupatee Ramgoonai**, **Sonny Mann** and the late **Sundar Popo**, while more contemporary acts to look out for include the smooth **Rikki Jai** (multiple winner of the Chutney Monarch competition), **Dil-e-Nadan** and **Chris "KI" Persad**. Perennial favourites **Ravi B and Karma** took the 2010 Chutney Monarch title with *Drinker*, a ridiculously catchy example of the so-called "rum songs" that the genre has become known for in recent years. Today, chutney is by no means the preserve of the East Indian community alone; big chutney acts regularly headline at Carnival fetes, while many black Trinidadian stars, from Machel Montano to Olatunji, employ chutney-style instrumentation in their music.

Steel pan

Said to be the only new acoustic instrument invented in the twentieth century, the **steel pan** evolved from the Trinbagonian propensity for using available materials as percussion instruments. During the Carnivals of the 1930s, tamboo bamboo-led kalinda music was supplied by bands of young men from deprived areas such as Port of Spain's Laventille and Belmont, who were unanimously viewed as "bad johns" or thugs by the more fortunate. With names such as Desperadoes and Invaders, these loosely organized bands supplemented the tamboo with **rhythm sections**, beating steel rods against anything from brake drums and buckets to dustbin lids to create a danceable beat. It was only a matter of time before someone realized that discarded saucepans or biscuit tins – and later the oil drums brought over by US troops – could be hammered into concave sections that produced rough notes; these early raw materials explain why steel drums are known as **pans**. Depending upon who you believe, the first pan was played at some point in the late 1930s either by **Winston Spree Simon** of the John John band (now Carib Tokyo), who tapped out *Mary Had a Little Lamb*, or **Neville Jules** of Hell Yard (now Trinidad All Stars) who managed the basic chords of a calypso called *Whoopsin, Whoopsin*.

By the end of the war, experimentation had produced basic pans with up to fourteen notes, and the 1946 Carnival was dominated by the ringing of steel bands. However, the associations of **violence** lingered, and the panyards that sprang up throughout the East–West Corridor were widely viewed – probably quite correctly – as seething dens of iniquity. Feuds were common, and in 1950 a bloody pitched battle between Invaders and Tokyo had Carnival revellers running for cover. Calypsonian Blakie documented the clash: "It was bacchanal/Fifty Carnival/Fight for so, with Invaders and Tokyo/ When the two bands clash/Mamayoe, if yuh see cutlass/Never me again/To jump in a steelband in Port of Spain."

Steel pan gets organized

Soon after the clash between Invaders and Tokyo, the violence tailed off and the movement gained respectability (and respect) as the music became more polished and complex. Soon, bands of up to 200 pannists were playing a sophisticated repertoire of classical pieces as well as calypso, and the nation's dedication to pan began in earnest. In 1950, the **T&T Steelband Association** (now **Pan Trinbago**; ⓦpantrinbago.co.tt) was established to promote and coordinate the movement, setting up a round of competitions that eventually led to the first annual Panorama tournament in 1963; twenty-odd years later, the steel pan was officially declared the national instrument.

These days, the pan calendar revolves around **Panorama**, a hugely popular affair that involves almost all of T&T's steel bands and attracts big crowds to its semi-finals and finals, held at Port of Spain's Queen's Park Savannah. To qualify for the event, bands must get through the preliminary stage, with judges visiting panyards in the various **regional zones**. Those that qualify take part in the semi-finals at the Savannah, and the final list battle it out on the Saturday before the main parade.

The steel band

Transforming an oil drum into a shiny, playable **steel pan** demands skill and experience. All pans other than the bass must first be **cut** to size, and a five-pound sledgehammer is used to beat the unopened end into a convex shape. The pan is then **heated** over a wood fire; oil is used to **temper** the metal, and a coating of **chrome** gives a better surface and a shiny finish. The **tuner** then takes over, marking the notes and beating them out with a hammer and chisel, an extremely specialized process that's usually achieved with the help of a keyboard. A finished chrome-coated tenor pan will sell for as much as US$1500, powder-coated versions around US$800.

In contemporary bands, different types of pan produce a variation of tones. The main melody is held by the **tenor** (or soprano) pan, which has the largest range of notes. **Guitar** and **cello pans** provide the background harmonies, and the booming **bass pan** underpins it all. Most contemporary bands are comprised of between fifty and two hundred volunteer pannists, who play one or two harmonic pans; with up to six instruments, bass pannists have to be pretty dextrous, twisting around to reach the right notes. And no steel band would be complete without its rhythm section or **engine room**, as the percussion section is known. In addition to a conventional drum kit, cowbells, shakers and scrapers, there is the **iron**, assorted bits of metal beaten with iron rods.

Each band is led by an **arranger**, who will adapt music from a variety of sources for the steel band. Though some arrangers work with more than one band, there are several long-standing relationships, such as Len "Boogsie" Sharp with Phase II Pan Groove or Pelham Goddard with Exodus. Though most bands used to play it safe and enter Panorama with calypsos familiar to audience and judges alike, many now enter original compositions, or even adapt recent pop hits.

Reggae

As in the rest of the Caribbean, **reggae** has made massive inroads in Trinidad and Tobago, and at Carnival time you'll even see the current hottest acts from Jamaica gracing the stage at soca fetes, usually as a guest performer in Machel Montano's set. There's also a lively **local reggae** scene, with artists such as **Marlon Asher**, **Prophet Benjamin** and **King David** leading the way, while local DJ families such as **Matsimela** play regularly at parties and clubs. Reggae has also lent its influence to soca, with many artists employing Jamaican vocal styles (and language and accent), while soca rhythms have become increasingly intertwined with dancehall from Jamaica; indeed, Jamaican artists usually release songs voiced on the most popular soca rhythm tracks of the year, either solo or in collaboration with Trini vocalists.

Rapso

A fusion of African-style drumbeats, soca melodies and spoken calypso-esque vocals infused with the militancy of 1990s hip-hop, **rapso** is a highly politicized genre that, while it has its followers, has always retained something of an underground feel. The genre's originator is generally considered to be **Lancelot "Kebu" Layne**, who released *Blow Away* in 1970 and *Get Off My Radio* in 1971. In 1976, "Mother of Rapso" **Cheryl Byron** became the first rapso artist to perform in a calypso tent, while **Brother Resistance** emerged as the "Father of Rapso" in the 1980s, and has become something of a spokesman for the genre, famously describing it as "the power of the word in the rhythm of the word". Rapso's popularity increased in the 1990s with the emergence of a host of new artists, though stalwarts such as Resistance, **Ataklan** and **3Canal** remain the movement's most popular proponents, fusing poetic, haunting lyrics that centre upon black empowerment and resistance to oppression with stinging, drum- and bass-dominated rhythms.

Ecology and wildlife

Joined to the South American mainland during the Ice Age when sea levels were lower, Trinidad and Tobago only became separate entities when movements of the Caribbean tectonic plates submerged the Orinoco Delta some 10,000 years ago. The islands owe their immense environmental diversity to this period of attachment, which has left them with many South American plants, animals and birds alongside the flora and fauna found elsewhere in the Caribbean. Few places of relative size harbour such variety.

A wide range of **habitats** support the wildlife; **Tobago** boasts the oldest protected rainforest in the western hemisphere along its main ridge of mountains, as well as marshes and lagoons in the western tip, a network of thriving offshore reefs and the bird sanctuaries of Little Tobago and the St Giles islands. In **Trinidad**, the rich wetlands at Nariva swamp are home to several plant and animal species found nowhere else in T&T, while Caroni Swamp offers easy access to mangroves and their inhabitants. The dry, treeless prairie at Aripo – the island's only remaining true savannah plain – sustains unusual plants and orchids as well as birdlife. Trinidad's hills are afforded some government protection, and contain three state reserves: the Northern Range Sanctuary, the Valencia Wildlife Sanctuary in the northeast and the Trinity Hills Wildlife Sanctuary in the southeast. However, there is only a handful of game wardens and rangers to defend the forests (and enforce the temporary hunting ban imposed in 2013), and with quarrying and industry constantly encroaching on virgin land, the island's wildlife is under constant threat. For more on the T&T environment, visit the **websites** of Environment Tobago (ⓦenvironmenttobago.net), Papa Bois Conservation (ⓦpapaboisconservation.org) or the Trinidad and Tobago Field Naturalists Club (ⓦttfnc.org).

Trees and shrubs

Although T&T's **woodlands** are disappearing at a significant rate, they still make up around 40 percent of the country's total land area. The various forest types include littoral woodland, deciduous seasonal woodland, rainforest and swamp forests; higher elevations see **montane** forest – wet and cool with plenty of epiphytic growth – while the stubby 2-metre canopy of **elfin** forest occupies only the highest mountain peaks.

About **350 species** of tree grow in T&T, including the exotically named pink bark, gustacare, crapaud, saltfishwood, sardine, purpleheart, bloodwood, hairy cutlet and the naked Indian, which gets its politically incorrect name from its peeling brown bark. Forests are mostly made up of **mora**, **teak**, **mahogany**, **cedar**, **cypre**, **Caribbean pine** and **balata**; the latter produces a milky latex used to coat golf balls. Immediately noticeable, the **bois cano** has large, deeply lobed leaves that dry into a distinctive claw shape; and the mighty 40-metre **silk cotton** or kapok tree (its fruits contain the cotton-like kapok) boasts an impressive girth of buttressed roots spreading elegantly to meet the ground – Amerindians used entire trees for their dugout pirogues. With its spectacular spreading branches, **samaan** are often planted as shade trees, while the **banyan** looks more like a collection of interweaved vines than a tree, as its boughs produce aerial roots that form secondary trunks when they reach the ground. The **tree fern**'s diamond-patterned trunk and top-heavy crown of fern-like leaves lend a primeval aspect to high altitude forests.

Ornamental trees

A host of **ornamental** trees turn T&T's forests into a patchwork of colour during the dry months (roughly Dec–May), when the intense orange-red flowers of the mountain **immortelle** compete with two varieties of **poui**, which shed their leaves to make way for cascades of dusky-pink or bright yellow blossoms. The **cassia** also produces prolific cascades of deep yellow or pink. Covering a flat, wide-spreading crown, the deep red **flamboyant** or poinciana blooms in August as well as April; during the dry season, half-metre pods full of rattling seeds dangle from the leafless branches.

Flowering sporadically throughout the year, the 15-metre **African tulip** or "flame of the forest" produces clusters of deep red blooms along outer branches; unopened buds in the centre of the flower are sometimes used as natural water pistols, as they contain a pouch of water which spurts out at speed when pressure is applied. Creating patches of mauve throughout Trinidad's forests, the crown of the **crepe myrtle** is usually smothered with blooms, while **bauhinia** or orchid tree and **jacaranda** add to the purple hues.

Fruit trees

Among the huge variety of **fruit trees**, the most easily recognizable are the many varieties of **mango**, with their rounded, dense crown of long, leathery leaves over a short trunk. **Banana** plants are not trees in the strict botanical sense; their huge, tattered leaves grow from a central stem of overlapping leaf bases. Covered by large purple bracts, the flowers hang from the main stem and eventually develop into fruit. **Plantain** trees are similar, with larger, less tattered leaves and bigger, more robust fruit. Equally easy to recognize, **pawpaw** (papaya) has a long hollow stem with large splayed leaves and fruit at the top.

Still grown in groves for export, **cocoa** is easily identifiable by its lichen-smothered trunk and dark green shiny leaves; the 20-centimetre ridged oval pods grow from the trunk and turn from light green to brown, yellow, orange or purple when ripe. Covered with a sweet white gloop, the beans inside can be sucked when raw, but are usually dried and roasted to make cocoa. **Cashew** trees, with their strongly veined oval leaves, are common; the familiar nut pokes out of the bottom of a sweet-tasting, pear-shaped red fruit, whose shell produces an oily liquid that is a skin irritant.

The lifeblood of many a craft vendor, the fruits of the **calabash** tree grow to more than 35cm in diameter and are hollowed out and made into bowls, bags and all manner of souvenirs. Employed as a vegetable but classified as a fruit, **breadfruit** was brought to the Caribbean by Captain Bligh aboard the HMS *Providence* as food for plantation slaves, and is common throughout T&T. With spreading branches decorated by large serrated leaves, the spherical fruits are lime-green and pockmarked.

COCONUT COUNTRY

Commercial plantations on both islands have made the **coconut** T&T's most prevalent palm. It's an incredibly versatile tree; the water and meat are consumed fresh at the jelly stage, while the flesh of older coconuts is grated and used in baking or immersed in water and strained to produce the coconut milk that flavours a thousand local dishes. Coconut oil is used in soap, cosmetics and cooking; the leaf fronds thatch roofs and make hats or floor mats; the husks are used to make floor buffers; and pieces of hard shell are made into jewellery and cups. Of the many ornamental varieties, the 30-metre **royal palm** is a graceful specimen with a grey, ruler-straight trunk; it's often used to mark out driveways. Similar but even taller at an average of 40m, the **cabbage** palm has thicker, messier looking fronds, while the squat, spiky-leafed **cocorite** is one of the most common forest species. The ultimate in tropical splendour, the **traveller's palm** is actually a member of the banana family – the name refers to mini-ponds at the base of the trunk that provide a convenient water source. Fronds fan out from the base in an enormous peacock's tail shape as high as 10m.

Its close cousin is the chataigne or **breadnut**, a similar tree with smaller, spiky fruits that are eaten roasted.

Coastal trees and palms
Trinidad's swamps of red, black and white **mangrove** trees, with their dense tangle of aerial roots, help protect coastal communities from hurricane surges, filter sediments that smother reefs and provide a nursery for fish and crustaceans. Common seashore plants include the wide-spreading **Indian almond** and **sea grape**, both with broad, deep-veined leaves that turn a pretty deep red as they mature. Definitely one to avoid, the **manchineel** tree grows to about 15m with a wide spreading canopy, yellow flowers and apple-like green fruits. All parts of the tree are extremely **poisonous**: even standing below a manchineel during rain incurs blistering from washed-down sap, and not all of those around T&Ts coastlines have an identifying warning plaque.

Plants and flowers
Of T&T's various **wild plants**, the **jumbie bead vine** produces distinctive red and black seeds used in craft items and as good luck charms; they are said to ward off evil spirits, and a bead kept in a purse will keep it filled with money. A variety of mimosa with scratchy stems, **ti Marie** is known as "the sensitive plant" for its ability to curl back its leaves at the slightest touch; you'll see patches of it on lawns throughout the islands.

The largest of the epiphytes that grow along tree branches, electricity wires and any available surface is the **wild pine bromeliad**, a spiky-leafed relative of the pineapple that produces a battered-looking red flower. These "air plants" are not parasites – they draw their nutrients from the humid, mineral-rich atmosphere – but water reserves trapped between the leaves (which provide a habitat for insects and frogs) can mean that smothered tree limbs sometimes collapse under their weight. Other epiphytes include 200 different species of **orchids**, which grow on living or dead plant or tree matter and in lowland savannahs such as Aripo in eastern Trinidad. In the lowland forests, distinctive epiphytes include the **monkey throat**, whose flower is a perfect primate facsimile, and the pendulous **jack spaniard**, with its trailing wasp-like petals; the common **lamb's tail** grows horizontally from large trees, and has attractive maroon-flecked green petals with a white and pink stamen.

T&T's 2300 varieties of **flowering plant** provide beds, borders and hedges with a splash of colour, and you'll often see several varieties of multicoloured **croton** leaves in between the blooms. The national flower is the **chaconia**, a spectacular crimson poinsettia which you'll see throughout the forests, but the ubiquitous **bougainvillea** is the most common ornamental, its red, white, orange, purple and pink papery bracts spilling out into intensely coloured clumps. Distinguishable by its protruding pollen-tipped stamen, **hibiscus** takes on an abundance of hues and shapes – the lacy **coral** variety has clusters of tiny curling red petals and a red frill at the end of the stamen. A dark-leafed shrub with clusters of small red flowers, **ixora** is another popular ornamental that flowers throughout the year.

Flamboyant **tropical flowers** are grown commercially in T&T and also flourish in the wild. Brush-like **ginger lilies** are one of the most common exotics; the deep pink or red bracts hide the insignificant true flower, and the shiny, banana-like leaves are used in flower arrangements. A close relative, the **torch ginger**'s deep crimson cluster of thick waxy petals makes an impressively showy head. However, the queen of local exotics – and the symbol of the PNM political party – are the 40 vividly coloured varieties of **balisier**, all members of the heliconia family, which include the aptly named **lobster claw** and the red, yellow and green **hanging heliconia**, which looks like a series of fish hanging from a rod. Equally prevalent are the artificial-looking **anthuriums**, a shiny, heart-shaped red, pink or white bract with a long penile stem or spadix protruding from the centre. The flashy **bird of paradise**, a blue and purple flower that resembles a bird's head graced by a deep orange crest, is rarer.

Wildlife

With more than 100 species of **mammal** roaming the forests and flats (not including T&T's 50,000-plus goats), hunting has long been a popular pastime and wild meat is consumed with gusto whenever available. The 2013 hunting ban looks likely to be extended indefinitely, but given the lack of enforcement (there are only a handful of rangers covering both Trinidad and Tobago), it hasn't had that much success in protecting the ever-dwindling species most favoured by lovers of "wild meat". Most hunters go after the most common animals; the smallest quarry is the herbivorous **agouti**, a rabbit-sized brown rodent that looks like a long-legged guinea pig and feeds on fruits and leaves; and its larger relative the **lappe** or **paca**, which has longer legs and a pattern of stripes and spots on its fur. Equally desirable for the pot is the **manicou** or **opossum**, an unattractive cat-sized marsupial with a rat-like tail and a long snout that forages for scraps and carrion. The nine-banded **tatoo** (armadillo) is increasingly rare, as is the brown-coloured **red brocket deer** (extinct in Tobago) and the **quenk**, an aggressive wild hog. Another threatened species, the metre-long **ocelot** wildcat has been extensively hunted for its beautiful spotted pelt.

Otters live in and around the Madamas and Paria rivers in Trinidad, but shy away from humans. Trinidad's cutest water-dwelling mammal, the herbivorous West Indian **manatee** or sea cow, grows up to 4m long and can live for fifty years. However, the destruction of its swampland habitat by development and by drainage for agriculture has decimated local populations, with around forty still living in the protected Nariva swamp.

The islands' largest **monkey** colonies also live in Nariva; with red-furred, hulking frames and a bulbous, bearded larynx, troops of up to fifteen **red howlers** defend their territory with the eerie, deafening roars that prompted their name. Smaller but extremely intelligent **weeping capuchins** live in the tree-tops in troops of up to twenty, and are able to use basic tools to crack open nuts as well as occasionally expressing their irritation at human intrusions by raining down a volley of sticks on curious heads. Around sixty species of **bat** inhabit T&T's forests and caves, most living on a diet of insects, fruit, nectar and pollen. The two notable exceptions are the vampire bat, which prefers a more gruesome food source, creeping up on sleeping livestock and drinking their blood, and the frog-eating bat, which distinguishes between poisonous and edible species by listening to mating calls.

Reptiles and amphibians

The largest of the seventy species of **reptile** is an endemic sub-species of the **spectacled caiman**, a 3-metre alligator with an elongated snout that inhabits swamps, rivers and dams, and feeds on fish and birds. Among the 47 different **snakes**, only four are venomous. With the girth of a man's arm and a length of up to 3m, the **fer-de-lance** is particularly aggressive, and is identifiable by its pointed head, yellow underside and chin, and orange-brown triangular markings. The **bushmaster** is slightly longer (up to 4m) with a burnt-orange skin distinctly patterned by dark brown diamonds, with smaller diamonds of orange within. Its venom can be lethal to the young, old or infirm, but deaths are incredibly rare and most bites afflict farmers working habitually in the bush; all hospitals carry antivenom. Both snakes are known as mapepire (pronounced "*mah*-pee-pee") and inhabit forest areas. The two varieties of poisonous **coral snake**, the common and large coral snake, are smaller, rarer and less aggressive; they're easy to spot, with black skin and red and white rings around the body. Known as macajuel (pronounced *makka*-well), **boa constrictors** – including anacondas – are T&T's largest snakes, and can grow up to 10m in length. Most are patterned with brown diamonds that provide camouflage. They are not venomous, but can easily crush a small mammal in their powerful coils.

Among more than twenty species of lizard are **geckos**, usually referred to as zandolie or ground lizards. The **twenty-four-hour lizard** gets its name from a local myth which warns that if you disturb one, it will attach itself to your body and remain there for 24 hours – at the end of which you die. The bright green, spiky-backed, herbivorous **iguana** is a favourite delicacy, especially if it's carrying eggs; unsurprisingly, it spends most of its time hiding from human captors in leafy tree-tops. The metre-long, dark brown **matte lizard** relies on speed to stay out of the cooking pot, raising itself onto its hind legs to accelerate to 11kmph in two seconds.

T&T's most common **amphibian** is the crapaud (pronounced "crappo"), a warty, hand-sized frog with a loud, booming croak. Another frog, the colostethus, provides a night-time chorus reminiscent of a demented guinea pig. Trinidad's only endemic species, the **golden tree frog**, lives in epiphytic plants that cling to the rainforest trees of the island's two highest mountains, El Tucuche and El Cerro del Aripo. In addition to the land turtle or morocoy, five species of **sea turtle** lay their eggs on T&T's beaches: the green turtle, the olive ridley, the hawksbill, the loggerhead and the giant leatherback (see p.142).

Birds

With more than 430 types of **birds** recorded on the islands, Trinidad and Tobago ranks among the world's top ten in terms of numbers of species, and offers the best birdwatching in the Caribbean. The national birds are the scarlet ibis (Trinidad) and the cocrico (Tobago), both of which adorn the republic's coat of arms. A native of Venezuela and best seen at the Caroni Swamp, the **scarlet ibis** typifies the eye-catching colours of local species, while the golden-brown, pheasant-like **cocrico** has a fleshy, bright red turkey-style wattle at its throat and a raucous, incredibly loud call that echoes through Tobago's hills in the pre-dawn hours.

The sugar-water feeders at most hotels are a great way to see smaller birds at close quarters. There are seventeen species of brightly coloured **hummingbirds** in T&T, of which the most frequently seen are the copper-rumped hummingbird and the white-necked jacobin, both with fabulous iridescent feathers. The most unusual hummer is the 6-centimetre **tufted coquette**, Trinidad's smallest bird and the third smallest in the world, with a red and yellow body, dark wings and a beautiful deep orange crest.

Both jet-black, the blunt-beaked **smooth-billed ani** and the **shiny cowbird**, with a sharper beak and beady yellow eyes, are the local equivalent of pigeons. The audacious

---

OILBIRDS

Squat, mottled-brown and whiskered, **oilbirds** have the honour of being the world's only nocturnal fruit-eating birds, and Trinidad supports eight breeding colonies. Spending the daylight hours inside the caves in which they nest, oilbirds are unusually gregarious; up to forty will huddle on a single ledge, squawking and picking through each other's feathers for parasites. Mature birds venture into the open only at night, using **sonar** to assist their manoeuvres through the forests in search of palm, laurel and camphor fruits, often travelling as far as 120km from the colony in each foray. Fruits are swallowed whole and the seeds regurgitated, and their in-flight consumption is an important agent of reforestation.

Oilbirds rear one brood of **young** each year, laying between two and four eggs over several days in nests constructed from regurgitated, cement-like matter that rapidly turns the snowy-white clutch a dirty brown. Both parents share the 32-day incubation, after which the blind, featherless fledglings emerge, remaining immobile for up to three weeks and feeding on partially digested fruit pulp. Development is slow; a patchy cover of downy feathers grows after 21 days, and young birds don't fledge until they are 100 to 120 days old.

A young oilbird weighs twice as much as a mature one, due to the high fat content that gave rise to its name. Amerindians and Capuchin monks used to boil the fledglings down for their **oil**, which they then used to fuel cooking fires and make flambeaux; Amerindians also called the oilbird *guacharo*, "the one who wails and mourns", on account of the rasps, screams, squawks and snarls that make up its call; an eerie sound that also inspired the bird's French patois sobriquet, *diablotin* – devil bird.

10cm black and yellow **bananaquit** is supposed to subsist on nectar, but has become a frequent visitor to hotel breakfast tables, dipping its sharp little beak into fruits and sweet preserves. Seen wherever there are cattle, white **egrets** roost on ruminating rumps in a mutually rewarding relationship that provides the egret with a constant supply of insects and the cow some relief from bloodsuckers.

In the forests and flats, frequently sighted birds include **white-bearded manakins**, which are one of several species of bird in Trinidad that perform intricate courtship displays in designated areas known as leks, intensely coloured **woodpeckers**, **antbirds**, **trogons** and **tanagers** – the palm tanager is a cool olive with black flecks on its wings, while the bay-headed variety is a brilliant emerald with a russet head. Various **honeycreepers** display dazzling hues of turquoise and black; the purple variety's near-black feathers only show their true colours in the sunshine.

Of larger birds, common varieties include multicoloured **toucans**, **parrots**, **yellow orioles** and the crow-like **crested oropendola**, black with a yellow tail, cream beak, beady blue eyes, a truly exotic call and a marvellous way of building nests: metre-long, teardrop-shaped constructions of dry grass that hang in groups from tree boughs. Though it can be hard to spot the **bearded bellbird**, you'll certainly hear its penetrating "bok, bok" call in the hill forests. Birds of prey include the **peregrine falcon**, as well as several kites and hawks, including the **ornate hawk-eagle**, the largest of the lot. The ubiquitous **vultures** – locally known as corbeaux – perform a necessary, if unsavoury, function by devouring dead animals.

Tobago sustains a few species not seen regularly in Trinidad, such as the **red-crowned woodpecker**, **rufous-tailed jacamar** and the **white-tailed sabre-wing**. The smaller island is also the best place to see **blue-crowned mot-mots** (locally called king of the woods), with deep orange breasts, green-blue heads and long flowing tail feathers. Offshore of both islands, **boobies** and **brown pelicans** trawl for fish, the latter diving from great heights into the sea and scooping up its quarry in its large pouched bill. However, if a **frigate bird** is around, smaller sea birds often lose their catch, as the frigate feeds on stolen goods snatched from the beak of more efficient fishers.

Insects and spiders

With 92 varieties of **mosquito** in T&T, and far too many kinds of **cockroach** (ranging from 7cm dark brown pests to the rare albino variety), you could be forgiven for doing your best to stay well away from the country's invertebrate life, but many species are vital to the local ecosystems. More than 600 varieties of **butterfly** flit between local flowers, ranging from the 2cm crimson-and-black red devil to the commonly seen bright blue 7cm emperor and the cocoa mort bleu, brown and mauve with eye-like spots on the wings.

Armies of black, brown or red bachac or **leaf-cutting ants**, with almost triangular heads and sharp, sizeable pincers, are divided into ranks. Large workers trim entire shrubs into coin-sized pieces and carry them on their backs to the nest, while smaller workers fend off any potential predators; the leaf-pieces are then shredded and chewed into compost for the cultivation of the fungus that feeds the colony. A single nest may discard as much as 20 cubic metres of waste material in five years, banking it up over the subterranean colony, which houses up to 2.5 million ants. Living in equally complex societies that can number one billion per colony, **termites** attach their large, irregular earthen nests to the sides of trees.

Aside from the spindly-limbed specimens that you'll see indoors, the largest common spiders are black and red **orb-web spinners**, about 8cm long including the legs, and which spin the classic hexagonal web. More unusual is the **trapdoor spider**, which conceals its forest-floor burrow with a hinged doorway, springing out to drag in passing prey. Ten species of **tarantula** range from a delicately hued violet and brown to hairy and black, and can measure between 8 and 15cm including the legs. Apart from a bird-eating variety, most are nocturnal insect hunters that construct their basic, messy-looking web tunnels on grassy banks or in dead wood.

ATTACK OF THE LIONFISH

The waters around T&T have seen an influx of the orange-and-white-striped **lionfish** in recent years, an invasive species with spectacular venomous spines that has made its way down the Caribbean chain from the south Atlantic, probably after having been released from private aquariums. Voracious eaters with no natural predators in Caribbean waters, lionfish spawn every three days and have had a devastating effect on the marine environment here, drastically reducing numbers of tropical reef fish such as parrot and snapper. Efforts are underway to control the population, with local divers co-ordinating culls and educating fishermen about how delicious lionfish are to eat, but little headway has been made thus far.

Marine life

Sediment flows from the South American mainland via the Orinoco River have prevented the build-up of extensive **reefs** around Trinidad, but the waters off Tobago, where visibility ranges from 12 to 50m, hold some of the Caribbean's richest reefs, though many are suffering the depredations of overfishing, pollution and the coral bleaching caused worldwide by rising sea temperatures. Among the sixty or so **coral varieties** found in T&T waters are rotund brains, patterned with furrowed trenches; branching umber elkhorn and staghorn; stalagmite-like pillar coral; and cool green star coral. Extremely striking are the groups of intricate **soft coral** sea plumes, sea whips and purple sea fans, while brilliant yellow **anemones** as well as red, brown, purple and green **sponges** provide a splash of colour, some growing up to three feet in diameter. Caribbean spiny **lobsters** and green or spotted **moray eels** lurk in the crevices between corals.

Sand flats and seagrass fields between the reefs host **spiny black sea urchins**; the spines of round white urchins are too short to puncture skin. Long, thin and off-white, **sea cucumbers** sift through the sea floor to feed on deposited nutrients, while **starfish** and **queen conch** snails move slowly along the seagrass blades, vacuuming up organisms that live there.

The reefs harbour a huge variety of multicoloured **tropical fish**, including parrot fish, electric-blue Creole wrasse, queen and French angel fish, striped grunts and spiny puffer fish – which balloon in size if threatened – as well as tarpon and trigger fish.

Of larger marine species, giant 7m **manta rays** are best seen around Speyside in Tobago; you'll also encounter smaller eagle, spotted and Atlantic torpedo rays, and southern stingrays. **Dolphins** and **porpoises** are common, and docile, 15m **whale sharks** are occasional visitors, feeding on plankton and small fish. Other large fish include reef, tiger and nurse sharks, grouper, dolphin (the fish not the mammal), kingfish (wahoo), tuna, blackjack, marlin, blue cavalli, sailfish, bonita and barracuda. During nesting season, T&T's beaches are also used as nesting sites by **turtles**, most notably giant leatherbacks (see p.142).

Books

The reviews below cover some of the best available books written about Trinidad and Tobago. All are readily available internationally and in T&T, where you'll also find many more specialized titles not listed here. Books that are especially recommended are marked with an ★ symbol.

FICTION

Michael Anthony *Cricket in the Road and Other Stories*. Concise, thought-provoking short stories, rich in descriptive detail. His novel *In the Heat of the Day* is centred on the industrial unrest that led to the 1903 water riots, while *The Year in San Fernando* is an acute portrayal of San Fernando in the 1940s, seen through the eyes of a teenage boy on a year's sojourn from his village home.

★**Robert Antoni** *My Grandmother's Erotic Folk Tales, Carnival* and *As Flies to Whatless Boys. Folk Tales* offers outlandish stories of life on Corpus Christi (aka Trinidad) under US military occupation during World War II, as told by a saucy 97-year-old to her grandson, while the powerful *Carnival* moves from New York to Port of Spain and the Trinidad rainforest, touching on love and the island's historical prejudices along the way. Perhaps his greatest work is the fantastic *Whatless Boys*, a magnificent *tour de force* that describes the journey to and settlement in Trinidad of a band of idealistic English pioneers led by a charismatic swindler. His earlier *Blessed is the Fruit* and *Divina Trace* are well worth checking out, too.

★**Kevin Baldeosingh** *The Autobiography of Paras P* and *The Ten Incarnations of Adam Avatar*. A bitingly funny satirical novel, *Paras* is a brilliant light read; *Adam Avatar* is much more powerful stuff, a retelling of Caribbean history from the inside by way of the central character's many incarnations, from an Amerindian to a white prostitute and a mixed-race slave-owner.

Valerie Belgrave *Ti Marie*. A romantic, passionate novel set in the late eighteenth century when Britain and Spain were fighting for control of Trinidad – a Caribbean *Gone with the Wind*, but far more intelligent and historically accurate.

Roslyn Carrington *A Thirst for Rain*. Love story set in the St Ann's foothills, centred around food seller Myra and her relationship with saga boy Slim, ex-stickfighter Jacob and teenage daughter Odile, with some fabulous descriptions of Port of Spain.

TRINBAGO'S LITERARY GREATS

Given T&T's diverse cultural heritage, opaque dialect and witty, imaginative use of language, it's no surprise that the islands boast a rich **literary heritage**. A radical 1930s journal featuring poetry and short stories by a host of young Trinidadian writers and intellectuals, the *Beacon* was at the forefront of the emerging literary tradition, but Trinbagonian literature really flourished after World War II. **Samuel Selvon**'s wryly humorous novels chronicle both the experience of growing up in Trinidad and the trials and tribulations of an emigrant in London, while those of **Earl Lovelace** are a lyrical celebration of Trinidadian life and culture, its "shacks that leap out of the red dirt and stone, thin like smoke, fragile like kite paper balancing on their rickety pillars as broomsticks on the edge of a juggler's nose" (*The Dragon Can't Dance*).

The late 1950s saw the appearance of Trinidad's most acclaimed novelist, Nobel Prize-winner **V.S. Naipaul**, who grew up in Chaguanas and Port of Spain, and won a scholarship to study English at Oxford University in 1950. He wrote his first book, *The Mystic Masseur* (1957), at the age of 23 while working for the BBC Caribbean Service in London, but it was his fourth, *A House for Mr Biswas*, that made his name in 1961. Naipaul's ironic treatment of the snobbery, corruption and small-mindedness of Trinidadian life has earned him an ambivalent reputation in his homeland, however. His brother **Shiva Naipaul** also garnered substantial literary acclaim with books such as *Fireflies* (1970) and *Beyond the Dragon's Mouth* (1984), before his sudden death of a heart attack at the age of 40 in 1985.

Trinidad's best-known poet, the Nobel Prize-winner **Derek Walcott**, was actually born in St Lucia, but lived in Port of Spain for decades, establishing the Trinidad Theatre Workshop there. An accomplished and prolific lyric poet, Walcott draws on the Elizabethan tradition, using both traditional rhyme and metre and free verse to explore issues of exile and identity and evoke the rich, heady atmosphere of the Caribbean.

★ **Earl Lovelace** *The Dragon Can't Dance* and other novels. A passionate examination of the motivation behind Carnival – if you only read one book about Trinidad, *Dragon Can't Dance* should be it. In *The Wine of Astonishment*, Lovelace highlights the persecution of the Spiritual Baptists, while *The Schoolmaster* offers a powerful and superbly handled allegory of colonialism. *Salt*, which won the Commonwealth Writer's Prize in 1997, is a stunning commentary on freedom from oppression, while *Is Just a Movie* explores the lives of residents of a small backwater village in Trinidad.

Shiva Naipaul *The Chip-Chip Gatherers*. A darkly funny tale of the machinations of the one rich man in a poor rural community. His novel *Fireflies* chronicles with empathy and ironic humour the moral, financial and spiritual decline of a rich and influential Indo-Trinidadian family.

★**V.S. Naipaul** *A House for Mr Biswas*. Mr Biswas – a newspaper journalist trapped by poverty into living with his domineering in-laws – struggles to establish his own identity. *In a Free State*, which won the Booker Prize in 1971, explores the changing roles and attitudes of people transplanted from their homelands, while *Miguel Street* paints a picture of community life in Trinidad through the eyes of a child. *The Middle Passage* looks at the effects of colonialism on five societies in the Caribbean and South America.

Elizabeth Nunez *The Limbo Silence*. The tale of a Trinidadian girl's efforts to integrate into an all-white school in Wisconsin during the Civil Rights movement. In *Bruised Hibiscus*, set in a Trinidadian village, the murder of a white woman reunites two childhood friends who are forced to relive memories of witnessing abuse by plantation owners.

★**Monique Roffey** *White Woman on a Green Bicycle*, *Archipelago* and *House of Ashes*. A beautifully written chronicle of an expat couple in Trinidad, *White Woman* describes the husband's passion for the country and its people alongside the wife's battles with racial politics, humidity and isolation, which she vents through writing letters to a wonderfully imagined Eric Williams. Via a boat journey from Chaguaramas to the Galapagos, *Archipelago* is a tender lament to a man coming to terms with the death of his infant son, while *House of Ashes*, set in the fictional island of Sans Amen, explores the events of 1990 in Trinidad. All are gripping and absorbing throughout.

Lawrence Scott *Ballad for the New World and Other Stories* is a clever collection evoking the experiences of a white boy growing up in pre-Independence Trinidad and in the colony, with ironic humour and sensitivity. Set on a leper colony off Trinidad's coast, *Night Calypso* revolves around the troubled life of an orphan who goes to live with the island's doctor.

★ **Samuel Selvon** *The Lonely Londoners*. A classic and powerful account of West Indian immigrants adjusting to the climate, racism and big-city life of 1950s London. Its sequel, *Moses Ascending* (Heinemann), is an ironic tale of an apathetic Trinidadian's experience of the Black Power movement and race relations in 1970s London.

★**Amanda Smyth** *A Kind of Eden*. A ruthless and gripping portrayal of a middle-aged British policeman working in Trinidad, whose various preoccupations have a devastating effect on his family when they visit Tobago together. Perhaps best read after you get home. Moving between the eponymous coastal village in Tobago, Port of Spain and Tamana in eastern Trinidad, her earlier *Black Rock* offers an interesting take on T&T just after World War II, with post-colonial racial politics at the heart of the action.

★ **Derek Walcott** *Omeros*. An extraordinary *tour de force* that draws on Homer's *Odyssey* to produce a vast Caribbean epic of the dispossessed. Many of the works in Walcott's *Collected Poems 1948–1984* evoke the sights and sounds of Trinidad, including the famous *Laventille*, dedicated to V.S. Naipaul.

HISTORY AND CULTURE

★**Stefan Falke** *Moko Jumbies: The Dancing Spirits of Trinidad*. Gorgeous coffee-table book capturing the beauty and energy of moko jumbies (stilt-walkers), from the Keylemanjahro School in Cocorite, from practice sessions to glorious Carnival shots.

James Ferguson *A Traveller's History of the Caribbean*. Concise and well-written overview that provides a good introduction to the region's history.

Patrick Leigh Fermor *The Traveller's Tree*. Written in the late 1940s, this classic account of a Caribbean tour has an interesting section on Trinidad, describing Port of Spain with an eagle eye and analysing the island's history, as well as its music and the "saga boy" fashions of the time.

James T. Houk *Spirits, Blood & Drums: The Orisha Religion in Trinidad and Tobago*. An anthropological study of the Orisha religion.

C.L.R. James *Beyond a Boundary*. Classic autobiographical book on cricket which extends into life and society in Trinidad in the 1920s.

John Newel Lewis *Ajoupa*. A marvellously idiosyncratic and enthusiastic account of the unique architecture of Trinidad and Tobago, illustrated by the author's superb line drawings. Hard to find outside Trinidad, but a must if you're interested in local architecture.

Peter Mason *Bacchanal! Carnival, Calypso and the Popular Culture of Trinidad*. A little dated, having first published in 1998, packed with interviews with the calypsonians and costume designers behind Trinidad's Carnival.

John Mendes *Cote Ce, Cote La*. The original dictionary of Trinbagonian words, recently updated and reissued, with sections on Carnival and proverbs and drawings by Carnival designer Wayne Berkley. Widely available on the islands.

JUMBIES IN TRINI FOLKLORE

Douens The malevolent spirits of unbaptized children, these sinister genderless waifs have backward-facing feet and hide their featureless faces beneath a wide-brimmed straw hat. They lurk in places where real children play; superstitious parents never call their child's name in the open, lest the douens remember it and lure the child away.

Jackalantern A mysterious light that misleads night-time travellers, luring them deep into the bush before vanishing.

La Diablesse An attractive female devil, La Diablesse wears the floppy hat and flowing gown of French colonial times, and lures men deep into the forest, never to return. At fetes, her frenzied dancing outshines the other women and attracts the men. The only way to distinguish her is by her feet; one is normal, the other a cloven hoof.

La Gahou Also known as *lugarhoo*, this spirit feeds on fresh blood. Iron chains slung about its body rattle and drag along the ground, and its sheaf of sticks functions as a whip; it can alter its form (usually becoming a jackass or dog) as well as changing size from minute to monstrous. A pair of scissors opened to resemble a cross and a Bible placed at the head of the bed are said to force the beast to revert to its human form.

Mama D'Leau Spirit and protector of rivers and lakes, Mama D'Leau sits naked at the edge of rivers, incessantly combing her long hair. Beneath the water, she has the lower body of a snake, which she uses to pull passing men to a watery death.

Papa Bois Tall and strong, his hair entwined with leaves, Papa Bois is guardian of forest trees, birds and animals. He imitates animal calls, leading hunters deep into the bush to become hopelessly lost.

Soucouyant This female vampire lives in villages as a reclusive old woman. At night, she sheds her skin to travel the country in the form of a ball of fire searching for victims, her skin kept in an overturned mortar bowl until her return at daybreak. She can only be stopped by dousing the skin in salt, which prevents her from re-entering it, or dropping piles of rice in homes and at crossroads; she is compelled to pick them up one by one until sunrise brings about her discovery.

Harvey R. Neptune *Caliban and the Yankees*. Fascinating account of the social and economic effects of the American bases at Chaguaramas and Waller Field during World War II, touching on everything from race and sexual politics to the response of calypsonians.

Colin A. Palmer *Eric Williams and the Making of the Modern Caribbean*. Contemporary take on the "father of the nation" and still the most influential figure in the republic's political history, from his days as a Howard University professor and author to his battle for an independent T&T and his years as the country's prime minister.

★**Alex Smailes** *Trinidad and Tobago*. Gorgeous coffee-table photo journal of Trinidad, with an incisive introduction to T&T history and culture by Jeremy Taylor and lovely reproductions of Smailes' photographs in the four sections, Carnival, Land, Water and People. The best visual souvenir on the market.

Vincent Tothill *Trinidad Doctor's Office*. The diaries of a Scottish doctor who signs up for a stint in Trinidad via the Colonial Office, this witty and often sad book offers a fascinating insight into Trinidadian society during the early twentieth century.

NATURAL HISTORY

Comeau, Guy, Hesterman and Hill *T&T Field Naturalists' Club Trail Guide*. Widely available in T&T, this is the definitive guide to hiking trails in Trinidad and Tobago with detailed descriptions and sketch maps, and useful sections on local geology and preparing for a hike.

Richard Ffrench *A Guide to the Birds of Trinidad and Tobago*. Definitive guide to T&T's birdlife, including information on habitat, habits, appearance and calls as well as a description of the islands' natural history and environment. The pocket-sized version with pictures and descriptions of 83 common species is handy for travellers.

Martin Kenefick, Robin L. Restall and Floyd E. Hayes *Birds of Trinidad and Tobago*. Newer than the classic French guide, with plenty of colour plates and detailed descriptions.

G.W. Lennox & S.A. Seddon *Flowers of the Caribbean; Fruits and Vegetables of the Caribbean; Trees of the Caribbean*. Slim and handy reference volumes with glossy, sharp colour pictures and concise accounts.

Lawson Wood *Diving and Snorkelling in Trinidad and Tobago*. Essential stuff if you've more than a passing interest in underwater T&T, with detailed descriptions of all the best dive sites on the islands.

Language

T&T's rich and varied vocabulary stems as much from a love of wordplay as it does from the republic's tumultuous history. Though English is the main language, Amerindians, the Spanish and the French have all left their mark, in both place names and common parlance, and in the Trinidadian village of Paramin in Trinidad, French Creole (or patois) is still spoken by elders. Meanwhile, Spanish surfaces in parang lyrics, and Hindi is widely used in Indian communities.

The nation's diverse ethnic mix has also influenced **Creole English**; Trinis will say "it making hot" as the French would say "Il fait chaud". Terms such as *pomme cythere* (golden apple) and *dou dou* (sweetheart, from the French *doux doux*) are commonplace, and French patois phrases are still part of the vernacular; *tout bagai* and *toute monde* are catch-alls meaning "everything". Hindi words, such as *dougla* and *aloo* (potato), have also entered the local lexicon.

Other idiosyncrasies include a habit of using the part to refer to the whole, calling an arm a hand, or a leg a foot – when someone breaks their arm, for example, they'll say "meh han break". People will also describe the afternoon as evening – it's common to be greeted with "good evening" at 3pm, while "goodnight" is used as a greeting.

Finally, bear in mind that language use here is often oblique and allusive. **Double entendres** are ubiquitous, especially in calypsos, with an endless supply of euphemisms – from "brush" to "hard work" to "saltfish" – employed to refer to sex or genitalia. If you're not well versed in local slang you'll need a Trini interpreter to appreciate the subtleties of many songs.

COMMON TRINBAGO EXPRESSIONS

Cockroach have no right in fowl party Don't involve yourself in situations where you're unwelcome or out of place.

Crapaud smoke yuh pipe You are in big trouble.

Every bread have it cheese Everyone, regardless of their background or appearance, will find a matching partner in the end.

De fruit doh fall far from de tree Children often turn out like their parents.

Get cage before yuh ketch bird Before you can ensnare a woman, you need a house to put her in.

If you play with dog, you must get fleas Hanging out with lowlifes will eventually rub off on you.

Man plans, God laughs It doesn't matter what you plan to do, things never work out the way you want them to.

Now yuh cookin' with gas When you finally understand or work out how to do something.

When cock get teeth Pigs might fly.

Yuh cyar play sailor an' fraid powder If you're going to be controversial you have to accept the consequences (a sailor mas traditionally includes a heavy coating of talcum powder on the face).

Zandolie fin' yuh hole Know your place and stick to it.

Glossary

Abir Pink dye thrown around by (and among) participants of the Hindu Phagwah festival.

Ajoupa Amerindian building with a palm-thatch roof and walls of clay and cow manure.

All fours Popular card game, often played for money.

Allyuh Everyone, as in "Allyuh not tired yet?"

Babash An illegal, extremely potent bootleg white rum, also called bush rum and mountain dew.

Bacchanal A rowdy event or social commotion, or just general scandal.

Bachac Large, black-brown leaf-cutting ant, which gives a painful nip.

Bad John Man of violent or criminal reputation, now a bit outdated.

Bamsie Bottom; backside, a staple of soca songs: "wine yuh bamsie".

Bandit A thief or mugger.

Bareback Term for a man who's not wearing a top.

Bath suit Swimsuit.

Bazodee State of confusion, usually caused by being attracted to someone of the opposite sex.

Beastly Used to describe an extremely cold beer.

Big yard Trinidad's largest panyard; the Savannah at Carnival time.

Blue food Root vegetables such as dasheen or tannia.

Blues The TT$100 dollar note.

Bobol Corruption, embezzlement; a **bobolee** is a person easily taken advantage of, as well as an effigy of an unpopular public figure which you'll see strung up on fences and at roadsides around Easter time, and which is treated to a piñata-like thrashing.

Boldfaced Being pushy or demanding.

Boof To lambast or scold someone: "He get a real boof for staying out last night".

Bounce Fist-to-fist greeting – you'll often be asked to "gimme a bounce nah?"

Brass band The bands that back live acts at fetes, usually featuring a good brass section; traditionally, soca and calypso songs hinge on a repeated brass refrain.

Break a lime To leave when a lime is in full swing, causing others to think about leaving, and often used to guilt-trip the person who wants to leave.

Broughtupsy Solid, proper upbringing – to have "no broughtupsy" is to have no manners and class.

Bumper Another word for backside, usually a woman's.

Bush Generic term for forests and undeveloped countryside. Also medicinal herbs used in a "bush bath" or "bush tea".

Buss To do something; eg to "buss a lime". Also describes an unsuccessful event ("De fete buss after Machel perform").

Cascadura Scaly black fish with folklore associations; if you eat it, you're destined to end your days in Trinidad.

Chip-chip Mollusc found on Trinidad's beaches; see **pacro.**

Chunkalunks Term of endearment, usually for a partner or a child.

Chupidee Something or someone idiotic.

Cocoa panyol/coco payol Originally used to describe Venezuelans who moved to Trinidad in the nineteenth century to work on the burgeoning cocoa and coffee estates, but often deployed to describe anyone or anything of mixed origin these days.

Commesse Confusion, controversy, scandal.

Cook up/cook out Food prepared in one pot, usually outside, such as pelau.

Coolie Derogatory term for someone of Indian descent.

Creole A broad term describing a person of mixed European and African descent born in T&T. Also classic Caribbean food, such as callaloo and *coocoo*.

Cut eye A nasty look, also a "bad eye".

Cutlass Machete.

Dingolay To wind down low or dance unreservedly.

Dotish Stupid, ridiculous-looking. Sometimes "dotishness" as well.

Dou dou Sweetheart.

Dougla Person of mixed Indian and African parentage. Does not have offensive connotations.

Dreevay Waste time.

Ease up To slacken, as in "ease up yuh mout'" ("be quiet").

East Indian A Trinbagonian of Indian descent.

Ent Used at the end of a statement to mean "is that not so" or "that's true isn't it?"

Fatigue Witty repartee.

Fete A large, open-air party or concert; the biggest are held around Carnival time.

Flambeaux A flaming kerosene torch used by oyster salesmen to advertise their wares.

Flask A half-bottle of rum.

Flim Trini pronunciation of film.

Free up Relax, let go.

Fresh water Yankee Mocking term for Trinbagonians who use foreign mannerisms picked up during trips to the US.

Friending Having a sexual relationship with someone.

Gallery Veranda or porch outside one's home; to "gallery" is to show off.

Get on bad To dance and jump up with abandon at a fete.

Ground provisions Root vegetable tubers (yam, dasheen etc).

Gyal/gyul Trini pronunciation of girl.

Hops Light, fluffy bread rolls.

Horning Two-timing, being unfaithful to your partner.

Horrors Lots of problems, bad vibes caused by anger.

Ital Rastafarian term meaning natural or pure, often used to refer to meatless food cooked with little salt.

Jackspaniard Large, aggressive wasp which delivers a vicious sting; also called a jep.

Jagabat Promiscuous woman.

Jamette Woman of questionable morals.

Jumbie Spirit or ghost, also a night person.

Jump-up Frenetic partying or a frenetic party.

Kaiso Old-time word for classic calypso music.

Kicksee Funny.

Lackeray Gossiping.

Laginlappe Pronounced "lan-nyap", a little extra, a bonus.

Las' lap Final parade of revellers on Carnival Tuesday before the abstinence of Lent begins.

Licks To lash or hit someone.

Lickser Person who gets free things through devious means.

Lime To socialize with friends on the street, in a bar, in a person's house, by a river, anywhere. T&T's favourite pastime.

Lyrics Flirtatious sweet talk, usually from a man to a woman.

Maaga Skinny, slim.

Macafouchette Leftovers from a meal.

Maco A busybody prying into other people's business; also used as a verb.

Make style Show off.

Maljo Evil eye.

Malkadi Epilepsy. Having a fit.

Mamaguy Verb meaning to fool someone with smart talk that makes false promises: "Don't try to mamaguy me!".

Mampy Fat woman.

Mas Short for masquerade, used to describe playing in a costume band at Carnival.

Mauvais langue Damaging gossip.

Melongene Aubergine, eggplant. Also called by its Indian name, *baigan*.

Navel string Placenta, buried by the superstitious under a fruiting mango tree to ensure a prosperous life. Also used to denote someone's roots or a place they frequent, as in "yuh navel string eh buried in Carnival fete yuh know".

Ol' talk Idle chatter.

One time Immediately, now.

Outside man/woman A person with whom one commits adultery.

Pacro Sea barnacle cooked up into "pacro water", a thin fishy broth said to have aphrodisiac qualities.

Pampalam Backside.

Pan The steel drum as a musical instrument.

Panyard Headquarters of steel pan bands.

Papa yo! An expression of surprise.

Pappy show From puppet show, meaning nonsense, something inconsequential and ridiculous.

Parlour Small grocery store.

Partna Commonly used by men to refer to their close male friends: "Me an me partnas making a lime".

Petit carem Dry spell in the middle of the rainy season, usually in September.

Picong The tradition of making fun of someone through an exchange of witty comments.

Piper Crack user.

Pitch oil Kerosene.

Posey Chamberpot. Sometimes placed on the stage by audiences at calypso tents to demonstrate displeasure with a performance; equally, used as a makeshift cup (filled with straight rum) during Jouvert.

Pot hound Skinny mongrel dog.

Pressure General term for stress or problems, as in "it real pressure, man".

Provision Root vegetables such as dasheen or tannia; a provision ground is where they're grown.

Puja Indian prayer or offering to the gods.

Puncheon High-proof rum.

Ras Dreadlocks or a person with them.

Real Plenty: "It have real people in the party!".

Reds Someone of African descent but with a light skin colour; also known as high brown.

Rucktion Confusion, bacchanal.

Saga boy Flashy dresser, now a little outdated.

Scruntin' Penniless, broke.

Sea bath To go for a swim in the sea.

Semi-demi Something unexpected, a little bit of magic.

Skin out To splay ones legs, usually when dancing.

Skin teet To smile.

Slackness Impolite, crude and low-down behaviour.

Sound system A crew of DJs operating the decks and providing the huge speaker boxes at fetes and parties.

Spranger Crack user, petty thief or volatile person.

Steups The Trini version of a "tut", a steups is kissing or sucking the teeth to indicate irritation, disapproval or derision.

Storm Getting into a fete without paying by climbing over the fence, sweet-talking the doorman, etc.

Stupidness The preferred term to describe ridiculous, slack, time-consuming actions or behaviour.

Sweet hand Used in reference to someone who cooks very well.

Sweet to bad Very good: "de curry duck was sweet to bad".

Sweetman A man who is financially supported by a woman.

Swizzle stick A whisk used for stirring callaloo or juicing fruits to make punch.

Tabanca The depression caused by the ending of a love affair. In extreme states, "tabantruck".

Tan-ta-na Excitement, confusion.

Tantie Aunt.

Tapia Hut made with thatch and mud walls.

Thick Pronounced "tik", and usually used to refer to the (pleasant) plumpness of a woman.

Ting A thing, woman or a euphemism for all kinds of eventualities – "tings a gwan".

Tittivay Waste time or stir up trouble.

Tobago love Disguising your feelings for a loved one, possibly due to finding it difficult to express your emotions; also the actions of a couple who quarrel all the time.

Tout bagai Everything.

Trace A road or street that once was or still is a dirt track.

Travel Using public transport.

Vaps To behave in an overexcited manner; or to indicate something that happens suddenly or a sudden change of mind/mood.

Vex Angry or annoyed.

Vex money Extra money to take out with you, in case you have an argument with your partner and have to pay your own way home.

Wajang A hooligan.

Wapie A card game.

Warahoon Person behaving in a wild or crazy manner.

Wassi Lewd, uninhibited behaviour and dancing at fetes; wining down to the ground.

Watless Worthless, no good.

We is we You are among friends.

Wine To dance by rotating hips and bottom in an erotic manner. Your "wining bone" is what allows you to move with suitable sensuality.

Yampie Matter that collects at the corner of the eyes after sleep.

Yard fowl Chickens raised in someone's backyard.

Zaboca Avocado.

Small print and index

A ROUGH GUIDE TO ROUGH GUIDES

Published in 1982, the first Rough Guide – to Greece – was a student scheme that became a publishing phenomenon. Mark Ellingham, a recent graduate in English from Bristol University, had been travelling in Greece the previous summer and couldn't find the right guidebook. With a small group of friends he wrote his own guide, combining a highly contemporary, journalistic style with a thoroughly practical approach to travellers' needs.

The immediate success of the book spawned a series that rapidly covered dozens of destinations. And, in addition to impecunious backpackers, Rough Guides soon acquired a much broader readership that relished the guides' wit and inquisitiveness as much as their enthusiastic, critical approach and value-for-money ethos.

These days, Rough Guides include recommendations from budget to luxury and cover more than 120 destinations around the globe, as well as producing an ever-growing range of ebooks.

Visit **roughguides.com** to find all our latest books, read articles, get inspired and share travel tips with the Rough Guides community.

Rough Guide credits

Editor: Greg Dickinson
Layout: Pradeep Thapliyal
Cartography: James Macdonald, Swati Handoo
Picture editor: Aude Vauconsant
Proofreader: Karen Parker
Managing editor: Andy Turner
Senior editor: Rachel Mills
Assistant editor: Sharon Sonam

Production: Nicole Landau
Cover design: Nicole Newman, Dan May, Pradeep Thapliyal
Editorial assistant: Freya Godfrey
Senior pre-press designer: Dan May
Programme manager: Gareth Lowe
Publisher: Joanna Kirby
Publishing director: Georgina Dee

Publishing information

This sixth edition published August 2015 by
Rough Guides Ltd,
80 Strand, London WC2R 0RL
11, Community Centre, Panchsheel Park,
New Delhi 110017, India
Distributed by Penguin Random House
Penguin Books Ltd,
80 Strand, London WC2R 0RL
Penguin Group (USA)
345 Hudson Street, NY 10014, USA
Penguin Group (Australia)
250 Camberwell Road, Camberwell,
Victoria 3124, Australia
Penguin Group (NZ)
67 Apollo Drive, Mairangi Bay, Auckland 1310,
New Zealand
Penguin Group (South Africa)
Block D, Rosebank Office Park, 181 Jan Smuts Avenue,
Parktown North, Gauteng, South Africa 2193
Rough Guides is represented in Canada by Tourmaline
Editions Inc. 662 King Street West, Suite 304, Toronto,
Ontario M5V 1M7
Printed in Singapore

© Rough Guides 2015
Maps © Rough Guides
No part of this book may be reproduced in any form
without permission from the publisher except for the
quotation of brief passages in reviews.
296pp includes index
A catalogue record for this book is available from the
British Library
ISBN: 978-0-24101-341-0
The publishers and authors have done their best to
ensure the accuracy and currency of all the information
in **The Rough Guide to Trinidad & Tobago**, however,
they can accept no responsibility for any loss, injury, or
inconvenience sustained by any traveller as a result of
information or advice contained in the guide.
1 3 5 7 9 8 6 4 2

Help us update

We've gone to a lot of effort to ensure that the sixth
edition of **The Rough Guide to Trinidad & Tobago** is
accurate and up-to-date. However, things change – places
get "discovered", opening hours are notoriously fickle,
restaurants and rooms raise prices or lower standards. If
you feel we've got it wrong or left something out, we'd like
to know, and if you can remember the address, the price,
the hours, the phone number, so much the better.

Please send your comments with the subject line
"Rough Guide Trinidad & Tobago Update" to
✉ mail@uk.roughguides.com. We'll credit all contributions
and send a copy of the next edition (or any other Rough
Guide if you prefer) for the very best emails.
Find more travel information, connect with fellow
travellers and plan your trip on ⊕ roughguides.com.

ABOUT THE AUTHOR
Polly Thomas has been travelling to the Caribbean since her teens, and lived in Port of Spain, Trinidad, for five years. As well as writing many articles about the region's food, music and travel attractions, she has authored guidebooks to Jamaica, St Lucia, Antigua and Barbuda, as well as T&T. She currently lives in London.

Acknowledgements

Huge thanks to all in Trinidad and Tobago, particularly Dexter, Aaron and Soleil and the Trini family: Lynette, Dale and Dean Lewis, Skye Hernandez, Gillian Jadoo, Anna Carlsson and Felizia Liverpool, and Daddy Frank, Eugene and Francine Romany. Many thanks also to Jillian and Jada Fourniller; Gillian Goddard; Gunda Harewood; Marcia, Arthur and the Guerrero family; Stephen Broadbridge; Pierro Guerrini; Patricia Turpin; Ean Mackay; Courtenay Rooks; Lorna and Steve Felgate; Porridge and Jeanelle Lopez; Angela Richards; Mark and Zena Puddy; Cynthia Clovis; Nova Alexander; Avion Hercules; Chris James; Lana Drysdale.

Readers' updates

Thanks to all the readers who have taken the time to write in with comments and suggestions (and apologies if we've inadvertently omitted or misspelt anyone's name):

John and Amanda Ewan; Steph Le Fevre; Andrew Gordon; Janna Grodecka; Marc Halpern; Josh Hart; Nick Hern; Alicia Kamm; Russ Peters; Steve Roebuck; Kathrin Sommer; Beth Woods.

Photo credits

All photos © Rough Guides except the following:
(Key: t-top; c-centre; b-bottom; l-left; r-right)

p.4 Wolfgang Kaehler/Corbis
p.5 Dave G. Houser/Corbis
p.9 Interpix/Alamy (t); Debra Wiseberg/Getty Images (b)
p.11 Bob Krist/Corbis
p.12 Vario images GmbH & Co.KG/Alamy
p.13 Bob Gibbons/Alamy (tl); Ian Brierley/Getty Images (tr); ANDREA DE SILVA/Corbis (c); Robin Chittenden/FLPA (b);
p.14 EyeOn/Getty Images (t); Sean Drakes/CON/Getty Images (c); Nik Wheeler/Alamy (b)
p.15 John Harper/Corbis (t); Tom Hanslien Photography/Alamy (b)
p.16 Christian Kober/Corbis (b)
p.17 FLPA/Alamy (t); Alison Wright/Corbis (c)
p.18 Norbert Probst/Alamy
p.20 Michele Westmorland/Getty Images
p.50 John de la Bastide/Alamy

p.53 EyeOn/Getty Images
p.106 All Canada Photos/Alamy
p.109 Dreamtours/Alamy
p.149 Ian Brierley/Getty Images
p.170 Sarabayphotography/Dreamstime.com
p.173 Tony Waltham/Corbis
p.190 RGB Ventures/SuperStock/Alamy
p.193 Dbimages/Alamy
p.248 Jeneil S/Getty Images

Front cover and spine Englishman's Bay, Tobago © Shaun Egan/AWL Images
Back cover Port of Spain Carnival © Travel Pictures/Alamy (t); French angelfish, Little Tobago © Norbert Probst/Corbis (bl); boat on Parlatuvier beach © Michele Westmorland/Alamy (br)

Index

Maps are marked in grey

Map symbols

The symbols below are used on maps throughout the book

Highway	Point of interest	Mountain peak	Church (regional map)
Main road	Post office	Mountain range	Mosque
Minor road	Hospital	Cave	Hindu temple
Footpath	Information office	Reef	Church (town map)
Ferry	Parking	Waterfall	Market
Waterway	Petrol station	Fortress	Building
Airport	Golf course	Museum	Stadium
Transport stop	Beach without facilities	Lighthouse	Park
Viewpoint	Beach with facilities	Bridge	Cemetery
Bank	Turtle nesting site	Swamp	Beach

Listings key

- Accommodation
- Restaurant/café
- Bar/club
- Shop

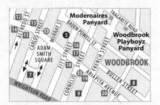